顧維理

民國八十九年

SAME BED, DIFFERENT DREAMS

A

Philip E. Lilienthal

■   ■   ■

B O O K

The Philip E. Lilienthal imprint
honors special books
in commemoration of a man whose work
at the University of California Press from 1954 to 1979
was marked by dedication to young authors
and to high standards in the field of Asian Studies.
Friends, family, authors, and foundations have together
endowed the Lilienthal Fund, which enables the Press
to publish under this imprint selected books
in a way that reflects the taste and judgment
of a great and beloved editor.

SAME BED, DIFFERENT DREAMS

Managing U.S.-China Relations, 1989–2000

DAVID M. LAMPTON

University of California Press
BERKELEY   LOS ANGELES   LONDON

University of California Press
Berkeley and Los Angeles, California

University of California Press, Ltd.
London, England

Lampton, David M.
   Same bed, different dreams : managing U.S.-China relations,
1989–2000 / David M. Lampton.
      p.   cm.
   Includes bibliographical references and index.
   ISBN 0-520-21590-7 (cloth : alk. paper)
   1. United States—Foreign relations—China. 2. China—Foreign
relations—United States.
I. Title.
E183.8.C5 L26   2001
327.73051—dc21   00-028712

Printed in the United States of America
08   07   06   05   04   03   02   01
10   9   8   7   6   5   4   3   2   1

The paper used in this publication meets the minimum requirements
of ANSI/NISO Z39.48–1992 (R 1997) (*Permanence of Paper*).

Dedicated to
The National Committee on
United States–China Relations,
Professor Michel Oksenberg,
My friends in China

Contents

PREFACE

The Chinese have an expression that captures the essence of a relationship between two people whose lives are intimately intertwined but who do not fundamentally communicate with each other: "same bed, different dreams" (*tong chuang, yi meng*). So it is with United States–China relations. The processes of economic and information globalization, along with the development of international regimes and multilateral organizations, have landed America and China increasingly near one another in the same global bed, but our respective national institutions, interests, leadership and popular perceptions, and the very characters of our two peoples, ensure that our nations have substantially different dreams. This has provided the underlying dynamic of the first decade of post–cold war U.S.-China relations and will continue to do so well into the twenty-first century.

This book reflects my unique opportunity to interact with Chinese people and leaders from the People's Republic of China (PRC), Hong Kong, and Taiwan for nearly thirty years as a scholar, as the head of a policy-oriented exchange organization, and as director of Washington think tank research programs dealing with China. These varied experiences account for this volume's eclectic mixture of academic analysis, personal account, and policy guidance. My first direct encounter with China was as a doctoral student in 1972–1973, when I interviewed brave refugees who had fled to Hong Kong to escape the terror of China's Great Proletarian Cultural Revolution. I undertook research in Taiwan a few years later, when the island was still under martial law and not much more congenial to foreign researchers than Communist China (where I conducted field research in 1982 while living in the city of Wuhan).

The most significant experience that has shaped this volume was my decade of work as president of the National Committee on United

States–China Relations in New York City. In that unique nongovernmental, nonpartisan organization, replete with splendid colleagues, I was able to interact with leaders and citizens at all levels of Chinese society (including in Hong Kong and Taiwan) during a particularly turbulent era in U.S.-China relations: 1988 to 1997. In this capacity I was able to spend extended periods of time with Chinese leaders and see them as they encountered America, and to observe U.S. leaders from different regions, economic sectors, and system levels as they tried to come to grips with the Chinese circumstance. I witnessed this interaction as the violence of Tiananmen in June 1989 pushed practically every political and cultural hot button in both nations. At various key points during the years that followed I was fortunate enough to spend considerable time with some members of the Chinese elite such as then Shanghai Mayor Zhu Rongji and former Shanghai Mayor Wang Dao-han (in mid-1990). Some of the key junctures that my tenure witnessed included the aftermath of June 4, 1989; successive congressional battles over most-favored-nation (MFN) tariff treatment for the PRC; the end of the Bush era and the rocky beginning of the Clinton administration; the reversal of President Clinton's China policy in the 1994–1996 period; the switch in political party control in the U.S. Congress in 1994–1995; the tensions in the Taiwan Strait of 1995–1996 and the direct popular election of Lee Teng-hui as president of Taiwan; the death of Deng Xiaoping in early 1997 and Jiang Zemin's rather uneventful transition to power; the reversion of Hong Kong to Chinese sovereignty in mid-1997; the summit diplomacy of 1997–1998; and the management of the relationship as the Asian financial crisis unfolded from mid-1997 to the end of the decade.

This extended exposure to China, its citizens, and its leaders, as well as to U.S. counterparts and the overall Sino-American interaction, has led me to several orientations that I wish to make explicit. Most important, this exposure has for me put a human face on the relationship; there is a human texture to decisions that others simply portray as cold, calculating, power-driven moves in interlocking domestic and foreign policy games. In meeting and dealing with many of the central actors that figure in the pages that follow (cabinet officers, White House staff, members of Congress, executive branch officials, local officials, business tycoons, and Chinese counterparts, including PRC dissidents), I have come to believe that simply watching their body language, listening to their questions, and attaching importance to what they are saying directly and below the surface is an indispensable supplement to documentary analysis and the assumption of interest-based real politik. Though realist assumptions about leadership behavior are central to the analysis that follows, my experience has led me to attach importance to what I have been told by principals, when that information is consistent with the documentary record, with the information provided by others, and with subsequent individual and system behavior. Leaders bring to the discharge of their duties biases, prejudices, goals, aspirations, and a will to survive that can never be disentangled from their decisions. While those involved in political and policy struggles may seek to hide such motivations, they do not *always* seek to do so and they often fail to do so.

I therefore attach importance to statements and sentiments that have come at me from a variety of directions in China. A notable example is the almost universally expressed desire of Chinese to economically, culturally, and politically resume their "rightful place" in Asia. In several conversations with a member of Deng Xiaoping's family, I asked why her father, when given the choice between slower economic growth and almost dangerously rapid expansion, invariably chose the latter. Her reply made clear the essential unity between Deng's personal mission, Beijing's domestic goals, Chinese nationalism, and PRC foreign policy: "In the mid-1970s, my father looked around China's periphery, to the small dragon economies [Singapore, Hong Kong, Taiwan, and South Korea]. They were growing at eight to ten percent per year and these economies had a considerable technological lead over China. If we were to surpass them and resume our rightful place in the region and ultimately the world, China would have to grow faster than them."[1]

This was not just the dream of an old man in his twilight years; it was (and remains) a vision shared across generations, walks of life, and system levels. One of China's most respected young economists of the 1990s said, "Developing countries always take risks. Without them you can never catch up."[2] Expressing this same sentiment, in 1986 dissident astrophysicist Fang Lizhi also found shame in China's economic position within Asia saying, "Industrial development lagged behind that in many other nations. Countries and territories [Hong Kong, Taiwan, and Macao] that were formerly at or below our level of development were now racing ahead of us."[3] Even in 1981, at the very outset of "opening and reform," when promotion of the "special economic zones" was a subject of heated internal debate, Xiang Nan, Fujian Province's first party secretary, spoke in favor of the zones saying, "Do we wish to constantly trail behind Taiwan?"[4]

Of course there are dangers that accompany the access to participants that I have enjoyed. One is that the observer equates the interlocutors' contemporaneous or post-hoc recollections with reality. Another potential pitfall is that I, as the outsider, may simply have been one piece in a larger political game the informant was playing and of which I was unaware. And perhaps most difficult of all to guard against, in developing relationships with persons central to the U.S.-China relationship in both nations, one unwittingly can develop stakes in those ties that overpower the objectivity of analysis. I have sought to guard against this, I acknowledge the dangers, and it is for the reader to judge whether the gains in understanding have justified the risks.

Beyond paying attention to what participants in the U.S.-China relationship have had to say, several other assumptions and orientations underlie the analysis that follows. First, America and China have enormous interests at stake in their bilateral relationship, many of which are held in common, but some of which are not. It is possible (though undesirable and unnecessary) that each will come to define the other as its adversary. Second, neither the United States nor China has been particularly deft in dealing with the other. Both nations can and must do better, though it will never be an easy task or a completely successful one. Third, the pace of political, economic, and cultural change in China has been staggering, given that the country only "opened" its doors in 1978. Taken as a whole, at the end of the twentieth century, the changes in China's economy, role in the world, and social circumstance had been largely in a positive direction from the perspective of American interests, and if both sides can manage the issue of Taiwan, they have a good chance of continuing in that direction. Finally, if we can understand the specific conditions, constraints, and perceptions shaping Chinese choices we would understand most Chinese behavior, even if we sometimes, perhaps frequently, do not find it particularly congenial.

This book recounts events in the first post–cold war decade of Sino-American interaction not so much to provide an exhaustive history as to extract from that progression of events lessons that should assist leaders in both nations to better manage the relationship in the future. I also hope that the book will assist citizens of our two nations to develop attitudes that will make a constructive relationship more likely in the twenty-first century.

In the course of writing this volume I have been aided by many people whom I must thank. I apologize for any errors of omission or commission.

I have dedicated this book to one organization, one individual, and my many friends in China; they have had a significant, positive influence on the U.S.-China relationship and on me, personally. Since 1966 the National Committee on United States–China Relations has been a leading constructive force in the Sino-American relationship through its untiring pursuit of one objective: mutual understanding between the leaders and peoples of the United States and China—nothing more, nothing less. I also dedicate this book to Michel Oksenberg, a person I have been honored to call a friend, a mentor, and a colleague since my undergraduate days at Stanford University. Mike inspired me to devote my professional life to the study of China, he taught me that knowledge brings with it the obligation to speak truth to power, and he gave me the confidence to surpass self-imposed limits. I will always be grateful for those gifts. Finally, this book is dedicated to my friends in China who have shared their knowledge with me and who also have labored to build a bridge between our two nations.

I worked with a number of people in the process of writing and producing this volume—each has contributed greatly to my understanding of the decade covered by this book and to the clarity with which I have attempted to convey that understanding. During the course of my research, I have had the pleasure of working with a number of extraordinary students at the Johns Hopkins Paul H. Nitze School of Advanced International Studies (SAIS): Amy Celico, Gregory May, and Tung Chen-yuan. Through the writing and production process, I have greatly benefited from the advice, encouragement, and assistance of Sheila Levine and Juliane Brand at the University of California Press, as well as Krista Forsgren Ahdieh and David Brown of SAIS and the staff at Impressions Book and Journal Services, Inc.: all of them pushed me to think and write as clearly as possible. In addition, I wish to thank Jan C. Berris and Professors Nicholas R. Lardy, Michel Oksenberg, and Ken Pomeranz for offering incisive and trenchant guidance for revision. And speaking of thinking clearly, I want to express my appreciation to Henry P. Sailer for his friendship and encouragement and for forcing me to think more logically throughout the period I labored on this book. I also benefited from the encouragement and inspiration of colleagues at The Nixon Center and the Sagaponic Think Tank.

Finally, I want to thank my wife and partner, Susan, who has supported and encouraged me every step of the way throughout our married life. I love her very much.

David M. Lampton
Washington, D.C.
May 2000

INTRODUCTION

The Big Picture

The U.S. talks of its leadership role. We would never say that.
Though we Chinese had Confucius, he taught only China, not
others. The role China can play will reflect its patience. Handling
any issue, China will not be impatient. So China won't attempt to
become the teacher.

> Vice Premier and Foreign Minister Qian Qichen,
> Diaoyutai, September 16, 1997

Many would argue that nonrecurring, broad historical forces
determine the course of relations among nations, including
wars.... But—and this is the fundamental point—leaders are
supposed to lead, to resist pressures or "forces" of this sort, to
understand more fully than others the range of options and
implications of choosing such options. This is what President
Franklin Roosevelt did when he convinced the American people
that the United States should help its allies fight the Nazis. I
believe this is what President Kennedy did during the Cuban
missile crisis when he resisted heavy pressure—public and
private—to attack the Soviet missile sites in Cuba. And I believe
this is what President Johnson and his associates, including
myself, should have done to resist the pressure—from the public,
the media, academicians, and the Congress—toward a military
solution to the problem of Vietnam.

> Robert S. McNamara, 1999

Cooperate if we can. Contend if we must.

> U.S. senator, July 1999

This book addresses two simple questions: Why is the relationship between the United States and China so difficult for Washington and Beijing
to manage? and How can it be handled more effectively? The book reaches
one simple conclusion: both nations can improve upon the diplomacy of

the first post–cold war decade, but their association will always be characterized by a complex mix of cooperation and contention, at best.

This book offers ideas, not an exhaustive recapitulation of every development in U.S.-China relations following the end of the cold war. The Tiananmen tragedy of 1989, which deeply affected American and Western views of China, enters but does not dominate the analysis. The violence of Tiananmen served as a catalyst for change in Chinese and American policies toward each other, giving shape and substance to growing anxieties and latent frustrations in both countries. But even if Tiananmen had never occurred, the bilateral relationship would have been a diplomatic challenge because of fundamental underlying considerations in China and the United States. This book addresses those factors.

THE DISSOLUTION OF THE
U.S.–CHINA GRAND BARGAIN

The story line in the chapters that follow is at once simple and profound in its implications.[1] In the 1970s and 1980s, President Richard Nixon and Chairman Mao Zedong, followed by President Jimmy Carter and Supreme Leader Deng Xiaoping, gradually constructed a grand bargain that helped stabilize Sino-American relations for nearly two decades (1972–1989). The terms of the bargain dealt with many policy issues, among them Taiwan, U.S. security alliances in the Asia-Pacific region and elsewhere, cooperation with respect to third parties (perhaps most notably Afghanistan in the 1980s), trade, and human rights. Some of the understandings of this period were committed to writing, while others remained largely unspoken. Nonetheless, they all were equally real.

The dimensions of the grand bargain were far-reaching. With respect to Taiwan, the strategic imperative for Sino-American cooperation led Mao, Deng, Nixon, and Carter all to agree that the island's status was an issue best placed in the background, to be dealt with later—Mao spoke in terms of a hundred years, Deng, fifty. This distant horizon allowed American and Chinese leaders to sidestep a problem for which they had no answer and to focus on cooperation elsewhere. Regarding U.S. security alliances, Beijing downplayed its anxieties concerning the U.S.-Japan security alliance and American pacts elsewhere because it saw them in the service of containing the Soviet Union throughout much of the 1970s and 1980s. In fact, Beijing actually favored stronger alliances between the United States and its allies. With respect to trade, both nations desired economic ties, but through the waning years of the cold war the commercial relationship in general and the trade imbalance in particular did not loom so large that it threatened to eclipse the security priority. And with regard to human rights, the Soviet threat allowed leaders in both Beijing and Washington to downplay the two countries' deep differences in this realm in the service of the more immediate objective of opposing Moscow.

It has become a cliché of post–cold war analysis to say that the gradual warming of Sino-Soviet relations in the latter half of the 1980s, capped off by the disappearance of the Soviet Union as a global power in 1991, dramatically weakened the rationale in both nations for subordinating latent frictions in the U.S.-China relationship. This is true, as is the assertion that the powerful effect of the violence and bloodshed in Beijing and elsewhere in China in 1989 acted as a solvent on the grand bargain. But, and here is the main point, as important as were the demise of the Soviet Union and the events in Tiananmen, a host of other developments contributed to Sino-American friction in the years from 1989 to 2000. It is the accumulation of these developments in the post–cold war era that has made U.S.-China ties so difficult to manage.

Among those factors are the following: First, the People's Republic of China (PRC) has simply been more successful at modernizing than almost any outsiders predicted in the 1970s and 1980s. As a result, China's interests have rubbed up against those of the United States more frequently and dramatically than was anticipated two decades ago. Without putting too fine a point on it, Americans were perhaps subconsciously comforted by the prospect of a China moving in the "right" direction, but not too rapidly. As some Americans became anxious about China's rise, many Chinese became concerned that the United States might try to keep China down.

Second, with respect to Taiwan, in the 1970s and for much of the 1980s, the island was under martial law, presided over by an authoritarian elite whose raison d'être was to rule a unified China. While the PRC and Taiwan might disagree about who ought to rule this union, their shared view of a single, united China provided a basis for stability. However, during the late 1980s, throughout the 1990s, and into the new century, leaders on Taiwan became progressively more responsive to the island's voters; Taiwan's economic and other achievements created a sense among its people that they were entitled to greater dignity and status in the international system; and as a multiparty political system developed, a new, more independent-minded identity took hold of the island's people. Beijing and Washington might wish to keep Taiwan on the back burner, but increasingly the island's people and leaders would not suffer this; a politically united China became a progressively less unifying concept across the strait. By the year 2000, mounting friction across the Taiwan Strait brought with it the significant danger of direct Sino-American military conflict.

Third, in post–cold war America and China, domestic politics have assumed a greater importance relative to international concerns; the effects of this inward turn have been reinforced by growing social and bureaucratic pluralism in both societies. That pluralism, along with a preoccupation with domestic politics and a shift in the character of political leadership in both countries from cold warrior to political technocrat and balancer, has diminished the capacity of each country's executive leadership to define and enforce international priorities. In the case of the United States, reflecting a process that started with the Vietnam War and gained steam with the Watergate scandal, Congress has come to play an increasingly assertive role in foreign policy.

Fourth, just as the cold war was ending and the United States and China, as well as other countries, turned their attention to economic growth, the confusing and profound process of economic globalization was taking hold. Labor-intensive production was being moved from around Asia to China, America's trade deficit with China relentlessly increased, and the population in each nation began to feel vulnerable to the economic decisions of the other in a way that had never before been the case. Moreover, in the realm of communication, an information revolution was under way. Instantaneous information, news, and images were shaping views on a scale and with a rapidity that had heretofore not been possible.

Finally, the 1991 Gulf War showcased another revolution that bore directly on U.S.-China relations—the revolution in military affairs, whereby new information-processing, sensing, and guidance technologies transformed the United States' ability to fight wars and permitted Washington to contemplate intervening in circumstances where it might not have dared before. Further, defense against missiles that had been deemed infeasible and undesirable in the 1972 Anti-Ballistic Missile Treaty appeared somewhat more feasible toward the end of the 1990s. As these capabilities were developed, China felt compelled to try to join the revolution; moreover, it became progressively more apprehensive as the gap between its own military capabilities and those of the United States widened throughout the 1990s. And as Beijing sought to deal with this new reality, China's smaller neighbors began to feel somewhat insecure, expressing their anxieties to Washington both openly and discreetly.

In short, the grand bargain of the 1970s and 1980s became the humpty-dumpty of the 1990s. The task, then, that has befallen leaders in both countries as we enter the new century is to try to fashion a new, persuasive rationale for Sino-American cooperation.

UNIFYING THEMES

Beyond the focus on the demise of the grand bargain, several strands of thought knit this volume together. These themes help make sense of the decade in U.S.-China relations that ended the twentieth century and can serve as guideposts as both nations enter the twenty-first century. They are as follows:

(1) *The relationship between China and the United States can be thought of as operating on three levels, each of which creates specific challenges for those who would manage that relationship:*

· The global level, characterized by international organizations and regimes (both worldwide and regional in scope), the operation of international markets, and the behavior of third parties

· The domestic level, characterized by governmental and civic institutions, internal politics, ideologies, and citizen opinion in China and the United States

· The level of individual political and societal leaders who have had a demonstrated impact on bilateral relations

When one considers the difficulty of reconciling the demands of the global system, domestic imperatives, and the idiosyncrasies and desires of specific leaders in both China and America, the productive management of Sino-American affairs becomes exceedingly difficult for both nations. This volume is organized around the challenges each nation has faced, and continues to face, on each of these levels.

(2) *Whether we are talking about officials in America's pluralistic political and social system or members of China's elite, each country's leaders confront two very different constituencies—one domestic, the other global.*

In both Beijing and Washington, various societal groups and government entities wield considerable power. These groups often have their own agendas and they apply pressure to influence policy. More and more, however, forces beyond each nation's borders also create pressures that are difficult to ignore. These forces, for example, are found in global markets, where the ebb and flow of money is ever more determined by the degree to which domestic policies conform to the demands of international investors and bankers.

Demands of the global system, however, go far beyond the realm of investment and banking. The United States, Europe, Japan, and the Third World urged that Beijing cease nuclear weapons testing and help stanch the spread of technologies of mass destruction. In the environmental arena, states near and far from China have demanded that Beijing limit emissions of greenhouse gases (thought responsible for global warming) and sulfur dioxide (which produces acid rain). In turn, at the December 1997 Third Conference of the Parties to the United Nations Framework Convention on Climate Change in Kyoto, Beijing spoke out for developing countries, arguing that because the United States was the largest greenhouse gas emitter, Washington had an obligation to make environmental technology and capital available to developing nations on favorable terms and to reduce its own emissions before poorer nations could be expected to do so. These demands for lower U.S. emission levels were perceived as a call for slower economic growth and were predictably resisted by many U.S. congressmen, citizens, and businesspeople.

Thus national leaders face the great dilemma of how to reconcile the demands of powerful domestic groups to maintain arrangements from which they have benefited with the demands of external constituencies. The latter, whether foreign countries, multilateral organizations, or multinational firms, often choose to provide or withhold cooperation or resources in areas of great concern to the Americans or Chinese. For example, Moody's Investors Services, a private investment-rating firm, evaluates the creditworthiness of financial entities around the world, and its findings dramatically affect the costs of borrowing for both nations and multinational corporations. In December 1997, Moody's downgraded South Korea's sovereign debt to "junk" status and, overnight, deepened what was already a serious regionwide economic crisis. In July 1998, the same firm merely announced the review of nine Chinese banks for a possible downgrade (that did occur), thereby negatively affecting Chinese equity values, raising transaction costs for the PRC's entire financial system, and discouraging potential Chinese borrowers from even entering the market.

This combination of domestic and international demands, each with internal and external consequences, is blurring the distinction between foreign and domestic policy. As one Chinese scholar put it, "Many things are unclear—what is the border between domestic and foreign affairs and between friends and enemies?"[2]

In China, where the leadership and citizenry alike see themselves as having only recently wrested control of their national destiny from the depredations of foreigners after more than a century of humiliation, demands by outsiders for internal change are particularly difficult to accept. Meanwhile, Americans, despite their Wilsonian impulses and self-image, also have proven ambivalent about delegating decision-making authority to international regimes such as the World Trade Organization (WTO), the United Nations, or multinational environmental regimes that may constrain their future economic or other prerogatives.

> (3) *Due to global economic interdependence and the resulting external demands, national leaders find fertile ground in their respective countries for nationalistic appeals.*

Leaders in both Beijing and Washington, especially aspiring politicians, are continually tempted to use domestic anxieties stemming from external demands to their own benefit by advocating assertive, unilateralist policies. In America, the temptation arises, in part, from a highly competitive, fragmented political system that features a continuous calendar of elections that, in turn, motivates an ongoing search by political figures and groups for issues with which to bludgeon electoral opponents. Mobilization of anxiety about external threats, real or imagined, is a cheap way to build coalitions and raise money.

In China, the temptation in part derives from the struggle for power in a system that lacks reliable and predictable mechanisms for political succession. But there are other reasons as well, one of which is that a leadership with a tenuous mandate must find ways to motivate a mammoth populace to undertake painful domestic changes while maintaining political stability and cohesion. Mobilizing anxiety about the outside world and acting as the agent by which past injustice will be redressed is one way to raise the threshold for internal pain and enhance regime support. A Chinese acquaintance, speaking about "America firster" Patrick Buchanan and his PRC analogue, Deng Liqun, commented, "You Americans have your fundamentalists and so do we." As the Chinese magazine *Strategy and Management* put it, "In the China of today, with economic reform pushing the country rapidly towards a socialist market economy, the chance of populism reemerging has certainly not diminished but has rather increased."[3] Certainly the anti-American demonstrations and violence in several Chinese cities in May 1999 in the wake of the U.S. bombing of the Chinese

Embassy in Belgrade had the effect of focusing popular attention on external events rather than internal problems, such as the potentially turbulent tenth anniversary of the June 4, 1989, violence.

At the same time that the politics of fear and nationalism has its attractions in both Beijing and Washington, it has some built-in restraints. If global markets and other countries believe that a nation's leaders are deferring tackling genuine internal problems or provoking conflict by diverting attention externally, those national leaders will pay a price through foregone investment and a declining ability to attract the support of other nations and international organizations. As we shall see, Bill Clinton unceremoniously retreated from his threats to end most-favored-nation (MFN, now called normal tariff relations or NTR)[4] status for China in 1994 for many reasons, one of which was the anticipated reaction of global financial markets, particularly the bond market.[5] That not a single traditional American ally would follow Washington's lead in so sanctioning China was another decisive consideration. In 1995 and 1996, China attempted to coerce Taipei to reduce its quest for more international breathing space by conducting missile exercises in the Taiwan Strait. At the same time, Beijing was busily reassuring both Western and Taiwan investors that its domestic reform policies had not changed and that it had not embarked down a reckless road to conflict.

Each society's leadership faces both internal and external contradictory pressures. On the one hand leaders are tempted to play the nationalism card, but on the other hand the world system will punish them if they push nationalism to the degree that global markets and investors become alarmed.

> (4) *China is a late modernizer of unparalleled scale, in many ways a growing economic, military, and political force. At the same time, however, its leaders and populace generally perceive themselves as a "victim" country—currently weak and poor and therefore entitled to treatment reflective of past wrongs and current conditions.*

The combination of perceived past injustices, current low per capita income, and high aspirations for future influence cause Beijing to come to discussions with a sense of present entitlement. Americans often come to discussions making demands.

From the American point of view, several considerations together make China different from earlier East Asian modernizers. As far as Washington is concerned, with respect to the textile industry, labor-intensive exports, nuclear weapons and related technology, and short-, medium-, and long-range missiles, China is not a typical developing country, but a force to be reckoned with. Further, American patience with the Asian development model (which includes state-directed investment, trade and investment barriers to defend local industry, and allocation of capital on the basis of personal and political, rather than economic, criteria) was exhausted by those economies in East Asia that preceded China down the road to modernization. Also, China's mere scale makes it hard to ignore inequities that were initially overlooked in earlier, and much smaller, modernizers (such as Japan, Taiwan, and South Korea). During the cold war, Americans could rationalize trade and financial inequities with the need to build a united front against the Soviet Union and its allies.

The Chinese see the present-day American impatience in a different light. They tend to see their modern history as a succession of attempts by outside powers to keep China down. Consequently America's demands for market access, a lower trade deficit, and limits on weapons exports are often viewed as changing the rules of the game in an effort to retard China's rise. The two nations' respective positions were well evidenced in the thirteen-year dispute over the terms of the PRC's entry into the WTO. Beijing demanded the more lenient entry terms of a developing country while Washington insisted that China be judged by a higher standard.

> (5) *One key to the productive management of the relationship between the United States and China is effective and secure political leadership in both nations. To that end, individuals are of enormous consequence.*

Notwithstanding the combination of globalization and domestic social and institutional fragmentation, the acts of individual leaders are not mere flotsam on the tides of history, global financial flows, and world intellectual and political currents. The teaching role of leaders—what James McGregor Burns called the transformative potential of leadership—is essential to the effective handling of the bilateral relationship.

Bill Clinton was almost one year into his second administration before he delivered a comprehensive speech (in October 1997) on China policy to the American people. Clinton's predecessor, George Bush, had a comparatively more integrated view of U.S.-China relations and certainly devoted more attention to the subject, but he, too, rarely shared his views systematically with the American people. The most notable exception was a little-publicized speech given at Yale University in May 1991,[6] long after the mass media and interest groups had seized the China policy initiative. The absence of presidential leadership simply means that diverse interest groups and the mass media fill the void. Foreign policy, one might say, abhors a conceptual vacuum.

Leadership matters in China too. Throughout the 1989–1996 period, Deng Xiaoping provided enough internal guidance to prevent the articulation of implacable hostility toward America. Yet with his health declining and a constellation of domestic opponents arrayed against him, and with his successor, Jiang Zemin, not yet secure, Deng was unable to move forward.

(6) *In the coming decades, the U.S.-China relationship will be the most enduring, broad-based foreign policy challenge that leaders in both Beijing and Washington will face.*

This will be the case for American leaders whether or not China achieves its economic and other national aspirations. For if the PRC cannot sustain fairly rapid economic growth and tolerable political cohesion, the world will face a highly nationalistic, resentful nation seeking to rationalize its failure by blaming it on the acts of others, notably the United States, and probably Japan as well. The world will be saddled with a country too weak to maintain domestic order and too chaotic to act responsibly abroad. On the other hand, if China continues to make progress, which I believe is the more likely scenario, it will demand an ever greater role in the making of global rules, while vigorously pursuing its own national agenda, one that includes significantly increasing its economic prosperity, comprehensive national power, and some form of reunification with Taiwan.

Making room for new powers in the international system has not been easy, as the nineteenth- and twentieth-century experiences with the rise of Germany and Japan amply demonstrate—although China is very different from these two nations, as is the world system into which it seeks to integrate. As the United States and other existing world powers contemplate the problems of accommodating new vigorous players, they should note that a modernized China fully participating in the global system also could constitute a powerful force to help resolve problems.

Handling the U.S.-China relationship will be no easier for Beijing. China faces the delicate problem of modifying the international order as it seeks to reassure foreign governments and world financial markets that it is responsible. Equally difficult, Beijing will face the challenge of pushing forward wrenching economic and social changes at home while achieving essential social and political stability in ways that do not outrage the rest of the world. We can expect incidents of tragic domestic violence in the future.

(7) *Finally, despite their important differences, China and the United States hold many common, as well as complementary, interests.*

The nature of these interests gives the relationship more durability than commonly is thought. That the relationship weathered four crises in the years from 1989 to 1999 and managed to move forward in the aftermath of each is cause for some hope, though not complacency.

China needs technology, capital, markets, and a sufficiently peaceful international environment that permits minimal diversion of resources to defense for at least the next decade, and probably considerably longer. America needs to sell its technology, import comparatively inexpensive goods, productively employ its capital, foster peace and stability in Asia (Korea, the Taiwan Strait, and the subcontinent), and effectively address a plethora of global issues, ranging from the spread of HIV, to the proliferation of weapons of mass destruction, to the need for peacekeeping operations. As the 1997–1999 Asian financial crisis demonstrated, the United States also increasingly needs China to be a responsible macroeconomic manager and engine of regional economic growth.

The question for the future, therefore, is this: Will our two systems build on common interests or will they allow divergent interests, the tyranny of domestic imperatives, and inevitable tensions to drive them ever further apart? Realism and prudence should guide expectations; idealism should shape aspirations.

PART I

THE FLOW OF EVENTS

TURNING POINTS

1989–2000

Around the middle of the 1990s, things became obvious for
Chinese scholars that the power structure in the post–cold war
era is *yichao duoqiang* [one superpower and several big powers].
People here [in China] realized that the leading position of the
U.S. would be unshakable and its comprehensive national power
would be unparalleled by any single country in the foreseeable
future. The U.S. has enough resources and influence to reach its
goals abroad. The only uncertainty is the will or the intention of
the U.S.

Jin Canrong, Beijing, April 2000

OVERVIEW

From the time George Bush was sworn in on January 20, 1989, until Bill
Clinton approached the end of his two-term presidency more than a
decade later, U.S.-China relations experienced four particularly tense periods during which the convergence of events, particular leaders, and international and domestic circumstances pushed the relationship in new directions. At these critical junctures, Chinese and American leaders considered
the costs of dramatically deteriorating bilateral relations and stepped back
from the precipice in order to halt the decline or move in more productive
directions. Nonetheless, each episode gave the relationship new substance
and an altered tenor.

Only through a painful, decade-long process was a new strategic foundation partially re-created, this time premised on the need for the two
countries to cooperate in the maintenance of regional stability and economic prosperity and the resolution of pressing global issues. Yet, at the
same time that they recognized the need to cooperate, each nation became
increasingly concerned about how the other would use its growing power.
And herein lies the management challenge for the twenty-first century:

how can both nations effectively manage a relationship whose hallmark is a mix of competitive and complementary interests?

The first seminal event in U.S.-China post–cold war relations was the violence in Beijing and elsewhere in China in 1989. This bloodshed changed perceptions of China in America and, before long, also changed Chinese views of the United States. George Bush and Deng Xiaoping were only able to take partially effective steps to insulate the relationship from the tragedy's fallout; each felt frustrated with the other.

The second critical moment was President Clinton's mid-1994 rejection of the link between human rights in China and MFN tariff treatment for the PRC, a linkage he had established just one year earlier.

The third turning point was the 1995–1996 Taiwan Strait military confrontation. At this point, the downward spiral in bilateral relations alarmed both Beijing and Washington to the point that they began a serious search for a more stable, strategically grounded relationship. By late 1997 the two capitals were talking about working toward a "constructive strategic partnership" in the twenty-first century. Summits in 1997 and 1998 were the immediate result of this mutual reassessment.

The final crisis considered here occurred in April–November 1999 with the coincidence of five developments: an initial failure to reach agreement on the terms of China's accession to the WTO in April; the bombing of the Chinese Embassy in Belgrade, Yugoslavia, in May; the release of a major congressional report (also in May) alleging that Beijing had been engaged in a long-term, broad, and highly successful program of espionage against the United States; a July statement by Taiwan's President Lee Teng-hui characterizing ties with the mainland as a "special state-to-state" relationship;[1] and a November bilateral U.S.-China agreement on the terms for China's accession to the WTO. The net result of these events was that both capitals quietly reduced the public use of the phrase "constructive strategic partnership," tensions in the Taiwan Strait rose, and both sought to make progress in the one area where it seemed possible—Beijing's accession to the WTO. Otherwise, both the United States and China sought to limit further deterioration and waited for an opportunity to move forward, with Beijing looking ahead to the election of a new administration in Washington—and in Taipei.

Of course a myriad other significant events affected bilateral relations during the first post–cold war decade, but the aforementioned were the hinge points. By the late 1990s these turning points had cumulatively brought the relationship to a new equilibrium, one of deep, mutual ambivalence, if not mounting distrust.

TURNING POINT ONE

George Bush Takes Office • Tiananmen • Preserving the Relationship

President George Bush closed his inaugural address by saying, "I see history as a book with many pages, and each day we fill a page with acts of hopefulness and meaning. The new breeze blows, a page turns, the story unfolds."[2] Little did he know in January 1989 how briskly the winds of Sino-American relations would blow, how fast the pages would turn, and how he would be torn between his impulse toward realism in foreign policy and his belief that "America is never wholly herself unless she is engaged in high moral principle."[3] Many things were on the president's mind that inaugural day and in the busy weeks that followed—the need for a balanced budget, the collapsing Eastern Bloc, the need to avoid conflict with an increasingly erratic Soviet Union.

Nonetheless, as Bush and his National Security Adviser Brent Scowcroft wrote nearly a decade later, the president "contemplated the possibility of a visit to China in the early weeks of the administration, and especially after one was announced for [Mikhail] Gorbachev. We wanted very much to meet with the Chinese leaders to review and enhance Sino-American relations before Gorbachev had a chance to speak with them. We anticipated that he might attempt a rapprochement between Moscow and Beijing, and would have liked to be certain it did not come at our expense."[4] However, given the press of other concerns, there seemed to be no justification for such an early trip, that is, until Japanese Emperor Hirohito died on January 7, 1989. "[T]his sad human event gave us the required opening."[5] The funeral was scheduled for February 24, and the new president arrived in Beijing the following day.

Concerns beyond Soviet diplomacy motivated the president to make his early trip to China. For one, it was thought that traveling to Asia before Europe (the reverse of what previous presidents had done) would be "a sign of priorities for the new era."[6] A second consideration was that this might be the last opportunity Bush would have to see China's aging supreme leader, Deng Xiaoping.[7] Finally, sentiment played a role as well. In a first-of-its-kind live television broadcast to the Chinese people from Beijing,[8] Bush spoke of his "homecoming" and fond memories of his days as chief of the United States Liaison Office in Beijing fourteen years earlier. Recounting that his daughter had been baptized in China's capital, he acknowledged "his general feeling of affection for the Chinese people." The Chinese interviewer, however, seemed as surprised as many Americans, saying,

"[Y]ou've decided to come to China so soon. Why now?" The president's response emphasized the need for the two nations to cooperate for global economic growth, to address global environmental issues, and to halt the spread of weapons of mass destruction: "It really has, because of China's importance and ours, a lot to do with world peace. And so, before much time went by, I wanted to reaffirm the importance that the United States places on this bilateral relationship, and I wanted to pledge to the Chinese leaders—and I've met the top four leaders in the last day and a half—that this relationship will grow and it will prosper."[9]

In a series of talks between Bush and General Secretary Zhao Ziyang, President Yang Shangkun, Premier Li Peng, Foreign Minister Qian Qichen, and Deng Xiaoping, items on the table concerned the prospects for and implications of *perestroika* under Gorbachev, the consequences of a stagnant economy in the USSR, future Moscow defense expenditures, Chinese reassurances that improved Sino-Soviet relations were not directed at the United States, and Chinese warnings to Washington to stay out of Chinese politics. Concerning the final point, Li Peng put it curtly, "To be more blunt, this smacks of interference in China's internal affairs, and we are not happy about it."[10] The point was also made by Zhao Ziyang when he said, "[I]f there are Americans who support those Chinese people who are opposed to the current policies of [our] government, they will hurt reform as well as Sino-U.S. friendship."[11]

In his talk with Deng Xiaoping, President Bush was struck by the aging leader's skepticism about the possibility of improved Sino-Soviet relations: "Mr. President, you are my friend. I hope you will look at the map to see what happened after the Soviet Union severed Outer Mongolia from China. What kind of strategic situation did we find ourselves in? Those over fifty in China remember that the shape of China was like a maple leaf. Now, if you look at a map, you see a huge chunk of the north cut away.... The strategic situation I have mentioned is very unfavorable for China.... This encirclement has continued from the Khrushchev period through Brezhnev to the present."[12]

During that February trip to China something else became apparent: an emerging contradiction between the importance the new president attached to ties with China and the moral sensibilities of the American people. In his January inaugural address he had observed that Americans were most comfortable when their foreign policy could also be viewed as one of "high moral principle." His trip to Beijing, however, inadvertently highlighted moral tensions.

Chinese astrophysicist Fang Lizhi, a well-known dissident, had been invited to a reciprocal banquet to be hosted by President Bush at the Sheraton Great Wall Hotel in Beijing, an affair senior Chinese leaders also were scheduled to attend. The dissident's name had been included on the proposed guest list sent *twice* by the U.S. Embassy in Beijing to the White House for approval. However, because Fang's name did not stand out to those scanning it back in Washington, the list was approved and the invitation was issued,[13] despite the fact that Fang's name and those of two other dissidents had been flagged by the U.S. Embassy in Beijing. After highlighting the names, however, the embassy did go on to say, "We nevertheless recommend that the three [dissidents] be invited."[14]

Predictably, the Chinese leadership wanted Fang uninvited, and the Western media viewed Fang's attendance as a moral test for the new administration. The initial Chinese position was that key PRC leaders would not attend if Professor Fang were present, since it was well known that Deng Xiaoping had a particular antipathy for Fang. Ever resourceful, the Chinese leadership unilaterally resolved the dilemma in its own way: the security services intercepted Fang on his way to the festivities and prevented him, his wife, and two accompanying Americans from attending, even though other dissidents did attend. By the time the astrophysicist's absence was noticed and understood by the American hosts, the party was over. Indeed, General Scowcroft only found out about it as he prepared for a postbanquet television interview.[15]

The White House blamed the ambassador in Beijing at that time, Winston Lord, for having put Fang on the proposed invitation list without making the controversial nature of the invitation clear to his superiors back in Washington and for thereby "irritating our [Chinese] guests."[16] This account is disputed by Lord, and the documentary record is clear that the White House was informed twice of Fang's invitation. It also is the case, however, that the embassy did recommend that Fang attend. In hindsight, the simple truth may be that the White House was not paying as much attention as it should have and that Lord, given his own personal commitment to human rights issues and symbolism, put the White House in an impossible position. Once Fang's name was on a written list, it was a no-win issue. If the White House scratched the name, that fact would become known and the administration would be accused of caving in to unjustified Chinese pressure and human rights insensitivity; if it kept the name on the list, the White House would offend China's supreme leader and undermine the principal purpose of the trip. In any event, the imbroglio contributed to Lord's alienation from the Bush administration and his increasingly critical posture thereafter. Lord was quoted a decade later in a Taiwan interview as having said, "He [National Security Adviser Scowcroft] used the Fang Lizhi incident to stab me in the back."[17]

Thus, even at this early hour in the Bush administration, clashes between the need to deal effectively with China's leaders and America's sympathy with dissent and the parallel gulf between the requirements of effective diplomacy and the reality of public relations in the global arena were glaringly evident. These contradictions were to overwhelm the relationship for much of the next decade.

Once back in Washington, the president filled out his Asia policy staff. By April he had put together a team with considerable China expertise, although each member knew that this president would be his own China desk officer. General Brent Scowcroft (who had been on the advance team for President Nixon's 1972 visit to China) was the assistant for national security affairs. China expert Richard Solomon would be assistant secretary of state for East Asia and Pacific affairs, and James Lilley (born in China) was accredited to Beijing as ambassador by mid-May. Douglas Paal, with Asia experience at the Central Intelligence Agency (CIA) and the Department of State, was appointed senior director for Asian affairs on the National Security Council (NSC). Thus, by May 1989, the United States had a president who was intensely interested in China policy, who already had a personal rapport with China's elite, and who had an experienced staff (for more, see Chapter 8). Of equal importance, he had a long-term, strategically grounded vision of China's economic, military, and global importance. Finally, American popular opinion of China was highly favorable, perhaps unrealistically so. In February 1989, public opinion surveys showed a 72 percent "favorable" perception of China (with 13 percent "unfavorable")—see table 6.

Then came the deluge—the June 1989 Tiananmen Square catastrophe in Beijing, turmoil in more than a hundred other Chinese communities, and globally televised suppression of students, workers, transients from the countryside, and Beijing citizens by the People's Liberation Army (PLA). The application of raw force was followed by a chilling manhunt for dissidents seeking to escape the public security dragnet. By July, the percentage of Americans holding a favorable view of China had dropped to 34 percent, and 54 percent now held unfavorable views (table 6). The televised violence constituted a blow to American popular perception of China from which the relationship had still not recovered a decade later. In his diary entry of June 5, 1989, President Bush noted that "[Representative Steve] Solarz on the left and [Senator Jesse] Helms on the right want us to move much more radically. Helms has always detested this relationship."[18]

The administration responded to the crackdown by imposing unilateral economic and other sanctions on the PRC and meeting with Chinese students studying in the United States. Over time, these sanctions came to be perceived by Chinese leaders and citizens alike as attempts to weaken the PRC. Deng Xiaoping and his colleagues repeatedly characterized the sanctions as a knot the Bush administration had tied and, therefore, would have to untie. Within the American government, "Tiananmen" (now global shorthand for bloodshed and repression inflicted by authoritarian governments) would soon drive a wedge between the executive and legislative branches on issues concerning China policy. This is the story to which we now turn.

President Bush and Chinese Leaders Respond to June 3 and 4

At about 9:30 A.M., Saturday morning, June 3, 1989, the Department of State's Operations Center informed Secretary of State James Baker that China was using lethal military force against demonstrators in Beijing—the carnage was being carried live on television. In the secretary's words, "Almost overnight, one of America's most striking cold war strategic successes was shaken to its core."[19] That same day in Washington, in a bit of understatement, President Bush said, "It's going to be difficult to manage this problem."[20] The problem was immediately made more challenging when it became known that Fang Lizhi had sought refuge in the American Embassy in Beijing and that the Chinese authorities were demanding that he be handed over to them, a demand no American administration could have met.

From the outset of the crisis, Bush saw his decisions on China linked in complex ways to other policy issues and domains. If he responded too softly to Beijing's crackdown, he would encourage the beleaguered communist regimes of eastern Europe and the Soviet Union to use force against their own domestic opponents, and he would embolden his policy opponents at home in America. On the other hand, if he reacted too harshly, he would feed the anti-Western nationalists and antireformist elements in Beijing and set back the process of reform that had struck him so intensely ("China has come a long way.")[21] during his February trip. Further, the president needed Beijing's assistance on other important issues, such as bringing peace to Cambodia, and he did not wish to drive China into Moscow's arms. In short, Bush had to find the delicate balance between expressing outrage and safeguarding "the underlying strategic relationship to the extent possible," as Secretary Baker put it.[22] The president also knew that China's leaders would react negatively to public castigation and that their saving face was a paramount consideration.

The president spoke with Richard Nixon at 8:00 A.M. Monday morning June 5 (see also Chapter 8), at which time the former president urged Bush not to recall Ambassador Lilley from Beijing and to "take a look at the long haul."[23] In addition to concurring with this advice, President Bush had had three policy steps in mind from the beginning of the crisis. Though the three impulses were sensible, taken together, they would prove nearly impossible to implement in the prevailing environment.

To start, the president moved to preempt popular and congressional overreaction by immediately imposing sanctions (on June 5 and June 20).[24] These included suspension of military-to-military cooperation and police equipment sales, suspension of military and high-level leadership exchanges, and the recommendation that new international financial agency loans to China be indefinitely postponed.

Second, at the same time that he imposed sanctions, the president tried to keep personal and direct channels of communication open with Beijing's leaders, particularly Deng Xiaoping. The president sought to phone Deng after the crackdown and was "rebuffed,"[25] though eventually Bush established direct contact with Deng through long and very personal presidential letters written on June 20 (answered in twenty-four hours) and July 21.[26] For many months thereafter, Bush used a "back channel" of communication with Jiang Zemin through Jiang's confidant and deputy director (later director) of the General Office of the Chinese Communist Party, Zeng Qinghong.[27]

Finally, President Bush sought to preserve his own primacy with respect to China policy. He saw this as his constitutional obligation to defend presidential preeminence in foreign policy against congressional encroachment. The day after Tiananmen, Bush made his position in this regard clear when he was asked at a press conference whether he would heed Congress's call for stronger sanctions against Beijing than those just announced: "I've told you what I'm going to do. I'm president. I set the foreign policy objectives and actions taken by the executive branch."[28]

From the opening hours of the post-Tiananmen era, therefore, George Bush was committed to a coherent but difficult-to-maintain course, a course that sought to preempt overreaction, maintain direct, personal communication with Beijing, and retain presidential control of foreign policy. A number of tensions were built into these objectives. How could Washington express outrage that would seem credible to Americans but not humiliate the Chinese leaders? The same sanctions that gained Bush credibility on Capitol Hill hampered communication with Beijing. But sanctions that proved ineffective in changing Chinese internal behavior simply fed the congressional appetite for stronger action. Furthermore, once imposed, sanctions (particularly those imposed by law) were difficult to lift, even should conditions change. Beyond sanctions, attempts to communicate personally with China's leaders seemed to critics at home to lend dignity to a leadership that, in their eyes, deserved none. The president's efforts to keep Congress on the sidelines of China policy only made Capitol Hill desire more involvement. Finally, congressmen who were genuinely frustrated by the difficulty of the situation and opposition Democrats who often were acting from partisan impulses both portrayed the president's policy as weakness in the face of callous, authoritarian rulers.

President Bush's dilemma became apparent in the second half of 1989 and in early 1990 when, for policy and parliamentary reasons, he vetoed two popular and bipartisan China-related bills. The first was a package of sanctions initially proposed in late June 1989 as part of the fiscal year 1990 Foreign Aid Authorization Bill (H.R. 2655) that later came to rest in the fiscal year 1990 State Department Authorization Bill (H.R. 1487). The proposed sanctions package codified the president's initial punitive measures of June 1989 *and added to them.* The White House resisted this legislation for several reasons, including objectionable provisions unrelated to China. However, one reason for administration opposition that did have to do with China policy was that the proposed legislation reduced the president's flexibility in foreign affairs: sanctions imposed administratively, as Bush had done, rather than mandated by law, would be easier to lift once conditions changed.

After five months of bitter negotiation, the White House and Congress agreed to provisions that allowed the president to waive the sanctions if doing so proved to be in the "national interest." However, at the last minute some non-China-related provisions were added to the bill carrying the sanctions package that were unacceptable to Bush. He vetoed it, leaving Congress with no sanctions bill at all as it adjourned in November 1989. In the end, a sanctions package was not passed and signed into law until February 1990 (PL 101-246), eight months after Tiananmen.

A second, more polarizing debate concerned the Chinese Student Immigration Bill. At the time of the events in Tiananmen, more than 33,000 Chinese students were enrolled in American institutions of higher learning (not including a large number of unmatriculated advanced scholars).[29] Many of these students and scholars protested the bloodshed publicly, some in front of the Chinese Embassy in Washington. With public security forces hunting for dissidents in China and Chinese students in America being photographed and subject to identification by PRC authorities, no American wanted to feel responsible for pushing Chinese youth back into the hands of China's police by sending them home once their visas had expired. In July, therefore, legislation was introduced in both the House (Pelosi, H.R. 2712) and the Senate (Mitchell and Dole, S.R. 358) to automatically extend the visas of Chinese students and scholars in America "without their having to register with the [U.S.] government."[30] The amendment attached to the Immigration Bill passed the Senate 97 to 0. Bush, who saw clearly the incendiary character of the Chinese student issue, particularly the arrest of Chinese students in the PRC, wrote in his July 21 letter to Deng Xiaoping, "If some way can be found to close the chapter on the students whose actions were those of peaceful demonstrators, that would help enormously.... If forgiveness could be granted to the students and, yes, to their teachers, this would go a long way to restoring worldwide confidence.... [I]t would give me the opportunity to make a statement supporting your decision."[31]

As in the case of the sanctions legislation, President Bush had anticipated congressional concern for Chinese students and had already declared that any request for a visa extension would receive "sympathetic review." Nonetheless, many in Congress argued that while the president's approach was consistent with theirs, their legislation offered greater protection to Chinese students because the students would not have to formally declare their desire to stay in the United States, thereby potentially calling themselves to Beijing's attention. Just before its adjournment in late November, Congress adopted the legislation by a vote in the House of 403 to 0. On November 30, 1989, however, the president announced he would pocket veto the legislation and, instead, implement the bill's provisions administratively. His action spawned the most bitterly contested veto fight in the Bush administration's tenure—California Republican Senator Pete Wilson even left his sickbed to fly to the Capitol and vote against the president.

In explaining his veto President Bush said, "I want to keep control of managing the foreign policy of this country as much as I can. And I didn't think that legislation was necessary."[32] As Kerry Dumbaugh of the Congressional Research Service has written, "The President was willing to prevent congressional initiatives to which he had no substantive objections."[33] In the end the White House prevailed in the Senate by the slim margin of four votes cast along party lines. What those who criticized the president did not understand was that the Chinese were more inclined to permit Chinese students to continue coming to the United States if there were no legislation—executive action is not legislation.[34] Ironically, those Chinese students in America calling for legislation were, in effect, proposing action that might deny their fellow students in China the same opportunities they had enjoyed.

The battles over the two bills produced an embittered Congress that was fracturing along party lines with respect to China policy. Other actions the president took magnified congressional (particularly Democratic) distrust. In July 1989, approximately a month after the smoke had cleared above Tiananmen, the president began to waive some economic and military-related sanctions by permitting the sale of four Boeing aircraft to the PRC. Three months later, in October, he took limited steps to revive work on the Chinese F-8 fighter aircraft upgrade project ("Peace Pearl") at Grumman Corporation on Long Island. Two months thereafter, on December 19, he waived a congressional ban on Export-Import Bank loans to firms engaged in business in the PRC and announced the export of three satellites to Beijing.[35]

Earlier that December, the president had dispatched his adviser for national security affairs, Brent Scowcroft, and deputy secretary of state, Lawrence Eagleburger, to Beijing to meet with China's senior leaders. This visit was not made public until the Americans were in Beijing on December 11—a public relations decision that in Scowcroft's words "made a mess of it."[36] Many in Congress took offense at remarks Scowcroft made while in the Chinese capital—to wit, "In both our societies there are voices of those who seek to redirect or frustrate our cooperation. We must take bold measures to overcome these negative forces."[37] For his part, General Scowcroft regrets that "none in the press saw fit to mention the highly critical comments in my toast about the Tiananmen events."[38] Although the trip was defensible in terms of keeping channels of communication open with Beijing and developing a road map out of the bilateral quagmire (see Chapter 7), it ran directly counter to the administration's declared policy of suspending high-level exchanges. As often happens in such cases, the trip's best justification could not be revealed—that it resulted in a vague understanding ratified by Deng Xiaoping that there would ensue a careful minuet of reciprocal bilateral moves. Beijing would take small strides forward and Washington would favorably respond—"the road map."[39]

For Bush, however, the December trip represented responsible policy and the prudent exercise of presidential prerogative. He put it best on December 10: "Congress jumps all over me, and the press is in a frenzy on the China trip.... I like this fight, because I'm convinced it's the right thing to do, and there's not a hell of a lot that Congress can do about it."[40]

In the end, the journey's fait accompli quality sowed further distrust in Congress and the mass media. This distrust was intensified by the revelation a few days later that General Scowcroft and Secretary Eagleburger had also visited China in early July, about a month after Tiananmen; the earlier trip had been unknown even to most of the White House staff and administration. In explaining the mid-1989 trip, Secretary Baker later remarked: "The idea was to make clear to the Chinese very privately that while their behavior was unacceptable and couldn't be ignored, the administration took no joy in imposing sanctions and was seeking ways to reconcile our estrangement. The Chinese had to be made to realize, however, that progress was impossible until they ceased their repression."[41]

By way of background on the first Scowcroft-Eagleburger trip, on June 24, Deng Xiaoping had answered George Bush's letter of June 20, saying that he accepted the president's proposal to send a personal emissary. Scowcroft knew the Chinese leadership better than any other senior executive branch official other than the president, he was authoritative, and he could make the trip without his absence being unduly noticed. Regarding his decision to send Scowcroft and Eagleburger (to represent the Department of State), the president's diary for June 24 describes his thinking: "This has been a very delicate matter—how to handle this relationship. China is back on track a little with the Soviets, and they could indeed come back in much stronger if we move unilaterally against them and cut them off from the west. Deng still worries about 'encirclement,' and so do I."[42] He concluded his entry for the day saying, "I take this whole relationship very personally, and I want to handle it [that way]."

Once in Beijing in early July, Scowcroft and Eagleburger met with Deng, among others, and the supreme leader made it clear that he felt the United States had "cornered" China during the months leading up to the June violence. He also asserted that America had been deeply involved in the disturbances and reiterated Beijing's view that how China handled its internal affairs was not a U.S. concern. Further, Deng declared that Washington's sanctions had injured Chinese dignity, and he concluded by saying that America had tied the knot and was duty bound to untie it. In response, the president's national security adviser said, "The president shares the feelings of the American people with regard to the recent events in China, but he also believes deeply in preserving the relationship between our two countries.... That has not been easy. It has not thus far been without cost, and it could, depending on events, become impossible for him. The actions taken by the Chinese government to deal with the demonstrators have produced demands by the American people and the United States Congress to take steps of our own to demonstrate our disagreement with those actions."[43]

The combination of the Scowcroft-Eagleburger trips, the president's fighting with Congress over legislation, and the modest erosion of sanctions proved a combustible mix in Washington. The president seemed to be weakening the sanctions he had imposed as Congress was locked in a struggle with him to maintain, and perhaps increase, them. He appeared to be conferring honor on those whose actions Americans found repugnant. Perhaps if the president had explained his larger strategy and rationale to Congress and to the American people, he could have created a better environment for his China policy. However, whereas the precondition for effective diplomacy with the American public is generally openness, the precondition with China in this case, as it often is, was secrecy.

Predictably, domestic political advisers urged Bush to distance himself from China policy. While this advice was understandable, without popular support on the issue, he left himself vulnerable to attacks from his opponents. The domestic political advisers prevailed, and the president's first comprehensive speech on China policy did not come until he addressed his alma mater, Yale University, in May 1991, almost two years after the violence in Tiananmen.[44] By then it was too late—there was substantial bitterness in Congress, and Democrats in and out of Congress were looking ahead to the upcoming congressional and presidential elections, when they could use the president's alleged insensitivity to human rights and his China policy to good advantage.

By early 1990 dissident Chinese students in the United States and motivated members of Congress such as California Representative Nancy Pelosi began to look for an avenue by which they could affect China policy,[45] and congressional Democrats sought a club with which to beat the Republican president. Such a weapon was readily at hand in MFN status for China. Under the terms of the Jackson-Vanik Amendment to the Trade Act of 1974, each year the president had to inform Congress of his intention to extend MFN tariff treatment to a "non-market" economy (read *communist country*); then the Congress had ninety days to reject (by majority vote of both houses) such an extension. In turn, the president could veto this congressional rejection, whereupon a veto override would require a two-thirds vote of *both* houses.

From the perspectives of Congress, the Chinese dissident students, and human rights interest groups, even if MFN tariff treatment for Beijing could not be terminated, the debate provided a highly visible podium from which to question the wisdom of the president's China policy every year and a way to deal themselves into China policy. Further, televised hearings provided opportunities for interest groups to mobilize members, and, perhaps, Beijing could be compelled to make at least a few token concessions. This was an annual opportunity that every Congress (whether controlled by the Republicans or Democrats) actively seized for the next decade.

Ironically, while the Bush administration was doing its best to insulate U.S.-China relations from the fallout of Tiananmen, the Chinese leadership viewed Washington with mounting suspicion. In a July 31, 1989, meeting in Paris between Foreign Minister Qian Qichen and Secretary of State James Baker, Qian fumed, "You know that China is not afraid of pressure. U.S. actions to pressure China have harmed China. China will not yield to pressure."[46] China's leaders, including Deng Xiaoping, accused the United States of providing much of the fuel that had propelled the 1989 antigovernment demonstrations in the first place. As Deng Xiaoping told visiting former President Nixon on October 31, 1989, the "United States was too deeply involved" in the student movement.[47] Indeed, this was the same point Deng had hinted at in his remarks to martial law troops on June 9, when he asserted that the Tiananmen incident was "the inevitable result of the domestic microclimate and the international macroclimate."[48] That China's most visible dissident, the astrophysicist Fang Lizhi, had been holed up in the American Embassy since the June crackdown (and was not allowed to leave the country until June 1990) only reinforced Chinese leaders' distrust of Washington. Moreover, this distrust was not to be found in the Chinese leadership alone—over time, it affected the Chinese intelligentsia too, precisely that segment of the society that Americans imagined themselves supporting.

Despite his disquiet with what he viewed as American encouragement of the Beijing demonstrations, Deng, like Bush, sought to insulate the relationship from the debacle at Tiananmen. In doing so, however, he faced vocal conservative opposition to continued domestic reform and to his open foreign policy. Those who had lost in the previous high tide of economic and political reform (particularly the party propaganda and organization departments and the state planning system) now saw an opportunity to regain influence, slow domestic reform, and further restrain U.S.-China relations. In the wake of the November 1989 Fifth Plenum of the Thirteenth Party Congress, party propaganda head Wang Renzhi called for a struggle against "bourgeois liberalization," a theme that even the cautious, newly appointed Party General Secretary Jiang Zemin had articulated the month before.[49] As one by one the Warsaw Pact countries broke free of the Soviet Union and established multiparty systems, China's leaders became even more wary of Washington's intentions for "peaceful evolution." The unexpectedly quick American victory in early 1991 in the Gulf War further exacerbated Beijing's sense of vulnerability.

Thus, from the earliest days after June 4, Chinese and American internal politics were on diverging paths, even though senior leaders of both countries attached great importance to sustaining ties. Deng and Bush were seen by their respective domestic opponents as soft on one another. Each hoped that the other would make some accommodation that would justify patience in the eyes of their domestic critics. As Deng Xiaoping explained to Richard Nixon on October 31, 1989, "Please tell President Bush, let's end the past, the United States ought to take the initiative, and only the United States can take the initiative. The United States is able to take the initiative.... China is unable to initiate. This is because the stronger is America, the weaker is China, the injured is China. If you want China to beg, it cannot be done. If it drags on a hundred years, the Chinese people can't beg [you] to end sanctions [against China].... Whatever Chinese leader makes a mistake in this respect would surely fall, the Chinese people will not forgive him."[50]

In Washington, President Bush (and later President Clinton), amidst increasing challenges from Congress, the mass media, and human rights interest groups, hoped in vain that some small response from Beijing would provide an opening for progress. However, such mutual accommodations would not be made in any serious way until 1996 and 1997. As James Baker put it, "For the remainder of 1989—and indeed the rest of the Bush presidency—the Chinese relationship essentially treaded water."[51]

George Bush and Deng Xiaoping were in similar predicaments. Each knew the importance of the bilateral relationship, each had been somewhat discredited by the other in the eyes of domestic opponents, and each was depending on the actions of the other in order to move forward. No one took decisive action—nor could they. Nonetheless, each leader deserves credit for keeping the relationship from degrading further and for continuing to think of it in a broad strategic framework. But, in the case of President Bush, his unwillingness to go directly to Congress and the American people with a compelling, sustained explanation of what was at stake in the relationship made his job virtually impossible. In all fairness, however, given public sentiment, ongoing Chinese actions, the media firestorm, and political partisanship, such an effort likely would have failed.

Moreover, the president had other things to think about—the collapse of the Soviet empire in eastern Europe, the Gulf War, the demise of the Soviet Union itself, and his prospects for reelection. In the grand scheme of things, preventing carnage in Europe and winning the Gulf War were interests that deserved priority, especially when progress on China policy was unlikely. One makes progress where one is able in politics. China was temporarily sinking on the American agenda.

Transition from the Bush Administration to the Clinton Presidency

While the U.S.-China relationship was, for the most part, treading water, the current of events in the rest of the world was moving swiftly. The Bush administration occupied itself with peacefully managing the process of the collapse of communism in eastern Europe and the Soviet Union—a collapse so thorough that by 1996 eleven of the twelve members of the Commonwealth of Independent States (CIS, the successor organization to the Soviet Union) had suffered anywhere from 20 to 65 percent decreases in GDP. American political currents were swift as well; the congressional elections of 1990 and the presidential election of 1992 came and went. Communism and Bush were out; democracy and Clinton were in. These developments in the United States and around the world aroused deep anxiety among Chinese leaders.

Other developments bothered Beijing as well. The union movement led by Lech Walesa in Poland was cause for alarm. That anxiety was further heightened by the fall of the Berlin Wall in November 1989, little more than two years after Ronald Reagan had stood at Berlin's Brandenburg Gate and called for Mr. Gorbachev to "tear down this wall." Most distressing of all at Zhongnanhai (the Chinese leadership's inner sanctum in the heart of Beijing) were the December 25, 1989, executions of Romanian dictator Nicolae Ceausescu and his wife. Ceausescu was Beijing's last kindred spirit in Europe, and Deng had seen him many times over the years, most recently in October 1988. Benjamin Yang recounts how Deng, Politburo members, and veteran cadres watched a videocassette recording of the Ceausescu executions in stunned silence: " 'We'll be like this,' said a voice from among the viewers, 'if we don't strengthen our proletarian dictatorship and repress the reactionaries.' 'Yes, we'll be like this,' said Deng, expressing his own opinion, 'if we don't carry out reforms and bring about benefits to the people.' "[52] With breathtaking speed, the Soviet Union's collapse culminated in Mikhail Gorbachev's declaration of an end to the USSR on Christmas Day 1991.

This history signified vastly different things in Washington and Beijing. In the United States the collapse of communism was seen as a vindication of Americans' belief in the universality of democratic values and their own persistence during the long cold war years. Moreover, in the American psyche the juxtaposition of Tiananmen and the collapse of communism everywhere except in China, North Korea, Vietnam, Laos, and Cuba transformed the PRC overnight from leading communist reformer to political atavism.

Beijing saw things in a different light. First, the regime's ability to keep the military and the Chinese Communist Party united contrasted sharply with the failed communist regimes to China's west. Further, by 1991 China's economic march forward had resumed after slow but positive growth in 1990 (3.8 percent in 1990 and 9.2 percent in 1991). Inflation had been reduced dramatically from 18 percent in 1989 to 3.1 percent in 1990. Foreign exchange reserves were rising: from $5.55 billion in 1989 to $11.16 billion in 1990 and $21.76 billion in 1991. Total foreign trade was growing at a rate of 3.4 percent in 1990 and 17.5 percent in 1991. In addition, *contracted* foreign direct investment (FDI) was expanding dramatically (rising 17.8 percent in 1990 and 81.8 percent in 1991), augmented in no small part by FDI from the rapidly democratizing Taiwan (up from US$224.26 million in 1990 to $471.89 million in 1991).

Although many inside the Beijing regime and broader Chinese populace resented the way Tiananmen had been handled and anticipated a "reversal of verdicts" on the demonstrators, China's leaders took overall satisfaction in their relative position. They were still in power and the economy was expanding; for them, political stability and economic growth were two sides of the same coin. Thus, while there had been moments of extreme anxiety among China's elite, particularly with the execution of the Ceausescus in late 1989 and the collapse of the Soviet Union,[53] Beijing did not view itself as a marginalized regime hanging on by its fingernails, though it did push very hard to break free of the sanctions and curtailment of high-level meetings initially imposed by the principal free-market democracies (G-7 nations) after Tiananmen.

These differing perceptions of China's circumstance provide the key to the next chapter in Sino-American interaction. Americans viewed China as a weakened regime that could be pushed into more humane treatment of its citizens and onto a path of democratic change. The superiority of American values (as demonstrated by the cold war victory), America's military and technological strength (as evidenced in the Gulf War), and China's growing dependence on exports to the United States in combination were perceived to give Washington tremendous leverage. In contrast, China's leaders believed that they were on the right track, and the fall of each communist regime to their west, combined with their own country's ongoing economic success, further convinced them of the wisdom, indeed the necessity, of their course. After they caught their breath in the wake of Tiananmen, Deng Xiaoping and his colleagues did not view themselves as prostrate before Washington.

It was in this setting that the 1992 U.S. presidential campaign was waged between incumbent George Bush and William Jefferson Clinton, the young Democratic challenger from Arkansas. Bush's campaign was centered on the twin issues of a slightly improving domestic economy and a record of foreign policy achievement—victory in the 1991 Gulf War (with 148 service members killed in action) and in the cold war. The Clinton campaign emphasized accelerated economic growth and job creation (with social equity), music to the ears of a population weary from lagging economic performance and the long twilight struggle of the cold war. Americans were searching for their peace dividend and looked forward to tending to domestic concerns—this was Bill Clinton's promise (see Chapter 7 for more).

Another central piece of the Arkansas governor's campaign platform was the accusation that the Bush administration was insensitive to human rights abuses around the world, most notably in China and in the former Yugoslavia. (Scenes of ethnic cleansing in Europe assaulted the American conscience on the nightly network news during the campaign.) The 1992 Democratic Party platform gave voice to both human rights aspirations and the belief that "[o]ne day [China] too will go the way of the communist regimes in eastern Europe and the former Soviet Union. The United States must do what it can to encourage that process."[54] This sounded like what in the era of John Foster Dulles in the 1950s had been called "rollback," the hope that communism could be pushed back from central Europe toward Moscow.

The 1992 campaign's dynamics of state-by-state trench warfare in quest of electoral votes led each candidate to take actions and adopt rhetorical postures that would make China policy difficult to deal with in the future. In September of that year, down by 19 percent in the national polls, President Bush made a last-ditch effort to woo voters in Texas (his home state) with a promise to General Dynamics Corporation factory workers in Fort Worth, Texas, of a contract for 150 F-16 fighters to be sold to Taiwan. Though the sale probably would have occurred eventually because of the deterioration in Taiwan's air force (and Clinton might well have promised to sell them if Bush hadn't done so), the timing of the sale was entirely driven by domestic political considerations. The Chinese were bluntly informed beforehand (including a meeting in the private quarters of the

White House) by the administration that electoral imperatives were the key consideration in the sale, not a change in Taiwan policy.[55]

In the meantime, Clinton saved some of his most incendiary rhetoric for attacks against the president's China policy, charging Bush with "indifference to democracy"[56] and having "coddled the dictators and pleaded for progress."[57] The central China policy commitment that Bill Clinton made in the election campaign was that he would find a way to link Chinese access to the American market with the improved treatment of its citizens.[58] Not surprisingly, F-16 fighter sales aside, Beijing's elite had a clear preference for Bush.

On November 4, 1992, Clinton took 43 percent of the popular vote and 68 percent of the electoral vote and immediately set about building a new administration. He was determined to focus primarily on the U.S. economy, directing only residual attention to foreign policy where he intended to emphasize increasing America's access to global markets, improving human rights in the post–cold war era, and halting the spread of weapons of mass destruction. Soon, however, he would find that in dealing with Beijing, attempts to pressure it on human rights diminished his capacity to achieve trade and nonproliferation objectives.

The Clinton Administration's Foreign Policy Objectives

During the transition to power, an American president can greatly enhance or diminish his chances for subsequent foreign policy success. In the few weeks before and after a president assumes office, he makes first impressions and demonstrates inner fortitude (or its absence) to enemies and friends alike. It is at the outset that priorities are established, institutions are organized, and personnel who will implement policy are selected (see also Chapters 8 and 9). Moreover, in dealing with foreign countries during such transitions, and especially China, one must not provide avenues by which divisions within one's own administration or between the United States and its allies can be known and exploited. From his earliest days in office, indeed even before his inauguration, Bill Clinton took steps that made the future management of U.S.-China relations exceedingly difficult. Part of the problem was that the Democrats had been out of power for twelve years and thus were wanting in recent foreign policy experience.

In November, shortly after his victory, Clinton met with George Bush and discussed China policy. Surprisingly, given his harsh campaign rhetoric, the president-elect told the press, "We have a big stake in not isolating China, in seeing that China continues to develop a market economy." This remark echoed what President Bush had been saying for more than three years and was greeted with a tentative sigh of relief by many in and outside of China.[59] At the same time, the human rights community was alarmed, and many in Clinton's own party (particularly on Capitol Hill) saw his remark as an early sign of indecision. Thus, even before his inauguration, Clinton inadvertently encouraged Beijing and anyone with an interest in China policy to push him—and push him they did.

While the administration's specific China policy was yet to be determined, Clinton did have one overriding commitment—whatever policy he pursued would have to be acceptable to Congress. He did not want to squander Capitol Hill votes that he would need for future budget and health care reform battles on China policy. Whereas Bush had a defined China policy and was prepared to fight Congress in its pursuit, Clinton had only vague inclinations and his basic definition of success was acceptability on Capitol Hill. To paraphrase a senior White House official, "From Clinton's perspective, he wanted peace with Congress and linkage could get it. [It was] a domestic issue."[60] He soon would find that getting a consensus on the Hill was difficult and that many in Congress (Democrats included) were not his allies but rather his competitors for power.

Just as one could discern George Bush's priorities from his initial personnel appointments, the bureaucratic structure of his administration, and his first trip abroad, one finds in Bill Clinton's earliest actions an indication of his priorities. The president established the National Economic Council (NEC), a new White House organization of equal rank to the National Security Council that was charged with pursuing the president's commitment to focus on the economy "like a laser" by ensuring that economic considerations were given full weight in foreign and domestic policy deliberations. The NEC was led by Wall Street investment banker Robert Rubin, who would become an effective player inasmuch as he developed closer ties with the president than most of Clinton's strictly foreign policy appointments. He would also provide the president a keen sensitivity to the powerful role of global financial markets, particularly the bond market. In the president's view, interest rates, along with public opinion polls, became key indicators of the administration's performance.[61] Rubin, with his Wall Street background, was a force within the administration who searched for a way to make the U.S.-China relationship work, for economic reasons.

The National Security Council was headed by Anthony Lake, a Mount Holyoke College professor who had briefly served in the Nixon administration (resigning in the wake of the Cambodian invasion) and subsequently in the Carter administration. Lake viewed the post–cold war era as one in which American power should be used not only to secure "realist" national interests but also to promote more democratic and humane governance around the world. Lake had never been to China, and, as he said in his first comprehensive foreign policy address delivered on September 21, 1993, at Johns Hopkins-SAIS in Washington, D.C., he considered the PRC akin to the "backlash states" of Iran and Iraq, albeit one that was seeking to liberalize economically. "[W]e may be able to help steer some of them [the backlash states] down that [democratic] path while providing penalties that raise the costs of repression and aggressive behavior."[62]

As secretary of state, the president installed Warren Christopher, a Los Angeles attorney who had once clerked for liberal Supreme Court Justice William O. Douglas. Christopher, a low-key, gentlemanly consensus builder, had been present as a young naval officer in Tokyo Bay at the time of Japan's surrender in 1945 and had served as deputy secretary of state under Jimmy Carter.[63] He vowed to get along with the president's adviser for national security affairs rather than engage in the kind of conflict he had witnessed between Secretary of State Cyrus Vance and Zbigniew Brzezinski in the Carter administration.[64] Christopher saw his principal opportunity as making a difference in the Middle East.

More than a decade earlier, in December 1978, immediately after the normalization of U.S.-China relations had been announced, Christopher had been sent to Taipei. He spoke at that time with Taiwan President Chiang Ching-kuo, explaining why Washington had established formal diplomatic relations with Beijing and informing Chiang that ties with Taipei would henceforth be "unofficial." His reception was memorable, and by his own account he was shaken. A news report described the scene as follows: "The Christopher party was met on arrival in Taipei Wednesday night by 6,000 to 10,000 angry demonstrators who hurled eggs, tomatoes, mud and rocks at the U.S. officials and smashed their automobile windshields with bamboo sticks. During their stay, a Taiwanese set himself on fire to protest the U.S. action and the newspaper *China News* said another chopped off his left index finger and wrote, 'I love my country' in blood on a piece of white linen."[65] From that time on Secretary Christopher never gave the impression that he enjoyed his China experiences much, whether in Taipei or Beijing.

As secretary of commerce the president appointed his friend and political confidant Ronald H. Brown. Ron Brown had been chairman of the Democratic National Committee during the Clinton campaign and in that role had helped purvey "red meat" denunciations of Beijing. However, at

Commerce, Brown would prove a powerful advocate for "commercial diplomacy," pushing American exports. Monitoring human rights and employment in the Anacostia section of Washington, D.C., was more of a priority for Brown than preaching about human rights in far-off Asia.[66] Similarly, at the Office of the United States Trade Representative (USTR), the president installed Mickey Kantor, a lawyer and his former campaign manager, who subscribed to the aphorism that former Ohio Governor Jim Rhodes once told me: "There are only three words in a politician's vocabulary—'jobs,' 'jobs,' and 'jobs.'"

Former Congressman Les Aspin was appointed secretary of defense. Aspin, occupied with guiding the Department of Defense through a force structure and budgetary review (the "bottom-up review"), a battle over homosexuals in the military, and arguments over the treatment of, and opportunities for, women in the armed forces, never figured prominently in China policy. Within a year he was succeeded by William Perry, who had extensive China experience, having gone to the PRC in September 1980 during the Carter administration to develop some of the earliest ties between the Chinese and U.S. military establishments. Although Perry had a highly developed and sophisticated view of China's strategic importance, he and Secretary Christopher vowed to have a cooperative relationship, and Perry carefully avoided intruding into foreign policy issues. Thus, Perry did not initially figure prominently in such matters until security and strategic issues became increasingly central in late 1993 and 1994, as concerns about North Korean nuclear development grew. In November 1993 Assistant Secretary of Defense Chas Freeman went to Beijing, and the following October the secretary of defense himself made the trip, in the process giving cabinet-level dialogue a boost and reestablishing senior-level military-to-military ties.

We should not forget the human network of personal staff and domestic advisers that Bill Clinton brought with him to the White House. Many of these individuals (e.g., George Stephanopoulos, who had been an aide to House Majority Leader Dick Gephardt, Gene Sperling, Bob Boorstin, Paul Begala, and Ira Magaziner, not to mention Hillary Rodham Clinton) saw themselves as the president's political antennae, guardians of ties to Capitol Hill, and custodians of his campaign promises, particularly his human rights commitments. Stephanopoulos, for example, is described by James Mann as "one of the [Chinese dissident] students' closest allies on Capitol Hill"[67] in the months following Tiananmen. These political advisers constantly emphasized how moving away from human rights commitments in either the former Yugoslavia or China would harm the administration's interests on Capitol Hill, among Democratic Party activists, and among the broader electorate.

Thus the seeds were sown in the early days of the Clinton administration for future dissent in Washington on China policy. The president had signaled uncertainty about his own commitments. He structured the cabinet and White House agencies so as to give great voice to the economic priority, and he staffed the economic-related agencies with close personal associates. At the same time, by appointing Lake to the NSC and Christopher to the Department of State, as well as by his choices of personal staff and political advisers, he ensured that human rights would be prominent on the agenda. In so doing the president guaranteed that he would always receive contradictory recommendations from his staff on China policy, and he was too busy and disinclined to sort it out—*until there was a crisis.* By the end of the administration's first year in office, the modus operandi was described by *Newsweek* as follows: "White House meetings were like 'college bull sessions.' Clinton seemed unwilling to set any clear objectives, and his top advisers—National Security Adviser Tony Lake, Secretary of State Warren Christopher and Secretary of Defense Les Aspin—could never agree on a course of action. Instead, Lake, who was trying to play honest broker, would present options to Clinton—who in turn became angry because he wanted consensus among his advisers. The result was more meetings."[68]

Most notably, a powerfully articulated strategic perspective was absent from this personnel mix. If the president could not provide a strategic point of view, it was incumbent upon either the adviser for national security affairs or the secretary of state to do so. When no one stepped into that role, the administration was without a means to assess competing foreign policy alternatives, credibly enunciate priorities to the Chinese, educate the citizenry, or fill the vacuum entrepreneurs in Congress were only too happy to occupy.

Nonetheless, from its earliest days, the Clinton administration knew it needed a China policy. Within eleven days of the president's inauguration, the National Security Council issued a Presidential Review Directive. This directive required the creation of an interagency working group (the Senior Steering Group, or SSG) to draft policy options and recommendations for the president before June 3, 1993, the date by which he had to inform Congress about his intentions concerning China's MFN status for the next year.

The Department of State was designated the lead agency, and the nominee for assistant secretary of state, Winston Lord (confirmed April 19, 1993), was put in de facto charge of the interagency group. Lord evinced both strengths and weaknesses in his role as head of a group composed of representatives from the NSC, CIA, Department of Defense, USTR, Department of Treasury, Department of Commerce, and the Office of the Vice President.

His strengths were considerable: having accompanied Henry Kissinger on his secret trip to Beijing in 1971 and having served as a long-time aide to Dr. Kissinger, Lord knew the intricacies of the bilateral relationship and the key Chinese personalities. Further, as the former chairman of the National Endowment for Democracy and one who had spoken out forcefully against the Tiananmen violence, his position on human rights gave him credibility on Capitol Hill. Finally, as discussed earlier in this chapter, he had been ambassador to Beijing from November 1985 until April 1989, when he left the Bush administration amidst friction over Fang Lizhi and the banquet invitation. In the new circumstances, that fight became a badge of honor for Lord.

Nonetheless, Lord had his weaknesses when it came to effectively dealing with Beijing in the post-Tiananmen context. His appointment sent a message of hostility to the Chinese leadership. Lord had written a tough piece in *Foreign Affairs* in the fall of 1989, calling the leadership "discredited" and predicting that it would not long endure—"transitional" was the word he used.[69] Thereafter, Beijing lost no opportunity to criticize Lord for his and his wife's (the author Bette Bao Lord) activism among Chinese intellectuals during his tenure as ambassador in China's capital. Lord's commitments to human rights organizations that boosted his credibility with Congress only heightened Beijing's anxiety.

Further, most of Lord's career had been spent with the Republicans, so some of the newly arrived Democrats in the executive branch saw him as an interloper, while Republicans in Congress did not completely trust him after his defection to the other side. Moreover, Lord had bureaucratic problems. His principal dilemma was that as an assistant secretary of state, he had little ability to command discipline among competing bureaucracies headed by persons who outranked him or even among his many bureau-level peers within the Department of State itself (see Chapter 7 for more).[70]

Finally, Lord was charged with developing a policy that would win consensus on Capitol Hill—this inadvertently gave the most vociferous elements on the Hill the whip hand. In the polarized setting that President Bush had left behind, those members of Congress who had endured more than three years of frustration (e.g., Senate Majority Leader George Mitchell and Congresswoman Nancy Pelosi) thought that their day for a tough China policy was at hand. They energized the process on the Hill, and getting consensus meant winning their support, or at least acquiescence. Pelosi's case was unusual: she was a very junior (first elected 1987) congressperson playing a central role with respect to a major foreign policy issue. This came about for several reasons: more senior members of the House had other concerns; Senator Mitchell supported her; her student immigration bill of 1989–1990 had almost accidentally become a cause célèbre and catapulted her into the public eye; and, finally, she deeply believed in the issue to begin with. Moreover, given that she represented the Eighth Congressional District in California, which had the highest percentage of Asian American residents (27 percent) of any district outside Hawaii, this issue made political sense for her.

It was in this setting of general Chinese distrust, bureaucratic weakness, and the need to win Hill support that Lord set about devising Clinton's *first* China policy.

TURNING POINT TWO

The Dilemma of Human Rights and MFN Linkage

From the third week of February 1993 on, the SSG's task was clear—develop an agreed-upon China policy before the June 3, 1993, deadline for the president to notify Congress of his intentions concerning renewal of China's MFN trading status. Although presidential guidance was vague, most participants assumed that unless Beijing improved its treatment of individual Chinese citizens dramatically, linkage of human rights–related conditions to the further extension of MFN was inevitable.

From February through early May of 1993, a Byzantine process of foreign policy development unfolded that involved endless working papers and meetings of departmental deputies and principals (secretary-level participants). The process was characterized by the lack of presidential involvement (until rather late), ceaseless negotiations with committed members of Congress, parallel attempts to obtain Chinese human rights concessions that would justify unconditional extension of MFN, and the development of conditions for MFN extension in the event that Beijing did not yield.[71] In tailoring conditions, Lord and the administration were looking—as President Bush had done—for a way to maintain presidential authority over foreign policy; thus they preferred an executive order to legislation. This search for conditions, however, was fatally flawed, driven as it was almost entirely by domestic politics. The search represented a failure to come to terms with the reality that the mere public articulation of such conditions would be construed in the PRC as an *ultimatum*, therefore unacceptable to the Chinese, whose national identity revolved around safeguarding national sovereignty (Chapter 6).

As the process of foreign policy development continued, government bureaucracies and particular interest groups sought to influence policy to their ends. Business interests found allies in the NEC, the USTR, the Commerce Department, the Treasury Department under Lloyd Bentsen (who had been more critical of MFN when he was chairman of the Senate's Committee on Finance),[72] and trade-related committees of the Congress. On the Hill, business interests received a sympathetic reception from the House Ways and Means Committee (Congressmen Dan Rostenkowski and free-trader Sam Gibbons) and the Senate Committee on Finance. Human rights and other interest groups who favored a get-tough approach found their avenues into the debate through the Department of State (Assistant Secretary of State for Human Rights John Shattuck), selected individuals on the National Security Council (Anthony Lake and Nancy Soderberg), highly motivated members of Congress, and some of the president's personal staff, as well as the mass media. Throughout the process Congress was energized by selective leaks from the intelligence community that fanned worries (many legitimate) about Chinese proliferation behavior[73] and by the powerful testimony of Chinese dissidents.

By early May, it was clear to Lord that the Chinese had not made the concessions (e.g., concerning prisoner releases, prisoner treatment, and cessation of jamming Voice of America broadcasts) that were needed to avoid the imposition of conditions for MFN extension. He flew to Beijing on May 3, 1993, for last minute talks but made no perceptible progress by the time he left on May 5.

Meanwhile, the Chinese were busy implementing a three-pronged strategy. The first step was to activate the American business community by holding out the lure of the China market and threatening to do business with U.S. competitors. Lucrative contracts were handed out during 1992 and the first quarter of 1993 to the Big Three auto companies, the Coca-Cola Company, ARCO, AT&T, General Electric, Motorola, and others. As a senior Chinese Foreign Ministry official put it to me with typical Cantonese directness, "The Chinese market is a big cake. Come early and you get a big piece. I hope our two countries have good relations, but it takes two to tango!"[74]

The second prong of Beijing's plan was to selectively release from confinement a few Chinese dissidents of interest to Washington.[75] Finally, Beijing made it clear that its continued cooperation on the UN Security Council (where Washington needed Beijing's help vis-à-vis the Korean nuclear proliferation problem and forging peace in Cambodia) depended on tolerably productive relations with Washington. Clearly the Chinese elite did not see itself as a supplicant to the White House, though it was willing to make some modest gestures in order to preserve China's growing economic interests, which were evident in its burgeoning $19.9 billion trade surplus with the United States in 1992.

It was in this setting that on May 28, 1993, President Clinton issued Executive Order 128590, released the required "Report to Congress Concerning Extension of Waiver Authority for the People's Republic of China," and delivered a speech in the White House Rose Garden concerning his MFN decision. The legally binding executive order established seven human rights–related factors as the conditions for extension of MFN for China beyond July 3, 1994. Failure to meet two of the conditions (pertaining to free emigration and prison labor exports) required the secretary of state to recommend to the president not to continue MFN waiver authority in mid-1994. Flexibility was built into the remaining five conditions, which pertained to the observance of the UN Declaration of Human Rights, protection of Tibet's distinctive culture, the humane treatment of prisoners, allowance of international radio and television broadcasts, and the release and accounting of prisoners held for the nonviolent expression of political and religious beliefs. The standard for determination was ambiguous: "In making this recommendation the Secretary [of State] shall also determine whether China has made *overall, significant progress*" (emphasis added).

In a single stroke, the president made what would prove to be several critical errors. First, he set the timer on a bomb that only Beijing could defuse: the Chinese would have to capitulate, or the bomb would go off. Thus, in essence, the president made himself hostage to Beijing. Second, his threat failed to take into account that he might need Chinese help on critical international issues such as the North Korean nuclear proliferation problem. Third, by publicly articulating the threat and setting a deadline, Clinton made the standard of his success the public humiliation of the PRC's leaders and the alteration of patterns of internal PRC governance—a price few nations would pay for market access, let alone one as proud as China. Fourth, he set the stage for a battle within his own administration over the primacy of economics versus human rights, although he was inclined toward the former. Fifth, the standard of compliance the president established ("overall, significant progress") was vague. This lack of clarity signaled to the Chinese that Clinton was not serious and simultaneously encouraged every relevant domestic interest group to pressure him to define the standard in a way most compatible with its own interests. Conversely, had the president established clear standards, those would have locked him into a position with little flexibility. It would not take the president and Winston Lord long to see that the concept of linkage was a course of folly.

The ink had hardly dried on the executive order linking MFN to human rights when the president began to express doubts. During a trip to Tokyo and Seoul in July 1993 he was advised about how to be effective in an Asian context from East Asians who were concerned about deteriorating U.S.-China relations. As the president's doubts grew, conflicts with Beijing multiplied. By mid-July, Winston Lord prepared a classified memorandum to the president calling for "comprehensive engagement," a policy that was approved in September and gave a name to a slow-motion change in administration policy. This change took about four years to reach the point that a Sino-American summit could be held in Washington in October 1997.

As for disputes, the second half of 1993 was the U.S.-China relations equivalent of a hellish Hieronymus Bosch painting. Washington imposed sanctions on Beijing in August for alleged missile-related transfers to Pakistan. That same month the U.S. Navy tracked and demanded inspection of a Chinese cargo ship (the *Yin He* [*The Galaxy*]) bound for Iran that U.S. intelligence agencies suspected of carrying chemical weapons "precursors" (which were not found once the ship was boarded in Saudi Arabia).[76] Also during this period, Congress expressed its opposition to Beijing as a possible site for the 2000 Olympic Games; for a variety of reasons the games were subsequently awarded to Sydney, Australia, further alienating popular Chinese feeling toward America. In the U.S. Senate, Alaska Senator Frank Murkowski proposed that the Taiwan Relations Act "supersede" the 1982 Sino-American Joint Communiqué concerning weapons sales to Taiwan, a move that about seven years later was resurrected by Senator Jesse Helms (see Chapter 8) in his "Taiwan Security Enhancement Act."[77] Had the maneuver by Senator Murkowski succeeded, it would have further weakened inhibitions on U.S. weapons sales to Taipei. Finally, in October, China conducted an underground nuclear explosion, despite President Clinton's unilateral call in July for a ban on such testing.

In the meantime, America's allies were taking full commercial advantage of the chill in Sino-American ties, leading Winston Lord to say two years later with considerable agitation, "We want European and Japanese and other help on nonproliferation, trade, or human rights. Good luck. We try very hard, they hold our coats while we take on the Chinese and they gobble up the contracts."[78] In November 1993, German Chancellor Helmut Kohl landed $3 billion in Chinese contracts, and the following April French Prime Minister Edouard Balladur visited China. Premier Li Peng told the visiting Frenchman that China planned to import $1 trillion worth of goods by the end of the century and that "France may get some of this expanded trade."[79]

Presidential doubts, a revised China policy ("comprehensive engagement"), deserting allies, an awkward and cool meeting between Presidents Clinton and Jiang Zemin at the November 1993 Asia-Pacific Economic Cooperation (APEC) meeting in Seattle,[80] and the desire for Chinese cooperation on international security issues fueled intense debate over the MFN conditions and increased presidential misgivings. These circumstances motivated many in the administration to look for the least damaging way out of the corner into which the White House and Department of State had painted themselves.

Several domestic developments set the stage for a reversal of Clinton's MFN policy. First, America's major multinational firms, the economic agencies within the U.S. government, and trade-oriented members of Congress from both parties (who traveled in record numbers to the PRC in 1993 and 1994) felt they had not been consulted adequately before the president made the initial decision in mid-1993 to link MFN to Chinese human rights. They vowed to articulate their pro-trade positions more forcefully now that a year later the issue was whether or not to deliver on the human rights–related threats.

Second, major foreign policy establishment organizations (such as the Council on Foreign Relations, of which Winston Lord had been president, and the Trilateral Commission) were criticizing the linkage policy, as was Lord himself. In a widely circulated April 1994 memo to Secretary Christopher, Assistant Secretary Lord wrote, "A series of American measures threatened or employed, risk corroding our positive image in the region, giving ammunition to those charging we are an international nanny, if not bully. Without proper course adjustments, we could subvert our influence and our interests."[81]

Finally, by spring 1994 even human rights organizations and Chinese dissidents in the United States were reassessing whether impoverishing Chinese workers through trade sanctions would promote people's rights in China. The respected Chinese dissident Liu Binyan was asked by former U.S. Ambassador to the United Nations Jeanne Kirkpatrick whether taking MFN away from China would encourage greater respect for human rights in the PRC. Liu's confused reply was telling: "Maybe we can find some middle way here, or some conditions on the MFN to make it renewed or just—I don't know how to—how to deal with that."[82]

In this chaotic state of affairs, Secretary Christopher traveled to Beijing via Australia (where Foreign Minister Evans publicly broke with Washington over China policy) and Tokyo (where he received no support from Prime Minister Hosokawa). His March 11–14, 1994, stay in Beijing was nothing short of an unproductive embarrassment, during which Clinton reportedly said, "What the hell is Chris doing there now?"[83] Consequently, control over China policy was effectively removed from the Department of State and from the SSG that Winston Lord had chaired since the administration's opening days; it now became the responsibility of a joint NSC/NEC team headed by Anthony Lake and Robert Rubin. In this arena, policy discipline could be more adequately maintained, and the influence of economic and strategic perspectives was greater than in the Department of State.

While Washington's strategy was unraveling, Beijing methodically exploited the openings. The PRC's relatively closed and hierarchical foreign policy decision-making process made it fairly easy to reach consensus and conceal any internal frictions that may have existed. More fundamentally, there was virtually no Chinese constituency for capitulation to American demands. With Deng Xiaoping's health deteriorating and succession politics underway, weakness in the face of American threats was not the way to achieve political ascendancy. Even intellectuals (who many Americans believed stood to gain from U.S. human rights pressure) could not support tactics that would only make their lives more difficult and their nation weaker. The only discernible internal constituencies urging any measure of accommodation upon Beijing were local governments and exporters in the PRC. They subtly expressed their hope that a resolution could be reached short of reducing their exports to the vast American market.

The essence of Beijing's strategy was to push the "big cake" (the Chinese market) under American noses. In April–May, Vice Premier Zou Jiahua came to the United States to attend Richard Nixon's funeral and to talk with President Clinton; he had a list of goods to be purchased if relations were good.[84] Simultaneously, Beijing nuzzled up to U.S. economic competitors in Japan and western Europe and sought to ensure that no other major strategic or economic player would join Washington were MFN to be withdrawn. The key to the Chinese strategy was to isolate America from its traditional allies. As one Chinese academic put it, "We welcome more 'nos' from Japan to the United States so China can align with other countries against the United States."[85] The Chinese calculated that if they took a harder line against Washington, American groups supporting a dissolution of the link between MFN status and human rights would be energized. Beijing believed that interest groups in the United States would pressure the president, and Chinese leaders had confidence in the president's inconstancy.

After one long year of struggle over the China MFN policy issue and with the deadline for a final decision at hand, at 5:10 P.M. May 26, 1994, President Clinton entered the White House press briefing room to make his announcement—making changes in his remarks right up until delivery. There he announced an end to the linkage policy he had proclaimed 363 days earlier. Despite some cosmetic, last-minute concessions from the Chinese, there was little to disguise the defeat:

> The Chinese did not achieve overall significant progress in all the areas outlined in the executive order.... The question for us now is ... how can we best advance the cause of human rights and the other profound interests the United States has in our relationship with China. I have decided that the United States should renew Most Favored Nation trading status toward China.... I am moving, therefore, to delink human rights from the annual extension of Most Favored Nation trading status for China.... I believe the question, therefore, is not whether we continue to support human rights in China, but how we can best support human rights in China and advance our other very significant issues and interests. I believe we can do it by engaging the Chinese.... We will have more contacts. We will have more trade. We will have more international cooperation. We will have more intense and constant dialogue on human rights issues.[86]

Such was the outline of "comprehensive engagement."

The decision to reengage China elevated economic and strategic considerations among the administration's priorities, but clearly focused on the former. However, the bilateral relationship would not be on relatively more durable footing until security considerations were elevated further, in Beijing as well as in Washington. This brings us to the third turning point in the post–cold war evolution of Sino-American ties: the July 1995—March 1996 confrontation in the Taiwan Strait. This friction reminded both sides that the U.S.-China relationship concerned more than trade and human rights. It is a relationship that, first and foremost, is about war and peace.

TURNING POINT THREE

The 1995–1996 Taiwan Strait Confrontation and Its Aftermath

The protracted Taiwan Strait missile exercise confrontation that culminated in the United States dispatching two aircraft carrier battle groups (sixteen ships) to the area near Taiwan in March 1996 was the next important episode in post–cold war U.S.-China relations. The speed with which events drew in the United States had a sobering effect on Beijing, Washington, and some quarters of Taipei as well. As then Secretary of Defense William Perry said, "We realized that things, if not attended to, could go quickly and seriously wrong."[87] This is a story of face lost in both Beijing and Taipei at the Clinton administration's hands, mutual misjudgments about reactions in Beijing, Taipei, and Washington, and divergent domestic politics and core interests in the three capitals. Taiwan had been the key stumbling block in U.S.-China relations from the beginning of the cold war through the 1970s, but it had temporarily receded as a prominent irritant after late 1982. In the mid-1990s the issue once again surged to the top of the Sino-American agenda, and it remains the most dangerous flashpoint in U.S.-China relations as we enter the twenty-first century. In order to understand the crisis, one needs some background.

In Taipei, from 1993 to 1995, President Lee Teng-hui was looking ahead to his presidential election campaign of 1996, from which he hoped to emerge as Taiwan's first president to be elected by universal suffrage, indeed, the first Chinese head of government to be so elected. Lee had long recognized the degree to which his constituents chafed under their isolation from the formal institutions of the international community at Beijing's hands—a deep resentment he shared. He was determined to break out of this imposed isolation through continuing and accelerating "flexible" and "vacation" diplomacy,[88] a technique whereby he and senior Taiwan officials seized any opportunity for travel and participation in multilateral organizations and events that would confer the appearance of officiality and international standing on Taipei. In 1994 and 1995, he visited a number of Southeast Asian countries and two Middle Eastern nations. President Lee also sought UN General Assembly membership for the island,[89] a futile effort given Beijing's Security Council veto. Should this latter attempt fail (which everyone including President Lee assumed would be the case), he would at least try to gain admittance to the functional organizations affiliated with the United Nations and other international bodies.

As a gambit in travel diplomacy, Taipei requested State Department permission for President Lee to spend one night in Hawaii during a May 4, 1994, refueling stopover en route to Central America and Africa. The State Department's reluctance to accommodate Lee in part derived from the fact that the White House already had its hands full with the fight with Beijing over MFN linkage and did not need more problems. Indeed, Lee's request struck some observers as timed to further complicate the Washington-Beijing relationship.

After embarrassing, friction-laden exchanges between Washington and Taipei, President Lee was not permitted to leave the airport, though he was free to deplane at a "dingy transit lounge at Hickham Air Force Base."[90] The State Department's fear was that President Lee might use a longer stay to give the appearance of officiality to U.S. relations with Taiwan—a fear borne out in his subsequent 1995 visit to Cornell University. Reportedly fuming in a sweater and slippers onboard his 747, President Lee refused to deplane and met the head of the American Institute in Taiwan, Nat Bellocchi, on board saying, "I can't get too close to the door of the plane, I might slip and enter America."

Although the State Department's decision represented an effort to reassure Beijing of the unofficiality of ties with Taipei, it appeared to many on Capitol Hill and elsewhere to be an overzealous, degrading, even supine, implementation of policy. The incident motivated Congress to become more involved in China policy, encouraged Taiwan (particularly the president's office and the Nationalist Party) to lobby Congress, contributed to an upgrading of relations with Taiwan later in the year, and ultimately forced the White House to allow a far more problematic trip to upstate New York in mid-1995. The incident in Hawaii became even more damaging in its retelling: eventually it became an accepted "fact" that the State Department would not even let President Lee off the plane—no way to treat a long-time friend of America, thought most on Capitol Hill. A furious Assistant Secretary Winston Lord, later testifying on the Hill, had the following exchange:

NEW YORK CONGRESSMAN GARY ACKERMAN: "He couldn't get off the plane!"

LORD: "He could. That's like the Energizer Bunny; we cannot stamp out that false rumor."[91]

More important, President Lee was understandably offended by his treatment; he not only got angry, he vowed to get even. Subsequently, in

1994 the public relations firm of Cassidy & Associates, already on retainer ($125,000 per month) by the Taiwan Research Institute (closely associated with the Kuomintang [Nationalist Party or KMT]), was given a grant of $2.5 million from the "Friends of Lee Teng-hui."[92] Liu Tai-ying, who then managed the KMT's economic enterprises and, like President Lee, is also a graduate of Cornell University, reportedly arranged for this money, a principal purpose of which was to obtain a visa for Lee Teng-hui to go to Cornell University for an alumni reunion. (Lee had received a Ph.D. in agricultural economics there.)

As this process was unfolding, a political earthquake hit Capitol Hill. In the off-year election of November 1994, both Houses of Congress emerged from the contest in Republican hands, something that had not happened since 1954. With the Democrats no longer dominant on Capitol Hill, and with the influx of new activist conservative members of Congress, a number of things occurred. First, Bill Clinton began to move toward the center of the American political spectrum, hoping to occupy the middle ground being abandoned by a right-leaning Congress that had just been elected and the left wing of his own Democratic Party—this process was called "triangulation." On the Hill, key committee chairmanships switched hands. North Carolina Republican Jesse Helms became chairman of the Senate Foreign Relations Committee (see Chapter 8). Ben Gilman of New York (who had traveled to Hitler's Germany in 1933 with his father and remembers the storm troopers to this day)[93] became chairman of the House International Relations Committee. Douglas Bereuter of Nebraska—a serious man who admits he is "interested in legislation"[94]—became chair of the Asia and Pacific Affairs Subcommittee. The new chair of the International Operations and Human Rights Subcommittee was Christopher Smith (see Chapter 8), who fiercely opposes abortion and is committed to expanding religious freedom and political rights around the world. These new Republican committee chairs were manning key legislative gates in the congressional foreign policy process: several came to their jobs already highly skeptical of, if not hostile to, the PRC. In addition, the new Congress was younger and much more inexperienced in foreign affairs than its predecessor. As Chairman Gilman himself noted, "[O]ne-half of the Congress has less than four years of institutional memory and little experience in foreign affairs."[95]

As 1995 began, therefore, President Clinton was trying to regain popular standing after his party's congressional defeat, and the political coloration of Congress had changed in ways that made the Hill even more receptive to Taiwan's concerns than usual. Now there was a truly partisan desire to tar Bill Clinton (who had flip-flopped on MFN) with the "soft on China" epithet that he had so effectively hurled against George Bush in the 1992 presidential campaign. And finally, Bill Clinton was getting tired of having to retreat in the face of Chinese demands, as he had done the previous spring on MFN.

In this setting, Congress and its committees went to work in January, as did the Taiwan lobbying machine. In March, the Senate Foreign Relations Committee unanimously approved a nonbinding resolution declaring that Taiwan should be given a seat in the United Nations; Speaker Newt Gingrich was on record, the month before, as saying that the people of Taiwan "have every right to be in the United Nations."[96] Since the United Nations is an organization composed of sovereign states, this would have constituted a fundamental shift in American policy had it been implemented. By May 1995, the House International Relations Committee sought to amend the Taiwan Relations Act to strengthen weapons sales to Taiwan and endorsed legislation declaring Tibet to be an occupied sovereign country,[97] contrary to both U.S. policy and the policy of every other nation. Also in May, by votes of 390 to 0 in the House and 97 to 1 in the Senate, Congress (H. Con. Res. 53) called on President Clinton to grant Lee Teng-hui a visa to visit Cornell University.

Despite Secretary Christopher's having said in February that such a trip would be contrary to U.S. policy,[98] and despite the secretary's having come very close in April to assuring Foreign Minister Qian Qichen that Lee would not be given a visa,[99] at the president's direction, the State Department announced on May 22 that a visa would be granted President Lee. Doing so ran against the State Department's own February testimony to Congress in which Winston Lord had declared that such an action would "reverse the policies of six administrations of both parties."[100] The president's decision followed a White House meeting with Senators Robb, Nunn, Lieberman, and Breaux on May 18, at which Robb had "complained that the administration was still refusing to grant Lee a visa to visit Cornell."[101]

The Chuck Robb–Bill Clinton connection calls for elaboration. Regarding their May 18 meeting, Senator Robb later said, "I told him [the president] we ought not to permit China to determine the visa policy of the United States.... Within minutes, it was clear that Clinton agreed."[102] Clinton and Robb had traveled to Taipei together for the National Day celebrations of 1985, as governors of Arkansas and Virginia, respectively. As Robb later recounted, "The President and Hillary and Lynda [Robb] and I had been to Taiwan at least once together as governors, and he was sympathetic to my suggestion [to grant Lee a visa]."[103] Indeed, prior to becoming president, Clinton traveled to Taiwan at least four times. (Over the years Taiwan has been meticulous in cultivating relationships with emerging American political leaders.)

Bill Clinton made the visa decision for three reasons. First, he saw no way to explain denying the president of a democratizing, friendly society permission to attend a private function at his alma mater. Second, the president was approaching his annual MFN fight and did not need added trouble in Congress over China. Finally, the margins of vote on House Concurrent Resolution 53 were so large that if he resisted, Congress might pass *legislation* (as opposed to a resolution) that would be even more damaging to the Sino-American relationship.

Whereas Americans can look at the preceding sequence of events and understand it as the incremental, unpredictable outcome of unanticipated electoral changes, the interplay of strong and weak personalities without the benefit of historical understanding, effective lobbying by Taipei, and domestic political calculations, Beijing saw it in a quite different light. It resembled a premeditated plot, a sequence of events that began with President Bush's sale of 150 advanced jet fighters to Taiwan more than two years earlier and continued with the upgrading of U.S.-Taiwan relations (the Taiwan Policy Review) in the fall of 1994.

Further, Beijing perceived the moves by Washington and Taipei as having taken place against the backdrop of its own flexibility and tolerance in the preceding period. In January 1995, Jiang Zemin had issued his "Eight Points" concerning Taiwan policy,[104] after having engaged in a tough internal debate with his own military over how flexible to be with Taipei. From Beijing's point of view, Jiang's Eight Points were a moderate call for the PRC and Taiwan to work toward a formal cessation of hostilities on the basis of a "one China" concept; Jiang, in part, stated that such consultations would be "on an equal footing." Moreover, Jiang's statement had followed earlier agreements whereby Taipei was able to remain active in the Asian Development Bank (admitted March 1986 as "Taipei, China"), a regional organization of which the PRC was a member nation, and to participate in the Olympic Games (1981) under the rubric of "Chinese Taipei Olympic Committee."[105] Indeed, with Deng Xiaoping's approval, Beijing had agreed to hold a senior-level cross-strait dialogue with Taipei (the Wang Daohan—Koo Chen-fu Talks); the first session was held in Singapore in April 1993.

It appeared to Beijing that its past flexibility had been repaid with moves by Taipei (and Washington) designed to further separate Taiwan from the mainland. In 1993–1994 Lee Teng-hui intensified efforts to gain

UN membership for Taiwan and continued "vacation diplomacy" with visits to the Philippines, Indonesia, and Thailand. In addition, in September of 1994 the United States modestly upgraded its treatment of Taiwan.[106] In April 1995, Lee effectively rejected Jiang's Eight Points by demanding that as a precondition to talks, Beijing drop its threat to use force—a condition no one in Beijing could accept for fear that the threat of force alone "deterred" Taipei from declaring independence immediately. Finally, as we have seen, early 1995 saw a spate of U.S. congressional resolutions and initiatives that brought into question Washington's prior agreements with Beijing concerning Taiwan.

The view from Capitol Hill was different. Congress was full of new members for whom talk of the "Shanghai Communiqué"[107] or a "one China" policy was ancient history, unfamiliar, or irrelevant given Taiwan's democratization. Simultaneously, voices in Beijing that momentarily had been stilled when Jiang issued his Eight Points, particularly the military, grew shrill in the wake of Bill Clinton's reversal of policy concerning the Lee visa. They argued that the dialogue approach with both Washington and Taipei was simply encouraging ever bolder departures from the status quo.

When the State Department granted a visa to Lee, Jiang Zemin's capacity to bear the political weight of critics at home was nearing the breaking point. That breaking point was reached when President Lee Teng-hui delivered his speech at Cornell on June 9, 1995. From Jiang's viewpoint, Washington had cut his political feet out from under him. As one extremely senior Chinese leader told a delegation of which I was a member (and I paraphrase), "The U.S. says that it wants to see negotiations and a peaceful settlement [of the Taiwan issue]. But I will spare you the diplomatic jargon and say frankly: although this is what you say, behind [our backs] you say the contrary. Americans say 'one China policy,' but actually ..."[108]

Opponents jockeying for advantage in the post–Deng Xiaoping succession had found an issue to be exploited, just as Bill Clinton had sought to capitalize on his characterization of George Bush as "coddling" Chinese dictators. National People's Congress (NPC) Chairman Qiao Shi, a rival to President Jiang, and apparently Politburo member Li Peng as well,[109] wielded the club of "soft on Taiwan" against Jiang. Further, the Chinese military, as the institutional repository of China's reunification aspirations, wanted bigger budgets and saw this as a chance to improve its case in that regard. Hot rhetoric, such as the following from Taiwan Democratic Progressive Party legislator (and former American professor) Parris Chang, stoked Beijing's hardliners: "We are institutionalizing our independence and the PRC is going to have to accept this reality."[110]

Following Lee's visit to the United States, Beijing launched a multidimensional response. First, already-scheduled (for the second half of 1995 and early 1996) military exercises near the Taiwan Strait were expanded and what the Chinese termed "missile tests" (aimed at two separate ocean impact areas) were included, along with mock beach landings. The first missiles flew during the week of July 21–28, 1995. About one month prior to this, on June 16, 1995, Beijing recalled its ambassador in Washington (Li Daoyu) and was in no hurry to approve the dispatch of former Tennessee Senator James Sasser to Beijing as Washington's new ambassador. (The approval was not obtained until September). Lastly, Beijing began to press for guarantees that Lee Teng-hui would not again visit the United States and that Washington would observe the one-China policy.[111] Over time, such assurances were given to various degrees and in various ways: Washington announced that possible future visits would be "rare, unofficial, and for a private purpose";[112] presidential letters were written to Jiang that have not been made public; there were conversations between the two presidents; a public statement was delivered by the secretary of state in 1998; and President Clinton while in Shanghai (June 30, 1998) said, "We don't support independence for Taiwan, or two Chinas, or one Taiwan–one China. And we don't believe that Taiwan should be a member of any organization for which statehood is a requirement." The bulk of these assurances, incidentally, were twenty-seven years old—Henry Kissinger had provided most in July 1971 during his first (the secret) trip to the PRC.[113]

An inaccurate image of the United States, its leadership, and the will of its citizenry also fed the hard-line approach in Beijing. The dominant view in Beijing was that Americans were preoccupied with domestic economic considerations and social problems and that Bill Clinton was too politically weak to allow any American blood to be shed abroad. One senior Chinese diplomat put it to me this way in August 1995, "It is bullshit that the U.S. will intervene. You did nothing in 1954 and 1958, Quemoy and Matsu, and you are doing nothing in Bosnia. This government and this president will not react. You are bluffing."[114] This mistaken view was so strongly held that Beijing did not attach much significance to the December 19, 1995, "passage of the aircraft carrier Nimitz and four escort vessels through the Taiwan Strait ... ostensibly to avoid 'bad weather,' "[115] the first such passage since 1979.

In early March 1996, Beijing announced a second set of tests and exercises: missile tests from March 8 to 15 directed toward offshore impact areas quite near Taiwan and additional live-fire exercises in the March 12–25 period. These missile tests and exercises coincided with the March

23 presidential election on Taiwan; they effectively closed large areas of international waters, created turmoil in Taiwan's financial markets, and drove capital abroad. Taipei's foreign exchange reserves fell 8.4 percent in March and the Taiwan government was forced to prop up the stock market with $3 billion.

In response, Washington took a number of steps, including issuing a White House statement on March 7, 1996, (already the 8th in Beijing) calling the Chinese military moves "reckless and provocative."[116] Further, after a meeting with Vice Foreign Minister Liu Huaqiu (described shortly) failed to halt the threats, the Pentagon disclosed on March 10 that President Clinton had ordered the dispatch of two aircraft carrier battle groups (the first of which was the "Independence," a name that carried unwanted connotations) to the waters off Taiwan; the vessels did not enter the Taiwan Strait itself. By this point, the popular press in Asia and in the United States was carrying headlines suggesting that conflict was likely. While neither Beijing nor Washington anticipated actual fighting,[117] both were very disturbed that relations could deteriorate so dramatically and rapidly.

Fortuitously, Chinese Vice Foreign Minister and Director of the State Council's Foreign Affairs Office Liu Huaqiu was in Washington as the missiles began to fly, and both sides seized the opportunity to talk. On the evening of March 7, Secretary of Defense Perry (along with Secretary of State Christopher and NSC head Lake) met Liu in the secretary's dining room in the Department of State, and Perry was "about as blunt as they come in contemporary diplomacy." There would be "grave consequences" if PRC weapons hit Taiwan.[118] Perry was very explicit: "As a former artillery officer, I understand very well, and the PLA understands very well, the symbolism of 'bracketing' a target. And as a technologist, I understand the very real possibility that a missile guidance system can malfunction."[119] Anthony Lake, Liu Huaqiu's nearest analogue in the U.S. government, met the next day with him in a northern Virginia retreat, and they "let their hair down."[120] Out of this exchange came a decision to invigorate engagement and to initiate a "strategic dialogue." Liu made it clear that cross-strait talks between Beijing and Taipei (suspended in mid-1995 in reaction to the Lee visit) could not be resumed until Taiwan had accepted the one-China principle. Mr. Lake decided to make his first-ever visit to the PRC during this period.

Following Lake's July visit to the PRC, the two governments announced an agenda of high-level exchanges that involved Secretary Christopher, senior arms control officials, and military personnel. His visit to China led Lake to a number of conclusions that he shared with me, among others. He found that one could not expect much from senior Chinese leaders unless one treated them with respect and spoke with them directly—face mattered. Second, China's economic transformation was truly phenomenal. Thus Beijing couldn't be pushed around. Finally, before issues could be effectively addressed with the Chinese, relations had to be put into a larger, strategic framework.[121] These were sound judgments, even though they came three and one-half years late.

The Taiwan Strait confrontation of 1995–1996 made clear to both governments the danger of mismanaged U.S.-China relations and the capacity of Taiwan to take actions that can produce Sino-American conflict, while underscoring the need for a strategic component to ties and ongoing discussions between each nation's senior leaders. Lack of familiarity breeds contempt and dangerous misjudgments about mutual intentions. Moreover, the tensions made the administration realize that it needed to be proactive in explaining its China policy to the American people, the mass media, and Capitol Hill.

Many in the executive branch reached one further conclusion: Taipei would not be particularly respectful of U.S. interests in its search for "international space." Indeed, a disturbing undercurrent could be discerned in the following remarks by one senior Taipei official in mid-1996: "No one else could achieve this [the congressional votes supporting a visa for President Lee], not Israel, not Britain! Clinton was under a lot of pressure ... The PRC, like us, read about it [Clinton's decision to grant the visa] in the papers."[122]

Consequently, on May 17, 1996, Secretary of State Christopher delivered an address in New York City before the National Committee on U.S.-China Relations and other organizations that, with remarkable durability, provided the China policy framework for the remainder of the first Clinton term and the entirety of the second.

> The United States and China share many interests that can only be served when our two countries deal constructively and openly with each other.... On some critical issues, we have deep differences. Our focus must be on the long term and we must seek to resolve our differences through engagement, not confrontation.... [T]he time has come to develop a more regular dialogue between our two countries. Holding periodic cabinet-level consultations in our capitals would facilitate a candid exchange of views, provide a more effective means for managing specific problems, and allow us to approach individual issues within the broader strategic framework of our overall strategic relationship.[123]

Two and a half years after the administration had adopted "engagement" as a concept, Christopher systematically defined it for the American people. Unfortunately, the president's own comprehensive statement was not to come for about another year and a half in a speech delivered on the eve of Jiang Zemin's fall 1997 visit to the United States.

Robert Dole, President Clinton's Republican presidential opponent in the November 1996 elections, chose not to seriously challenge the new formulation of China policy; indeed, he broadly concurred, though he did argue for more support for Taiwan, including missile defenses. Once the general election was out of the way and Bill Clinton had been reelected to a second term with a 49 percent plurality, he met with President Jiang at the APEC meeting in Manila on November 24, 1996. There they agreed, in principle, to a 1997 summit meeting in Washington (which occurred in October 1997 and went smoothly) and a presidential visit to China in 1998 (which occurred in June 1998 and also was successful). These are stories to which we return in future chapters.

One additional observation is important in light of subsequent developments involving Taiwan. Because the Clinton administration viewed Lee Teng-hui's pressure to go to Cornell as provocative and his speech there as unnecessarily inflammatory, the administration went to considerable lengths to reassure Beijing in the visit's aftermath. In August 1996, Secretary Christopher met Vice Premier and Foreign Minister Qian in Brunei and gave him a letter from President Clinton to President Jiang, inviting the Chinese leader to Washington and articulating principles very close to what later became known as the "Three No's."[124] In short, Taipei's efforts to end-run the administration by going through Congress could, and did, produce results Taiwan does not savor, as would be seen again in the summer of 1999. Indicative of the dilemma that the United States faces, however, it was the attempt by Beijing and Washington to develop a "constructive strategic partnership" in 1997–1998 that was part of the motivation for Taipei to seek firmer defense commitments from Washington in 1999. This is the story to which we now turn.

TURNING POINT FOUR

The April–November 1999 Convergence of Domestic and International Events

The most important outcome of the new strategic dialogue and summitry was that at their October 1997 meeting Presidents Clinton and Jiang issued a "Joint Statement" that committed both nations "to build toward a constructive strategic partnership" in the twenty-first century.[125] While spelling out the content of "constructive strategic partnership" was left for the future, the slogan nonetheless conveyed the sense that the United States and China shared more interests than divided them and that the security dimension of the relationship was being taken seriously. This spirit carried through President Clinton's June 1998 summit trip to the PRC. But soon after the mid-1998 summit a number of developments at home and abroad worked together to substantially delegitimize the concept of "constructive strategic partnership" in *both* nations.

Nineteen ninety-eight ended and the new year began with the Chinese leadership worrying that the cumulative effects of a lagging domestic economy (seen in sustained deflation, a dangerously weak banking system, sagging economic growth, softening exports, and mounting unemployment), sporadic unrest in rural areas, endemic corruption, five impending sensitive anniversaries (the most worrisome being the tenth anniversary of Tiananmen), and a somewhat emboldened dissident community in the wake of Bill Clinton's visit could precipitate domestic social and political instability. To prevent such instability, the regime began a systematic campaign to lock up potential political organizers, particularly members of a nascent political party called the China Democratic Party (established June 25, 1998).

Reflective of the human rights situation in China in 1999, in April Washington again sought a resolution condemning Beijing's human rights practices from the UN Human Rights Commission in Geneva. But the U.S. administration could not get a single additional country to cosponsor the resolution, and delegates reportedly burst into applause when the vote against Washington was announced.[126] In contrast, the year before, with summit diplomacy, Washington had eschewed seeking such a resolution. The 1999 attempt had more to do with the administration's efforts to calm roiled congressional waters and to satisfy restive human rights groups than it did with any realistic assessment that the resolution would be adopted. The attempt did, however, strengthen the growing chorus of anti-American voices in the PRC.

Another systematic crackdown, this on members of a very large quasi-religious meditation organization of citizens called the Falun Gong, also hurt Sino-American relations. More than ten thousand members of the Falun Gong, most well known for its organized morning physical exercise programs, had managed to surround Zhongnanhai on April 25, 1999; its leader, Li Hongzhi, was ensconced in New York City, seemingly leading the movement over the Internet. By quietly and peacefully surrounding the leadership compound in Beijing, the demonstrators were expressing their dissatisfaction with local authorities who were opposed to the group.[127] The public security forces and the elite were shocked that all their domestic intelligence capabilities had not forewarned them of a demonstration of such magnitude at the very seat of Communist Party power. In the United States, the net effect of this repression was to further weaken the notion that engagement with China was producing human rights change in the PRC and to raise the question of how one could have a partnership with a country that, in the words of former CIA Director James Woolsey, locks up "middle-aged people who like to do breathing exercise."[128]

The second stream of events that helped precipitate a reassessment by both capitals of the U.S.-China association were developments in the Federal Republic of Yugoslavia (FRY). There, in February–March 1999, ethnic cleansing by Serbs of Albanians in Kosovo Province generated pressure among America's European NATO allies and Washington to somehow intervene to stop the actual and anticipated carnage. Because Beijing and Moscow saw the violence in Kosovo as a domestic (as opposed to international) conflict, they were unwilling to support UN-sanctioned intervention, thereby encouraging the United States and its appalled European allies to turn to NATO as the instrument of intervention. On March 24, after the mid-March collapse of the Rambouillet Peace Conference in France, NATO began bombing targets in the FRY without UN authorization in an attempt to force Yugoslav President Slobodan Milosevic to stop the ethnic cleansing by Serbs.

The intervention fanned Beijing's fears that a resurgent United States was putting humanitarian intervention above the traditional concept of state sovereignty and that it planned to use its bilateral security alliances as its preferred tools. Indeed, in a speech in Chicago on April 22, British Prime Minister Tony Blair did establish this as his doctrine.[129] The Chinese could see such a doctrine being applied to future secessionist movements in their own country—that is, in Taiwan, Tibet, and Xinjiang.

Even more worrisome to Beijing than the allied military campaign waged against the FRY from March 24 to June 20, 1999, was the fact that there were *no* American combat casualties in the war itself (though two helicopter pilots died in a training mishap in Albania). NATO waged its war exclusively from the air. The idea that the United States and NATO could intervene in the internal affairs of another country outside the area of the North Atlantic Alliance itself, circumvent the United Nations (where China had a veto), and do so with virtually no casualties, led the Chinese to reassess both their own military vulnerability and the need for a faster pace of military modernization; to their dismay, it appeared that their armed forces were even further behind the Americans in 1999 than they had been in 1991 at the time of the Gulf War.

The third stream of events concerned the April visit of Premier Zhu Rongji to the United States and Beijing's hope to reach an agreement on China's accession to the WTO. As Zhu explained to a congressional group, which I accompanied to Beijing on the eve of the premier's U.S. visit,[130] he faced domestic opposition to his trip because of both the economic concessions he was proposing and widespread displeasure in China with the ongoing Kosovo intervention. Nonetheless, after considerable debate, Jiang Zemin ordered that the trip go forward.

On April 7, 1999, just before the premier's arrival in Washington, President Clinton delivered a comprehensive address on China policy, suggesting that a WTO accession deal was imminent. It soon came to light that Beijing had made unexpectedly far-reaching concessions in agriculture, services (particularly financial services), telecommunications, and general market access. Nonetheless, a few hours after his speech and discussions with Premier Zhu, President Clinton decided not to proceed with the agreement at that time.

Primary among the president's reasons was his fear that he could not obtain the necessary congressional support to win permanent MFN status for the PRC—an essential ingredient of the deal between Beijing and Washington. Specifically, as Senator Joseph Biden later explained in a Senate Foreign Relations Committee Hearing on August 4, 1999, he had informed the president's advisers that there was virtually no chance Congress would approve permanent MFN treatment for China given that a report from the House Select Committee on U.S. National Security and Military/Commercial Concerns with the People's Republic of China (the "Cox Committee") was about to be released alleging years of Chinese spying and theft of U.S. nuclear and other secrets.[131] In addition, Vice President Gore was pursuing his year 2000 presidential election campaign bid and counting on labor union support, a critical consideration because organized labor generally opposed Chinese membership in the WTO—indeed organized labor was deeply skeptical of WTO itself, with some unions already on record as opposing the PRC's accession.

The net effect was that even though President Jiang and Premier Zhu had braved domestic opposition and pushed the Politburo hard to get the concessions they hoped would achieve China's accession to the WTO, the United States rejected (at least temporarily) the offer. Clinton did so hoping that the delay in reaching agreement would wring further concessions from Beijing and allow U.S. business to do some of the heavy political lifting essential to win congressional support. For Zhu and Jiang, however, the rejection gave lower-level bureaucratic opponents of WTO entry who had not already been won over or silenced more time to oppose the concessions that had been offered and strengthened the hands of those in China who said that Washington was more interested in keeping China down than reaching a deal.

With Jiang and Zhu already on the defensive, a fourth development further strained relations and put the Chinese who were arguing for engagement with the United States in an even more defensive crouch. On May 7, a B-2 stealth bomber, flying from Whiteman Air Force Base in Missouri, dropped precision-guided munitions on the Chinese Embassy in Belgrade, destroying it. The embassy had been misidentified as a legitimate Serb military target, in part because U.S. and NATO targeters were having to hit so many targets they got sloppy.[132] Three Chinese citizens were killed and more than twenty injured. As events unfolded, Beijing found it hard to accept Washington's insistence that the bombing was accidental because, for one thing, many pieces of ordnance had hit the intelligence section of the embassy and, for another, American diplomats had previously been to the embassy location that the administration asserted was not properly identified on the maps used for targeting. Perhaps most fundamentally, the Chinese had been so impressed by the prowess America had shown in high-tech warfare in the Gulf War and in the Kosovo war up to that point that they simply found the explanation of mistake incredible.

Over the following days, a series of events compounded the blunder. To start, a seemingly casual apology delivered by President Clinton on May 8 on an airport tarmac as he visited storm-damaged Oklahoma mistakenly conveyed to Chinese the impression that the United States did not take the bombing incident too seriously. This belief persisted despite the facts that the secretary of state and the U.S. ambassador to China also had quickly made more formal apologies and President Clinton had followed up his airport statement with both a letter and an attempted phone call to President Jiang that was not initially taken. Chinese sensibilities were further offended when the apology was linked to an explanation that asserted that unfortunate errors happen in war and that Yugoslav President Milosevic was the real culprit. Informed that China had called the bombing "barbaric," Clinton bristled, "It wasn't barbaric. What is barbaric is what Milosevic has done. It's tragic. It's awful. What is barbaric is the intentional 'ethnic cleansing' that he has provoked for a decade now."[133]

The outrage the bombing provoked among the Chinese populace and elite gave rise almost immediately to anti-American demonstrations (with considerable Chinese government facilitation) in many locations throughout the PRC. The U.S. consulate general's residence in Chengdu was burned, tons of rocks were hurled at the U.S. Consulate in Shenyang, notable protests occurred outside the U.S. missions in Shanghai and Guangzhou, and dramatic and sustained demonstrations occurred at the U.S. Embassy in Beijing on May 8–10. For a few tense hours U.S. Embassy personnel were in serious doubt that security would be adequate to prevent the mission from being overrun; classified and sensitive materials were destroyed as a precaution.[134] Subsequent testimony before the Senate Foreign Relations Committee by Assistant Secretary of State Stanley Roth made it clear how angry the American side was at the treatment of its diplomatic personnel and "the role that the Chinese government played, or failed to play, in handling the anti-American reaction that took place throughout China."[135]

Among the most disturbing aspects of the Chinese government's response to the bombing and subsequent demonstrations were that the Chinese people were not initially informed of the U.S. apologies (officials claimed the expressions of regret were so superficial that they would have further inflamed the enraged populace), the PRC citizenry was not informed about Milosevic's ethnic cleansing and therefore simply saw U.S./NATO intervention as aggression, and the Chinese authorities not only helped transport demonstrators to the Beijing protests but police seemed indifferent to the damage inflicted on U.S. property. (Again, the subsequent Chinese explanation was that by allowing a "controlled" reaction, a bigger explosion was averted.) Parenthetically, in subsequent conversations with Chinese intellectuals, it is clear that at least some came to feel misled by their government. As one put it to me in mid-2000, some Chinese students "thought they were manipulated by the Chinese media. They now want their own point of view."[136]

People's Daily carried a blistering set of authoritative "Commentator" articles calling the bombing a "flagrant attack," "deliberate," "a willful murder," "a bloody atrocity," "new gunboat diplomacy," and a "barbaric crime."[137] The United States was told, at the top of the mass media's lungs, that "[t]he Chinese people are not to be humiliated" and "China is not to be bullied."[138] Predictably, editorial opinion in the United States responded that the "veil" had finally been lifted on Chinese hostility toward America.[139] Almost immediately, the Beijing leadership suspended discussions on WTO accession with Washington, ended human rights dialogues, and stopped approving U.S. Navy port calls in Hong Kong; later U.S. military aircraft landings in Hong Kong also were halted.

After delay on the Chinese part and interagency negotiation in Washington, on June 17 Under Secretary of State and Presidential Special

Envoy Thomas Pickering personally delivered to Beijing an explanation for the bombing error, an explanation that was deemed "unconvincing."[140] In providing this explanation Washington was trying to address the "four demands" that Beijing had articulated in order to get relations back on a more normal course—an apology, a full and public accounting of how the accident occurred, "punishment" of those responsible for the bombing tragedy, and compensation for lives and property.

Within six weeks of the bombing, and after severe internal debate, it became clear that the dominant portion of the PRC elite wished to achieve enough of the demands so that a skeptical public and leadership hardliners could be convinced that Beijing was justified in resuming more normal relations with Washington.[141] By late June the "road map" back was understood by both sides: a quick resolution of the compensation issue (a compensation agreement regarding bombing victims was announced July 30) and something that would provide political cover for the Chinese elite to get back to business with America. Subsequently, Washington agreed to pay $28 million for property damage, $4.5 million to the families of killed and injured, and in April 2000 fired one CIA operations officer involved in the targeting.

Just as a path began to appear out of the dense fog of events, on July 9, 1999, Taiwan President Lee Teng-hui made a statement to *Deutsche Welle* that cross-strait relations were "state-to-state or at least special state-to-state" in character.[142] For Beijing, this assertion was very close to the formal declaration of independence that the PRC had threatened for many years could elicit the use of force against Taiwan. Were force employed, the implied and explicit obligations of the United States under the Taiwan Relations Act of 1979 would have been tested once again, as they had been in 1995 and 1996. In order to avoid the no-win choice of stumbling into conflict with China on the one hand or being seen to abandon a democratic friend of long-standing on the other, the Clinton administration sent Assistant Secretary of State Stanley Roth and the NSC's Kenneth Lieberthal to Beijing to urge caution, discourage the use of force, and assure Beijing that the U.S. government still adhered to the one-China policy. Simultaneously, the head of the American Institute in Taiwan, Richard Bush, was sent to Taipei with the same message for Lee Teng-hui, with a subtext that the United States was deeply concerned that policy had been so radically changed without consultation with Washington.

A few tense, uncertain weeks followed while Beijing's leaders were closeted in their summer policy confab at Beidaihe in North China trying to decide what to do with respect to all these foreign policy problems, as well as the domestic scene. Beijing's desires to continue to focus on domestic economic and social problems and development, a promise to the PLA of more resources, a step-up in PLA Air Force sorties in the strait, and ever so slight "clarifications" from Taipei were where the situation stood as the summer of 1999 ended.

Unsurprisingly, cross-strait dialogue was a casualty. Former Shanghai Mayor and Chairman of the Association for Relations Across the Taiwan Strait (ARATS) Wang Daohan (see Chapter 8) aborted what would have been the highest-level visit to the island since 1949. Beijing, it seemed, had decided to elevate tension a bit, to talk less to Taipei, but not to respond in a way that would bolster pro-independence sentiment and candidates prior to the island's March 2000 presidential election. Beijing would wait and see what the year 2000 election in Taiwan brought and staunchly refuse to deal with President Lee in the meantime. In the end, the candidate Beijing most feared, the Democratic Progressive Party's Chen Shui-bian, won when the Nationalist Party split, a set of developments beyond the scope of this volume but pregnant with consequences for the future management of U.S.-China relations.

Beijing's relative restraint, Lee Teng-hui's July 9 statement that sowed further distrust between Washington and Taipei, and the administration's quick disassociation from those remarks paradoxically made it easier for the United States and China to resume more productive ties. One reflection of this was that after exhausting, last-minute negotiations in Beijing against the backdrop of intense business community pressure on the U.S. administration, on November 15, 1999, the PRC and the United States agreed on terms for China's accession to the WTO, terms very much like those rejected the previous April (see Chapter 4).

Nonetheless, the Sino-American relationship had changed due to this accumulation of events. The differences set the scene for managing relations as the twenty-first century began. To start, Taiwan had become the most difficult and prominent problem to manage once again. Next, distrust between the U.S. executive branch and the Taiwan government was high, and the tendency of Taipei to end-run the administration by going to Congress had grown. And finally, in both the United States and China those who believed that there was a fundamental strategic conflict between the two countries had been strengthened and Chinese nationalism had become more anti-American in character.

CONCLUSIONS

In the decade that followed the end of the cold war, four turning points together brought U.S.-China relations to a different place than they had been on George Bush's inauguration day in early 1989. By the end of 1999, the warm embrace of George Bush and Deng Xiaoping and the "partnership" of Bill Clinton and Jiang Zemin seemed like old pictures in a family album; they evoked memories but were strangely detached from the moment. The events of the 1989–2000 period had convinced many in both societies that this relationship was at best a mixed bag of competitive and complementary interests, and it would remain so for a very long time (see Chapter 9). While optimists in both nations could hope to build toward a true partnership, the immediate task was to seize opportunities to advance common interests whenever possible and avoid deterioration to open rivalry.

To the degree that post–cold war developments foster more realistic expectations in the two nations, they are all to the good; to the degree that present circumstances foster frustrations and the possibility of demagoguery in both nations, they hold danger. That George Bush Sr. ran for president in 1988 as a friend of China and his son George W. Bush felt compelled to run for president a decade later calling Beijing a "competitor" shows how much had changed.

With the chronological road map laid before us, in the next two chapters we turn to the substantive foreign policy issues that dominated the 1989–2000 period. These issues mobilized powerful interests in both the United States and China, thereby generating considerable conflict as well as nurturing impulses toward cooperation.

2

SECURITY ISSUES

MAO ZEDONG TO HENRY KISSINGER: [Regarding a hypothetical Soviet attack on China] And then you can let them get bogged down in China, for half a year, or one, or two, or three, or four years. And then you can poke your finger at the Soviet back.... KISSINGER: Mr. Chairman, it is really very important that we understand each other's motives. We will never knowingly cooperate in an attack on China.
MAO (INTERRUPTING): No, that's not so. Your aim in doing that would be to bring the Soviet Union down.
KISSINGER: That's a very dangerous thing. *Laughter.*
MAO: The goal of the Soviet Union is to occupy both Europe and Asia, the two continents.
KISSINGER: We want to discourage a Soviet attack, not defeat it. We want to prevent it.

Mao Zedong's residence, February 17–18, 1973

The third task [after opposing hegemonism and reunifying with Taiwan] is to step up economic construction, that is to step up four modernizations construction.... National defense construction, without a certain economic foundation, is no good.

Deng Xiaoping, January 16, 1980

As to the real state of China's defense establishment, due to our sharply lower ratio of defense spending to GNP since the 1980s, we are severely short on resources. This has sharply affected our defense construction and building of the military force, leaving us with a weak defense economic base, slow weaponry renewal, poor technology, a steadily widening gap with the weaponry of developed nations, poor military infrastructures, and relatively declining serviceman income.

Wu Fangming and Wu Xizhi, Academy of Military Science, February 1996 [during tensions in the Taiwan Strait]

If China cannot feed its people no one else can help. If we feed and improve their livelihood, provide big markets, this is a great contribution to the world. Some talk of a China threat. Starving Chinese are a threat! North Korea doesn't have a big population and it wants assistance, but the international community can't satisfy their requests. So, you can imagine if China was plunged into crisis—a real China threat!

Vice Premier and Foreign Minister Qian Qichen,
Beijing, September 1997

More often you, the United States, go from the specific to the general. You think if you [China] do well on human rights, IPR [intellectual property rights], then we'd be friends. Chinese are just the opposite; if we are friends we can deal with specifics easier.

Chinese scholar, June 20, 1998

The wholesale theft of all of our important nuclear secrets is an act of foreign aggression against the United States. It is the espionage equivalent of Pearl Harbor.... If China gets away scot-free with its violation of our nation's most important secrets, it will be an act of national spinelessness that sends a message to Beijing—American companies are too addicted to profits and politicians too dependent on corporate campaign donations to act in our own national interest when confronted with a dire threat.

Former Clinton adviser Dick Morris, June 1, 1999

PUTTING ISSUES INTO CONTEXT

I have suggested that U.S.-China relations from 1989 to 1999 were characterized by a sequence of turning points at which warring personalities, incongruent domestic politics, clashing national interests and strategies, unpredictable external events, and often inaccurate perceptions converged to push bilateral relations in new directions. But the decade can also be understood as a period in which several recurrent issues dominated the bilateral agenda: security, economic and trade relations, and individual rights and governance (human rights). The principal security issues were big power and alliance relations, the priority to be accorded the traditional concept of sovereignty, proliferation and arms control, technology transfer, and Taiwan. The trade, economic, and human rights issues are addressed in Chapter 3.

That the security issues enumerated above provided the focus for Sino-American security relations in the first post–cold war decade reflects a number of developments:

· With the USSR's decline and eventual demise in 1991, the Soviet threat that had unified the United States and China vanished. Thus bilateral issues that had been subordinated for years rose on the agendas of *both* nations.

· China's economic, diplomatic, and military growth throughout the 1980s and 1990s meant that U.S. and Chinese interests increasingly overlapped, at times fostering cooperation and at others generating friction.

· As the threat of a global nuclear disaster receded with the cold war's end, the United States became more concerned with the proliferation of weapons of mass destruction to unfriendly or unstable nations and terrorist groups. The March 1995 sarin gas attack by a Japanese doomsday cult on the Tokyo subway, along with the bombing of the World Trade Center in New York two years before by Middle Eastern terrorists, made Americans feel vulnerable. Consequently, Beijing's sales of weapons and technology in unstable regions and to pariah states became of ever greater concern to Americans.

· Changes were occurring in Taiwan that made that island more attractive to Americans and, at the same time, more assertive in seeking a role of dignity in the world community. Both considerations alarmed the PRC. Consequently, as the 1990s unfolded it became increasingly difficult for Beijing and Washington to manage the Taiwan issue in a mutually acceptable way.

In the post–cold war era practically every facet of the U.S.-China relationship had a duality. Americans saw growing exports to China as positive, but they viewed the mounting U.S. trade deficit and leakage of critical technologies to the PRC as negatives. With regard to proliferation, the Chinese seemingly helped Washington in North Korea while hindering it in Pakistan. From the Chinese perspective, dualities obtained as well. The United States was China's largest single export market, but Washington frequently sought to use that leverage (through unilateral sanctions) to promote internal change in the PRC and other non-trade-related goals. In the realm of technology, the United States exported more technology to China than any other nation yet continually imposed limitations on technology transfer. Finally, Washington's security role in Asia helped moderate Tokyo's acquisition of military power, but China saw that the U.S.-Japan security alliance could intervene in the Taiwan Strait. Thus, for both China and the United States, the bilateral relationship's strengths were also its dangers.

These dualities made the management of the relationship in both countries inseparable from domestic politics, as Chinese and American proponents of stronger bilateral ties sought to highlight the positives of such ties, while their opponents relentlessly underscored the negatives. A principal challenge that leaders faced, therefore, was to manage the domestic friction these dualities generated in each nation and to weld a new, post–cold war consensus in both nations about why Sino-American cooperation was in the net security interest of both nations. By the decade's end skepticism in both nations seemed to be on the rise.

BACKGROUND: SECURITY AND THE SINO-AMERICAN AGENDA

When President Nixon met Mao Zedong for the first time in February 1972, both men knew what had brought them together. Each believed that his nation stood to gain leverage in its dealings with Moscow if a closer association could be forged between Beijing and Washington. Henry Kissinger has written that he and the president shared "the same fundamental judgment: that if relations could be developed with both the Soviet Union and China the triangular relationship would give us a great strategic opportunity for peace."[1] For China, the need to gain a degree of deterrence against Soviet pressure along its borders was foremost in the minds of Mao Zedong and Zhou Enlai. As Mao put it to Nixon, "The issue of the international situation is an important one." "The small issue is Taiwan, the big issue is the world."[2]

The Americans, too, had a longer-range objective in mind. As Richard Nixon put it in an October 1967 article in *Foreign Affairs:* "Taking the long view, we simply cannot afford to leave China forever outside the family of nations, there to nurture its fantasies, cherish its hates and threaten its neighbors.... For the long run, it means pulling China back into the world community—but as a great and progressing nation, not as the epicenter of world revolution." Nixon hoped to bring China into the family of nations, thereby promoting behavior compatible with U.S. interests.

President Carter came to office in 1977 with personal experience of a war-wracked China; in 1949, as a young submarine officer, he had visited Qingdao and other Chinese ports.[3] The new president took a broader view of the bilateral relationship than had his predecessors, attaching more weight to economic potential than they had. Nevertheless, like Nixon and Kissinger, Carter believed that China's "permanence and strategic importance in international affairs were evident."[4] Writing in his diary on May

16, 1978, Carter noted, "We all agreed that a better relationship with the PRC would help us with SALT [the Strategic Arms Limitation Talks]."[5] Also like Nixon and Kissinger, Carter subscribed to the longer-range objective of involving China constructively in the international system and thereby giving her a stake in the global community compatible with American interests.

The anti-Soviet rationale was central to Deng Xiaoping's thinking, as it had been for Mao Zedong. To this end, Deng opposed Vietnamese[6] aggression in Cambodia in order to break what he saw as Moscow's intention to surround the PRC in an arc from Vietnam, through India, to Afghanistan.

Yet, at the same time, Sino-American cooperation to further China's economic and technological modernization motivated Deng in a way it had not Mao. Deng made economic development the top priority. A China that was weak economically would be ineffective in opposing "hegemonists," reuniting Taiwan, or building a strong national defense. As he said in 1984, "Our political line is to take the four modernizations [agriculture, industry, science and technology, and national defense] as the key point, from beginning to end to not let go of this, unless another world war arises."[7]

By the time the U.S.-China agreement on normalization was reached in late 1978, both sides therefore had multiple motives. Gaining leverage in dealings with Moscow was central for China and the United States. For Washington, constructive involvement of the PRC in the international community was also pivotal. For Beijing, gaining American cooperation in economic development was paramount. On the basis of these initial objectives, the 1980s were remarkably successful for both countries. By the end of the decade, trade and economic ties had grown at the rate of 17.4 percent annually; the 1989 dollar volume of trade was 381 percent above the 1980 level. Furthermore, the threat from Moscow had receded with Mikhail Gorbachev's rise to power (1985) and his trips to the United States in late 1987 and 1988 and to Beijing in May 1989. Finally, China was becoming an active member of the international community and multilateral organizations, thereby addressing both American desires for integration of the PRC and Chinese aspirations for recognition and international dignity. These achievements, however, created many of the policy issues that dominated the 1990s and are the topic of this and the next chapter.

SECURITY ISSUES

Throughout the 1990s, leaders and citizens in America and China remained uncertain about one another's current and long-term intentions and future capabilities. Each nation saw its historic task in different terms—the United States to maintain, perhaps to enhance, its preeminence in the post–cold war era, and China to regain its "rightful place" in the family of nations.

Those two strategic objectives still obtain as we enter the twenty-first century. China's leaders and citizens alike see their nation as resuming its historic central role in East Asia and feel that no decisions should be made that affect their interests in the region without first consulting Beijing—*consultation* meaning obtaining Chinese assent on key issues. In contrast, Washington's policy, as set forth in February 1995 in *United States Security Strategy for the East Asia–Pacific Region,* is as follows: "The United States has been the pre-eminent Pacific power since World War II ... [and the U.S. interest has been and remains] the prevention of the rise of any hegemonic power or coalition."[8] China's desire to regain a position of power and influence in Asia and America's desire to preserve its own pre-eminence need not inevitably result in conflict, but these differing priorities must be carefully managed, for they do produce tension.

Since the fall of the Berlin Wall, five key factors have contributed to Sino-American security controversies:

(1) China's defense strategy changed in the period immediately preceding the end of the cold war. Since the Taiwan Strait tensions of 1995–1996, the PLA has made a contingency of conflict in the Taiwan Strait (possibly involving the United States) a principal focus of its own modernization.

(2) The United States and China have somewhat divergent views concerning the desired character of the international order, with Washington seeking to strengthen its bilateral alliances and Beijing seeing the UN Security Council (where it has a veto) as central. During the 1990s, successive American interventions (Iraq, Somalia, Haiti, Bosnia, and Kosovo) suggested that Washington was elevating human rights issues over state sovereignty, a position sure to be worrisome to most Chinese.

(3) China's economy grew extremely fast throughout most of the 1990s. That growth raised questions in American minds: How rapidly will the PRC's mounting economic strength be translated into military might and how will that strength be exercised? For their part, the Chinese wondered whether the United States would seek to retard the PRC's progress.

(4) China sees itself as weak militarily compared with the United States; this makes Beijing reticent to be transparent about its military

capabilities and plans, which, in turn, feeds worst-case analyses in many quarters of America and among some of the PRC's neighbors, notably Taiwan, Japan, India, and Vietnam.

(5) Finally, the United States is a global power with global interests. Consequently, Americans judge China's behavior in terms of its effects on the complex network of U.S. interests and concerns around the world, rather than merely from a bilateral standpoint. Beijing tends to judge American action in terms of its immediate effects on China's security and aspirations for unification.

Counterbalancing these factors are *incentives* for U.S.-China cooperation in the security realm. For instance, the quixotic North Korean regime generally has inadvertently fostered cooperation between Washington and Beijing in the post–cold war decade, inasmuch as each saw Pyongyang's erratic behavior as a potential catalyst for catastrophe. As one Chinese official remarked to me, "With friends like this [North Korea], who needs enemies?" Moreover, leaders in both countries realize that increased Sino-American tension would require increased defense expenditures and thereby reduce monies available for domestic priorities. Another consideration that fosters Sino-American security cooperation is a desire not to see a robust, much less nuclear, Japanese military that would create anxiety among neighbors in the region. And finally, U.S.-China cooperation in the wake of the Indian and Pakistani nuclear detonations of May 1998 demonstrated that both Washington and Beijing desire to avoid a destabilizing nuclear arms race on the Indian subcontinent.[9] Thus, national security is a complex mix of shared, parallel, and conflicting interests, mutual suspicions and uncertainties, and domestic politics that create incentives for both conflict and cooperation.

One can also point to specific instances of security-related cooperation. For instance, when Washington sought UN authorization for specific military and peacekeeping operations, President Bush and, later, President Clinton generally found Beijing at least minimally supportive in key Security Council votes until the end of the 1990s. In 1990–1991, prior to the launch of the ground war in Iraq, for instance, China voted with other permanent members of the UN Security Council in favor of sanctions against Baghdad, casting an "abstention" only on the resolution authorizing the use of force to eject Iraq from Kuwait. On subsequent Security Council votes concerning interventions in Somalia, Haiti, and the former Yugoslavia, Beijing's permanent representative frequently expressed concern about such operations but did not choose to cast a veto, until 1999 when

Beijing blocked an extension of peacekeeping forces in Macedonia. Later that year, Beijing also grudgingly went along with the G-8 position on the termination of the Kosovo conflict. China consistently has been motivated by two contradictory impulses in this regard: the desire to be a responsible member of the big power club and the desire to stand against big power interventionism—abstention frequently becomes the middle path.

China's Changing Concept of Security

In the 1960s (particularly during the United States' escalation of the war in Vietnam in 1964–1965), fearing a Soviet or American attack on China's industrial capacity, Chairman Mao Zedong located much of China's factory production in inaccessible interior rural and mountainous areas—"the Third Front."[10] Mao proposed to defend these facilities through a "people's war" in which the hypothetical invader would be ground down in a protracted battle of attrition fought on Chinese territory.

After Mao's death and the ascent of Deng Xiaoping, the normalization of Sino-American ties, and the gradual thawing of Sino-Soviet relations in the 1980s, China's leaders made a new strategic assessment at an enlarged meeting of the Party Central Military Commission in mid-1985: the probability of large-scale war involving China was low, the number of military personnel could be reduced by one million, and PLA modernization would be pursued within the framework of overall economic development as the first priority.[11] Further, in 1978–1979, Deng and his colleagues adopted an approach to economic growth and cultural change premised on China's increasing involvement in the Western world. China's coastal cities, not its hinterland, figured into the initial stages of this development effort most prominently. The concept of a Third Front no longer made sense. Instead, defending China's industrial and financial structure along the coast became a principal objective. The focus of security attention correspondingly shifted from China's west to its east and from the land to the sea and air. As one Chinese strategic analyst described:

> Besides, if one were to take into account the important fact that its economy is increasingly getting integrated into surrounding areas, and that much of it is focussed on coastal regions—highly vulnerable to military attacks—China's need to keep military conflicts away from its borders becomes all the more urgent. China's main economic centres, comprising almost 56.3 per cent of its GDP, are concentrated in the coastal regions, making it all the more imperative for the country to defend them. The whole process of modernization would be seriously jeopardized if the economies of the coastal areas were destroyed. It is therefore

necessary to build up its navy and air force to deter external enemies so that conflicts do not spread into Chinese territory.[12]

This changed concept had another important dimension—the center of gravity of the PLA's concerns shifted from preoccupation with superpower threats to the dangers that lurked on its periphery. "The whole geographical framework changed, with China's security interests focussed on the surrounding areas."[13] Rather than worrying about a massive land invasion by a superpower, the issue became how to defend China's claims in the South China Sea, wage possible combat in the Taiwan Strait, defend territorial claims against Vietnam and India, and defend China's coastal cities from naval and air attack. Further, all of this had to be accomplished in a much more high-tech environment where remote sensing, rapid data transmission, precision guidance, and electronic warfare were becoming progressively more important—the revolution in military affairs.[14]

This shift in priority has had and will continue to have implications for the PRC's defense budget, for the size of its military, for the kinds of capabilities and equipment its military leadership believes it needs, and for its operational doctrines: "After the demise of the cold war the strategy changed. China's military leaders reached a consensus that to safeguard the country's economic achievements, the Chinese army should engage the enemy outside of its territory. And since wars in the post–cold War era are probably going to be high-tech local conflicts, China has to arm itself with high-tech equipment."[15]

Some of the implications of this new military thinking were reassuring to China's neighbors and to the United States—others were not. For example, throughout the 1980s China's official defense spending *declined* in inflation-adjusted (and some years in absolute) terms, though no credible Western analyst of the Chinese military budget takes the official figures at face value.[16] PLA manpower fell by about one million troops in the 1985–1990 period.[17] Deng Xiaoping's purpose when the 1985 decisions were made was to trim the PLA by ridding it of poorly trained and unneeded land army forces, upgrading the training and equipment of the troops that remained, along with that of the air force and navy, and conserving scarce budgetary resources for broad, civilian economic and technological development. If China modernized its economy in the 1980s and 1990s, this would permit the military to more rapidly and effectively modernize in the period beyond 2000. This was to be a "strategic transformation" with the objective of creating a military force able to fight a "people's war under modern conditions."[18] At the Fifteenth Party Congress in September 1997, Deng Xiaoping's successor, General Secretary Jiang Zemin, made a further commitment to reduce the land army by 500,000 persons over three years, though some considerable percentage of the PLA's personnel reductions went into the People's Armed Police (PAP). For China's neighbors, the constrained military spending and the personnel reductions were welcome, while the eventual goal of military modernization and offshore defense raised anxieties.

In trying to implement this policy of strategic transformation throughout the 1980s and 1990s, China's military leaders faced a painful contradiction. On the one hand, the military was to slash personnel and operate on a shoestring budget; on the other hand, it was to modernize and emphasize expensive naval and air forces. In the long run, broad economic development would strengthen all Chinese capacities, including those of the military. In the short run, however, China's military would have to wait for significantly more money, and, in the words of General Liu Huaqing (China's most senior uniformed officer) to former Secretary of Defense Robert McNamara and a group of senior retired military officers I accompanied in 1994, the armed forces "have had great patience."[19]

Consequently, throughout the 1990s, China's military searched for justifications for increased allocations. Although the PLA's role in the Tiananmen suppression of 1989 accounts for some of the subsequent increases in the PLA's official budget (though inflation ate away at gains from 1989 through the mid-1990s), other unrelated developments also bolstered the PLA's case for more money. These developments indicate that the Chinese often are reacting to events they did not foresee, rather than initiating and methodically implementing a finely honed military development strategy.

One such development was America's quick victory in the Gulf War of 1991—a pyrotechnic display that destroyed Iraq's army that had better Soviet-style equipment than China's. The Gulf War made it clear to the Chinese military and civilian leaders just how central information (intelligence), air and naval capabilities, and the integration of air, land, and naval forces had become in modern warfare. These were capabilities in which China's military was sorely deficient. A second, decisive consideration was America's dispatch of two aircraft carrier battle groups to the Taiwan Strait in March 1996, a display that made the inadequacies of China's military very apparent. As one Chinese defense analyst explained to me, "The Gulf War and the Taiwan Strait crisis did speed up defense modernization. The Gulf War had a large-scale impact on the PLA in terms of the kind of warfare and the Taiwan crisis made more convincing the pace of military modernization."[20] And finally, the U.S.-NATO air campaign intervention in Serbia and Kosovo (March–June 1999), contrary to initial Chinese expectations, did bring Serb leader Slobodan Milosevic to the negotiating table with zero loss of lives of American combatants. *People's Daily* put it as follows on June 1, 1999: "With the hegemonist lust of the United States swelling like never before, international relations will depend more on strength. A weak country has no foreign relations, and a country [that] lags behind is vulnerable to attacks. China must rise in vigor, and increase its economic and defense strength, as well as national cohesiveness."[21]

One final consideration arguing for higher PLA budget allocations was corruption and increasing entrepreneurship by PLA units and commands as they sought to generate revenue independent of the central budget. Because the PLA's official budget was constrained by the priorities of broad national development throughout the 1980s and much of the 1990s, military organizations literally went into business on a broad scale; some of this business activity involved weapons exports[22] as well as nonmilitary ventures including hotel ownership, gas stations, transport companies (using naval ships), and shoe polish factories. This phenomenon fed corruption and smuggling, weakened fighting unit readiness, sometimes ran at cross-purposes with China's formal diplomatic commitments, and diminished central control of the military establishment.

In the mid and late 1990s, Beijing attempted to reduce the PLA's commercial activity and to replace some of the lost revenues with regular budgetary appropriations.[23] The initial efforts met with only partial success, so by mid-1998 Jiang Zemin and Premier Zhu Rongji had launched a much more vigorous effort to get the PLA out of business, commerce, and smuggling. While it was essential for the central government to get control of military financing by increasing central budget allocations to replace some of the self-generated local revenue that was to be curtailed, to many Western observers this increased central appropriation for the PLA looked like a real defense spending increase. Nonetheless, if the late-1990s efforts succeed, this may help to bring the PLA under greater civilian control and should make it somewhat more transparent.

Although Beijing's attempts to modernize the military seemed natural to the Chinese for a number of reasons, some of the PRC's neighbors and some Americans viewed these plans and gradually mounting capabilities with concern. Demonstrating this wariness, one very senior former U.S. defense official asked a senior Chinese military officer in 1998, "No one expects an attack on China from the sea, so how is this [modernization of the navy and air force] defensive?"[24]

With respect to the perceptions of its neighbors, China has had ongoing border and offshore disputes with several neighboring states (the ASEAN nations, India, Russia, the Republic of Korea, and Japan) and has had a long history of conflict with others as well. Each neighbor looks at mounting Chinese power and Beijing's new strategy with memories of the past. Even if China's current purposes are benign, its growing capabilities could permit the future redefinition of purposes in dangerous ways. It is no surprise, therefore, that when the Hindu Nationalist Party (BJP) in India gained power in 1998, its defense minister, George Fernandes, defined China as a primary Indian defense concern—the threat from "across the border to the north."[25]

In the late 1980s and 1990s, China's neighbors began to adjust in different ways to the prospect and the reality of gradually mounting Chinese military power. In many cases this adjustment was multidimensional, with capitals simultaneously improving diplomatic relations with Beijing (Russia, South Korea, India, Japan, and the ASEAN countries); purchasing or developing more (and more advanced) weapons (Singapore, Indonesia, Malaysia, Taiwan, Thailand, and India); enhancing security relations with the United States (Singapore, Indonesia, the Philippines, and Japan); and trying to bring Beijing into multilateral security dialogues such as the ASEAN Regional Forum.

In America, the specter of rising Chinese power and its evolving military strategy created a new cottage industry devoted to defining the "China threat" and trying to generate popular and elite support to address it.[26] Richard Bernstein and Ross H. Munro's *The Coming Conflict with China* was the most widely distributed, and among the most weakly constructed, of these polemics. The opening sentence of the book reads: "The People's Republic of China, the world's most populous country, and the United States, its most powerful, have become global rivals, countries whose relations are tense, whose interests are in conflict, and who face tougher, more dangerous times ahead."[27] But expressions of concern were not limited to Americans and the PRC's neighbors. Bao Tong, former Premier Zhao Ziyang's senior-most political adviser in the late 1980s, voiced the concerns of those beyond China's borders: "[China] has already gone mad twice in the last 40 years. You have to ask yourself a question: What will it do on the international scene? Is it a source of stability or a potential source of instability? When it doesn't have enough power, its attitude will be restrained. But once it develops and becomes strong, what kind of role is it going to play without a complete structural change?"[28]

This, however, is only part of the story. The United States and China had, and continue to have, somewhat different perceptions of the desired world order in the post–cold war era.

U.S. and Chinese Views of the New International Order

America feels most comfortable in a leadership role, and China prefers an international system in which power is more dispersed. *Liberation Army Daily* put it this way: "Only by exerting mutual constraints can power reach an equilibrium and an equilibrium [of] power can be the only foundation for the stability of an international safe environment."[29] In a world of comparative balance among powers, Chinese leaders believe they have the greatest room to maneuver—they are able to play powers off one another. As one Chinese analyst said to me, "The United States wants a unipolar world and we want a multipolar world. This limits our [U.S.-China] cooperation. . . . The United States wants to intervene and we do not want this to happen very often."[30] A Chinese international relations scholar put it differently: "Since Li Hung-chang [a modernizer in the second half of the nineteenth century], we have tried to manage the world through geopolitics, balance of power, barbarians against barbarians. We still want to use Russia to affect the United States. Developing countries against developed countries."[31]

This Chinese desire contrasts with America's post–cold war notion that its leadership is "indispensable" in establishing international rules of the road and enforcing them. Saddam Hussein's invasion of Kuwait (1990–1991), the breakdowns in Somalia (1991) and Haiti (1993–1994), and the ethnic cleansing of Slobodan Milosevic in the former Yugoslavia (1991–1995 and 1999) were taken to be notable examples of the kind of savagery that would persist and even grow worse without American intervention and leadership. President Bush's notion of a "new world order"[32] and the Clinton administration's repeated reference to America as the "indispensable nation"[33] were expressions of this widely shared American belief (see Chapter 6).

Chinese concerns about American post–cold war assertiveness, however, were more than theoretical ruminations about U.S. intervention in distant third-world nations; Beijing's anxiety also sprang from Washington's (particularly the U.S. Congress's) increasing reliance on unilateral sanctions. The United States had aimed these sanctions at China and many other nations. During "President Clinton's first term alone, the United States imposed new unilateral economic sanctions, or threatened legislation to do so, 60 times on 35 countries that, taken together, make up about

42 percent of the world's population."[34] By 1998, two-thirds of the world's population (seventy-five countries) was subject to American economic sanctions.[35] Between 1995 and 1998, at least thirty-six U.S. states and cities also imposed sanctions on "offending" governments abroad (see Chapter 7).[36] Predictably, the rest of the world did not feel it needed America's moral instruction—certainly not proud civilizations like Russia, France, and China. Given the perceived humiliations at the hands of the West, the Chinese were resentful, a feeling one friend revealed: "The U.S. is too self-confident.... we see it saying 'the end of history;' 'the U.S. the sole remaining superpower.'" Then, recounting a conversation with an American in the early 1990s, this person went on to say that he was told, "We are the victor, we are the winner; we have the right to choose on China, free to exert pressure, free to give most-favored-nation or not to give it."[37]

Beijing had other specific grievances as well. To start, Washington's immediate response to the 1989 Tiananmen tragedy was to impose economic, political, and technology transfer sanctions on China (many of which were still in place a decade later). In his sanctions announcement of June 5, President Bush prohibited future weapons sales to the PLA and froze a $550 million upgrade of Chinese jet fighter aircraft approved by the Reagan administration in 1986, "Peace Pearl," a project being undertaken by Grumman Corporation.[38] One Chinese general explained, "Before 1989 [the U.S. and Chinese militaries] had big steps forward and we sent the Qian [fighter] to be upgraded. But after June 4 [it was canceled], so we were forced to go to the Russians and purchase [military equipment] from them. Economically, we went to the Japanese and European markets. China and the United States lost from U.S. sanctions."[39] This, along with repeated sanctions in the proliferation realm, suggested to the Chinese military and its civilian leaders that Washington wished to hinder the PRC's rise and either prevent or delay the emergence of a competing power.

Beijing's disquiet was further heightened by an incident in August and September 1993 on the high seas involving a Chinese ship, the *Yin He* (*The Galaxy*), carrying a load bound for Iran. As discussed in the preceding chapter, the vessel was believed by American intelligence officials to be carrying ingredients for chemical weapons. However, once the ship was inspected with U.S. observers standing by, no such cargo was found. The result left the Americans embarrassed and the Chinese publicly offended that the United States demanded inspections of ships on the high seas going to foreign ports. "You couldn't find anything, but [you issued] no apology," one Chinese scholar complained to me.[40] In a subsequent White

House meeting with a visiting Chinese delegation, one U.S. official attempted to characterize the *Yin He* incident as an example of "Sino-American cooperation" in antiproliferation work. The reaction of the PRC guests was one of disbelief.

The Chinese image of an assertive and interventionist post–cold war Washington was reinforced by other developments as well. Anthony Lake, assistant to the president for national security affairs, delivered the Clinton administration's first major address on global strategy, entitled "From Containment to Enlargement," on September 21, 1993, at John Hopkins-SAIS in Washington.[41] Lake defined U.S. policy in such ideological terms that Beijing's suspicions that Washington intended to flex its muscles and hasten the passing of all nondemocratic regimes were heightened (see Chapters 1 and 6).

Differing Assessments of National Power

China's immense population (about 1.3 billion people in 1999) is significant in many ways. First of all, the PRC's large scale dramatically affects the way both nations' leaders look at China's present circumstance and future potential. When one speaks with Chinese leaders, they are strikingly preoccupied with domestic concerns. In the day-to-day management of a population so vast, garbage removal, education, and urban social order are the things that elicit their most impassioned and thoughtful responses. Foreign policy frequently is a diversion, a problem that can get in the way of their efforts to focus domestically. For them, China's 270 million poor, 70 million of whom are living in absolute poverty, are an economic drag and moral problem, an ongoing threat to social order, and a sign of China's weakness.[42]

Yet when Americans look at China, particularly at the coastal skylines or the per capita incomes in Shanghai and Beijing (that in 1997 were where Hong Kong's income was in the early 1970s and Taiwan's was in the 1980s), they see a giant in the making.[43] Americans are mindful that the population of only the mainland's relatively modernized coastal areas is more than 380 million—more than half again the combined populations of Japan, North and South Korea, Singapore, and Taiwan. From this vantage point, even a partially modernized China represents a huge competitive force with large resources to meet a variety of ends, some compatible with U.S. interests—others not.

The fact that Chinese tend to see themselves as currently weaker than outsiders do has important consequences. For example, in 1993 the International Monetary Fund (IMF) concluded "that China's economy was about four times larger than the previous most widely quoted figure and thus only slightly less in absolute size than that of Japan."[44] The World Bank said China was the third largest economy in the world in May of that year. In reaching this conclusion, the IMF and the World Bank applied a methodology that used assessments of the actual purchasing power of the Chinese currency (RMB), rather than simply using the prevailing exchange rate to convert Chinese currency into U.S. dollar figures. There is much uncertainty about applying this methodology to China given the PRC's weak statistics and other conceptual problems.

China's leaders believe that such figures overestimate their nation's current real economic capabilities. Then, when this "larger economy" is extrapolated into the future using China's average growth rate (9.3 percent) during the first two decades of reform (1978–1997), the China of the twenty-first century becomes the world's largest economy (in aggregate, though not in per capita terms). Beijing's leaders are flattered and simultaneously horrified by this conclusion. This projection is at such variance with the problems of daily governance they encounter that they see it as little more than an attempt to justify cold war era alliances, exaggerate Chinese power, and increase the price Beijing must pay for entry into global organizations, such as the WTO. Such overblown estimates provide the economic underpinning for constructing a China threat, in their view. This brings us to China's military self-conception.

At the time of this writing, China's capacity to project military force at any distance beyond its borders is extremely limited, though Beijing's reach is growing with an expanding missile force. Moreover, the PRC's vulnerability to American power is great. Indeed, given China's few intercontinental ballistic missiles (ICBMs) and the accuracy of the U.S. force, it is far from clear that Beijing even had a secure second-strike capability in 1999. These considerations create several problems in the Sino-American security relationship. The first is that this imbalance exacerbates the Chinese tendency for secrecy. Washington argues that Beijing should be more forthcoming about its military budgets, its procurement plans and activities, changes in doctrine, and force location. "Transparency," say the Americans, creates confidence in surrounding societies, and if China's neighbors have confidence they will not need to acquire the military means by which to meet a Chinese threat that does not exist.

However, transparency is a very different matter for the strong than for the relatively weak. While exaggerating to make a point, a Chinese military officer said to me: "Sure the United States would like transparency with respect to nuclear forces. You have thousands of warheads and we only a small fraction of that. If you had confidence about what we had you could destroy our entire force, with most of your force remaining unexpended after an attack" (paraphrase). Another Chinese analyst commented, "The U.S. also uses military transparency as part of its military deterrence policy [meaning the United States lets China see its modern military systems as a deterrent]. China should also have some military transparency in the future, but China should proceed step by step. China cannot have as much military transparency as that of the U.S., because China's defense forces are much weaker than those of the U.S."[45] It is significant, therefore, that in November 1995 China issued its first arms control white paper and in July 1998 its first defense white paper, entitled *China's National Defense.*

This difference of attitude between strong and weak powers is reflected in other security-related areas as well. With respect to the Strategic Arms Limitations Talks (I and II), for example, the Chinese have steadfastly refused to participate until Russia and the United States reduce their thousands of warheads to a level that begins to approach the 200 to 450 that China possessed in the late 1990s.[46]

Finally, while theater and national missile defenses may be practical for an economically booming U.S. society fearful of relatively small attacks by rogue nations or groups, such systems could reduce the potency of China's fledgling nuclear deterrent and conventional missile force. This, in turn, could force Beijing to spend even more money to acquire the capability to penetrate such defenses. In short, that China is militarily weaker than the United States means that certain frictions in the security realm are inevitable.

American and Chinese Perspectives on Global and Regional Power

Washington and Beijing have very different ways of looking at the world. Washington clearly has global interests, whereas currently Beijing is a regional power with mounting influence in the world. Beijing tends to view its interests on a country-by-country basis and from a regional perspective, although this is changing as China's economic and security interests expand. The regional perspective is evident in the very organization of China's Ministry of Foreign Affairs as compared to the U.S. Department of State. In Beijing, regional bureaus dominate the Foreign Ministry and policy is conceived largely in terms of bilateral relations with particular nations; countries closest to China with the most direct influence on PRC interests generally receive the most attention.[47] As a Shanghai professor explained: "The Foreign Ministry puts [functional problems] in the International Law and Treaties Department. One weak point is that on specific [functional or technical] issues it is very preliminary and it has no deep understanding and [this problem should be] settled in the future. So, sometimes, we can't raise a specific prescription to problems, so we list vague principles. This is a problem we should settle. You, the United States, take care of the world and we take care of the surrounding areas. But the world demands that we strengthen the study of specific issues. For example, biological weapons, we have weak knowledge of this."[48] This analyst went on to explain, "We don't have functional bureaus too much.... My impression is that they [the Foreign Ministry] don't have real experts in non-proliferation. We need people who understand the technical experts.... And we have to coordinate with the military which is difficult."[49]

Within the U.S. foreign policy apparatus, by way of contrast, functional bureaus responsible for nonproliferation, export control, free trade, human rights, and energy and the environment are significant policy players. Particularly in the first Clinton administration, the influence of functional bureaus and experts often transcended that of geographically defined units. In the American policy process, functional bureaus are more concerned with how China's behavior affects "their" issue than with China as a whole, or even U.S.-China relations.

Moreover, the United States' numerous global security alliances (NATO, the U.S.-Japan security alliance, defense pacts with the ANZUS/Australia, the Philippines, Thailand, and South Korea, not to mention bilateral commitments) require that it remain credible. Because the United States has commitments around the world, it is essential that American purposes be taken seriously in order to avoid unnecessary challenges that might trigger subsequent expensive U.S. involvements. The very nature of these commitments has thrust upon Washington the role of "global policeman," a role about which Americans are ambivalent and that the Chinese reject. Beijing, by way of contrast, is party to no external alliances. In summing up the difference between the two systems, one Chinese observer put it to me this way in June 1996: "China is most concerned with its own internal development and the United States is most concerned with trying to maintain international order. Therefore, our agendas are different."[50]

One instance illustrates how these divergent national perspectives create Sino-American friction. Throughout the 1980s and 1990s, the United States saw China's clandestine assistance to Pakistan's nuclear and missile programs as inimical to America's national interests and contrary to its nonproliferation and missile control policies. In reaction, on several occasions Washington imposed sanctions on Beijing (and Pakistan). From Beijing's perspective, however, India was a rival power with which China had fought and won a brief border war in 1962, which had been nuclear weapons capable since 1974, and which became a declared nuclear weapons state in May 1998. To Beijing, Pakistan was a stabilizing counterweight to New Delhi's ambitions; a nuclear-capable India and a nonnuclear Pakistan constituted an inherently unstable circumstance on China's border. Consequently, in Chinese eyes, transferring nuclear and missile technology to Islamabad was both a measure to restore strategic balance to a region dangerously out of equilibrium as well as a financially profitable enterprise. In this instance, as in many others, whereas Beijing tends to look at localized interests and effects, the United States worries about the global effects of localized behavior. For China, stability on its border was at stake; for Washington, its global commitment to nonproliferation was the issue.

This difference in regional and global perspective, however, is changing gradually as China acquires increasingly far-flung interests and becomes more involved in global institutions and dependent upon distant regions for strategic commodities. Throughout the 1980s, for example, China was basically self-sufficient in petroleum. By November 1993, however, the PRC had become a net oil importer,[51] with most of its oil imports coming from Indonesia and a small amount from the Persian Gulf. Yet as its economic growth continues China will not only need more oil imports but also want to diversify its sources to avoid a dangerous dependency on any single unstable area. Predictably, China is increasingly turning toward the Persian Gulf, Central Asia, and places further afield such as Venezuela and Sudan. In turn, as the PRC's linkages expand, so do its vulnerabilities, and these vulnerabilities create the need for new policies.

For example, nuclear technology and conventional weapons transfers to Tehran seemed like cost-free export earners in the 1980s, but by 1997 they had become a threat to the stability of China's own Persian Gulf oil imports. It was only then that Beijing agreed with Washington to cease worrisome nuclear and conventional weapons and technology transfers to Iran. Herein lies the central hope for more compatibility between U.S. and Chinese security interests in the future. As Beijing acquires global stakes, its concerns hopefully will more often converge with Washington's. On the other hand, China's oil thirst and other strategic interests will at times drive Beijing to do business with regimes of which Washington disapproves—for example, Iran, Iraq, Sudan, and Libya.

This brings us to proliferation.

The Proliferation of Weapons and Technologies of Mass Destruction

Background and Context. Beijing has a mixed nonproliferation record, as does Washington. On the positive side, throughout the 1980s and 1990s China agreed to participate in most of the major multilateral arms control regimes. These have included the International Atomic Energy Agency (1984); the Biological Weapons Convention (1984); the Limited Test Ban (1986); the Non-Proliferation Treaty (1992) and its indefinite extension (1995); the Chemical Weapons Convention (1993); and the Comprehensive Nuclear Test Ban Treaty (1996). In 1992 and 1994 Beijing affirmed and reaffirmed its intention to observe the "guidelines and parameters" (though not Annex revisions adopted since 1987) of the Missile Technology Control Regime (MTCR, created April 1987), a nontreaty group of twenty-nine members (with three adherents: Ukraine, China, and Israel) that sets standards governing the transfer of missile and missile-related technologies (capable of delivering weapons of mass destruction) to entities outside the group.[52] In addition, China agreed to join the Zangger Committee (1997) and that same year also agreed to a list of nuclear export controls very similar to that of the Nuclear Suppliers Group (founded in 1992, having thirty-four members as of 1999) that establishes guidelines for NPT export control provisions. Finally, in the course of the October 1997 Washington summit between Presidents Bill Clinton and Jiang Zemin, the U.S. administration was given assurances by Beijing concerning a halt in nuclear (and some missile) cooperation with Iran. Assistant Secretary of State Winston Lord said in 1996 of the Chinese nonproliferation record, "If you look at China's position now versus 10 or 15 years ago when they were saying nuclear weapons were good for you, in effect, they have come a long way."[53]

Nonetheless, as of mid-1998 China was not a member of four major export control groups: the Australia Group (biological and chemical weapons), the Missile Technology Control Regime, the Nuclear Suppliers Group, and the Wassenaar arrangement (conventional weapons and dual-use goods), which became effective in September 1996. The reasons for China's reticence to join these organizations are complex in each case. With respect to MTCR, for example, Beijing views missile defenses (not covered by MTCR) with almost as much alarm as offensive missiles.[54] Consequently, if the United States pushes ahead with regional missile defenses, Beijing already has indicated it might no longer feel constrained from offensive missile exports.[55]

Another positive development in China's nonproliferation record involved North Korea. During the 1992–1994 crisis concerning North Korea's effort to acquire nuclear weapons, Beijing helped bring the North Korean nuclear program under (tenuous) international supervision in the 1994 Framework Agreement, though some Clinton administration officials believe China gets more credit than it deserves in this respect.[56] Further, in the 1996 to 1998 period, Beijing modulated its food and resource shipments to North Korea in an attempt to moderate Pyongyang's behavior, thereby seeking to stabilize a seriously deteriorating situation in the DPRK.[57] China's principal interest in the Korean peninsula throughout the 1990s was to avoid three things: a nuclearized peninsula, war that would destabilize the entire region, and a tide of North Korean refugees in Northeast China, fleeing bloodshed, starvation, and pestilence. Washington, with 37,000 troops on or near the 38th parallel separating North from South Korea, shared Beijing's aversion to a breakdown on the peninsula. Looking to the future, however, were the two Koreas to reunify, the Chinese probably would prefer to have the U.S. troops leave the peninsula.

Beijing has also shown a dark side in its dealings in the realms of proliferation and technology transfer. Of greatest concern to Washington has been documented Chinese behavior contributing to the spread of technologies of mass destruction (and the means of their delivery)[58] to states located in explosive regions, some with erratic leaders and highly nationalistic populations (i.e., Iran, Iraq, Libya,[59] Algeria, and Pakistan). Further, Washington has expressed ongoing concern (in the 1998–1999 Cox Committee Report) about American technology and production processes transferred to China for civilian uses being diverted to military end users (particularly in the high-performance computer, guidance, encryption, jet engine, and precision machine tool areas).[60] Finally, there is ample evidence that counterintelligence at U.S. weapons and energy laboratories was inadequate from the late 1970s until 2000, though many of the allegations of Chinese espionage have generated more heat than light; few disciplinary actions and prosecutions have been possible,[61] with the former head of counterintelligence at Los Alamos National Laboratory, admittedly not a disinterested party, saying of charges against one Chinese-American suspect that ethnicity had been "a major factor" in the accusations that were "built on thin air."[62] More disinterested analysts, including a Stanford University team, said that the Cox Report contained "sloppy research, factual errors and weakly justified inferences,"[63] charges denied by U.S. Senate Select Committee Staff Director Nicholas Rostow.

Judging the accuracy of charges against this individual, Wen Ho Lee, will need to await the outcome of court proceedings that as of mid-2000 promised to be protracted.

Several considerations provide the context for Chinese behavior in the area of proliferation. First, well into the 1990s China had virtually no formal export control structure, though in 1995, 1997, and 1998 Beijing began to issue regulations on controlled chemicals, control of nuclear exports, administration of arms exports, and control of nuclear dual-use items and related technologies.[64] Further, much of China's weapons and weapons-related manufacturing industry was put on a profit-and-loss basis during the economic reforms of the 1980s. The combination of profit motive and inadequate mechanisms of control was one reason for Chinese sales to fringe regimes.

Second, like Washington, Beijing has found that from time to time weapons sales and technology transfers can solidify relations with significant countries. For example, in 1986 (as Washington discovered in 1988) China sold between twenty and twenty-four CSS-2 intermediate-range missiles to Saudi Arabia—a transaction that not only made money for Beijing (perhaps $2 billion)[65] but also helped induce Riyadh to recognize the PRC and sever official ties with Taiwan in July 1990. According to Professor John W. Lewis, Hua Di, and Xue Litai, when the question of whether to sell the missiles to Saudi Arabia came to Deng Xiaoping for a decision, he simply asked, " 'How much money did you make?' The Poly Technologies [the arms export company] officer answered, 'two billion dollars,' and Deng replied, *'bu shao'* [not little]. The matter was thereby closed."[66] With respect to other weapons sales (such as cruise missiles) to Iran, Beijing has sought to solidify relations with a nation that may be an important future energy supplier and at the same time improve relations with a nation that, if so motivated, could conceivably help foment rebellion among China's Muslim population in its periodically unstable West.

Third, China has sought to use weapons sales and technology transfers to Pakistan not only to undermine its rival India but also to induce Washington to reduce weapons sales to Taiwan. Beijing will use every bit of leverage it has to halt weapons sales to Taipei.

Finally, in the case of missiles, although China agreed to observe the guidelines and parameters of the MTCR in 1992 and 1994, it did not become a *member* of the regime. Consequently, when members of MTCR would periodically change the rules, Beijing was placed in the awkward position of being asked to observe strictures it did not help draft.[67]

Several other factors are critical to understanding the nature of Sino-American interaction in the nonproliferation area—namely, uncertainties, legal injunctions, and inconsistent American behavior.

Uncertainties. Due to the covert nature of many proliferation and technology transfer activities and the intelligence systems used to verify their occurrence, U.S. intelligence gatherers often are not certain what has happened, when it occurred, and what it may signify. For example, the 1999 Cox Committee Report on Chinese espionage and technology acquisition is littered with qualifiers such as "[the] Select Committee judges that," "could choose," "may be tested," "is aware of reports," "[the PRC] could further accelerate," "could have a significant effect," "it is possible or even likely that," and so on.[68] Moreover, an independent review panel commissioned by the director of Central Intelligence to look at the same evidence concluded, "We believe it is more likely that the Chinese used US design information to inform their own program than to replicate US weapon designs."[69] Further, much technology is "dual use" equipment or material—that is, having legitimate civilian uses as well as potential military applications. Consequently, the pattern in almost every dispute with Beijing over proliferation has been Chinese denial that the alleged activity occurred, or that it exceeds agreed-upon guidelines, or that the end user intends to employ the product for military or other unapproved purposes. These denials have been paralleled in Washington by inter- and intra-agency debates over what occurred and how certain analysts may be.

The Washington bureaucracies most concerned with proliferation (the National Security Council; the departments of Defense, State, Commerce, and Energy; the Nuclear Regulatory Commission; the Arms Control and Disarmament Agency; intelligence agencies and relevant congressional oversight committees) use conduits in the mass media such as the *Washington Times* to leak partial data and alarming (or reassuring) stories to shore up their respective positions. In so doing each participant may hope to affect the annual MFN debate, pending or desired future legislation, executive branch actions, summit meetings, or election campaigns, as well as hope to retard the spread of weapons of mass destruction. For example, in May and June 1998, with President Clinton on the eve of his first, controversial visit to the PRC, Congress preparing for its annual consideration of MFN, other China-related legislation pending, and congressional election fever heating up, intelligence agencies began to hemorrhage information. Much of the data was conflicting or dubious. For example, the *New York Times* reported, "A classified report by the Central Intelligence Agency concluded that the companies, Loral Space and Communications and

Hughes Electronics, did not reveal information to China in 1996 that could harm national security.... But the intelligence arm of the State Department found just the opposite.... The State Department's assessment ... parallels the previously reported conclusions of a Pentagon Agency.... The conflicting judgments of government intelligence and security analysts muddy an already complicated inquiry by House and Senate committees."[70]

Between Chinese secrecy, the uncertainties of intelligence, the multiple uses of technology, and the confusion created by interagency fights and domestic politics, it has often been difficult to assess the soundness of U.S. accusations or the true irresponsibility of Chinese actions. One thing is clear, however: the mid-1999 charges of Chinese espionage were part of a larger process of deteriorating U.S.-China relations as the decade ended (see Chapter 1).

Legislation. In the United States, a number of laws have been key to nuclear nonproliferation policy and arms and technology export control throughout the post–cold war decade: the Atomic Energy Act of 1954;[71] the Nuclear Non-Proliferation Act of 1978; the Foreign Assistance Act of 1961 and the Arms Export Control Act as amended by the 1976 Symington Amendment, the 1977 Glenn Amendment, and the 1985 Pressler Amendment; the Export Administration Act of 1979 (which expired in September 1990 but continued to be implemented under Executive Orders 12730 in 1990 and 12924 in 1994 and lists "controlled countries" of which the PRC was one in 1999);[72] the Omnibus Trade and Competitiveness Act of 1988 (concerned with "the national security effects of proposed mergers, acquisitions, and takeovers of U.S. companies by foreign interests");[73] and the 1994 Nuclear Proliferation Prevention Act.[74]

The legal framework for policy regarding chemical and biological weapons is complex as well; it includes the Export Administration Act, the Arms Export Control Act, the Iran-Iraq Arms Non-Proliferation Act of 1992, and various executive orders, as well as the Chemical Weapons Convention and the Biological Weapons Convention. Finally, there is a body of U.S. law that pertains to missiles and missile technology under the Arms Export Control Act and the International Traffic in Arms Regulations.

The aforementioned laws have some conceptual features in common—namely, that documented actions of foreign countries that are deemed by Washington to have fostered the spread of weapons and technologies of mass destruction and the means of their delivery require that the United States impose sanctions on the offenders. Sanctions usually involve one or all of the following: tightened technology export controls, prohibitions against American firms buying goods or services (such as satellite launches) from sanctioned business entities, prohibitions against the export of specific products to China or specific end users, and the cutoff of aid and other financial benefits to offenders. Oftentimes these sanctions have no sunset provisions and sometimes do not allow for the issuance of a presidential waiver (i.e., exception), and therefore, once imposed, they become very difficult to remove. Thus the sanctions can become an "all sticks, and no carrots" approach to foreign policy. Domestic export offenders can be hit with penalties that include fines, imprisonment, loss of export privileges, revocation of export licenses, and seizure of illegal exports and their means of conveyance.

American exporters often resist sanctions because foreign suppliers of roughly equivalent items may exist for the Chinese, and the U.S. firms simply lose sales. This is one reason the 1999 Cox Committee Report called for reestablishing "new binding international controls on technology transfers."[75] In other cases, sanctions may affect the ability of Americans to buy goods or services from the PRC—for example, the purchase of Chinese launch services for American satellites. Chinese payload delivery is 15 percent less expensive than the American, Russian, French, Ukrainian, and Japanese alternatives.[76] American business, therefore, is disadvantaged by sanctions on Chinese launch services because it is forced to use higher-priced, less available alternatives. Ironically, in such cases, Americans are hurt twice by China's documented and suspected proliferation behavior: once with the transfer itself and again by the U.S. sanctions imposed to punish Beijing. In 1996 Assistant Secretary of State Winston Lord vented his frustration with this conundrum in the context of a spring 1996 dispute over Beijing's sale of some $70,000 of ring magnets to Pakistan, magnets that could be used to process uranium: "But we have got to weigh credibility in Beijing about our firmness, maintaining a productive dialogue with them on these issues, maintaining U.S. domestic support, promoting non-proliferation above all costs, following U.S. law, no matter how crazy it is. And I would say to sanction $70,000 worth of exports with huge sanctions which cut off our exports to China does not seem to be the most effective way to go about it, but we will apply the U.S. law."[77]

That U.S. firms and jobs are affected by each sanction decision motivates a plethora of domestic interest groups who try to minimize the frequency with which sanctions are invoked and the magnitude of the harm done. This gives rise to endless political conflict, policy inconsistencies, and assertions that political leaders such as President Clinton have been subject to undue pressure from companies with large export interests.[78]

American Inconsistencies. Inconsistency in American nonproliferation policy stems from a number of sources beyond those just discussed. These include America's divergent interests with respect to various countries (different treatment for friends and rivals), changing administrations and congresses in Washington, and the struggle between functional and regional bureaus and among cabinet-level departments. Nonetheless, the fundamental origin of U.S. policy inconsistencies is the conflict among American economic and security goals and among economic objectives themselves—for example, between immediate profit and long-term economic competitiveness. As former Under Secretary of Commerce Jeffrey A. Garten put it, "In dealing with big emerging markets like China, the U.S. faces excruciating tradeoffs. On the one hand we have overwhelming commercial goals. On the other, we have to be careful about transferring technology, first because there could be unintended military consequences, and secondly because we could be transferring our competitiveness."[79]

More broadly, the United States has been inconsistent in its fidelity to the goal of nonproliferation and to its nonproliferation policies. For example, Washington assisted Britain in obtaining nuclear weapons, was only slightly less helpful to the French program, and turned a blind eye to Israel's acquisition of such weapons.[80] On the other hand, it also is true that the United States twice induced Taiwan to stop its nuclear weapons development effort.[81] Finally, throughout the 1990s, Washington did little beyond private expressions of dissatisfaction to halt Tel Aviv's transfer of conventional American military technology to Beijing contrary to U.S. law and bilateral agreements. Only in April 2000 did Secretary of Defense William Cohen publicly rebuke Israel for proceeding to sell one of possibly four early-warning aircraft to Beijing. At the same time, there were rumblings in the U.S. House of Representatives about holding up a portion of U.S. military aid to Israel until Tel Aviv canceled the sale. Washington was particularly concerned that these airborne radar platforms would reduce Taipei's tactical air advantage over the Taiwan Strait.[82]

Moreover, the United States' position as the world's leading weapons exporter since 1991 further erodes Washington's moral standing on nonproliferation. (China has been the fourth to sixth most prolific exporter of weapons since 1985.)[83] In Beijing's view, a U.S. F-16 aircraft can deliver weapons of mass destruction as easily as a Chinese missile. Further, it is worth noting with respect to the Indian nuclear program that conducted an initial "peaceful" nuclear detonation in 1974 and then weapons tests in May 1998 that 1,300 Indian nuclear scientists had, over the years, been trained in the United States. Abdul Kalam, the force behind India's bomb development, spent four months training in the United States.[84] Moreover, America extended India "subsidized loans and research grants for both applied and pure research in this area,"[85] though such activity was curtailed after the 1974 test. The United States can be linked to Pakistan's missile program as well. NASA trained Pakistani rocket scientists at the Wallops Virginia Flight Facility.[86] Thus, for China and much of the world, the implicit U.S. position can be translated as follows: some countries can be trusted with weapons of mass destruction and their means of delivery, while others cannot, and this trust will shift as American attitudes, interests, and policies change.

When it comes to issues of nonproliferation, a pattern can be detected in the U.S.-China post–cold war relationship. The United States accuses China of weapons and technology transfers that violate agreements or that are, in Washington's view, ill advised; Beijing denies it; Washington threatens and sometimes invokes sanctions; those sanctions are rolled back as U.S. domestic economic interests raise a cry while competitors elsewhere are filling the vacuum; and eventually the Chinese make a limited (often verbal) pledge to refrain from future behavior they deny having undertaken in the first place. Sometimes China remains faithful to these pledges, but oftentimes Washington is uncertain. This general dynamic, however, has been accompanied by overall progress as Beijing has joined the principal international agreements on arms control and built an export control structure that may become increasingly effective over time.

A Case Study in Nonproliferation and Technology Transfer: Satellite Launches. One case is particularly illustrative of the complex problems both sides have faced in dealing with proliferation and technology control in the post–cold war decade—the issue of American satellites launched on Chinese carrier rockets. This case demonstrates how intertwined domestic politics, our respective nations' ties with India and Pakistan, American proliferation anxieties, and Chinese concerns about Taiwan have become. It also illustrates the difficulties presented by dual-use technologies and the difficult trade-offs among security and economic objectives.[87]

The issue revolves around whether to permit American satellites to be launched on Chinese carrier rockets and, if so, under what conditions. In the 1980s and 1990s PRC boosters were a relatively inexpensive means for American companies to put some payloads into space; by 1998 the PRC held 9 percent of the international commercial satellite launching market,[88] and it saw the launch business as a major commercial opportunity.[89] Although provisions (and a 1988 agreement with Beijing)[90] exist designed to safeguard the U.S. satellite's technology prior to launch (such as putting it in a "black box," "embedding" critical technologies in the satellite, and presumably guarding the technology around the clock when it is in the PRC), there have, nonetheless, been serious concerns that classified information and technologies (related to encryption, guidance, separation, warhead delivery, and rocket reliability) can find (or have found, according to a 1999 congressional report)[91] their way into Chinese (particularly PLA) hands, perhaps after a mishap, through people associated with the commercial transaction, through the international insurers of launches, or as a result of poor on-site security by the Department of Defense and its contractors. In the latter case, for example, "Both the Defense Department monitors [of in-China satellite launches] and industry representatives have complained about the quality of work and the conduct of some members of the contractor security forces. . . . The Defense Department monitor indicates that the solicitation of prostitutes became so intense that he was approached by a PRC foreign affairs officer who was assigned to the launch to report that one of the [American] guards had been soliciting prostitution in front of the local police department."[92] Beyond fears about a possible loss of technology to the PRC, Washington also worries that Beijing might re-export it to terrorists or rogue nations.

Some in the American defense and security establishments, as well as in Congress, also worry that U.S. satellite companies and their insurers might inadvertently or intentionally assist the Chinese in making their rockets more reliable to safeguard their $200 million satellites. On the other hand, as U.S. Commerce Secretary William M. Daley argued in 1998, high-tech exports are the United States' comparative advantage in the global economy and the key to creating high-wage jobs for Americans. Without such exports the United States would be unable to achieve the production scales that allow it to preserve its primacy in high-tech products and in R&D. To further complicate matters, although immediate sales may be in the interest of U.S. firms, the technology transfer involved could decrease American economic competitiveness over the long run. Clouding this discussion is the lack of certainty about what the PRC may have obtained and how long it might take to translate such information into deployable systems or products.

In 1988, against this background of commercial interest and national security concern, President Reagan approved U.S. satellite launches on Chinese carriers.[93] In response to the 1989 bloodshed in China, President Bush, who had carried on Reagan's satellite policy, imposed sanctions that included the requirement that satellite launches on Chinese rockets receive a presidential waiver (justified as in "the national interest") in each instance. The first such launch waiver was approved in December 1989, much to the dismay of the Bush administration's human rights critics, who viewed the decision as backsliding on post-Tiananmen sanctions. Throughout the four-year Bush administration a total of three waivers were issued covering the launch of nine satellites.[94]

The inconsistency of waiver issuance during the Bush presidency reflected changes in Washington's perception of Beijing's proliferation behavior. In May 1991, because of alleged and documented PRC missile, missile technology, and other disquieting transfers to Iran and Pakistan, the Bush administration announced restrictions on high-tech trade with Beijing. However, on September 11, 1992, because of commercial pressure, the need for greater satellite communications capacity, and Beijing's assurances in a February 1 letter from Foreign Minister Qian Qichen that it would abide by the MTCR,[95] the president issued new launch authorizations.[96] In the waning days of the 1992 presidential campaign, vice presidential candidate Al Gore was particularly critical of those waivers, saying in a speech at the Goddard Space Flight Center, "President Bush really is an incurable patsy for those dictators he sets out to coddle."[97]

Campaign rhetoric notwithstanding, the new Clinton administration continued the Bush policy and replicated the stop-and-go pattern of linking approvals of satellite launch waivers to Chinese nonproliferation behavior, issuing a total of eight waivers for eleven launches through early 1998.[98] By July 1993, seven months into the Clinton administration, the White House had approved three satellite launch authorizations, but the next month it imposed sanctions on Beijing because of the PRC's sale of missile technology to Pakistan. At issue was whether M-11 short-range ballistic missiles had been shipped from China to Pakistan (in the immediate aftermath of President Bush's November 1992 decision to sell fighter jets to Taiwan) or just missile parts. Had complete missiles been sold, that "would have called for far stricter measures, including the end of all satellite exports [to China]."[99] Thereafter, no satellite waivers were issued until February 2, 1996, when three approvals were granted. These approvals should have confused the Chinese about the U.S. commitment to nonproliferation, coming at a time when Washington was concerned about prior Chinese missile exercises near Taiwan, the ongoing transfer of missile technology to Pakistan, and the sale of ring magnets to Islamabad. The net effect probably confirmed Beijing's suspicion that in the end economic interests would trump proliferation concerns in Washington.

In 1996, however, the story began to assume complex domestic overtones in the United States. A Chinese rocket (launch waiver issued by President Bush in September 1992) carrying a Loral satellite exploded shortly after launch on February 15, 1996, destroying the $200 million satellite and killing an estimated one hundred Chinese living in a nearby village with falling debris[100]—there had been two earlier launch failures of Hughes-manufactured satellites, one in 1992 and the other in 1995. Two American firms (Loral Space and Hughes Electronics) played some role in helping the Chinese ascertain the cause of the mishap. The two firms' involvement had been prompted by international insurers who hesitated to continue covering launches on unreliable vehicles.[101] During consultations in April–May 1996 between the U.S. companies and the Chinese (and in a subsequent report), there *may* have been some transfer of protected technology.

A number of issues ran through this saga of satellite launch waivers, as they run through most technology export decisions: How should national security and economic considerations be balanced and what should be the trade-off between short- and long-term economic interests? To what degree was the threat of satellite waiver disapproval (a sanction) effective in inducing Beijing to be more responsive to U.S. proliferation concerns? Were sanctions counterproductive? Was it feasible to expect that only civilian Chinese end users employed whatever technology was legitimately transferred? In the case of communications satellites, for example, what could be done if the PLA (or PLA front organizations) leased some of the frequencies from third parties who "owned" the satellites? Could satellite technology be fully protected in a black box or by being embedded in larger structures, and what would happen to sensitive technology in the case of accident? Finally, how could the approval process be accelerated so American firms would more expeditiously know whether or not their commercial plans were viable? American business has expressed ongoing concern that the approval process is so cumbersome that it is disadvantaged in the competition with foreign firms whose governments have less rigorous export control standards and faster approval processes. In addition, the ever present threat of sanctions and their on-again, off-again application make U.S. suppliers unreliable in the eyes of foreign purchasers.

Against the backdrop of these issues and in the midst of a battle between the Department of State and Department of Commerce over control of commercial satellite licensing, in March 1996 President Clinton decided to shift the lead in licensing commercial satellite launches (including satellites with nine critical technologies that could be used for military purposes)[102] from the Department of State to the Department of Commerce.[103] The shift in jurisdiction, it was hoped, would expedite approvals and make the process more transparent, while leaving the departments of State and Defense still able to review all license applications with an eye toward national security concerns; if they had worries there was an elaborate appeal process. The decision took effect in November 1996, *after* the general election.[104] This attempt to streamline the satellite-licensing process was something that many in Congress had urged since 1990 and that corporations such as Loral, Hughes, Motorola, and Martin Marietta (later Lockheed Martin Corporation) had promoted, in part because under Commerce Department jurisdiction more favorable tax treatment was generally given.

For the next two years, little was heard concerning this issue. Then, in February 1998, President Clinton issued a launch waiver for another Loral Space and Communications satellite. This approval came against a backdrop of resentment in some quarters of the U.S. national security apparatus at having had the lead for approving launch waivers transferred to the Commerce Department: the resentment, in part, stemmed from the Commerce Department's decision not to have any U.S. government officials monitor several launches in the PRC,[105] as well as from the pattern of perceived Chinese behavior during the preceding two years or so. The PRC's two sets of intimidating missile exercises near Taiwan in mid-1995 and March 1996 did not help matters. In addition, there were continuing reports of Chinese transfers of missile and missile-related technology to Pakistan, Iran, and Libya. (There were accusations that China had agreed to supply Iran with gyroscopes, accelerometers, telemetry equipment, and nearly four hundred tons of chemicals used to produce nerve agents.)[106] Lastly, for about a year there had been ongoing investigations into whether or not people (some associated with the PLA) acting on Beijing's behalf had illegally contributed campaign funds to congressional and presidential coffers (see Chapter 7). All of this political tinder was lying around, just waiting for an enterprising reporter, bureaucrat, or congressman to ignite it.

Ignition occurred on April 4, 1998, when the *New York Times* carried an investigative report on the Loral and Hughes 1996 postcrash investigation, alleged technology transfer, and President Clinton's February 1998 Loral launch waiver. Thereafter, anonymous leaks, confessions, and information surfaced. By May and June 1998 hearings were being organized in both the House and the Senate. The Senate Select Committee on Intelligence (the Shelby Committee) agreed to lead an investigation on the transfer of satellite technology and related issues on May 21, 1998, with its extensive report issued a year later.[107] On June 18, 1998, a Select House Committee (chaired by Representative Christopher Cox of California) was created (by a vote of 409 to 10) with a budget of $2.5 million to investigate U.S. technology transfers to China. On January 3, 1999, the Cox Committee finished its classified report and, after months of wrangling with the White House, released the three-volume unclassified version on May 25.[108]

Much of the mass media and Clinton administration detractors argued as follows:

(1) During the 1996 presidential campaign an unscrupulous fund-raiser for the Democratic Party named Johnny Chung had accepted money from Lieutenant Colonel Liu Chaoying, the daughter of China's then ranking military officer, General Liu Huaqing.[109] Colonel Liu worked for China Aerospace, a PRC state enterprise that had a direct interest in promoting the use of Chinese rockets for American satellite launches.[110]

(2) The chairman of Loral Space and Communications, Bernard L. Schwartz, the largest personal contributor to the Democratic National Committee in the 1996 election cycle,[111] may have influenced President Clinton to approve the 1998 Loral launch waiver. Further, it was argued that Loral Space stood to gain from Clinton's making the Commerce Department the lead agency for issuing civilian satellite licenses in 1996.

(3) Loral Space and Hughes Electronics had inappropriately conveyed sensitive information to the Chinese rocket program in the 1996 postcrash investigation, thereby providing Beijing the ability to strike U.S. cities with more accurate missiles. In a joint hearing of the House International Relations and National Security Committees on June 17, 1998, data were presented asserting that from 1990 to 1996, 25 percent of Chinese rocket launches blew up. But from 1996 to 1998 the Chinese had had a perfect record in ten launches,[112] a record of reliability that the Chinese thereafter used to advertise their Long March rockets in search of future launch customers.[113]

All of this eventually came down to an assertion that U.S. national security had been compromised and America's China policy was for sale for campaign contributions—both foreign and domestic. This had allegedly occurred because the administration had been in a headlong rush for campaign cash and had placed too high a premium on U.S. commercial success rather than national security. An explosion of partisan rhetoric immediately ensued; Dana Rohrabacher (R-Calif.), chair of the House Science Subcommittee on Space and Aeronautics, said, "It takes the wind right out of your lungs.... If this is true, it is the worst technological betrayal of the American people since the Rosenbergs. This is nothing less than a catastrophe for the security of our nation."

Into this seething cauldron yet another ingredient was added: five unexpected nuclear test detonations on May 11 and 13, 1998, made India the sixth declared nuclear state. Six *claimed* Pakistani tests followed on May 28 and 30, 1998, making it the seventh declared nuclear state. Further, in the months preceding these nuclear tests, both New Delhi and Islamabad had been testing missiles that could loft nuclear warheads to each other's principal urban areas.

China's past nuclear and missile cooperation with Pakistan suddenly assumed ominous overtones. One line of thought in the United States was that China's assistance to Pakistan had alarmed India to the point of testing nuclear weapons. In this view, the facts that India's Hindu Nationalist Party (the BJP) had long been committed to India's acquisition and testing of such weapons and that the BJP had just taken over the reins of power seemed a mere coincidence. Democratic India being bullied by Communist China made for a gripping headline in the American debate about China policy.

Clinton administration detractors were weaving all these strands into a large tapestry. The tapestry's threads were commercially driven (and campaign contribution-driven) decisions to loosen export controls, illegal foreign and domestic campaign contributions to sway decisions, and PRC collaboration with Pakistan that violated nonproliferation agreements and past assurances to Washington and fueled democratic India's fears. Each link in this chain of assertions was weakened by unproven assumptions and debate over the evidence and its meaning. However, that did not make the picture any less damaging in the short run, often the only time horizon that matters politically. By the time the accuracy of these overlapping and complex charges could be assessed, the November 1998 congressional elections would be over.

In this atmosphere, the House of Representatives passed a bill (in a bipartisan vote of 364 to 54) prohibiting further satellite exports or reexports to China. After the bill had survived threats of veto and had made it through a more skeptical Senate, Congress passed the National Defense Authorization Act for fiscal year 1999, which in October 1998 became Public Law 105–261 (the Strom Thurmond National Defense Authorization Act). It included a "sense of the Congress" clause that "the United States should not export to the People's Republic of China missile equipment or technology that would improve the missile or space launch capabilities of the People's Republic of China"; in addition, the act instructed the administration to move regulatory control back to the Department of State from the Commerce Department.[114] Shortly thereafter, the Clinton administration rejected an export license application for a $450 million Hughes Electronics Corporation satellite to a Chinese-Singapore consortium, in part to signal seriousness to Congress and the Chinese, in part to send a message to Hughes that the administration was displeased with how it had discharged its earlier obligations concerning technology transfer, and in part because of concerns that the Chinese military would benefit from particular information necessary to successfully complete this particular launch.[115]

In late 1998 and early 1999, amidst the rancorous and partisan impeachment proceedings against President Clinton, the story became more embroidered still, with the Cox Committee issuing a classified report (January 3, 1999), the later declassified portion of which (released May 25, 1999) asserted that China had engaged in protracted and exhaustive efforts to obtain American military and commercial secret and proprietary technologies. Charges included penetration of the U.S. Energy Department Laboratory at Los Alamos, New Mexico, and compromise of U.S. nuclear warhead secrets. In turn, U.S. policy on technology transfer to the PRC was further tightened, Republicans had a campaign issue to use in the upcoming presidential campaign of 2000, and the Chinese predictably denied acquiring prohibited information. The Cox Committee Report justifiably called attention to security and counterintelligence lapses at U.S. laboratories and elsewhere, but it provided considerably less evidence as to what actually had been lost, how useful it might be, and when, if ever, the losses would find their way into the Chinese arsenal. Nonetheless, these 1999 accusations became another piece in the mosaic of a deteriorating U.S.-China relationship and contributed to the atmosphere that made it very difficult for Bill Clinton to agree to terms for China's entry into the WTO in April. (See Chapters 1, 4, and 7.)

Impact of U.S.-Chinese Security Conflicts on the Bilateral Relationship

The preceding case study illustrates how conflicts in the nonproliferation and technology transfer domains can color the entire relationship. Without understating the legitimacy of these concerns, they can become brushes with which the opposition party paints an unattractive portrait of the occupant of the White House. The uncertainty that often surrounds what the Chinese have done and the inconsistency of executive branch actions allow U.S. domestic political forces (in both parties) to conjure up the most damaging scenarios and use them to bludgeon the administration. Foreign policy then becomes hopelessly intertwined with partisan politics. Further, Congress passes laws that are nearly impossible to implement or are counterproductive, then proceeds to blame the party occupying the White House for failure to do so. Finally, the case study illustrates several additional features of the relationship that make effective management difficult.

First, U.S. law pits America's commercial interests against the most cautious understandings of U.S. national security, setting off endless struggles among interest groups and bureaucracies. Commercial interests generally argue for selling something unless the harm is demonstrable and there are no alternative foreign suppliers. By way of contrast, single-issue interest groups (e.g., the Wisconsin Project) and bureaucracies responsible for antiproliferation policy wait for their opportunities to make a case for restricting such transactions. These interest groups and their congressional and bureaucratic allies save their accusations for the strategic moment when the mass media are focused on some news peg, whether it is a presidential trip to China or the annual review of MFN. This process creates a pattern of oscillating friction, stop-and-go policy, and general uncertainty.

Second, the U.S. laws that mandate sanctions often generate results that damage the integrity of the government in the eyes of its own citizens or the credibility of U.S. policy in the eyes of Beijing. Policymakers who must implement such laws may seek to overlook evidence or lift sanctions shortly after they are imposed to minimize economic damage to U.S. interests. As President Clinton mentioned in a moment of candor at the White House, "What always happens if you have automatic sanctions legislation is it puts enormous pressure on whoever is in the executive branch to fudge an evaluation of the facts of what is going on."[116]

Third, Chinese foreign policy is created in a system principally organized by geographic region, a system in which the military has its own separate channels to the top. Beijing often lacks functional expertise on many issues and the Foreign Ministry can be ineffectual in controlling the PLA. Chinese in the foreign and national security establishments recognize these problems, but solving them is another matter, though the export control structure was getting stronger by the close of the 1990s.[117]

Fourth, Chinese security interests (e.g., maintaining balance between India and Pakistan) may not accord with America's perceived interests (opposing proliferation at all costs). Beijing considers U.S. arms sales to Taiwan as being as sensitive to its interests as America considers proliferation activity to its.

Finally, although I have focused on points of friction with China during the 1995–1999 period, progress was made toward nonproliferation goals as well. During that time period, Beijing agreed to the indefinite extension of the Non-Proliferation Treaty, agreed to the Comprehensive Test Ban Treaty, and offered assurances on curtailing nuclear and missile cooperation with Iran. Moreover, in 1999, when the U.S. Senate rejected the Comprehensive Test Ban Treaty, Beijing declared its intention to proceed with its own ratification of the pact. The record, therefore, has been a combination of progress and ongoing conflict. The past is prologue to the foreseeable future. As for American firms, they can expect actual and alleged technology transfers to China to come under increasing scrutiny as PRC power grows, as the Lockheed Martin Corporation found out in spring 2000.[118]

Taiwan

Taiwan has been yet another focus of long-standing security concern. Although Taiwan is more than a security issue in U.S.-China relations, its security implications are serious. If China and the United States were to clash militarily in the early twenty-first century, the Taiwan Strait would be the most likely location. As Mao put it to Henry Kissinger on October 21, 1975, "A hundred years hence we will want it [Taiwan] (gesturing with his hand), and we are going to fight for it."[119] As seen in the preceding chapter, Washington, Beijing, and Taipei are each becoming more alarmed with the security implications of the Taiwan tangle.

The missile crisis in the Taiwan Strait in 1995–1996, one of the turning points discussed in the preceding chapter, should constitute a flashing yellow light in the management of U.S.-China relations, as should the tensions set off by President Lee Teng-hui's call in July 1999 to consider mainland-Taiwan ties to be a "special state-to-state relationship," and as should the March 2000 election of former independence advocate Chen Shui-bian to be president of Taiwan. The Taiwan issue is addressed here (as well as in Chapter 5) because, for Beijing, preventing the de jure separation of Taiwan from the mainland is inextricably linked to regime legitimacy and, therefore, survival. It is an issue over which Beijing might very well engage in combat, even if it stood to lose, and in its 1998 white paper

China's National Defense, Beijing declared that selling weapons to Taipei "threatens China's security."[120] For Washington, Taiwan also is a security issue. If conflict broke out in the Taiwan Strait it could directly involve U.S. forces. As a matter of U.S. law as written in the 1979 Taiwan Relations Act (TRA),[121] a peaceful resolution of the tensions in the strait is linked to American interests in regional stability. In any case, the outcome of a possible future crisis in the strait would have great bearing on the fate of the U.S. security presence and alliances throughout East Asia and would affect Washington's global credibility. The importance of managing this issue properly cannot be overstated; however, doing so will be difficult for Washington and Beijing for three sets of reasons, discussed in the following paragraphs. DIFFICULTIES IN·MANAGING TAIWAN ISSUE:

Neither Beijing nor Washington Controls Taipei. As members of both Taiwan's Kuomintang (KMT) and Democratic Progressive Party (DPP) never tire of saying, the island's people are determined to control their own fate, and they have considerable resources to do so. The island possesses Asia's fourth largest modern military to protect it from its potential attacker, which is approximately one hundred miles away. Taiwan had more than $98.6 billion in foreign exchange reserves as of July 1999 and is the world's fourteenth largest trading economy.

Furthermore, political and social trends underway on the island since the 1980s have made Taiwan's citizens and government much more assertive in proclaiming their autonomy and pursuing their interests abroad. Throughout the first half of the 1980s, Taiwan President Chiang Ching-kuo brought "Taiwanese" (as opposed to mainlanders who had come to the island around 1949) into the ruling KMT and into the government itself in substantial numbers. By the time of his death in January 1988, Taiwanese constituted nearly 67 percent of the KMT's membership.[122] Chiang's successor, Lee Teng-hui, is a native Taiwanese. (Over time Beijing came to speak of him as culturally Japanese, reflecting not only Lee's upbringing in Japanese-colonized Taiwan and subsequent study in Japan, but also perhaps the PRC's own effort to question even Lee's credentials as a Chinese.)

Thereafter, under Lee Teng-hui's leadership Taiwan evolved into a multiparty, increasingly competitive democracy; the principal rival to the ruling KMT became the DPP that had written into its charter (in 1986) a commitment to the island's independence. Following local elections in November 1997, DPP officials headed cities and county governments in which 72 percent of the island's population resided, with KMT officials administering areas with only 22 percent of the population.[123] Although the

DPP's numbers were reduced somewhat by the late-1998 elections in which the KMT recaptured the Taipei mayor's office, all of this (and popular frustration with "black money," corruption) made the DPP a serious (and ultimately successful) contender to capture the presidency in the year 2000 election. Taiwan's democratization, combined with the end of the cold war and the emergence of many post-Soviet states, created a sense among Taiwanese that they deserved a dignified and meaningful international role and that the world might be receptive to their yearnings. As many citizens of Taiwan looked to America, they saw a traditional ally, a nation historically receptive (particularly the Congress) to the Wilsonian concept of rights of self-determination, and a nation dismayed by what it had seen in Tiananmen Square in June 1989.

Further, throughout the 1980s and 1990s, the political/cultural identity of Taiwan's people changed dramatically. In 1992, 44 percent of the population saw itself as "Chinese," whereas by 1998 that percentage had dropped to 16.7. Conversely, in 1992, 16.7 percent of the population defined itself as "Taiwanese"; by 1998 the corresponding number was 37.8 percent. Those defining themselves as both Taiwanese and Chinese grew from 36.5 percent of the population in 1992 to 39.5 percent in 1998.[124] Reflecting both his own sense of identity and those of his constituents, President Lee Teng-hui said in late August 1998, "I'm a Taiwan person first and a Chinese person second. All of us came a long time ago from mainland China, and we spend our lives here. So we love this place. But of course, we are all Chinese as well."[125]

Several factors account for this shift in how Taiwan's people perceive themselves. The first was that between the 1980s (when travel to the mainland was first allowed) and 1998, Taiwan residents made more than 13 million visits to the mainland for business, pleasure, and family reunions. By and large, these visitors were not attracted to what they saw, socially or politically, though they realized that there was money to be made on the mainland.[126] In addition, as the mainland observed Taiwan's people developing an identity of their own separate from mainland China and saw Lee Teng-hui and the DPP making more vigorous efforts to establish a separate identity for Taiwan in the international community, Beijing did two things that heightened the estrangement. It employed coercive (Beijing would call them "deterrent") methods (e.g., the missile exercises of 1995 and 1996 and a gradual missile buildup thereafter)[127] and openly resisted efforts by Taipei to establish official, or semiofficial, ties abroad. In an earlier era, when Beijing did not perceive so much separatist momentum, it had agreed to what it deemed appropriate Taiwan participation in the Asian Development Bank and in the Olympics. The more recent actions designed to isolate Taipei, however, only further alienated an increasingly prosperous, assertive, and democratic Taiwan populace. More and more, to the people of Taiwan, Beijing's policy appeared to be all sticks and no carrots.

From Beijing's perspective (and, I believe, that of the PRC citizenry more broadly), the changes on Taiwan have absolutely nothing to do with its claim to the island. The mainland believes in its historical sovereign claim, which also was recognized by the Cairo Declaration of November 26, 1943. Further, the Chinese position that Taiwan is a part of China was "acknowledged" (*chengren*), not "recognized," in the Three Communiqués with Washington (of 1972, 1978, and 1982), as well as in innumerable other statements U.S. officials have made since the early 1970s.

During his June–July 1998 trip to China, President Clinton publicly offered the assurances that came to be known as the "Three No's," most of which Henry Kissinger had privately said to Zhou Enlai in July 1971: "We don't support independence for Taiwan; or two Chinas; or one Taiwan, one China."[128] Unlike Kissinger, Clinton went on to say, "And we don't believe that Taiwan should be a member in any organization for which statehood is a requirement."[129] Herein lies the policy problem facing Beijing and Washington in the post–cold war era, as it pertains to Taiwan. Both Beijing and Washington have based their relationship on the acknowledgment of a vague "one China" vision that increasingly is not shared by the people of Taiwan. Speaking with his advisers in October 1976, Kissinger foretold the dilemma to which the United States is now dangerously close: "For us to go to war with a recognized country where we have an ambassador over a part of what we would recognize as their country would be preposterous."[130]

The United States supports and expects a "peaceful settlement" across the Taiwan Strait, and although there is no formal U.S. commitment to defend the island in the event that peace breaks down, there is a bias in that direction built into the TRA. The United States has not concerned itself with the substance of the final resolution across the strait, choosing instead only to say that whatever the resolution is it should be peaceful. The principal deviation from this measured posture was an off-the-cuff response by President Clinton to an audience question at Peking University on June 29, 1998. In that response he said: "Now, when the United States and China reached agreement that we would have a one China policy, we also reached agreement that the reunification would occur by peaceful means, and we have encouraged the cross-strait dialogue to achieve that."[131] The White House immediately sought to correct this, and though people in Taiwan were alarmed by the implication that the administration was endorsing "reunification" (as opposed to "resolution"), Washington has been, and remains, committed to a process, *not a particular outcome*. Beijing, on the other hand, is committed to defending its one-China vision to preserve its own legitimacy by any means necessary, although peaceful means are preferable; *it is committed to a broad outcome*, not a process. Further, Washington finds it difficult to defend a one-China vision against which increasingly powerful forces on the island are working. This brings us to Taiwan's lobbying in the United States.

Domestic Politics in the United States and China Are an Important Consideration in the Taiwan Issue. With the exception of Israel, no foreign entity has been as effective at lobbying the United States as Taiwan. This has been the case since the 1940s and 1950s.[132]

With about two-thirds of the Taiwan cabinet (as of 1996) having received advanced education in the United States,[133] and Taiwan consistently among the top five sources of foreign students enrolled in American institutions of higher education, Taipei has a deep reservoir of people who have studied in America and understand it well. President Lee Teng-hui studied agricultural economics at Cornell University. The head of Taiwan's Institute of International Relations in 1998 and the former director-general of the Government Information Office, Yu-ming Shaw, taught at Notre Dame. The heads of two prominent think tanks in Taiwan taught at American universities, and Taiwan's National Security Council has several staff members who have studied and taught in the United States. Hung-mao Tien, Chen Shui-bian's foreign minister, taught at the University of Wisconsin. Indeed, the pattern of long-time Taiwanese residents of the United States returning to serve the Taiwan government is common. Ma Ying-jeou, elected mayor of Taipei in 1998, went to Harvard University and widely capitalized on that fact during his election campaign. Consequently, Taiwan's leaders understand how the American system operates, have extensive personal and institutional ties to the United States, and communicate effectively in the American political and cultural idiom.

Beyond its own human infrastructure, Taiwan has not shied away from spending substantial money to retain the best American political, public relations, and legal talent money can buy. For example, sometime after he was defeated in the presidential race of 1996, the law firm of former Senate Majority Leader Robert Dole reportedly accepted a monthly retainer of $30,000 from the Taipei Economic and Cultural Representative Office for Mr. Dole to provide "strategic advice and counseling," an arrangement that was perfectly legal.[134] In 1997, Taipei was reported to have fourteen

U.S. law firms under retention—Beijing had one. Similarly, Beijing has ties with one U.S. public relations firm, while Taipei has many PR advisers.

The Taiwan government is not the only Taiwan entity to effectively articulate its viewpoint in the American setting; the island has other, less well known access points to the United States, one of which is a separatist organization called FAPA (Formosan Association for Public Affairs). A registered U.S. nonprofit organization founded in 1982, FAPA is composed primarily of persons of Taiwanese ancestry. Over the years some members of Congress have received political and other support from FAPA. In FAPA's own words, its first purpose is "[t]o seek international support for the right of the people on Taiwan (Formosa) to determine their future status."[135] One of its 1998 publications was titled *Towards De Jure Independence!*

Moreover, Taipei has followed a long-term strategy to influence rising U.S. political and intellectual leaders. Taipei brings promising local American politicians to Taiwan early in their careers (Bill Clinton went four times before he became president), and congressional trips to Taipei are legendary for their frequency and hospitality. In academic circles, in the first half of the 1990s, the island became a major source of funding for China studies in the United States.[136] Many U.S. China scholars, including this author, have traveled to Taiwan as guests of various government-associated entities over the years. Moreover, some of Washington's most active think tanks have received money from Taiwan sources, with government money sometimes being passed through Taiwan "donor" corporations.

Finally, on the economic and trade fronts, Taiwan has been tireless in sending "buying missions" to individual U.S. states, using commercial transactions to augment generalized support for Taiwan. Every year from 1987 through 1997, Taiwan imported more goods from the United States than did the PRC, even taking into account U.S. exports to mainland China transshipped through Hong Kong (see tables 1 and 3).[137]

All of the foregoing activity is legal and has been successful not only because it is skillfully executed but also because it builds upon the most fundamental resource Taiwan has in dealing with Americans: the people of Taiwan have a remarkable story to tell, particularly when combined with the inherent American preference for the underdog. A bedraggled military force defeated by communist forces in 1949, led by General Chiang Kai-shek, fled to the poor island of Taiwan. There, Chiang's legions established an authoritarian government, gained U.S. economic support and military protection, and began to transform the island from an impoverished backwater into one of Asia's wealthiest, free-market societies (in 1952 per capita GNP was US$196 and in 1997 it was more than US$13,000). Moreover, after Generalissimo Chiang's death, and with U.S. encouragement, the island gradually established a competitive party system under the leadership of Chiang Kai-shek's son (Chiang Ching-kuo) and his successor, Taiwanese-born Lee Teng-hui.

It is against Taipei's sophisticated performance on the American stage that the PRC's efforts in the mid and late 1990s to increase its own clout with Congress and U.S. officials must be viewed. Into the 1990s, Beijing labored under a deficient understanding of the U.S. political system. China believed that the executive branch was more important than Congress. After all, neither President Nixon nor President Carter had consulted Capitol Hill before dramatically changing policy toward China in the 1970s. Reinforced by their understanding of their own system, Beijing's leaders saw Congress as a sideshow, not one of three independent and constitutionally coequal branches of government. Consequently, Beijing always preferred dealing only with the Department of State and the White House. Emblematic of this was a conversation I had with a very senior Chinese official in early 1995. I told him that he had to expect that Congress would put irresistible pressure on President Clinton to grant a visa to Taiwan President Lee Teng-hui to visit the United States unofficially. His paraphrased response was, "This will not happen; I have been assured by the Department of State and your secretary of state."

Three sets of events served to gradually break down this simplistic image. The first was the annual congressional debate over MFN from 1990 on, which is discussed at length in the next chapter. Second, with Taipei's encouragement, Congress pushed very hard for President Clinton to treat Taiwan with more dignity, which by September 1994 resulted in a modest change ("upgrade") in U.S. policy. Third, in May 1995, Congress called upon Clinton to grant Lee Teng-hui a visa to visit Cornell by overwhelming votes of 396 to 0 in the House and 97 to 1 in the Senate, and the U.S. president agreed to do so on May 22. This constituted a high-voltage shock to Beijing and resulted in the 1995–1996 Taiwan Strait missile confrontation.

The Chinese capital's newfound appreciation of Congress manifested itself in a number of areas, including Beijing's late-1995 creation of a Central Leading Working Group on the U.S. Congress.[138] For his part, Chinese President Jiang Zemin wished to augment efforts to understand the U.S. Congress, and thereafter he met often with visiting U.S. legislators, at least once taking time away from senior leadership summer meetings at Beidaihe to see particularly important U.S. congressmen. Further, in early 1997 some Chinese think tank scholars began discussing the creation of a data bank on members of Congress in order to help in understanding the legislators' voting records and constituencies. Beijing also encouraged more members of the legislative branch to travel to China, believing that a firsthand introduction to the country would help reduce harmful stereotypes. The new interest in Congress was also reflected in a substantial augmentation of the Congressional Liaison Office's personnel in the Chinese Embassy in Washington that occurred in 1995.

Together these activities constituted a significant effort to compete with Taiwan, something not lost on Taipei's officials, who said, "They [Beijing] never cared about Congress. Now they're learning from us."[139] While it remains unclear what other forms of influence Beijing may have sought to exert on Congress during the 1996 election cycle (with Senator Fred Thompson asserting that "high-level Chinese government officials crafted a plan...to subvert our election process."),[140] such alleged efforts may have germinated in this context.

In the PRC, the Taiwan issue also bleeds into domestic politics. One particular example will suffice to illustrate this. In late January 1995, Jiang Zemin issued his comparatively flexible "Eight Point Proposal" on Taiwan, which called on Taipei to accept the one-China principle and conclude an agreement to formally cease hostilities. However, when President Lee quickly rejected this overture and President Clinton agreed to issue the visa to Lee about five months later, Jiang appeared weak to domestic critics. With an increasingly frail Deng Xiaoping and succession politics at full throttle, domestic political competitors sought every opportunity to gain advantage over Jiang Zemin. For example, Qiao Shi (chairman of the National People's Congress and member of the Standing Committee of the Politburo) seized on Jiang's setback on Taiwan to criticize him and Foreign Minister Qian Qichen and thereby improve his own political prospects.[141]

The PLA, particularly a group of influential retired officers, wrote Jiang Zemin and demanded that a tougher line be taken on Taiwan. As one Chinese scholar commented to me, "The Chinese military is quite different from the U.S. military that takes orders from the civilians. Power comes out of the barrel of a gun.... To the military, it [Taiwan's separation] is a shame of 50 years' duration."[142] In short, Taiwan is a litmus test for those who aspire to leadership in Beijing, much as the capacity to deal with Moscow was a litmus test for aspiring U.S. leaders during the cold war.

China Uses the "Taiwan Lens" in Viewing Policy Issues and the American Presence in Asia. Chinese suspicions of American intentions vis-à-vis Taiwan color Beijing's view of every U.S. action in the region, including America's overall security posture in the Pacific. Beijing often tries to use U.S. concerns in one policy area (e.g., proliferation) to extract concessions on Taiwan. So, for example, beginning in late 1992, after George Bush agreed to sell 150 F-16s to Taiwan, every time Washington protested some actual or suspected transfer of missile-related technology or nuclear technology to Pakistan, the Chinese response was simple—though Washington's charge was unwarranted, the issue could be discussed more productively if Washington were willing to curtail (or at least "discuss") weapons sales to Taipei. It is also notable that the Chinese transfer of M-11 missiles to Pakistan dates from late 1992, following the U.S. sale of F-16s to Taipei. Later in the 1990s, particularly in the context of President Clinton's 1998 visit to China, Beijing sought to link its joining the MTCR as a full member to Washington's weapons sales to Taiwan.

Taiwan also is a lens through which Beijing views the U.S.-Japan Security Treaty. Beijing's sensitivity to the alliance has varied over time (see Chapter 5); it is greatest when Beijing-Tokyo ties are strained and Beijing is worried that the United States might seek to contain the growth of Chinese power, conditions that prevailed in the mid and late 1990s, for example. But lurking in the recesses of the minds of Beijing's elite has been the thought that Japan and the United States might cooperate militarily to prevent reunification with Taiwan. Because Japan was the colonial occupier of Taiwan from 1895 to 1945, leaving quite a cultural imprint, and Lee Teng-hui is more comfortable speaking Taiwanese and Japanese than Mandarin, Chinese suspicions are constantly aroused. Similarly disturbing to Beijing is that 1997 public opinion polls in Japan showed that more Japanese than Americans believed "Taiwan is an independent country" (64.3 percent and 59.9 percent respectively).[143]

When Beijing considers the issue of U.S. troops on the Korean peninsula, it finds their presence acceptable as a stabilizing deterrent, for the time being. However, in the event of a possible Korean reunification, at least one line of thinking in Beijing would prefer U.S. troops to depart. There are many reasons for this attitude. Traditionally, China's foreign policy desire is to have buffer states between its own border and strong foreign forces. Beyond this is the consideration that a postreunification U.S. presence on the Korean peninsula could be used to support possible intervention in Taiwan.

In brief, the more that the PRC suspects that the U.S. presence in Asia is directed toward intervening in the Taiwan problem, the more China will favor the removal of U.S. forward-deployed forces. Anxieties concerning Taiwan affect Beijing's view of almost every security issue in the region.

In the year 2000 and beyond, the Taiwan issue will continue to present five overall policy problems for the United States, and by implication, China:

(1) The principal long-term question is this: How many resources will the United States be willing to expend to maintain the current fabric of implied commitments to the people of Taiwan in the face of China's increasing power and Taiwan's increasingly distinct identity? Beijing cannot help but believe that American long-term interests lie more with it than Taipei, and herein lie the seeds of miscalculation—that in the final analysis Washington would not come to Taiwan's military rescue in the event of armed conflict in the strait. This line of reasoning led Beijing to be surprised by the 1996 dispatch of two U.S. aircraft carrier battle groups to the seas off Taiwan and could lead to a similar miscalculation in the future.

(2) Beijing (particularly the PLA) concluded from the Taiwan Strait confrontation of 1996 that it must acquire the military capability to inflict unacceptable costs on Taipei if it is to deter Taiwan from moving toward de jure independence. Part of China's effort toward that end has included a gradual buildup in Chinese short-range and intermediate-range missile capability and naval forces.[144] This buildup has had a number of consequences, including mobilizing congressional support for Taiwan,[145] frightening Asian neighbors, and reenergizing Taiwan's search for unilateral security through theater missile defense, more weapons purchases from the United States, the acquisition of more offensive capability, and, conceivably, nuclear or other weapons of mass destruction.

(3) How can the United States work to deter China from coercive actions without simultaneously emboldening some in Taiwan to act provocatively?

(4) How can the U.S. executive branch effectively convey to Taipei the need to be cautious in its dealings with the PRC and enhance cross-strait cooperation when the U.S. Congress frequently gives the people of Taiwan signals of more unconditional support?

(5) How can the United States best meet the requirements of the TRA with respect to weapons sales? Put differently, how can it comply with the law, meet Taiwan's legitimate security concerns, and avoid triggering a localized or regional arms race?

Washington and Beijing are not alone in their problems. Taipei must come to terms with a central reality—its economic plans and security needs run counter to its emerging political identity. If Taipei does not work with Beijing to develop a politically stable and cooperative relationship, it stands to lose much: it will be unable to fully realize the economic potential of ties with the mainland, its own investment environment will be relatively insecure, and it will be a less attractive partner for others in the Asia-Pacific region. More ominously, conflict is possible. IN THE END IT IS UP TO TAIPEI.

CONCLUSIONS

In the post–cold war era, American and Chinese conceptions of their security are neither identical nor entirely divergent.

Both nations want stability in the Asia-Pacific region and the world so that they can pursue their respective domestic priorities. Each generally finds nuclear proliferation not in its interests. China and the United States wish to avoid conflict over Taiwan, though both may be willing to fight under certain conditions. Neither country wants to see a remilitarized Japan that would set off an Asian arms spiral. On the Korean peninsula, both Washington and Beijing have not only desired stability but also have had reasonably compatible approaches to achieving it—the four-party talks and preventing Pyongyang from obtaining nuclear weapons capability. Nonetheless, it is true that Beijing often frets that Washington will resort to force against Pyongyang. For its part, Washington is never sure how much pressure Beijing applies to North Korea to be more cooperative.

These significant areas of agreement, nonetheless, leave ample room for ambiguity and divergence. For instance, China's attitude toward an American military presence in the Pacific and the U.S.-Japan security alliance varies over time, and largely depends on U.S. policy toward Taiwan and Beijing's confidence in that policy. With respect to Korea, while U.S. troops in a divided Korea may be stabilizing, there is no reason to think Beijing wants U.S. troops in a *unified* Korea that butts up against its border. On the Asian subcontinent, the U.S. and China both desire stability between India and Pakistan, but throughout the 1990s they did not agree on what policies were conducive to achieving that stability. Beijing tended to believe that stability was best achieved by assisting Pakistan acquire military power adequate to deter Indian attack.

Finally, as China grows economically and more of its assets are located along the coast, we can expect it to acquire capabilities to protect itself ever further from its shores. However, in acquiring those capabilities, Beijing will simultaneously acquire the ability to threaten others in the region, including Taiwan.

Therefore, the task of managing the security dimension of the U.S.-China relationship is twofold: (1) to identify and develop areas of cooperation that will compensate both sides for the frustrations encountered where they disagree and (2) to manage the Taiwan problem so that it does not shatter the entire fabric of Sino-American ties and produce conflict.

3

ECONOMICS AND HUMAN RIGHTS

Our policy will seek to facilitate a peaceful evolution of China
from communism to democracy by encouraging the forces of
economic and political liberalization in that great country.
    Warren Christopher, confirmation hearing, January 13, 1993

The United States maintains a triple standard. For their own
human rights problems they shut their eyes. For some other
countries' human rights questions they open one eye and shut the
other. And for China, they open both eyes and stare.
    Chinese Finance Minister Liu Zhongli, March 20, 1994

Do we love trade more than we loathe tyranny?
    Patrick J. Buchanan, May 1996

The Treasury Department is always the most important in any
country. Meeting a treasury secretary makes you think you will
become rich.
    President Jiang Zemin upon meeting Treasury Secretary
    Robert Rubin, Beijing, September 26, 1997

In other villages, probing ineptly for the peasants' conception of
human rights, I had sometimes asked whether there was anything
they felt was absolutely their right and something they deserve to
have. The answer often came quickly and without hesitation: "Yes,
roads."
    Anne Thurston, *Muddling toward Democracy*, 1998

I feel that on issues such as human rights and religious freedom, it
is better to engage Chinese leaders directly, without public
condemnation.... Once you state a critical view publicly, then the
Chinese government, even if it wants to change, would find it
more difficult.
    His Holiness the Dalai Lama, New York City, April 30, 1998

A third Clinton administration official said that however
infuriating U.S. officials find repression of political dissent, they
also value Beijing's cooperation on such issues as North Korea's

nuclear and missile programs, the arms race in South Asia, and containing the Asian financial crisis.

Washington Post, January 1999

OVERVIEW

During the first post–cold war decade, particularly its first half, Washington and Beijing each thought that growing economic ties provided human rights leverage over the other. Many U.S. policymakers and interest groups acted on the assumption that economic sanctions and threats and Beijing's growing dependence on the American export market could be parlayed into more humane governance in the PRC. Beijing did not agree, believing its huge economic potential gave it leverage over Washington. For most of the decade China was a very fast growing, large export market for the United States. Premier Li Peng put it with his usual bluntness in 1996: "If the Europeans adopt more co-operation with China in all areas, not just in economic areas but also in political and other areas, I believe the Europeans can get more orders from China."[1]

Nonetheless, economic leverage did have its utility for Washington in gaining Chinese concessions in some economic and nonproliferation disputes. By 1999 a clear lesson had emerged: economic levers were often effective tools to achieve economic ends and sanctions sometimes were useful in achieving nonproliferation objectives; however, such measures were least effective in the domain of individual rights.

The economic story, however, is important beyond simply the money to be made and the leverage each side tried to extract from the economic association to achieve other ends. During the 1990s, the Sino-American economic relationship provided the essential glue that held the countries together while Washington and Beijing attempted to rebuild a new, broad-based rationale for long-term cooperation after the demise of the Soviet Union had gravely weakened the previous, anti-Moscow rationale. By the last quarter of the 1990s, both Beijing and Washington were trying to build toward a "constructive strategic partnership" in the twenty-first century, but making headway was proving exceedingly difficult due to the mix of competitive and complementary security interests discussed in the preceding chapter and the human rights differences documented in this chapter.

Most fundamentally, the United States' and NATO's use of force against Yugoslavia in 1999 (see Chapters 1 and 2) signaled to Beijing that

Washington (and Britain) had elevated concerns about human rights above those of sovereignty in determining whether to intervene in foreign countries and, further, that the United States was willing to use instrumentalities other than the United Nations (i.e., NATO) to conduct such actions ever farther from NATO's own territory. This doctrine ("the New Strategic Concept") hit at the core of the Chinese sense of security.[2] Nonetheless, common economic interests and the security costs of breakdown kept the United States and China minimally cooperating throughout the 1990s.

ECONOMIC AND TRADE ISSUES

The Growing Importance of Economic Issues in Bilateral Ties

Economic and trade issues were not the primary motivations for thawing relations in the early 1970s for either Beijing or Washington. As Henry Kissinger told Mao Zedong in February 1973, "Our interest in trade with China is not commercial. It is to establish a relationship that is necessary for the political relations we both have."[3] Nonetheless, by the late 1970s and throughout the 1980s, two trends converged to make economic considerations more potent for both sides. To start, in the 1980s economic ties grew rapidly, with the value of two-way trade expanding nearly fourfold in the decade and utilized ("actualized") U.S. foreign direct investment (FDI) in the PRC growing from virtually zero in 1980 to $284 million in 1989. China was even becoming a player in the U.S. Treasury notes and bond market (see table 2).

Second, with security concerns receding in the late 1980s and early 1990s, domestic economic growth rose on the agenda of both nations. The end of the cold war allowed America to try to restructure its anemic economy and increase international competitiveness, thereby gaining high-wage export-related jobs. Similarly, Deng Xiaoping and his reform-minded colleagues saw their regime's legitimacy after the decade of the Cultural Revolution residing in their ability to put goods on the shelves.

The expansion of economic ties brought with it both positive and negative consequences for each country and Sino-American relations. Positively, at the start of the Bush administration, an estimated 100,000 American jobs were dependent on merchandise and goods exports to China (not including "service" exports), and by the second Clinton term (1997) that number had gone up by about 50 percent.[4] By 1999, China had become America's fourth largest trade partner, rising from tenth place in 1989.[5]

For selected American multinationals, China was of great consequence by the mid to late 1990s. The Coca-Cola Company held 26 percent of the carbonated soft drink market in China by 1997.[6] As of January 1, 2000, 335 of the 503 jetliners operating in China were Boeing airplanes.[7] For Motorola the market in China and Hong Kong accounted for 10 percent of global sales in 1998, ranking below the United States (41 percent) and Europe (21 percent) but ahead of Japan (7 percent) and the rest of the Asia-Pacific region (7 percent).[8] Proctor and Gamble, S. C. Johnson and Company, and Gillette had similarly captured substantial shares of the personal care product market by 1998. Finally, China's satellite launch capacity was important to U.S. satellite makers and telecommunications companies that faced a global shortage of inexpensive, reliable launch capacity. For example, if the ill-starred Iridium global telephone system of sixty-six stationary orbit satellites was to be sent aloft expeditiously, it required three Chinese launches for six of the satellites. In mid-1998, there was a global three-year wait for launch space. It is for this reason, and others, that in May 1999 President Clinton approved the export of two Iridium system satellites to China for launch, despite the domestic uproar over security concerns discussed in the previous chapter.

Beyond the aggregate growth in economic and trade ties, another, more significant transformation was underway in the 1990s. Companies that had first invested in China in the late 1970s and 1980s (personal care products, beverages, fast food, and pharmaceuticals aside) generally saw it as a low-labor-cost export platform to produce products for markets outside the PRC, particularly the United States. Indeed, it is this foreign-invested export production (moved from other locations in Asia) that accounts for much of the subsequent U.S. trade deficit with the PRC. Further, even if these early investors saw their China presence as an entrée for eventual domestic sales, they expected that the domestic market potential was some years in the future.

However, by the 1990s, foreign investors increasingly came to view China as a huge and increasingly real potential consumer market. Although the PRC still had 800 million poor peasants, it also had an enormous coastal and urban population that was quickly acquiring buying power and sophisticated consumption preferences. In 1996, per capita GDP in Shanghai was 22,275 RMB (or about US$2,700 at the time) and Beijing's per capita GDP was about 15,000 RMB (or US$1,800). In Beijing in 1998, the average private firm "bosses" made around $8,000 annually and typically enjoyed the accoutrements of middle-class status: cell phones, microwaves, personal automobiles, and foreign travel (often to Southeast

Asia). Whereas in the late 1980s 95 percent of airline passengers in the PRC were foreigners and only 5 percent were PRC citizens, by 1998 this percentage had been reversed.[9]

Consequently, China represented a strategic decision for many of the United States' largest multinational corporations. The American auto industry (Ford, GM, and Chrysler), for example, competed fiercely for entry into the auto assembly and auto parts arenas, believing that their foothold in the China market was a key to maintaining production scales that would keep them competitive in the twenty-first century. Similarly, with the emergence of an interdependent world financial system, insurance companies such as American International Group, Metropolitan Life, New York Life, and Chubb, among others, saw huge potential in the Chinese market, where about 35 percent of the GDP was saved yet there was no place to productively put this savings.

As Americans and their international competitors focused on the Chinese market, the PRC had to make internal adjustments. According to a September 1996 report by the Development Research Center of the State Council, "The issue of 'foreign companies crowding China's market' has two aspects: problems created by imported goods and problems created by goods produced by foreign-invested enterprises being sold in the domestic market.... The two situations are different in that the former mainly involves China's import and tariff protection policies, and the latter involves our foreign capital utilization policy. Currently, the latter is the more controversial of the two."[10]

Throughout the 1990s, the PRC became progressively more dependent on foreign trade and particularly on the U.S. market. In 1989, 24.4 percent of Chinese exports went to the United States (including those transshipped through Hong Kong); by 1998, the corresponding figure was 38.7 percent (see table 2). Further, by 1998, the Chinese were reporting, "It is estimated that 3 percent out of every 10 percent of China's economic growth is the result of exports."[11] Simultaneously, the United States was becoming an increasingly important source of FDI for the PRC, supplying 9.4 percent of total contracted FDI in the first nine months of 1997 (compared with 5.4 percent in 1991).[12] China's increasing reliance on the U.S. market and financial resources, despite efforts to diversify to markets like South Korea (with which Beijing normalized relations in 1992), reflected the demand of a strong U.S. economy hungry for inexpensive imports, weak economies elsewhere throughout the 1990s, and the movement of export capacity from Hong Kong, Taiwan, and South Korea to China's mainland. Nervous about such dependence on a single market, PRC trade authorities sought to diversify into Russia, Latin America, elsewhere in Asia, and Africa, but by 1998 were saying, "It is still an arduous and long-term task for China in its opening up of diversified markets."[13]

By 1998, cumulative, utilized American FDI totaled $18 billion in more than 24,000 enterprises, according to Chinese sources,[14] and about $21 billion by year-end 1998, according to Western sources (see table 2). This investment was important not only in terms of its dollar amount, but also because of the technology, management expertise, and marketing networks that accompany it. American-invested enterprises on China's mainland, compared with the investments of East Asians, have consistently been more modern, higher-technology, longer-term projects. Overseas Chinese investment in the PRC, which constitutes the bulk of FDI, has tended to be low-tech and highly mobile from one country to the next—"hit and run" money. The Chinese acknowledge this, with Ministry of Foreign Trade and Economic Cooperation (MOFTEC) Minister Shi Guangsheng saying in June 1998, "U.S. companies here are comparatively more advanced in technologies and have better management, with higher-quality products, and thus they are widely welcome by the Chinese side."[15] Further, for a regime seeking to absorb vast numbers of displaced and unemployed workers, the 250,000 Chinese citizens working in American-invested firms in 1998 were a significant consideration, not to mention the several million Chinese workers producing exports for the United States in indigenous firms.

The Political Uses of Economic Ties

China's reliance on the U.S. market and FDI carried with it the potential for miscalculation in Washington. Some in Congress, organized labor, and the human rights community looked at that reliance and assumed that the threat to limit Chinese exports to the United States provided them leverage with respect to their grievances with the PRC. Trying to use this leverage to achieve broad political change in the PRC, rather than more limited improvements in the areas of economics and security, proved exceedingly difficult. In order to understand this miscalculation, we must turn to the American political scene, though that topic is discussed in greater detail in Chapter 7.

The growing importance of economic ties with China, combined with receding security concerns (in the aftermath of the cold war) and the mobilizing effect of Tiananmen, increased Congress's role in making China policy. The U.S. Constitution vests Congress with significant powers in the trade arena (e.g., to set tariff levels). In contrast, when security is the dominant concern, as it was during the cold war, constitutional prerogatives and the need for quick response favor presidential dominance. Thus, moving from a *security*-centered to an *economics*-centered relationship with Beijing put the relationship more substantially into the congressional domain.

In the American system economic and trade disputes exist within closely intertwined *legal* and *political* contexts. With respect to the former, several broad areas of law were relevant in the 1990s, with the most important being the Jackson-Vanik Amendment to the Trade Act of 1974. That legislation requires that the president notify Congress each year of his intention to extend most-favored-nation status to a "non-market economy" and can set off a complex executive-legislative branch interaction, such as that described in the preceding chapters. President Jimmy Carter had agreed with Beijing in the 1979 Agreement on Trade Relations between the U.S. and PRC[16] to extend MFN to Beijing; this was approved in a joint resolution of Congress in January 1980.

Thus the legal context created an annual opportunity through the MFN debate for politicians and interest groups to demonstrate their commitment to American values and to promote their concerns. The combination of the 1989 wave of freedom sweeping the communist world and the Tiananmen violence made China the poster child for a broad variety of single-issue U.S. interest groups. Members of Congress were free to raise any concern they wished pertaining to China policy (human rights were prominent), and the president was forced to respond. And even if MFN continued for China, as it did throughout the 1990s, Congress might be able to extract some other concession from the executive branch, the Chinese, or both in the process.

In the early 1990s the economic insecurity of many Americans provided a powerful way for entrepreneurial U.S. politicians to connect Chinese problems and abuses to American concerns. By 1999, trade concerns were also being linked with the security and technology transfer issues discussed in the preceding chapter. In speaking of American trade policy, and connecting the Chinese trade surplus with the United States and China's defense modernization, the admittedly immoderate Patrick Buchanan put it this way: "Free Traders are Traitors" and "You're walking very close to the line of treason."[17]

American Economic Grievances

Former U.S. Trade Representative Mickey Kantor pointed to the intimate ties between foreign and trade policy, on the one hand, and domestic policy, on the other, when he said, "Trade and international economics have joined the foreign-policy table. Clinton is the first President to really make trade the bridge between foreign and domestic policy."[18]

With respect to economic relations throughout the 1990s, the linchpin issue was the growing U.S. deficit with the PRC. According to U.S. government figures, in 1988 the United States had a $4.244 billion trade deficit with the PRC. By 1997 that gap had increased more than twelvefold to about $53 billion (see table 3), and by the following year it was $60.85 billion.[19] Every year since 1983, the United States has run a trade deficit with the PRC; the deficit's average annual rate of growth from 1987 to 1996 was about 36 percent, though the rate of increase generally has been declining as total trade has expanded. Economists usually downplay the importance of bilateral trade surpluses and deficits. In China's case most argue that much of the surplus is accounted for by a number of considerations: the relocation of export production and assembly from the newly industrializing countries to the PRC; value added by intermediaries such as Hong Kong; U.S. export controls on its own companies; flawed trade statistics that make Hong Kong a distorting factor; and Chinese production of goods no longer made in America.[20] *However, politicians are not economists!* For them, the mounting trade deficit with the PRC raises "fair trade" and industrial job loss concerns, some of which are justified. Illustrating the gap between economic analysis and political perception and interest, economist Nicholas Lardy points out, "[T]he trade deficit with China primarily reflects its openness to foreign investment, not unfair trading practices."[21]

Once the issue became one of fairness and jobs, every specific trade dispute incited debate. As Senator Donald Riegle Jr. (D-Michigan) rhetorically asked me at a June 1991 Senate Finance Committee hearing, "Why are we sending all of these jobs out of the country, $15 billion worth net in a 12-month period to China, when we have got literally millions and millions of people in this country unable to find work even at the level of the minimum wage?"[22] Clearly the trade deficit was a major concern to many in Congress—yet America's trade-related grievances went far beyond that.

American businesspeople chafed at the lack of transparency of Chinese trade rules, arguing that they often did not know what rules affected their operations in China; many regulations there remained unpublished (this began to change as the 1990s progressed), and administrative discretion in their interpretation and enforcement often was (and remains) capricious at best. With Chinese judges often beholden to local Communist Party and political authorities who have a stake in a ruling in favor of the Chinese side, impartial and speedy dispute resolution has been an ongoing concern. When Americans won court cases, they often did so because they played the game the Chinese way. One attorney who won several cases in Chinese venues was reported to have been so successful because "[h]e just invites some very powerful people in Beijing to come sit in the front row."[23] There was also the issue of national treatment of American firms—would U.S. firms be treated equally with PRC firms under Chinese law? If the truth were told, foreign firms were ambivalent about being treated in the same manner as domestic firms. Finally, market entry has been an ongoing problem for those doing business in China, particularly in securing unimpeded access to the Chinese consumer for America's most competitive industries (agriculture, financial services, distribution, etc.).

All of the above generalized concerns underlay the specific trade frictions of the 1990s: intellectual property rights (IPR), textiles, market access, *laogai* (prison labor) exports, and China's protracted negotiations (13 years) with Washington over terms of accession to the General Agreement on Tariffs and Trade (GATT), reconstituted as the World Trade Organization on January 1, 1995. We will examine two illustrative issues here (IPR and *laogai* exports), saving discussion of WTO for the next chapter in which global regimes and economic flows are discussed.

Intellectual Property Rights. The worldwide piracy of intellectual property is a critical concern for much of American industry. Such losses to the American software industry alone totaled an estimated $11 billion in 1998. According to the Business Software Alliance and the Software Publishers Association, almost $1.2 billion of this loss was in China.[24] The music recording industry faces similar problems. The Recording Industry Association of America reported in 1996 that its lost revenue through compact disc (CD) piracy in Japan was $500 million annually, "more than the $300 million the American record industry says it is losing annually from the far more well-known piracy in China."[25] Other U.S. industries suffer as well, such as pharmaceutical and chemical manufacturers and developers and producers of products where brand identification is key. In China, Kellogg's Cornflakes has faced bogus trademark and packaging competition and Sun Microsystems has faced trademark copying, as have Pabst Blue Ribbon and Delmonte.[26] Piracy in the publishing industry is extensive as well. On several occasions Deng Xiaoping's youngest daughter, Xiao Rong, complained to me that in-China sales of her book, *Deng Xiaoping, My Father,* suffered because of widespread unauthorized duplication.

Beyond the issue of industry losses, the IPR controversy affects two related issues. First, American industries are hesitant to move intellectual property–intensive products and manufacturing processes to China if IPR protection is inadequate. Second, the insecurity resulting from the

inadequate protection of intellectual property becomes one more constraining consideration in export control decisions in the United States.

Although there are fair criticisms that the affected American associations inflate IPR loss figures (by multiplying the estimated number of illegal items produced by each item's retail sales price *in the United States,*
a price Chinese consumers could not afford), the scale of IPR theft in the
PRC was significant throughout the decade of the 1990s. American concern in this area was signaled as early as the 1979 Agreement on Trade Relations (article 6). Since that time, IPR theft has grown progressively more
intolerable. As the bilateral trade deficit grew from the mid-1980s on,
Americans became ever more concerned about the competitiveness of U.S.
industry and increasingly frustrated with Chinese barriers to penetration
of their market. The theft of IPR became a symbol for the inequity of the
trade relationship and a metaphor for a wide range of Chinese behavior.
Inflaming the situation, local Chinese entrepreneurs, sometimes associated with PRC military or civilian officialdom and often enjoying the capital and marketing support of businessmen from Taiwan and Hong Kong,
produced and sold unauthorized versions of IPR-intensive U.S. products
outside of China. A substantial percentage of these phony copies found
their way to Asia, Latin America, Canada, and the United States, thereby
despoiling additional markets.[27] By one 1995 U.S. estimate, 95 percent of
pirated CDs produced in South China were exported.[28]

Sino-American interaction vis-à-vis IPR has taken on many dimensions, but for the most part Americans have been frustrated and the Chinese have been confused and resentful—confused because, as one Chinese
associate put it to me, "Regarding IPR, from our side we can't figure out
why it was so prominent in 1995. From our perspective it should be in our
economic talks with the WTO and trade deficit. It became number one for
you, USTR [the United States Trade Representative], but not that important to us."[29] In this remark, one can see two key aspects of the Chinese
view. First, at any given moment, there are several issues at dispute in the
economic domain (e.g., the trade deficit, WTO membership, and IPR). For
the Chinese, all issues are negotiable, meaning that meeting a U.S. concern
in one area should be linked to American concessions in other areas, but
for the Americans, IPR protection was almost a nonnegotiable issue of
fairness that need not be traded off for progress in other domains. Second,
the remark betrays the Chinese frustration at how the American system
keeps coming up with issues with which Beijing often is unprepared to
cope and little understands. Additionally, Beijing generally feels that it is
not being given the time to adjust to international trade standards that the
earlier modernizers, Hong Kong, Taiwan, and South Korea, received.

On the positive side, beginning in the early 1980s China sent many State Council law drafters and legal scholars abroad to study issues of IPR protection. The result was the rapid development of a legislative and regulatory IPR framework and participation in the principal international organizations in the field.

> China passed the Trademark Law in August 1982 (revised 1993), the Patent Law in March 1984 (revised 1993), the Copyright Law in September 1990, and the Computer Software Regulations in October 1991. In addition, the General Principles of Civil Law, adopted in April 1986, recognized the rights of individuals and legal entities to hold copyrights, patents, and trademarks. This enactment and a subsequent Civil Procedure Law passed in April 1991 enabled Chinese citizens and legal entities, as well as foreigners and foreign enterprises and organizations, to demand in Chinese courts that infringements be halted and that courts award claimants compensation for damages. In the international arena, China was accepted as a member of the Geneva-based World Intellectual Property Organization (WIPO) in April 1980. It joined the Paris Convention for the protection of Industrial Property in December 1984 and the Berne Convention for the Protection of Literary and Artistic Works in October 1992.[30]

The recurring problem, however, has been policy implementation. Mounting American IPR losses have followed each agreement. For example, estimated losses to software piracy were 93 percent larger in 1996 than they had been in 1994, and they more than doubled in 1997.[31] This discrepancy between the purposefulness with which Beijing has constructed a legal and regulatory framework and the modest results of policy implementation has been the focus of American policy and ire. This frustration is clear in House Minority Leader Richard Gephardt's (D-Missouri) remarks to the Detroit Economic Club on May 27, 1997: "China has said to many of our companies that if they want to sell there, they must produce there. Then they have ordained that in order to build factories there we must transfer our technological knowledge to them. Business is being blackmailed into giving China the means and the trade secrets that will make them an economic powerhouse. And in return they will continue to pirate our music, software, and videos."

Several factors account for the gap between declaratory policy in Beijing and actual policy implementation throughout the PRC. To start, the technological sophistication and buying power of Chinese consumers is outstripping the genuine progress in the regulatory and legal fields—and technology itself is moving very rapidly. Further, there are many Chinese governmental organizations with overlapping and competing jurisdictions when it comes to enforcement.[32] Moreover, corruption in and out of government is a mounting problem. And finally, the Chinese population has a limited understanding of the concept of intellectual property, and, as in other developing nations, such awareness takes considerable time to develop. On the day in late February 1995 when China and the United States signed an IPR agreement concerning CD piracy, I went to a kiosk in the city of Harbin and asked whether a CD I wanted to purchase was pirated. Thinking my only concern was quality, the salesperson unabashedly replied, "Yes! But, it is a high quality fake!"

The U.S. government has taken two broad approaches to address the IPR dilemma in China: (1) provide Chinese officials a sense of urgency by threatening trade sanctions on a scale comparable to claimed losses and (2) work cooperatively with the Chinese to further develop adequate legal and implementation structures. This two-pronged approach has not entirely resolved the problem, but it almost certainly has improved the situation beyond what it otherwise would have been. It also is interesting to note that some American brand-name firms have concluded that the unauthorized use of their brand can have an upside—it promotes their product in a country where consumers are not yet wealthy enough to buy the genuine article, thereby retarding the development of competing, indigenous Chinese brands. In a perverse way, piracy of U.S. products retards the development of vigorous Chinese competitors and brand names.

International experience suggests that a solution, if one exists, resides in several developments that either have not occurred in China or are in their infancy: the gradual institutionalization of the rule of law and an independent judiciary, the development of clearly defined property rights, and the emergence of indigenous innovators and stakeholders who themselves have an interest in the enforcement of intellectual property laws. In 1999, for example, Microsoft Corporation won a judgment against Yadu Science and Technology Company in Chinese courts, and a local supplier of software whose sales had suffered because of the piracy was pleased with the judgment as well, arguing that "the most hard-hit victims of software piracy are Chinese software companies."[33]

America's two-pronged approach to the IPR infringement problem in China has relied principally on the threat of targeted penalties aimed at holding hostage key Chinese exports to the United States. The statutory bases for this approach are found in the 1974 Trade Act and Special Section 301 of the Omnibus Trade and Competitiveness Act of 1988. Under the provisions of Section 301, an annual list of nations failing to provide adequate protection for American IPR is compiled. Some of these countries may be designated "priority watch," a label that hopefully leads to negotiations with the offending party to agree on measures to resolve the complaint. A serious or recalcitrant IPR violator can be designated a "priority foreign country." Such designation leads to the invocation of a six-to-seven-month deadline for improvement, with failure to comply setting the stage for the possible imposition of penalties proportional to the claimed IPR losses sustained by American industry.[34]

On this unilaterally defined legal basis, an important part of U.S.-China IPR interaction has taken place, involving repeated moves toward the imposition of 301 sanctions and last-minute agreements between Beijing and Washington. Because IPR was an American grievance, it was the Office of the United States Trade Representative (USTR) that took the lead in raising the issue. Beyond the USTR's statutory responsibility and the fact that the USTR is highly responsive to Congress, other factors played a role in determining the vigor with which the issue was pursued. Washington was most motivated to pursue the IPR issue with Beijing when three events converged: (1) the United States had recently experienced a rapidly increasing bilateral trade deficit, in percentage terms, (2) elections were imminent, and (3) MFN renewal was coming up for discussion by the Congress and the outcome seemed uncertain.

These factors converged with particular force in the 1991–1992 and the 1995–1996 periods. In 1990 the bilateral trade deficit was up about 60 percent over the preceding year, and the following year intense negotiations over IPR issues began, reaching a conclusion in 1992, a general election year. Similarly, in 1994 (a landmark election year) the bilateral trade deficit was up 43 percent, IPR negotiations reached a climax in early 1995, and the dispute was rekindled in 1996 (also a general election year). In short, while genuine grievances and interests lay at the core of American IPR protection efforts, the timing of disputes and the intensity with which they were pursued had a great deal to do with domestic politics.

After the adoption of the Omnibus Trade Act (with a section known as "Special 301") in 1988, the United States put the PRC on a "priority watch list" in order to give Beijing time to begin to meet Washington's expectations. By 1991, however, after experiencing two successive years of 60-plus percent increases in the bilateral trade deficit, with little relief from Chinese IPR violations, and facing a fierce battle over MFN in the Congress, the USTR placed China on the "priority foreign country list." On January 16, 1992, just before Washington imposed threatened sanctions in the $300–500 million range, Beijing promised to protect computer software, books, sound recordings, pharmaceuticals, and agrochemicals and to extend the duration and scope of patent, copyright, and trade-secret protections. Soon thereafter, the two concluded the U.S.-China Memorandum of Understanding (MOU) on Intellectual Property Rights.

In December 1994, the Clinton administration launched another Special 301 investigation of Chinese IPR practices and on February 4, 1995, announced the imposition of punishing sanctions in the $2.8 billion range. Beijing reacted by declaring, "For such a big country as China, [the sanctions of] $2.8 billion dollars doesn't account for too much."[35] Moreover, Beijing stated its intention to retaliate equally, saying that American consumers had more to lose than Chinese, and protesting that the kinds of changes Washington requested amounted to intervention in China's internal affairs. The latter charge was correct and will become more common as China's internal practices increasingly affect the rest of the world. In announcing its intention to impose sanctions, the USTR used the plight of CD plant workers in Huntsville, Alabama, to illuminate the unfairness and outrage Americans felt. When USTR Mickey Kantor was asked whether Deng Xiaoping's failing health and succession problems in the PRC might not account for some Chinese recalcitrance, he replied, "That's China's problem, not our problem. We have U.S. workers and their jobs at stake, here."[36]

By the end of February, the two sides reached an agreement, with Mme. Wu Yi, then Chinese Foreign Trade Minister, signing an MOU "detailing measures to be taken to enforce and upgrade the protection of intellectual property rights."[37] However, in December 1995, looking ahead to a general election year and still confronted with mounting IPR violations, particularly the unauthorized duplication and mass sale of CDs, USTR Kantor (Bill Clinton's former campaign manager) demanded that Beijing close twenty-nine offending CD production facilities (nineteen of which were in the freewheeling southern province of Guangdong).[38] This time even a street vendor in Beijing in the fall of 1995 was promoting pirated software sales by saying, "You better buy now before the next crackdown."[39] For the next seven months, Beijing and Washington were locked in dispute, with the USTR threatening sweeping sanctions potentially reaching $3 billion to take effect in mid-June 1996.[40] The acting USTR, Charlene Barshefsky, announced on June 17 that the United States was satisfied with China's moves (including the public steamrolling of allegedly illegally duplicated CDs) to effectively implement the 1995 IPR Enforcement Agreement. One ought to note an irony that Michel Oksenberg observed, namely that the Chinese have sometimes enforced IPR agreements by engaging in behavior "we chastise as human rights violations but accept because [it] serves our interest."[41]

Results of the IPR agreements have been mixed. In its *1998 National Trade Estimate,* the USTR reported increased enforcement efforts in the PRC, more training of regulators, and greater cooperation within agencies and among jurisdictions in China. Nonetheless, the estimated cost of software piracy generally has continued to climb, as has the incidence of trademark counterfeiting and piracy. In addition, in fiscal year 1997, the U.S. Customs Service seized $14.49 million in counterfeit merchandise from China (ranking number one in seizures) and $5.96 million from Taiwan (ranking number two in seizures).[42] There is no end in sight for this problem.

This experience teaches several lessons. First, the IPR issue reflects several current conditions in China: a lack of institutional and legal development, an absence of public understanding about the issue, local corruption, transnational organized crime, and an indigenous community with a weak interest in IPR enforcement. Until a critical mass of Chinese firms and individuals have a real stake in IPR protection, intellectual property–exporting countries will face severe problems. But such awareness is slowly growing. One example is Shandong's Tsingtao Brewing Company, a firm selling a globally branded beer. In 1996, it was trying to revoke the intentionally similar trademark of a South Korean beer being sold in Taiwan.[43]

Second, focused, targeted sanctions will heighten Beijing's IPR protection efforts, provided the threats are aimed at high-value Chinese export sectors and the penalties are proportionate to credible loss estimates. Third, even as China becomes more developed, the institutional gains that are made in IPR enforcement and public understanding are likely to be offset by the increased technical and financial capabilities of its people to pirate, as has happened in the Western world. Finally, Taiwan and Hong Kong are often part of the IPR violating network associated with the PRC.

The Laogai (Prison Labor) Issue.[44] The problem of Chinese prison labor has more political resonance in America than actual economic consequence for the United States. Although figures are scarce and unreliable, in 1997 Senate testimony, the commissioner of the U.S. Customs Service, George Weise, cited a Chinese figure of $100 million for the value of all global export goods made in PRC prisons in 1988.[45] If *all* these goods went to the United States (highly improbable) and all were made by "forced" or "slave" labor (as distinct from voluntary prison labor), then their value would have constituted about 1.2 percent of total Chinese exports to the United States.

Far more economically significant than *laogai* exports in the 1990s were such trade issues as nonscientifically based public health import standards for U.S. fruit and grain exports to the PRC; repeated Chinese textile industry efforts to evade quota agreements through mislabeling, fraudulent invoicing, and transshipment through third countries; limited market access; and IPR infringement (problems addressed during Vice Premier Zhu Rongji's 1999 trip to the United States and partly resolved by the November 1999 bilateral WTO accession agreement with Beijing). But the "slave" labor export issue illustrates how coalitions among economic, political, and human rights groups in the United States can be built and appropriated by politicians who are genuinely concerned by a problem or see that issue as politically useful. As we will see, the prison labor issue also illustrates how the drive for revenue among Chinese bureaucracies, poor regulatory structures, and corruption lead not only to entrepreneurial activity but also to lawless domestic and international activity. It further illustrates that when the Ministry of Foreign Affairs and MOFTEC come up against their own internal security apparatus, they frequently lose, foreign policy consequences notwithstanding.

In politics, the person or group that defines the issue first, gives it a name, and puts a human face on it, reaps political rewards. China's use of prison (or forced or slave) labor to make some exports for the U.S. market became widely known in 1991. That year, the U.S. Congress was frustrated with the Bush administration, and a fierce battle over continuation of unconditional MFN for China was underway. Further, the trade deficit with China had jumped more than 60 percent from that of the year before. In this setting, a marriage of convenience was made between liberal and conservative forces both in and out of the Congress.

In 1990 Senator Jesse Helms (R-North Carolina)—whose broader role in China policy is discussed in Chapter 8—took on the "slave labor" issue by requesting that the General Accounting Office report on the subject. In April of the following year, Asia Watch, a New York–based human rights group, issued a report on the problem entitled *Prison Labor In China*, a compilation of Chinese documents on various aspects of prison labor enterprise.[46] Armed with these studies and stimulated by the tireless efforts of Hongda (Harry) Wu, a former prisoner in the Chinese penal system and author of *Laogai: The Chinese Gulag* (1992), a bipartisan coalition emerged.[47] This alliance among congressional conservatives, liberals, and human rights groups was a classic Capitol Hill marriage, bringing together strong congressional personalities who agreed about virtually no other issue. Congressman Frank Wolf (R-Virginia), Congressman Sam Gejdenson (D-Connecticut), Congresswoman Nancy Pelosi (D-California), Senator George Mitchell (D-Maine), Jesse Helms, and many others on Capitol Hill joined in the effort to make China's continued MFN status conditional on many things, including cessation of prison labor exports to the United States.

In this coalition, one sees the fusion of human rights organizations; the humanitarian concerns of Americans regarding prisoners of conscience; members of Congress motivated by a mélange of humanitarian and political concerns; and organized labor determined to stem import competition (with the AFL-CIO leasing space to Harry Wu's Laogai Research Foundation). As Wu said, "Obviously, the AFL-CIO does not appreciate having goods coming into the United States that are made by unsalaried prisoners in China."[48] These interests and impulses were further strengthened by the general American perception that China was amassing ever larger trade surpluses as well as by latent anticommunist sentiment. Asia Watch's Holly Burkhalter, testifying before the Senate Finance Committee in June 1991, hit all the chords.

> Asia Watch recently released new information about the problem of forced labor, which I believe you are familiar with.... This is a problem of unprecedented severity and the fact that the authorities [in China] are deeply involved in pushing the labor reform gulag to produce items for export is deeply, deeply distressing because it suggests that MFN may actually be inadvertently subsidizing the cruel use of prisoners—many of them political prisoners—to produce items that Americans are now buying, without ever knowing, of course, how they are being produced.... And apparently, the [U.S.] Customs Service is not yet quite convinced that forced labor is occurring and that items are entering this country.[49]

The statutory basis for the issue in U.S. law is Section 307 of the Tariff Act of 1930, which prohibits the importation into the United States of goods produced with convict labor. In the context of the frictions with China in the 1990s, Americans generally viewed this prohibition as a human rights provision, although the initial impulse behind the legislation in the 1930s had been much different. American labor understandably did not wish to compete with foreign products made by virtually cost-free prison labor. Parenthetically, and without asserting moral equivalence, it is interesting to note that several U.S. states[50] (including Florida, Oregon, and California) export goods made in penal institutions. Further, as with Jackson-Vanik, this example shows how legislation, once adopted, persists, providing perpetual opportunity for legislators and interest groups to bend a law's original intent to fit current concerns. Protectionist legislation of the 1930s can become human rights legislation in the 1990s.

In order to gain support from the Senate on MFN and from the public five months prior to the November presidential election, in mid-June 1992 President Bush began to toughen up the administration's China policy along a number of fronts, including technology transfer, illegal textile shipments, IPR infringement, and prison labor exports. The president's promise to adopt a tougher China policy prompted a long negotiation with Beijing, which ended in the August 7, 1992, signing of the MOU on Prison Labor Products whereby China undertook not to export such items to the United States and to permit inspections of suspected production sites by U.S. officials.

However, after just two such site visits to suspected prisons, the Chinese refused to permit further visits. This resulted in charges of bad faith by Washington; in the understated words of one government official, "Initial implementation of the MOU was spotty."[51] It was not until a January 1994 visit to China by Treasury Secretary Bentsen that the U.S. government was told that U.S. Customs officials would be permitted to inspect five prisons suspected of violating the prohibition against prison exports.

Subsequently, in March 1994, the two sides negotiated a Statement of Cooperation to improve implementation of the MOU. Once again, even this modest concession was extracted from the Chinese in the setting of another looming decision (this time by the Clinton administration) about whether to renew China's MFN status. In the president's 1993 decision to link future MFN status to "overall, significant progress" in human rights, he had made one of the inflexible conditions implementation of the MOU on Prison Labor Products.

In effect, Beijing "sold" the same concession twice—it signed the memorandum on prison labor exports in 1992 and it again made the same promises to ensure continuation of MFN in 1994. Even after this, the PRC Ministry of Justice continued to resist U.S. access to prisons for which the Chinese felt there was "insufficient evidence" and access to "reeducation through labor" (*laojiao*) facilities, not considered "prisons" by the PRC. Predictably, the U.S. Congress remained unsatisfied, and the following July the House passed a bill titled the China Policy Act of 1995. Among other things, it asserted that the PRC "continues to engage in discriminatory and unfair trade practices, including the exportation of products produced by prison labor."[52] The act died in the Senate.

This issue, like so many in U.S.-China relations, is like Lazarus—it rises periodically from the grave, in part, because Chinese compliance often is debatable and, in part, because the symbolism of the issue is so useful politically. An issue is particularly useful when the actual scope of the problem is unknown or, better yet, unknowable. The unknown, when combined with legitimate skepticism concerning Chinese compliance, makes it difficult to refute any charge, no matter how unlikely it may be. In July 1997, for example, Representative Christopher Cox (R-California) introduced the Laogai Slave Labor Products Act of 1997 (H.R. 2195), which passed the House by a vote of 419 to 2 in November and was adopted by amendment into Senate Bill S. 2057—the Defense Authorization Act of 1999—which became Public Law 105–261 in October 1998. The bill's principal effect was to appropriate $2 million for hiring additional U.S. Customs Service personnel for fiscal year 1999 to monitor Chinese imports that violate the prohibition against goods made with forced labor. The bill expressed the "sense of the Congress" that the president should seek to renegotiate the 1992 memorandum on prison labor exports and other similar agreements.

This brief look at two trade issues, IPR and prison labor exports, by no means exhausts the trade and economic conflicts of the post–cold war decade. From these two cases, however, several general observations can be made.

First, decentralization of the Chinese economy and polity has led to ambiguous results. Economic and political decentralization have unleashed latent Chinese entrepreneurship, multiplied the points at which the two nations can construct mutually beneficial economic arrangements, and provided the basis for the growth of a middle class and civil society. Nonetheless, it also has meant that China's lower-level government units, localities, and individual entrepreneurs are much more able to resist central control and develop corrupt practices (e.g., prison wardens and their superiors in Beijing seeking to make money by selling prison-made goods abroad for hard currency, with other officials turning a blind eye, with their hands out). The remedies to these problems lie in further marketization in the PRC, more transparency in decision making and regulation, and better and more independent regulatory and legal institutions. These features will take a long time to develop; on Capitol Hill time is measured by two-to-six-year election cycles, and in the PRC the calibration is very much longer.

Second, the distinction between *internal* and *external* is vanishing, particularly in the economic realm—a topic to which we return in the next chapter. For China to solve the IPR problem is to acquiesce to external demands for changes in its judicial and legal systems, concepts of ownership, and regulatory institutions. Similarly, the demands concerning prison labor exports require providing foreigners access to penal institutions, something China has been loath to do. For a regime that has defined its legitimacy as protecting national sovereignty and keeping foreigners out of internal affairs, demands made logical by economic globalization appear to be fundamental intrusions.

Third, there is a direct connection between severe conflicts in one sector of the bilateral relationship and the capacity to resolve problems in other sectors. In 1993 and 1994, when the United States was threatening to withdraw MFN tariff treatment from the PRC unless certain human rights–related conditions were met, managing the prison labor issue and other areas of the relationship was virtually impossible. One cannot attack the roots of the relationship and expect the leaves to flower.

Finally, while Chinese authorities say outwardly that they will never bow to foreign pressure, they are constantly evaluating the costs and gains of acquiescing to demands, whether foreign or domestic. At the same time, they are assessing the foreigner's resolve. American threats with respect to economic issues have been relatively effective because the Chinese have believed that Washington has had the will and the capacity to implement them—Americans are capitalists, after all! U.S. economic threats also have been more credible because it is easier to quantify the damage one is suffering and to specify proportional retaliation. Moreover, although economic threats and demands may have implications for the domestic system, they are not explicitly aimed at changing the nature of domestic governance. In short, targeted economic threats have a greater chance of working than broad threats directed at producing political change. This brings us to the intersection of economics and human rights.

HUMAN RIGHTS

To understand a central element of the American experience, visit Ellis Island in New York harbor. There, in the high-ceilinged, beige-tiled great hall, millions of predominantly European immigrants who came to U.S. shores in the nineteenth and twentieth centuries began the transition to becoming Americans. Some Chinese passed through this gateway, though most came across the Pacific to the West Coast. Among the newcomers were people fleeing economic decline, unrest, cultural and religious persecution, and political oppression, while others simply were in search of a better life with more economic opportunity. This history gives the United States several defining characteristics as it deals with the rest of the world, particularly in the human rights area (see Chapter 6 for more). Two are of central importance: ethnic politics and the idiom of U.S. foreign policy.

Ethnic group politics is central to U.S. foreign policy, with those who left the "old country" taking a special interest in those who stayed behind. James Schlesinger notes the degree to which the United States' policy toward Cuba has been influenced by Cuban immigrants in Florida and New Jersey, how Middle East policy has been influenced by Israel's supporters, how policy toward Haiti has been affected by the Congressional Black Caucus, and how "NATO expansion too, has been driven by concern over the politics of appealing to voters of East European origin."[53] Immigrant groups traditionally have used the many points of access to the American political system, particularly the U.S. Congress, to shape U.S. policy toward their native land. In this sense, the dissidents who fled China in 1989 (or stayed here after their academic programs had concluded) and founded groups to influence congressional attitudes toward Beijing were merely following a well-trodden path. I will never forget testifying before subcommittees of the House Committee on Foreign Affairs on the same panel as Zhao Haiqing, the chairman of the National Committee on Chinese Student Affairs of the Independent Federation of Chinese Students and Scholars. Zhao concluded his oral testimony with the moving prose of an unnamed 15-year-old Chinese boy who died in the June 1989 violence in the PRC.

> I hear the call of democracy. It is ringing in my mind. I can feel the sparks of freedom. They are burning in my heart. Like our thinkers of the past who dared to dream, I must follow in their steps. I, too, am prepared to bleed, and I will give my life as they did for this, our beloved land. Goodbye forever, my mother, my country. I shall go plant democracy in this, our beloved land. Thank you for nourishing me, for bringing me up, for making me what I am. I give you my love. I leave you my respect. Goodbye forever, my mother, my country. I have become a spark. I am fire seed who shall go to ignite the light of freedom. May it glow forever to reflect the virtue of my countrymen. Goodbye forever. Goodbye, my mother, my country.[54]

The second defining characteristic is the American foreign policy idiom. Unlike discourse in Europe, *national interest* has rarely been enough to justify foreign policy, except when national survival is thought to hang in the balance. Americans are most supportive of a foreign policy when its pursuit arguably serves both U.S. interests and ideals.

One need not retreat to the theory of Abraham Maslow about the "hierarchy of human needs" (where physiological and security imperatives are met before self-actualization needs) or "Asian values" arguments (suggesting individual liberty is not a priority in Asia) to understand why widely shared Chinese attitudes are distinct from Americans' views.

China's modern domestic history has been tumultuous, whereas America's has been relatively calm, with the glaring exception of the Civil War. About one-third of China's history has been characterized by a fragmented national polity.

In the twentieth century alone, China's people have endured at least five cataclysmic periods, most of which have been self-inflicted, when millions lost their lives: the civil wars of the 1915–1949 period, the Japanese invasion of the 1930s and 1940s, land reform in the early 1950s, the policy-induced famine following the Great Leap Forward of the late 1950s, and the Cultural Revolution decade of 1966 to 1976. The Chinese did not know peace throughout Mao Zedong's long life (1893–1976). Some Chinese still alive today have endured all of these tragedies. The result is that the Chinese people, for now at least, place a very high value on *order* and *economic advancement.* Not an order that justifies abuse, but one that fosters development, cohesion, and strength. As one Chinese villager recounted to a foreign interviewer when looking at a postcard of the Statue of Liberty, "I don't suppose it means the same to me as it does to you. For us, it doesn't mean freedom. It means opportunity."[55]

Further, although Confucianism contains elements that support responsive and humane governance,[56] China's political tradition, long before communism, has placed emphasis on a strong central, executive power, not decentralization and limited government—rule by man not rule of law. China is far less ethnically diverse than America, and the average educational levels are more uneven and far lower than in the United States. In the mid-1990s the illiteracy rate in China for persons over 15 years of age was about 19 percent, the average length of schooling was 5.6 years, and only 2 percent of the population was college educated. In contrast, in America about 82 percent of the population graduates from high school and about 24 percent are college graduates.[57]

All of these facts make a difference, a difference apparent not so much in the long-term aspirations of the Chinese and American peoples, as in immediate agendas. As the Deputy Secretary of State Strobe Talbott put it in 1996, "Poverty, underdevelopment, and stagnation are not alibis for tyranny, but they are obstacles to freedom."[58] As the collective memory of past disorder fades, as broad educational levels rise, as a middle class desirous of protecting its interests grows stronger, and as the PRC becomes more integrated into the world and familiar with its norms, the agendas of successive Chinese generations will progressively diverge from those of their forebears. Although Chinese patterns of governance, much less national interests, will never fully converge with American preferences, the

Chinese search for liberty and opportunity, within the framework of order and prosperity, will proceed.

Another distinction helps place the U.S.-China controversy over individual, human rights in perspective. Americans generally are oriented to the present, meaning they are inclined to look at a current situation and compare it to the standards that prevail that day in the United States. By this measure, China's treatment of its citizenry is dismal. In contrast, Chinese tend to recall their starting point. Americans talk about their political and social system without acknowledging that the United States also went through a development process; only in 1920 were U.S. women given the right to vote. One student at Peking University posed a question to President Clinton in June 1998 that provides a glimpse of a widely shared Chinese view: "In your address just now, you made a very proud review and retrospection of the history of America's democracy and of human rights. And you have also made some suggestions for China. Of course, those sincere suggestions we welcome. But I think I recall one saying; that is, we should have both criticism and self-criticism. So now I'd like to ask you a question. Do you think in the United States today there are also some problems in the area of democracy, freedom and human rights, and what has your Government done to improve the situation?"[59]

Furthermore, in the Chinese view, Americans often do not look at the evolution of their own views about China. How is it, for example, that Americans could be enthusiastic about Mao Zedong's "no flies in China" in the first half of the 1970s, while at that time urban youth still were in forced exile in the far reaches of China's hinterland because Beijing ordered them reeducated? Yet, two decades later, the same Americans were critical of a Deng Xiaoping who brought those young people back to their homes, reunited families, and opened up economic and educational opportunity for them, including study in the United States. Those inscrutable Americans.

These divergent orientations are reflected in specific bilateral human rights conflicts and in the contending approaches that the two governments have taken. In the first post–cold war decade, the global discussion of human rights norms occurred in the following contexts: the 1948 Universal Declaration of Human Rights; the June 1993 UN World Conference on Human Rights (and the regional preparatory conference held earlier that year in Bangkok); repeated attempts by Washington (1990–2000) to have China condemned by the UN Human Rights Commission in Geneva; and Beijing's 1991 and 1995 publication of human rights white papers.[60]

In the final analysis, three *sets* of questions have provided the focus of human rights debate between China and the United States and within America itself:

(1) What is the specific content of internationally recognized human rights norms? Do these standards vary by culture and level of development? What is the appropriate balance between economic, social, and collective rights on the one hand and individual political and civil rights on the other?

(2) Is state sovereignty a limiting factor as one state (or the international community) seeks to correct human rights abuses in another state? As discussed in the two preceding chapters, the U.S. and British elevation of human rights above sovereignty in deciding whether to intervene in another country's domestic affairs is a core strategic issue between the United States and China as they enter the twenty-first century.

(3) What tools are most effective in addressing human rights problems? It is in this domain that economic relations and human rights concerns most obviously intersect.

The Evolution of Human Rights Issues in U.S.-China Relations

From 1989 to 2000 human and individual rights concerns occupied varying positions on the American priority list. A review of this period leads me to conclude that the effective management of Sino-American ties and individual rights progress in China are best promoted when human rights is *not* the first agenda item and when U.S. interaction with China focuses on long-term development. Of course, events of the magnitude of June 4, 1989, can create such furor in the United States and elsewhere that concerns about human rights overwhelm all other priorities, interests, and perceptions (see Chapter 6).

Looking first at U.S. *priorities*, at the very outset of the Bush presidency in 1989 it was unclear how much longer the Soviet Union would last. At the National Security Council and other meetings in February, March, and early April of 1989, President Bush's advisers were divided: some thought that Mikhail Gorbachev was trying to win "breathing space" to salvage the USSR and drive a wedge into NATO, while others believed that a more "fundamental shift" was on the horizon. No one was predicting the rapid collapse of the entire Soviet system.[61] Consequently, security considerations initially dominated the administration's thinking about the bilateral relationship with China (as they had for Presidents Nixon, Ford, Carter, and Reagan).

However, under the cumulative impact of the events at Tiananmen and their aftermath, the collapse of the Warsaw Pact countries, the fall of the Soviet Union, and the election of Bill Clinton, big power security concerns temporarily receded and issues pertaining to economics, human rights, and proliferation started an indecisive competition for primacy during most of Clinton's first term. This indecisive competition produced confusion at home and in the PRC as to whether Washington had priorities, or just a laundry list of grievances. As Clinton's Assistant Secretary of State Winston Lord said to Secretary Christopher, "How do we reconcile our competing goals in a post cold war agenda when security concerns no longer lend us a clear hierarchy?"[62]

Toward the end of Clinton's first term, however, the cloud of confusion began to lift somewhat. Having seen the Chinese assist in defusing the crisis of 1993–1994 with Pyongyang over its nuclear program, having endured the mid-1994 reversal on MFN, and having stumbled into confrontation in the Taiwan Strait in 1995–1996, President Clinton made a remarkable admission in July 1996: "After I was here and thought about it and had a chance to assess the Chinese and the Chinese leadership and the nature of the changes going on in China and the way they looked at the world and us, I concluded that [previous policy] was simply not right."[63] Thus the security priority once again gained ascendancy, albeit in an altered form and with a much heavier economic component. This shift, in turn, affected where human rights issues were placed on the agenda and how they would be addressed.

The period from 1989 to 2000 can be understood as a time when Washington tried two broad approaches to promoting human rights in the PRC. The first approach, termed *engagement*, focused on interacting with Beijing in ways that supported the social, economic, and structural changes already underway in China in order to bring PRC behavior into increasing alignment with international norms over a protracted period. The term engagement is rightly associated with a classified memorandum written by Winston Lord to President Clinton in mid-July 1993 that called for "comprehensive engagement" and was adopted that September; as Lord subsequently put it to me, "The president wanted a broader framework" for dealing with China.[64] However, the term was not entirely new. In his inaugural address President Bush had spoken of a "new engagement" in interpersonal relations, between branches of government and with other nations, saying, "To the world, too, we offer new engagement."[65] The approach emphasized positive inducements, dialogue, and closed-door diplomacy rather than public stigmatization and openly delivered threats, and assigned high value to economic cooperation.

The second approach, the *punitive* approach, focused on the obvious abuses of individual and group rights in the PRC and employed sanctions and shame as the tools of choice. This approach sought to employ economic ties as a lever to extract human rights concessions from Beijing, with concessions often defined as improved conditions (justice) for identifiable individuals.

Relatively few participants in the policy process would consider themselves exclusively in one camp or another, preferring to see themselves as "realists." Even fervent "engagers" recognize the need for force and credibility and the need to employ unilateral sanctions in the economic and proliferation realms on occasion. Conversely, even those most inclined in the punitive direction recognize that ignoring long-term structural change is futile.

Having said this, though, the human rights battle of the 1990s raged between two groups whose center of gravity in policy terms was very different. The engagers argued that only through economic growth, the emergence of a middle class, and institutions built on an educated populace, could lasting human rights progress be made. Adherents of the more punitive approach rejoined that one had to be concerned about the immediate circumstance of people facing torture and unjust incarceration and that only with a more liberalized polity was sustainable economic growth and social stability possible. Finally, they argued, Beijing's dependence on positive economic performance for legitimacy and the PRC's dependence on the U.S. export market provided Washington enormous leverage.

It was in the context of these inclinations that President Clinton in May 1993 linked the continued extension of MFN to "overall, significant progress" in specific human rights areas (e.g., prisoner accountings and more humane treatment, religious expression, preserving Tibet's cultural heritage, permitting international broadcasts to reach Chinese citizens, and implementing the 1992 bilateral agreement concerning prison labor) in his Executive Order 128590. This context also helps account for the absence of U.S.-China state visits during the first Clinton term. The implicit theory was that the combination of threatened economic pain and public shame would prove powerful levers over Beijing in the human rights domain. A further implicit assumption was that the Chinese regime was "transitional," as Wintson Lord put it, later explaining to me that, "I was over optimistic about Li Peng going. If you told me Li Peng [would be] there ten years later I would [have been] surprised."[66]

By the end of 1993 and throughout 1994, however, there were clear signs of a troubled policy. In February 1994, John Shattuck, the assistant secretary of state for human rights and humanitarian affairs, met with Chinese dissident Wei Jingsheng (who had been released from jail the previous September) in Beijing, only to have Wei incarcerated the next month. In March of that year, Secretary Christopher traveled to the PRC, publicly criticizing Beijing's noncompliance with the Clinton administration's MFN linkage demands at every stop on his way across the Pacific. In Canberra, he said, "They [Beijing] have heard from me before and they'll hear from me again that overall significant progress [on human rights] will be necessary before the most-favored-nation treatment can be extended."[67] Predictably, when Secretary Christopher arrived in Beijing, he received the cold shoulder, and more dissidents were arrested. By May, President Clinton felt compelled to break the linkage between Beijing's MFN tariff status and its individual rights performance that he had established the previous year.

What accounts for this humiliating U.S. policy reversal? The administration faced three insuperable problems. First, it was making a threat, but it lacked credibility. The absence of credibility derived from Beijing's assumption that American business pressure to continue MFN tariff treatment would prove decisive. The administration was also divided with Commerce Secretary Ron Brown and the other economic agencies pursuing a policy best described as commercial diplomacy. Winston Lord put it to me this way: "My complaint is that once the president chose policy, it is up to the White House to maintain discipline or you lose leverage over the Chinese. Once the Chinese saw the economic agencies cutting up [the president's policy], and the president not reining them in, we lost all leverage with the Chinese."[68] Moreover, the September 1993 embrace of "comprehensive engagement" at the same time Washington was threatening Beijing (along with Assistant Secretary Lord's distancing himself from the punitive approach) told the Chinese that there was a lack of resolve in the administration. Finally, the president was seen as weak, having vacillated and retreated in the face of prior foreign policy challenges during his first term—Somalia, Bosnia, and Haiti.

Second, the United States was without allied or any other external support. America's friends would simply pick the carcass of deserted U.S. commercial opportunity in China; even Hong Kong and Taiwan argued against damaging trade ties in the name of pursuing human rights.

Lastly, the Chinese had strong incentives for resisting U.S. pressure. Beijing believed it could prevail and call the administration's bluff. Jiang

Zemin was in the midst of positioning himself for the post–Deng Xiaoping era, and he dared not capitulate to external pressure. And, most fundamental, no government can permit its internal political character to be held hostage to the tariff levels of another nation, no matter how important exports to that market may be. Certainly China would not capitulate to such a threat given its history of foreign encroachment, the fact that the regime's legitimacy increasingly hung on nationalism, and the very simple notion of face—you don't back down to publicly articulated threats, period.

Nonetheless, the failure of MFN linkage did not lead to an immediate and clearly stated adoption of comprehensive engagement. It took two more years for the president to survey the wreckage of his policy, for external events to make clear the cost of continuing the punitive approach, and for the White House and Department of State to achieve the consensus necessary to clearly articulate a new policy. Further, Congress, in its dealings with the China issue, had to reach a certain point of exhaustion before it became more pliable, and a full articulation of comprehensive engagement had to await demonstrations that there were high security costs to Beijing's noncooperation.

It was not until May 17, 1996, therefore, that Secretary of State Christopher delivered a landmark address, declaring that high-level exchanges on a regular basis with PRC leaders were essential and that progress on security and economic issues should not be held hostage to human rights differences.[69] Although the general election of 1996 and the transition to the second Clinton administration would delay the full implementation of the new policy, Secretary Christopher's speech signaled the direction for China policy for the remainder of the Clinton presidency.

Reflecting this shift, the president's national security adviser, Anthony Lake, who three years earlier had lumped China together with "backlash states," made his first-ever visit to the PRC in July 1996 to pursue "strategic dialogue." Following his four-day trip, Lake's transformation was stunning; he now spoke of the need to treat Chinese leaders with respect and dignity, observed that the economic transformation in the PRC was truly astounding, and gave expression to the fear that too much human rights pressure was counterproductive.[70] "You can do it better [make progress on human rights and other issues] when not every issue becomes, in itself, so confrontational that in effect they [sic] Chinese leaders cannot afford to make a compromise because then we'll look as if we have steamrolled them and then will do so on every other issue."[71]

Consistent with this "new" perspective, China's minister of defense, Chi Haotian, the chief of staff of the PLA at the time of the Tiananmen bloodshed, visited the United States in December 1996; early in Clinton's second term, President Jiang Zemin visited the United States, and during the October 1997 summit both sides agreed "to build toward a constructive strategic partnership."[72] In June–July 1998, President Clinton traveled to China for a follow-up summit, where he was officially received on the perimeter of Tiananmen Square itself, much to the dismay of the American human rights community. In justifying the largely successful trip, the administration emphasized China's strategic importance, focusing on the PRC's pivotal role in maintaining stability on the Korean peninsula and on the subcontinent, where India and Pakistan had just tested nuclear devices, and in cooperating to maintain macroeconomic stability in financially troubled East Asia.

Only with the clear ascendance of the engagement approach and the broadened security rationale that carried with it a large economic component, did the Chinese begin to make limited gestures to assuage Washington's human rights concerns. Although from time to time individual dissidents of high priority to Washington had been released since 1989, it was only in 1997, just before the Washington summit, that Beijing signed the International Covenant on Economic, Social, and Cultural Rights. Following that, in March 1998 Vice Premier Qian Qichen expressed Beijing's intention to sign the International Covenant on Civil and Political Rights, doing so in October of that year.

Further, only in this context did China agree to work with the United States in the field of legal and judicial cooperation. In November 1997 Minister of Justice Xiao Yang came to the United States, and in the 1997 and 1998 summits there were general agreements to cooperate in the "rule of law" realm. With respect to subsequent cooperation in the legal field, the greatest obstacle became congressional unwillingness to appropriate money, not Beijing's resistance.

Finally, it was in this context that Jiang Zemin agreed to the live, nationwide broadcast of two events during the June 1998 Beijing summit at which President Clinton was critical of China's human rights record. The first was a joint press conference on June 27, where Clinton said, "I believe and the American people believe that the use of force and the tragic loss of life [at Tiananmen] was wrong";[73] the second, a speech at Peking University two days later, where the U.S. president said, "But true freedom must mean more than economic opportunity. In America, we believe that freedom itself is indivisible."[74] Also, prior to the Beijing summit the PRC released two internationally known dissidents, Wei Jingsheng and Wang Dan, sending them into exile in America.

However, there is a difference between tactical and strategic human rights changes. The tactical release of a dissident here and there and the signing of an international covenant from time to time are welcome, but they do not necessarily lead to more durable and comprehensive improvements. Long-term economic and social development often is the essential foundation upon which durable change and improvement rests.[75] As Stanley Lubman points out in his essay "Sino-American Relations and China's Struggle for the Rule of Law," fundamental change will be linked to changes in the governing system itself, the development of independent judicial and legislative institutions, the gradual accretion of legal codes, social, economic, and educational development, and changes in Chinese legal culture.[76]

Critics of China tend to ascribe the deficiencies of the legal system entirely to communism. In fact, such deficiencies reflect the interaction of current institutions with long-standing tradition. "[T]he dominant attitudes [of Chinese traditionally] discouraged persons from taking their disputes to courts, and a venerable tradition of emphasizing compromise in the context of long-standing relationships continues to exert its influence."[77] While more recent research on traditional legal practice calls some of these characterizations into question,[78] it nonetheless is true that significant changes in China's individual rights situation will not occur principally because of U.S. pressure or expressions of concern. Rather, they will reflect the exposure of the Chinese people to the outside world, the degree to which the Chinese leadership feels secure, the concerns of a growing middle class in China, and the painstaking construction of a judicial and legal system. Americans frequently flatter themselves unduly in assuming that their threats and rhetorical expressions have much impact. Expressions of concern are imperative, but they are not the locomotives of change.

The Spectrum of Human Rights Issues in Bilateral Relations

Human rights-related issues in China during the first post–cold war decade fall into several categories: individual rights concerns, group rights issues, and problems germane to specific geographic areas, particularly Tibet and Hong Kong. At the beginning of the decade, conflicts over the fate and treatment of specific Chinese dissident figures dominated the bilateral human rights discussion. However, as the decade unfolded, the issue of group rights became increasingly prominent. Moreover, many in Washington began to support the proposition that working together with the Chinese to develop legal and judicial institutions might be more productive than stigmatization and coercion. When the fate of individual dissidents was at issue, it often proved more effective to address the problem quietly.

Underlying these developments during the 1990s were two other, instrumental developments in Western thinking vis-à-vis human rights, developments that may be key to the future U.S.-China relationship. The first was that many in the United States and among its Western allies began to believe that the need for humanitarian intervention could, on occasion, prove so compelling that violations of traditional norms of state sovereignty and the UN Charter were justified. This evolution in thought led naturally to a second development: many Americans began to view the ability of the people of Taiwan to determine their own destiny free of compulsion as a human rights issue. The fusion of humanitarian intervention as a priority and the Taiwan issue will make management of the Taiwan issue more difficult in the future. The following is not simply the expression of a frightened Chinese propaganda apparatus, but rather a reflection of more broadly shared views in the PRC: "But unlike the old cold war, the new cold war, launched by the United States under the banner of 'safeguarding human rights' and 'global democratization' at a time when it is lording it over the world, is more hegemonic and smells stronger of gunpowder. The initiators of the new cold war, no longer satisfied with the general ideological struggle and infiltration or peaceful evolution, now brazenly interfere in other countries' internal affairs, trample on their national sovereignty, and seek to impose their own standard of human rights and 'well-behaved ID card' or be put on the 'black list.'"[79]

Individual Human Rights. The category of individual rights issues pertains to the fate of specific persons (e.g., Fang Lizhi, Hongda [Harry] Wu, Wei Jingsheng, Wang Dan, and Bishop Zeng Jingmu, to mention only a few). Beyond strictly humanitarian considerations, individuals and their courageous stories provide a vehicle by which human rights organizations, politicians, and others can mobilize their bases politically, financially, and otherwise.

Nonetheless, a Sino-American poker game with individuals as chips has its downside. For instance, it has become routine before or after each summit or very high level meeting to release (usually into exile) a few individuals: after the 1997 summit Wei Jingsheng was released, and prior to Premier Zhu Rongji's 1999 visit to the United States Gao Yu was released. Preparations for very high level meetings become an implicit bargaining game in which the lives of individuals are traded for concessions in a variety of unrelated domains. This process does little or nothing to fundamentally change broader conditions in China and may even create an environment that encourages "hostage taking" for subsequent release while discouraging Sino-American cooperation that might have a more profound impact over time. Finally, the resolution of an individual's case often results in exile, which the regime views as a convenient way to remove troublesome people from the country, but which may not be the desire of that individual or his or her family.

Group Human Rights. By group rights I have in mind several issues. One is the treatment of infants and young children in Chinese orphanages, a topic that became a major concern in 1996 after the January airing of the British Broadcasting Corporation documentary *The Dying Rooms.* Human Rights Watch/Asia released a report on the same topic in January 1996 titled *Death by Default.* The published report alleged that a Shanghai orphanage "selected unwanted infants and children for death by intentional deprivation of food and water."[80] This was done, the report asserted, because China's "one child policy" had led to an increased number of abandoned children (often females) and because orphanage capacity was insufficient to accommodate demand. In the report's words, "[I]t was the ruthless arithmetic of the situation, the impossible disparity emerging between orphan supply and institutional capacity, which conspired to exacerbate further China's already staggering orphanage mortality rates during the prosperous 1980s and 1990s."[81] In effect, it was alleged that the Chinese authorities had in place a policy that limited orphanage beds so that "excess" children were permitted, or helped, to die at the Shanghai Children's Welfare Institute and, by implication, at other PRC institutions, and that this "deliberate starvation, torture, and sexual assault, continued over a period of years."[82]

A related issue involves repeated indications over the first post–cold war decade (and before) that female fetuses are disproportionately aborted and girl infants sometimes killed or left to die as a result of implementing the one-child policy in a society heavily biased toward male offspring. Indeed, demographic data in China indicate that 114 to 117 male children are born for each hundred females, though there probably are unreported female births.[83] Beyond the moral costs of this phenomenon, significant social problems stemming from the growing gender imbalance lie in store for the PRC. In this vein, the October 1994 Law of the People's Republic of China on Maternal and Infant Health Care, a watered-down version of a previously proposed eugenics law, is deeply disquieting to many in the West, suggesting that termination of pregnancies can be used to select out "undesired" attributes from the population. Indeed, the long-term social and moral costs of scientific possibility is a problem confronting not just the Chinese, but the entire world as well.

A third issue pertains to periodic charges that some Chinese organizations and citizens have traded in human organs harvested from executed prisoners. The February 1998 arrest of two Chinese citizens in New York accused of conspiring to sell organs, plus reports dating back to 1993, are indication that this repugnant commerce does indeed exist.[84]

A fourth group rights issue, particularly of note in the second half of the 1990s, concerns labor rights and fair labor standards—the right to form free labor unions and charges of poor working conditions. Beyond the ethical issues, American free labor wants as level a playing field as possible in the global economy, desiring not to compete with low-cost Chinese labor, even if those PRC laborers prefer the conditions of the industrial sweatshops to the muck of rice paddies. As for U.S. businesses, by-and-large they have a quite laudable record of providing good working conditions in the PRC, as Doug Guthrie documents in his exhaustive study of Chinese enterprises with foreign participation.[85] Nonetheless, American multinationals generally have resisted the imposition of "codes of human rights conduct" and other voluntary principles for business activity that organized labor, human rights groups, and the Clinton administration have from time to time sought, as in 1995. The Chinese government looks at this push for international labor standards as just another attempt to preserve U.S. economic dominance and to interfere in domestic governance.[86]

A related set of issues concerns labor and environmental standards in international trade. Among the controversies are whether there should be an internationally set floor on wages, whether there should be minimal standards applied to the production of export goods in terms of environmental impacts, and whether nongovernmental organizations and other citizen groups should have a role in WTO policymaking. These controversies burst onto the global scene in late November and early December 1999 as a WTO ministerial-level meeting was convened in Seattle, Washington, to establish the terms for a new round of trade liberalization negotiations. The talks were marked by protests and street violence and concluded with no agreed-upon future agenda. Beijing (not then a WTO member) and Washington were on opposite sides of these issues.

Representative Tom Lantos (D-California) pretty well summed up the Chinese group rights issues of concern in a February 1994 hearing of a subcommittee of the House Committee on Ways and Means:

There are forced confessions and torture by police and prison authorities. Chinese prisons are filled with thousands of political and religious prisoners who committed the crime of trying to practice the universal basic freedoms of speech and assembly. And you will be hearing later today concerning the most outrageous anti-Christian violence which is occurring in China.... Prisoners are used as slave labor for China's huge export market. Coercive birth control practices continue, including forced abortions and forced sterilizations.... Restrictions on emigration remain in place for dissidents, and the regime also practices on a large scale, Mr. Chairman, internal exile.[87]

All of the above phenomena occur in China, though with what frequency we cannot be sure. Nonetheless, it is useful to consider these abuses from the perspective of U.S. interest group politics. For each of the examples in the preceding paragraphs, some U.S. political or social organization (and often more than one), from religious conservatives to organized labor, finds its values offended. The organizations also find in these human rights abuses powerful symbols they can utilize to mobilize their support bases in the competitive and adversarial political and fund-raising processes. The combination of genuine abuses of unknown magnitude in China, the offense taken by Americans, and the strength and usefulness of the resulting image as a mobilization device means that the human rights issue will be a long-lasting fixture of U.S.-China relations.

Another key consideration has given the human rights debate between China and the United States a murky quality. Even when abuses occur and are documented, often one cannot be sure whether the acts have been sanctioned by central government policy or instead represent the behavior of local officials or citizens acting illegally or overzealously (or both). One example involves the trafficking of some 100,000 illegal emigrants per year—a lucrative enterprise (more than $3 billion per year by one estimate)[88]—where local officials, in league with "snakeheads" (thugs who smuggle Chinese nationals abroad and keep them in indentured servitude), buy off corrupt immigration and customs agents along the coast. Marlowe Hood writes, "Official malfeasance has reached dimensions unprecedented during Communist rule and bolsters migrant smuggling in a least three ways, one direct and the other two more difficult to quantify. Its obvious role is in facilitating the organized, illegal exit of Chinese citizens from the PRC, an exodus that the local government has very little incentive to stop, and arguably a good reason to tolerate, given the vast amount of remittances and investment flowing back into the region, $100 million annually in Changle alone, according to local officials."[89]

Further, there is an international dimension to the problem of trafficking, with criminal networks in Taiwan and Hong Kong playing a prominent role. "All of the at least 37 smuggling vessels with would-be migrants on board apprehended in or near North American waters by U.S. law enforcement from mid-1991 through mid-1994 were somehow linked to Taiwan."[90] The same pattern is seen in the trafficking of women for purposes of prostitution.[91] Indeed, the problem of corruption of the customs and immigration authorities and external organized criminal involvement had become so pervasive by 1998 that President Jiang Zemin had to order the formation of a new antismuggling police force. Clearly, much happens in China that Beijing opposes.

This point is also illustrated by national population control policy. Much, but by no means all, of the abuse arises from the interaction of rigid birth quotas passed down the system, some zealous local officials anxious to comply, and new technology (e.g., sonograms) that makes selective abortion of female fetuses possible. Again, Beijing opposes the resulting infanticide, sex selection, and child abandonment that results but cannot entirely evade responsibility for the foreseeable consequences of its policies.

The preceding is not to say that all human rights abuses in China are simply a result of local officials, international organized crime, decentralized authority in the absence of clean government, or weak judicial institutions. Rather, it is to say that the decentralization and marketization of Chinese society (which Americans applaud) can produce illegal and indefensible results in the absence of a legal and regulatory system that takes a long time to construct. In addition, because China's central government feels compelled to maintain the façade of control, it hesitates to even measure the scope of abuse, fearing that to do so is to acknowledge how much has slipped from its grasp.

Human Rights in Hong Kong and Tibet. Hong Kong became an object of concern to human rights proponents when Great Britain and China agreed in the 1984 Joint Declaration that as of July 1, 1997, the colony would revert to Beijing's sovereignty. In the aftermath of the 1989 violence in China and as tortuous and conflict-laden negotiations between London and Beijing proceeded thereafter, Americans, particularly in the U.S. Congress, increasingly feared that Hong Kong's social and economic freedoms were at risk upon reversion (see Chapter 5). This concern was stoked by articulate and brave advocates for political pluralism and the rule of law in Hong Kong, including British Governor Christopher Patten (sworn in July 1992), Martin Lee, head of the United Democrats of Hong

Kong (after October 1994 the Democratic Party), and many other key figures such as Christine Loh, Elizabeth Wong, and Emily Lau.

From 1990 on, however, a paradox emerged in which some members of the U.S. Congress proposed to promote human rights in China and Hong Kong by threatening to take MFN away from Beijing, a move that even Hong Kong's most ardent promoters of human rights (including Martin Lee) opposed. In May 1993 Governor Patten told a National Committee on U.S.-China Relations audience in New York: "I think it is impossible to cancel MFN, impossible to heavily constrain MFN, without damaging Hong Kong. I just don't know how you do it. So I feel particularly strongly, and I've been saying this to congressional leaders this week, that those people who think that they can somehow help Hong Kong by attaching what happens in Hong Kong to renewal of MFN should really think again. You can't help Hong Kong by hurting Hong Kong's economy."[92]

Three years later, only one year before reversion, again in New York to a National Committee audience, Patten said:

> How do you show your continuing interest [in Hong Kong on the eve of the reversion to the PRC]? Well, if I may say so ... not by failing to renew MFN; not by applying conditions to MFN. I make that point not as a spokesman for China. I am not a propagandist for China's human rights record; not a propagandist for China—China's record on weapons proliferation or—on intellectual property. I make it as somebody who wants to protect and defend Hong Kong's interest, and at a time when we're going through this particularly difficult transition, it would make our job incomparably more difficult, the job of safeguarding a free society—if our economy was to be hit for 6 during the next 12 months.[93]

Hong Kong's democratic party leaders were torn between two impulses. On the one hand, they were tempted to use America's economic leverage to coerce Beijing into further liberalization at home and with respect to Hong Kong. On the other hand, they feared that to support such measures would hurt the territory's economy, Hong Kong citizens, and presumably their own political prospects by tarnishing their "patriotic" credentials with Beijing. Further, it was apparent to most Hong Kong citizens that not only would a poor and struggling China stripped of MFN transship less through Hong Kong, but a poor unstable China would be a constant threat to the enclave itself; the worse things got on the mainland the worse things would be in their city.

Given all of these considerations, Congress took a different, and ultimately more productive, approach. Senator Mitch McConnell (R-Kentucky) introduced a bill in September 1991 that eventually became the United

States–Hong Kong Policy Act of 1992. The act did four things: (1) it obligated the U.S. government to ensure that the functional equivalents of the legal agreements, representation, and exchanges that linked Hong Kong and the United States in the colonial era were in place by reversion; (2) it specified America's tangible interests (economic and otherwise) in Hong Kong; (3) it enumerated the indicators Washington would use to evaluate the territory's human rights and other conditions after reversion; and (4) it indicated that if Hong Kong's condition along these dimensions deteriorated, then the city's favorable treatment under the act also could be affected by presidential order. Basically, the act conferred benefits, defined U.S. interests, provided guidance for monitoring, and did not make any specific, noncredible, and incendiary threats.

While Beijing delivered a pro-forma protest about the act constituting interference in China's internal affairs, the legislation never became a point of major contention. Part of the reason for this muted response was that, first, Americans had demonstrable economic and other interests at stake in the reversion process, and Beijing recognized that; second, Washington did not make specific threats; and third, the act offered clear benefits to Hong Kong, which would soon be an official part of the PRC.

Overriding all of this, however, was that Beijing had an enormous self-interest in Hong Kong's successful reversion. Its interest derived from the fact that the reversion was a test of the "one country, two systems" model Beijing was trying to sell to Taipei. Indeed, the model had been introduced by Deng Xiaoping in September 1981 in connection with Taiwan, and only subsequently was it applied to Hong Kong.[94]

Four additional considerations were also important. First, over one-half of the foreign direct investment that came into the PRC throughout the 1980s and the first half of the 1990s came via Hong Kong.[95] Second, the legitimacy of Jiang Zemin's regime would be enhanced or diminished by its ability to govern Hong Kong as well as, or better than, the colonial British had previously. Third, the PRC had about two thousand China-funded enterprises in Hong Kong itself.[96] And finally, Hong Kong constituted a critical link in Sino-American trade, with 43 percent of Chinese exports to the United States and 27 percent of imports to the mainland from America transiting through the Hong Kong Special Administrative Region (HKSAR) in 1997.[97]

Thus, Chinese interest in a smooth reversion process contributed to the ease of transition, as did reasonable U.S. policy. In April 1997 House Speaker Newt Gingrich appointed the chairman of the Subcommittee on East Asia and the Pacific, Doug Bereuter (R-Nebraska), to head a task force to monitor the Hong Kong reversion and its aftermath and to deliver quarterly reports to the House based on twice-yearly trips to the HKSAR. In its first three reports, the task force's operative judgment was "so far, so good," though the second and third reports called for "closer attention" to rule of law.[98] In 1999 several issues in this regard did become prominent, most notably controversy over the Hong Kong court's ability to rule on immigration issues.

In sum, American expressions of concern and interest in Hong Kong have been positive and have not proven to be major irritants in bilateral relations. Indeed, these expressions probably were net positives. Despite all the Western concerns about reversion prior to mid-1997, as the twenty-first century concluded, Beijing's sovereignty had not been disruptive. Indeed, most of the problems that hit Hong Kong in the late 1990s had to do with the Asian financial crisis (see Chapter 4) that began in Thailand in July 1997—the same month Hong Kong reverted to China.

The Tibet Autonomous Region (TAR) and the American role with respect to this troubled Himalayan expanse twice the size of Texas do not present the same positive story as Hong Kong. U.S. posturing (principally by Congress) has maximized Chinese fears and defensiveness and created unrealistic expectations for American involvement among Tibetans.[99] The United States never has formally recognized Tibet as an independent, sovereign state, nor has it recognized the Fourteenth Dalai Lama—widely admired around the world as a spiritual leader of the Tibetan people (and winner of the 1989 Nobel Peace Prize)—as a head of state. As Warren Christopher put it in his January 13, 1993, confirmation hearing, "I don't foresee the United States taking any action such as unilateral recognition, for example, of Tibet because of the high cost it would invoke in other areas."[100] Further, tangible U.S. interests are negligible in Tibet. Lastly, Tibet's location is so remote that expressions of American support rarely have been backed by genuine commitments, except in the 1950s and 1960s when the United States[101] ran "black operations" in the mountain redoubt and provided other support to the Tibetan movement over the years.[102] Recently declassified U.S. government documents and a fascinating study by former CIA officer Kenneth Knaus reveal Washington's past involvement in the Tibetan movement for independence.[103] Those actions included financial support of the Dalai Lama[104] and Cultural Revolution–era discussions between U.S. and Taiwan officials about how unrest in China as a whole and the cause of independence in Tibet might be promoted.[105]

Past U.S. behavior and ongoing political rhetoric concerning Tibet have convinced Beijing that America's interest there derives more from a desire to split and weaken the PRC than to promote spiritual values or human rights. Beijing asserts that it is bringing the blessings of modernity to a primitive people who were exploited under the old monastic order of traditional Tibet. One child of a very senior Chinese political personality with whom I spoke in the early 1990s talked in impassioned terms about the alleged brutality of the old order—"using skin to make lampshades" and the practice of dismemberment.

The Tibet issue is complex. There are disputes over whether or not (and the degree to which) Tibet historically has been independent of China; the geographic extent of Tibet itself ("Greater" or "Ethnographic" Tibet, with a population of about 6 million and covering much of southwestern China, versus the TAR, covering much less territory, with a population of about two million); and the human rights conditions that characterized traditional Tibetan society. As well, there has been debate within and outside the Dalai Lama's own movement about whether autonomy within the Chinese state or true independence from Beijing ought to be the goal. In short, Tibet has been a tangled issue about which Americans have little knowledge, and the executive branch's formal policy (though not actual behavior) has been consistent throughout the post-1949 period—that Tibet is part of China.

Amidst this complexity, however, are genuine human rights concerns that have fueled repeated efforts by the U.S. Congress, human rights organizations, and many philanthropic groups to come up with proposals. The first issue is the treatment of the Tibetan religious establishment—its monks, adherents, and monasteries.[106] The second is the gradual dilution of Tibetan culture and way of life, due to the twin and interconnected phenomena of modernization and Han in-migration.

It was appalling to travel to Lhasa and its environs in the early 1980s and see the towering mountainsides littered with the ruble of what were once thousands of monasteries. The few monasteries left standing in the early 1980s had virtually no monks in them, nor were they recruiting novitiates to replace elders who died; the numbing hand of Communist Party control in the monasteries was evidenced everywhere.

The situation in the TAR during the Cultural Revolution (1966–1976) and in succeeding years was so grim that in 1978 the post–Mao Zedong regime sought improvements, and Chinese Communist Party General Secretary Hu Yaobang and Vice Premier Wan Li traveled to the region in May 1980. Hu issued a "Six Point" reform program,[107] ordered a dramatic reduction in Han officials in the TAR, and promoted more liberal religious, economic, and social policies.

However, with the fall of Hu Yaobang in January 1987, demonstrations ("riots") in Tibet in 1987, 1988, and 1989,[108] and growing dissatisfaction with Beijing's poor handling of the selection of a new Panchen Lama (the tenth had died in 1989) in 1995, Beijing tightened policy in the region and the inward movement of Han Chinese resumed.

The Chinese are faced with a dilemma. To start, because prior to 1949 the Dalai Lama embodied both religious and secular authority in Tibet, the reverence with which Tibetans regard him to this day is not only an assertion of religious freedom but also, in Beijing's eyes, a declaration of political independence. The Chinese cling to this view, despite the Dalai Lama's assertion that if he returned to Tibet he would assume only a religious (not political) role. Beijing believes that the reverence with which his Holiness is regarded in the TAR would make it impossible for him to separate his religious role from political authority. Nonetheless, as long as Americans see suppression of religion in Tibet and know that Beijing prevents the Dalai Lama's return to his people, they will define Tibet as a human rights problem and will respond accordingly.

Second, the TAR's monasteries are both religious institutions and repositories of organized independence sentiment. Consequently, when the Chinese relax controls on religion and allow monasteries to grow and recruit novitiates, Beijing and its officials in the TAR soon are confronted with growing challenges by the ranks of monks and TAR citizens to their sovereignty. When Beijing clamps down on these expressions of independence sentiment, its actions are viewed in the TAR and abroad as a violation of individual rights, as well as an attack upon religion.

Another significant dilemma is the flow of long and short-term migrants of Han Chinese ethnicity into the TAR from elsewhere in the PRC. The confusion surrounding this issue is great. Chinese demographic statistics often are problematic, and in this case they do not include those persons who are "temporarily" in Tibet (but whose household registration is elsewhere) in the permanent population figures. With freer internal migration in the post-1978 period throughout the mainland, many Han Chinese have come to the TAR in search of economic opportunity or to work on a variety of construction projects, some of which are of dubious economic value to the indigenous population and/or ecologically destructive; in addition there are a large, but unknown number of PLA troops posted in the region. This influx of Han Chinese has produced increasing domination of the urban economy, cultural change, conflict, and repression in the wake of what was called the Third Forum in Beijing in July 1994.[109]

Service establishments and light industries are now dominated by Han Chinese. Chinese truck in watermelons from other provinces, and stone cutters from Fujian are to be found doing the fine work on restored and new buildings. Given the generally noncommercial and nomadic nature of Tibetans, Chinese have come to dominate the urban economy (particularly in Lhasa and Shigatse) and urban areas assumed an increasingly Chinese character throughout the 1990s. While the vast pastoral regions of Tibet have a far less pronounced Chinese presence, if any, it is the cities and urban centers where religious, cultural, and political life are most organized, where most westerners visit, and where religious and social repression are most acute. It is the combination of political and religious oppression and systematic cultural dilution that has constituted the principal contours of the Tibet human rights issue in American politics.

While U.S. administrations repeatedly have seen Tibet's circumstance as tragic but peripheral, the Chinese regard Tibet as a core strategic concern. The region's importance derives from Beijing's belief that if it were to allow independence or grant a high degree of autonomy to Tibet, it would immediately be subject to pressure for similar latitude from Xinjiang Autonomous Region (with a large, periodically restive Muslim population), Mongolia, other minority areas within China, and Taiwan. In short, for Beijing, Tibet is central to the edifice of unity. Throughout successive Chinese dynasties, the falling away of a regime's periphery has been a prelude to its demise. Finally, to the Chinese it is the destiny of Tibet to be dominated by one or another big power—in the past, Britain, India, and even Russia, have all competed with China in this respect. In addition, given that Tibet is the strategic high ground on the subcontinent, the Chinese would rather they occupy it than India.

So in the Chinese view Tibet (unlike Hong Kong) is an area in which Americans have no concrete, legitimate interest and about which they have little capability or will to do anything. In Beijing's view, were it to capitulate to U.S. concerns, core Chinese interests (national unity and security) would be compromised. Washington is left with rhetoric.

Rhetoric brings us to the reality of pluralized U.S. politics, in this case Congress, the mass media, the émigré Tibetan lobby, and single-issue interest groups. Many institutions and political organizations have found in the Dalai Lama, his movement, and his people a powerful symbol of religious freedom, self-determination, and human rights. Consequently, Congress passes resolutions every year calling for presidents to see the Dalai Lama on his visits to the United States (as both Presidents Bush and Clinton have done), tying MFN tariff treatment to preserving Tibet's heritage and culture, the establishment of various emissary and bureaucratic positions in the U.S. government with which to push the Tibet issue harder with Beijing, assistance for Tibetan refugees and scholarships for Tibetan students, and the conferral of more officiality on the Dalai Lama and his movement.[110]

All this might represent a useful legislative-executive branch dynamic were it not for three considerations. First, such behavior encourages Tibetans in the belief that the United States might actually come to their assistance at some point. The 1956 Hungarian uprising and the unfulfilled expectation of U.S. assistance is a sad reminder of what can happen in this regard.

Second, these resolutions and legislative initiatives (some of which refer to Tibet as an "occupied country")[111] feed Beijing's predisposition to believe that the real objective of U.S. policy is to split and weaken China and thereby reinforce the PRC's inclination to further clamp down on the TAR. In short, it is far from clear that some expressions of American humanitarian impulses are having humanitarian effects on the ground in Tibet.

There is one further consideration. The Dalai Lama is a moderating element within his own movement. In his speech to the European Parliament in June 1988 in Strasbourg he called for China to accord Tibet a high degree of autonomy within the PRC.[112] In the spectrum of opinion among his followers, the Dalai Lama and his elder brother Gyalo Thondup are moderates, in favor of both dialogue with the Chinese and the U.S. policy of engagement.

However, the Dalai Lama's flexibility and moderation are not uniformly supported within the Tibetan exile community in the United States or among his fellow Tibetans in Dharamsala, the Dalai Lama's redoubt in northern India. Some generally younger Tibetans support a more aggressive, and in some cases violent, approach. If the Dalai Lama died without resolution of the Tibetan issue, the Chinese almost certainly would seek to determine the identity of the next Dalai Lama (as they did when the Tenth Panchen Lama died in 1989). Such a selection would have little or no legitimacy in Tibetan eyes and the initiative within the Tibetan exile community could easily flow into more violent hands. The Chinese would be faced with mounting violence, they would retaliate, and in any event, the process of cultural dilution would continue or accelerate in Tibet. In the end, the two million Tibetans in the TAR and their culture almost certainly would be the losers. Such developments would send tremors throughout the U.S.-China relationship as Congress and the American public reacted.

This suggests, therefore, that those well-meaning members of Congress, émigré organizations, and human rights organizations that either explicitly or implicitly support Tibetan independence may well be contributing to the least desirable outcome. The most desirable, *feasible* goal is a more genuinely autonomous Tibet, with less in-migration of Han people, within the framework of the Chinese state. However, in an adversarial, pluralized system Washington finds it difficult to defend a policy that is realistic, but not ideal. The benefits of symbolic politics to the players in the U.S. political process can come at the expense of the people they wish to help.

CONCLUSIONS AND LESSONS LEARNED

Why have U.S.-China relations, as outlined in the last two chapters, proven so difficult to manage, and what accounts for the successes that have been achieved?

First, the cold war era's defining challenge, avoiding a nuclear Armageddon, no longer served as an organizing principle for foreign policy in the United States after the 1991 collapse of the Soviet Union. Without this discipline, policymakers lacked an accepted rationale by which they could establish geographical or issue-based priorities. Consequently, in the first half of the first post–cold war decade, particularly during Bill Clinton's initial term, Washington made commitments to such varied and arguably peripheral areas as Haiti, Somalia, and (more debatably) the Balkans, while simultaneously permitting periodic and dangerous slides in relations with Japan, China, and Russia. In terms of issues, it was impossible for either participants in the policy process or outside observers to determine overall administration foreign policy priorities: it was "commercial diplomacy" at the Department of Commerce and other economic agencies, proliferation or human rights (or both) at the Department of State (depending on which bureau one listened to), market access at the USTR, conventional security cooperation at the Defense Department, and the "China threat" in some corners of the national security and intelligence apparatus.

Having no priorities, in turn, sent the same signal to both congressional opponents and Beijing—the administration would not fight for anything. Indeed, as he started his first term, Bill Clinton made congressional acceptance of his China policy the principal criterion of success. As a result, he was challenged on his China policy repeatedly by Capitol Hill. Further, without priorities the Chinese never knew what it would take to actually improve relations, fearing that satisfaction of one U.S. demand would simply inspire others.

Only in the last part of the first Clinton term was a sense of priority regained. That priority was reflected in the reaffirmation of the primacy of security, the broadening of the concept of security to include economic stability and growth, and the assertion that an environment of security and economic cooperation fostered human rights progress in China over the long run. Paradoxically, human rights are most effectively promoted by putting other issues first.

A second conclusion emerges from the first. When the foreign policy apparatus has a broad array of functional bureaus competing equally with the geographic bureaus to make policy, as was more nearly the case in the Clinton administration than previous U.S. governments, priorities become blurred and policy becomes insensitive to the actual localities in which it must be implemented. Catharin E. Dalpino, the former deputy assistant secretary of state for democracy in the Bureau of Democracy, Human Rights, and Labor (1993–1997), put it crisply after her experience: "The administration should take democracy promotion out of the functional orbit of the policy agencies and base it in the regional bureaus."[113] She goes on to note that often the needs of democracy promotion are at odds with the needs of advancing human rights; the one needs slow, quiet, institution building and the other thrives by calling global attention to perceived deficiencies.

A third lesson pertains to unilateral American sanctions as tools of foreign policy. Unilaterally imposed U.S. sanctions aimed at the PRC have been most effective in the economic area, sporadically effective with respect to proliferation concerns, and generally ineffective in the human rights domain. The reasons for this variable success lie in the specificity of the demand being made, the likelihood that Washington can carry out the threat effectively, and the difficulty the Chinese would have complying. Economic sanctions applied for economic ends often can be precisely targeted and the United States has considerable leverage by virtue of the high percentage of Chinese exports destined for America.[114]

At the other end of the continuum, American human rights demands on China are often diffuse ("humane treatment for prisoners" or "respect for Tibet's cultural heritage"), compliance with such demands is difficult to measure and to monitor, and allied support for such efforts has been virtually nonexistent. Finally, using economic threats to achieve human rights objectives can create so much collateral damage to allies and nationalistic backlash among those you are seeking to assist that sanctions become demonstrably counterproductive. As Richard Haass puts it, "Sanctions alone are unlikely to achieve desired results if the aims are large or time is short."[115]

Finally, from the Chinese perspective there are two kinds of issues in U.S.-China relations: those concerns where U.S. interests are obvious, genuine, and large, and those that seem to derive more from the American political process, its need for symbolic issues, and its desire to change China's system. The United States often has been effective in achieving results in the first domain, and almost without success in the latter.

PART II

THE GLOBAL LEVEL

4

GLOBAL INSTITUTIONS AND ECONOMIC FLOWS

[The Chinese] are pushing the envelope with nuclear help to Pakistan. But at least there is an envelope, which did not exist 10 or 15 years ago on proliferation. Their actions could be much worse.

U.S. Defense Secretary William Perry, 1996

In 1987, the last major world economic crisis, most Chinese just watched and said, "This is not our business." Some people even said that crisis proved the weakness of capitalism and was good for us. Now there is a sense that if you have a problem, we have a problem too. A totally different mentality has come about here within a decade.

Zhou Mingwei, Shanghai Foreign Affairs Office, 1998

[The Asian financial crisis] indicates the failure of the Asian way of development. Big government, export oriented. It matters a lot for China. The tigers had provided reference and provided Chinese leaders a reason to resist American pressure.

Chinese professor of international relations, 1998

It is also in China's interest that the international financial system should be reformed to cope with the risks related to globalization of financial markets and liberalization of the financial system of developing countries. A new system with closer monitoring of financial transactions in world markets and institutionalized risk control and crisis management systems would help China to avoid similar crises [to the Asian financial crisis] on its way towards further opening.

Fan Gang, economist, National Economic Research Institute and China Reform Foundation, May 1998

The result [of growing international capital mobility] has been a pattern of competitive liberalization over the last decade in which China and its neighbors in Southeast Asia—not to mention other latecomers around the world—have, on the whole, responded in accommodating fashion to the demands of global capital.... There is a *private* conditionality driven by market forces that operates

similarly to the *official* conditionality imposed on developing
countries by foreign governments and MEIs [multilateral
economic institutions].

Thomas G. Moore and Dixia Yang, 1999

INTRODUCTION

In June 1998 I delivered a lecture at Nanjing University, and a student in
the audience asked me: "China has not devalued its currency, even though
we face heavy export competition from other nations in East Asia. China
is a poor country, so what is a fair burden for China to bear in the face of
the East Asian financial crisis?" In posing this question, the young woman
captured the central issue confronting Chinese and American leaders as
they seek to manage the bilateral relationship in the post–cold war era.
What are the respective obligations of great powers to the larger international community when they are at different stages of development? And
what constitutes the rational pursuit of self-interest when one's own interests are so intricately intertwined with those of others?

This chapter and the next will examine U.S.-China relations from the
perspective of the global system, a system in which nation-states coexist
with transnational institutions and impersonal economic markets that
show little regard for national borders. This chapter focuses on the emergence of transnational regimes and institutions and the rapid development
of globe-spanning markets in which goods, services, financial resources,
and information move with ever greater speed. Chapter 5 addresses the
United States and China in relation to third parties (Taiwan, Hong Kong,
Russia, and Japan) that complicate management of the bilateral relationship. These two chapters taken together grapple with the fundamental tension in the global system as the twenty-first century dawns—the integrative forces of global institutions, the communications and information
revolutions, and markets as they contend with the balkanizing forces of
self-regarding states in pursuit of security, wealth, and power.

The United States and China have found reconciling these divergent
forces difficult, both within and between themselves. In the United States,
its pre– and post–cold war global dominance has created a national habit of
acting unilaterally. At the same time, America has also promoted global institutions, alliances, ad hoc coalitions, and economic interdependence, particularly when it benefits from them.

China's historic inability to effectively exercise sovereignty due to internal disorder and external domination has made its leaders fierce guardians of national sovereignty and has made the country itself a more circumspect player in international institutions and regimes and more ambivalent about the unalloyed virtues of interdependence. At the same time, Chinese leaders recognize that the PRC's access to world markets and financial resources throughout the 1980s and 1990s has helped fuel dramatic economic and social development. Moreover, global institutions and regimes in which Beijing plays an important role have been tangible expressions of China's national greatness. And finally, in the mid-1990s, Beijing came to understand that international institutions could influence and constrain the United States in ways the PRC could not accomplish alone. This realization, for example, lies at the heart of China's support for the supremacy of the United Nations as the United States used NATO as the preferred instrument of intervention in Yugoslavia in 1999.

Further, each nation has specific concerns about the other in the context of global institutions and interdependence. Americans wonder if China will be a nondisruptive member of the current international community willing to share the "fair" burdens of growing power. The Chinese are anxious about whether existing global regimes and institutions historically dominated by the West will prove willing to take into account their concerns, interests, and unique circumstances and whether Chinese regard for sovereignty will be respected by an interventionist-minded United States. Turning to the global economy, Americans desire a level playing field, while the Chinese fear that equal rules for contestants of unequal strength work to their disadvantage.

The challenge for the United States and China in the coming decades, therefore, is to continue to develop rules and effective transnational institutions in which both nations feel ownership while preserving the essential elements of sovereignty. This will not be an easy task for either nation. Failure is possible, but it is not inevitable.

CHINA, THE UNITED STATES, AND GLOBAL INSTITUTIONS AND REGIMES

China and the United States would not participate in global institutions and regimes unless leaders in both nations generally perceived that their interests were thereby being served. Those interests are defined differently in each country, and each country's goals shift over time. China's objectives in joining international organizations have been broadly governed by four desires:

(1) To gain international recognition and status

(2) To prevent decisions adverse to China's vital interests and infringements on its internal governing capacity

(3) To play a role in constraining the behavior of other international actors

(4) To maximize the inflow of international resources for its modernization

Consequently, there is a somewhat passive, reactive posture to Chinese participation in many international organizations. Beijing does not usually beat the gongs to mobilize international organizations to intervene in an international crisis or resolve a global issue. A notable exception occurred in mid-1998 when Beijing asked the five declared nuclear powers to convene in Geneva to discuss how to react to the nuclear detonations of India and Pakistan. That the detonations took place on the PRC's borders was a major motivating consideration. Similarly, China played an unusually assertive (and constructive) role in joining with the IMF early in the Asian financial crisis to try to stabilize the Thai and Indonesian economies. Nonetheless, these are exceptions that underscore the more general pattern.

In contrast to China, the United States' participation in international organizations and regimes is shaped by its extensive global commitments. America's global alliance system, worldwide dispersion of investment, and resource dependencies mean that it currently has more interests to protect internationally than does China. America's history reinforces an activist tendency, with one central twentieth-century learning experience being that war and social breakdown elsewhere draw the United States in (see Chapter 6). Consequently, Washington seeks to actively enlist the international community's assistance more often than Beijing.

Thus the real question for the future is this: as China develops, acquires increasingly far-flung global interests, and becomes increasingly entangled in global institutions and regimes, will its perceptions of its international interests become more compatible with those of the United States? There is no assurance that this will be the outcome, but the trends of the first post–cold war decade leave room for optimism.

China's Growing Role in International Organizations and Regimes

In 1977, the year after Mao Zedong's death and the year before Deng Xiaoping and his colleagues adopted the "reform and opening policy," the PRC was a member of 21 international governmental organizations (IGOs) and 71 international nongovernmental organizations (INGOs). By 1995 China had joined 49 IGOs and 1,013 INGOs;[1] and by 1997, the numbers had increased to 52 IGOs and 1,163 INGOs.[2]

International Financial and Trade Organizations. After joining the Bretton Woods institutions of the World Bank and the IMF in 1980,[3] Beijing became an active participant in the governance of these organizations and in 1992 became the largest recipient of World Bank funds.[4] By mid-1999 China's cumulative borrowings from the World Bank had grown to about $33.2 billion, about one-third of which was from the International Development Association (IDA), the bank's concessional lending window.[5] By mid-1999, however, China's economic progress had made it ineligible for continued IDA financing. China also joined the Asian Development Bank (ADB) in 1986 and became the number three borrower in 1997 (after the Republic of Korea and Indonesia), having borrowed a total of $8.166 billion as of year-end 1998.[6] In 1992 Beijing accepted the Basle Capital Accord standards for bank capital adequacy and four years later joined the Bank for International Settlements.

As for trade groups, in 1980 Beijing joined the World Intellectual Property Organization, and in 1983, the Multifibre Agreement. In November 1984 China was granted permanent observer status in GATT and in July 1986 applied to "recover" (*huifu*) its membership in GATT (which became the WTO on January 1, 1995). China joined the Berne Convention for the Protection of Literary and Artistic Works in 1992.[7] In addition, China has been an active member of the Asia Pacific Economic Cooperation (APEC) forum since it was admitted (as were Taiwan and Hong Kong) in November 1991.

Arms Control Agreements and Regimes. While Mao Zedong was alive, Beijing's rhetoric suggested that it believed proliferation was a solution rather than a problem. At the time of Chairman Mao's death in 1976, and for a considerable period thereafter, China tested nuclear devices in the atmosphere, refused to join the International Atomic Energy Agency (IAEA), and declined to be a party to the Non-Proliferation Treaty (NPT). Beginning in 1982, however, Beijing progressively joined the principal arms control regimes and multilateral organizations concerned with security, as explained in detail in Chapter 2.[8] In November 1995, Beijing published its first white paper in the national security area, *China: Arms Control and Disarmament,* and in July 1998 issued its second, *China's National Defense.* These documents were Beijing's initial, limited steps toward greater transparency on security issues. Further, Beijing joined the ASEAN Regional Forum on security (ARF) in the mid-1990s as a full dialogue partner. Though generally positive, China's participation in ARF has been unsettling at times, as Beijing's reticence to make progress on conflicting South China Sea claims has become evident to her Southeast Asian neighbors.[9] Taken as a whole, however, these moves were motivated by improved relations with the West, a gradual reduction in international tensions, encouragement by third-world nations, a desire to minimize defense expenditures, and an increasing interest in the stability of the international system as a backdrop for its own development.

Understandably, but less reassuringly, Beijing has steadfastly refused to become a party to the strategic arms reduction discussions between the Soviet Union/Russia and the United States until Moscow's and Washington's strategic stockpiles are roughly comparable in size to China's. Throughout the 1990s Beijing's nuclear arsenal remained consistently (and very considerably) smaller than the respective arsenals of Moscow and Washington.[10] While China had about 430 warheads, of which an estimated 18 were intercontinental ballistic missiles (ICBMs), only in the year 2000 did Russia ratify the Strategic Arms Reduction Talks II (START II; the U.S. did in 1996), which called for reductions in both Russian and American strategic arsenals down to the 3,000–3,500 deployed warhead level by January 1, 2003.

Missile defense systems also are an item of contention between the United States and China. As the first post–cold war decade progressed, Americans became increasingly concerned that weapons of mass destruction (delivered by missiles) might fall into more hands and into the possession of unstable and erratic nations or groups, particularly North Korea, Iran, and Iraq. U.S. military planners became progressively more concerned about the vulnerability to missile attack of the U.S. homeland and American troops stationed abroad.[11] The more Washington became enamored with missile defenses for itself and its allies (e.g., Japan and possibly the Republic of Korea), the more Beijing became concerned that the United States would nullify the effectiveness of China's relatively small nuclear deterrent and provide missile defenses to Taiwan, thereby giving Taipei an umbrella under which to perhaps pursue greater autonomy.

So although Beijing's posture on joining the principal nonproliferation and arms control regimes became progressively more positive throughout the 1980s and 1990s, nonetheless, like the United States and the Soviet Union before, Beijing is driven by the logic of deterrence in the direction of force growth and modernization. Whether or not and how to deploy missile defenses will be an early-twenty-first-century decision with enormous consequences for U.S.-China relations. Beijing will keep a wary eye on Japan's acquisition of such systems and is unalterably opposed to Taipei's acquisition of increasingly capable missile defense systems. Interestingly, by mid-1999 Beijing was calling upon Washington to continue observing the terms of the 1972 Anti-Ballistic Missile (ABM) Treaty, arguing (just as the United States did in the 1970s) that missile defenses are destabilizing and promote arms races.

International Environmental Regimes and Agreements. Beijing was one of the first nations to sign the 1992 Convention on Biological Diversity, an agreement that came in the wake of the Rio Earth Summit. President Clinton signed it in 1993; the U.S. Senate, however, subsequently curtailed consideration of ratification. The Montreal Protocol on Ozone-Depleting Substances (ODSs), a second important international environmental agreement of the period, was adopted in 1987 and ratified by the PRC in 1991. China has "championed the ODS phase-out campaign,"[12] though "the key to Chinese accession and implementation was the international community's willingness to finance the Chinese implementation effort" and the PRC's desire to export appliances that would have to meet international standards to be salable.[13] Though the PRC did not reach its 1996 ODS reduction target (and in fact became the world's largest producer of ODSs in 1995) because of "rapid economic growth and a slow start in phase-out," the World Bank has nonetheless praised China as a "model of international cooperation" in the area.[14] Other observers are somewhat more critical of the Chinese effort, saying that local officials are not cooperating.[15] With this criticism as background, in late 1999 the State Environment Protection Administration reported that the PRC would accelerate the timetable for achieving ODS reduction and called for additional international assistance to accomplish this.

While some environmental issues have fostered Sino-American and broader international cooperation, others have not. In this vein, "greenhouse gas" emission is likely to become a growing point of contention as Beijing remains more concerned about economic growth and ameliorating its "own" pollution problems, while the United States becomes increasingly concerned about the global effects of carbon emissions. The two nations (reflecting the broader split between developed and developing countries) are at odds about the allocation of costs in addressing climate change. At the Kyoto Meeting of December 1997 in which the Kyoto Protocol was drafted,[16] China (along with India, Brazil, and many other developing nations) was active in pushing to exempt developing countries from greenhouse gas reduction targets, thereby putting the burden to act first and effectively on the developed nations. As China becomes an ever greater carbon dioxide emitter, U.S. dissatisfaction with the Chinese stance is likely to grow. The World Bank estimates that by 2020, if China remains on its present course, it will emit about three times the tonnage of carbon into the atmosphere that it did in 1995;[17] the PRC will surpass U.S. carbon emissions early in the twenty-first century.

Human Rights Organizations and Regimes. Since 1988 China has been a signatory to the Convention against Torture and Other Cruel, Inhuman, or Degrading Treatment or Punishment, which by any fair estimation Beijing has not faithfully observed. In 1992, then Premier Li Peng declared that "China agrees that questions concerning human rights should be the subject of normal international discussion." The year before this statement Beijing issued its first-ever white paper, titled *Human Rights in China;*[18] two more were issued in 1995 and 1997. As discussed in the preceding chapter, under considerable international pressure and against the backdrop of the U.S.-China summits in late 1997 and mid-1998, Beijing signed the International Covenant on Economic, Social, and Cultural Rights and the International Covenant on Civil and Political Rights. Further, China has been active since 1982 in the UN Human Rights Commission headquartered in Geneva. Throughout most of the 1990s and into the new century, however, Beijing's energies at that commission were largely expended in resisting U.S. attempts to have the PRC condemned for its human rights abuses (1991–1997 and 1999–2000).

U.S. and Chinese Citizenship in International Organizations

The rate at which China joined international organizations in the 1990s was striking. The acid test, however, is not the number of organizations and regimes the PRC has joined, but rather the nature of its participation. Here, Beijing's post–cold war record has been mixed but on the whole encouraging inasmuch as the trend has been toward greater multilateral participation, more frequent compliance, and a closer fit between the institutional structures and personnel of the world community and China's domestic apparatus.

China's active participation in international organizations and regimes has been most positive when the PRC has been integrally involved in writing the rules and when the international community has made tangible economic contributions to facilitate implementation of agreements. Beijing's involvement has been less praiseworthy in cases where it has not been a full member of the institution or regime, it has had no role in drafting or interpreting the rules, international economic assistance has not been provided, compliance would harm powerful domestic groups, it has no parallel institution to act as an interface with the world community, and agreement would lock China into a position of permanent inferiority along an important dimension. Indeed, several of these *same* considerations would also help explain America's behavior in international organizations. For the most part, China's actions are not inscrutable.

With respect to the United Nations, for instance, from 1971 to April 2000, China cast only four vetoes in open session of the Security Council[19] (not including nineteen vetoes pertaining to the selection of the UN secretary general), though it blocked votes in closed sessions, and in 1998 it threatened publicly to veto a resolution that would have authorized NATO's use of force in Kosovo.[20] By way of contrast, the United States cast twenty-four vetoes from 1986 to 1995 and two more in 1997, though both American and Russian vetoes became a rarity after the cold war.

Of note, however, is the PRC's 1997 veto of a UN plan to send 155 military observers to monitor a peace agreement in Guatemala because of Guatemala's diplomatic ties to Taiwan. This motivation rankled most UN General Assembly members, and when it became clear that China's veto would be undone by a "uniting for peace" action in the General Assembly, China lifted its veto rather than be defeated.[21] Similarly, in February 1999, the PRC vetoed a UN resolution to extend the mandate for a peacekeeping force in Macedonia because Macedonia had switched recognition from Beijing to Taipei.[22] Taipei paid a reported $1 billion or more for this switch of recognition.

These instances aside, the PRC generally has adopted a method of articulating its position on controversial items and then abstaining if its views cannot prevail, as it did in June 1999 when it abstained on a 14-to-0 vote authorizing the UN to become involved in the Kosovo peacekeeping operation. Indeed, from 1990 to 1996 Beijing cast nearly 65 percent of all the "abstention" votes of the five permanent members of the Security Council.[23] From the perspective of U.S. interests, however, China has a lower *General Assembly* voting coincidence with the United States than with any other permanent member of the Security Council.

The methods by which Beijing pursues its interests and its points of sensitivity require comment. The PRC generally believes that the imposition of economic sanctions violate national sovereignty and may legitimate possible future punitive actions directed against China itself. Beijing has similar reservations concerning multilateral military interventions. Nonetheless, despite misgivings about UN prosecution of the Gulf War in 1991 and UN interventions in Somalia (1993–1994) and Haiti (1993), China either supported or abstained on key votes in the Security Council in all three cases. However, this support or lack of opposition did have a price tag. In the case of the Gulf War, for example, Beijing parlayed its abstention into a White House meeting for Foreign Minister Qian Qichen and American agreement not to oppose World Bank loans to the PRC, thereby diminishing Beijing's post-Tiananmen isolation. In dealing with Beijing, there is no free lunch. One Latin American diplomat provided a summation of the Chinese modus operandi in the Security Council: "They never take part in the give and take of preparing resolutions.... If they can, they let others weave together a resolution, then say they can live with it. They do not waste any time on things that are not fundamental to their interests."[24]

China first participated in UN peacekeeping operations (PKO) in 1990, when it sent observers on UN missions.[25] Since then, Chinese peacekeepers have gone to the Middle East, Namibia, elsewhere in Africa, Cambodia, and East Timor. In mid-1997, Beijing agreed in principle to participate in peacekeeping standby arrangements involving observers, police, engineers, and medical personnel. However, Beijing places emphasis on obtaining the consent of countries where PKO forces are sent, and it reflexively opposes uninvited intervention. For example, a key in winning Beijing's support for sending a UN force to East Timor in late 1999 was that the Jakarta government "invited" the peacekeeping troops, notwithstanding the fact that the Indonesian government was under intense pressure to do so.

In its interaction with the World Bank, China has been an exemplary citizen, at least in part because it has been the bank's largest borrower since 1992. Former World Bank President Barber B. Conable Jr. summed up his view of Chinese participation in the bank during his years as president (1986–1991) as follows: "China has been quite exemplary in meeting obligations. The Bank hasn't had to make reform or adjustment loans to China because their own self-imposed constraints are totally in keeping with the World Bank's."[26]

With respect to the IMF, the PRC has benefited from its advice and standby credits during periods of economic retrenchment, high inflation, and foreign exchange difficulty. China repaid its first credit tranche from the IMF in early 1994. Authors Jacobson and Oksenberg comment that in the IMF and the World Bank, "China's has been a voice for moderation and pragmatism."[27] Similarly, Nicholas Lardy notes, "When China joined the

IMF in 1980, its foreign exchange system was distorted.... Over the next fifteen years China undertook important reforms of its foreign exchange system.... This example suggests that China has established a credible record in meeting the obligations inherent in membership in major international economic organizations."[28]

China's record of compliance with human rights, arms sales, and technology transfer commitments, however, has been less pristine than its record with the keystone international economic organizations. Chinese adherence to the 1984 Convention against Torture and Other Cruel, Inhuman, or Degrading Treatment or Punishment has been regularly breached (as an international review suggested in 2000), and Beijing's alleged and actual transfers of nuclear, missile, biological, and chemical weapons technology to Pakistan, Iran, and other states of concern to Washington have pushed the NPT, MTCR, and other international agreements to the limit, if not clearly exceeded them, as discussed previously.

China, as reported by the Rumsfeld Commission, "has carried out extensive transfers to Iran's solid-fueled ballistic missile program. It has supplied Pakistan with a design for a nuclear weapon (before it signed NPT) and additional nuclear weapons assistance. It has even transferred complete ballistic missile systems to Saudi Arabia (the 3,100-km-range CSS-2) and there is considerable evidence of transfers to Pakistan (the 350-km-range M-11)."[29] In his 1997 report to the Senate Select Committee on Intelligence, the director of Central Intelligence reported that in 1997 Iran received Chinese chemical and missile assistance and that Beijing was working on two previously contracted nuclear facilities there. By the end of 1997, however, Beijing had pledged to Washington not to engage in any new nuclear cooperation with Tehran.[30] With respect to Pakistan, "Chinese and North Korean entities continued to provide assistance to Pakistan's ballistic missile program in 1997."[31] Having said all this, it is necessary to distinguish between transfers of technology that are unwise and contrary to American interests and those violating international agreements. Chinese behavior has clearly fallen into both categories. For its part, Beijing would point to U.S. weapons sales to Taiwan as proliferation acts contrary to its interests and to a bilateral agreement (the August 1982 Joint Communiqué).

The 1997 CIA assessment goes on to note that in that year "China took a number of steps to strengthen its control over nuclear exports ... in line with its May 1996 commitment not to assist unsafeguarded nuclear facilities."[32] In May 1997 Beijing issued the *Circular on Issues Relevant to Enforcing China's Nuclear Export Policy*, providing guidance for all Chinese entities on nuclear-related dual-use items in the form of a comprehensive control list. That action was followed up in September of that year with the issuance of *Regulations on Controlling Nuclear Exports* and the following year with regulations on the *Control of the Export of Dual-Use Nuclear Materials and Related Technology.*[33] The key provisions of the September 1997 regulations were as follows: nuclear exports were to serve only peaceful purposes; recipients must be subject to IAEA supervision; there could be no transfers to third parties without Beijing's prior approval; and "nuclear exports shall be managed by no other unit or individual that is not designated by the State Council," implying that previous transfers had occurred without State Council authorization.[34] As part of the gradual development of a control structure, the Foreign Ministry's Arms Control and Disarmament Department began to play a progressively more important role so that the foreign policy implications of arms and technology transfers could be assessed before damage to Chinese external relations occurred.[35]

Thus, prior to 1997, Beijing's compliance with agreements concerning transfers of technologies and weapons of mass destruction was dubious at best. In fact, China was entirely outside the international arms control regime as the 1980s began. From late 1997 on, however, China's performance improved as its resolve to conform to arms agreements appeared to increase. Yet it is unclear even as we enter the twenty-first century whether Beijing has reliable control over the transfer process or whether it might subsequently seek to use the threat of transfers to extract concessions in other areas or express its dissatisfaction with U.S. behavior in other realms (particularly Taiwan). Nonetheless, despite these uncertainties, at the conclusion of the 1990s Beijing was developing an export control structure that offered the hope of more responsible future behavior. Indeed, Beijing had come so far in its policy that its 1998 white paper *China's National Defense* declared, "The task for the international community to strengthen non-proliferation mechanisms has become even more pressing now."[36]

This trend in Chinese arms control behavior raises two questions: What accounts for this positive movement? and What accounts for Beijing's failure to observe commitments in certain areas?

With respect to the first query, throughout the second half of the 1990s Beijing's thinking gradually began to shift toward recognizing that security cannot be achieved solely through unilateral action, though some serious analysts like Alastair Iain Johnston have argued this change is more rhetorical "adaptation" than genuinely internalized ("learned") behavior.[37] As the 1998 defense white paper stated, "Security is mutual."[38] Also, as Bates Gill notes, Beijing's behavior is increasingly "shaped by the intricate web of international dependencies, commitments, status relationships and security realities which China faces."[39] Nonetheless, there is a contending, long-standing school of thought among Chinese defense thinkers that asserts that states with advantage seek to maintain their advantages and use negotiations to lock the adversary into a position of permanent inferiority. If one examines U.S. arms control behavior throughout the cold war and after, U.S. negotiating behavior also can be understood as a means to accomplish this. In both China and America, therefore, there is tension between notions of using negotiations to achieve "common security," locking in advantage, and unilaterally achieving security. These contending impulses are reflected in the negotiating behavior of both countries.

In response to the second question, aside from the money to be made (the PRC exported arms worth $2.5 billion between 1993 and 1995, though the volume has dropped considerably since then),[40] Beijing, like Washington, uses arms exports to court countries it deems strategically important.[41] Pakistan, for example, has (until recently, perhaps) seemed to be China's Israel. In addition, relations with Iran have become increasingly important as Beijing worries about the security of growing oil imports from the Middle East and the effect of Muslim fundamentalism on its insecure western territories.

Two other considerations help account for some of China's worrisome arms transfers. First, Beijing's efforts to build an export control structure and give a more prominent role in decisions to the Foreign Ministry is evidence of a central problem—the Chinese military and the arms-producing corporations (which are not identical to the PLA and sometimes are competitors with the military for sales abroad) have not been under the full, unified control of the central leadership in all instances. A June 1997 RAND report asserts that "there currently is no hard evidence that this trade [in weapons other than those of mass destruction] is directed by the senior political leadership in Beijing,"[42] although there is ample evidence of senior leadership approval of some of the key sales. President Jiang Zemin's June and July 1998 orders to the Chinese military to halt business activities (involving perhaps 18,000 firms), saying that they were a huge source of corruption and lax discipline certainly is suggestive.[43]

Second, in some cases China excuses its noncompliance in one area (e.g., weapon and technology sales to Pakistan) with what it views as Washington's noncompliance in another area (e.g., U.S. arms sales to Taiwan, where Beijing believes Washington has violated its 1982 Joint

Communiqué with the PRC). Regarding missile technology control, Chinese analyst Liu Huaqiu said, "we believe that as a first step, the United States should halt the sale of F-16s to Taiwan. This will help China and the United States cooperate in halting missile proliferation."[44] In sum, the reasons for Chinese noncompliance revolve around money, the weakness of central control mechanisms, corruption, the recipient's strategic importance, and seeking leverage over Washington or others in the international community.

A clear pattern can be discerned in China's expanded participation in the institutions of global governance, its good citizenship in some, and deficient performance in others: it seeks to maximize resource inflow and minimize obligations. Further, Beijing will withhold compliance on agreements of high value to Washington in order to secure agreements of high value to itself. It will also use its membership in international organizations to deny Taiwan the chance to bolster its international identity. This kind of four-color picture of Chinese behavior contrasts with the stark black-and-white images of the PRC as a rogue regime that often shape discourse in America.

There are numerous examples of China's interest-driven pattern of behavior. In 1978, for the first time China sought aid from the UN Development Program and by the late 1980s was the program's largest recipient of funds. The following year, Beijing successfully sought to have its annual UN assessment rate reduced from 5.5 percent of the organization's budget to 0.79 percent. As of 1999 its support was down to 0.72 percent, according to Samuel Kim,[45] although China does pay its bills—unlike Washington, which was $1.6 billion in arrears at one point in 1999.[46] By 2000, the PRC's contribution is scheduled to rise to 0.995 percent.[47] In this scenario, by the year 2000 China will still have 20 percent of the UN's veto power and more than 20 percent of the world's population while supporting less than 1 percent of the organization's budget.

As the PRC's economy and national power grow, Beijing will be expected to accept heavier international burdens, even as the United States may be ambivalent about the PRC playing a larger role. The dilemma will be that the outside world's assessment of China's capability to support international undertakings will likely exceed its own evaluation. This consideration is behind Beijing's rejection of the purchasing power parity methodology that enlarges the assessment of China's economic size and strength. Chinese leaders and advisers with whom I have met assert that "China should contribute according to national strength."[48] While this is a reasonable principle, there is likely to be disagreement over how to measure the PRC's strength and the perceived disproportion between

China's rights, privileges, and power in international organizations and its financial and other contributions.

Behind these matters, however, rests a nagging question: Does China accept the legitimacy of the current rules and norms of international organizations and regimes or will it seek to alter them once admitted? Thus far, the answer seems to be that the mere act of seeking admission to current global institutions represents Beijing's willingness to acknowledge their legitimacy and be a member of the club. As long as China sees more to be gained from being in the club than standing outside, this will remain the case. It therefore was encouraging to be told by one Chinese policy analyst in 1996, "China is realistic about regimes. China doesn't want to change them unilaterally. In the long term China will ask for change in unfair rules, but it won't seek to change them unilaterally."[49] Ironically, in 1999 China found itself defending the UN Security Council as the only international organization legitimately capable of authorizing intervention in Yugoslavia. In its defense of sovereignty and UN Security Council prerogatives, Beijing has been driven to reinforce the traditional norms of the international community and the UN against a Washington and London that at century's end seem to wish to change them.

Thus, although there is a general disposition in Beijing to join the world's principal multilateral institutions and regimes, China's membership in each instance presents both the United States and the PRC with difficult choices. An examination of two international organizations is instructive.

In the case of the Missile Technology Control Regime, Washington has been internally divided over whether having the PRC in the club is in U.S. interests. Likewise, Beijing has apprehensions about the regime and the benefits of joining. The second case study concerns the thirteen-year-long discussion with Beijing about accession to the WTO. This is a case in which, *in principle*, both capitals agreed that PRC membership was desirable, but it nonetheless took substantially more than a decade to reach agreement, with the principal point of dispute being the price to be paid for Beijing's entry.

China and the Missile Technology Regime. The MTCR is not a treaty; it is an agreement among twenty-nine member states to restrict transfers of nuclear-capable missiles and related technology. China is not a member. The controls are based on "Guidelines" and an "Equipment and Technology Annex."[50] Since its formation in April 1987 the agreement has been broadened to include missile delivery systems for all kinds of weapons of mass destruction.[51] The MTCR does not cover other categories of systems capable of carrying weapons of mass destruction (such as fighter aircraft) or other "conventional" weapons and defensive missile systems. MTCR member states use their own domestic legal systems to deal with exports that contravene regime rules. The member states set standards, and those standards change over time. Because Beijing is not a member, it plays no role in shaping the rules it is expected to observe by virtue of its 1992 and 1994 pledges.

China's alleged and documented missile and technology cooperation with Pakistan and Iran caused continual conflict between Beijing and Washington in the 1990–1998 period. Disputes centered on whether the technical characteristics of the transferred missiles or technology were in contravention of the regime (range and throw weights) and whether Beijing was bound by changes made in regime rules after it had agreed to observe them: "The PRC has not agreed to adhere to revisions to the Guidelines and Annex that have been adopted since 1987."[52] With these ongoing disputes in the background, it seemed to officials in the U.S. National Security Council and Department of State preparing for the 1998 Beijing Summit that getting China into the MTCR would be one way to reduce some conflict with the PRC and achieve more compliance.

To this end, in early to mid-1998, officials responsible for China and counterproliferation affairs at the NSC and the Department of State began to explore Beijing's interest in becoming an MTCR member. One possible inducement for Beijing was enhanced Sino-American commercial (satellite launch) and scientific space cooperation. This initiative was taken despite the reluctance of some current and former executive branch officials who feared that Chinese membership in MTCR might provide Beijing access to sensitive technical information. As bilateral discussions proceeded, factions of the intelligence and defense communities in Washington began to leak information about the proposed cooperation, asserting that such cooperation might assist the PRC in the development of its missiles. The resulting discussion became entangled in the controversy over Chinese launches of American satellites discussed in Chapter 2.

Consequently, a move that the administration had designed to promote Chinese adherence to nonproliferation norms was being portrayed as a way to provide Beijing with access to sensitive American technology. Were this the case, one would predict that Beijing would have seized the opportunity to become a member of the club. It did not. Indeed, the irony becomes even more rich given that the May 1999 Cox Report implicitly criticizes Beijing for not being a member of the MTCR; truth be told, many of those leveling that criticism would vigorously oppose such membership if the executive branch pursued it or China wanted to join.

Beijing had long distrusted the basic purpose of the regime, believing that it was designed to constrain those weapons about which Washington was most concerned while excluding from regulation those about which Beijing was most anxious (i.e., F-16 fighter aircraft sold to Taipei) and had the greatest commercial value for the United States. As Liu Huaqiu, senior fellow at the Program on Arms Control and Disarmament at the China Defense Science and Technology Center in Beijing, commented in 1995: "We believe that missile technology control regulations should be built on fair, reasonable and [a] complete foundation. Therefore, we recommend that the 'regulations' be expanded into a treaty whose limitations extend to aircraft, all participating countries having equal rights and obligations. Clearly translating the above recommendation into reality will be no easy matter."[53] The Chinese obviously had in mind prohibiting aircraft sales to Taiwan.

Yet in America, any attempt to further constrain weapons sales to Taiwan would run into a congressional buzz saw. In 1982, the United States agreed to Taipei's proposed "Six Assurances," one of which was that "[t]he United States will not consult the PRC about future arms sales."[54] Moreover, the executive branch is bound by the Taiwan Relations Act of 1979 to "make available to Taiwan such defense articles and defense services in such quantity as may be necessary to enable Taiwan to maintain a sufficient self-defense capability." Consequently, any agreement with Beijing that looks like an attempt to constrain sales to Taipei would generate enormous political heat in Washington, particularly on Capitol Hill.

For its part, Beijing has had a long-established strategic relationship with Pakistan and was (and remains) reluctant to circumscribe its latitude in dealing with Islamabad. This mirrors Washington's historic unwillingness to make its relationship with Tel Aviv the subject of discussion with others. Moreover, one can speculate that China's defense industry was reluctant to constrain the export of one of its few products (missiles) for which there was actual international demand (its annual arms sales fell from $1.108 billion in 1993 to a mere $170 million in 1997).[55] In comparison, the United States sold $10.84 billion in weapons abroad in 1997 alone.

At the Beijing Summit in 1998 President Clinton suggested to President Jiang Zemin that the United States would welcome China's membership in the MTCR. The Chinese replied that they would "actively study" joining the regime,[56] but Beijing is unlikely to do so until its concerns regarding Taiwan and possible U.S. missile defense plans are addressed. Paradoxically, as mentioned above, there are many in the American security community who fear technology leakage to the PRC were it to join the regime and therefore hope that Beijing studies MTCR membership for a long time. Finally, American skeptics have their counterparts in Beijing, where there are fears that if China joins it will reveal its technological weaknesses. As so often happens, those in each society who resist more co-operation can become one another's greatest allies.

Negotiating China's Accession to the World Trade Organization. A broad goal shared by two parties can easily prove difficult to attain when they are driven apart by the discussion of specifics and the intervention of seemingly unconnected political, economic, social, or other events. Consequently, a major challenge for American and Chinese foreign policy leaders is to foster the alignment of the political stars in both countries and seize the moment when that alignment occurs. Political phases in both the United States and China are rarely compatible. And so it was for thirteen years after Beijing applied to formally "recover" its membership in GATT in 1986.

During the mid and late 1980s, when China was undergoing a break-neck pace of reform that fanned internal and external optimism, the PRC expected that it would "rejoin" GATT relatively quickly. However, China's economic problems of the late 1980s and early 1990s,[57] combined with the global reaction to the 1989 Tiananmen Square violence and the belief among GATT-contracting parties that eastern European countries had been admitted in the 1970s under excessively lenient terms,[58] made that impossible.

Consequently, by the time serious GATT accession talks resumed in 1991, the context for China's entry had changed. The United States and other countries were uncertain whether reform in the PRC would proceed. The U.S. trade deficit with Beijing doubled from 1989 to 1991 (and showed every sign of continuing to expand), and there were acrimonious annual debates in the U.S. Congress over MFN renewal for China. In January 1993 a new administration took office in Washington, and President Clinton was determined to use economic leverage to secure political change in the PRC and to show solidarity with a tough-minded Congress in its dealings with Beijing, as we have seen in preceding chapters. All this conspired to make Washington a tough negotiator in the 1990s.

Developments in China also made it a tougher negotiator in the 1990s. In the second half of the 1980s, GATT entry generally was defined as a foreign policy issue in Beijing. There was a tight circle of decision makers composed largely of the foreign policy elite; they were a group that could not be "blocked by opposition from industry."[59] In any event, Deng Xiaoping was in the wings as the ultimate arbiter. Moving into the 1990s, however, sectors of Chinese industry became progressively more apprehensive about what global competition would mean for them, and Deng Xiaoping's weakened health and subsequent death in 1997 removed him from the scene as a final arbiter. Also, Beijing's frustrations with Washington's successive attempts to humiliate it on the human rights front multiplied. These grievances included linkage of human rights to MFN status (1993–1994), 1993 congressional resolutions urging that the 2000 Olympics not be held in China, and successive attempts in Geneva to seek condemnation of China's human rights record by the UN Commission on Human Rights (1991–1997 and 1999). Further, some in the U.S. human rights community,[60] and even United States Trade Representative Charlene Barshefksy, suggested that there should be (or objectively was) linkage between China's human rights behavior and its accession to the WTO.

Moreover, 1990 to 1997 was a period in which the struggle for primacy in the post–Deng Xiaoping era was underway. Deng's health was deteriorating, and General Secretary Jiang Zemin's position as successor was not absolutely assured. Soviet-trained Premier Li Peng exerted an important influence over foreign policy, inasmuch as he headed the Leading Small Group on Foreign Affairs. As concurrent head of the State Council, Premier Li was subject to the pressure of industrial ministries that would be the first to feel the pinch of global competition were China to enter GATT/WTO, particularly under strict conditions. In ever greater numbers, state-owned enterprises (SOEs) were losing substantial sums of money (with losses growing from 34.9 billion RMB in 1990 to 74.4 billion in 1997)[61] due to growing competition from nonstate enterprises and imports and rising input costs resulting from progressive price deregulation. The need to stanch these losses, and a host of other developments including demographic growth and rural-urban migration, was causing growing unemployment and underemployment.[62] By 1997, the problem had become so serious that Chinese citizens were driven to gallows humor, which they shared with foreigners. "Chairman Mao," I was told, "sent us down to the countryside [*xia fang*]; Deng Xiaoping sent us into the sea of business [*xia hai*]; and Jiang Zemin? He has sent us on furlough [*xia gang*]."

This is the backdrop for the years of tortuous WTO accession discussions (1986–1999) between Beijing and Washington, with the United States as the lead negotiator among the trade organization's contracting parties. Throughout the 1990s, both capitals agreed that Chinese membership in the WTO under appropriate terms would be good for the global system and for one another. Nonetheless, the question remained, What was an appropriate price for both parties to pay in order to achieve PRC entry? The issue sparked disagreement and divisive conflict both between the two nations and within the borders of each.

In China, the State Economic and Trade Commission's Yu Xiaosong explained, "There are different opinions in different levels of the government on WTO."[63] Two groups represented each end of the spectrum of opinion in the mid to late 1990s. The first viewed China's accession to the WTO as highly desirable and something for which China should be willing to pay a significant price. People such as Representative for Trade Negotiations Long Yongtu, who Premier Zhou Enlai sent to the London School of Economics in 1973–1974, and MOFTEC Vice Minister Sun Zhenyu believed that China's participation in the WTO would greatly aid their efforts to promote China's integration into the world economy. Long and Sun were joined in this view by Premier Zhu Rongji in early 1999, as discussed shortly. They wished to use China's sovereign undertakings as a member of the WTO to gain leverage over the industrial ministries, SOEs, and provinces that resisted global competition.

Allies of the reformers in this battle were export-oriented provinces like Guangdong that had high concentrations of export industries and foreign investment. Guangdong, for example, accounted for 39.7 percent of China's exports in 1996 and believed it would benefit from WTO protections in foreign markets and could weather the tides of foreign economic competition. Further, China's most competitive industries believed they would do well in a more open, competitive environment.[64] A large inducement for both the pro–WTO entry forces and the fence-sitters was the prospect (though not assurance) of permanent NTR for China from Washington upon the conclusion of an accession agreement, and there was the lure of the WTO's multilateral dispute resolution mechanism that might help reduce China's vulnerability to U.S. unilateral trade sanctions.

Pro-accession forces also argued that China's entry into the WTO would facilitate cross–Taiwan Strait economic intercourse, particularly if Taipei entered as well, as it was likely to do shortly after Beijing's accession. Taipei had resisted the "Three Links" (*san tong*)—that is, direct cross-strait transportation, trade, and postal services. In this line of thinking, if both Taiwan and China's mainland were members of the WTO, Taipei might be induced or required to conduct cross-strait ties in a more WTO-compatible manner.

There were, of course, fence-sitters in this argument. When I spoke with officials in Shanghai such as Mayor Xu Kuangdi, they admitted to ambivalence about WTO entry. Huge foreign direct investment and export volume (in 1996 Shanghai accounted for nearly 9 percent of China's exports) inclined them toward paying a price for WTO entry, whereas the relatively high concentration of SOEs in the city inclined them in the opposite direction. The cost-benefit analysis was complex, as one Chinese scholar recounted.

> Shanghai is more supportive [of WTO entry] than Beijing [as a municipality]. Our high buildings are full of foreign companies. Three-thousand foreign companies have one telephone and one representative. If we open accounting, law, insurance, those offices will each take five or ten rooms, so now [under that circumstance] no buildings will be empty. So, Pudong [Development Zone in Shanghai] is in favor [of WTO entry]. Even some SOEs favor national treatment, because it would mean taxes on them would be cut from 30 percent to 15 percent. But the interior provinces have to pay little tax [in any case], so it is not necessary to cut taxes for them. So, the coastline is more eager to be in WTO. And, Guangdong Province has few SOEs.[65]

Margaret Pearson reported that "many officials of the Ministry of Finance and the SPC [State Planning Commission] favor accession to WTO in the long term, but believe it should be carried out under terms more favorable to China's industrial interests than is now foreseen, or than as advocated by many MOFTEC officials."[66] To complicate things further, MOFTEC itself was of several minds. As one Chinese academic put it to me, "The bureaucracy [MOFTEC] has an interest in regulation of trade. MOFTEC has licenses and quotas and they sell them and make money.... Much of MOFTEC is opposed and provincial and municipal [bureaus] are monopolies, so they are opposed."[67] There often has been one further consideration at the local level: if there is no "national treatment" for foreign firms, then the "privileges" foreigners are granted by local officials can be conferred for a price (corruption or "rent seeking") rather than granted as a matter of right and law.

At the other end of the spectrum were those who directly opposed WTO accession for China. This group included many economic planners; industrial ministries (particularly those most protected behind a wall of price subsidies, those least technologically modernized, and those most overstaffed such as electronics, automobiles, petroleum refining, machine tools, and instruments);[68] militarily sensitive industries; cash cows such as telecommunications; agricultural interests (particularly citrus); some services;[69] and provinces with high densities of SOEs, relatively little foreign direct investment, and low levels of exports. Speaking harshly of the SPC (which reform-oriented Premier Zhu Rongji renamed the State Development and Planning Commission and downgraded in comparison to the State Economic and Trade Commission in 1998), the scholars Wang and Fewsmith report that it "had a strong institutional interest in resisting, deflecting, and enervating the market-oriented reform policies put forth by reform-minded leaders."[70] One of the principal reasons for SPC opposition was its fear that adopting GATT/WTO norms "would result in the loss of its regulatory power over the economy."[71]

To discern even more clearly what has been the primary resistance in China to WTO entry, one need only compare the respective demands of Chinese and U.S. negotiators. The PRC continually asked for an accession agreement that recognized China as a "developing country," if not in name then at least by providing long transition times for vulnerable or sensitive sectors to adapt to global competition. The United States steadfastly refused to accept this categorization for the obvious reasons that China was the world's eleventh largest trading power in 1998, had a global trade surplus of about $43.6 billion in that year, was a major competitor in the global satellite launch business, and was a superpower exporter of textiles, shoes, and sporting equipment. The PRC is not your run-of-the-mill developing country. Were China categorized as such under WTO rules, it would be entitled to more time to fully comply with organization requirements.

Unsurprisingly, China's least competitive economic sectors were the ones most persistent in their demands for long transition times. As one prominent Chinese economist said to me in mid-1998, "Trade issues, WTO, are all domestic politics. The least competitive, least penetrated sectors are the most protectionist."[72] Agriculture is a protectionist element in many political systems, China included, and as trade has been decentralized in the PRC, local governments have become even more protective of their agricultural constituents. Peasants freed from simply growing grain have invested in crops such as oranges, and they vigorously sought to protect their new groves from Florida's competition.[73] Telephone callers to a live call-in show with China made precisely these points to me in 1999.

Turning to industry, given the structure of the political system that China essentially imported from the Soviet Union in the early 1950s, heavy industry and provinces with heavy industrial concentrations have great, though declining political clout. These industries fear global competition the most. In fact, among the most significant moves that the Jiang Zemin–Zhu Rongji leadership made at the Ninth National People's Congress in early 1998 to advance reform was to remove many of the heavy industrial ministries from the State Council.[74] Their skeletal planning functions were instead lodged in a reinvigorated State Economic and Trade

Commission, and some ministries were converted into corporations.[75] In this way, Jiang and Zhu removed some of the most economically recalcitrant forces from government decision making. Simultaneously, representation on the Central Committee of coastal, trade-oriented provinces increased, with over 70 percent of the Politburo of the 1997 Fifteenth Central Committee closely associated with coastal areas, nearly triple the percentage in 1982.[76]

Nonetheless, U.S. demands for market access for service, agricultural, telecommunication, and direct sales companies, as well as demands for lower levels of tariff and nontariff protection, threatened many economic sectors, bureaucracies, and regions. For example, three PRC economists estimated that trade liberalization would cost about 11.2 million Chinese their jobs in protected industries (in 1994), with the biggest losses occurring in agriculture, particularly among wheat growers.[77] Even under the best of circumstances, simultaneously taking on so many domestically powerful constituencies would be hard for Beijing's leaders. And, in a China with high and expanding unemployment, a decelerating rate of economic expansion as a result of the Asian financial crisis in 1997–1999, and mounting fears about what global integration meant to domestic economic sovereignty, the late 1990s was not the most propitious of times. As one Chinese analyst put it, "If [there had been] no Southeast Asia financial crisis we would have moved faster in trade liberalization."[78] The real surprise, therefore, is that President Jiang and Premier Zhu were willing to try to reach agreement on the terms of China's WTO accession by making major, contingent concessions in early 1999, a complicated story to which we shall return shortly.

Points of domestic resistance notwithstanding, Beijing made some concessions and policy changes earlier in the 1990s that moved China generally in WTO-compatible directions. The average tariff rate declined from about 43 percent in 1994 to 17 percent in 1997.[79] Moreover, in 1994 China eliminated its dual exchange rate and dual currency system and continued to widen the areas in which foreigners were permitted to invest in China. In 1996 the PRC's currency became convertible for trade, though not capital movements. One year later, in 1997, "China promised to sweep away all its restrictions on so-called trading rights within 3 years after WTO entry"[80] and offered concessions on intellectual property protection, local content requirements for exports, and export subsidies. Thus, despite many economic problems, Beijing moved forward even before 1999, although erratically, reflecting shifting economic and domestic political circumstances.

The politics of Chinese accession to the WTO has been no less complex in the United States, bringing into play considerations of U.S. economic health, relations between the congressional and executive branches, the divergent views of various U.S. interest groups, the personal and political standing of the president, and electoral strategies. The American business community, for example, is a complex political web, with fault lines separating exporters from importers and small businesses from large businesses. This was seen in the 1995 battle over IPR, where the National Retail Federation opposed the imposition of sanctions on the importation of Chinese goods, saying, "We support stronger protection for intellectual property, but this shouldn't be at the expense of the American consumer"[81]—and retailers! The issue of the terms of WTO entry for China, therefore, set off a complex dynamic of discussion among various business sectors. They adopted a mantra that was supposed to project unity: We support China's WTO accession on "commercially meaningful," "commercially viable," or "commercially acceptable" grounds.[82] Nonetheless, every subset of the business community had a somewhat different threshold of acceptability.

Beyond the divergent views within the U.S. business community itself, however, a far more complex topography of political conflict existed, and continues to exist. Among members of the Democratic Party (e.g., Richard Gephardt), as well as some independents and Republicans, there is a deep-seated belief that trade liberalization has worked against America's working men and women, particularly those in industrial and unionized jobs. Reacting to a large annual trade deficit in 1995 to which Mexico and China contributed substantially, the then nominally Republican Pat Buchanan simplistically asserted, "We just lost 2.2 million jobs last year."[83]

A few facts have shaped the views of many Americans toward trade liberalization agreements. In 1990, around 36 percent of U.S. imports were produced in nations whose wage levels were at most one-half of those in the United States; in 1978, only one-fourth of U.S. imports had been produced in such low-wage nations. Further, U.S. employment in manufacturing dropped by approximately 300,000 in the two decades between 1970 and 1990.[84] Additionally, after the North American Free Trade Agreement (NAFTA) was signed in 1994, many in organized labor claimed that by 1998, 500,000 jobs in manufacturing had been lost.[85] NAFTA became a symbol to many in organized American labor of what trade liberalization without tough labor and environmental standards could do to domestic manufacturing jobs.

As unions in the labor-intensive manufacturing sector surveyed the situation in the early 1990s, therefore, they saw themselves competing with low-wage foreign economies. Moreover, these competitors were rapidly moving up the industrial learning curve. Unions were losing industrial jobs and dues-paying members.

In the wake of the violence at Tiananmen in 1989, there was a superficial plausibility to organized labor's assertion that China's low wages, poor working conditions, and human rights violations ("slave labor" as discussed in Chapter 3) largely accounted for China's competitive advantage, the rising U.S. trade deficit, and loss of industrial jobs. Subsequently, labor unions and human rights groups began calling for tough labor standards to be a part of any pursuit of trade liberalization with China. This sentiment led House Minority Leader Richard Gephardt (who wished to win a Democratic majority in the House so he could become Speaker) to sponsor a bill that would require prior congressional approval before the United States supported the admission of the PRC to the WTO and would "provide for the withdrawal of the United States from the World Trade Organization if China is accepted into the WTO without the support of the United States."[86] Supporting this tide, from 1996 to 1998 the Washington director of Human Rights Watch/Asia argued in various congressional hearings that "by focusing on the WTO, Congress could effectively link trade with China's abusive [human rights] behavior."[87] Ultimately the broad spectrum of domestic opposition affected the latitude the administration felt it had in negotiating with Beijing over WTO accession and accounts, in part, for President's Clinton's decision not to conclude an agreement with visiting Premier Zhu Rongji in April 1999, the story to which we turn now.

Chinese Premier Zhu Rongji was scheduled to visit the United States in the spring of 1999. As the time for that journey approached, those planning the trip in each capital became increasingly concerned about the specifics of the visit's agenda. Each side needed "deliverables," results that would justify the trip, move the relationship forward, and give some tangible content to the pursuit of a "constructive strategic partnership." A number of considerations gradually made it clear in early 1999 that the biggest opportunity for substantial, mutually beneficial gain was to agree on terms for China's entry into the WTO.

By early 1999, focusing on WTO made sense for Beijing because new foreign direct investment was declining, foreign banks had greatly tightened up on lending to China, and SOE reform was moving slowly (with nonperforming bank loans to floundering state enterprises mounting).[88]

State-owned-enterprise reform was bogged down because of already high unemployment, slow domestic economic growth, prolonged price deflation, and fear of social instability. Premier Zhu was coming to believe that only a genuine move toward reform, such as getting into the WTO, would reassure foreign investors, make China more efficient and genuinely competitive internationally in the future, and break the hammerlock of those domestic forces dragging their feet on SOE reform. The premier hoped to use international commitments to overcome domestic opponents and promote fundamental reform.[89] Further, Taiwan was ready to enter the WTO, and it would take progressively more of Beijing's political capital to persuade other nations to indefinitely delay Taipei's accession in order to ensure China's prior entry.[90] A meeting in mid-January 1999 with U.S. Federal Reserve Chairman Alan Greenspan was decisive in Zhu's thinking. It was at this time that Zhu publicly made known his desire to vigorously push for China's WTO entry in 1999.[91]

In Washington, the Clinton administration was also looking for areas where meaningful progress could be made, although in late 1998 and very early 1999 there was not much expectation that Beijing would be willing to make the broad and wrenching concessions that would be necessary with respect to agriculture, tariffs, market access, and service industries. As the trip drew nearer, however, it became clearer to Washington that the Chinese were serious about making the moves necessary to maximize chances of WTO entry. A short time before Premier Zhu's arrival in the United States, Beijing indicated its willingness to reduce barriers to U.S. agricultural exports, enhance access for U.S. banks and insurance companies, further cut tariffs, make concessions on U.S. participation in the domestic telecommunications industry, and permit foreign participation in product distribution in the PRC. The president of the Emergency Committee for American Trade, a "big-business lobby," said that Beijing's concessions were "a true breakthrough."[92]

The late-hour concessions set off a flurry of last-minute negotiating, with President Clinton, on the eve of Zhu's Washington arrival, further fanning the flames of optimism by saying, "The bottom line is this: If China is willing to play by the global rules of trade, it would be an inexplicable mistake for the United States to say no."[93] Over the next twenty-four hours, however, with Zhu Rongji then in the U.S. capital, Clinton decided to say "not yet" to Beijing's WTO accession.[94] The reasons for the seeming turnaround are to be found in the domestic atmosphere. First, Congress was out of session, and the White House was worried about what the popular and Capitol Hill reaction would be to a forthcoming congressional report on alleged technology leakage to the PRC and Chinese espionage. Parts of the report, *U.S. National Security and Military/ Commercial Concerns with the People's Republic of China* (otherwise known as the Cox Report), had been leaked upon the premier's arrival in the United States. Senator Joseph Biden (D-Delaware) put it this way to an August 4, 1999, Senate Foreign Relations Committee panel before which I testified: "If any of you think that the president of the United States could have successfully concluded the WTO negotiations, no matter what the Chinese said, in light of the 'stealing of all our secrets,' you all are, with due respect, rookies and not the pros I think you are."[95] Senator Biden had told political advisers in the White House who were pondering whether to proceed with a WTO deal that if they proceeded, "Congress would crucify them."[96] Nonetheless, others on Capitol Hill did not share his view; on April 13, senators on the Finance Committee "berated the administration" for failing to reach agreement with Beijing on WTO.

Another complicating factor was organized labor's opposition to WTO entry for the PRC. Members of Congress responsive to labor unions and Vice President Al Gore, running for president himself, knew they needed labor support in the upcoming year 2000 general election campaign. Labor was particularly concerned about protecting domestic industries (e.g., steel) from Chinese export surges and "dumping" (the export and sale of goods below their cost of production, usually done to gain market share unfairly), and the textile industry had its anxieties that textile quotas would be phased out by 2005. And finally, there was further domestic clamor by human rights groups arguing that signing off on China's WTO entry when it was locking up dissidents was inappropriate.

The bureaucratic forces lined up on both sides of the issue were as follows. The National Security Council, Department of State, USTR, and CIA favored a deal; the White House political staff, the Treasury Department, and the National Economic Council argued that the White House needed to continue to protect vulnerable American industries, that the depth of business community support for the agreement was unclear, and that the congressional response was problematic— better to wait and try to secure a better deal before the end of the year. In the end, Clinton, supported by Treasury Secretary Robert Rubin,[97] went with the wait-and-see analysis, hoping he could get a better offer from Beijing if he delayed the process, figuring he would have more time to judge Congress, and expecting that business thereby would have time to turn up the political heat on Capitol Hill. Commerce Secretary William Daley explained that in the prevailing political atmosphere of the United States, a good deal was not sufficient—

the president needed a super deal: "The reality is that a basically sound deal simply is not good enough.... We need to be able to defend a deal— on Capitol Hill and across the country—by demonstrating that it is fully in our national economic interest.... But even the best commercial deal may not be enough for some. There are those in Congress and elsewhere who have raised the bar in recent months."[98]

All the while that Premier Zhu Rongji was in the United States, he was an astute observer of this unfolding drama. In a remarkable CNN interview aired on April 13, he commented as follows:

> INTERVIEWER: You at one point in the last few days, I believe to members of Congress, described President Clinton as lacking courage, suggesting that he gave in to political concerns in the United States [about possible terms for the PRC's entry into the WTO]. Is that your view of the President? Is he weaker, politically, than you expected?
>
> PREMIER ZHU RONGJI: I don't think we should look at this as a matter of courage. Rather, it's a judgment of opportunity. And this reflects his assessment of the domestic political situation in the U.S. And I believe that he should make up his mind and come to some conclusion, based on the views of Congress and on popular opinion in the United States. And I do believe he will make the right decision.[99]

As explained in Chapter 8, in coming to the United States Zhu had accepted substantial domestic political risk, and indeed there had been several Politburo and Politburo Standing Committee meetings over whether the trip should proceed. Some senior Chinese leaders were opposed to the trip because of its economic implications; others resisted because of the recently begun NATO air war (without UN Security Council authorization) against Yugoslavia aimed at stopping Belgrade's military campaign of ethnic cleansing and repression in Kosovo. In a March 31 meeting with the premier that I attended in Beijing shortly before his departure for the United States, he was quite direct in telling the visiting congressional delegation that he faced domestic opposition to his forthcoming trip and that China had made about as many concessions on the WTO question as was possible. My notes recount the following:

> We have made great concessions and the USTR [i.e., Charlene Barshefsky] believes our concessions we have made were impossible three to five years ago.... USTR thinks the agreement is acceptable, but as a result of pressure from Congress, the USTR is tougher and tougher. If she [USTR] gets an inch she takes a yard.... I expected to reach agreement but yesterday she came to our meeting with a different tone. Why? Because Congress put too much pressure on the negotiations. Our side has

made maximum concessions on market access.... even your negotiators believe we made enough [concessions], but they still won't sign.... If we can't reach agreement in the next three to five years, well, say good-bye to WTO.... I can tell you, Americans won't accuse Mrs. Barshefsky of trading away principles. Chinese people will accuse Zhu Rongji of trading away principles.[100]

Unable to secure a WTO agreement during his trip, Zhu returned to a skeptical home audience, a divided leadership, and empowered opponents in the military, propaganda bureaucracies, and economic institutions affected by the proposed concessions. He became vulnerable on three counts: (1) there were those ministries and sectors of the economy (particularly agriculture and telecommunications)[101] that felt his concessions had exceeded what had been agreed to prior to his departure and that even the agreed-upon concessions had been too sweeping; (2) that Washington had rejected Beijing's concessions proved that Americans did not really want China to become a full-fledged member of the international community; and (3) in early May, less than a month after the premier's return from the United States (and Canada), the United States tragically bombed the Chinese Embassy in Belgrade (killing three Chinese nationals and injuring more than twenty others), instantly making it more difficult still for PRC leaders who argued for conciliation and compromise with Washington.

As described in Chapter 1, Chinese crowds stoned the American Embassy in Beijing, demonstrated in front of most U.S. government buildings in China, and burned the U.S. consul general's residence in Chengdu, thus making it even more difficult for the Clinton administration to adopt a flexible posture on WTO entry for Beijing.

In short, what Bill Clinton thought (or hoped) in April was a brief delay in reaching a WTO accession agreement with Beijing looked, by the end of June 1999, like a failure to reach closure when he had a chance. The domestically driven actions and reactions of each side weakened each one's ability to make the compromises necessary to reach a final agreement. Domestic pressures made Clinton hesitate and then a combination of unpredictable international events and domestic forces made proceeding even more difficult. As one Chinese scholar observed in June 1999, "The Clinton administration seems in very bad coordination. President Clinton had missed a very good opportunity when he balked at signing the WTO package with the visiting Chinese premier in April. When the momentum is lost, it is very difficult to pick it up again."[102]

In the months after May, a series of hurdles had to be cleared before it was even possible to resume WTO negotiations: compensation for lives and property lost in the embassy bombing had to be addressed, tempers had to cool, both countries had to rebuild a minimal domestic consensus to resume WTO negotiations where they were left off (and there was dispute about where that was!), and difficult issues such as permissible levels of foreign ownership in Chinese telecommunications, textiles, protection against dumping, and access for financial services firms still had to be re-solved. After marathon bargaining in Beijing, the two sides reached agree-ment on November 15, 1999. This set the stage for a year 2000 battle be-tween Congress and the White House over extending permanent NTR to China, a story beyond this volume's scope, other than to observe that on May 24, 2000, the U.S. House of Representatives, by a vote of 237 to 197, approved permanent NTR treatment for China, after a bruising struggle that pitted the business community against organized labor and various human rights, environmental, and antiglobalization groups.

The long saga of the WTO negotiations brings us to a conclusion simi-lar to the one that the discussion of the MTCR brought us to—namely, that the PRC is willing to join global regimes and international organiza-tions and play a constructive role in them, but the more important and di-visive issue for both the United States and China is the price to be paid for Beijing's entry. For both sides, when one gets into the details, the costs can be too high. At a minimum, the negotiations to fix that price can be ago-nizingly long.

THE UNITED STATES AND CHINA IN THE GLOBAL ECONOMY

Overview

Beyond global regimes and international institutions, another dimension of the global scene has become exceedingly important in the post–cold war era: the emergence of global markets and financial flows. The global mar-ketplace is proving a powerful influence on Sino-American relations. To recount the sequence of developments in the Asian financial crisis as it played out from 1997 to 1999 is to recount why the management of U.S.-China relations is complex and why economic globalization creates both major frictions *and* opportunities for cooperation.

As we enter the twenty-first century, we enter a world in which inse-curities in one corner of the globe can almost instantly amplify insecuri-ties elsewhere. This is a world in which changing currency values in China, Hong Kong, and Taiwan can affect America's prospects for stable growth and employment and the average citizen's most fundamental sense of economic well-being. This is a world in which economic forces beyond a leader's control can become a litmus test for that leader's competence. And, in a related vein, this is a world in which global investors can "run out the doors" of national economies at the first whiff of problems, whether founded or not. As Singapore's Lee Kuan Yew said in early 1998, speaking of Indonesian President Suharto's search for a vice president, "If the market is uncomfortable with whoever is the eventual vice president, the *rupiah* will weaken again."[103] This is a world in which Chinese communists hedge the risks in their own financial system by buying large volumes of U.S. Treasury instruments and American multinationals hedge lagging growth and profits in one part of the world by turning to frontier economies such as China. And, this is a world in which a China that historically has denounced the interference of others in its domestic affairs now makes recommendations to the U.S. Federal Reserve about its interest rate policy. In short, this is a world in which the human motivations of fear and greed drive national political leaders to cooperate where possible and to struggle to defend themselves and their systems where necessary.

The growth of commerce between China and the United States in the 1980s and 1990s and the Asian financial crisis of 1997–1999 affected Chinese and American thinking and behavior. For much of the 1990s, China and the United States were the engines of economic growth in East Asia. The need for parallel, if not coordinated, policies became increasingly apparent—exchange rate policy is one example. This need for cooperation, in turn, added a new component to the rationale for positive Sino-American relations.

Nonetheless, both nations are ambivalent about the phenomenon of economic interdependence. While global financial flows into the PRC during the 1980s and 1990s brought technology, modern management techniques, growth, and jobs to China, the sudden flight of capital out of much of East Asia in 1997 and 1998 heightened Beijing's sense of vulnerability. These fears found expression in analyses such as, "[I]dle money is flowing unscrupulously and going on a rampage in the world. It relies on modern information technologies for fund transfer at an extremely high speed to carry out speculative activities, make trouble, and engage in profiteering."[104] On the one hand, some PRC constituencies became more resistant to economic reform and globalization; on the other, some became more convinced than ever that the PRC had to reform its financial system to avoid suffering the same fate as other East Asian financial systems: "It is normal to have doubt and worry, but is it possible to ward off others' aircraft carriers by building a few rows of wattled walls? Moreover, cannot the small sampans be replaced by aircraft carriers? Besides, not all Chinese enterprises are small sampans. Liu Chuanzhi, president of the Lian Xiang [Legend] Group, said that 'only if we allow others to get in can we really stand with them on the same starting line. Protection cannot make enterprises grow larger.' "[105]

Chinese ambivalence about economic globalization and growing interdependence was mirrored in America. In the United States, China's importance as an engine of Asian growth was suddenly recognized, as was its capacity to help stabilize the region through management of its own economy and currency. At the same time, however, while the Asian financial crisis and the globalization of trade and finance strengthened U.S.-China relations in some ways, in others they created division. Beyond the obvious U.S. concerns with the trade deficit ($11.4 billion in 1990 and $60.8 in 1998;[106] see table 3), issues involving technology transfer, IPR, employment, and labor and environmental standards had become more abrasive, as discussed in preceding chapters.

Globalization of trade and finance has made management of the bilateral relationship more difficult for three primary reasons. First, political leaders often are forced to respond to the hysteria of millions of dispersed buyers and sellers worldwide. Markets are moved by individual greed and fear, and both of these impulses respond to misinformation and misperception as quickly as to fact. When financial markets move there is no global decision maker to which one nation's leadership can appeal or against which one can threaten retaliation. Yet these uncontrollable market shifts create political opportunities and challenges to which leaders of every state must respond, and respond rapidly, given today's twenty-four-hour-a-day global markets.

Second, within each society, economic and financial globalization creates domestic winners and losers, with those groups trying to influence government policy to their advantage. As the politicians of each nation respond to these domestic constituencies, they frequently create conflicts with their economic partners abroad.

Finally, Washington has found that to threaten economic reprisal against Beijing is to threaten inadvertent damage to third parties the United States does not wish to harm but who have become linked to the PRC economy through globalization. This collateral damage can outweigh the gains sought through economic reprisal, a topic that is addressed in detail in the next chapter.

Let us now look at each of these three factors.

The Asian Financial Crisis and the Global Herd Mentality

On Thursday, October 23, 1997, the currency crisis that had in preceding months bludgeoned exchange rates and equities markets in Thailand (baht down 37 percent), Malaysia (ringgit down 24 percent), Indonesia (rupiah down 33 percent), the Philippines (peso down 23 percent), and Singapore (dollar down 9 percent) hit Hong Kong. The Hang Seng Index dropped 10 percent in a single day. Bank rates in the HKSAR trebled in two days. Interest rates in the HKSAR rose steeply, as the Monetary Authority attempted to defend its dollar from speculators, in turn driving down the Hang Seng Index another 23 percent during the last week of October. By October 27, the spreading fear had hit Wall Street, with the Dow Jones Industrial Average dropping 554 points. Not surprisingly, this echoed back across the Pacific, sending the Hang Seng Index yet lower. Other Asian markets also took their cue from Wall Street.

These mutually reinforcing declines gave rise to several common fears throughout the region. Among these were that capital from the United States and elsewhere would slow to a trickle, domestic growth would slow as the cost of money went up and as already weak banking structures were further undermined, and the region might be driven into a cycle of competitive currency devaluations, as each nation sought to maintain its export volume. As Minoru Makihara, president of Mitsubishi Corporation, put it, "If China starts a great export drive—and if they devalue—this would have a damaging effect on the global economy."[107]

By early November 1997, the contagion of fear once again hopped the Pacific: Brazil (and its creditors) became worried that it might be forced to devalue its currency in order to maintain export competitiveness. As one investment banker stated, "The Government has started taking the necessary steps to avoid a devaluation, but if foreign markets like Hong Kong continue to dive, there may be little that can be done."[108] Caught in a process in which fear in one area of the globe stoked fear in another, Thailand and the rest of Southeast Asia began to consider the possibility that China might devalue its currency and that their already weak position would further deteriorate. "China can make everything we do now—only cheaper."[109]

By late November, the contagion had spread further, with South Korea asking for IMF assistance to rescue its currency from the accumulated ills of crony capitalism in the banking system, excessive industrial concentration, and sluggish exports. This gave rise to a series of further blows, as already weakened Japanese banks, which held substantial amounts of South

Korean assets and debt, pulled the Japanese yen down further, and as major Japanese brokerage houses either failed or reached the brink of failure, leading, in turn, to rumors of hidden mountains of bad loans in Japanese bank portfolios.

The previously scheduled APEC senior leaders meeting of November 25, 1997, was devoted almost exclusively to the mounting economic tragedy. Yet this meeting seemed so divorced from the reality that Asian citizens saw on the streets that one currency specialist in Singapore suggested that the meeting's conclusions were "like calling the second world war a minor disruption to the social fabric of Europe."[110] By the end of the month, the Russians were also alarmed; rising interest rates necessary to prop up the ruble threatened to kill off what little growth they had. Domestic and foreign investor confidence in Russia was thus weakening both because of Russia's *own* domestic economic and political situation and because world investors were shying away from emerging markets generally.

Beijing had its own anxieties, particularly beginning in September 1997: China feared it might have to draw on its approximately $130 billion in foreign exchange to defend the Hong Kong dollar (*gangbi*) against speculators who sought to break the peg to the greenback established in 1983.[111] President Jiang Zemin, who was on the eve of his long-sought state visit to America (making him the first Chinese head of state to do so since 1985), did not wish to appear unable to defend what had heretofore been East Asia's most stable currency. More specifically, were the U.S.-Hong Kong dollar peg to fall and the *gangbi* to devalue, Beijing would face the charge that it was a weaker steward of Hong Kong's prosperity than the recently departed British. Even more tangibly, PRC investors with more than US$14 billion in Hong Kong[112] and Hong Kong investors with $99 billion in the PRC (with more coming each day)[113] were tightly wrapped in each other's financial embrace.

It was in this context that Beijing announced its willingness to back the Hong Kong dollar and to help Thailand (as early as August 1997) by promising a $1 billion contribution to an IMF loan package.[114] Notably, Beijing moved before the United States. Eight months later, China pledged to provide Indonesia with a grant of $400 million, again as part of an IMF package.[115]

As the days passed from September to December and into early 1998, Beijing also worried that Southeast Asian nations were becoming stronger export competitors at the same time that their demand for Chinese exports was collapsing. During 1998, however, China's exports held up better than many had anticipated; nonetheless, Beijing did face mounting competition in its own markets—South Korean steel exports to China, for example, grew 32.4 percent faster in the first half of 1998 than during the same period the preceding year. "Inexpensive East Asian goods, led by steel and textiles from South Korea, [were] pouring into China."[116] China's efforts during the previous eight years to diversify its exports within Asia and to reduce its dependence on the American market were likewise threatened. The U.S. market loomed ever larger—with all exporters in East and Southeast Asia hoping to use shipments to the United States to fuel their own growth. For example, former Shanghai Vice Mayor Sha Lin told me in March 1999 that it was only the 34 percent growth in exports to the United States in 1998 that compensated for his city's export declines elsewhere.[117] Chongqing, China's largest municipality, with lots of foundering state enterprises and large unemployment, was not so lucky: in 1998 the city's exports declined 36 percent, with its exports to Hong Kong falling 60 percent, those to Japan, 50 percent, and exports to South Korea, 40 percent.[118]

An equal source of anxiety for Beijing was the prospect (and later reality) that as the Asian economies spiralled downward, economic growth in the PRC would slow, making only more apparent the glaring weaknesses of its banks, SOEs, and urban property bubbles. With respect to the latter, for example, 70 percent of new office space in Shanghai's Pudong Development Zone was standing idle in 1998.[119] In January 1998 Shanghai Mayor Xu Kuangdi said, "What has happened in Southeast Asia gives us a wake-up call."[120] Meanwhile, all of this was occurring just as China needed high growth rates to absorb the millions of workers soon to be shed in the ongoing restructuring of the state enterprise sector, as agreed to at the September 1997 Fifteenth Party Congress. Capital Iron and Steel Corporation is illustrative of the problem—it employed 135,000 staff to support fewer than 15,000 workers making steel.[121]

No less worrisome, Hong Kong accounted for 58.21 percent of FDI in the PRC, while Taiwan accounted for 8.52 percent, Japan, 8.11 percent, and Singapore, 3.53 percent during 1979–1996. South Korea had also been a growing source of FDI. As each of these areas became more strapped, however, and as other overseas investors lost confidence in China's economy, due to slower growth in the PRC or worker instability, or both, the flow of "actualized" FDI into China could (and in 1999 did) slow, as contracted future investment had been doing since it peaked in 1993.[122] In the case of Taiwan, for example, the island's FDI commitments to the PRC in July 1998 were down 12.8 percent over year-earlier levels.[123] Such a loss of investment, of course, would make it only more difficult to keep growth, employment, and the pace of SOE reform on track. Not all these concerns fully materialized, but they clearly drove Chinese policy. With respect to attracting FDI, for instance, Beijing announced that "China has promptly adjusted its investment policy to offer preferential treatment to foreign capital and is courting multinational corporations heavily."[124] And eventually it was this need to keep FDI flowing into the PRC that tipped Beijing in the direction of reaching agreement with Washington on terms of accession to WTO in late 1999, despite the pain of the necessary concessions.

Finally, if Beijing could not maintain prosperity in Hong Kong (where, between August 7 and December 31, 1997, the Property Index had fallen by over 35 percent) and sustain a high rate of domestic growth at home, what attraction would "peaceful reunification" and "one country, two systems" have for the people of Taiwan? For Beijing, in short, a great deal was at stake during the last quarter of 1997 and thereafter—international prestige, foreign investment, domestic stability, economic prosperity, and the sacred mission of reunification with Taiwan. Each concern was ensnared in a financial crisis not of Beijing's making, nor, in large part, within its control.

What was the gunshot that began this stampede? Economic historians will likely debate the question, but the rough contours of the process are clear. As Donald Tsang, financial secretary of Hong Kong, explained in July 1998:

> There were some who thought that the capital inflows of more than US$200 billion in the region would never stop. But when international banks panicked and withdrew funds, net capital outflows from the Asian Five [Korea, Indonesia, Malaysia, Thailand, and the Philippines] amounted to some US$109 billion, or roughly 10% of their GDP. The result was a chain reaction of collapse in Thailand, Indonesia and then Korea.
>
> According to data from Nomura on 8 Asian countries, total funds raised through bank loans amounted to 92% of GDP, compared to 71% from the stock market and only 22% from the bond market. Given this over-reliance on short-term funds, it was not surprising that Asia suffered a sharp liquidity shock. Once bank credit shrank and stock markets collapsed, overseas investors could not diversify into domestic bond markets even if they wanted to. The only alternative was to withdraw their capital.[125]

One could add that money was fleeing because the reality of weak banks, bad loan portfolios, nontransparent bookkeeping, lax banking regulation, cozy relationships between lenders and borrowers, excessive short-term debt denominated in major currencies, and trade deficits in multiple East Asian countries was dawning on foreign investors all at once. Moreover, China's emergence as a powerhouse exporter represented an ever more competitive force for several of the previously successful Southeast Asian economies. These conditions, of course, had existed to various extents long before. Suddenly, the logic of the herd that earlier had led foreign investors to ignore risks in Asia now led them to ignore all the strengths that heretofore had contributed to the "Asian miracle."

By early and mid-1998, it was becoming progressively clearer that the process of economic decline would have severe political repercussions in some of the affected countries. As steep currency devaluations occurred, political instability began to rear its head. In May, the thirty-three-year rule of Indonesian President Suharto came to an end following widespread riots. By the summer of 1998, workers in South Korea were beginning to challenge newly elected South Korean President Kim Dae Jung's tough economic reform policies. By the fall, Malaysian Prime Minister Mahathir was under assault as well, though both Kim and Mahathir survived.

While the markets and the citizenry were punishing these nations' leaders, the IMF was imposing stringent fiscal and regulatory conditions before providing them with desperately needed liquidity for their banking and financial systems. This, in turn, gave rise to both unemployment and protests that external forces (particularly U.S. financial interests and the IMF, which was perceived in many quarters as an arm of Wall Street) were interfering in internal affairs and bailing out foreign financial service firms while impoverishing domestic citizens. Meanwhile, American corporations that had wanted into the Asian financial service and other sectors for decades now saw the opportunity to gain entry on relatively cheap and favorable terms. For its part, the U.S. government was supportive of this desire and used its influence over bailout support to promote this objective in Korea and elsewhere. That action, of course, fed resentment and nationalism in the region.

As local currency values fell, the affected countries raised interest rates to attract capital; as interest rates rose, growth slowed further. Slowing growth, tighter credit, and mounting unemployment all fed the potential for, and reality of, political instability. This instability, in turn, made these countries even less attractive as sites for foreign investment. Finally, as their currencies fell, the real debt repayment burden on these nations' large, foreign currency–denominated debt became progressively more onerous. Much of this foreign debt, however, was owed to non-American financial institutions, with Japan holding about 30 percent of the lending to the most affected Asian economies,[126] thus worsening the already weak state of Japan's banking system.[127]

Specifically, Japan's banking system was burdened with an excessively high proportion of bad loans and stock portfolios that had shrunk as the Nikkei Index fell during the 1990s. Faced with these troubles, Japanese banks tightened up on lending both domestically and regionally, slowing both domestic and regional growth yet further. As this psychology of austerity spread in Japan, a citizenry that already saved a substantial percentage of its income began to save even more of certain kinds of assets, with postal savings growing by 8.6 percent in early 1998.[128] This placed yet a further drag on regional consumption and, consequently, on demand. Meanwhile, the Liberal Democratic Party (LDP) government of Prime Minister Hashimoto had raised the consumption tax by 2 percent in April 1997,[129] in the mistaken belief that Japan was on a growth trajectory. This further reduced domestic consumer demand. Throughout the process, moreover, the factionalized politics of the ruling LDP and the need to win support from smaller political groupings made Tokyo slow to respond to declining demand with the adoption of stimulatory policies.

Thus Japan, Asia's richest economy, was not part of the solution to regional deflation—it was a very big part of the problem. Consequently, by the spring of 1998 the United States and China had become the two principal engines of growth left in the Pacific basin. They needed to cooperate, or at least adopt parallel or reinforcing policies, if worse global financial difficulty was to be avoided. The United States welcomed China's decisions (announced in late 1997 and during the first quarter of 1998) to boost its domestic growth through infrastructure spending, to support the Hong Kong dollar, and not to devalue its currency in 1998 and 1999. For its part, China was pleased that by the fall of 1998 the United States had begun to stimulate its own economy through an interest rate cut. Indeed, Beijing wanted the United States to move even more aggressively in that direction, with the *People's Daily* reading like the *Wall Street Journal*, observing that "[t]he U.S. interest rate cut can help reduce the currency pressure on developing countries and ease the spreading financial crisis." The only complaint was that "It is a wise action, but it [the cut] is too small."[130]

For Washington, less buying power in East Asia and lower-cost exports to America threatened to worsen what already was a large, rising, and politically combustible trade deficit with the region, and particularly with China. Lower Asian purchasing power, for instance, led to an expectation that commodity exports to the region (e.g., corn and pork) would fall in 1998, thereby pushing commodity prices down and hurting American and European agricultural export revenues. By the end of 1997, U.S. agricultural exports to Indonesia had fallen more than 15 percent; those to Taiwan and South Korea, nearly 12 percent; and those to the PRC, about 2.5 percent. Meanwhile, the U.S. trade deficit with the PRC reached $53 billion in 1997 (see table 3), and $60.8 billion a year later.[131] In part, the mounting deficit accounted for Washington's unwillingness to make substantial concessions to Beijing to secure a WTO agreement, concessions that might be subject to domestic political attack.

Despite Washington and Beijing's respective fears about the economic downturn in Asia, they were engaged in a financial embrace in several areas. Beijing had invested billions of dollars of its foreign exchange in U.S. Treasury Bonds (see table 2);[132] these bonds provided a safe harbor for some financial reserves. For Washington, meanwhile, these assets were part (though a relatively small one) of the flow of cheap money that kept U.S. interest rates low and liquidity in the U.S. housing market high. In an irony of world finances, poor, socialist China was financing wealthy, capitalist America. Indeed, in a rare moment of candor in international relations, Treasury Secretary Robert Rubin suggested to China's financial leaders in late 1997 that it would "make more sense to use these reserves to import capital equipment."[133] For their part, American multinationals had invested in excess of $21 billion on the mainland as of 1998 (see table 2); an economic downturn there would hurt their sales in China's domestic market. Finally, a slowdown in China, with rising unemployment due to SOE reform, might well make Beijing more resistant to financial service reform and even more skittish about market access.

Then there was Taipei, ever on the prowl for opportunities to gain a more respected, official place in the international community and looking for ways to limit its growing economic dependence on the PRC. With respect to its own international status, in late 1997 Taipei seized on the currency crisis to bring its approximately $90 billion of hard currency reserves into the service of its pragmatic diplomacy. A leading figure of the Kuomintang (Nationalist Party) suggested that Taipei might be willing to extend South Korea a $10 billion loan of stabilization funds if such funds could be provided under the auspices of an international financial organization like the IMF.[134] In January 1998, Taiwan Premier Vincent Siew traveled to the Philippines and Indonesia, and Vice President Lien Chan met with Lee Kuan Yew in Singapore. Both sought to translate Taiwan's foreign exchange reserves into diplomatic status and commercial opportunity. As to Taiwan's efforts to undermine Beijing, there were some in both Washington and Beijing who suggested that Taipei devalued its currency in October 1997 in order to compound Hong Kong's difficulties maintaining the *gangbi*'s peg to the greenback and to force a PRC devaluation that would undermine Beijing's credibility.[135] This, the logic went, was an effort to further erode the attraction of the "one country, two systems" concept.[136] The significance of the monetary turmoil, thus, reached well beyond the economic realm.

Winners and Losers in the Global Economy

Domestic politics in China and the United States are dissimilar in many respects, but in one respect they are the same: squeaky social and political wheels get the grease. And in the global economy, in which abrupt changes can render entire economic sectors obsolete, there are lots of squeaky domestic wheels. Since domestic losers cannot appeal to the global economy to mitigate their pain, they must adapt to the market itself and turn to their own elites and institutions to help cushion blows. In some cases, disgruntled constituencies urge that the government protect them entirely from the need to change. Politicians also are confronted with the attacks of political opponents who profess that they could manage, or avoid, dislocations more effectively than incumbents. So while politicians are attempting to respond to the riptides of the global economy, they must do so with one eye on the social, economic, and political vultures circling at home.

The struggle to adapt to the global economy can give rise to enormous frustration and insecurity. Native Indonesians attack fellow citizens of Chinese ancestry for their alleged financial misdeeds and disproportionate wealth, and simultaneously topple the three-decade-old Suharto regime. These attacks on overseas Chinese in Indonesia, in turn, give rise to PRC citizens' demands that Beijing do something to assist their ethnic brethren abroad.[137] South Korean workers strike to protest the industrial, fiscal, and financial restructuring that the global economy and its multilateral executor, the IMF, impose. Japanese popular dissatisfaction produces successive governments in Tokyo. Chinese workers demonstrate because the forces of global competition have shuttered their plants. And, of course, some members of the U.S. Congress demand a say in whether to admit China to the WTO because they fear the executive branch will not drive a hard enough bargain on behalf of American workers. In Seattle in late 1999, organized labor, environmental, and human rights groups from around the world assembled to pressure WTO member nation trade ministers to take their concerns more fully into account.

Chinese and American winners and losers in the global economy will constantly shift. Despite these shifts, however, it is possible to describe some of the principal winners and losers in each society, as the twenty-first century begins. Some losses are absolute, as in declining real income, while others are relative, such as not keeping up with those groups against which one judges oneself or simply fearing that future job security depends on forces far beyond the individual's control. The losers will try to be heard as the winners seek to protect and enhance their gains.

In China and the United States alike, globally noncompetitive domestic industries and the workers they employ regularly appeal to their governments for protection. About 57 percent of the PRC's urban workforce was still employed in SOEs in 1996, while in 1997 and 1998 alone, 1.8 million Chinese textile workers lost their jobs.[138] Ironically, textile workers in America weren't happy either. U.S. Commerce Secretary William Daley was confronted in Fall River, Massachusetts, by one such worker, a lingerie mill employee opposed to the PRC's entry into WTO, who said, "We're losing our jobs left and right to China."[139]

The sought-after protection can be achieved by hidden or open subsidization, tariff barriers, harassing suits or administrative actions against imports (antidumping), nontariff barriers such as quotas or prohibitions on imports, capricious product health or safety standards, and boycotts. In *both* China and the United States, however, as tariffs have receded as a means of protecting sensitive domestic sectors, nontariff measures (such as antidumping suits) have increased in prominence. In 1998, for instance, China's hard-hit steel and petrochemical industries were leading the charge for relief from what they alleged was South Korean dumping. In the United States during the 1990–1998 period, similarly, there were forty-five U.S. International Trade Commission Title VII investigations conducted with respect to China, over half of which were judged "affirmative," meaning that a basis was found for referring the matter to the Department of Commerce for action. Most of the referrals, in turn, resulted in actions against the offenders. These investigations covered products ranging from hand tools to chemical compounds and dinnerware to roofing nails.[140] Indeed, one of the final sticking points in the November 1999 WTO accession negotiations between Washington and Beijing was the length of time the United States would be permitted to use its antidumping legislation to the disadvantage of China's exports, with Beijing agreeing to a surprisingly long time.

The issue of nontariff measures and dumping, however, is more complex than thus far described. As Ken Pomeranz argues, a country that allows low occupational safety and environmental standards is providing a hidden subsidy to its firms by transferring costs that are properly those firms' to society as a whole or to the entire global system. In short, it is not immediately apparent how the costs of production can be objectively established in the current international economic system and whether or not costs vary by a nation's level of development.

In a related domain, there usually is conflict between a nation's exporters (who wish to have a relatively low exchange rate to make their products cheaper abroad) and its importers (who wish to have a strong monetary unit that makes imports cheaper for domestic consumers). Amidst the severe export competition of 1998, therefore, it is unsurprising that an executive at the Shanghai Hudong Shipyard, a facility that did not receive a single order in the first six months of 1998 "despite cutting the price of its ships by 30% and trimming its work force by 20%," said, "If the yuan is not devalued, we won't be able to avoid making a loss this year."[141] Of course, devaluation of the yuan in 1998 would have put additional strain on the rest of the Asian economy and damaged the emerging idea that economic cooperation between Washington and Beijing was a manifestation of "constructive strategic partnership." This meant little, however, at the Hudong Shipyard.

Winners and losers also change as local and global markets rise and fall. As this occurs, the pattern of political pressures within and between nations changes. With the decline of the Japanese yen at least marginally eroding the comparative position of some of China's exports throughout 1998, for example, Beijing pressured Washington in June 1998 to buy yen and thereby prop up its value—making Japanese exports more expensive, and therefore less competitive, than Beijing's. The PRC had indirectly threatened that if Washington failed to comply with its request, it might have to devalue the yuan, setting the stage for further economic destabilization. As President Jiang Zemin explained in June 1998: "The economies of the world are increasingly interrelated. So there ought to be a common standard that it is inadvisable [for the United States] ... to commend the efforts of one country [China] for maintaining the value of its currency while giving tacit approval ... to another country [Japan] which devalues its currency."[142]

In short, the political dynamic of winners and losers within and between countries in the global economy is almost entirely understandable in terms of material interest, market behavior, domestic political considerations, and national power. Conceiving of China as a communist society in economic terms leads analysis astray.

Nonetheless, even though culture and ideology are not necessary to explain PRC global economic behavior, culture and ideology can become convenient lightning rods for the frustrations that arise within individual economies. So, for example, in the second half of 1997 Malaysian Prime

Minister Mahathir Mohamad blamed his country's economic woes on international speculators, particularly George Soros, and reportedly stated, "We are Muslims, and the Jews are not happy to see the Muslims progress.... The Jews robbed the Palestinians of everything, but in Malaysia they could not do so, hence they do this, depress the *ringgit*."[143] Likewise, in Indonesia in 1998 and 1999, wealthy citizens of Chinese extraction became targets of their fellow frustrated (generally Muslim) neighbors who were generally poorer and resentful.

Another related complication in managing U.S.-China relations in the global economy stems from the increasingly multilateral character of criminal activity and the involvement, on occasion, of the Chinese military.[144] Domestic criminal networks worldwide are becoming more globalized. Criminal syndicates operating in cooperation with increasingly organized Chinese networks ship illegal products (human beings, narcotics, and other illicit materials) to the United States via South China, Hong Kong, Southeast Asia, South and Central America, and Russia.[145] In the late 1990s, organized Chinese crime was shipping illegal migrants through the relatively poorly regulated territories of Guam, the Virgin Islands, and Puerto Rico.[146] Likewise, intellectual property violations frequently involve Taiwan capital, equipment, and high-tech components; manufacturing in the PRC; and distribution through Hong Kong. In Japan, Chinese gangs involving individuals from both the PRC and Taiwan have even the notorious Yakuza (Mafia) in awe of their ruthless quest for money.[147] And finally, human smuggling also often has a "greater China" (Hong Kong-PRC-Taiwan) dimension.[148]

CONCLUSIONS

Characterizations of China as a rogue regime standing angry and isolated outside (or being disruptive within) international organizations and regimes have little basis in fact. A striking pattern of Chinese behavior in the post–cold war era has been the degree to which the PRC has joined and cooperated with global institutions of governance. China has become progressively more involved in most international regimes and has developed internal organizations, regulations, and increasingly skilled personnel that allow it to deal more easily and effectively with the international community. These internal organizations and experts generally have, in turn, become constituencies within the PRC for openness and internationally acceptable behavior.

When China joined the Bretton Woods institutions, for example, it developed the internal organizations and skilled personnel to deal with those institutions. Those same individuals eventually became some of the most articulate advocates inside China for more open economic structures and, in the wake of the Asian financial crisis, called upon the world to build new financial structures (particularly with respect to financial flows) to provide additional stability in the future.[149] Indeed, the dominant part of China's ruling elite concluded from the Asian financial crisis that the PRC had no realistic choice but to proceed with economic opening and structural reform, albeit gradually and with particular caution in the area of financial system change.[150] This lesson accounts for the startling trade concessions the PRC made in its effort to secure membership in the WTO during Premier Zhu Rongji's April 1999 visit to the United States; it accounts as well for the rigorous terms of China's accession that Beijing and Washington agreed to in November 1999.

With respect to arms control, in the second half of the 1990s, Beijing established internal organizations and regulatory structures and cultivated a corps of skilled professionals to deal with the international community in this area. Even in the realm of individual rights, where Beijing's behavior often remains reprehensible, it has conceded that human rights are a legitimate area of international concern. Domestic laws and regulations are being promulgated that make more adequate protection of individual rights conceivable.

Nonetheless, China's compliance with international agreements has been inconsistent, reflecting both Beijing's perception of its own interests and objective difficulties in ensuring faithful implementation. Predictably, China's compliance has been best when an international institution or regime provides resources, the regime or international institution does not offend powerful domestic constituencies, Beijing perceives it will pay a large international price by virtue of noncompliance, or when the elite sees no leverage to be gained through noncompliance. Finally, most Chinese leaders wish the PRC to be viewed as a responsible member of the big power club whenever possible.

Americans viscerally view (and explain) what they do internationally in terms of domestic constraints, but they rarely appreciate that Chinese behavior also cannot be understood apart from domestic considerations. Yet when they view China's behavior in international settings, Americans see only Beijing's position, not the underlying domestic pressures that account for that behavior. For instance, when the Chinese led the charge against developing countries agreeing to cap their greenhouse gas emissions at the Kyoto Meeting in December 1997, this, in part, reflected the pressures of the energy-inefficient state enterprises that employed over half of the urban workforce. Many of these facilities are going under and, quite predictably, resist the imposition of additional costs, as do the localities that depend on them for employment and tax revenue. Indeed, the U.S. government did not ratify the Kyoto Protocol in 1998 for precisely the same reason that Beijing does not wish to be bound by greenhouse gas emission caps: each feared that doing so might retard domestic economic growth. China's behavior is not necessarily in U.S. interests, but it is understandable by reference to many of the same considerations Americans use to explain their own actions—constituencies, interests, and institutions.

Turning to the less tangible but extremely powerful realm of the global marketplace, the degree to which China's trade and financial behavior manifests the same patterns and responds to the same stimuli as other nations is remarkable. China seeks to preserve its competitive position through currency values, hedges against uncertainty by acquiring foreign exchange reserves and foreign securities, and protects industries and constituencies that are most central to its economy and politics. Americans may not always find Chinese behavior in their interests, but again, such behavior is understandable and largely predictable.

Political leaders in China and the United States, therefore, face several tasks: they must try to prevent domestic social and economic cleavages from becoming too large, help domestic losers acquire the skills necessary to compete and soften the costs of transition, create incentives for foreign economic partners to engage in patterns of behavior that mitigate domestic problems, tackle transborder organized criminal activity, and avoid demagoguery themselves. If U.S. and Chinese leaders do not succeed at managing the adjustments of their domestic systems to the global economy they will find it difficult to manage their bilateral relationship in the years ahead.

5

THE DILEMMA OF THIRD PARTIES

MAO ZEDONG TO HENRY KISSINGER: I am going to heaven soon....
And when I ... see God, I'll tell him it's better to have Taiwan
under the care of the United States now.
KISSINGER: He'll be very astonished to hear that from the
Chairman.
MAO: No, because God blesses you, not us. [Mao waves his hands.]
God does not like us because I am a militant warlord, also a
communist. That's why he doesn't like me. He likes you.
KISSINGER: I've never had the pleasure of meeting him, so I don't
know.

> Mao Zedong's residence, October 21, 1975

How do you penalize the Empress Dowager without hurting the
people? The only way in an earlier era was to burn down the
Summer Palace.

> Very frustrated senior Hong Kong official, May 1992

QUESTION TO HONG KONG GOVERNOR CHRISTOPHER F. PATTEN: How
do you rebut the Chinese accusation that the reason the Hong
Kong Government started democratization is a plot to destabilize
Hong Kong after 1997?
GOVERNOR PATTEN'S REPLY: We do to some extent find ourselves
staggering wearily from one conspiracy theory to another! What's
Britain's interest in Hong Kong? Britain's interest is to manage
the transfer of sovereignty in as decent and honorable a way as
possible.... One reason why we want to do that is that old British
idea—I think you understand it as well—of honor. I remember
once trying to explain to my opposite number, Director Lu Ping,
Lu Ping of the Hong Kong/Macao Affairs Office, who I think has
spoken to this Council [the National Committee on U.S.-China
Relations], that to a British politician, particularly one who had
lost his seat in a general election [like me], the notion of "face"
was completely meaningless! On the other hand, the idea of
trying to lay down Britain's last colonial responsibility as
honorably as possible—now that meant something!

> Q&A with Governor Patten, New York City, May 6, 1996

We understand that in principle you will not renounce the right to use force. We want you to understand that we will defend Taiwan. Period.

> Speaker of the House Newt Gingrich, Shanghai, March 1997

Any program of engagement must recognize the reality that China's rapid rise as an economic, political, and military power inevitably poses challenges to other Pacific powers, and in particular to the United States and Japan and to their security alliance.... But even though China has itself profited from this stability, China believes that this alliance and these [American forward-deployed] troops are directed against it.

> Ashton B. Carter and former Defense Secretary
> William J. Perry, 1999

A WEB OF RELATIONSHIPS

Relationships with third parties are central to the dynamics of the U.S.-China relationship. Historically, a principle of Chinese statecraft was to avoid dealing with foreign nations (particularly adversaries) as a group, preferring to deal bilaterally in order to exploit the differences among outsiders to one's advantage. The nineteenth-century modernizer Li Hongzhang explained this proclivity as a way to "neutralize one poison with another."[1] Similarly, given America's worldwide interests and its many global alliances, its dealings with Beijing are rarely devoid of third-party considerations.

Third-party relationships can facilitate or complicate the management of United States-China relations. When both Washington and Beijing view an important third party as a common problem, their cooperation provides an overarching, sometimes strategic rationale that allows them to subordinate other irritants in the bilateral relationship. One example in this regard is dealing with North Korea's attempts to become a nuclear power in the 1990s, an outcome both sought to avoid through parallel efforts. Conversely, when Chinese or American ties to a third party are seen as problematic for either country, that relationship can become a source of irritation and sometimes conflict. As seen in Chapter 2, relations with Pakistan have been emblematic in this regard. Even when both Beijing and Washington have generally productive links to a particular third party, managing the three-way relationship can prove trying, as is often the case with Japan.

It frequently is said that the United States is a global power and the PRC a regional power. This is misleading because not all regions are equally important to the two nations and because China's reach is increasing. The PRC is embedded in an important region pivotal to America's security and economic interests. Many of China's fourteen immediately adjacent neighbors, as well as South Korea, Japan, the Philippines, and Taiwan, are entities that have substantial bearing on U.S. interests. Some of these are societies with which the United States has had long-standing and often tumultuous relationships in the twentieth century alone—Vietnam, Japan, Russia, and North Korea. The Chinese live in a tough, important neighborhood. Eight of China's neighbors' armed forces rank among the world's top eleven in terms of manpower or expenditure size (Russia, Japan, India, North Korea, South Korea, Pakistan, Vietnam, and Taiwan).[2] Three of China's neighbors are declared nuclear weapons states (India, Pakistan, and Russia). Four other neighbors could acquire nuclear weapons in a relatively short period if the decision was made to do so (Japan, North Korea, Taiwan, and South Korea). Four nearby neighbors were among the top fifteen trading entities in the world in 1998 (Japan, Hong Kong, South Korea, and Taiwan).[3] And finally, China is culturally wedged between states dominated by Islam, Hinduism, and Christianity.

Consequently, many relationships in Asia involve the United States, the PRC, and a third party. These triangular relationships are often difficult to manage, and the way in which they are handled has great bearing on the interests of both America and China. In addition, as the PRC's power grows, the scope of its global relationships expands accordingly, thereby multiplying the instances in which U.S.-China relations have to be managed in the context of third (or fourth) parties.

In contrast to the preceding chapter, which dealt with the complexities introduced into the management of bilateral relations by the relatively new features of the global system, this chapter addresses a problem as old as the nation-state system itself—managing relationships among self-regarding, power-maximizing states and nonstate actors. We open by examining the U.S.-China relationship as it relates to Taiwan and Hong Kong—ongoing delicate triangular management dilemmas. After exploring the complexities of these two unique situations, we turn to two more conventional third-party international relationships—that is, with Russia (the former Soviet Union) and Japan.

BEIJING, TAIPEI, AND WASHINGTON

Chapters 1 and 2 demonstrated that the PRC-Taiwan-United States relationship has been a recurrent source of instability and friction in both

Sino-American ties and within the region. Managing this triangular relationship has required that all three capitals understand what is intolerable to the other two and then act in accordance with that knowledge. This has not been an easy task for any of the three inasmuch as contending social and political groups in each society have divergent views of their interests, the ultimately achievable goal, and the risks attached to following different paths. Gross mismanagement and misperception in any of the three capitals could result in severe friction—conceivably war.

Opportunities for misperception abound. Beijing may sometimes believe Washington is bluffing when it threatens intervention if Taiwan is attacked without provocation. Taipei may mistakenly perceive that Beijing will not jeopardize its internal economic development and cross-strait economic ties to assertively press its sovereignty claims or that Washington will defend the island irrespective of what it does. And Washington might believe Beijing doesn't have the capacity or the will to attack Taiwan. Indeed, it is this latter misperception that worries Chinese leaders greatly. As Premier Zhu Rongji put it in March 2000: "Some people have made some calculations about how many aircraft, missiles and warships China possesses, and presumed that China dare not and will not use force based on such calculations.... People making such calculations don't know about Chinese history. The Chinese people are ready to shed blood."[4]

Taipei will continue to employ every means at its disposal to ensure that the United States is an explicit, unconditional guarantor of its security and to expand its scope for dignified, meaningful international activity. These goals are advanced by sophisticated lobbying, only part of which is included in the Taipei Economic and Cultural Representative Office's $1.2 million annual budget for contracts with fifteen U.S. firms to "help open doors," in the words of Taiwan representative Stephen Chen.[5] The island will continue to cultivate the U.S. executive branch and the U.S. Congress, while playing one off against the other—generally having more confidence in Capitol Hill than the White House. In a June 24, 1999, meeting Taiwan President Lee Teng-hui approvingly observed to the group I was with that the U.S. Congress was the repository of commitment to America's tradition of freedom and liberty, whereas the executive branch, he critically observed, often was more concerned with short-term interests and power.[6]

Beijing sees the United States and Japan as the key players in the Taiwan issue, knowing that if it can prevent Washington and Tokyo from supporting an independent Taiwan, it is highly unlikely that other major powers would do so. The PRC seeks to build and maintain a big power fence around the changing identity on Taiwan, and it therefore attaches great importance to President Clinton's public articulation of U.S. policy in this regard during his June 1998 trip to China: "[W]e don't support independence for Taiwan, or two Chinas, or one Taiwan-one China. And we don't believe that Taiwan should be a member in any organization for which statehood is a requirement. So, I think we have a consistent policy. Our only policy has been that we think it has to be done peacefully."[7]

For the same reason, Jiang Zemin's failure to secure such a statement from Tokyo during his late-1998 visit to Japan was a disappointment to Beijing. A secondary, but key objective for Beijing is to reduce arms transfers to the island (particularly American weapons sales, as was envisioned in the August 17, 1982, Joint Communiqué between Washington and Beijing),[8] thereby reducing Taipei's capacity to resist cross-strait negotiations. A tertiary objective is to induce Washington to pressure Taipei to come to the table, though Beijing is ambivalent in this respect because it wants U.S. involvement only when it serves PRC purposes. All of these objectives came into clear focus in 1999 in Beijing's response to President Lee Teng-hui's July 9 call for "special state-to-state" relations between Beijing and Taipei,[9] discussed later in this chapter and in Chapter 1.

The essence of the American management problem is to deter *both* Beijing and Taipei from behavior that would cause peace to break down in the Taiwan Strait. This double deterrence is essential to American interests and regional stability because it is exceedingly unlikely that the United States could remain uninvolved if conflict erupted, although America could live with any peacefully determined outcome between Beijing and Taipei. Pending such a peaceful resolution, accomplishing double deterrence requires Washington to maintain its credibility with both Beijing and Taipei and to forego the domestic political gratifications that constantly tempt it, particularly the Congress, in directions pleasing to Taipei but unsettling to Beijing.

However, politics and policymaking in all three capitals constantly endanger the prospect of subtle management of the triangular relationship. Political leaders in Beijing will be tempted to play the "Taiwan" card in domestic politics when they are weak and in need of popular support or military backing. In Washington, the combination of partisan politics, tension between the White House and Congress, Beijing's heavy-handedness (whether through missile exercises, election-eve threats, or international isolation), and the genuine popular receptiveness to appeals for Taiwanese rights of self-determination creates a sympathetic environment for Taipei.

As for Taiwan, competitive politicians on the island continually seize the electoral gains to be made by appealing to the changing Taiwanese identity. In August 1998, for example, Taiwan President Lee Teng-hui stated, "Taiwan's destiny isn't China's to decide. It's for the 21 million people on Taiwan to decide their destiny."[10] For Beijing, by way of contrast, Taiwan's destiny is for 1.3 billion Chinese people to decide. As one of China's most senior military officers told me in 1997, "The most important thing is not popular opinion on Taiwan, but only the opinion of the whole country. New York can't decide for New York. I am a general; I am blunt."[11]

Politics aside, technological change will also make it difficult to manage this three-way relationship. For instance, growing North Korean, Iraqi, and Iranian missile capabilities have generated substantial U.S. commitment to developing a theater missile defense (TMD) system to be deployed to protect American troops and allies abroad, as well as a national missile defense system for the American homeland. Taiwan, reacting to Beijing's 1995–1996 missile exercises, the steady growth of the PRC missile force,[12] and PRC threats in 1999, has expressed interest in acquiring TMD. Further, earlier generations of Patriot Missile systems sold to Taiwan with antiaircraft capabilities are constantly being upgraded and becoming a more potent (low-altitude) antimissile system. Additionally, the 1999 National Defense Authorization Bill called for a U.S. Defense Department study of "the architecture requirements for the establishment and operation of a theater ballistic missile defense system in the Asia-Pacific region" to protect "key regional allies."[13] This phraseology was meant to include Taiwan.

The PRC vehemently objects to such a scenario because it would presumably degrade (probably only modestly) its capacity to strike Taiwan, could tighten Washington-Taipei security linkages (through the possible flow of early warning data and command-and-control requirements), and would further involve the United States in an internal Chinese problem. From the perspective of some Americans, Taiwan participation in TMD would enhance security (and thereby confidence) on the island, such systems would seem self-evidently defensive and a response to Beijing's growing missile force, and U.S. sales to Taipei would help lower the per unit costs of a TMD system for Washington. While the configurations and price of such systems currently are unknown, costs will be very high, perhaps requiring items such as Aegis seaborne systems at an approximate cost of more than $1 billion per ship—this is big business as well as security.[14]

Possible ways out of the TMD conundrum that Washington faces are to simply not talk about selling Taiwan a system that does not yet exist, seek restraint from Beijing in its own missile development in the strait area (which might cool Taipei's ardor to buy an expensive system of uncertain value), assist Taiwan in developing its own system (though this would be very expensive), and develop a sea-based system that remains under U.S. control and is dedicated to a broader regional mission.

There is a further consideration, however. If Taipei loses faith in the American security relationship and does not have access to foreign military equipment and technology, it may seek to achieve deterrence of the PRC by rekindling its apparently terminated nuclear weapons project (a project that may have started as early as the 1960s and extended to the late 1980s). Were that project rekindled, it would not only dangerously escalate tensions in the Taiwan Strait, but would also leave U.S. nonproliferation policy in tatters.

In contrast to the tensions created by politics and technology, there are factors that tend to moderate conflict, most notably cross-strait economic and people-to-people ties.[15] In late 1998 the volume of Taiwan capital actually invested in the mainland (i.e., realized investment) was $20.86 billion; pledged Taiwan investment in the PRC totaled $40.16 billion; and around 40,600 Taiwan companies were doing business on the mainland.[16] Much of this Taiwan investment in the mainland produces exports to the United States; the shoe industry is a notable example.

While such economic integration is an enormous asset for maintaining a fabric of common interest across the strait, it has also created problems in managing the relationship in all three capitals. For Washington, unilateral economic trade sanctions against Beijing have become less desirable because in imposing them on the PRC, one inadvertently hits Taiwan firms located on the mainland whose output was destined for the American market. Goods that previously came to the United States from Taiwan firms on the island now come from Taiwan firms in the PRC. This development has contributed substantially to the increasing PRC trade surplus with the United States.

For Taiwan, increasing economic dependence on trade with, and investment in, the PRC raises the difficult issue of becoming overly dependent on one's chief security threat. For example, Taiwan had perhaps a $90 billion cumulative trade surplus with the PRC at the end of 1998.[17] On the other hand, while one might worry about such export dependence, failing to achieve adequate production scales for its industry to remain competitive is also a threat to Taiwan's economic base. That challenge can be most readily met by tapping the Chinese market.[18]

Conversely, for the PRC, as investment from Taiwan increases (about 7.2 percent of cumulative foreign capital invested on the mainland had come from the island by late 1998),[19] the more PRC constituencies (localities, companies, and individuals) become dependent on those flows continuing. Predictably, these constituencies argue for restraint toward Taiwan, though their actual influence is unclear. In short, while economic interdependence across the strait is a factor for stability and cooperation, it also complicates the management of the relationship in each capital.

BEIJING, HONG KONG (LONDON), AND WASHINGTON

Prior to the violence in Tiananmen Square in June 1989, while David Wilson was governor of the Royal Crown Colony, the Hong Kong government and the Foreign Office in London were worried that the United States, through good intentions, but bungling execution, might complicate the ongoing discussions with Beijing over reversion of the territory to Chinese sovereignty on July 1, 1997. London and the Hong Kong government wanted Washington to express its support for progress in the reversion negotiations; to assure them that U.S. law would be modified to maintain continuity in U.S.-Hong Kong economic, intergovernmental, and cultural relationships in the postreversion period; and to otherwise stay in the background.

Given that U.S.-China relations under Presidents Reagan and Bush were generally quite positive from December 1984 (when the Joint Declaration of the Government of the United Kingdom of Great Britain and Northern Ireland and the Government of the People's Republic of China on the Question of Hong Kong was signed) to June 1989, what amounted to a common desire on the part of London and Beijing presented no particular problem for Washington. That Margaret Thatcher was Britain's prime minister (1979–1990) further reduced anxieties in Washington, though some observers, both British and American, noted that her remarks were not always taken well by the Chinese. While China viewed the nineteenth-century agreements by which Britain came to govern Hong Kong as illegitimate "unequal treaties," Prime Minister Thatcher had intoned at a Hong Kong press conference in 1982, "You know that treaties are made to be kept.... [I]f a country will not stand by one treaty, it would not stand by another treaty."[20]

With the military crackdown in June 1989 in Beijing, however, the management of this multiparty relationship changed. London and Hong Kong sought firmer support from the Americans. This, along with a growing democracy movement in Hong Kong and the subsequent arrival of Chris Patten as governor, led Beijing to become increasingly suspicious of London's motives, believing Great Britain sought to leave behind a destabilizing fifth column in 1997 and to "internationalize" a bilateral issue. The PRC became correspondingly more anxious about unwanted American intrusion into its internal affairs and the possibility of British-American collusion.

One way Hong Kong Governor David Wilson sought to restore battered confidence in Hong Kong after June 1989 was by committing the territory to build a huge, modern airport to replace the aging, insufficient Kai Tak facility in Kowloon. This project (which eventually cost US$20 billion[21] when it was completed in 1998) was "[o]n a scale with the rebuilding of Kuwait after the Gulf War."[22] Even prior to the 1989 Tiananmen bloodshed, the then Jardine Matheson "Taipan," Brian M. Powers, explained to me how airport expansion was central to the economic health of the city and the confidence of the business community as July 1, 1997, approached. A community that will not invest in itself lacks confidence, and a community without confidence has little future. Economically, the new airport was needed to handle the growing throughput to and from the rapidly expanding South China export machine; from 1985 to 1990 reexports were growing at an average annual rate of 29 percent.[23] Politically, the project became a tangible expression of the departing government's confidence in Hong Kong's economic and political future. Finally, as part of the confidence-building enterprise, and in order to show that Hong Kong could act with "a high degree of autonomy," the project was undertaken with a minimum of consultation with Beijing.

Initial intentions aside, the fight between the Hong Kong government (and London) and Beijing that followed the airport's announcement did not inspire confidence within the territory or abroad. As Wilson's successor, Christopher Patten, later noted, the airport controversy "undermined him [Wilson] politically."[24] The more London and Hong Kong sought to act on their own in order to reinforce the territory's autonomy, the more Beijing was driven to assert its interests and reiterate that nothing of significance could occur without PRC approval. London and the Hong Kong government were reluctant to consult with Beijing, knowing full well that consultation would be turned into a protracted negotiation. There was also the issue of pride—the British feeling that they had been good stewards of Hong Kong's interests for 150 years, that they would continue to be such without Beijing's instruction until their departure, and that, in Prime Minister Thatcher's words, Britain had a "moral" obligation to its soon-to-be former subjects.

Beijing's predictable reaction fed the worst British, American, and Western fears about the PRC's propensities to meddle. Beijing had not been meaningfully consulted before the airport project was announced, and given the baseline Chinese distrust of the British, the activities of many Hong Kong citizens in support of demonstrators in Beijing in May and early June 1989, and the very large anti-Beijing demonstrations in the territory after the bloodshed on June 4 (involving about one-sixth of the colony's population), the PRC was extremely wary. Consequently, Beijing (usually in the person of Lu Ping, head of the Hong Kong and Macao Affairs Office) raised a series of objections concerning the airport's financing, subcontracts, China's possible liability for financial obligations after reversion, how the territory's financial reserves would be used, current and future tax rates (with Beijing taking the low-tax, pro-business perspective!), and, most important, the need for London and the colonial government to obtain Beijing's agreement before making commitments that would entail obligations extending beyond the handover date of July 1, 1997. In effect, Beijing wanted prior consultation on major decisions made *prior* to reversion—something Britain and the Hong Kong government were loath to do.

For many Hong Kong citizens (and for many in Washington and London), Beijing's interventionism brought into question two pillars of the PRC's 1990 Basic Law (the city's post–July 1, 1997, miniconstitution): "Hong Kong people administering Hong Kong" and the HKSAR having "a high degree of autonomy."

All the while, the forces of democratic pluralism were getting stronger in Hong Kong under the leadership of Martin Lee and many others. Their key issues from 1989 on were the percentage of the Legislative Council (LEGCO) to be elected (as opposed to appointed), the definition of voting constituencies, and the time period over which liberalization would be achieved in Hong Kong. The growing democratic impulse in Hong Kong, the endless negotiations with Beijing over the airport, and the mounting domestic criticism of his government for being too accommodating to Beijing led Prime Minister John Major (who succeeded Margaret Thatcher in 1990) to look for a way to more credibly associate his government with a tougher, pro-democratic line toward the PRC.

Major's frustration reached its zenith when he had to resolve the airport issue by being the first Western leader to travel to post-Tiananmen China (September 2–4, 1991), though Japanese Prime Minister Kaifu had visited the PRC the month before.[25] While in Beijing, Major met Prime Minister Li Peng, the person indelibly associated in the West with the June

1989 violence (see Chapter 8). Mindful of those in Britain and in Hong Kong who were critical of his trip (Martin Lee had accused Britain of "appeasement"),[26] Major countered, "I raised the treatment of religious believers in Tibet and elsewhere, and I raised the detention of people in China for expressing the freedom of expression, predominantly student demonstrators. I asked Prime Minister Li Peng to take a personal interest in all these cases."[27]

London's need to deal with Beijing to secure Hong Kong's economic and political future meant that Governor Wilson *and* Prime Minister Major were both subject to increasing domestic attack. It was in this environment that, on April 25, 1992, Major named Chairman of the Conservative Party Christopher F. Patten (Major's 1992 campaign manager, who lost his own seat in Parliament the same year and to whom Major was indebted) to the post of governor of Hong Kong. Patten arrived in Hong Kong as the twenty-eighth (and final) governor on July 9, 1992, the first strictly political appointee to ever hold the post. Patten, himself, saw that he would present a problem for the Foreign Office. He said, "The notion of a politician arriving in the job with, conceivably, his own questions and his own ideas was bad enough; what was worse was to have a politician senior enough to have a direct line to the Prime Minister and the Foreign Secretary. With a former cabinet minister as Governor, policy was clearly more likely to be initiated in Hong Kong than in London or Peking."[28]

A skilled orator and an attractive politician, Patten was dedicated to taking a tougher, pro-democratic line in negotiations with Beijing. Such a stand was seen as worthy of support in Britain and essential to restore confidence in post-Tiananmen Hong Kong as it approached reversion five years hence. Patten's approach was also welcome in the halls of the U.S. Congress and in the American mass media—though many American professional diplomats and sinologists were torn between appreciation for Governor Patten's values and goals and a belief that his approach would make Beijing all the more intractable. Patten's decision not to stop in Beijing on his way to taking up his post in Hong Kong was a straw in the wind for the next five years. He later explained this decision: "The politics of going to Peking before I had arrived in Hong Kong and appearing (not least since the Chinese would leak their side of any meeting) to sell out Hong Kong's freedom and democracy for agreement on an airport would ensure that when I did arrive in the territory, I would be the lamest ever of lame ducks."[29] This decision along with his flesh-pumping, populist style maximized Beijing's anxiety. The more credibility Patten had in London, Hong Kong, and Washington, the more distrust he inspired in Beijing.

Patten brought one other, little-noticed attitude to his governorship. In May 1989, on the eve of the Tiananmen violence, when Chinese democratic impulses were most evident, Patten had visited Beijing to attend meetings of the Asian Development Bank in his then capacity as minister for overseas development. At the time, he described Beijing as "a city bubbling with excitement and intoxicated with hope."[30] After hearing the soothing words of Foreign Office China experts and having heard Zhao Ziyang speak reassuringly about the demonstrations, Patten left Beijing "convinced ... that the demonstrations would end peacefully."[31] When the demonstrations ended instead in violence, one senses that Patten's views of both China experts (particularly in the Foreign Office) and the PRC's leaders were forever altered.

On September 1, 1992, not long after Patten's arrival in the territory, a small group of Americans, of which I was a member, met with him at Government House. At that time, the governor was preparing for his maiden address to LEGCO (to be delivered on October 7, 1992). He told us that he was striving to find a balance between "the present and Chinese limits," and that it was his intention to fill in the ambiguities in the 1984 Sino-British Joint Declaration in a way that increased the democratic character of Hong Kong. While he would "stick with [agreed-upon] numbers" in terms of the evolution of Hong Kong's electoral system, "he would redefine the rules of election in each category" in ways that expanded the universal character of the franchise.[32] This political reform package would be announced with minimal consultation with Beijing. As I left that breakfast with Governor Patten I thought to myself that he was an admirable, articulate person, but that he had no idea that the speeding vehicle he was driving would soon run head-on into the Great Wall—and he wasn't wearing a seat belt.

In his October 7 address to LEGCO,[33] Governor Patten announced his intention to accelerate the pace of electoral change without having reached any agreement with Beijing. Indeed, China's chief negotiator on Hong Kong, Lu Ping, subsequently told me that Beijing had received a text of Patten's speech with so little time to react that it was clear that the PRC's input was not genuinely desired. This set the stage for increased criticism from Beijing, and from there the relationship rapidly descended into name-calling. "Buddha's serpent," "villain for one thousand years," "pirate," "prostitute," and "tango dancer" were among the more memorable epithets Beijing hurled at the governor in the aftermath of his LEGCO address and over the years that followed.

The essence of Patten's political reforms was that a greater percentage of members of the LEGCO would be elected by procedures approximating

universal suffrage than had been envisioned in the Sino-British negotiations and understandings, the voting age would be lowered, and there
would be a clear separation between legislative and executive authority.
The entire transition process prior to Patten had been built on the notion
of *consultation* between the British and Chinese. For most westerners *consultation* means, "I'll tell you before I act; I will take into account what you
say; but I will proceed as I deem fit after having considered your point of
view." For the Chinese, *consultation* tends to mean, "You won't move
ahead until I agree." Patten's unilateral moves were, by Beijing's definition, both not consultative and inconsistent with the letter and spirit of
prior understandings over the preceding eight years.

Further, Patten was beefing up LEGCO's status relative to the executive
branch in the Hong Kong political structure. The Chinese preferred to in-
herit an executive-led system such as the British had maintained in the
colony for the preceding century and one-half. Consequently, in March
1993, warning the United States to "stay out of the row,"[34] Beijing announced that it would replace Hong Kong's LEGCO elected under Patten's
reform rules at the moment reversion occurred—12:01 A.M., July 1, 1997.
Upon reversion, a Provisional Legislature would take LEGCO's place until
new elections, consistent with Beijing's views of the original Sino-British
understandings, could occur.[35]

This situation provides insight into the general problem of managing
third-party ties in Sino-American relations. The combination of tangible
American interests in the Hong Kong transition (30,000 U.S. expatriates
living in the territory, 1,200 American firms, at least $12 billion in U.S. FDI
in the city as of 1996)[36] and the symbolic utility to U.S. politicians of seeking to involve themselves in the Sino-British dispute made it unlikely that
Washington would remain on the sidelines as the tension-laden reversion
process unfolded.

In the context of the long and complex relationship between the United
States and Great Britain, there was an overlay of British sentiment that
the not-too-subtle Americans, in their enthusiasm, might upset delicate
and sophisticated arrangements painstakingly worked out with Beijing.
And yet London and the Hong Kong government did want Washington's
support. Conversely, the dominant impulse of many Americans was to admire Governor Patten's values and style, though some steeped in Chinese
history and culture wondered whether his brashness was not working to
the detriment of his democratic objectives. Admiration, an inclination to
support one another, and a mutual wariness were the contending senti-

ments of the American-British relationship in terms of Hong Kong in the 1990–1997 period.

Beyond government, however, there were other key players, particularly the democratic activists in Hong Kong. Among them, there was a belief that if left to their own devices the British would sacrifice democracy in the territory to a smooth transition and England's long-term economic interests with Beijing. Consequently, Martin Lee (head of the United Democrats of Hong Kong, later the Democratic Party) assiduously cultivated support on Capitol Hill, particularly with the membership and the staff of the Senate Committee on Foreign Relations and Senator Mitch McConnell. During some of this period a young American activist worked tirelessly on Lee's staff. Thus forces within the democratic community in Hong Kong played no small role in shaping the U.S.–Hong Kong Policy Act of 1992 (the McConnell Bill). Five years later these same groups helped facilitate the April 1997 withdrawal of U.S. government funding from a LEGCO delegation visiting the United States because it included two individuals who had been named to the future Provisional Legislature—a body that had no legitimacy in the eyes of some of Hong Kong's democratically elected legislators and most members of the U.S. Congress (see Chapter 8 for more). China responded to that withdrawal of funds by saying the action "will make it [the U.S. Congress] the laughingstock of the world."[37] The *Hong Kong Standard* carried an article entitled "Legislature Faces Puerile Obstacles."[38]

At the same time, however, Martin Lee feared that the U.S. Congress, in its enthusiasm to support democracy in Hong Kong and human rights in both the territory and in the PRC, might withdraw MFN status from Beijing, thereby harming Hong Kong's economy and citizens. On trips to the United States from 1990 on, Lee made it clear that the withdrawal of MFN status would not be welcomed by Hong Kong's already anxious citizenry, including many of its democratic activists.

For the Chinese, the close historical association of the United Kingdom and the United States, along with Washington's visceral support for faster democratization in Hong Kong and the connections between the democratic forces in Hong Kong and Capitol Hill, all fanned distrust of the British, the Hong Kong democratic forces, and the United States. In its darker moments, Beijing professed to believe that Washington's behavior betrayed an "attempt to fill in the space left by Britain's withdrawal, use Hong Kong to contain the mainland and hinder China's development … probably a chessman move by the United States in its chessboard strategy."[39]

The Beijing, Hong Kong (London), and Washington relationship went through three phases:

(1) Before the June 1989 violence in Beijing, Britain and the PRC both wanted the United States to guarantee the continuity of U.S. commercial, intergovernmental, and cultural involvement with Hong Kong after the July 1, 1997, reversion of the city to Chinese sovereignty as the HKSAR. Both sides basically wanted the Americans to keep up ties, keep investing, keep quiet, and not rock the boat!

(2) After the Tiananmen Square crackdown, London sought a more visible (but noninterventionist) U.S. commitment to the territory's future and the democratization process, while simultaneously hoping that Washington would not go so far as to totally alienate Beijing and complicate matters. Both London and the Hong Kong government thought that if there were no U.S.–Hong Kong Policy Act to placate angry members of the U.S. Congress, then the chances for MFN revocation by Congress would increase, a far worse alternative in their view. Consequently, London and the Hong Kong government tacitly supported a moderate version of the U.S.–Hong Kong Policy Act of 1992 (discussed in Chapter 3). In speaking of the U.S.–Hong Kong Policy Act working its way through Congress in May 1992, a most senior member of the Hong Kong government described to me the delicate balancing act: "[The act] is well intentioned, and there is a need. We don't want MFN taken away. Our public position [on the act is] that it's a matter for the U.S. Privately, we have anxiety, that though it is well intentioned it will hurt us. The Chinese want us to intervene against it in Congress. To take a public position against the bill in Washington would hurt us on MFN [continuation]."[40]

Further, from 1990 to 1997 the Hong Kong government openly urged Washington to resist the impulse to punish Beijing's human rights infractions in ways that would devastate Hong Kong, most notably by opposing MFN withdrawal from Beijing. Indeed, those elements of the U.S. executive branch, Capitol Hill, and the business community that favored MFN extension welcomed the participation of Hong Kong in the battle because, particularly with Governor Patten's democratic credentials, one could argue that one favored *both* human rights and democracy in China and Hong Kong *and* business with China.

For its part, Beijing was convinced that the Americans and British were working hand-in-glove to make the reversion as difficult as possible and leave behind a political fifth column—the democratic parties and loyal bureaucrats in the civil service—and that, further, London was "playing the international card on Hong Kong" by seeking U.S. support for Governor Patten's political reform package.[41] The Chinese position on the U.S.–Hong Kong Policy Act was articulated to me in May 1992, when a senior Chinese official in the territory said, "The Chinese Government opposes the McConnell Bill. We don't want this problem internationalized. Hong Kong is an international economic center, not a political center. You don't have a need for this act."[42]

(3) The last of the three stages took place in the postreversion period. Once established on July 1, 1997, the new HKSAR government led by shipping magnate C. H. Tung welcomed U.S. economic involvement in Hong Kong and sought to minimize political anxieties in Washington, while still proceeding to dismantle the Patten LEGCO and electoral reforms discussed previously. Tung's first major trip abroad was to the United States in September 1997. Beijing remained remarkably restrained in talking about Hong Kong, and even granted port access to the HKSAR by the United States Navy, though in the wake of the bombing of the Chinese Embassy in Belgrade in May 1999, Beijing temporarily ceased approving such visits, a move that cost local service providers in the HKSAR considerable income. Nonetheless, from late 1997 on, as the economic crisis in Asia deepened, overall there was "a tangible switch in Hong Kong to viewing Beijing as a source of support as opposed to a negative force."[43]

By 1999, a new equilibrium had been established among Beijing, Washington, and Hong Kong, at least for the time being. Hong Kong's biggest postreversion problems in the 1997–1999 period were not interventionism by Beijing, but an epidemic affecting chickens in late 1997 and early 1998 and the impact of the Asian financial crisis. C. H. Tung noted in an interview in January 1998 that every problem he and his administration had confronted since reversion had been unexpected a year earlier and that all of the problems that had been anticipated earlier—particularly fears of possible PRC repression, manipulation, or meddling—had not materialized. Ironically, he said that he found himself hoping for a little *more* interaction with Beijing and that even the head of the Hong Kong and Macao Affairs Office in Beijing "doesn't want to come here—nothing to do."[44]

Shortly after Tung made these remarks, U.S. Congressman Doug Bereuter of Nebraska, chairman of the Speaker's Task Force on the Hong Kong Transition that visited the HKSAR, gave a general "so far, so good" evaluation to the transition, noting that there was one principal nagging question: "Are Hong Kong officials subtly anticipating what Beijing desires and not in all instances vigorously pursuing the autonomy they have out of fear they will upset Beijing?"[45] This was something to consider, but a worry far different from the general prereversion expectation of glaring, heavy-handed Beijing interference. Time will tell, whither Hong Kong. The answer will never fail to influence Sino-American relations.

Lessons of Taiwan and Hong Kong

A comparison of the Hong Kong and Taiwan cases yields at least two lessons of note with regard to the challenges of managing third-party interactions in the Sino-American relationship. The first lesson is that the U.S. Congress can be a decisive and important player that sometimes acts in ways that are helpful and sometimes in ways that are not. When a third party does not like U.S. executive branch policies or tendencies with respect to China, it can cultivate support on Capitol Hill to immobilize or change them. With respect to Hong Kong, Martin Lee built extensive support on Capitol Hill and played a key role in motivating and shaping the adoption of the 1992 U.S.–Hong Kong Policy Act and in getting Capitol Hill to come out clearly against the Provisional Legislature. In the case of Taiwan, President Lee Teng-hui probably never would have been granted a visa to visit Cornell University in mid-1995 had there not been overwhelming votes in the House and the Senate forcing President Clinton's hand. These votes represented the outcome of spontaneous sentiment on Capitol Hill *and* sophisticated lobbying by Taiwan. Similarly, it may well be that in mid-1999 President Lee would not have made his "special state-to-state" declaration if he had not been confident that he had support on Capitol Hill.

Second, third parties themselves often are fragmented, with each faction seeking out that part of the American political system that it views as most sympathetic to its cause. For instance, while Martin Lee focused throughout the early and mid-1990s on the mass media, sympathetic members of Congress and congressional staff, and human rights organizations, the Hong Kong government and the Hong Kong business community (persons such as Ronnie Chan, Victor Fung, and Eric Hotung) devoted more attention to the American business community, the executive branch, and members of Congress concerned with trade. Of course, the result of this fragmentation can be that the Americans are unclear about what the third party actually wants and who speaks for it.

The Hong Kong and Taiwan cases provide an interesting contrast, particularly with regard to President Lee Teng-hui getting a visa to visit Cornell University in May 1995. In that instance, nearly all Taiwan-oriented forces were pushing the U.S. government in one direction. There was little discernible tension among them—beyond a few persons (often in Taiwan's Foreign Ministry) who distrusted Lee and worried about Beijing's angry response to a high-profile visit. It seemed that Taiwan spoke with one voice, and Congress listened. As for Hong Kong, extremely credible residents of the territory were on all sides of the issue, a reality that, in the end, elicited a more thoughtful and nuanced policy response from Washington.

Finally, it is notable how passive and reactive Beijing generally was in shaping the perceptions of key players in the American political process. Indeed, it was only after what it regarded as the 1995 Taiwan visa debacle that Beijing seriously turned its attention to beefing up its congressional liaison function. However, as soon as it did so, Beijing immediately became the target of allegations that some of its attempts were inappropriate or illegal (see Chapters 7 and 8).

WASHINGTON, BEIJING, AND MOSCOW

As we saw in Chapter 1, even before he took office, George Bush and his national security adviser, Brent Scowcroft, were primed to go to China. Their motives included the desire to solidify relations with Beijing before Mikhail Gorbachev traveled there later in the year.

More generally, throughout the 1989–1991 period, Bush was careful to avoid taking actions that would foster disadvantageous Sino-Soviet cooperation. This, in part, accounts for Bush's relatively restrained reaction to the bloodshed in and around Tiananmen Square. As we saw in Chapter 1, during his February 1989 trip to the PRC, much of the president's time with Deng Xiaoping and other Chinese leaders was consumed with exploration of one another's views of Gorbachev, his reforms, and the future foreign policy posture of Moscow.[46] Even with the demise of the Soviet Union in late 1991, the Russian polity and landmass continued to be a concern (and opportunity) to both nations; such considerations have created, and continue to create, opportunities for mutual diplomatic maneuvering. As American global power and dominance grew throughout the 1990s, both

Moscow and Beijing came to perceive a shared interest in somehow creating another international power pole to offset U.S. advantage. As Moscow's news agency ITAR-TASS put it in June 1999 in reference to the visit of Chinese Vice Chairman of the Central Military Commission Zhang Wannian to the Russian Far East: Zhang "supports 'the policy toward creating a pole which should ensure the protection of our states against encroachment by [an]other party.' "[47] Russian Defense Minister Igor Sergeyev put it this way when meeting his Chinese counterpart Chi Haotian in Kazakhstan in March 2000: The two countries' defense ministries "are flagships of implementing the political agreements of our leaders."[48]

The most dramatic event in the cold war's protracted end was the collapse of the Soviet Union and its transformation into the nominally democratic Russian Federation under Boris Yeltsin in December 1991. In 1991 much more than politics changed in the region. Suddenly, the USSR that had covered 22.4 million square kilometers[49] became the Russia that covered 17 million square kilometers.[50] The USSR that in 1989 had an ethnic makeup of about 50 percent Russians became the Russia that in 1994 was ethnically 83 percent Russian.[51] The Soviet Union that once had a 7,000-kilometer border with the PRC became the Russia that now had a *mere* 4,300-kilometer border with China,[52] with three new states (Kazakhstan, Kyrgyzstan, and Tajikistan) emerging from the old USSR to complicate Beijing's management of its northwestern frontiers. The USSR that had 12,200 strategic nuclear warheads[53] became the Russia that by January 1998 had 6,680.[54] And perhaps most poignant of all, life expectancy for males in Russia dropped from 63.4 years in 1990 to 56.5 in 1996.[55]

Among the most consequential changes for U.S.-China relations was the disappearance of a common enemy. The anxiety that Beijing and Washington had shared concerning Moscow since the 1960s had provided a rationale for productive bilateral ties since the initial days of Richard Nixon's first administration. Indeed, in his earliest conversations with Mao Zedong and other Chinese officials, Henry Kissinger repeatedly sought to reassure them that America would not welcome Sino-Soviet war,[56] telling Chairman Mao on February 17–18, 1973, for example, that "[i]f they [the Soviet Union] attack China, we would certainly oppose them for our own reasons."[57] The shared Soviet threat had made it logical for Nixon and Kissinger to make it clear to Moscow in 1969 that an attack against the PRC was not in American interests,[58] to share sensitive, high-resolution satellite pictures of Moscow's force dispositions along the Sino-Soviet border with Beijing in October 1971,[59] as well as to later share data on Soviet missile tests gathered in western China in jointly established facilities.[60] As Kissinger put it to Chinese UN Ambassador Huang Hua in December 1971, "But we would be prepared . . . to give you whatever information we have about the disposition of Soviet forces. . . . You don't need a master spy. We give you everything (handing over his file)."[61]

In addition, this shared anxiety prompted Washington to agree to sell Beijing certain categories of "nonlethal" military equipment in 1980 and to broaden the categories of military items sold thereafter, particularly in the Reagan administration when Caspar Weinberger was secretary of defense.[62] Indeed, the Ford administration had started down this road in 1975–1976, most notably with its covert support of British Rolls-Royce jet engines being sold to the PRC.[63] The Soviet threat also provided the rationale for the explicit cooperation between the two capitals to support the mujahideen "freedom fighters" who were resisting the invading Soviet army in Afghanistan from 1979 to 1989.[64] This cooperation included the CIA's purchase of 107-millimeter rockets from the PRC and their transfer into mujahideen hands,[65] as well as the purchase of thousands of Chinese mules to transport the goods.[66]

The sense of common threat had other effects as well. Such effects are nowhere so well demonstrated as in the attitudes and behavior of the early Reagan administration toward Taiwan. President Reagan came into office well disposed toward Taiwan, having said on August 25, 1980, "It is absurd and not required by the [Taiwan Relations] Act that our representatives are not permitted to meet Taiwanese officials with fairness and dignity."[67] The trouble this position could cause in U.S.-China relations, however, became immediately apparent in a flap over whether a representative of Taipei would attend the January 20, 1981, inauguration ceremonies as an "invited guest." The situation was finally resolved with the "disinvitation" of the prospective Taiwan guest. Regarding the situation, Secretary of State Alexander Haig subsequently observed that "it seemed imperative to me that the Administration recognize that American relations with China was among the most important strategic questions of our times."[68]

The demise of the Soviet Union and the seeming end of that threat as the decisive consideration in U.S. policy toward China, however, has not meant the end of triangular politics among Moscow, Beijing, and Washington in the post–cold war era.[69] In the course of Boris Yeltsin's April 1996 trip to the PRC, the two nations announced "their resolve to develop a strategic partnership of equality, mutual confidence and mutual coordination toward the twenty-first century."[70] Yeltsin was so enthusiastic that he observed, "Our communists . . . are fanatics. But here, they are pragmatists."[71] Both nations had multiple objectives in this upgraded relationship, one of which was to gain leverage over Washington. With Sino-American ties deteriorating because of missile exercises in the Taiwan Strait in mid-1995 and March 1996 and Chinese alarm at the strengthening of the U.S.-Japan alliance, Beijing saw gains to be made from moving closer to Moscow. As one Chinese strategic analyst in Shanghai put it, "If we don't have good relations with the U.S. we can have them with Moscow."[72] The difficulties in U.S.-China relations in 1999 reinforced this logic.

Beijing's policy toward Russia has its origins primarily in domestic Chinese needs. Nonetheless, trying to gain leverage over Washington through their bilateral interaction is a significant consideration for both Beijing and Moscow. Washington ought not play into this game by being overly concerned about the Sino-Russian "strategic partnership," because as a matter of strategic reality, as well as diplomatic tactics, there are limits to how far genuine cooperation between Beijing and Moscow can proceed under late-1990s conditions. As Walter A. McDougall put it in 1993, "A Russo-Chinese détente is not impossible, but except for the monetary savings to be gained from reducing frontier deployments, neither country has much the other needs. What Russia and China need is the capital, technology or markets of Japan and America."[73]

Beijing's relations with Moscow and Washington reflect its domestic interests, the broad economic reform strategy it has implemented since the late 1970s, general concepts of international relations, and a larger strategic architecture that has governed Chinese foreign policy since General Secretary Hu Yaobang enunciated China's "independent foreign policy" at the fall 1982 Twelfth Party Congress. The concept of independent foreign policy represented a decision to readjust the PRC's previous tilt toward the United States and to pursue a multidirectional, balanced, and economically grounded foreign policy.[74] As one PRC foreign policy official told me, China has "no problem making our foreign and domestic tasks mesh."[75]

Three facets of China's domestic reform strategy were critical from the viewpoint of Sino-Soviet (later Sino-Russian) relations: (1) China's defense budget would be severely constrained for a decade or two, as discussed in Chapter 2; (2) conflict along the PRC's borders had to be minimized so that domestic economic development could proceed in a secure external environment that permitted minimal defense expenditures, and good relations with Moscow could provide access to less expensive military technology; and (3) China's heartland areas would initially be disadvantaged by the focus on coastal development and therefore forced to look for their economic opportunities in contiguous areas (for China's northeast and west, the Russian Far East, Siberia, and later the central Asian states were the targets of opportunity).

These interlocking domestic and foreign policy considerations account for the fact that from 1982 Beijing consistently has sought to improve relations first with Leonid Brezhnev (in his last months of life), then with Mikhail Gorbachev, later still with Boris Yeltsin, and thereafter with Yeltsin's successor Vladimir Putin. These were four vastly different leaders, in their politics as well as their personalities, but this had relatively little to do with Chinese calculations. Hu Yaobang put China's flexibility on policy toward the Soviet Union this way: "[F]or politicians, hatred is something which they can forget after a night's sleep. I do not agree with the view that it is difficult to move the piled-up resentment between China and the Soviet Union."[76]

Though Sino-Soviet relations had started their gradual thaw under Brezhnev and Gorbachev in the 1980s, it was not until the collapse of the Soviet Union and the rise of Yeltsin that some of the most significant progress was made. Once the new Russian president had stabilized his position in Moscow, Yeltsin traveled to China in December 1992. The trip produced accords on commercial relations, nuclear power cooperation, the purchase of military equipment and technology, and border military forces.[77] The 1992 accords provided China's inland provinces near the Russian border (Heilongjiang in particular) a chance (or a hope) to profit from expanded trade opportunities. In the beginning hopes were realized with trade increases in 1992 and 1993: total two-way Sino-Russian trade peaked at 4 percent of the PRC's total trade and 7 percent of Russia's in 1993 (see table 4).[78] Since then, however, Sino-Russian trade growth was a disappointment to both sides, dropping considerably as a percentage of total trade for each by 1996. In December 1996 China and Russia agreed to boost two-way trade to $20 billion by the year 2000, but by 1999 it was merely $5.7 billion; clearly the year 2000 goal would be missed by a very wide margin.[79]

In addition to trade, the military agreements made in 1992 held the prospect for the PLA to acquire badly needed and relatively advanced military equipment and technology at fire sale prices, including advanced fighter jets, missile and antiaircraft systems, submarines and surface ships, cruise missiles, and bombers, among other items.[80] The 1992 military-related accords were followed up in November 1993 when Russian Defense Minister Pavel Grachev signed a five-year military cooperation agreement that focused on China's acquisition of military know-how and technology.[81] By 1999, Beijing was shopping for even newer aircraft, dangling the prospect of purchases in front of the noses of Russia's beleaguered aircraft industry.[82]

Parenthetically, although these purchases did not rapidly and dramatically shift big power relations, the actual and planned acquisitions have had a number of perceptual and practical consequences. The purchases, for example, have increased Taiwan's alarm about its own capacity to maintain air superiority over the strait and its ability to break a blockade that could be imposed by the PRC. Among the nations surrounding China, in the Philippines for example, there is concern about greater power projection by Beijing. And with respect to America, greater Chinese capacity to inflict damage on the U.S. Navy and other U.S. forces in the region looks like an effort to raise the costs of any possible intervention in the Taiwan Strait and thereby deter such a move by Washington. Moreover, the presence in China of up to 2,000 Russian scientists and technicians working on defense-related new technologies increases Washington's concerns about possible breakthroughs that could alter calculations.[83]

As the above events unfolded, security was enhanced by gradually resolving most territorial issues between Russia and the PRC. In April 1996 and April 1997, Russia, China, and the three central Asian states of Kazakhstan, Kyrgyzstan, and Tajikistan (the "Shanghai Five") agreed to confidence-building measures along their respective borders, including a reduction in armed forces in the boundary region.[84]

While Beijing's principal motivations for improved relations with Moscow stem from the considerations enumerated above (trade, technology, military items, and security), the post–cold war era in U.S.-Russian relations also has created tensions that Beijing's leaders believe they can exploit to gain leverage over Washington and to weaken post-Tiananmen sanctions. The crux of the Chinese analysis since the early 1990s has been that there is an inherent conflict between Moscow and Washington that limits their ability to cooperate: "Since Russia is 'no longer what it was' and dares not break up with the West, it is forced to make concessions in a weak-kneed fashion.... Once it has recovered sufficient to stand on its feet, its conflicts with the West, especially with US hegemonism, are bound to sharpen. It will not accept the attempts of the United States to build a 'unipolar world.' "[85]

There are four categories of either latent or actual Russo-American friction that Beijing believes it can exploit. First is Russian frustration with the level of Washington's economic and technical assistance since 1991; it has been far less than Moscow had hoped for. For instance, Freedom Support Act funding for Russia from the U.S. Agency for International Development (and USAID transfers through other U.S. agencies) peaked in 1994 and then fell off every year thereafter, even as Russia's economic difficulties deepened. By 1998 such expenditures were a mere 8 percent of their 1994 high.[86] In Chinese words, "Moscow feels more and more that the Clinton administration's willingness to help Russia is only a means to make Russia bow and scrape before the United States."[87] By late 1998, in the wake of Russia's drastic devaluation of the ruble and President Clinton's visit to Moscow, it was clear that assistance from Washington was to be minimal and consist mostly of humanitarian aid (3.1 million tons of food).[88]

Second, China believes that America's strategic goal is to keep Russia weak and encircled. The natural Russian resentment that flows from this can be utilized by Beijing. Most notable in this regard was the December 1997 NATO decision to enlarge NATO to include three central European states (Hungary, the Czech Republic, and Poland)—this was achieved in March 1999. As the NATO alliance moved eastward, Moscow saw it aimed at Russia, much as Beijing fears the strengthening of the U.S.-Japan alliance. Similarly, NATO's spring 1999 intervention in Kosovo against the Serbs, over Russian opposition, again created a shared interest in Moscow and Beijing, as they both tried to make the UN Security Council the sole legitimate organ capable of sanctioning international intervention.

Third, the Chinese perceive that Russian nationalism has been offended by the "U.S. attempt to 'play a leading role' in the world."[89]

And last, the United States has resisted all Russian attempts to assert privileges or rights in the newly independent states of the former Soviet Union. Collectively, these considerations create resentment in the former superpower that Beijing hopes it can exploit to its advantage in dealing with both Washington and Russia.

Even limited cooperation with Moscow is of value to Beijing for the following reasons: First, the Russia link affords a way to secure relatively advanced military and military-related technology inexpensively, one example being a gas-centrifuge plant to produce low-enriched uranium.[90] In the 1992–1996 period, Chinese purchases of advanced weapons and technology from Russia ranged from US$1 to $2 billion annually, making Russia Beijing's main weapons supplier and making the PRC an extremely important export market for the Russian arms industry.[91] In early 2000, the news agency TASS reported, "Russia's annual revenue from the sale of arms in recent years exceeded one billion dollars [annually], or nearly one-fifth of the total value of trade turnover between the two countries. China buys up to 40 percent of Russia's total arms exports."[92] As the Russian newspaper *Nezavisimaya Gazeta* put it,

"Moscow is ready to assist China's transformation into a first-class military power. Especially considering the fact that Beijing is ready to pay for that in freely convertible currency."[93]

Second, the Russo-Chinese relationship provides the United States additional, but not necessarily compelling, incentives to curtail its technology sanctions against Beijing. Paraphrasing one interviewee in the late 1990s, "[Y]ou are losing chances to sell China weapons."

And finally, both Russia and China distrust the United States' cold war alliances (NATO and the U.S.-Japan alliance respectively) and the post–cold war tendency of American and NATO interventionism, whether it be in the former Yugoslavia, Iraq, or North Korea. Given the United States' post–cold war ascendancy, Beijing and Moscow are drawn together by their shared views on sovereignty, independence, and multipolarity, "all anti-American code words."[94]

In their positions as permanent members of the UN Security Council, Moscow and Beijing have sought to restrain the exercise of American power under UN auspices, making it more difficult for the United States to employ force and sanctions in Bosnia,[95] Iraq,[96] Kosovo, and Macedonia. Part of Beijing's concern has been the tendency for the United States to act using NATO and to seek UN endorsement for independent NATO actions. In October 1998, for example, Chinese dissatisfaction (along with Russian disquiet) reached a boil with both countries threatening to veto[97] any UN Security Council resolution on Kosovo that would endorse NATO military retaliation against Belgrade.[98] In response to the U.S. and NATO decision to possibly use force and win subsequent UN approval, China's ambassador to the UN, Qin Huasun, said on October 24, "Such [an] irresponsible act does not befit the peaceful atmosphere surrounding the question of Kosovo and will not help solve the issue.... Furthermore, it has violated the purposes, principles and relevant provisions of the UN Charter, as well as international law.... It is a contempt and a challenge to the authority of the UN and the Security Council."[99]

Worse yet, from the Chinese and Russian perspectives, by spring 1999, without UN endorsement, NATO had launched a sustained, intense bombing campaign, hitting not only the site of Balkan conflict (Kosovo), but the Yugoslav capital of Belgrade as well. The *People's Daily* said, "The massive air strikes against the Yugoslav Federation launched by NATO headed by the United States mark the first time in its 50 years of existence that NATO has militarily intervened in the internal affairs of a non-NATO sovereign state without UN Security Council authorization.... The military intervention launched by NATO ... violate[s] Article Five of the

North Atlantic Treaty which lays down that military action 'must be strictly authorized by the United Nations or the Organization for Security and Cooperation in Europe.'"[100]

In this setting, Russian Prime Minister Yevgeny Primakov turned back from a March trip to the United States in mid-air (when the bombing was imminent). Chinese Premier Zhu Rongji came under domestic pressure to postpone his April 1999 trip to the United States (see Chapters 4 and 8), in part for the same reason. On March 31, 1999, he told a congressional group in Beijing, of which I was part, "We [Chinese] also have a congress and public opinion. We have seen the use of force against Yugoslavia ... and many people here say don't go to the United States."[101]

Thus both Russia and China chafe at the U.S. tendency to intervene using non-UN instrumentalities of which Moscow and Beijing are not members, and then to later seek UN endorsement or, worse yet, circumvent the United Nations entirely. Moscow and Beijing's roles as permanent members of the Security Council allow them to act together on the basis of this resentment. United States Secretary of State Madeleine Albright gave voice to the thought that bothered both Russia and China: NATO, she said, is "our institution of choice" for "defending western values on the continent."[102] In this ongoing debate over the role and scope of NATO activity, former Soviet President Mikhail Gorbachev asked, "Would NATO be willing to bomb Chechnya, or Russia for that matter? Or bomb Tibet, and risk a full-scale response from China?"[103]

Looking more broadly at the Russian-Chinese partnership, in 1998, one Chinese strategic analyst defined that partnership in the following terms:

> Defense of each other's national dignity and legitimate rights and interests through consultations over and coordination in international affairs. On the issue of NATO's eastern extension, which involves Russia's security interests, China "understands Russian anxieties" and holds that "NATO's action should meet the aspirations of all the countries in the region and benefit world peace." In April 1997, Russia cast a crucial vote of abstention, when deciding the issue of whether China's human rights conditions should be put on the agenda of the International Human Rights Convention, thereby frustrating the attempt of certain countries [the United States] to intervene in the internal affairs of China under the pretext of human rights.[104]

Finally, Russia has desired to become more active in economic and security issues in East Asia, viewing itself as the "double-headed eagle," looking both east and west. At the same time Beijing has been alarmed at strengthened U.S. military alliances in the region, fearing that those actions are directed at the PRC itself. The most notable cause for this alarm has been the strengthening of the U.S.-Japan alliance in 1996, the subsequent issuance and adoption of alliance "Guidelines," and agreement between Tokyo and Washington to cooperate on TMD research, which Beijing opposes (more on this shortly).[105] In this atmosphere both Beijing and Moscow have sought to emphasize a "new security concept," the key features of which are peaceful settlement of disputes, promoting dialogue, and branding alliances cold war relics. As one Chinese analyst commented, "The new [security] concept is not only advocated by China but also firmly supported by Russia."[106]

While not welcoming such cooperation between Moscow and Beijing, many (but by no means all) analysts in Washington fundamentally believe there are genuine limits to it. In the final analysis, the recurrent antagonism between Russia and China will outweigh their incentives to cooperate, unless American policy forces them together. Even the Chinese and Russians are clear about the limits to their cooperation, with one Chinese observer putting it this way: "Like all other matters in the world, Sino-Russian partnership has also two sides. It is indeed pregnant with a huge potential for cooperation and a promising future. But it is also confronted with many difficulties and obstructions."[107]

In 1995 some Russian analysts asserted that China was the nation's most serious, long-term national security challenge,[108] and suspicion still separates the Chinese and Russians, as one particularly discovers in visits to the Russian Far East. A number of factors breed Russian distrust and anxiety, including the illegal migration of from 300,000 to possibly 2 million Chinese into the Russian Far East (though such numbers are unreliable and perhaps exaggerated);[109] the business and trading acumen of the Chinese; the export in the early 1990s of inferior light industrial products made in China to Russia; and the fact that some 37 million people live in the bordering Chinese province of Heilongjiang, while only 8 million Russians inhabit an area two-thirds the size of the United States on their side of the eastern border.[110] In 1996, as Boris Yeltsin was on his way to Beijing, he stopped in the Russian Far Eastern border city of Khabarovsk, where he noted, "In the Khabarovsk region alone there are 180,000 living illegally, mostly Chinese citizens."[111]

One main point of friction between the countries is that Russians and Chinese compete for scarce jobs, smuggling to and from China, and that the Russians see their territory as a vacuum that a vast Chinese population could fill. With a long legacy of conflictual cross-border dealings in the Far East, Sino-Russian cooperation cannot be assumed. One local Russian official summed up the prevailing view for me: "As for the Chinese ... all their promises even at the highest level do not work, they simply do not keep them."[112]

Five considerations make the prospect of long-lasting Russo-Chinese cooperation dubious, unless Washington forces them together:

(1) A group of Russian military officers and security analysts believes a long-term policy of selling China high-tech weapons works against Moscow's own security interests, particularly when Russia cannot afford to modernize its own military forces.[113] As one Russian scholar put it, "In whose interests is it to increase China's military potential? The people who are profiting from arms deliveries to the PRC probably hope that these weapons will be aimed against other states, not against Russia. But what guarantee is there ... ?"[114]

(2) Russian-Chinese economic relations have not developed at the pace necessary to achieve the joint goal (agreed to in December 1996) of two-way trade of $20 billion by the year 2000, as explained earlier in the chapter.[115]

(3) Moscow would like to increase its influence on the Korean peninsula, but Beijing has resisted this attempt, as have both Koreas and the United States.

(4) China's ascendancy irritates the bruised Russian postimperial psyche. Russians cannot be happy to read an authoritative Chinese analyst write that "[i]n international affairs the West often looks on Russia as a state 'defeated in the cold war,' and denies it equal status.... In the circumstances, it is most important for Russia to have an equitable, trust-based relationship and consolidate cooperation with another great power, China, which stands up for its sovereignty and independence."[116] A country that still clings to the view of itself as a teacher of China is unlikely to welcome the proposition that it now needs its student to stand up for its sovereignty and independence.

(5) Beijing cannot have been comforted to have joined Moscow in denouncing U.S.-NATO intervention in Yugoslavia in March–June 1999, only to have Russia vote in the UN Security Council to endorse the occupation of Kosovo to oversee refugee return and postwar reconstruction, leaving Beijing to be the lone abstention from a 14-to-0 vote in the Security Council. From a Chinese viewpoint the Russians simply aren't reliable.

Latent conflicts aside, Beijing will derive what benefit it can from bilateral ties by seizing the chance to inexpensively upgrade its military weaponry and acquire technology, while hoping to keep Russia from upgrading relations with Taiwan or selling weapons to Taipei (as Moscow reiterated its agreement not to do during Jiang Zemin's November 1998 visit).[117] China will also attempt to minimize the security problem along the border and use the Russian card whenever possible to exert pressure on Washington. Nonetheless, Russia is a secondary consideration for Beijing, and is likely to remain so for the foreseeable future. If it becomes a primary consideration for the PRC, it will be either for reasons of conflict with Moscow or dramatically worsened relations with Washington.

From the American perspective, the most troublesome areas of Sino-Russian cooperation are weapons and technology transfers and the desires of Beijing and Moscow to reduce Washington's sway in multilateral forums such as the UN Security Council. Beyond these problematic areas, however, the objectives of U.S. policy should remain threefold: to ensure that both China and Russia have larger economic and technological stakes with the United States than they have with one another; to not allow its bilateral political relations with Moscow and Beijing to dramatically deteriorate simultaneously; and to make it clear that China and Russia each pose a greater long-term security threat to one another than the United States presents to either of them.

Robert Legvold provided a harsh summary of Russian influence on China, the United States, and Japan in the post–cold war era when he said, "If one thing stands out ... it is how seemingly marginal Russia and its new neighbors have become to the central concerns of the other three powers."[118] That may be indicative of big power assessments in the first post–cold war decade, but America is well-advised *not* to view it as a permanent condition. China does not, and keeps a wary eye trained on her northern neighbor. A number of possible positive or negative developments in Russia could change such an assessment considerably. For instance, as Legvold reminds, "If, for any number of reasons, order within or between these (post-Soviet) societies collapses, the misery and mayhem likely to follow will not halt at the old Soviet borders."[119] Conversely, Russia will not be forever weak.

WASHINGTON, BEIJING, AND TOKYO

As the Chinese survey the post–cold war security situation in East Asia, they see problems and potential for conflict in the following areas: the Korean peninsula; with Japan over islands in the East China Sea (Diaoyutai, or Senkakus);[120] the Taiwan Strait; and over conflicting maritime claims in the South China Sea involving a number of ASEAN nations and Taiwan.[121] In each of these instances Japan is a significant consideration. In addition, given the U.S. alliances with Japan, the Republic of Korea, and the Philippines, as well as Washington's complex relationship with Taiwan, the United States also is involved in each of these situations to a greater or lesser extent.

Of all the problematic international relationships of consequence in East Asia, none is more sensitive than that between Japan and China.[122] In Chinese hearts, the Japanese imperial army's invasion and atrocities during World War II, combined with Tokyo's unwillingness to candidly acknowledge them thereafter, are never far below the surface. To anyone who watches the visitors at the Nanjing Holocaust Museum and similar memorials to victims of the Japanese invasion in Harbin or other northeastern Chinese cities, it is apparent that these feelings run deep.

In Japan, anxiety concerning rising Chinese power, resentment at Beijing's repeated references to Japanese World War II behavior in China (and the Japanese feeling that China will never let an apology be the end of it), and apprehension that Washington may switch strategic partners in Asia are ever present. And finally, Beijing worries that the United States and Japan, as long-time allies, will gang up on China, particularly should conflict break out in the Taiwan Strait or over the Diaoyutai (Senkaku) Islands. A Hong Kong criticism of Beijing's restraint in responding to Japanese activities on the disputed Diaoyutai Islands in late 1996 reveals how intertwined trilateral relations and domestic politics in each society can become: "What we want to examine is whether or not our attitude of 'glossing over things to stay on good terms' [with Japan] has resulted in an erroneous judgment by Japan, believing that China wants to utilize Japanese loan[s] and technology, and utilize Sino-Japanese relations to resist U.S. economic threats against China, and resulted in Japan's being more arrogant and even losing its senses."[123]

The strain on Sino-Japanese relations was evident during Chinese President Jiang Zemin's November 1998 visit to Japan.[124] He had hoped to accomplish three things: to obtain an unequivocal, *written* apology by the government and people of Japan for the invasion of China in the 1930s and 1940s; to receive assurance that Japan would not intervene in the Taiwan Strait in the name of the U.S.-Japan security alliance; and to have Tokyo repeat the Three No's (regarding Taiwan) that President Clinton had a few months earlier uttered in Shanghai. He failed in each regard. So jarring were these results that by the time Jiang left Japan, a Hong Kong Chinese newspaper was reporting that Chinese Foreign Minister Tang Jiaxuan (a Japan expert who had been sent to Tokyo at the last minute to try to produce an agreement before Jiang's arrival) was repeatedly being denounced by persons in his own ministry for his "fawning" behavior and "incompetence, betrayal, and shame."[125]

From the American perspective, the perplexity of managing the U.S.-Japan-China relationship is that Japanese fears are aroused when Washington's relations with Beijing become too strained or too intimate. This is also the case for Beijing when it views U.S.-Japan relations. Thus the three-way relationship is a very delicate balancing act. Yet productive Sino-Japanese-American ties are the key to the long-term stability of the region. Ultimately, East Asia will remain stable only as long as these three major powers have minimally productive relations and cooperate on important regional issues.

Early in the Clinton administration, Japanese government personnel (particularly in the Ministry of International Trade and Industry), although soft-spoken, were merciless in criticizing what they perceived as Washington's needless antagonism of Beijing; they were fearful that the PRC's isolation would only make Beijing more uncooperative in the region. However, by the time of President Clinton's June 1998 summit in Beijing, and his decision not to stop in Japan as part of the itinerary, Tokyo was afraid that Washington was in an overheated embrace with the PRC, leaving Japan in the cold. Secretary of State Albright had to make a hurried postsummit stop in Tokyo to reaffirm the "unshakable friendship" between Japan and America.[126]

Beijing is equally ambivalent. Consequently, it is exceedingly difficult for the United States to maintain a stance that is equally reassuring to both Beijing and Tokyo. Within these mutual insecurities, however, lies the key to the most productive course for U.S. policy—to maintain better relations with both Tokyo and Beijing than they are capable of achieving between themselves and to foster a three-way dialogue whenever possible. Before further analyzing this delicate trilateral relationship in the post–cold war era, we must understand the nature of Sino-American-Japanese ties during the preceding decade.

Background

Sino-American-Japanese cooperation reached its zenith with the announcement of normalization of U.S.-China relations in late 1978 and the signing of the China-Japan Peace and Friendship Treaty that same year.

The latter agreement included an antihegemony clause that was aimed at Moscow. In April of the following year, Beijing announced it would not extend the Treaty of Friendship, Alliance, and Mutual Assistance with Moscow that had been signed by Chairman Mao Zedong and Stalin when the Chinese leader was in Moscow in February 1950. These acts, combined with Moscow's November 1978 signing of a security treaty with Hanoi and the USSR's invasion of Afghanistan the following year, only served to reinforce Sino-American-Japanese relations.

In the late 1970s and early 1980s, Japan, the PRC, and the United States were, in effect, strategic partners working together against Soviet dominance. Two Chinese strategic analysts describe Beijing's thinking about the U.S.-Japan alliance and growing Japanese strength during that period: "China no longer perceived the increase in Japanese defense capacity in negative terms. Instead China both publicly and privately encouraged the Japanese to develop their independent military force."[127] As another Chinese analyst in Beijing's intelligence community put it, "In [the] 1970s, the [U.S.-Japan alliance] took its eyes off China and turned to deterring threat from the former Soviet Union, then China had no need to oppose it."[128]

In 1989, with the June 4 violence, Gorbachev's visit to Beijing, and the Soviet withdrawal from Afghanistan, however, China became progressively more concerned about American and Japanese objectives in East Asia and with respect to Taiwan. This concern was aggravated by the West's post-Tiananmen sanctions, the Clinton administration's gradual upgrade of relations with Taiwan in 1994–1995, and the anti-PRC tone of the first Clinton administration. By April 1996, Beijing had become wary of possible "containment" purposes to which the now strengthened U.S.-Japan alliance could be put in an era of growing PRC power: "In [the] 1990s, the alliance is no longer completely directed against China [as it had been in the 1950s], but [it] put Taiwan into its defense scope, though in an opaque way, violating China's sovereignty, therefore, China has every reason to lodge a stern protest against it."[129]

Beijing began to talk about the U.S.-Japan security alliance as a "relic" of "cold war thinking," and as China's anxieties increased, Beijing began to nuzzle up to Moscow. In more candid moments, Chinese analysts were very clear, saying, "China's relations with both the United States and Japan sunk to the lowest ebb since the 1970s. Given the circumstances, China began to seek a closer relationship with Russia, which was beleaguered with the pressure of eastward expansion of NATO. In April 1996, China and Russia released a joint statement, declaring they would form a 'strategic collaborative partnership.' "[130]

In the post–cold war era three sets of issues have shaped, and will continue to shape, interaction among Beijing, Tokyo, and Washington. The first is the U.S.-Japan alliance and its implications for possible conflicts on the Korean peninsula and across the Taiwan Strait. The second involves the nature and capacities of Japan's military (self-defense) force and whether Tokyo will acquire antimissile defenses. The third concerns the management of each country's domestic economy in an economically interdependent world. In the aggregate, these forces have resulted in a Sino-Japanese relationship that one Chinese scholar calls "competitive co-existence."[131]

The U.S.-Japan Alliance

The most succinct expression of Beijing's view of the U.S.-Japan security alliance[132] in the post–cold war world was given by a Chinese government analyst when he said, "But the bottom line is that almost every time when they [Washington and Tokyo] strengthen their alliance, China's national interest is damaged in one way or another. Under the circumstances, China has to stand up for itself."[133] When they speak candidly and off the record, Chinese leaders and analysts sometimes recognize that Japan's inclusion under the U.S. security umbrella means that Tokyo need not acquire its own comprehensive defense (including nuclear) capacity, which is reassuring to Japan's neighbors.[134] Nonetheless, in the years since the end of the cold war, Beijing has come to view the alliance with increasing skepticism. Rather than seeing it as the cork in the bottle of Japanese remilitarization, Beijing has come to see the pact as a hard eggshell protecting an embryo of growing Japanese military power and as a beachhead for intervention in the Taiwan Strait.[135] Against this backdrop, some (but not many) in Beijing are looking for more collaborative ways for the United States, Japan, and China to interact, as an alternative to the strengthening of the U.S.-Japan alliance.

In the 1950s and 1960s, the principal targets of the U.S.-Japanese alliance were the Soviet Union, China, and North Korea. In the 1970s and 1980s, the target was the Soviet Union. However, with the demise of the USSR in 1991, the concomitant Chinese modernization, the strained U.S.-China relationship (1989–1996 and 1999), and mounting Chinese fears about Taiwan's "pragmatic foreign policy," Beijing worried in the 1990s that the U.S.-Japan alliance was aimed at containing China and separating Taiwan from the mainland.

One good example of the interplay of these forces was the April 1996 strengthening of the U.S.-Japan alliance (the Clinton-Hashimoto Declaration) and the subsequent September 1997 issuance of the U.S.-Japan Defense Guidelines and their approval by the Japanese Diet in spring 1999.[136]

In 1994, instability in North Korea (DPRK) was a major issue in Northeast Asia. The isolated regime was believed to be building nuclear weapons and to be in steep economic decline; plus, it appeared politically unstable in the wake of the July 1994 death of Kim Il Sung, the DPRK's godlike leader of more than forty years. The United States confronted the possibility of conflict on the Korean peninsula, a conflict that could have erupted through the preemptive actions of a desperate Pyongyang or because American or Republic of Korea (ROK) forces felt compelled to destroy the germinating nuclear capability. If conflict erupted on the peninsula, American forces, supplies, and logistical support from U.S. bases in Japan would be critical to any military campaign.[137] And yet when Secretary of Defense William Perry and American policymakers and planners looked at the nature of the U.S.-Japan security alliance, it was unclear exactly how helpful Tokyo might be due to the restrictions imposed by Article Nine of Japan's constitution.

U.S.-Japan relations were already at a low ebb in the 1991–1996 period for several reasons: friction had arisen over the level and form of Tokyo's Gulf War support and trade conflicts; Japan was outraged over the September 1995 rape of an Okinawan schoolgirl by American military personnel; Japan had a new socialist prime minister; and Liberal Democratic Party support for bases was weakening. Thus it was uncertain how long the United States would have continued access to its major base in the Japanese islands—Okinawa.[138] Amidst all the uncertainties, Washington policymakers were sure that if war broke out on the Korean peninsula and Japan refused to assist the United States, all popular support for the U.S.-Japan alliance would quickly evaporate in America. Further, if the U.S.-Japan military alliance ended, support in the rest of Asia for having a forward American presence would also crumble. Consequently, in the fall of 1994 Washington and Tokyo began discussions about how to strengthen the U.S.-Japan alliance and define areas of cooperation *before* conflict erupted on the Korean peninsula, and thereby improve U.S.-Japan relations across the board. It was a complex, protracted discussion.

The negotiations moved considerably forward in November 1995 when Defense Secretary Perry "proposed the main outlines of the reaffirmation agreement to Japan's Prime Minister Tomiichi Muruyama" in Tokyo. "President Clinton had essentially settled the agreement when he met with Prime Minister Ryutaro Hashimoto in a February 1996 meeting in

California."[139] President Clinton, having deferred a trip to Japan scheduled for November 1995 due to a budget fight with Congress, rescheduled his visit for April 1996. Although the president's trip was scheduled with other considerations in mind, the trip and its centerpiece, the U.S.-Japan Joint Declaration on the Alliance for the Twenty-first Century, occurred in a context far different than initially anticipated. The summit took place in the wake of China's March 1996 missile "exercises" near Taiwan. This conjunction of events, along with Washington's dispatch of two aircraft carrier battle groups to the seas off Taiwan in March, created a new and ominous context for the strengthening of the alliance from the PRC's vantage point. Beijing came to believe that Tokyo-Washington security cooperation was now aimed at the PRC and provided a means whereby the two countries could intervene in the Taiwan Strait if need be. China's leaders were particularly worried by the U.S.-Japan Joint Declaration's call for the alliance to study "regional contingencies"[140]—what they viewed as a code word for Taiwan.

In the wake of the April declaration, Tokyo and Washington worked on drafting U.S.-Japan Defense Guidelines that would provide greater specificity as to the types of cooperation Washington could expect from Tokyo in the future. The Chinese watched these discussions closely. In early 1997, as the negotiations proceeded, there was a spate of books (among them *The Coming Conflict with China*), popular articles, and calls in the United States suggesting that containment of China was the appropriate policy approach. Chinese analysts and political leaders connected these "dots" and behavior (including the September 1994 upgrade in ties with Taiwan, the May 1995 Lee Teng-hui visit to Cornell University, the March 1996 movement of aircraft carriers, the April 1996 Joint Declaration, and popular rhetoric) and saw a clear picture of containment and intervention in the Taiwan Strait—with the U.S.-Japan security alliance as the cornerstone. Alarm and distrust were aggravated by the fact that President Nixon, more than twenty years earlier, had assured Premier Zhou Enlai that "[w]e will, to the extent we are able, use our influence to discourage Japan from moving into Taiwan as our presence becomes less."[141]

From an American point of view, while the U.S.-Japanese alliance has the functional purpose of maintaining balance and stability through reassurance rather than designating a geographic enemy (the PRC or Russia), there is ambiguity in whether alliance provisions would be activated in the case of conflict in the Taiwan Strait. Some American planners see this ambiguity as a further deterrent to Beijing; yet it may simultaneously embolden Taipei, or some independence-minded groups on Taiwan, to make unwarranted assumptions about Washington's and Tokyo's support. Gauging the U.S. congressional and executive branch reactions in the event of hostilities in the Taiwan Strait is difficult. Given the strong Japanese aversion to war, the constitutional impediments to Tokyo becoming involved, and the difficulty Tokyo usually has making tough decisions, confidently forecasting Japanese reaction to such a contingency is close to impossible.

Given these perceptions in the PRC, Washington should not foresee a future in which Beijing applauds the U.S.-Japan security alliance. At best, Washington, Beijing, and Tokyo should endeavor to keep the alliance from becoming a destabilizing factor in the triangular relationship, and Washington should do all it can to encourage three-way discussions between the respective governments—something that Beijing has resisted, for fear of being the odd man out in any such setting. When all is said and done, however, as the U.S.-Japan security alliance was progressively strengthened throughout the latter half of the 1990s, as Taipei's actions in pursuit of sovereign identity became progressively clearer, and as U.S.-China relations deteriorated in 1999, Beijing's anxieties mounted. The PLA's *Liberation Army Daily* said in June 1999, "When explaining the scope of the peripheral situation [to which the alliance was applicable], the United States and Japan have never specifically stated that it does not include Taiwan; this shows that they have unspeakable conspiracies regarding China's Taiwan."[142]

Japan's Military Capabilities

In the same way that Beijing's view of the U.S.-Japan alliance has changed in response to threats from other quarters, so has its attitude toward Japan's self-defense (military) forces. In late 1997, a very senior military officer expressed a widely held Chinese view to me: "Japan wants to be an ordinary country. What does that mean? Japan still has obligations stemming from its war crimes. It is to have only Self Defense Forces, not other forces."[143] In short, China remains adamantly opposed to an increase in Japanese military power.

The most notable departure from this worry about Japanese military power occurred shortly after the normalization of Sino-Japanese diplomatic relations, when then Premier Hua Guofeng visited Japan in 1980. At that time, Hua not only expressed appreciation for "Japan's efforts to strengthen its alliance with the United States," but also stated that "[a]n independent and sovereign state should have the right to maintain its own defense so as to safeguard its independence and sovereignty. As to what Japan will do, we do not interfere in its internal affairs."[144] The following year, with Ronald Reagan in the White House and Zenko Susuki as prime minister of Japan, Beijing was openly supportive of Tokyo's desires to increase its air and sea capabilities in the "surrounding area" and to "help reduce the financial burden of U.S. forces in Japan."[145] This reflected Beijing's great concern in the wake of Moscow's invasion of Afghanistan and uncertainty as to how the USSR would react to tense Sino-Vietnamese relations in the wake of China's 1979 "defensive counterattack" against Vietnam.

However, such expressions of support for Japanese military modernization had a brief life span. A series of developments in the mid-1980s led Beijing to become ever less supportive of Japanese military modernization and burden sharing with the United States. Key among those developments were Leonid Brezhnev's indication in 1982 that he wished to improve relations with Beijing and Mikhail Gorbachev's more credible signal in that direction delivered in a July 1986 speech in Vladivostok in which he called for "good-neighborliness."[146] These signals, and Deng's own desire to redirect resources toward domestic economic development, made him receptive to Moscow's overtures. Using Japan and the alliance to offset a hostile Moscow was becoming less necessary.

Simultaneously, as Japan's trade surplus with the PRC grew in the early and mid-1980s (according to PRC figures), trade friction between Beijing and Tokyo also mounted (see table 5).[147] Finally, throughout the 1980s, a series of Japanese actions suggested to the Chinese that Tokyo desired to downplay its World War II atrocities. As usual, this sensitive issue inflamed Chinese popular opinion and resulted in anti-Japanese demonstrations in the PRC in the fall of 1985.

Thus by the end of the 1980s and throughout the 1990s, a combination of economic, nationalistic, and strategic frictions converged to make Beijing much less supportive of Japan's military power. To the degree that Beijing saw value in the U.S.-Japan alliance, it was because the United States was viewed as a restraint on Tokyo's need to acquire its own comprehensive, autonomous military capacity.

It is in this light of post–cold war era suspicion of the U.S.-Japan relationship that Beijing now views all Japanese military procurements as well as U.S.-Japan cooperation in weapons research and development. As *Liberation Army Daily* put it in 1999, "Japan for its part will draw support from its military alliance relationship with the United States to further speed up its pace in becoming a military power."[148] As we have seen, by the 1990s a number of cooperative gestures between the United States and Japan led

China to believe in "the possibility that the U.S. security structure, particularly the U.S.-Japan alliance, may become an instrument of containing China rather than curbing any other major powers in the region."[149] Any U.S.-Japanese development (as agreed to in 1998[150] and 1999) and deployment of missile defenses, even if primarily designed to cope with a North Korean threat,[151] are seen by the PRC as detrimental to its security interests. Even if such defenses ultimately are ineffective, they force Beijing to devote more resources to missile modernization and enhancement, thereby diverting resources and further alarming neighbors. In addition, the transfer of technology to Japan could assist Tokyo in developing other offensive systems—in particular, missiles—of concern to the PRC.[152] Finally, "Beijing views the ability to attack U.S. bases in Japan as a key part of its strategy to deter U.S. intervention in a conflict with China, although this is rarely acknowledged by Chinese strategists."[153] Indeed, it is precisely this possibility that is part of the U.S. motivation for TMD in the first place.

Given the proliferation of regional missile threats, as described by the July 1998 Rumsfeld Commission (the Commission to Assess the Ballistic Missile Threat to the United States), U.S. security policy was driven in the direction of missile defenses (both theater and national missile defense) in the late 1990s. And although the combination of cost and technological uncertainty may make construction of workable national and theater missile defenses a protracted process, Japan likely will participate, and others in Asia, South Korea and (particularly) Taiwan, may give consideration to these systems as well. The 1999 National Defense Authorization Bill called on the Department of Defense to study the "the architecture requirements" for a regional TMD that could include "key regional allies" (i.e., Taiwan).[154] The move in the late 1990s toward national and regional missile defenses will likely prove to be one of the most important elements in the Sino-American-Japanese interaction in the early twenty-first century. If Beijing sees Washington, Tokyo, and Taipei acquiring the means to blunt its own modest missile force and enhance security cooperation, there is no reason to believe Beijing will not expand its capacities to a level sufficient to overcome those defenses. Indeed, Beijing applies the logic that Moscow and Washington applied when they agreed to the 1972 ABM Treaty—that missile defenses are inherently destabilizing and offensive, providing a shield behind which nations can pursue provocative policies. As the PLA put it in 1999, "[T]he United States and Japan will pursue absolute military superiority, in a bid to be able to attack other countries without being attacked themselves."[155] This line of thinking and dynamic could spark a regional arms race.

Economic Interdependence

Economic interdependence is a growing consideration in the management of U.S.-Japan-China relations. One example illustrates the complexity of this management problem that increasingly confronts each capital.

As discussed in Chapter 4, a central feature of the economic turbulence in Asian economies in the late 1990s was currency depreciation. By July 1998 China's neighboring exporters had all witnessed dramatic currency depreciation since mid-1997.[156] Most important of all to the PRC, by July 1998 the Japanese yen had depreciated by 17 percent since mid-1997 (41 percent since April 1995).[157] At the same time, China's Premier Zhu Rongji had staked his reputation on no devaluation of the RMB in 1998, and there was a widespread belief that were Beijing to depreciate its currency, Hong Kong would be unable to maintain its peg to the U.S. dollar (7.8:1). Further, it was widely believed that were China and Hong Kong to devalue, it would set off another round of devaluations in the region and globally, with Russia and Latin America the next potential victims. As domestic demand sagged throughout East and Southeast Asia, exports to the West, and in particular the United States, became even more important. The U.S. and European markets alone could not absorb all these exports forever.

While China's exports did not immediately suffer as much from its neighbors' 1997–1998 currency depreciations as one might initially have predicted (though they did in 1999), Beijing was particularly concerned that the Japanese currency not devalue below the 150-yen level; this would have presented too much price competition to all the other Asian economies, including the PRC's. In June 1998, the yen was pushing against that mark, and Beijing felt that Tokyo was once again trying to export its way out of economic doldrums rather than stimulating its own domestic demand and tackling its internal financial problems. Japan's financial illnesses were multifaceted, but they centered on the banking system—which reported problem-loan portfolios of US$600 billion.[158]

Consequently, on the eve of President Clinton's June 1998 visit to China, Beijing implied that if Washington did not intervene in the foreign exchange markets to stop the yen's slide, the PRC would reconsider its commitment not to devalue the RMB. The very thought of an RMB devaluation sent shudders through world markets, with one MIT economist saying, "If China goes, we'd have a Great Depression in Asia."[159] On Friday, June 12, China's ambassador to the United States, Li Zhaoxing, asked the G-7 to support the yen, and the following Monday NPC Chairman Li Peng criticized Japan for the yen's drop. On Wednesday, June 17, the U.S. Federal Reserve and the Bank of Japan intervened in the foreign exchange markets to the tune of about $4 billion, and the yen rose about 5 percent in response.[160] Welcoming this move, the PRC reciprocated by reaffirming pledges not to devalue the RMB. Beijing's policy of restraint won it (temporary) respite from U.S., particularly congressional, criticism in other policy areas.

Economic interdependence has added yet another, and increasingly important, dimension to the Sino-American-Japanese interaction, beyond the traditional security domain. Tokyo, Beijing, and Washington are each finding that the economic policies and behavior of the other two are vital to their own domestic economic well-being. For this reason, each party seeks to build either implicit or explicit coalitions with one or both of the other two to advance its economic interests. In the new world of economic interdependence allegiances shift rapidly. One day China and the United States are allies with respect to the Japanese exchange rate, and that same day, Japan and China are aligned in persuading Washington to maintain most-favored-nation treatment for Beijing. With increasing numbers of Japanese-invested factories in the PRC dependent on the U.S. export market, closure of the U.S. market to Chinese exports means closure of American markets to the Japanese.

LESSONS IN THIRD-PARTY MANAGEMENT

Third-party relationships can be complicating considerations in the management of bilateral ties between the United States and China. A number of conclusions can be drawn from the preceding examples.

First, in a three-way relationship it is exceedingly difficult to communicate with one party without affecting the behavior and perceptions of the third party, sometimes adversely. For example, prior to conducting missile exercises in the Taiwan Strait in March 1996, Beijing did not anticipate the muscular response that the United States adopted in sending two aircraft carrier battle groups to the region. In sending those forces, Washington conveyed clearly to Beijing that America's level of commitment to Taiwan's security was high. In the process of communicating this, however, Washington also inadvertently communicated to Taiwan a greater degree of support than was intended. Indeed, it was partially the need to offset this misunderstanding in Taipei that led President Clinton to artic-ulate the Three No's in Shanghai two years later. This was an attempt to tell Taipei that the United States was not writing it a blank check to engage in provocative independence-minded activity. This move, in turn, led Lee Teng-hui to begin to contemplate his "special state-to-state relation-ship" statement of July 9, 1999, to shore up his position in the face of the Beijing-Washington cooperation that he found threatening. And, in turn, Beijing at first suspected that, somehow, Washington and Taipei had colluded in Lee's statement, which, in fact, had caught the United States by surprise.

A second conclusion involves the role of the U.S. Congress in making U.S. commitments more or less credible. In the case of Hong Kong's rever-sion to the PRC, for example, Congress played a broadly constructive role by reinforcing executive branch messages about the importance of Amer-ican interests in the city without threatening specific, possibly counter-productive measures. Indeed, by mid-1997 Beijing had a relatively relaxed attitude toward the U.S. Hong Kong Policy Act, with then Vice Premier Zhu Rongji saying, "I said to Mr. Gingrich that although the U.S. House of Representatives has adopted [a law to monitor Hong Kong], for that I can't criticize you. But it is entirely unnecessary to adopt such an act. It is not the U.S. but China that cares the most about Hong Kong."[161]

On the other hand, in cases like Taiwan (and Tibet, as seen in chapter 3), the expression of congressional opinion often has been at cross-purposes with executive branch policy. This sows confusion in Beijing and creates the chance for miscommunication, with potentially tragic consequences. The solution to the problem is not the unattainable aspiration that the two branches always agree. Rather, a very high value should be attached to congressional and executive branch unity, when it is at all achievable.

Third, a clear lesson to be drawn from the U.S.-China-Russia relation-ship is that there is a difference between genuine national interests and rhetoric. In the 1970s and early 1980s, the United States and China had common bedrock interests in opposing the Soviet Union. The "strategic partnership" between Moscow and Beijing in the mid- and late 1990s has no such fundamental basis, except a shared apprehension of U.S. domi-nance. This suggests that Washington should pursue the following course: maintain better relations with both Moscow and Beijing than they are able to achieve between themselves and not be overly alarmed by the level of cooperation they have achieved in the late 1990s, beyond the obviously important area of weapons sales.

Finally, the case of U.S.-China-Japan relations suggests two conclusions. First, as in the case of the U.S.-China-Russia triangle, Washington's objective should be to maintain better relations with Tokyo and Beijing than either can sustain with the other. At the same time, Washington should encourage three-way cooperation that fosters regional stability. And second, economists and finance ministers will play an ever larger role in the management of the relationship and in the overall management of global relations.

PART III

THE STATE AND CIVIL SOCIETY LEVEL

6

THE STORIES WE TELL OURSELVES

National Myths and the Mass Media

All nations live by myths. That is, they paint a picture of the past that satisfies their present needs but does violence to the historic record. Some myths are beneficial. They are those that strengthen a nation's confidence in having been, and being, able to do what the tasks of the moment demand of it.... Other myths are pernicious. They draw from a distorted reality lessons for the understanding of the past and the charting of future action which please collective emotions but lead judgment and action astray.

Hans J. Morgenthau

The end of the cold war and the emergence of newly independent states in eastern Europe have the potential to enlarge dramatically the family of nations now committed to the pursuit of democratic institutions, the expansion of free markets, the peaceful settlement of conflict and the promotion of collective security. For the sake of both its interests and its ideals, the United States has *a special responsibility* to nurture and promote these core values.... As the sole superpower, the United States *has a special responsibility* for developing a strategy to neutralize, contain and, through selective pressure, perhaps eventually transform these backlash states into constructive members of the international community [emphasis added].

Anthony Lake, assistant to the President for National Security Affairs, Spring 1994

I've seen the book "The Coming Conflict with China" and Samuel Huntington's "The Clash of Civilizations." It's ridiculous. For more than 150 years, China has been subjected to foreign aggression and we have suffered egregiously. China's still got a long way to go to become a developed country. Even when China becomes strong and developed, China will never get involved in aggression against other countries or interfere in other countries' internal affairs.

Then Vice Premier Zhu Rongji, interview, May 1997

249

If the last few decades teach anything, it is that American influence—our ability to change the actions and nature of other governments—is magnified by our ideological assertiveness.

Gary L. Bauer, president, Family Research Council, October 1997

Indignant college students and the masses to the south and the north of the Chang Jiang [Yangtze River] and inside and outside the Great Wall are successively staging demonstrations [to protest the U.S. bombing of the Chinese embassy in Belgrade, Yugoslavia]. . . . They shout: "China cannot be bullied, and the Chinese nation cannot be bullied."

People's Daily, May 10, 1999

INTRODUCTION

Understanding post–cold war U.S.-China relations requires one to first look at how the people of both nations perceive themselves, their modern relationship, their respective histories, and the necessities that these widely shared beliefs create for today's citizenry and leadership. Divergent historical experiences and the conceptions of national role to which those experiences give rise create conflicting Chinese and American foreign policy impulses. While there are diverse views and self-perceptions among citizens and leaders within both countries,[1] there also are some very widely shared understandings within each nation. We turn to those shared, broad national understandings that are reflected in the discourse of citizens and the behavior of leaders, and that are conveyed to citizens and leaders via the mass media.

Their national experience has created a sense among Americans that their values of democracy and freedom are universal, global entitlements and that the United States has an obligation to promote those values abroad. The fall of the central European and Soviet communist regimes in 1989 and thereafter only served to reinforce this belief, though the ethnic and religious strife that followed in parts of south central Europe, the Caucus states, Africa, and Indonesia cast a few shadows on this generally sunny belief. The sense of American obligation is fortified by a sense of self-interest. Americans' understanding of twentieth-century history is that when their values or interests were under assault in the far corners of the globe, the conflicts often grew until the United States was drawn into them from the sidelines. Thus Americans are predisposed to conclude that it is better to intervene early rather than to be drawn into large-scale conflict later, under more disadvantageous circumstances. This was a central lesson of both World War I and World War II. Nonetheless, what Americans may view as prudent involvement may be viewed by others as unwarranted and unwise intrusion.

Another part of the American self-conception is that power confers responsibility. In his second inaugural address, President Clinton said, "America stands alone as the world's indispensable nation"[2]—a recurring formulation of the Clinton administration. Although many Americans are publicly more humble, this theme, "indispensable nation," captures a deeply held belief. Americans are inclined to believe that their nation's unique capacity to act at a great distance from its borders creates a moral imperative to do so. In a world where tragedy is broadcast live from remote regions to every American living room, the sense of broad, global interests and moral imperatives gives rise to debates over when, under what circumstances, and how the United States should bring its power to bear on distant problems and unfolding tragedies. Public opinion polling in 1999 by Potomac Associates reveals that Americans in general (and more informed elites in particular) rate maintaining peace and stability as their primary goal, followed in a near dead heat by the twin priorities of seeking economic benefits from trade and working to improve human rights in Asia.[3]

A final component of Americans' perception of their place in the world is the belief that U.S. motivations and foreign policy toward China and other countries have been more magnanimous, different in kind, than the motivations that animated other Western powers in the Age of Imperialism. The Chinese do not have such a benign understanding of U.S. behavior in the past or today.

China's nineteenth- and twentieth-century experience has been entirely different than that of the United States: for much of that period it has been the playground for foreign intervention and encroachment. China's domestic situation during the last 160 years has been marked by warring factions and numerous self-inflicted tragedies, yet through it all several overarching beliefs have held China's people together: the sense of a long and glorious past, unjust treatment at the hands of foreigners from 1840 to 1949 (and beyond), a desire to regain international respect and equality, an imperative for territorial reunification, and a wish to reaffirm their collective greatness as a people and nation. Succinctly, therefore, as China enters the twenty-first century, it carries the self-image of a "victim" nation, albeit a nation with aspirations finally on a path toward greatness restored. This victim complex, coupled with China's aspirations and growing power, creates a sense of entitlement—a combination that makes Beijing prickly in its dealings with the United States.

Beyond the foregoing broad stories of national experience that make up each nation's vision of itself lies the realm of stories nations tell themselves and other nations on a daily basis. In this context the mass media are critical in that they reflect the underlying social values, historical lessons, and social and political organization of each nation. They mirror and reinforce the national experience and interpret events through the prism of that experience. Further, the American dominance of global media and communications means that the American "story" often becomes the story of record. This reinforces the sense of victimization among many Chinese. As one member of the Standing Committee of the Politburo put it to me, "Facts are no longer facts. Now we have TV sets, the world is smaller, so who has greater communications has greater influence. So all men are not created equal."[4]

DIVERGENT VIEWS OF HISTORY

The U.S.-China Relationship in Modern Times

The radically different perspectives from which Chinese and Americans view their interaction in the nineteenth and twentieth centuries has been observed frequently by such persons as John King Fairbank, Foster Rhea Dulles, Warren Cohen,[5] Wang Jisi, and many others. In the latter part of the 1990s, Wang Jisi, the director of the Institute of American Studies at the Chinese Academy of Social Sciences in Beijing, put the historical relationship in the following terms:

> In the People's Republic of China (PRC), textbook interpretations describe the history of the United States as a world power in negative terms. Toward the end of the nineteenth century, the United States as a leading imperialist country joined major European powers ... in a worldwide contest for hegemony. It soon began to play a significant role in Asia by pronouncing the "Open Door" doctrine in 1899 and 1900, which was designed to dominate China alone by squeezing out the other imperialist powers.
>
> Political observers and educators in the PRC have never accepted the American textbook cliché that the United States has been inspired by its revolutionary tradition.... Although there are some variations and moderation of this line, no one of political weight in China would actually portray the United States as playing a generally constructive role in maintaining world peace.... In the bilateral relationship, US hostility toward the PRC is manifested in an incessant effort since 1949 to separate

Taiwan from other parts of China. A more sinister American plan has been to sabotage the Communist regime by encouraging political dissension and promoting Western-type democracy within China. This plan is referred to as the "strategy of peaceful evolution."[6]

The predominant view in the United States has been that American missionary involvement in China from the early 1800s until the communist takeover in 1949 was largely a philanthropic and humanitarian undertaking that left behind many enduring legacies, particularly in the educational and medical fields; Chinese point to the patronizing aspect of such missionary work. Americans assert they never had "treaty ports" in China; the Chinese remember that Washington did not relinquish extraterritoriality until 1943. Americans see their Open Door Policy dating from 1899–1900 as an attempt to prevent China from being carved up into commercially impenetrable foreign colonies; Chinese believe that the Americans were more concerned about maintaining their own commercial access and having the privileges that extraterritoriality conferred. While Americans view their "nonrecognition" of Japanese aggression in China during the 1930s as standing up for China's territorial integrity, Chinese see inaction until 1941 (when the United States was brought into the war by the attack on Pearl Harbor and needed the Chinese to tie down Tokyo on another front).

Chinese are by no means oblivious to the benefits that missionary involvement in China brought or to periods of Sino-American cooperation, such as during World War II in the Pacific. Indeed, I saw one Chinese leader weep while recalling that period of Sino-American cooperation and comparing it to the friction of the 1990s. Nonetheless, the dominant Chinese sentiment is that while the United States speaks in the voice of transcendent values, it acts principally according to its interests. John K. Fairbank put it with clarity:

> Unfortunately for us, a proud people when weak do not enjoy receiving help. The American attitude toward China during the century of the unequal treaties was consciously acquisitive but also benevolent. . . . We were proud of our record, indeed a bit patronizing toward the imperialist powers, of lesser virtue. Inevitably, however, the Chinese experience of Sino-American relations was different from the American experience. We found our contact with China adventurous, exhilarating, rewarding in material or spiritual terms. Americans who did not like it could avoid it. China, on the other hand, found this contact forced upon her. It was a foreign invasion, humiliating, disruptive, and in the end catastrophic. . . . Out of the mix of past-Sino-American relations, Chinese today can stress American imperialism [or its late-twentieth-century cousin, hege-

mony] where we see mainly our philanthropy, exploitation where we see American aid to the Chinese people.[7]

Given these differing historical perspectives, it is unsurprising that American and Chinese views of Washington's post–June 1989 impositions of economic and other sanctions against the PRC were very different. Americans thought they were striking a blow for the Chinese people against a repressive elite, whereas Chinese (intellectuals and the working class alike, not to mention leaders) quickly concluded that the U.S. sanctions simply were one more attempt to slow China's economic development—another try at keeping China down. In the wake of the bombing of the Chinese Embassy in Belgrade in May 1999, for instance, one distressed older Chinese intellectual wrote, "Overnight, we are regarding each other as the main 'threat.' Here in China, I find the ill feelings towards the United States surprisingly widespread, from taxi drivers to university students. The general theme is that we are being bullied and humiliated because we are too weak. The young people ... are talking about the 'heroic days' of the Mao Zedong era when the Chinese nation, although poor, dared to defy the imperialists, etc."[8]

As Washington pushed for sanctions to punish the human rights infractions of the Communist leadership in 1989 and thereafter, it simultaneously pushed for market opening and protection of intellectual property rights, the same combination of commercial pressure and high-minded rhetoric that the Chinese had experienced prior to 1949. To Americans, these drives for commercial access and respect for property rights represented a legitimate demand for a "level playing field" for foreign investors, reciprocal access to offset an ever-growing trade deficit with the PRC, and part of the march toward "rule of law." Rule of law was the ground on which human rights values and commercial interests found reconciliation in the American mind. For the Chinese, this was but a recurrent pattern— Americans articulate high principles but simultaneously seek to turn Chinese weakness to their commercial advantage. Americans believed or rationalized that their pursuit of economic interests was part of their larger pursuit of normative values and the noble cause of China's integration into the established world order.

The 1989–2000 period is characterized by a pattern of Chinese compromise in the face of U.S. economic and security demands but resistance to concessions in the human rights domain. This pattern reflects the Chinese sense that Americans were serious about their economic and security interests, yet not nearly as determined when it came to their humanitarian impulses. The Chinese are predisposed to see American moral protests as simply a means of exerting pressure in the pursuit of more tangible economic and security interests—as bargaining chips. As one Hong Kong source put it when the PRC "postponed" U.S.-China discussions on trade issues (WTO entry) and arms control and nonproliferation, and "stopped" the human rights dialogue, in response to the U.S. bombing of the Chinese Embassy in Belgrade in May 1999, "The two 'postponements' are two issues with which the United States are most concerned and the one 'stoppage' is the bargaining chips [*sic*] of the United States in dealing with China in all fields."[9]

These widely shared Chinese views of America generate some assumptions that have been ably summarized by one of China's most articulate observers of the United States:

· The United States wants to maximize its national power and dominate the world.

· It is easier to deal with the United States and seek its cooperation when its power is on the decline.

· Americans believe in "the law of the jungle," seeing no other nations as equal partners and attempting to prevent them from rising up.

· Compared with other advanced capitalist countries, the United States has a much stronger concept of racial and cultural superiority, and tends to use ideological and cultural tools, in addition to economic and military strengths, to expand its influence.[10]

Chinese Victimization, Nationalism, and Patriotism

During the post–cold war era, China has been strained by two opposing impulses: the push toward growing global interdependence and the internal pull to avoid dependence.

On the one hand, the PRC's drive to become involved in a variety of international governmental and nongovernmental organizations and regimes suggests that it has an interest in joining these mechanisms of international intercourse as a full and *equal* member. Indeed, it is such equal involvement that will constitute the final redress for past injustices. Yet most global institutions were established before the PRC was a full participant in the international community, and therefore institutional rules were not devised with China's interests, sensitivities, or unique conditions in mind. This consideration predisposes Chinese leaders to be extremely cautious about which organizations they seek to enter and the terms upon which Beijing agrees to enter them (as discussed in Chapter 4).

On the other hand, China's "century of humiliation" (from the mid-1800s to the mid-1900s) has created a deep sense of victimization among the Chinese people, a feeling shared by leaders and followers alike, with President Jiang Zemin telling a group of which I was a part, "Looking at China's modern history, I see suffering and bullying."[11] One Chinese analyst explained the implications of these feelings:

> Indeed, China's attitude toward the existing international order is one of ambivalence. On the one hand, China is integrating itself into the world community speedily and with fascinating enthusiasm, which itself is an indication that the existing order is not that detrimental to China's interests and goals.... On the other hand, it will take a long time for China to lay down the burden of "victim country." To be sure, patriotism is mobilized in this country to maintain national unity. Besides, many factors today are still relevant to the "victim mentality": Hong Kong has just been returned to China's sovereignty with ambivalent feelings of the Western countries; Taiwan is seen by many Chinese as being separated by the United States since 1949. American sanctions against Beijing after June 4, 1989, have not been totally lifted; China is singled out by Americans for accusations of human rights violations despite enormous progress in China in recent years; Japan's unrepentant attitude toward World War II constantly reminds the victimization of China in its recent past.[12]

The combined sense of victimization and the reality of increasing Chinese nationalism and the various forms it can take are another key issue. At the "soft" end of the continuum of Chinese nationalism is patriotism, a sentiment that can foster social cohesion without veering off into threatening external behavior. The idea that "patriotism is mobilized ... to maintain national unity" is how Beijing describes the character of prevailing nationalism in the PRC.[13] At the "hard" end of the nationalistic continuum is what Allen Whiting refers to as aggressive nationalism—that which "arouses anger and mobilizes behaviour" externally.[14] Somewhere in between patriotism and aggressive nationalism one finds "assertive nationalism"—to a Western ear, Chinese protestations of patriotism can sound assertive. Yet from the Chinese perspective, "The higher the Chinese people hold the banner of patriotism, the more China will be able to accelerate its development, the closer the people of all nationalities in China will be united, and the more the Western nations' attempt to contain China will fail."[15]

A central issue for the future management of U.S.-China relations, therefore, is this: Under what conditions is China likely to move from patriotic to assertive, and on to possibly aggressive nationalistic behavior? The broad answer to this question, drawing heavily on Allen Whiting's research,[16] is that Chinese behavior will progressively move toward the aggressive end of the nationalism spectrum the more of the following conditions prevail (many of these conditions, for example, existed when demonstrators in Beijing and other Chinese cities protested against, and in some cases vandalized, American diplomatic establishments in the wake of the May 1999 bombing of the Chinese Embassy in Belgrade):

- When China's elite is warring amongst itself over substantive issues and when leadership cohesion and stability is low

- When the global balance of power is seen as disadvantageous to China

- When the United States is challenging Chinese interests across a wide range of issues, as was the case throughout the first half of the 1990s and in 1999

- When "leftist" ideology or the Chinese military, or both, are domestically ascendant

In such periods, the propaganda apparatus and popular sentiment drift into the following lines of thought: "The United States is a country composed of immigrants and it should have the combination of outstanding culture characterized by harmony and affinity. However, when the descendants of Anglo-Saxons, with the pirate spirit, embarked on the North American continent, they started the inhuman killing of the Indians ... and started the evil history of trading black slaves and Chinese."[17]

American Views of China: Past and Present

There is much written about how Americans have viewed China during the nineteenth and twentieth centuries and what this says about how Americans view themselves.[18] Several key findings of this literature are germane to current considerations, though they are not this chapter's principal topic. First, American motivations with respect to China always have been a strong alloy of what T. Christopher Jespersen calls "economic enticement" and "spiritual and economic salvation"[19]—meaning simply that Americans tend to rationalize economic intercourse with China with improvement (as they see it) of the spiritual and political lives of the Chinese people.

A second enduring component of the American view of China has been that Americans hold, seemingly simultaneously, two images of China—one benign and constructive, the other malevolent and threatening. Harold Isaacs described this phenomenon eloquently.

> The name of Marco Polo is scratched onto the mind of almost every American school child. Attached to it are powerful images of China's ancient greatness, civilization, art, hoary wisdom. With it in time comes a heavy cluster of admirable qualities widely attributed to the Chinese as people.... Genghiz Kahn and his Mongol hordes are the non-Chinese ancestors of quite another set of images also strongly associated with the Chinese: cruelty, barbarism, inhumanity; a faceless, impenetrable, overwhelming mass.... In the long history of our associations with China, these two sets of images rise and fall, move in and out of the center of people's minds over time, never wholly displacing each other, always coexisting, each ready to emerge at the fresh call of circumstance.[20]

In the recent period, the decisive "fresh call of circumstance" came with the June 1989 tragedy in Tiananmen, when the American popular attitude toward the PRC changed overnight—from 72 percent "favorable" in February 1989 to 58 percent "unfavorable" six months later. Indeed, favorable views of China had not recovered a decade later.[21] Another "call of circumstance" came in May 1999, when demonstrators unleashed violence against American diplomatic establishments in China in the wake of the embassy bombing in Belgrade. By 1999, 60 percent of Americans considered the PRC a "serious threat," whereas two decades earlier (in 1980), only 18 percent did.[22]

In short, the American belief that our endeavors, business and otherwise, in China can bring both economic benefit and moral purification, along with the two-sided image of a friend/foe China, are nothing new. For their part, Chinese view Americans with ambivalence, appreciating periods of cooperation and resenting prior coercion. This mélange of images in both nations creates ample room for domestic politicians in both China and America to paint powerfully motivating pictures for their respective domestic purposes. In the United States, politicians can call today's Chinese leaders "Nazis"; in Beijing, the elite can accuse America of a desire to foster "peaceful evolution," to keep China weak, and to bully, harass, and humiliate the Chinese nation. Similarly, the Chinese mass media used the epithets *Nazi* and *fascist* to denounce the United States for the bombing of the Chinese Embassy in Belgrade. These enduring conceptions of Americans and Chinese were the trunks upon which their post–cold war thinking was grafted.

American Post–Cold War Conceptions of Foreign Policy

Americans emerged from the cold war era holding several notions about their country's role in the world:

- American political and economic "values" reigned triumphant at what Francis Fukuyama called the "end of history."[23]

- The United States needed to remain active in world affairs—hopefully at a low cost in terms of lives and money.[24]

- Washington needed to direct its energies toward "protecting American economic interests and maintaining a global military, economic and political position."[25]

Nonetheless, though Americans thought about the world in these terms, the more important point is that they *preferred* to think about domestic issues (see Chapter 7). Bill Clinton, both as candidate and then as president, shared these views and the implicit priority among them; Clinton promised to focus on the economy "like a laser."

However, the promotion of democratic ideas and morals abroad is a time-tested method for gaining political support. So despite his domestic focus and priorities, on June 3, 1992, presidential candidate Bill Clinton said, "It is time to put America back on the side of democracy and freedom. I hope the Congress will move quickly to enact legislation [conditioning MFN treatment for China on Beijing's human rights behavior]."[26] Nonetheless, at the same time that the Democratic Party's platform linked human rights to MFN status for China, it also made it clear there were other goals the United States sought to advance through ties with Beijing. It called on the PRC for "greater access for U.S. goods, and responsible conduct on weapons proliferation."[27] Clearly Clinton and the Democratic Party had a laundry list for Beijing: they wanted political change, humane governance, access for American goods, and PRC behavior that was consistent with American security interests, particularly as it related to weapons of mass destruction and their means of delivery—incidentally, this list was not so different from that of Clinton's incumbent adversary, George Bush, though the way each proposed to advance the objectives was quite different.

Clinton, like most American political office seekers, had no incentive to prioritize his goals or specify what the cost of achieving them might be. Only the harsh reality of governance forced him to gradually define his actual priorities.

Once the Clinton administration assumed office on January 20, 1993, the combination of a new idealistic staff, a desire to enact campaign promises, and a need to placate a Congress deeply frustrated with what was seen as George Bush's deference to Beijing (see Chapters 1 and 8), led the new president and his team to simultaneously seek to achieve every China policy goal articulated in the recent campaign. Once the Chinese made it clear that any attempt by the United States to coerce Beijing with respect to political change would severely compromise U.S. economic and security interests, however, the president chose to give primacy to security and economic objectives after the agonizing domestic policy struggle chronicled earlier. Yet at the start of the new administration, the president had no incentive to choose—his aides did not wish to choose and his administration was simply not effectively organized to make such choices (see Chapter 9).

The administration's inability to organize itself in terms of foreign policy is clearly reflected in its America-centric "enlargement" policy, which was articulated by the president's assistant for national security affairs, Anthony Lake, in a speech in September 1993. Lake's statement was everything that a policy statement should not be: it was largely rhetorical; it did not represent a consensus within the administration; it raised expectations in Congress, and it generated excessive anxiety in the PRC.

> First, America's core concepts—democracy and market economics—are more broadly accepted than ever. Over the past 10 years, the number of democracies has nearly doubled. Since 1970, the number of significant command economies dropped from 10 to 3.... Democracy and market economics are ascendant in this new era, but they are not everywhere triumphant.... But it is wrong to assume these ideas will be embraced only by the West and rejected by the rest. Culture does shape politics and economics. But the idea of freedom has universal appeal. Thus, we have arrived at neither the end of history nor a clash of civilizations but a moment of immense democratic and entrepreneurial opportunity. We must not waste it.[28]

The tenor of this initial foreign policy statement (which links "democratic and entrepreneurial opportunity") is perhaps best expressed in Lake's discussion of China in a section of the address that was called "The 'Backlash' States":

> Every dictator, theocrat, kleptocrat, or central planner in an unelected regime has reason to fear their subjects will suddenly demand the freedom to make their own decisions.... Such reactionary "backlash" states are more likely to sponsor terrorism and traffic in weapons of mass destruction and ballistic missile technologies. They are more likely to suppress their own people, foment ethnic rivalries, and threaten their neighbors.... Our policy toward such states, so long as they act as they do, must seek to isolate them diplomatically, militarily, economically, and technologically.... We cannot impose democracy on regimes that appear to be opting for liberalization, but we may be able to help steer some of them down that path while providing penalties that raise the costs of re-

pression and aggressive behavior. These efforts have special meaning for our relations with China.... That is why we conditionally extended China's trading advantages [MFN], sanctioned its missile exports, and proposed creation of a new Radio Free Asia. We seek a stronger relationship with China that reflects both our values and our interests.[29]

Lake's remarks left much unexamined—for example, Was normal trade (MFN) simply advantageous for China or a mutually beneficial economic relationship? and Was it possible to obtain Beijing's cooperation on missile (and other technology) exports while actively promoting political system change in the PRC? The overarching message of the address was that American values were going to drive policy to a greater extent than they had under George Bush and that a principal purpose of U.S. policy was to produce systemic change in the PRC.

Anthony Lake's remarks were not isolated and quixotic, but rather reflections of presidential and congressional views and popular attitudes. The early Clinton administration put vigorous human rights advocates into a variety of positions. The post of Special Assistant to the President and Senior Director for Democracy was created within the National Security Council with Morton Halperin as the occupant. In the summer of 1993, Halperin wrote in *Foreign Policy* magazine that "[p]eople are coming to view constitutional democracy as the only legitimate form of government.... The United States should take the lead in promoting the trend toward democracy.... Thus, when a people attempts to hold free elections and establish a constitutional democracy, the United States and the international community should not only assist but should 'guarantee' the result."[30] To put it delicately, Beijing was wary.

Beyond the rhetoric lay the administration's initial policy decisions regarding China—to condition MFN extension on Beijing's human rights behavior; to impose sanctions in a variety of areas; and to push for the creation of what eventually became Radio Free Asia, similar to Radio Free Europe. Speaking with a very high level group of Chinese diplomats and government officials in April 1993, one well-known American columnist and political commentator expressed his view this way: "Rome was great not because of its trade balance but because of its power, its culture, and its law.... We will pursue democracy even if it hurts us economically. This is the ethos of the Radio Free Asia program."[31]

Many Chinese expressed the following sentiment to me during this period: "We Chinese were so ideological during the Cultural Revolution. We have abandoned that. But now, in the wake of the cold war, you Americans are so ideological." In early 1993 one senior Chinese diplomat put his understanding of U.S. policy in the following terms: "The pillar of your policy is democracy and you will use levers.... This gives people the impression that ideology is being injected into economic relations. If you do that, will it be realistic?"[32]

If one considers the verbiage and behavior coming out of Washington during the first two years of Clinton's first term in light of the historically derived Chinese sensitivities enumerated above, some of the problems in the relationship are easily discerned. Historically, the Chinese have feared external efforts to change their system; such change seemed to be Washington's explicit declarative goal. The Chinese suspected that when forced to choose between ideological goals and economic interests, Americans would, in the end, choose the latter—and we did. The Chinese vowed to use every economic and security lever they possessed to force that choice upon the administration—earlier rather than later. Premier Li Peng put it very clearly three months after the new Clinton administration took office: "President Clinton says his first priority is the economic revitalization of the American economy. If he misses out on the Chinese market, it won't help his efforts to revive the economy. So, please convey this message when you return."[33]

The collapse of the administration's effort to link trade and human rights in mid-1994 (see Chapters 1 and 3), the growing desire for Chinese assistance in preventing North Korean acquisition of nuclear weapons, and the need to preserve stability in the Taiwan Strait (1995–1996) cumulatively provided the Clinton administration with incentives to specify its foreign policy priorities more clearly, indeed to reorder them. From mid-1994 on, the administration increasingly emphasized the primacy of security and economic interests. Thereafter, those for and against a more cooperative posture toward Beijing made their principal arguments in terms of American security and economic interests. Instead of focusing on human rights violations, the skeptics of "engagement" asserted that China's military modernization, repeated efforts to gain American high technology, alleged efforts to buy influence in the U.S. electoral system, and unfair trade practices represented real threats to American security and economic interests.

In the wake of the 1996 presidential election this line of attack became pronounced. The activist core of the Republican Party was searching for new, powerful issues to be used in order to secure a larger majority in the Congress during the off-year elections of 1998 and to lay the foundation for the year 2000 quest for the White House (see Chapter 7). As Republican strategist William Kristol put it, "The issue of China dovetails neatly with the looming problem of national defense."[34] In another setting, Kristol pointed to the power of China as a "wedge issue," an issue that helps draw a sharp line between oneself and the opposition.

As we have seen, there is a repetitive quality to the themes of American and Chinese thinking about one another. Further, the views, rhetorical formulations, and actions of one side have fed the anxieties of the other. In turn, as we shall see in the chapter that follows, these anxieties have provided political opportunity to politicians in both systems. The mass media also have been central in this dynamic. In China and the United States, albeit for far different reasons, the mass media are not simply reporters of fact. Rather, they see themselves as guardians of the core values of their respective societies. Moreover, the media represent forums in which politicians and opinion leaders vie to attract popular attention and political support. The media are therefore not simply observers of the U.S.-China relationship; they are active players in it.

THE AMERICAN AND CHINESE MASS MEDIA AND THE GLOBAL MEDIA FISHBOWL

Much as the United States and China have their own distinctive national self-conceptions and understandings of their bilateral relationship, they also have distinctive mass media structures that inform their respective citizens about the other society. Instead of trying to evaluate the content, coverage, and accuracy of each nation's media, I focus principally on another set of questions: How do the structure, operation, and conceptualization of each nation's media machine help account for the difficulty in managing the U.S.-China relationship? and How do these considerations practically guarantee that there will be mutual misunderstanding in the future? The sources of built-in conflict fall into three areas: (1) the power of instantaneous media images; (2) a free, foreign press working in a highly constraining system; and (3) differing understandings concerning the press's role in the United States and in China. In addressing these questions, it is wise to keep in mind the following observations by *Los Angeles Times* correspondent Jim Mann:

> [S]tories in the American media tend to be governed at any given time by a single story, image or concept. In the 1950s and the 1960s, the "frame" was of China as little blue ants or automatons. In the 1970s, following the Nixon administration's opening, the frame was of the virtuous (entertaining, cute) Chinese.... In the 1980s, the frame was that China was "going capitalist." And for most of the 1990s, the frame was of a repressive China.

The reduction of China to a one-dimensional frame affects coverage of China in many ways, both direct and indirect.... The problem for media coverage is that China itself changes far less than do the one-dimensional American frames of it.[35]

Powerful Global Images

News coverage tends to be one of two types: event-driven or trend stories. Event-driven media coverage concerns itself with dramatic events and powerful visuals. Trend stories tend to be more complex, of less immediacy, and, due to the evolutionary character of their subjects, often less visual. Television particularly tends to be event driven, and it is television that creates the most enduring and potent images. Americans most frequently get their news from television.[36] This accounts for a constant refrain among both the Chinese and China experts that news coverage of the PRC tends to be superficial, simplistic, and to ignore many central subjects. In short, it is hard to get good coverage of a trend story (such as the gradual transformation of China) in an event-driven medium, and in a medium in which the length of the average sound bite has dropped from about twenty seconds to seven or eight seconds in the last twenty years.[37] In this respect, the proposition that coverage of China lacks balance and depth has less to do with journalistic bias against the PRC than the nature of the story (which is long term, complex, and "exotic" in character) and the limitations of one of the primary vehicles by which it can be conveyed.

This brings us to the "CNN effect." This term captures a complex reality in which powerful, real-time images of unfolding human events and tragedy are potentially directed into every electrified home in the world, setting off demands for a policy response by governments, markets, and multinational organizations globally. The impact of media imagery on a society is a function of the clarity of the images, the degree to which individuals identify with them, and the percentage of the population exposed to the imagery. When clear, high-impact images hit a huge percentage of a country's population, the resulting popular demand for response puts pressure on politicians to act. In trying to build support for NATO's intervention in Kosovo, for example, British Prime Minister Tony Blair was in Chicago and gave graphic witness to the CNN effect: "No one in the West who has seen what is happening in Kosovo can doubt that NATO's military action is justified. Bismarck famously said the Balkans were not worth the bones of one Pomeranian Grenadier. Anyone who has seen the tear-stained faces of the hundreds of thousands of refugees streaming across the border, heard their heart-rending tales of cruelty or contemplated the unknown fates of those left behind, knows that Bismarck was wrong."[38]

By all these measures, the violence in and around Tiananmen Square in June 1989 was an extraordinary event in the annals of global media coverage. In the weeks and days leading up to the night of June 3–4, 1989, Chinese students and other PRC citizens were giving television interviews with reporters from around the world—making their aspirations for the future immediately tangible to the world. The powerful images that were provided during the period leading up to the repression, the crackdown itself, and the manhunt for dissenters thereafter did more than create a sense of human identification between those in Tiananmen Square and viewers around the world—they provided images so memorable that they are still used repeatedly as lead-in footage to news and documentary broadcasts more than a decade after the events themselves. Among those images are students in the midst of a hunger strike; the "Goddess of Democracy"; the unidentified, solitary man facing off a tank; and the harrowing nighttime scene of tanks racing through the crowd as the crackdown proceeded.

No less important than the images, however, were the amount of time that the network news programs devoted to coverage of the events and the number of persons exposed to those images. One study of network news coverage during this period reported that "China received just 64 minutes of airtime the year before (1988), while in 1989, the year of Tiananmen, news on China totaled 881 minutes."[39] Further, the percentage of Americans who closely followed the unfolding tragedy was unusually high. A 1998 study published by the National Committee on U.S.-China Relations, the Kennedy School at Harvard, and American University reported that recent media pieces on China received the attention of only about 10 to 15 percent of the American public.[40] Even seemingly newsworthy events like the tensions in the Taiwan Strait in 1996 were followed "very closely" by only 19 percent of Americans—President Clinton's trip to China in 1998 drew an audience of 14 percent.[41] "The exception was in 1989, when nearly half [47%] of the American public closely followed the events in Tiananmen Square."[42] As one 1992 Harvard study noted, "This worldwide real-time audience had existed on a few rare occasions before, for such events as the Americans' landing on the moon in 1969."[43] The combination of the power of the images and the duration of the public's exposure to them (combined with other sources of information) produced the aforementioned overnight shift in public opinion toward China in the wake of June 4.

Paradoxically, while great numbers of Americans were exposed to these powerful images, the general Chinese populace had little visual exposure to Tiananmen. The central government prevented such coverage from reaching most Chinese viewers. There was virtually no access in the country except at a few international hotels with CNN or other international news sources; the relatively few satellite receivers in China at the time were concentrated along the coast. Consequently, when I visited China in September 1989 and spoke with Chinese leaders and citizens, I was struck by the lack of comprehension of the effect that this sustained, live television coverage of Tiananmen had abroad.

Parenthetically, mounting numbers of Chinese are gaining access to the global media. For example, in 1997 there were 1.4 million Internet users, in June 1999 there were about 4 million, and by 2000 the number had reached 9 million, a number equal to the users predicted for 2002 less than a year before.[44] With respect to Internet accounts, "many of those accounts are shared by 10 or 20 people."[45] In mid-1999, I was told that 90 percent of students at Peking University had Internet accounts, and by the end of that year nationally there were 520 Internet service providers and 1,000 Internet content providers.[46] Moreover, in 1997 CNN reportedly was received in 1.4 million Chinese households. Despite a 1993 State Council ban on privately owned satellite dishes, in 1996 in Shanghai alone it was estimated that 8,000 individuals had such dishes and the number of new customers was growing by 100 a month.[47] On a 1999 trip on the Yangtze River, I was struck by the number of satellite dishes atop remote village homes. That same year, an estimated 45 million homes in China had access to Hong Kong–based Phoenix Satellite Television, through individual dish and local cable systems.[48] The number of Chinese listeners to Voice of America can run as high as *60 million.*[49] As a consequence of these trends, China's leaders are being forced to become more sensitive to the domestic and international impact of media coverage; but they were not in 1989!

Americans, however, are not the only ones who can be affected by powerful visual images. Nor should they think that a "plugged-in" China inherently weakens the links between Chinese citizens and their government. The May 1999 U.S. bombing of the Chinese Embassy in Belgrade created powerful visual images that were constantly replayed and reprinted in the PRC media; this information was made available to the Chinese people through the expanding infrastructure of global communication just described. Those images included pictures of the smoking hulk of the bombed-out embassy, grieving relatives of the dead, the return of the victims' bodies to their homeland, and their bodies lying on autopsy tables.[50] The result, along with some active measures by Beijing, was to mobilize tens of thousands of citizens into the streets of Beijing, Chengdu, Shanghai, Hangzhou, Shenyang, Guangzhou, Xiamen, and Xian to demonstrate against the American government, in some cases violently. In short, if powerful visual images of Tiananmen ended Americans' honeymoon with China in 1989, powerful visual images of Belgrade ended what was left of that honeymoon for the Chinese people a decade later.

A second important characteristic of the CNN effect is that once such an event occurs, it tends to persist. The images persist until an equally powerful set of images displaces them. By their very nature, such events are infrequent. In the case of American perceptions of China, one set of powerful images transformed those views in early 1972 when President Nixon visited the PRC—Nixon shaking hands with Zhou Enlai and the presidential motorcade driving through central Beijing on a wintry day. Such images, reinforced by Deng Xiaoping's 1979 visit to a Texas rodeo wearing a ten-gallon hat and Ronald Reagan's April 1984 trip to the PRC, were not supplanted until the events of June 1989. And these new images were highly negative.

Since that time, there has been no event that has generated sufficiently positive images to overpower those of Tiananmen, though the Clinton administration and the Chinese self-consciously tried to create visual records during the 1997 and 1998 summits and the 1999 visit of Premier Zhu Rongji to the United States (see Chapter 8) that would cumulatively do so. In speaking of the president's purposes in going to China in June 1998, one U.S. executive branch figure said, "The president was trying to get the U.S. people beyond Tiananmen and desired to get footage of a varied China, to get beyond APCs [armored personnel carriers] and bodies on stretchers."[51] With respect to his October 1997 visit to the United States, President Jiang Zemin had a "core audience of about 10 percent," a far cry from the audience for the Tiananmen violence.[52] Similarly, Beijing sought to use what proved to be the smooth transition in Hong Kong to this end as well in mid-1997. Nonetheless, as of mid-1999, public opinion polls showed very little improvement in China's favorability rating (see table 6).[53]

The bombing of the Chinese Embassy in Belgrade has likewise created an enduring set of images. With the images of the wrecked embassy and of the Chinese killed by the bombs, Americans have created new, strong, and negative visual images that are likely to persist in the PRC. And the Americans came away from this tragic incident with a troubling image too—their ambassador peering through the shattered windows of the U.S. Embassy in Beijing (see photograph in photo section).

A Free Press Working in a Constrained Environment

The way Beijing has treated the foreign press generally and the methods the PRC has used to get its story out have been counterproductive, though as the 1990s ended there were small, easily reversible signs of improvement. In the final analysis, there is a fundamental conflict between Mao Zedong's still operative concept of the press as mouthpiece of the Communist Party (dating back to the chairman's seminal Talks at the Yenan Forum on Art and Literature of 1942)[54] and the needs of both a pluralizing Chinese society and foreign journalists trying to perform according to their professional standards and meet the commercial pressures to which they are subject back home.

When Western journalists are first posted to China, they generally are excited at the prospect of being there; many have spent months or years in language and academic preparation for their assignment. However, their treatment once in the PRC often alienates them, with bugging of apartments, harassment of informants, withdrawal of press credentials, security "tails," occasional raids, and even more infrequent expulsions as examples.[55] This has negatively affected the resulting coverage.

Beijing's method of managing news is another consideration that works against PRC interests. For example, in periods of *crisis* news interest is highest. A crisis can be defined as a severe problem, in a situation of imperfect information, under conditions of time compression. It is at precisely such times that foreign journalists are under the greatest pressure to obtain news. Also, it is at precisely such times that Chinese officials talk the least. The 1998 National Committee on U.S.-China Relations report on U.S. coverage of the PRC referred to previously, for example, observed that "during the Taiwan Strait crisis [March 1996], Beijing uniformly denied interview requests. In such situations, it would be more conducive to accurate and balanced coverage if Chinese officials briefed reporters, explaining the relevant context and history, and answered questions about China's policy and position."[56]

The Harvard Barone Center study cited earlier provides another interesting example of how Chinese officialdom's refusal to communicate can bias coverage of the PRC, in this case Tiananmen-related coverage: "The China coverage was somewhat hampered by the fact that the conservatives in the Chinese government refused to talk to the press, and the only officials who did talk, even surreptitiously, to the press favored the reformist faction. This led to false optimism at one point that the reform faction might win the struggle."[57]

The PRC can be assured of one thing: in circumstances such as these, whether it is Taipei or the politically disaffected domestically who are speaking, they will present their side of the story in the most effective manner possible. During the June 4, 1989, crisis, the official system became largely uncommunicative, leaving the field to those most motivated in the Chinese system to communicate. If Beijing does not get its story out, others will fill the gap, particularly domestic dissidents. Further, if official Chinese sources have nothing credible to say, the media will be driven to observers entirely outside of the Chinese system, who may or may not be informed or unbiased—such sources may be international nongovernmental organizations, foreign observers of China, or Taipei. So little information was available on what was happening in China on June 4–5, 1989, for instance, that I had reporters *in Beijing* calling me *in New York City* asking for news about what was going on in the Chinese capital!

There are many reasons Chinese officials hesitate to make themselves accessible to the foreign press, particularly in times of crisis. To start, Chinese officials do not value, indeed fear, a free flow of information, having been brought up in a system in which access to information was a privilege, not a right, and usually not in their interest either. They come to believe that the system is doing the media a favor by providing any information, and that therefore it is not incumbent on the system to make access to that information either easy or inexpensive. For example, in 1996 the Foreign Ministry announced that it would stop providing official English translations of statements at its twice-weekly press briefings, with the press spokesman saying, "You ask the questions in Chinese—that's what we will do as of September 1," to "improve the working efficiency."[58] In October of the following year, however, the ministry quietly resumed providing English translations. The initial response could be justified— most countries hold press briefings in their native tongue and Americans in China should be able to speak Chinese. Yet the fact remains that it is in the regime's interest to be understood in the English-speaking world when it chooses to speak.

Moreover, the Chinese system usually develops its "position" on an event only after considerable internal "consultation." Consequently, there is a lag between when the press needs a response and when the system can generate one. Also, Chinese officials simply assume (sometimes with good reason) that their views will be put in the worst possible light by Western media. And finally, the price a Chinese official might pay for a serious misstep is greater than the price to be paid by officials in many other systems.

A related problem concerns what one might call "the service orientation" of the Chinese information bureaucracy. In the West, the breaking story waits for no one. In China, the bureaucracy has its own schedule (although this is gradually changing). This was seen during Hong Kong's reversion to Chinese sovereignty in mid-1997. This was a global story, with thousands of foreign reporters in town, and China had a rather good story to tell the world. But the PRC was not well prepared to tell *its* story. "For example, during the Hong Kong handover, the Chinese news agency set up a hot-line, but it closed every day at 5:00 p.m.; 'anti-handover' forces, on the other hand, were well-prepared to explain their position to the media at any time."[59]

Similarly, the costs of satellite time, ISDN lines, telephones, translation or interpretation, and office space are all very high in the PRC. There are explanations for this situation, but the effect is to make it more difficult and expensive for foreign news agencies to cover China in depth. Due to the high costs and general difficulties of setting up shop in the PRC, foreign media organizations "parachute" in journalists from time to time (often in connection with a major event or leadership visit). Usually the temporary visitors do not have any particular China expertise, and this can negatively affect the quality and accuracy of reporting. Thus the PRC frequently disadvantages itself; it would receive more knowledgeable and favorable coverage if it lowered the barriers to media entry and increased the access of reporters.

Access, however, is not only discouraged by the factors just listed; active methods are used to limit the possibilities for journalists to ferret out the darker aspects of Chinese society. Active discouragement includes making it difficult for reporters to travel to remote localities or gain access to particular "units," the surveillance of both reporters and their informants, the punishing of informants, and the fact that the foreign reporter must often bear the expense of PRC officials who are required to accompany him or her and whose presence generally inhibits informants. In September of 1997, I was in Beijing with the editor of the *National Interest*, Owen Harries, and other journal editors at a meeting with a number of resident foreign journalists. Harries recounts, "I asked a group of Western correspondents how thuggish they considered the regime to be these days. Offered a choice between Louisiana in the 1950s and Mussolini's Italy, they all opted for Louisiana."[60]

Whether the Chinese methods are comparable to those of Louisiana or Italy in bygone eras is not as important as the fact that their net effect is to alienate the reporters who are the medium through which China is portrayed to the rest of the world. This treatment not only alienates journalists but also has the perverse effect of driving them into the arms of the system's greatest domestic critics—those who are willing to take great risks to get their story out. If reporters can't talk to Chinese officials or representative citizens, talking to the disaffected can become the principal avenue open to them. Moreover, talking to dissidents can become the "lazy" journalist's way out—it is easier than trying to get access to sources through the regular Chinese bureaucracy. As Steve Mufson of the *Washington Post* put it, "Dissidents have no *waiban* [foreign affairs office]."[61]

The desire to limit foreign press access brings us to perhaps the greatest barrier to effective and accurate portrayals of China in the United States. There is a great cultural and political division between the two countries on the proper roles of the mass media. The PRC's definition of the legitimate role of the mass media becomes the crystallization of everything foreign reporters find objectionable about the system, a metaphor for the larger system. Conversely, the sometimes subtle anti-China bias that many Chinese perceive in the American press feeds their image of China as a "victim" and their deeply held sense that the West always tries to humiliate China.

The Media's Role in Market-Driven and Politically Driven Systems

The author Orville Schell neatly encapsulates the dilemma facing both a Chinese press in a changing domestic environment and the foreign press trying to document the maelstrom: "The dilemma of the overseas press corps in China grows out of China's own dilemma: that it is a nation and a society caught between contradictory systems, between an older theoretical underpinning of Marxism-Leninism and a new overlay of market-driven free enterprise and competitive practice. But what hobbles China's own indigenous press from developing and what keeps the status of the overseas press corps in a state of inescapable ambiguity is the notion that 'the press' ought to 'partner' with the Party and the state in promoting its agenda."[62]

In the West, particularly in the United States, the journalist's job is to inform the public, as objectively as possible, without any particular agenda. While this standard may not always be achieved, it is the professional's definition of the goal. One system characteristic that works at cross-purposes to this standard is the need for news organizations to succeed as revenue-producing enterprises (which can reward sensationalism, airing graphic images without providing context, and a focus on short-term drama rather than long-term trends). As one Senate Foreign Relations Committee staffer put it in early 2000: "Good news is bad news. Complicated news is no news. Bad news is good news. The best news is simple bad news!" In a more scholarly analysis, the Harvard Barone Center study concluded with respect to Tiananmen coverage, "The need to fill a 24-hour news hole, to beat the competition, to justify the costs of sending extra people to Beijing—all this ended up driving much bad information into the public record."[63] There is the added difficulty of conveying a complex story in a short period of time on a topic for which viewers have little context. Nonetheless, objectivity, without agenda, is the ultimate goal of mainstream news coverage.

In the PRC, the standard for evaluating the performance of journalists and the media is far different than in the West. The Chinese are straightforward in acknowledging this distinction.[64] Their view, in part, has its origins in the Confucian (and Leninist and Maoist) notion that a principal role of leadership is to consciously structure the belief systems of followers in directions supportive of collective state goals and policy. The leaders must educate the populace in ways conducive to the maintenance of power, the implementation of government policy, and the preservation of social solidarity. In China, the *word* (both spoken and written) traditionally has been, and remains, very important. Donald Munro recalls the Chinese traditional aphorism that "[t]hrough the use of force one causes men's mouths to submit; through reasoning one causes their minds to submit."[65] My notes on the remarks of one Chinese journalist in mid-1998 convey the political purpose of the PRC media neatly: "Media are the instruments to construct spiritual civilization, promote policies and stability, and promote the economic progress of the people. Media plays a key role in implementing Party policies. Media is social engineering and is a major weapon of political battle and is a mouthpiece of the government. It is to help build socialist government and create popular awareness and help government keep power and convince people of policies and to spread ideology and policies. It is to help the Party and the government run the country and avoid things that lead to crime, violence, or social disorder."[66]

Many contrasts can be drawn from these two widely divergent conceptions of the press, but several are central. One is that Chinese media are part of the official governing structure, while American news organizations overwhelmingly are not—indeed U.S. journalists often see themselves in an adversarial posture. Another difference involves the purpose of news. In the PRC, exposing the dark side of Chinese society is *not* traditionally seen as compatible with the promotion of social solidarity, whereas U.S. news organizations reserve their highest accolades for those who bring light to the dark corners of politics and society—at home and abroad. And finally, in its interaction with Chinese media and propaganda personnel, the American press is faulted for not helping to improve the atmosphere of U.S.-China relations—something that American journalists deeply believe is not their role. As one American journalist put it, "Journalists do not see their role as facilitating U.S.-China relations nor do they see their role as disrupting such relations. [It is] irrelevant!"[67] As Professor T. K. Chang put it, "Americans look at news as good, per se, and Chinese look at the consequences of news."[68]

These very different conceptions of the role of the mass media mean that an adversarial relationship will persist between the Chinese government and the Western media into the foreseeable future. The nature of this relationship will lead Chinese authorities to treat the foreign media in ways that are not always in Beijing's own best interests. Such treatment affects the breadth and tone of coverage, both directly and indirectly. As one Chinese official explained the relationship between the foreign media and the Chinese authorities in mid-1998, "Slowly Chinese leaders come to understand the need to work with the U.S. media, meet deadlines, etc. But, many remain deeply skeptical of institutional bias [in the U.S. media]."[69] Another Chinese analyst of the U.S. press put it this way:

> My study of July–October [1995] issues of the *Washington Post* shows that during the period the newspaper published 202 stories about China and 79 of them about Harry Wu and the so-called human rights abuses. The others dealt with the so-called harassment of delegates to the Fourth World Conference on Women which was convened in Beijing in September, Chinese military threats to its neighbours, China's poverty, corruption and smuggling.... But the picture the American people get from their press about China is a country plagued with human rights' abuses, baby killings, forced abortions, women trafficking, labour camps, beggars, harassment of foreigners and China's military threats to its neighbors.
>
> Such an irresponsible and unfair coverage of China will not only turn many American people away from China but also make reform-minded Chinese people very much suspect the ultramotives [*sic*, ulterior motives] of the American press.[70]

In the same way that Chinese believe that there are deep institutional biases in the way U.S. mass media portray China, there is ample evidence that Chinese media frequently convey a highly distorted portrait of America. One analysis of programming on the PRC's Central Chinese Television

(CCTV) compared the portrayal of the United States to that of other foreign countries: "CCTV also gave two to four times more attention to disaster and accident news from the United States than it did in its coverage of other countries: approximately 17.6 percent of stories on the United States focused on disasters in 1996, compared to 4.4 percent for other nations. News reports concerning crime and law also had a much higher profile in CCTV's coverage of the United States, compared to its investigation of such topics in other countries; about 5.9 percent for the United States in 1996, but only 1.3 percent for other nations that same year."[71]

Similarly, in their coverage of the March–June 1999 NATO air campaign against the Belgrade regime of Slobodan Milosevic, the Chinese media emphasized NATO's intervention in a "civil war" within a sovereign country but not the ethnic cleansing that precipitated the NATO action in the first place. Further, in the wake of the May 7, 1999, bombing of the Chinese Embassy in Belgrade, the pages of *People's Daily* were covered with assertions that the tragedy was "deliberate," and stories were replete with descriptions such as "willful murder," "blood debt," "archcriminal," "lunatics," and "prevarication."[72] Because the Chinese press is a reflection of Chinese government policy to a considerable extent, such portrayals of the United States are particularly disturbing to Americans—coverage reflects an official intentionality that cannot be said to characterize the Western press.

Having said this, there is a reform-era evolution toward growing numbers of media and information outlets in China, with foreign news becoming increasingly available. By the late 1990s, only about 30 percent of the more than 2,000 newspapers in China were Communist Party organs. As well, in the late 1990s there were an estimated 1,000 cable stations nationally and 980 television stations at different levels, with the number of TV stations quadrupling between 1985 and 1995.[73] Moreover, commercial logic increasingly drives editorial decisions, as a Xinhua (New China News Agency) editor explained in 1998: "Government subsidies to media are drying up. *Xinhua* subsidizes only 30 percent of *Xinhua's* expenditures. So how to sell more print and ads? So, this has brought more masters to the Chinese media."[74] Chinese television today is awash in advertising, the majority of which carries messages rather inconsistent with the propaganda apparatus's objectives. Book publishers and cash-starved government offices that are their patrons are constantly pushing at the limits of the acceptable.

Moreover, some Chinese leaders, particularly Premier Zhu Rongji, believe that a press with more initiative can possibly be a useful partner with the government that can help ferret out domestic wrongdoing. By the close of the 1990s this concept sparked a debate that had been latent since 1989 when, for a brief period of time, Chinese media had sided with the Tiananmen demonstrators: should the mass media be an organ of the Communist Party or "for the people"? One PRC-oriented paper in Hong Kong described the debate as follows: "Zhu Rongji's theory of media oversight has been much discussed in political and press circles. Some hold that Zhu Rongji's view that the media is 'the public mouthpiece' echoes that of the elder in PRC press circles and former *People's Daily* Director, Hu Jiwei, that 'a newspaper should be more for the people than the party.' "[75]

Such debate may appear encouraging to Americans. However, even if the utilitarian view of a free press were to gain strength, increased press freedom would not necessarily be considered a fundamental right, but rather a useful tool. The gulf between the Chinese and American conceptions of the role of the media is very wide and probably will remain so for a long time.

The Tactical Use of the Press

Although the goal of journalists in the United States may be to tell a story of importance with objectivity to large numbers of people, the U.S. mass media nevertheless provide an arena wherein domestic policy and power contenders wage their battles. The weapons are selective, distorted leaks and carefully scripted, contrived events. Media become the vehicle by which policy agendas are formed and articulated, coalitions are built, and power struggles are waged.

In an off-the-record session, one respected U.S. observer of American politics discussed selective leaks about, and partisan attacks on, China from a variety of sources in Washington's bureaucracy and on Capitol Hill: "It is an attempt to frame U.S.-China relations, and this is an attempt to define Bill Clinton as a craven, immoral leader." Similarly, the U.S. national security community hemorrhaged information every time (from 1990 to 2000) the administration and Congress girded up for their annual battle over MFN treatment for Beijing or some other divisive China policy issue such as the Taiwan Security Enhancement Act proposed in 1999. The media in China provide an arena for conflict as well, although this is sometimes more difficult to discern or interpret from the outside. But one example would be the great lengths to which President Jiang Zemin went to use his 1997 trip to the United States to bolster his domestic position through film (*Across the Pacific*) and in a book (*History in Focus*) in both English and Chinese.[76]

CONCLUSIONS

There are important ideologically derived tensions in U.S.-China relations, none more central than the Chinese quest for control over their internal affairs and the deeply held American belief that China's internal governance is also the United States' proper concern.

Writing about policy toward China in 1948, George Kennan staked out one position in the ongoing American debate over priorities, sovereignty, and intervention—a view that I believe the experience of the first post–cold war decade reaffirms: "It is a traditional principle of this Government [the United States] to refrain from interference in the internal affairs of other countries.... Whoever proposes or urges such intervention should properly bear the burden of proof (A) that there is sufficiently powerful national interest to justify our departure ... from a rule of international conduct which has been proven sound by centuries of experience, ... and (B) that we have the means to conduct such intervention successfully and can afford the cost in terms of the national effort it involves."[77]

Departure from this practice, as occurred to a certain extent in the first three years of the first Clinton administration's China policy (and on a broader global basis thereafter), had a number of results, some unwelcome. Notably, it made the Chinese uncooperative with respect to other issues such as proliferation, reduced U.S. credibility when threats were not carried out, often worked to America's economic disadvantage, and had little discernible effect on the overall human rights situation in China (see Chapter 3). And finally, the U.S. effort to achieve human rights improvements without allied support called into question the wisdom of American leadership in a broad international context.

A more effective strategy, and one that fits well with the American self-conceptualization, is to recognize that economic and security interaction with the PRC ("engagement") will gradually be reflected in internal changes in China. Pursuit of legitimate American economic and security interests will have broader and positive consequences, over a probably rather long period of time.

A second conclusion relates to the globalization of the mass media. Because the media deliver powerful, real-time images to the world's population, and because Beijing has a declining capacity to insulate its citizens from such images, PRC leaders will increasingly be selected for their ability to deal with the media and to avoid situations that create powerful, long-lasting, negative pictures of China. President Jiang Zemin and Premier Zhu Rongji are the PRC's first national-level leaders to be comparatively media sensitive in the global information age.

Zhu, for instance, both as Shanghai mayor and later as premier, has dealt very effectively with the foreign press, as demonstrated in his successive trips to the United States, Japan, Europe, and Hong Kong. For example, his press conference of March 19, 1998, following his designation as premier was handled masterfully from a public relations perspective. When asked by a *Time* magazine correspondent whether China-wide popular elections for state president and premier were future possibilities, Zhu began his response by saying, "I saw my picture on the cover of the latest issue of *Time*, which seemed to be better looking than the one on the cover of *Newsweek* that was published several days ago. So, I'd like to thank you. [laughter] But I did not blame *Newsweek* in the least because I am not that good looking. [laughter].... As to when such elections will take place, it is now hard for me to predict."[78] Zhu's media skills were equally on display during the premier's trip to the United States in April 1999.

Similarly, Shanghai Mayor Xu Kuangdi has been remarkably effective in dealing with, and in being relatively accessible to, the foreign press. Prior to and during his November 1996 visit to America, he received the kind of press coverage that American politicians crave: he was portrayed, correctly, as an erudite lover of Mozart and Tchaikovsky, good books, and efficiency. A *New York Times* reporter painted him as a thoughtful iconoclast, recounting how some years before, when then Shanghai Mayor Zhu Rongji had asked him to head Shanghai's State Planning Commission, Xu replied, "But I don't believe in planning."[79] Many of China's young local leaders, like Dalian's mayor, Bo Xilai, and Zhuhai's mayor, Liang Guangda, have also dealt very effectively with the Western media.

When one looks at emerging local Chinese leaders, particularly in cosmopolitan coastal cities, one finds a gradually expanding pool of persons who are skillful in dealing with the mass media. One late-1990s example of this was the elevation of former Shanghai Vice Mayor Zhao Qizheng to be spokesman for the State Council. One of the first challenges he faced in his new post was to respond to 1999 Cox Committee charges of Chinese espionage. To do so he set up an Internet demonstration for international journalists to show just how much sensitive scientific information already was in the public domain.[80]

A third conclusion is this: because of the vast differences between the two nations' mass media systems and the divergent economic, political, and value systems in which they are embedded, each nation's coverage of the other will be a source of ongoing friction. China's domestic coverage of the United States is highly skewed and politically driven, though market forces will change that somewhat over time. The inadequacies of American coverage are also numerous and have several sources. Television media, particularly in a crisis, focus viewer attention on a single issue and place; it is like looking at China through a straw. The view provided is real, but there is no peripheral vision. In June 1989, to most Americans, China equaled Tiananmen Square. Perceptually, there was no China beyond the range of the camera lens.

The other principal problem with American news coverage of China is that, like most American reporting of events in the United States, it tends to focus on the negative. In that sense, there is no more bias in American coverage of China than there is in coverage of the United States itself. The problem arises, however, in the fact that the average American does not have the contextual knowledge of China that he or she has of the United States. Therefore, there is no broad context in which to place the negative information. Thus both the narrow focus of China reporting, particularly in television, and the concentration on negative news have an inherently distorting effect.

A final, broad conclusion can be drawn, and it leads us into the following chapter on the interplay of domestic politics and foreign relations. In American politics mass media attention is indispensable for candidates, and "red meat" political rhetoric calling for the realization of American ideals can frequently attract such coverage. While this may help a candidate get elected, it does not necessarily make it easier for the victor to responsibly govern. The experience of the first Clinton administration suggests that the aftermath of trying to deal with unworkable campaign promises relating to China can last more than three years, by which time a new general election campaign has begun. The combination of off-year and general election campaign competition, values-driven and partisan rhetoric, a mass media searching for stirring remarks, and the time required for a candidate to free himself or herself of such rhetoric after winning the election means that policy is rarely free of the dangers of rhetorical excess. This brings us to domestic politics in both nations.

Newly elected President George Bush and Senior Leader Deng Xiaoping talk over lunch, Beijing, February 26, 1989. A trip designed to consolidate bilateral relations ended up underscoring human rights frictions as the dissident astrophysicist Fang Lizhi was prevented from attending a presidential banquet at which senior Chinese leaders were present. Photo courtesy George Bush Presidential Library.

His Holiness the Dalai Lama meets with National Committee on U.S.-China Relations (NCUSCR) team to discuss its report on conditions in Tibet, October 1991, New York City. (From left: Richard Holbrooke, Harold Saunders, the author, the Dalai Lama, Dwight Perkins, Sidney Jones, Jan Berris.) Photo courtesy Jan Berris, NCUSCR.

Journalist and activist Dai Qing speaks with author at New York City meeting sponsored by NCUSCR, January 21, 1992. Photo courtesy Jan Berris, NCUSCR.

In April 1993 Mr. Koo Chen-fu, chairman of the Straits Exchange Foundation in Taiwan (left), and his counterpart Mr. Wang Daohan, chairman of the mainland's Association for Relations across the Taiwan Straits (right), signed four agreements at historic talks in Singapore. Photo courtesy Straits Exchange Foundation, Taipei, Taiwan.

Christopher Patten, the last governor of Hong Kong, visits the United States to argue that one cannot help Hong Kong by inflicting economic damage on the PRC that reverberates in the territory. New York City, May 1993. (From left: Christopher Patten, the author, Robert Levinson, and Barrie Wiggham, Hong Kong Commissioner for Economic and Trade Affairs). Photo courtesy NCUSCR Archives.

In May 1994 a NCUSCR team traveled to Beijing to facilitate resumption of military-to-military exchanges and cross-strait dialogue. (From left: General William Richardson (ret.), Admiral David Jeremiah (ret.), former Secretary of Defense Robert McNamara, and General Xu Xin, former vice chief of staff of the PLA.) Photo by David M. Lampton.

Taiwan President Lee Teng-hui campaigning for president in Taiwan's first island-wide popular election for the post in early 1996. In the wake of PRC missile exercises, Lee won handily. Photo courtesy TECRO News Bureau, Hsieh Hui-chuan.

In the wake of the 1995–1996 tensions in the Taiwan Strait, a NCUSCR team sought to promote greater mutual strategic understanding between China and the United States. (From left in the foreground: Admiral David Jeremiah (ret.), former Secretary of Defense and Energy James Schlesinger, Vice Chairman of the Central Military Commission General Zhang Wannian, and General Xu Xin.) September 1996, Beijing. Photo courtesy Elizabeth Knup, NCUSCR.

Presidents Bill Clinton and Jiang Zemin review People's Liberation Army troops on the perimeter of Tiananmen Square at the welcoming ceremony, June 27, 1998, Beijing. Photo courtesy New China News Agency.

Author meets Premier Zhu Rongji prior to the premier's conversation with Aspen Institute–sponsored congressional delegation, March 31, 1999, Beijing. During this meeting shortly before Zhu's visit to the United States, WTO entry, human rights, and other issues were discussed. Photo courtesy State Council, People's Republic of China.

U.S. Ambassador to China James Sasser surveys damage to his embassy in Beijing in the wake of large-scale and violent demonstrations to protest the U.S. bombing of the PRC Embassy in Belgrade, May 1999. Photo courtesy Harry Hays, through the United States Information Agency.

7

THE SEAMLESS WEB
Domestic Politics and Foreign Relations

Henry Kissinger to Deng Xiaoping: In this respect, we have to
keep in mind—and I'm being very frank with you—a very
complicated domestic situation. For the United States to take
strong actions in crises, it is necessary to do so from a position of
having demonstrated to our people that we have exhausted every
avenue for peace. I think Chairman Mao, last year, said the United
States plays complicated games, and China too plays complicated
games, but more energetically (*laughter*).

Meeting between Henry Kissinger and
Vice Premier Deng Xiaoping, Beijing, November 26, 1974

Even if presidents make a sincere transition from a campaign
perspective to a governing one, they are unlikely to be believed if
they begin from so far out in left or right field. It will seem as if
they are only playing politics. And their leadership cannot be
effective if Presidents are always in the position of having to prove
that they mean what they say.

From *Our Own Worst Enemy,* by I. M. Destler,
Leslie H. Gelb, and Anthony Lake, 1984

Our two systems and leadership are different. Your leaders draw
their strength from society and the people whereas our leaders
draw their strength from the confidence of their superiors. Your
Secretary of State Christopher misled [the Ministry of Foreign
Affairs about Lee Teng-hui receiving a visa to visit the United
States in 1995] and we told our leaders he would not be granted a
visa. You can imagine how I felt. My leaders lost confidence. My
parents grow rice in Northern China. I will return home and grow
rice with them.

Paraphrase of a very senior Chinese official, November 1996

The human rights problem is easier to understand than economics
and proliferation. Many of us [American politicians] understand
the hypocrisy of our demands and our own lack of purity, but
symbolism is important and the release of Wei Jingsheng was
good. But those kinds of symbolic actions will make it possible for

better informed [American] political and economic leadership to
make progress in other areas.

> U.S. senator to visiting Chinese delegation, December 1997

This agreement [on permanent normal tariff treatment for China]
has become like fly paper for the accumulated frustrations people
have about things in the world that they don't like very much; or
that are spinning beyond their control; or that they feel will have
an uncertain result. And that's the world we're living in.

> President Bill Clinton, White House, May 9, 2000

INTRODUCTION

One central failing in the way leaders in Beijing and Washington have
dealt with one other has been that while each side has recognized the constraints that its own political circumstance imposes on it, it has had little
appreciation for the constraints that limit the other side. Daily requirements for political survival and the priority of domestic agendas have been
central foreign policy drivers in *both* capitals.

In China as well as in the United States, a leader's losses or gains abroad
affect his or her domestic position. Consequently, foreign policy is designed
with an eye to domestic consequences, as we have seen in every chapter of
this book. American and Chinese politicians use the outside world as a prop
in their respective domestic theaters, hoping to convert perceived foreign
policy successes into improved domestic fortunes. Jiang Zemin used the
1997 Washington summit to bolster his standing at home in the immediate
post–Deng Xiaoping period, as Bill Clinton added some gravity to a presidency floundering in domestic scandal in mid-1998. And in May 1999, the
PLA, the propaganda apparatus, and individuals who had lost in previous
rounds of political struggle in Beijing used the U.S. bombing of the Chinese
Embassy in Belgrade to shore up or advance their positions.

Americans freely admit the connection between domestic politics and
foreign policy, and the contradictions to which that link gives rise. In contrast, Chinese often argue that their leaders are somehow above the domestic fray when making foreign policy decisions and that there is a correspondence between the requirements of domestic policy and the
effective conduct of foreign affairs. As one Chinese foreign policy official
told me, China has "no problem making our foreign and domestic tasks
mesh."[1] To some extent this is true, but to a large extent it is not.

This chapter focuses on the factors in both countries that create a tight link between domestic politics and foreign policy: rising pluralism, the emergence of a new type of leadership, changing balances between national and local institutions, and broad national agendas. In looking at these topics, the struggle for power, organizational politics, and coalition building are never far beneath the surface—in either country.

DOMESTIC POLITICS AND FOREIGN POLICY IN A BROAD CONTEXT

Politics

When thinking about the PRC, American policymakers and citizens tend to overemphasize differences between the two systems and downplay the many important similarities. China, we are told, is "communist," "totalitarian," "authoritarian," or "centralized," whereas America is "democratic" and "pluralistic." Although there are genuine, highly significant differences, one overriding similarity explains a great deal—the political task itself.

Three definitions capture the essence of politics, whether in China or in America. For political scientists, politics is "the authoritative allocation of values [ethical values and valued things] for a society."[2] Harold Lasswell points out that politics concerns itself with "who gets what, when, [and] how."[3] And in the prose of Ambrose Bierce, politics is revealed as "[a] strife of interests masquerading as a contest of principles. The conduct of public affairs for private advantage."[4] Together these definitions remind us that politics is an inescapable, universal social function.

Political leaders in China, like their American counterparts, have limited political *capital* with which to influence key domestic institutions and constituencies. In each country this capital can be spent or accumulated on both domestic and foreign policy issues. Therefore, whether it is Deng Xiaoping or Jiang Zemin, George Bush or Bill Clinton, the political leader must be engaged in a ceaseless process of calculating how much scarce political capital to spend on foreign policy versus domestic policy and where in each domain to spend it. It is unlikely, for instance, that when President Jiang Zemin and Premier Zhu Rongji are involved in a serious fight to end the military's heavy involvement in commerce and control the PLA's smuggling activities (as they were in 1998–1999), they would choose to offend those same interests further by making concessions on a litmus test issue such as Taiwan. The intensity of that particular domestic struggle was revealed in October 1998, when Premier Zhu Rongji, on national Chinese television, stated, "A large quantity of petroleum has been smuggled into our domestic market, almost crushing our entire petroleum industry. Smuggling is not something that every boss of a private enterprise can take a share of, and those bastards have [*sic*] all have links with the army as well as public security and national security setups."[5] Similarly, when President Clinton needed thirty-four votes in the U.S. Senate to survive a possible removal vote in early 1999, he did not risk antagonizing Democratic Party liberals in the Senate by pushing ahead with generous terms of entry into the WTO for Beijing. In the more distant past, presidents Kennedy, Nixon, and Ford all postponed progress in U.S.-China relations to second terms that either never came or were not completed.

Thus to understand the relationship between domestic developments and the behavior of China and the United States toward one another at any given moment, it is essential to know the political capital that each leadership believes it possesses and how it has decided to expend that capital. For example, in explaining Jiang Zemin's slow response to Washington's granting of a visa to Lee Teng-hui in May 1995, one Chinese analyst said, "Jiang Zemin simply did not have the political capital to decide alone, he had to build a consensus and this took time."[6]

Pluralism and Social Complexity

With Armageddon-like external threats seemingly reduced in the post–cold war era, America's deeply embedded pluralism, and the growing pluralism of Chinese society and government, domestic politics has become an increasingly formidable consideration in the making of foreign policy in both countries. As Richard Solomon aptly put it, "[T]he influence of senior political leaders [in China] has been somewhat diluted."[7] The days when leaders such as Richard Nixon and Mao Zedong could radically redirect the bilateral relationship in splendid isolation are over.

Mounting social and governmental pluralism increases the need for political leaders to spend their capital maintaining domestic political cohesion and discipline and building coalitions. Further, social and political pluralism make the context for resolving difficulties in the bilateral relationship arduous and offer endless opportunities for misunderstanding. Chinese leaders, for example, sometimes find it difficult to distinguish a remark made by a congressman on C-SPAN television from an authoritative reflection of U.S. government policy. As U.S. Ambassador to China James Sasser put it, "Some of the older [members of the Chinese] leadership don't understand that simply because a senator gets up on the floor of the Senate and says some uncomplimentary things about China that that's not necessarily government policy."[8] Indeed, Deng Xiaoping spoke for himself on American pluralism during his 1979 trip to the United States when he asked in exasperation, "How many governments do you have? We can only deal with one government."[9]

Yet it is not always the Chinese who, through unfamiliarity, simply attach undue import to what they hear—sometimes they are told by very credible people simply not to believe the executive branch. So, for example, in the midst of sensitive negotiations in 1993–1994 over whether President Clinton would withdraw MFN tariff treatment from the PRC unless Beijing improved its treatment of individuals, one very senior member of the U.S. House of Representatives told a visiting senior Chinese delegation, "I have some bad news for you today and some good news. The bad news is that President Clinton has promised to take MFN away from you unless you improve human rights. The good news is that President Clinton does not keep his promises." The Chinese were shocked that one part of a government would so undermine the credibility of another.

Similarly, with respect to China, U.S. national security officials had difficulty determining whether the sale by some PLA-affiliated company of spare parts that cost $14 each to Pakistan that could be used to fabricate nuclear weapons reflected a decision by the Politburo to promote proliferation, an unauthorized attempt by lowly officials to make money (corruption), insufficient regulatory mechanisms, or ignorance. Part of the trick in managing bilateral relations for both nations, therefore, is discerning genuine policy from the normal chatter and unruly behavior of pluralized polities.

The China emerging from its decade-long Cultural Revolution hibernation in the mid- and late 1970s had little knowledge about a late-twentieth-century American society dominated by interest groups, checks and balances, and the mass media. Chinese leaders were predisposed to view the U.S. Congress in the same light as they viewed their own rubber-stamp legislature—supine. As time has passed, however, the Chinese have had to learn that the U.S. Congress, the mass media, and interest groups do play an important role in American policymaking.

For its part, the United States has been slow to grasp the implications of the gradual pluralization of Chinese society and its political institutions in the years since Mao Zedong's death in 1976. Mao's successor, Deng Xiaoping, never had the same latitude to unilaterally change foreign policy that Mao Zedong enjoyed. And in turn, Deng's successor, Jiang Zemin, has been further constrained. With the progressive decentralization of power, authority, and economic resources in the PRC, Americans must now build vertical and horizontal relationships throughout Chinese society and government.

With Mao there was one-stop shopping for policy decisions and implementation. Now, as we enter the twenty-first century, obtaining a favorable central decision from Beijing is only the beginning of the challenge—having it implemented involves endless negotiation and haggling with innumerable levels of bureaucracy, political authority, and, increasingly, other societal groups.

And no less important, with rising Chinese nationalism, Washington is finding that popular attitudes in the PRC affect policy, albeit not as measurably as in poll-driven America. Americans are sadly mistaken, for example, if they think that the Chinese demonstrations against U.S. diplomatic facilities in May 1999 after the bombing of the PRC Embassy in Belgrade, Yugoslavia, were simply government-managed riots. Rather, the government was, in part (and only in part), trying to surf a wave of popular anger.

Another consideration has been the growing complexity of civil society in the United States and the much more gradual emergence of civil institutions in the PRC. In America of the 1950s and 1960s, there were relatively few nongovernmental organizations (NGOs) with foreign policy missions, and they often derived their clout from their close, albeit informal ties to government: the Council on Foreign Relations is a good example. More recently, NGOs in the United States have multiplied, often *marketing* themselves as opponents of "the establishment." They often have large memberships composed of those most unhappy with current policy.

On a far smaller scale, quasi-NGOs are making their appearance in China as well, adding to the complexity of domestic Chinese politics. Though generally weak and peripheral in the late 1990s, as Chinese NGOs grow in number and haltingly gain momentum, they increasingly will interact with, and feed off, their U.S. counterparts, and vice versa.[10] For example, the Chinese writer, journalist, and activist Dai Qing has established an organization for distributing information on the environment and has taken an active role in challenging the Three Gorges Dam project, writing books and giving interviews to foreign journalists, as explained in the chapter that follows. This opposition helped fuel the decision of the Board of Directors of the Export-Import Bank of the United States (May 30, 1996) to rule that the bank could not issue a letter of interest for the Three Gorges Dam project because it was inconsistent with the bank's environmental guidelines.[11]

Returning to pluralization in America, in late 1998 the number of lobbyists registered with the Secretary of the U.S. Senate was 18,590.[12] There were more than 7,500 trade associations and professional societies in the

United States, of which 2,300 trade associations, professional societies, and labor unions had their national headquarters within twenty miles of the Capitol in 1998.[13] And finally, hundreds of America's NGOs and multinational corporations have headquarters or sizable public affairs and government relations offices in Washington. Each organization seeks to influence policy most germane to its own interests and concerns—usually with little thought given to the broader issues, interests, and tradeoffs among them. To American antiabortion groups, abortions in China are of as great concern as are abortions in the United States. For the environmental movement, carbon dioxide emissions, whether from Canton, Ohio, or "Canton," China, are equally problematic. From the human rights perspective, abuses of prisoners in Los Angeles, Shanghai, and Tibet are morally equivalent.

Consequently, an increasing number of NGOs, from Human Rights Watch/Asia to Worldwatch, are focusing on China because its size and pace of modernization ensure that it is often the largest example of problems facing humankind. Not only do the PRC's huge dimensions make it a logical focus for such attention, but its communist political system also makes it a politically attractive target. This attractiveness has been further increased by the collapse of favorable public opinion about China in the wake of Tiananmen (table 6) and the tendency for "American opinion on foreign affairs to devolve into a reification of domestic preferences."[14] China's scale, political character, and American opinion, therefore, fit neatly with the fund-raising imperatives of some NGOs and interest groups. NGOs often, though by no means always, eschew (or seek to limit) U.S. government and corporate funding, fearing that to take money (or too high a percentage of the organization's budget) from those sources would compromise perceptions of their integrity. Consequently, these organizations often are driven to rely on one or two types of sources for revenue: wealthy patrons with a "cause" or many small contributors that have to be motivated to make modest donations. To support a large budget through small contributions means that the organization must motivate a huge number of dispersed persons. This, in turn, places a premium on finding sensational issues to pursue. Similarly, big contributors are looking for dramatic causes worthy of their largesse.

The result is that NGOs can be driven toward rhetorical excess. Thus one finds organizations like Human Rights Watch/Asia issuing a report entitled *Death by Default*[15] about orphanage abuses in China, and Worldwatch issuing a report entitled *Who Will Feed China?*[16] Such reports are not necessarily false, indeed are often helpful, but they often lack balance because moderation does not mobilize congressional action, contributor support, volunteer activism, or media attention.

Despite the periodic lack of balance in presenting their viewpoints, NGOs in the United States usually do represent entirely legitimate concerns. Yet on occasion they operate in a questionable fashion. In December 1997 I received a letter from an elderly woman in California who had been sent an unsolicited letter by an organization called the Selous Foundation in Washington, D.C., asking for a contribution. The pitch calling for contributions was as follows:

> You must act now. The reason is simple—and ominous: the Red Chinese have bribed and bullied the corrupt Panamanian government to give them virtual control of our Panama Canal! That's right. Communist China, the same regime that willingly butchers its own citizens and has allegedly—and illegally—donated millions of dollars to Bill Clinton's 1996 presidential campaign now operates the critical bases at both ends of the Canal.... But the Chinese go the Soviet's [*sic*] a step better. Rather than rely upon traitors in the CIA to give them American military and technology secrets, the Communist Chinese government sets up and finances phony corporations to do the dirty work.... Our national security is being compromised. And unless I can count on you to sign and return your EMERGENCY PETITION TO BILL CLINTON ... along with your most generous *tax-deductible donation* of $15, $20, $25, $50, $75, or $100 to the Selous Foundation ... the Communist overlords in Peking will win the Panama Canal. We can and must stop them. I hope I can count on your support.[17]

This letter is inaccurately based on the Panamanian government's contract with one of Hong Kong's largest, most well-established companies—Hutchison Whampoa Limited (HWL)—to operate two ports, one on either end of the canal. In 1997 HWL had market capitalization of US$25.5 billion, employed 30,000 persons worldwide,[18] and operated major ports around the world, including the Port of Felixstowe (Europe's fourth largest), Freeport Harbour Company in the Bahamas, Hong Kong International Terminals, and Shanghai Container Terminals.[19] Its chairman, Li Ka-shing, started his career in Hong Kong in the 1950s making plastic flowers, and the firm he controls has roots in a British firm established in 1868.[20]

In mid-1997, HWL was accused by some members of the U.S. Congress and competing American firms of having "unfairly beat three American competitors to win two lucrative port deals on the Panama Canal."[21] In mid-May, a Senate Foreign Relations Committee staff report was issued, and while it said the bidding process on the port concessions was "unorthodox" and "lacked transparency," it concluded, "To date, however, US officials have not found evidence that suggests Panama did anything illegal." In 1997, and again in 1999, some members of Congress, most notably Senate Majority Leader Trent Lott, said that they saw U.S. national security at risk.[22] The aforementioned mid-1997 Senate staff report spoke to this issue as well, saying, "Although there is not a direct national security threat to the Panama Canal, there is a business monopoly concern."

Whatever the merits of the charges of anticompetitive business behavior, there was no reasonable basis for any of the charges being made by the Selous Foundation. Indeed, far from falling under communist control, Panama resisted Beijing's attempts to pressure it into ending diplomatic relations with Taiwan; Panamanian President Ernesto Perez Balladares told Beijing (the fifth largest canal user) that if Beijing didn't like this decision they could stop using the canal and go around Cape Horn.[23] One is left to conclude that the Selous Foundation's charges may have had more to do with fund-raising than national security or reality. More broadly, some of the congressional charges about future Panama Canal security seem politically driven, remaining impervious to the overwhelming bulk of the information available to the Congress.[24]

Turning to the PRC, in an arguably totalitarian system such as Mao Zedong's China, one often did not have to look far beyond the chairman's whims to explain much domestic or foreign policy.[25] However, the story of China after Mao is a story of the gradual pluralization of a society and its domestic and foreign policy processes. Foreign policy in the PRC gradually is coming to reflect popular attitudes, divisions within the political elite and bureaucracy, and the behavior of an increasingly active business community with a complex, and sometimes tenuous, connection to the central government.[26]

More specifically, the economic, cultural, and security connections between the Chinese people and the outside world are becoming increasingly close, and there is growing scope for ties that are largely independent of the United States and China. If one, for example, is seeking to understand how an American citizen of Chinese ancestry, Johnny Chung, was caught up in accepting several hundred thousand U.S. dollars from a Chinese military/business agent (most of which apparently ended up in Chung's pocket) and why he escorted several PRC business groups into the White House, his own explanation reveals the pluralization occurring in China: "[T]hey [the Chinese businesspeople visiting the White House] wanted 'what most Americans want from our system—influence and the ability to develop relationships with important people.' The photographs they had taken with the president and first lady were worth 'gold,' he said, because 'in China such photographs project a great sense of importance.'"[27]

The pictures were advertising in the personal relations–oriented Chinese business world and the transitional PRC economy.

LEADERS, POLITICAL INSTITUTIONS, AND LOCALITIES IN THE UNITED STATES AND CHINA

Leaders

Using the vocabulary of James MacGregor Burns, there has been a gradual evolution in the United States, China, and perhaps globally away from dominant "transformational" leaders, or leaders who try to change their followers, epitomized by Mao Zedong and Franklin D. Roosevelt, to more "transactional" leaders like George Bush, Jiang Zemin, and Bill Clinton. Transactional leaders seek to find sustainable balances among the perceived needs of different followers or constituencies.[28] For them, foreign policy is a natural extension of domestic politics, and domestic politics often is the eternal struggle to achieve balance.

In the PRC, another remarkable transformation occurred in the last two decades of the twentieth century, a change toward a more engineering-oriented, problem-solving generation of leaders. As of June 1999, of the twenty-four full and alternate members of the Politburo, seventeen had engineering and scientific backgrounds.[29] When one speaks with central leaders such as Jiang Zemin, the conversations in which they become most engaged are those that have a technical component. Jiang, for instance, becomes animated when talking about bridge and overpass design or urban sanitation. With Zhu Rongji, the Port Authority of New York and New Jersey and similar regional authorities elicit considerable interest.

An important transformation is also occurring at the lower echelons of the Chinese leadership. In his 1998 study of leadership change in Shanghai, Shi Chen reveals that from 1983 (and particularly from 1991) on, increasing numbers of municipal leaders were in their fifties (as opposed to their sixties or seventies), had joined the Communist Party after the 1949 revolution, and had been in charge of research institutes or economic enterprises or had been professionals (often engineers) rather than individuals who had risen along bureaucratic or political career tracks. Shi Chen concludes by stating, "The party technocrats who now lead China appear to have much in common with their counterparts in other countries. They, too, share in the vision of a market economy and modernization, of rationalization and the creation of formal institutions, and the promotion of science and technology."[30]

Each society, therefore, is promoting leaders who tend to judge foreign policy in terms of its effects on their capacity to achieve domestic objectives and maintain domestic political balance.

Institutions

One origin of the close connection between America's internal political battles and its posture abroad is the structure of its federal political system of checks and balances. Foreign policy power in the United States is divided among institutions just as power is with respect to domestic affairs. The president is commander in chief, but without congressional support (or at least acquiescence) he finds it hard to sustain protracted military combat abroad. The executive branch implements trade law, but the Congress sets tariff levels. The president negotiates treaties, but the Senate must ratify them. The executive branch implements policy, but the legislative branch can investigate that implementation in areas as diverse as alleged illegal Chinese campaign contributions in the 1996 election or technology transfer to the PRC in 1998–1999. And finally, few foreign policy principals in the executive branch can escape the necessity of confirmation by the U.S. Senate, the key exceptions being the president's White House staff.

In China, institutional considerations are equally important, albeit different. In the Stalinist institutional political-economic system of the pre-1978 period, inland areas, heavy industries, the planning apparatus, and the propaganda and security structures were dominant. Since that time, coastal areas, light industries and services, markets, and a freer flow of information have been the new priorities; individuals, institutions, and localities associated with the old system generally have been the losers. Predictably, the last quarter of the twentieth century has been a struggle between the old institutions that gained from the old priorities and those institutions, regions, and groups advantaged by the new ones.

Inland provinces with aging heavy industrial bases have sought to shut out the competitive goods from new domestic coastal industries and from abroad. And heavy industries, such as steel, petrochemicals, and machinery, throughout the 1990s were exceedingly hesitant to enter the WTO world where they would quickly be exposed to global competition. As Shirk pointed out in 1984, "The Ministry of Machine Building is an important source of protectionist pressures in the Chinese system."[31] These same protectionist forces remain evident in 2000. The Chinese periodical *Management World* (Guanli Shijie) explained:

> The issue of "foreign companies crowding China's market" has two aspects: problems created by imported goods and problems created by

goods produced by foreign-invested enterprises being sold in the domestic market.... As China thoroughly opens up to the outside world, foreign companies directly investing in this country are moving away from labor intensive processing enterprise.... we have now entered a phase marked by the massive influx of multinational companies and foreign capital.... Most of these investments are internal-oriented; their products are not destined for foreign sales but are mainly sold in the Chinese market, and, therefore, there is increasing market conflict with China's own existing industrial enterprises.... The reason their [foreign multinational] market shares have become such an important issue is that their goods do have substantial market shares in certain sectors, and many domestic enterprises are under siege; they are facing production shrinkage and are on the verge of collapse. This is especially true for cosmetics, detergent, beverages, beer, tires, and some machinery and electronic products.[32]

China's petroleum industry provides an example of a vast, strategic sector of the Chinese economy that has grown up in the cocoon of economic protection and is now unable to withstand external competition. Consequently, domestic consumers, seeking to acquire cheaper petroleum products, collude with smugglers and local officials to import better-quality, lower-cost Middle East products, thereby undermining legal authority and sapping central revenues: "China's oil industry is a large sector employing almost 10 million people in the whole country. Should oil workers be laid off or the state seal oil wells and rely upon imported oil only, how many more unemployed people would the country face? ... That is why [Premier] Zhu [Rongji] has decided to intervene in the market by administrative means and let the country's oil industry survive.... However, many people believed that the state has introduced a policy of protecting the backward and a policy that could hardly stimulate the country's oil departments to study ways and means of lowering the production cost."[33]

There are other remnants of the prereform Stalinist system. As we saw in the preceding chapter, the propaganda apparatus still tries to maintain its control over the mass media. It also is very concerned about the Internet, undertaking Sisyphean efforts to limit its content available in the PRC. In January 1996, for reasons of both cash and ideological control, the State Council attempted to force Dow Jones, Bloomberg, and other foreign economic information services to route their dispatches through the New China News Agency (Xinhua)—something that was both impossible to implement and unacceptable to the foreign companies.[34] By October of the following year, the policy was relaxed. Similarly, the public security and state security structures traditionally have been responsible for rooting out challenges to Communist Party control and eliminating the bacteria of foreign political and cultural infection. The fact that these organizations' arrest of political dissidents complicates the Foreign Ministry's dealings with the West does not concern them.

And finally, with regard to China's legislature, although the National People's Congress (NPC) still does not play a highly significant role in policymaking, in the future one can expect its deliberations to become increasingly relevant. The NPC has periodically expressed nationalistic positions (particularly on territorial issues such as the Diaoyutai Islands, the South China Sea Islands, Taiwan, and the U.S. bombing of the Chinese Embassy in Belgrade) that may have marginally constrained Chinese elite actions. However, there is no reason to think that if China succeeds in developing a more potent legislature that it will facilitate foreign policymaking or make such policy more compatible with American interests.

Moving from the broad characteristics of the political institutions to the particular organization of power, the question of who holds strategic bureaucratic positions in what kind of structure is critically important in both nations, as discussed in Chapter 8. In the United States, the tenure of Assistant Secretary of State Winston Lord during the first Clinton term illustrates some of the organizational dynamics and pitfalls.

When the Clinton administration came into office in early 1993, Lord was nominated as assistant secretary. He had the responsibility for interagency coordination of China policy, which meant reevaluating past policy, making recommendations for the future, and dealing with Congress and the Chinese. It soon became clear, however, that his rank and influence were insufficient to command the compliance of the other thirty officials of equivalent or higher rank in the Department of State at that time, much less the many other cabinet-level officers and their deputies outside the department. Some historical and numerical information makes the problem clear.

In 1960 (see table 7), the Department of State had five regional (geographic) bureaus and ten functional bureaus (e.g., Bureau of International Organization Affairs, Bureau of Economic Affairs, etc.). In 1980 these respective numbers were five and thirteen; by 1990 there were five regional and eighteen functional bureaus; and by 1998 the respective numbers had grown to six and nineteen. Looked at in terms of personnel at the assistant secretary and the deputy assistant secretary (DAS) levels, in 1960 there were fifteen assistant secretaries in the department and eighteen DASs; by 1998 the corresponding numbers were twenty-five and seventy-eight. In terms of power, this bureaucratic growth has meant that being an assistant secretary is not what it once was in terms of access to the secretary of state, let alone the president. Further, geographic bureaus have lost ground relative to functional bureaus.

In the Department of State an additional consequence of the shift in the bureaucratic center of gravity toward functional bureaus (such as Political/ Military Affairs, Economic and Business Affairs, or Oceans and International Environmental and Scientific Affairs) is that such bureaus tend to develop universal norms and standard operating procedures to deal with all countries that touch upon their interests. In contrast, a regional bureau tends to be sensitive to the particular character of "its" country and region.

These trends of enlargement and specialization have been broadly replicated in other cabinet-level agencies with China-policy stakes such as the Department of Treasury, the Department of Defense, and in the far-flung intelligence community. As Jack Downing, head of the CIA's Directorate of Operations, said in 1999 when talking about the post–cold war emphasis on new CIA centers for counterterrorism, counternarcotics, counterproliferation, and counterintelligence, "[T]he line divisions [covering geographic areas] were being starved."[35] Moreover, there have been new (variably potent) competitors for influence, such as the National Economic Council, as discussed in Chapter 1.

The net effect of this organizational constipation and growth (combined with more specific problems like the unsuccessful spring 1994 Christopher trip to China and the then-imminent mid-1994 decision on MFN renewal) was that power flowed toward the White House during the first half of 1994. While Assistant Secretary Lord remained involved, the seat of decision and initiative moved away. He put it to me this way: "The White House was engaged in China policy, more and more meetings were kicked to a higher level, as appropriate with MFN, and I was always there. It is a little simplistic to say I was thrown into the dustbin and the White House took over. I wanted more White House involvement. The economic people were more important and the White House took the lead. The NEC [National Economic Council] felt left out before."[36]

In China, influence over six organizational levers is key to political supremacy and foreign policy control, with the posts of general secretary, chairman of the Central Military Commission, and the presidency being most important. With respect to foreign policy, one must simultaneously control the Foreign Affairs Leading Small Group, the Foreign Propaganda Leading Group, and the Taiwan Affairs Leading Small Group—interagency coordinating bodies that oversee the flow of information and options to the Politburo and monitor subsequent policy implementation. Although Jiang Zemin had gained control of all three major positions by 1993 (when he was named president of the People's Republic of China), he also had to deal with the reality that as long as Deng Xiaoping was alive, Deng remained the legitimate final arbiter of disputes, even without holding any formal position. Only at the Fifteenth Party Congress in September 1997, following Deng's death, could Jiang more fully wield the power of the three paramount positions. And not until the March 1998 Ninth National People's Congress was it clear publicly that he had also gained control over the three most important foreign affairs–related small groups, principally the Foreign Affairs Leading Small Group.[37] In 1998 a consultant to China's foreign policy leadership explained:

> Now [with Deng dead], Jiang Zemin is head of the Foreign Affairs Leading [Small] Group. The problem in 1993–1997 was that Jiang's power base was not well consolidated. Jiang was in charge of U.S. and Taiwan policy, but the structure gave [Premier] Li Peng [as head of the Foreign Affairs Leading Small Group] the right to speak his opinions. So the structure was inconsistent.... So, before the 15th Party Congress, this split was very difficult.... But now we see Jiang is the leader of the Taiwan Leading Small Group and the Foreign Affairs Leading Small Group.... Jiang's position was difficult, he had no strong power ten years ago [1989]; ten years ago people didn't listen to him. After Deng passed away his position was more, but the structure [remained a problem] until the 15th Party Congress and the Ninth National People's Congress.[38]

Only after Jiang had consolidated his power in 1997 and 1998 and had pushed Premier Li Peng to the margins was he able to take risks on his own, such as his vigorous implementation of summit diplomacy with the United States in late 1997 and mid-1998.

Turning from a consideration of executive to that of legislative power, one of the central trends of the last twenty-five years in the United States has been increased congressional involvement in foreign policy, a trend with origins in the era of the Vietnam War and the Watergate scandal. This greater congressional involvement reflects many things, including a more domestically oriented national agenda, popular and legislative branch skepticism of White House power, and the expansion of the congressional bureaucracy. With respect to the latter, for example, in 1972 professional congressional staff persons numbered 14,588; by 1997, that number was up by about 26 percent, to 18,423.

As a consequence of the increased prominence of Congress, an ever larger number of organized groups seek to influence it. According to *Independent*

Sector, an organization working to strengthen the nonprofit (or third) sector, in 1977 there were 1,123,000 nonprofit, tax-exempt organizations in the United States; by 1996 that number had grown by about 36 percent to 1,530,000. While most nonprofit organizations have no China-related interest, many do. And although many nonprofit organizations are prohibited by tax law from lobbying, their "educational efforts" often are aimed at Capitol Hill. The combination of a proliferation of third-sector organizations and an expanding number of professional staff serving Congress means that almost every organized interest group in America has a well-cultivated point of access to the legislative branch. At various junctures in the 1990s, for example, if one wanted to defend human rights in Hong Kong, you went to Ellen Bork on Senator Jesse Helms's Foreign Relations Committee staff. If one wanted to advance the cause of human rights in Tibet one went to Paul Berkowitz on the staff of the House Committee on International Relations. If your concern was abortions and right-to-life issues, it was Joseph Rees in the office of Representative Christopher Smith of the Subcommittee on International Operations and Human Rights (see Chapter 8).

Such developments are taking place against a broader spectrum of change in American political life. As Hedrick Smith explained in his classic *The Power Game,*[39] American electoral politicians have become entrepreneurs. This development reflects the increasing cost of election campaigns, the need to buy ever more expensive media time to gain name recognition, and the weakened condition of the political parties that no longer control all the purse strings. These political entrepreneurs are constantly in search of *issues* that will win organized interest group support, mobilize activist campaign workers, win campaign contributions from dispersed small donors, and command media attention.

In electoral politics, generalized *public opinion* is not central; what *likely voters* think is. Particularly in off-year elections and primary campaigns, *likely voters* in each party are heavily weighted toward activists, persons who are often off the political center. As Senator John McCain put it, "If the great center doesn't [vote], extremes rule the political process."[40] In mobilizing such individuals, using foreign policy as a metaphor for domestic issues (such as abortion, religious freedom, or the environment) can be effective. The convenient thing about using foreigners as motivational devices is that no matter what one says about them, they can't vote and such attacks can energize one's own activist base of support.

It is Congress's increased importance in the American system and the tendency for some on Capitol Hill to use China as a metaphor for domestic issues that account for Beijing's 1995 decision to put added emphasis on influencing Congress.[41] As one Chinese scholar defined the effort, "We've tried to model ourselves on Israel or Taiwan, not get into trouble."[42] The full range of means by which such influence may have been sought was the subject of congressional investigations from mid-1997 into 1999, but one of the primary ones was simply getting members of Congress to travel to the PRC and experience China themselves.[43] Despite such efforts, however, the PRC in 1997 was considered by such observers as American Ambassador to China and former Senator James Sasser to be "the worst lobbyist" in Washington.[44] In 1997 the PRC still had only one registered lobbying firm—Taiwan had fourteen.[45]

Localities

States, provinces, and localities play a significant role in U.S.-China relations in three main ways: To start, they provide the initial experiences that persons who later become national leaders draw upon when, and if, they move to the capital. Second, to some extent localities go their own way in dealings abroad. And finally, localities articulate their own interests in the national policy process. Often the motivation for local involvement is economic.

Looking first at the experience localities provide future national leaders, Bill Clinton's emphasis on economic issues in the U.S.-China relationship has been a reflection of his prior experience as governor of Arkansas, where economic development was a primary concern—his state ranked forty-sixth in per capita personal income in 1992. As James David Barber said in his classic on presidential character,[46] a politician's initial "independent political successes" tend to be replicated throughout his or her subsequent career. It is no accident, therefore, that the Bill Clinton who found that emphasis on local economic development in Arkansas led to political success carried this lesson with him to Washington. In the same way, Jiang Zemin's economic successes in Shanghai shaped his view of appropriate priorities and survival strategies once he moved into national politics in Beijing. More broadly, in China, there has been a striking increase in "the proportion of central committee members taken from the local regions," with the percentage rising from 25 percent in the Thirteenth Party Congress (1987) to more than 60 percent in the Fourteenth (1992).[47] Of further significance, 70 percent of the Politburo elected by the Fifteenth Central Committee (1997) consisted of persons who had their origins or substantial work experience in five coastal provinces or two coastal, provincial-level cities. In 1982, only 24 percent had this background.[48]

From the late 1970s on, local governments in the United States and China have increasingly played the role of economic development agencies, particularly in foreign trade, by seeking outlets for their localities' products abroad and soliciting inward-directed foreign investment. In the course of these development efforts, localities have established numerous independent relationships abroad, including some between the United States and China. Governor Jim Rhodes of Ohio, for example, was a pioneer in this regard, signing the Ohio-Hubei Commercial and Cultural Agreement in October 1979.[49] By 1998, sister-city arrangements between the PRC and the United States totaled seventy-eight, linking such diverse places as Red Wing, Minnesota, with Quzhou, Zhejiang Province, and Shanghai with San Francisco.[50] The latter relationship was arguably the most active. In the late 1970s and most of the 1980s, then San Francisco Mayor (later Senator) Dianne Feinstein worked with then Shanghai Mayor Wang Daohan, and his successors Jiang Zemin and Zhu Rongji, to establish and develop ties that shaped not only local relations but also the thinking of these individuals long after they moved to their respective national capitals.[51]

In the PRC, the decentralization of foreign trade, revenues, and economic development authority has made local governments ardent promoters of U.S.-China economic links and links between Chinese localities and localities around the world. Cheung and Tang describe how the Chinese provinces of Liaoning, Jilin, and Shandong each have sought to shape Beijing's relations with South Korea in pursuit of their economic interests, and how trade-and-export-oriented Shanghai and Guangdong Province have pushed for more moderate, economically oriented relations with Washington than other localities.[52]

Taiwan is an important element in the U.S.-China local relationship in that the island has been a tireless cultivator of political support in American states and municipalities. Every year from 1989 to 1999, Taiwan imported at least 25 percent more in dollar volume of American products than did the PRC, although these numbers are somewhat skewed because of the large volume of U.S. exports to China that are routed through Hong Kong and therefore escape official count.[53] Taipei extracts every ounce of political mileage possible from each purchase by sending buying missions around the United States to publicly sign contracts and solidify support among local politicians. The PRC has never extracted this kind of political goodwill from its "big ticket" imports, much less smaller purchases. In 1996, the *New York Times* reported, "In recent years, 23 state legislatures have passed pro-Taiwan resolutions, some of them calling for membership in the

United Nations,"[54] a position contrary to Washington's longtime stance on UN membership for Taiwan. In a related vein, a study center set up in North Carolina reportedly "receives grants from Taiwan interests."[55]

The expansion of local government involvement in international affairs has complicated the management of U.S.-China ties. In New York City, for example, in the wake of the 1989 Tiananmen violence, then Mayor Ed Koch suspended all municipal-sponsored "sister city" exchanges with Beijing Municipality. He also renamed the intersection in front of the Chinese Consulate at Forty-second Street and Twelfth Avenue "Tiananmen Square"—a name it still retains in 2000. One of his successors, Mayor Rudy Giuliani, often refused to meet with visiting senior Chinese leaders for a number of reasons, including fear that the New York City human rights community would exact a political price. Also, with respect to Giuliani, when reports of corruption in China reached him, they were something that, as a crime-busting local prosecutor prior to becoming mayor, he did not wish to be associated with. On more than one occasion the visit of a very senior Chinese leader to New York City was arranged to find a face-saving formula that would avoid making it obvious that the mayor was refusing to meet them.

In the economic realm, both generally and with respect to China, U.S. localities have periodically considered imposing (and more rarely adopted) unilateral economic sanctions. These efforts have, in turn, given rise to arguments over whether such measures are unwarranted intrusions on the federal government's primacy in foreign affairs, a debate that reached the U.S. Supreme Court in a case brought against the state of Massachusetts in March 2000.[56] In May 1997, for example, New York City Council Speaker Peter Vallone proposed a measure that would have required the city to withdraw deposits and investments from banks that did business with fifteen specific countries (including the PRC) accused of persecuting Christians. Moreover, the proposed legislation would have banned the city from procuring goods and services from firms commercially active in the prescribed nations. New York City's budget is America's fourth largest after the federal budget and those of New York state and California.[57] In the course of debate, one city council member argued, "Just like in South Africa and in Northern Ireland, New York City can stand as a leader in the battle for human rights around the world."[58] Ultimately, while the measure was not adopted because of heavy business opposition, defeating the proposed sanctions required a huge expenditure of effort. In a related vein, nongovernmental organizations have sought to pressure state pension funds to withhold investments in Chinese projects of which they disapprove.[59]

Thus institutions in the United States and China form part of the backdrop for understanding the difficulties of managing the bilateral relationship. There is a constant struggle for political advantage within and among those institutions and among their current and aspiring leaders. Also important to our understanding are the experiences that shape the thinking of the leaderships, with many of those experiences acquired in the localities of the two nations. Finally, such localities are constantly interacting with one another and seeking to nudge national policy in directions most congruent with their own respective local interests.

BROAD NATIONAL AGENDAS

In addition to leaders, institutions, and localities, broad national agendas also play a role in the shaping of foreign policies. These agendas are not necessarily imposed top down on the citizenry—though Mao Zedong assuredly had such power. Rather, they often emerge from the indefinable yearnings of populations whose leaders try to sense what goals can generate popular support and catapult them to, or maintain them in, power. Leaders are often followers who discern which way the national crowd is moving. The Chinese have a word for such people—*feng pai*, or "breeze watchers."

It is therefore instructive to look briefly at PRC history from 1949 to 1978 from the perspective of the national agenda thereafter. There were several bright spots in communism's first thirty years of rule, including restoring national sovereignty, creating a basic infrastructure for modernization, dramatically increasing life expectancy and literacy, and gaining some measure of global prominence. Yet these achievements were purchased at considerable cost, and gigantic problems remained. In 1979 the PRC remained among the most desperately poor nations on Earth—ranking about number 160 in the world in per capita income; in 1975, 568.9 million Chinese people in rural areas were in poverty.[60] While the calculations are subject to wide variation because of assumptions concerning exchange rates and GDP measurements, in 1979 China had about 6.4 percent of its GDP in foreign trade, compared with the United States' 17 percent and the Soviet Union's 14 percent. Finally, only in 1974, twenty-five years after the communist victory, did the average Chinese's diet have what the World Bank considered to be the minimal daily nutrient availability.[61]

More damaging than this modest record of progress, however, was the price at which it had been secured. Every peasant and urban resident alike had scars from the preceding three decades of domestic political, social, and economic turmoil and deprivation. Chinese political history from 1949 to

1978 was an uninterrupted series of mass movements and incessant political struggle. A high percentage of rural families lost at least one relative during the policy-induced famine of the late 1950s and early 1960s.[62] Few urbanites escaped suffering during the decade of the Cultural Revolution (1966–1976), a decade that saw, at least in its initial stages (1966–1967), the national suicide rate increase significantly. As Marshall Lin Biao noted in March, 1967, "Many people have committed suicide or been killed."[63]

In short, by the time Deng Xiaoping came to power in the late 1970s, the Chinese Communist Party and its supreme leader, Mao Zedong, had not achieved central elements of basic popular aspirations. Among those aspirations were the desires for individual and family security, minimal social stability, international respect and national strength, and an improving personal material circumstance. Deng Xiaoping's genius lay in his recognition of this elemental fact and in his capacity to push the system in directions that made achievement of these objectives possible. He understood that China's communist leaders needed to "carry out reforms and bring benefits to the people," if they hoped to survive.[64] Five days before the June 4, 1989, violence in Beijing, Deng told two "responsible central comrades" that "[w]e need to establish a real and new third leadership. The leadership must be credible to people and the party.... In our [Deng's] second generation, I was the leader of the group. However, we were a group. With this group, people were basically satisfied because we implemented the open door and reform policy and proposed the policy of four modernizations.... The third leadership needs to make the party credible to people and also to make some concrete achievements. The closed-door policy is no way.... In that situation, the economy cannot be developed, the people's life cannot be improved, and national strength cannot be reinforced."[65]

Thus Deng Xiaoping recognized and powerfully articulated China's implicit broad national agenda in the late 1970s and was able to focus on the domestic economy, maintain basic social stability, and minimize distracting problems abroad in order to forge an elite and popular consensus in the 1980s and 1990s. Individual Chinese leaders and citizens might disagree about *how* best to pursue these objectives, but the objectives were widely shared while Deng remained alive, and thereafter. Relations with America were (and are) evaluated against these goals. To the degree that ties with Washington promote national strength, they are welcome; to the degree that they make achieving domestic progress more arduous, ties with the United States are viewed as problematic. Doubts lurk in the back of Chinese minds about whether the United States really wants the strong, stable, and prosperous China about which President Jimmy Carter and all of his successors have spoken.

Emerging from the cold war, the United States also had a broad national agenda that was powerfully driven by domestic concerns and a diffuse popular consensus. The successful politicians (such as Bill Clinton) were those who were most able to identify with, articulate, and build a coalition around this implicit national agenda. Foremost in the minds of most Americans was the heavy defense burden they had shouldered for about forty-five years and genuine domestic problems. In the wake of the early-1991 Gulf War victory, economic and social problems dominated American thinking. A March 1992 Gallup Poll reported that "almost three quarters (73 percent) of Americans mention some aspect of the economy as the nation's most important problem."[66] Among those economic and social issues of most concern were the budget deficit, health care, education, social and family decay, and declining competitiveness as reflected in industrial job loss. While not isolationists, Americans were less willing now to play the role of solitary global policeman, though the role of "global leader" still held its attractions.[67] By late 1991, the Gallup Poll revealed that "Americans (82%) want the U.S. to concentrate on internal issues, and scale down our international involvements."[68] When they did get involved abroad, post–cold war Americans expected their allies to share the burdens.

Throughout the 1990s, these trends were reflected in reduced support for military spending and actual reductions in U.S. military spending. An October 1991 Gallup Poll revealed that "[h]alf of Americans (50%) feel we are spending too much money on defense. Only one in ten (10%) says the defense budget is too low; the remainder—36 percent—say it is about right."[69] In fiscal year 1989, U.S defense expenditure in constant (fiscal year 1999) dollars was $374.3 billion, 5.5 percent of GDP; eleven years later, in fiscal year 1999, defense expenditure was $258.6 billion, which represented 2.9 percent of GDP—the lowest share of U.S. economic output since 1940.[70] Similar trends are apparent if one looks at the composition of federal outlays for the budget category "international affairs." In 1991 federal outlays for international affairs were $15.851 billion, or 1.2 percent of total federal outlays. In 1997 (in current dollars) federal outlays for international affairs were $15.228 billion, or 1 percent of total federal outlays.[71]

Emerging from the cold war, therefore, Americans had many things on their minds, but least of all was foreign policy. When interest in matters of foreign policy was aroused, it generally was because of the perceived linkage between the domestic economy and international concerns. Although Americans did wish to promote their values abroad, they wished to do so at minimal cost (in blood and money). Sanctions appealed as an instrument of power because they seemingly were inexpensive means to

promote righteous ends and often also could be sold as a method to redress inequitable trading relationships thought to be hurting the domestic economy.

In sum, the bilateral relationship between the United States and China
reflects the broad leadership, institutional, and public opinion patterns in
each country at any given moment. A brief case study illustrates this
point.

THE DIFFICULTY OF ALIGNING POLITICAL STARS: A CASE STUDY

The story of the first seven years of the post–cold war era (1989–1996) in
U.S.-China relations is simple, yet complex. The period was one in which
the domestic political cycles of the two nations generally were out of sync;
when one national leadership was in a position to move forward in the bilateral relationship, the other was not. It is precisely the rarity of favorable
alignments that makes political leadership so critical. It takes vision, skill,
and courage to help engineer and then seize those rare moments—moments that are often not obvious until the opportunity has been seized, as
Richard Nixon did in 1971–1972.

In the first six months of 1989, immediately following President Bush's
inauguration, both Beijing and Washington were prepared to move forward to develop relations, but then the Tiananmen violence took place. In
the immediate aftermath of the tragedy, the Bush administration made an
attempt to restore stability to the relationship, but its efforts alienated
both Congress and the mass media, as we saw in Chapter 1. Further, the
administration's need to impose some penalties on Beijing to maintain its
own credibility alienated a Chinese leadership that was immobilized by its
own internal discord. By the end of 1989, the unresponsiveness of Deng
Xiaoping and his colleagues, combined with collapsing regimes in eastern
Europe and then the Soviet Union, quickly diverted Washington's attention from U.S.-China relations. Moreover, the collapse in eastern Europe
and the Soviet Union made Beijing even more reticent to accommodate
the United States on issues of internal governance.

By the time developments in Europe and (now) Russia had settled down
somewhat in 1992, the United States was involved in a highly contentious
presidential campaign between President Bush and his democratic challenger, Governor Clinton. In a campaign notable for its inattention to foreign affairs, China policy was an issue, in part accounting for the sale of
F-16 fighter aircraft to Taiwan. Once Bill Clinton had won the election, he
went through the period of policy review and uncertainty customary for

new administrations. This was followed by an attempt to implement a more punitive policy toward the PRC and deliver on his campaign promises to link MFN tariff treatment with China's human rights behavior. In May 1994 that policy approach collapsed, and the "engagement policy" gradually emerged. But by the time the Clinton administration was even remotely able to move forward, Deng Xiaoping's health was faltering, succession contenders were reluctant (and politically unable) to be accommodating to Washington, and increasingly the Taiwan issue was injected into the stew.

To further complicate matters, as a result of the November 1994 U.S. election, the party leadership of both houses of Congress shifted from Democratic to Republican, bringing persons who were far more skeptical of China into the chairmanships of key congressional committees. Jesse Helms (North Carolina) became chairman of the Senate Foreign Relations Committee, and Benjamin Gilman (New York) became chairman of the House International Relations Committee (see Chapter 8).

It was only in mid-1996 that the domestic stars of both nations began to come into conjunction. The March 1996 Taiwan Strait confrontation made the fundamental security costs of continued deterioration in the bilateral relationship painfully evident to both sides, and as the year progressed, both Jiang Zemin and Bill Clinton became progressively more confident of their own domestic political futures. The failure of past policy, the increasingly apparent costs of deteriorating ties, and more secure leaders in both capitals were the essential ingredients for improved relations. With the alignment of these stars, the twin summits in Beijing (1997) and Washington (1998) were conceived and delivered.

A brief look at one of the periods in which the domestic political stars of the two nations were out of alignment illustrates the more general problems that continually affect management of the bilateral relationship.

Post-Tiananmen Stalemate: Bush and Deng

In a late-1996 speech in Harriman, New York, President Bush's former assistant for national security affairs, General Brent Scowcroft, explained how the combination of domestic politics in the United States and China, along with broader global developments, made restabilizing U.S.-China relations after Tiananmen nearly impossible. Scowcroft used his December 1989 (second) visit to Beijing as the point of departure. The first visit had been so secret that the U.S. ambassador to Beijing at the time, James Lilley, was recalled to Washington to be informed of it, face to face.[72] Scowcroft explained as follows:

[My second trip to China after June 1989 resulted] from a message from former President Nixon who had visited China [in November and] who said that Beijing wanted to restore relations. I brought a roadmap and they agreed on a set of reciprocal releases and steps for 1990 that were to be implemented over several months to a year, "to walk the cat back." The set of moves was to end in a visit by Jiang Zemin to the United States. Then it all stopped, I believe, because of the fall of the Ceausescus in Romania, which Chinese leaders thought was a solid regime. Then we [the Bush administration] go into the [1992 presidential] campaign, Clinton campaign remarks about coddling dictators, MFN conditionality, and the succession in China. Romania still affects their [Chinese] thinking about stability.

Ironically, the December 1989 trip made it much more difficult for the president to proceed in developing the bilateral relationship thereafter. To begin with, the acknowledgment of the two 1989 trips made it apparent to Congress and the American public that the administration's practice of diplomacy was at odds with the president's June 1989 suspension of all high-level exchanges with the PRC.[73] As Scowcroft recounts, "Unlike our earlier trip [in July 1989], there was no need to make this [December trip] a secret operation. We did, however, hope to keep it at a very low profile, since it was bound to be controversial. It was here that we—I—made a mess of it. We did not want to give advance notice of the trip because of the danger that Congress would demand an explanation of what we were about and why.... [C]ontroversy in Washington at its very beginning would not enhance the prospects for success."[74]

The visual record of the visit was devastating from a public relations perspective; a photograph of General Scowcroft toasting his Chinese hosts according to protocol conveyed an image of conviviality that neither existed nor was intended. As Scowcroft subsequently put it:

CNN happened to be in Beijing at the time, and the Chinese proposed extensive media attention. That was the last thing we had in mind, and after some discussion we agreed that camera crews would be permitted only at the initial meeting and at the outset of the session with the Chinese leadership. Following that script, there were cameras at the protocol meeting immediately on our arrival at the state guesthouse. However, as the ritual toasts began at the end of the welcoming dinner given by the foreign minister [Qian Qichen], the television crews reappeared. It was an awkward situation for me. I could go through with the ceremony and be seen as toasting those the press was labeling "the butchers of Tiananmen Square," or refuse to toast and put in jeopardy the whole purpose of the trip. I chose the former and became, to my deep chagrin, an instant celebrity—in the most negative sense of that term.[75]

In the December 1989 trip we see two fundamental dilemmas that confronted the Bush administration in terms of domestic politics. First, to try to restore communication and constructive relations with Beijing required quiet initiatives; however, such diplomacy eroded public support as soon as it became known, as was almost inevitable. Second, the domestic political needs of PRC leaders in the media age clashed with those of the White House. The PRC wanted as much positive media coverage as possible to demonstrate to its citizens and the rest of the world that China's post-Tiananmen isolation was ending; the White House needed to avoid conveying this impression. During this period it was not only government officials who tried to avoid public connection to the Chinese regime. Prominent U.S. citizens and senior nongovernmental delegations often engaged in long, embarrassing, and tension-laden negotiations with Chinese hosts to ensure that they would not be photographed with individuals like Premier Li Peng. This process further demeaned Chinese leaders and hosts, and further alienated those already suspicious of the United States. In turn, Chinese leaders had their parallel sensitivities that further estranged them from Americans, which we will explore in detail in Chapter 8. One such instance in the second half of the 1990s included the unwillingness of Communist Party functionaries to have very senior political leaders publicly receive a well-known American China scholar who had criticized Chairman Mao Zedong and China's human rights situation.

The June–December 1989 period saw mounting conflict between the administration and Congress on China policy. A focus of particular controversy was the previously mentioned (see Chapter 1) bill by Congresswoman Nancy Pelosi to waive the requirement that Chinese students and scholars return home after completion of their studies, the Emergency Chinese Adjustments of Status Facilitation Act (H.R. 2712). Bush pocket vetoed the legislation in November and administratively implemented safeguards, thereby setting off a wave of congressional and media backlash.

Starting in 1990, the annual consideration of China's MFN status became the preferred instrument by which Congress (and the human rights and Chinese dissident communities) sought to shape China policy for the rest of the decade. Kerry Dumbaugh writes, "In 1990, Congress amended the Trade Act of 1974 with new procedures for disapproving presidential actions, replacing those deemed unconstitutional in 1983 by the Supreme Court.... Thus, 1990 was the first year that joint resolutions of disapproval were sanctioned as the method for Congress to disapprove presidential recommendations on China's MFN status."[76] Legal opportunity coalesced with congressional frustration. And Chinese students and dissidents meeting in Cambridge, Massachusetts, in January, joined by Congresswoman Nancy Pelosi and congressional aide (and later Clinton political adviser) George Stephanopoulos, hit on the strategy of trying to shape policy in the context of a debate over MFN status for Beijing.[77]

A very junior congresswoman from California, Pelosi, in alliance with Senate Majority Leader George Mitchell, ignited this political prairie fire, notably in major hearings on MFN status for China in May 1990 before the House Committee on Foreign Affairs. In those hearings she noted:

> Many members of Congress and China experts have called repeatedly on the president to send a clear and principled message of outrage to the leaders in Beijing. He has missed every opportunity to do so. He missed an opportunity by vetoing the bill to protect Chinese students; he missed an opportunity by intervening personally on the veto override; he missed another opportunity by authorizing the Scowcroft visits and the resumption of U.S. support for World Bank lending. And now, the president has renewed most favored nation status to China, missing yet another opportunity to send an unequivocal message of U.S. condemnation to the Chinese regime who ordered the massacre in Tiananmen Square and the ensuing repression.[78]

In China, the domestic environment made it exceedingly difficult for Deng Xiaoping and his colleagues to take actions that would have muted the punitive impulse in Washington. Deng had his conservative opponents, who were all too ready to charge him with appeasement.[79] Even as President Bush fought with Congress to adopt less coercive policies toward the PRC, to Beijing he still looked punitive. In a July 2, 1989, meeting with General Scowcroft, Deng Xiaoping told him that "[w]e have been feeling since the outset of these events more than two months ago that the various aspects of U.S. foreign policy have actually cornered China. That's the feeling of us here."[80] While the administration saw itself as paying a price for its moderation, Beijing saw Washington as bullying. At one point Scowcroft told Deng, "Congress and much of the U.S. press have attacked him [Bush] for not acting strongly enough."[81] Further, the tolerance and restraint from Beijing that Washington needed to move away from a sanctions-oriented policy looked to Chinese leaders like the kind of weakness that proved lethal to communist regimes in eastern Europe. And finally, given the escalating demands from Congress, Beijing could not be assured that concessions would not simply produce further demands.

Deng Xiaoping's behavior was also shaped by other aspects of China's domestic circumstance. In Beijing, the events in Tiananmen Square had set off a debate over reform in general, the PRC's relationship with the world, and a reconsideration of what went wrong in Tiananmen and what needed to be done in order to avoid similar situations in the future. Some of these questions did not begin to be resolved until fall 1992, at the landmark Fourteenth Party Congress. This party congress had been preceded in February of that year by Deng Xiaoping's "southern tour" (*nanxun*) to Wuhan, Shenzhen, Zhuhai, and Shanghai,[82] which had been, in the words of one Foreign Ministry official, undertaken because Deng "opposed the economic policy [of his opponents] and he did the same as Mao by going to the provinces to gain support."[83]

During his trip south, which went largely unreported at the time due to opposition among the elite, Deng said that to depart from reform and opening would lead the people to "overthrow whoever does so," that retreating on reform and opening would "give rise to civil war." He continued, "Therefore, the military and the state power must safeguard this path.... The fast development which our country has achieved in just a decade or so has delighted the people and impressed the world.... To put it simply, the bottom line is that there will be no change in upholding this line."[84]

The Fourteenth Party Congress that followed the southern tour in the fall of 1992 was notable for a number of reasons. Its decisions ratified Deng's southern tour impulses and guidance. The congress called for a *socialist market economy* with "survival of the fittest" enterprises;[85] urged cadres to guard against "leftist tendencies" (meaning radical, xenophobic, and antimarket policies); and made personnel changes that brought Zhu Rongji to the Politburo Standing Committee along with other more open leaders. Provincial leaders who had a greater economic stake in the open policy joined the Politburo, and some of Deng's most virulent critics (Yao Yilin and Song Ping) lost their positions. The Central Advisory Commission—the organizational perch from which conservatives had criticized Deng's policies of reform and opening—was abolished.[86] Jiang Zemin's position as chairman of the Central Military Commission (a post to which he had been promoted in September 1989) was strengthened by the dismissal of a competitor on the commission, Vice Chairman Yang Baibing, and many new military leaders were brought into the Central Committee with Deng and Jiang's patronage.[87] And finally, the propaganda apparatus that had been so vocal during the preceding three-plus years in criticizing Deng Xiaoping and the open and reform policies saw several of its leaders lose their positions, most notably the director of *People's Daily*, Gao Di. Professor Richard Baum sums up the impact of these changes by saying, "The removal of the ... hard-liners left the voices of political and ideological orthodoxy significantly weaker at the party center."[88]

The Fourteenth Party Congress of October 1992, therefore, marked an important signpost along the route to reaffirming Deng Xiaoping's reform and opening policies and moving the old generation gradually toward the sidelines. However, it took nearly three years of post-1989 battle for the Chinese political system to reaffirm those policies—an indication of the magnitude of the forces that raged during that period. This accounts for Secretary of State James Baker's evident frustration in effectively communicating with Beijing during that time. "The Chinese, unfortunately, seemed utterly oblivious to our concerns."[89] They were; they had other, domestic priorities.

By late 1992, when Beijing's reformists had consolidated their positions to a considerable extent, the United States was in the throes of the 1992 general election. Soon thereafter a new administration, with new priorities, took over in Washington. By the time the Clinton administration began to straighten its policy out in 1994, Beijing was into a more intense phase of its succession process. In Washington, the opposition Republicans had seized control of Congress, a position from which they could more potently challenge White House China policy. It is, in short, very difficult to get the political stars—the cycles of politics—favorably aligned in both countries.

CONCLUSIONS

This examination of the interplay between domestic politics and the management of the U.S.-China relationship produces several conclusions.

To start, the American political system is built on entrepreneurship, as is its economic system. The United States is a free market political system in which the currency is votes and the products are issues. Political entrepreneurs in search of issues with which to win votes (and the media attention necessary to reach voters) must identify dramatic problems for which their proposed remedies seem to be plausible solutions. The historical American interest in China distinguishes it from most other nations of the world in terms of U.S. attention and therefore makes it more politically useful than many other potential foreign policy concerns. Further, China combines a scale, complexity, residual communist ideology, and obscurity that makes it a stage upon which Americans can act out their greatest hopes and their worst fears. Among the actors on this stage are what Pat Buchanan once termed "a great coalition of human rights activists, Christians appalled at China's persecution of fellow Christians, a right-to-life movement sickened by Beijing's barbaric population policy, union members concerned over export of factories and jobs and foreign-policy realists who see in China a rising menace to Asian peace and America's position in the Pacific."[90] There are, of course, other actors, many in the realms of education and nonprofit organizations, who find their impulses for world betterment served by constructive involvement with China.

Second, weak executive leaders, whether in Beijing or Washington, make it extremely difficult to effectively manage bilateral ties. Whether it is a succession struggle in Beijing or an impeachment inquiry in Washington, senior leaders whose domestic clout has been reduced invite encroachment upon their management of the relationship. Leaders facing challenge may find it expedient to use frustrations with the relationship to advance their own domestic prospects. Only a Bill Clinton secure in the knowledge that he would have a second term was able to agree to a summit with Jiang Zemin in late 1996. And only a Jiang Zemin who had consolidated power after Deng Xiaoping's death was strong enough to take domestic political risks.

Moreover, to be effective in China, certain strategic institutions or key power levers must be under the senior leader's control. When the Foreign Affairs Leading Small Group was under Premier Li Peng's sway, as it was throughout the post-Tiananmen period until late 1997, Jiang Zemin's already limited capacity to move the relationship forward was further circumscribed. And finally, when there is not a strong leader to impose some order over competing interests, as Deng Xiaoping did in 1992 and Jiang Zemin increasingly did from 1997, the bureaucracy below is frozen in the paralysis generated by conflicting signals and uncertainty.

Third, as China becomes a more pluralized society it is becoming a "more normal" polity inasmuch as its decisions increasingly reflect the pulling and hauling among increasingly institutionalized bureaucracies, territorial administrations, social groupings, and even public opinion. One foreign ministry official told me, for example, that "every province in China has a representative office [*daibiaoqu*] in Beijing, though unlike America they don't lobby the Congress, they lobby the executive. In China now they lobby less for money and more for favorable policy."[91]

Fourth, the pattern of institutional design in the policymaking system matters. For instance, the functional departments at the U.S. Department of State have proliferated to the point that a secretary of state's span of control is too broad, which in turn creates the ever present dangers of policy inattention, perpetual bureaucratic wrangling, and sending mixed messages to governments abroad and to Congress. Even though functional concerns are legitimate and important, unless the geographic bureaus play integrative roles, foreign policy is likely to be increasingly chaotic or simply to become the responsibility of the White House, where the capacity for policy coherence is greater and presidential commitment more easily obtained.

Finally, political cycles have enormous impact on the U.S.-China relationship. In the United States, it is the calendar of off-year and general elections; in China it is the irregular rhythm of succession, and the more regular schedule of party congresses. In both societies, leaders must hoard their political capital for these events that invariably affect the two nations' interactions. As with the business cycle, it cannot be assumed that there will be a frequent, positive convergence of the political calendars of the two nations.

PART IV

THE INDIVIDUAL LEVEL

8

PEOPLE COUNT

I would also like to say in a personal sense—and this to you Mr.
Prime Minister [Zhou Enlai]—you do not know me. Since you do
not know me, you shouldn't trust me. You will find I never say
something I cannot do. And I always will do more than I can say.

> President Richard Nixon, speaking with Chairman
> Mao Zedong, Zhongnanhai, February 1972

So the question is, what can I do as an individual. So I am back to
what can we do—education.... The worst dangers China faces are
population and the environment. The worst problem is for China
to become a world burden.... We want a moist southern breeze to
blow up and help China reform.... If I must choose, economics
first, politics later.

> Dai Qing, New York City, January 21, 1992

Personalities matter. It matters in the conduct, formulation, and
implementation [of foreign policy]—the Foreign Minister [Qian
Qichen] is key. Foreign Minister Qian is one of the most capable
foreign ministers on the globe today. Firm and intelligent.

> White House official, February 1997

One congressman asked: "I just want to know, if you've accepted
Jesus Christ as your personal savior." The [Chinese Deputy
Foreign Minister] looked stunned, and he said "no." The whole
table almost fell on the floor. The congressman was quite serious.
That was his litmus test.

> U.S. Ambassador James Sasser, recounting a 1997
> conversation between a U.S. congressman and the
> Chinese Vice Minister over a banquet in Beijing

I had a talk with my old friend, Mr. Maurice Greenberg. I told him
that while I was Mayor of Shanghai, I had permitted AIG
[American International Group] to establish a branch in Shanghai,
and at the time, I was called a traitor by a certain person in a
responsible position. But after AIG came to China, not only did
AIG do very well, our Chinese insurance companies also learned a
lot about insurance operations and management from AIG, and
they developed more rapidly than before.

> Premier Zhu Rongji, New York City, April 13, 1999

CONGRESSMAN MEEKS: Do you like China?
CHINESE WOMAN: Of course I do. I'm Chinese!
          Encounter between young migrant woman from
          Anhui Province and Congressman Gregory Meeks
          (D-New York), Spring 2000

INTRODUCTION

Thus far we have examined the U.S.-China relationship from two vantage points: the level of global systems and the national level, particularly institutional arrangements, domestic politics, and beliefs that define both China and America. Each level adds a layer of complexity to management of the bilateral relationship. Consequently, the capacity of a single leader, or small groups of individuals, in either country to fundamentally alter the trajectory of the relationship is circumscribed.

In both the United States and the PRC, the ability of an individual to alone determine the relationship has declined since the 1970s. In China, the system has moved through the eras of Mao Zedong,[1] Deng Xiaoping, and Jiang Zemin. Mao's proclivities were usually determinative, Deng's inclinations were extremely important, and Jiang Zemin (along with his colleague Premier Zhu Rongji) must spend enormous energy building and maintaining coalitions and support for his policy.[2] As seen in Chapter 4, for example, President Jiang Zemin and Premier Zhu Rongji had to spend nearly seven months rebuilding a consensus on China's WTO entry offer after the previous consensus was shattered by Premier Zhu's abortive April 1999 trip to the United States and the subsequent bombing of the Chinese Embassy in Belgrade.

The United States also has witnessed a progression toward leaders who are less able to dominate China policy. President Nixon and Henry Kissinger single-handedly negotiated a new relationship with Beijing. Jimmy Carter controlled the U.S. terms of negotiation with Beijing on normalization until he was forced to acquiesce to the congressional version of the Taiwan Relations Act. And their successors have had to manage an increasingly complex bilateral relationship in an atmosphere where national institutions, social forces, and global markets have an increasing impact. Moreover, the disciplining effect of the cold war has vanished. As Robert Sutter put it, "[T]he post–cold war period has seen substantial changes in the way foreign policy is made in the United States. In general, there has been a shift away from the elitism of the past and toward a much greater pluralism."[3]

Nevertheless, despite the limited capacity of leaders and individuals to determine the course of the relationship, their influence has been, and remains, significant. A subtext throughout this volume has been that *leaders and individuals in both China and the United States count*. Further, individual leaders in third-party governments (see Chapter 5), people like Taiwan President Lee Teng-hui or Hong Kong Governor Christopher Patten, have had an enormous impact on the bilateral relationship. In the final analysis, crisis decisions and circumstances requiring nonroutine decisions often provide the opportunity for individuals to leave the deepest imprint.

There are at least four broad ways in which individuals in both China and the United States have been involved in the development or implementation of foreign policy and in shaping the broader context in which U.S.-China relations have been managed. To start, there is the category of individuals who have been constitutionally empowered to play a leadership role in each society. In China, by "constitutionally empowered" I mean those individuals the Chinese refer to as the "core" and "nuclear core" leaders; in other words, the "supreme leader" and relevant members of the Politburo and its Standing Committee.[4] In the United States one must put in this category not only the president but also the assistant to the president for national security affairs, the secretary of state, the secretary of defense, and other cabinet-level officials who intermittently shape foreign policy (e.g., the secretary of the treasury or the U.S. trade representative).

The second category comprises individuals who control the "strategic passes" of their respective policymaking systems. These individuals may or may not be specifically mandated to play a role in the development and management of the U.S.-China relationship. Nonetheless, by virtue of their strategic position in the larger system they exercise influence should they choose to do so, or should the issue under discussion fall into their domain. Key congressional committee chairmen, for example, fall into this category in the U.S. system.

Third, there are those individuals in each society whose wisdom is sought by the senior leadership and policy community irrespective of their formal position—the informal advisers, the "elders" in China. These are the Clark Cliffords, Henry Kissingers, James Schlesingers, Carla Hills, Leonard Woodcocks, and Wang Daohans of their respective systems.[5]

Finally, there are those individuals who have no government position but who employ their distinct power (intellectual, organizational, political, or economic) to shape the bilateral relationship or the broader context in which such management occurs. In the United States, business, labor, other interest group, think tank, and civic organization leaders fall into this category. In China, emerging civic organization leaders such as Dai Qing and political dissidents such as Wei Jingsheng[6] (who since the late 1990s has been in the United States in effective exile) are two examples.

In this chapter, I have selected a few notable examples of each of these four categories of individuals. In choosing them, I do not intend to convey uncritical moral or policy endorsement. Rather, the criteria for selection were that the individual has had a demonstrable and important impact on the relationship and that I generally have had some rather direct interaction with the individual, however limited. The latter criterion is both a strength and weakness. To the degree that I have met, known, or dealt with either the principal or his or her staff, I at least have the sense of them that can only come through interaction. It is that very interaction and personal investment, however, that can create blind spots—a desire to emphasize the positive, for example. It is for the reader to judge where those blind spots may be, taking into account that most of the people discussed below have acted on a very broad stage and that a total evaluation of each would require a different standard from that applied here.

One more preliminary word—in China and America the skills needed for national leadership in one era are not necessarily those required in another. The era of radio rewarded different skills than the age of television, and the cold war required different skills than the murkier era that has followed it. At the start of the cold war, the United States was fortunate to have a generation of practical, organizationally adept strategists such as Paul Nitze, Clark Clifford, George Marshall, James Forrestal, and George Kennan. These individuals helped America conceptualize the new era and build the structures to pursue a fairly coherent, broad, and durable national security strategy. Once the strategy and apparatus were in place, more modest individuals carried out the process of implementation—persons such as Dean Rusk in one era, and Warren Christopher in another.

With the end of the cold war, strategists who could build organizations and sell their vision to a U.S. Congress, public, and allies searching for a new framework of association were once again needed. This stage was portrayed aptly in the 1997 words of Bill Clinton: "Presidents are the custodians of the time in which they live as well as the instruments of the visions and dreams they have.... So the first thing I had to start with was, you know, we don't have a war, we don't have a depression, we don't have a cold war."[7]

THE ELITE FOREIGN POLICY LEADERSHIP ROLE

Leadership in Washington

In the American foreign policy and national security system the president generally is the principal foreign and national security policy leader. The president must select a team that possesses a diverse range of skills, in addition to modifying the extant policymaking structure to suit his tastes, strengths and weaknesses, and sense of priorities. Presidential personnel and organization-structuring decisions are intensely personal. During the 1989–2000 period, the United States had two presidents, George Bush and Bill Clinton, who possessed quite different sets of skills, priorities, political bases, and temperaments and who consequently developed somewhat different institutional structures, policy processes, and staffing patterns for their administrations. They also made radically different decisions about how to allocate their own time and with whom to surround themselves.

George Bush. As mentioned in Chapter 1, Bush not only cared about foreign policy, having been director of Central Intelligence, the U.S. permanent representative to the United Nations, and the second head of the United States Liaison Office in Beijing (October 1974–December 1975), but also defined the U.S. relationship with China in personal terms. He knew Chinese leaders personally and, just as he did elsewhere in the world, he managed the relationship through people he knew. It was no accident that one of his first post-Tiananmen reflexes was to try to phone Deng Xiaoping.

President Bush's secretary of state, James A. Baker III, was not particularly interested in China and wisely deferred to a president for whom that country was a very high priority. "From the instant of his inauguration," Baker said, "[Bush] took an unusually personal interest in China policy and drove its development to an unprecedented degree."[8] "China was obviously going to be one of the President's personal priorities since he had served as head of our liaison mission there in the 1970s."[9] The secretary of state concentrated mainly on other regions of the world, and on Europe, Russia, and the Middle East in particular. Of George Bush's interest in the PRC, Baker went on to say, "In the case of China policy, however, it's fair to say that very few policy initiatives were generated either by State or the National Security Council staff during my tenure. There was no real need. George Bush was so knowledgeable about China, and so hands-on in managing most aspects of our policy, that even some of our leading Sinologists began referring to him as the government's desk officer for China."[10]

George Bush was of the World War II generation that thought of the world in geostrategic terms, and he selected persons of similar temperament and experience to advise him. Brent Scowcroft, the president's national security adviser, friend, and subsequent coauthor,[11] had been a U.S. Air Force Lieutenant General, an associate of Henry Kissinger in both government and business, President Ford's assistant for national security affairs, and centrally involved in the China initiatives of the early and mid-1970s. Scowcroft too had a personal connection to the U.S.-China relationship.

George Bush's coming of age in the World War II generation facilitated his communication with the Chinese. One Chinese interviewee put it this way in comparing the ease with which George Bush dealt with the Chinese to the later Clinton interaction: "Bush saw Deng less than Clinton sees Jiang. George Bush and Deng both were of the World War II generation, geopolitics, they thought along the same line. I don't know if it is true, but Jiang came back from the United States, then said that he felt there was a generation gap. Clinton is 51 and Jiang is 24 years older."[12]

These proclivities, personalities, priorities, and work styles came together to create a particular policy context for the Bush administration. The president was interested in, and involved with, China policy. He was in close proximity to a trusted lieutenant (Brent Scowcroft) who shared his views regarding China and who could ride herd on policy in the bureaucracy. The State Department (often a policy competitor to the National Security Council) was headed by a personal friend of the president, James Baker, who had virtually no desire to compete for influence over China policy. To further tighten the White House hold on China policy, James R. Lilley, CIA station chief at the Liaison Office in Beijing during Bush's time as representative there, became ambassador to Beijing. Lilley, born in north China's port city of Qingdao, was raised in China and speaks the language well, served as national intelligence officer for China, worked at the National Security Council, and was ambassador to the Republic of Korea for President Reagan.[13] This, therefore, was a setting in which the chances for policy coherence and control were comparatively good.

In terms of China policy, therefore, the Bush administration was in a relatively strong position—it had presidential attention, a capacity to think strategically, an unusually noncompetitive Department of State, and a relatively experienced foreign policy team with many members who felt "ownership" in the U.S-China relationship.

At the same time, however, the administration and the president were deficient in two key areas. The first difficulty was that the president rarely sought out the role of public educator. Some of his foreign policy aides subsequently spoke of their frustration at their inability to persuade him to deliver a comprehensive explanation of the administration's China policy to the American people until long after the vacuum of public pronouncement had been filled by administration opponents. A second problem stemmed from the president's ardent defense of executive branch primacy in foreign policy. Particularly in the context of the emotionally charged debate over China policy in the wake of Tiananmen, Bush's zealous defense of presidential authority made him appear deaf to congressional and popular outrage. This intensified congressional backlash. Nonetheless, given the mood in Congress at the time, particularly the intense partisanship of Senate Majority Leader George Mitchell (D-Maine), the argument could be made that any presidential conciliation simply would have fed more extreme demands from the Hill.

There was another, related problem when it came to dealing with Congress, and in this respect Bill Clinton proved more astute. While George Bush appointed excellent ambassadors to China with genuine China expertise (e.g., James Lilley and Stapleton Roy), these individuals did not interact with Congress extensively, though Lilley was more active in that regard than Roy. When Bill Clinton appointed his emissary to Beijing, it was a former member of Congress, Tennessee Senator James Sasser. While Sasser started with less knowledge about China than many of his predecessors, in times of waning domestic support for China policy, influence on Capitol Hill was probably more important. Here Sasser was comparatively effective. Moreover, the ambassador-designate spent a great deal of time studying China even before his posting because of the protracted confirmation process he faced.

Bill Clinton. Turning to President Clinton, there are stark contrasts between his administration's proclivities, personalities, priorities, and work styles and those of George Bush. To a much greater extent in his first term than in his second, Clinton did not see foreign policy as a priority. In contrast to Bush, Bill Clinton moved China policy as far away from himself as he could, calculating that there were no political gains to be made in this policy area, until late in his second term when his attention turned to his legacy and China came to assume importance in that regard. In his first term, however, the president in effect assigned an assistant secretary of state (Winston Lord) to come up with China policy and then implement it. In pushing a policy concern so far away from himself (physically and in hierarchical terms), the president signaled to other powerful political actors that working on that issue was not a priority. This put the subordinate responsible for China policy in the untenable position of trying to shape the behavior of cabinet superiors who did not agree with that policy. Consequently, discipline broke down, foreign interlocutors became confused and truculent, and domestic political opponents saw cracks into which wedges easily were driven.

A second consequence of the president's clear preference for domestic issues was that China policy, when addressed, was filtered through the lens of domestic political concerns. For example, whereas George Bush to a considerable extent judged a China policy initiative by whether it advanced strategic interests or specific foreign policy objectives, Bill Clinton's reflex was to consider domestic reaction and implications, and whether it would receive congressional acceptance. By making congressional approval a principal definition of success Clinton transferred tremendous initiative from the executive branch to Congress and threw China policy into an arena dominated by domestic, often parochial, political concerns. In addition, the issues germane to China policy that most attracted Clinton's attention were those items that had a domestic resonance—human rights and economics (particularly trade issues).

The new bureaucratic agencies that the president created reflected these concerns as well—the National Economic Council in the White House, a special assistant to the President and senior director for democracy in the National Security Council (Morton H. Halperin), and a substantially strengthened Bureau of Human Rights and Humanitarian Affairs at the Department of State. Predictably, senior administration personnel were quite different than those who had characterized the Bush administration. A college professor specializing in international relations at Mount Holyoke College, Anthony Lake, who had broken with Henry Kissinger over the Cambodia invasion of 1970, was selected as assistant to the president for national security affairs.[14] Warren Christopher, a Los Angeles attorney, previously deputy secretary of state in the Carter administration, who had served as law clerk to Justice William O. Douglas in 1949–1950, became secretary of state. To a greater extent than in George Bush's administration, these men reflected the idealistic thread in the American foreign policy tradition.

Most fundamentally, the fact that the president simultaneously elevated *both* the economic and human rights priorities on his agenda by building and staffing bureaucracies to reflect those priorities meant that Bill Clinton constantly received conflicting advice. He generally found support for the economic priority among his close friends, Robert Rubin at the NEC and Commerce Secretary Ron Brown. Among his political advisers, the secretary of state, his assistant for national security affairs (until the last part of the first term), and First Lady Hillary Rodham Clinton he generally found support for the human rights priority. By process of elimination, the relative priority attached to security was reduced, as reflected in real declines in the defense budget every year of his first term.[15] That he generally received conflicting advice interacted negatively with Clinton's own decision style—to defer choice until developments forced it upon him.

The problem with this style of leadership was that on any given policy issue Clinton's opponents could see his tendency to vacillate and wait until the last moment to make a decision. This invited every domestic and foreign actor to fight policy at each step, believing that if they could be the last to gain the president's ear and mobilize their constituents, they could prevail. Thus to a remarkable degree the policy experience of the first Clinton administration reflected the character of the president. In interviews with members of the first administration, one State Department official succinctly summed up the frustration that was then felt across the political spectrum within government: "Decisions are never fully made, so the MFN decision does not denote a long-term strategy.... There is an inability of the government to sort out domestic needs from foreign needs. So, you get conflict avoidance and a desire for harmony.... This is management by miasma, chew the fat, nothing happens, commission papers.... Most routine decisions go to big groups, where anyone has a voice. So, by the end, only in a crisis do you get a decision."[16]

This feeling was not limited to Washington; it also was found at the most senior levels of the American diplomatic establishment in China, with one senior U.S. diplomatic official remarking to me in 1994: "There is a problem in the administration policy-making process and it starts with the president. There still is no real control in policy making.... There is no capacity to decide anything. They can't get it together. They can't get it together to lift sanctions and they are way out of synch with both Congress and people, and they can't decide on a new ambassador."[17]

According to his aides, the president had a willingness to allow debates to extend indefinitely. Howard Paster, Clinton's early first-term congressional liaison, was "amazed at Clinton's willingness to allow these extended debates where they essentially talked to death the inevitable. Clinton was always trying to pick out a new course."[18] Such meetings generally had an aimless, unstructured, seminar quality about them; one left a gathering as unclear about future action as when one entered.

Such presidential fickleness and procrastination was reflected in several instances: Clinton's fiddling with his MFN "delinkage" speech up till the moment of delivery on May 26, 1994; the delivery of a speech on the morning of April 7, 1999, that seemed to signal a determination to move ahead on WTO entry for China,[19] then the backing away from that position over the next twenty-four hours; and finally, the reevaluation of the administration's WTO position yet again as Premier Zhu Rongji mobilized the American business community to support entry for Beijing in the course of the next few days (Chapters 1 and 4).

Leadership in Beijing

In the same way that U.S. presidents set, or fail to set, priorities for the Sino-American relationship, so do PRC leaders. Three Chinese leaders' commitment to Sino-American ties in the 1989–2000 period molded the course of Beijing's overall policy: Deng Xiaoping, General Secretary Jiang Zemin, and Premier Zhu Rongji. Deng's role in keeping the relationship from deteriorating beyond repair from 1989 until his death in early 1997 has been addressed earlier. Here we focus instead on Jiang's and Zhu's roles in post–cold war Sino-American ties—their propensity to take risks on behalf of the relationship and their recognition that Beijing needed more effective ways to communicate with the U.S. Congress, the mass media, and the public.

To reiterate, however, this assessment is through the comparatively narrow lens of their impact on the bilateral relationship, not broader issues of whether or not their governance of China meets the moral and practical tests that one might apply. Therefore, an evaluation of Jiang Zemin that examines his deferral of political reform issues and the legitimacy-weakening lurches back into China's political past with the mass campaign against the quasi-religious group Falun Gong and the Three Emphases Movement (*san qiang yundong*) in 1999–2000 would lead to a less favorable assessment than that provided in this chapter. Indeed, as the first years of the twenty-first century unfold, the current leadership's reticence to move ahead with further, deep-going political reform may stand out as its single biggest failing—with the most far-reaching implications.

Jiang Zemin and Zhu Rongji are much more cosmopolitan, more creatures of the media age, and more willing to consider calibrating their actions to the American milieu than was their immediate predecessor, Deng Xiaoping. These attributes have been reflected in a number of ways, but most importantly in the degree to which Jiang and Zhu have sought to build constituencies in the United States that will support productive U.S.-China relations. Moreover, they have dealt directly with the U.S. Congress and sought to use the U.S. mass media to communicate directly with the American public from the earliest days after the June 4, 1989, tragedy. Both Jiang and Zhu have assumed domestic risks in pursuit of these objectives and have sought to put a human face on the Chinese regime, cultivating bases of support in the U.S. system in a way that would never have occurred to Deng or those of his generation. This is not to say, however, that they have always done so. On issues of Taiwan policy and domestic dissent they often have shown little regard for the U.S. domestic context.

Jiang Zemin and Zhu Rongji. Early after Jiang's move from his position as first party secretary in Shanghai to Beijing, where he was designated the "core" leader by the Fourth Plenum of the Thirteenth Central Committee in June 1989, he used Zhu Rongji, then mayor of Shanghai, as a vehicle by which U.S.-China relations could be improved to a limited extent.[20]

In the months that followed the violence in and around Tiananmen Square, both the Chinese and American governments were looking for a way to restore high-level contact. Both governments were receptive to a suggestion from the National Committee on U.S.-China Relations that Shanghai Mayor Zhu Rongji (accompanied by several other Chinese mayors and former Shanghai Mayor Wang Daohan as senior adviser) make a twenty-day, eight–city/metropolitan area visit to the United States in July 1990. The journey's purpose was to meet with senior American officials, members of Congress, the mass media, and civic leaders, with the delegation meeting the President's Adviser for National Security Affairs Brent Scowcroft, the deputy secretaries of State and Commerce, and leading members of Congress.[21] This suggestion worked well in light of Bush's post-Tiananmen ban on all exchanges at or above the ministerial or cabinet level; in the Chinese system the mayor of Shanghai (a provincial-level city) occupies the rank of "minister," while in the American system a mayor is a mayor. Zhu also was a close associate of General Secretary and Chairman of the Central Military Commission Jiang Zemin.

In coming to the United States one year after the Tiananmen bloodshed, Mayor Zhu assumed several risks in his own political system. In eastern Europe, communist regimes were tottering, and the U.S. press was enamored of Mikhail Gorbachev. Zhu, already well known in the United States as a man who could get things done—"one stop chop Zhu"—was widely referred to in the Western mass media as "China's Gorbachev." While Americans considered this an approving appellation, it won Zhu no plaudits back home, since Gorbachev was viewed by the Beijing elite as a traitor to the proletarian cause. In a nationally televised interview on *The*

MacNeil/Lehrer NewsHour, Robin MacNeil asked the mayor if he was China's Gorbachev, and Zhu replied, "No, I am China's Zhu Rongji."[22] Further, the fact that no widespread lethal violence had occurred in Shanghai during the spring of 1989 was something to be praised in the United States, yet such comparisons with the tragedy in Beijing, again, would win Zhu few friends in the Chinese central government.[23] Finally, given the hostility of Americans at the time to the Beijing regime as a whole, Zhu could not be sure how he would be received in the United States and how, in turn, this would look to his countrymen upon his return. As it turned out, during his visit to America there was only one rather large and disruptive demonstration. It occurred in San Jose, California, and Zhu ignored it with a studied nonchalance.

While in the United States, in a systematic effort to effectively reach as many Americans as possible, Zhu did what no PRC leader before him had done. First, he almost never read a speech and he often spoke in English—moves that alone awakened his audiences from their usual somnolence. He was willing to go even further and appear live on the national media and answer unscripted questions. And finally, Zhu asked to meet as many members of Congress as possible (twenty-four in all), including those most vociferous in their opposition to China's policies; he held a private meeting with Congresswoman Nancy Pelosi. Almost a decade later, Zhu recalled these meetings with members of Congress.[24] In his public appearances, he generally did not wait passively for the uncomfortable human rights question to come to him. Instead, he usually seized the initiative in his opening remarks by saying something along the lines of, "I know you Americans are concerned with human rights—so am I. Let me tell you about my experience of human rights as mayor of Shanghai." Further, Zhu never went into a meeting without knowing with whom he was speaking, attempting to understand that audience's concerns, and having figured out a way to identify with them on a human level.

The response to this 1990 visit was positive, and the reviews he received generally were excellent. This trip by no means transformed the bilateral relationship, but it was part of the process by which it was eventually stabilized, and this was possible only because Deng Xiaoping, Jiang Zemin, and Zhu Rongji were willing to accept personal political risks in pursuit of improved ties.

This brings us to Jiang Zemin. Early on he recognized that China needed to learn more about the American political system and that Beijing had to more effectively deal with the U.S. Congress. Former Political Counselor at the Chinese Embassy in Washington Chen Youwei recounts:

"[W]hen Ambassador Zhu Qizhen went back to Beijing in December 1990, Jiang Zemin told him that Deng had asked Jiang himself to handle U.S.-China relations. Jiang said he carefully read Embassy cables from Washington and would like to establish direct contact with [the] Embassy. Jiang hoped to know more about the USA. He questioned Zhu [Qizhen] about American politics.... Six months later, when Zhu was going back to Beijing again, he asked me to draft a lengthy analysis with 17 pages about the political system and power structure of the USA, and submitted it to Jiang. Jiang later said it was helpful for understanding America."[25]

Having a clearer understanding of the United States was helpful to Jiang because he also was willing to assume periodic risks in order to more effectively present China's case to Americans. He made such efforts during his fall 1997 summit trip to the United States; in his decision to allow the live, unedited broadcast to the Chinese and American peoples of a joint news conference he held with Bill Clinton on June 27, 1998, during Clinton's trip to China; and in his early April 1999 decision to proceed with Zhu Rongji's scheduled visit to the United States despite the opposition of several Politburo members and much of the Chinese cognoscenti.[26]

To put such risks in context, some background is necessary. Bill Clinton's May 1995 decision to authorize the issuance of a visa to Taiwan President Lee Teng-hui, coming on the heels of the Republican Party congressional victory in the November 1994 off-year election (see Chapter 7), galvanized Jiang to emphasize research on the U.S. Congress. He became determined to make more contacts with legislators by inviting more of them to visit the PRC. Just one example of this commitment is the fact that in 1996, 85 or 86 members of Congress visited the PRC, while the following year 101 did so, with President Jiang meeting most of them personally.[27] The numbers of congresspeople visiting China prior to this had been considerably less, though reliable data are scarce. Moreover, the Chinese Embassy's congressional liaison office was strengthened by placing the Oxford-educated Foreign Service Officer Shao Wenguang in charge of a staff that had expanded from four to twelve in 1995–1996.[28] Nonetheless, this operation still remained small in comparison to Taipei's. It was in the context of this increasing sensitivity to Taipei's influence in the United States and the role of the U.S. Congress that alleged efforts to influence American elections *may* have germinated.

The attempt to influence Congress reveals a fundamental shift in Jiang's approach as compared with that of earlier PRC leaders. Previously, Beijing's assumption was that the executive branch managed and shaped the domestic political environment in America; therefore China would deal with the executive branch. However, the combination of a more powerful post–cold war Congress and a president who initially was somewhat disengaged from foreign affairs meant that Beijing could no longer rely on the executive branch to manage the American domestic setting—Beijing and Jiang himself would have to become more proactive.

This analysis is nowhere so well evidenced as in Jiang's own approach to preparing for his fall 1997 trip to the United States and in his behavior while in America. To begin, President Jiang gave a number of print and broadcast interviews (*Time* and the *Washington Post*)[29] and held a news conference in the Great Hall of the People prior to his departure[30]—something that previous ranking Chinese officials had not done to any significant extent. Indeed, Jiang had assumed earlier risks by giving *U.S. News & World Report* and Barbara Walters interviews in the first six months of 1990, which was not an easy period to be subjected to open-ended questioning by the American media, given reaction to the Tiananmen violence. Indeed, some of his early remarks about Tiananmen being "much ado about nothing" did not carry the message of erudition he hoped to convey to the American audience, but rather insensitivity.

Further, in the months leading up to Jiang's 1997 trip to the United States, a torrent of Chinese scholars visited New York and Washington (many connected with Jiang Zemin) and quizzed Americans concerning the themes Jiang should emphasize, persons he should meet, how he could maximize favorable media coverage, and what progress could be expected in bilateral relations.

Early on, a key question became whether President Jiang should accept an invitation to deliver an address and respond to questions at Harvard University. Much of the advice that these Chinese visitors received (from Henry Kissinger among others) was that a different venue might be less risky, particularly considering the size of the Chinese dissident community in and around Cambridge, Massachusetts. One person solicited for advice referred to Harvard as "the lion's den."[31] As the time for the visit drew nearer, the question of whether to go to Harvard kept resurfacing, indicating to me that some of those Chinese giving advice were worried that their counsel to avoid Cambridge was being ignored by Jiang. The president wanted to go to Harvard for many reasons, but one was that he was an intellectual and, in his mind, Harvard was the pinnacle of American academia.[32] That Taiwan President Lee Teng-hui had gone to Cornell University two years earlier may also have given his decision a dimension of one-upmanship.

In the end, Jiang did go to Harvard. Replying to one query about China's leaders having dialogue with their own people and the Tiananmen bloodshed, he made an oblique statement that won him some credit (perhaps mistakenly) with Americans looking for a softening line on the Tiananmen demonstrators. "It goes without saying that, naturally, we may have shortcomings and even make some mistakes in our work."[33] The risk paid off, increasing President Jiang's confidence in his own instincts concerning U.S.-China relations and winning him generally decent mass media reviews.

In two subsequent meetings at which U.S. Ambassador James Sasser and I were present, Jiang made reference to his Harvard appearance—it obviously affected him deeply. In January 1998 he said, looking over to Ambassador Sasser seated to his right, "My success in coming to the United States owes a lot to your ambassador and at the end of the Harvard visit he [Sasser] was relieved."[34] In a separate meeting, with evident pride and camaraderie, Jiang remarked, "I went to Harvard with [Ambassador] Sasser and many Americans tried to dissuade me—but I went! There was noise, but I raised my voice and it was stronger."[35]

In another example of risk taking, Jiang forged ahead with his support of the planned visit of Premier Zhu Rongji to the United States in early April 1999 in the face of substantial elite (and some popular) opposition. According to a well-connected Chinese interviewee, "[T]he Standing Committee of the Politburo met and there was a long, tough debate, with many Members of the Standing Committee arguing that Zhu should postpone his trip to the United States because of the bombing of Yugoslavia and [the decision of the United States to seek condemnation of China at] the United Nations Human Rights Commission. The attack was strong and it was only Jiang Zemin weighing in and making the decision to pay attention to overall U.S.-China relations that kept the trip on track."[36]

This account parallels what Zhu Rongji told a delegation of which I was a member when we met with him in Beijing a few days prior to his departure for America. At that time the premier said, "We have our political problems too. We also have a Congress and public opinion. We have seen the use of force against Yugoslavia and an anti-China resolution at the United Nations and many people here say, 'don't go to the United States.'"[37] Subsequently, in his April 8, 1999, joint press conference with President Clinton, Premier Zhu put it this way: "But President Jiang Zemin decided that I should come according to a schedule, and he is number one in China so I had to obey him."[38]

Once in the United States, Zhu faced a situation in which the hoped-for centerpiece of his visit, the basic completion of an agreement with Washington on the terms of Beijing's accession to the WTO, seemed to be vanishing before his eyes. This was due in part to President Clinton's doubts that the U.S. Congress would provide necessary support (Congress would have to approve permanent NTR for Beijing) and his political advisers' concern about the opposition of American organized labor and some in the human rights community to any likely agreement. With respect to organized labor, the executive branch was loath to estrange unions from Vice President Al Gore who was counting on their muscle for his year 2000 presidential bid. Premier Zhu immediately grasped that he would have to mobilize the U.S. business community, opinion leaders, and members of Congress to create an environment in which Clinton would see conclusion of the WTO accession agreement to be in *his own* interests.

After the seeming breakdown of negotiations on April 7–8,[39] the Chinese leader hit the hustings—what Beijing media termed the "tour of communications"[40]—where he addressed business and opinion leader groups. The premier argued that China had made unparalleled concessions in its bid to enter the WTO and that countries other than the United States would reap the commercial benefits if this effort failed because of timidity in the White House.

While the WTO accession agreement that finally was worked out in November 1999 required a great deal more than the acumen Zhu demonstrated in the United States, this is a clear example of how a strong, savvy national leader who understands his interlocutor's domestic constraints counts. In this case, Zhu adeptly played to U.S. interest groups and mass politics. As Zhu explained in a CNN interview aired April 13, 1999, "[S]o far I've already been to five cities, including New York, and tomorrow we have still to go to Boston—I've had an opportunity to come into contact with a good array of people in the United States, including members of Congress and people from the business community and members of the press.... And I think that this bodes well for a continuing progressive development in U.S.-China relations. And I feel that all the people we've met certainly would be supportive of China's accession to the WTO."[41]

Carrying the story forward to its denouement, as seen in Chapter 4, in November 1999 Jiang Zemin once again had to weigh in with a split Politburo to win acceptance for China's final, successful offer to the United States for terms of accession to the WTO.[42] In short, while one can certainly say that Jiang has been timid on issues of political reform in China, and indeed repressive in his reaction to the development of independent social and political organizations in the PRC, his record has been one of considerable boldness when it has come to U.S.-China relations.

Li Peng. Senior leaders, by design or chance, can be the lubricant reducing friction and creating possibilities for progress or they can be an obstacle. The case of former Premier Li Peng is instructive in this regard. Concerning the different attitudes that Jiang Zemin and Li Peng had toward the United States, former Embassy Counselor in Washington Chen Youwei reports the following:

> Even in the most critical times, Jiang's attitude toward America was more prudent and moderate than Li Peng's. In September 1989, Li made a personal attack on President Bush in an interview with a French correspondent. He said that from Dulles to Bush, the US government has persistently pursued an unchanged policy aimed to overthrow China's socialist system. A few days later, the *Guangming Daily* carried an article that assailed Nixon by name. Zhu Qizhen then was deputy foreign minister in charge of China-US relations. He wondered [whether this signaled] a new tendency in China's US policy. So when he met Jiang the next day, he raised the question. Jiang's answer was not, he didn't know that, personally he disagreed to [*sic*] attack Nixon publicly.[43]

To Americans, Premier Li Peng became the incarnation of the regime that had crushed the Tiananmen protesters because his was the voice that declared martial law in Beijing in May 1989. Li Peng's self-image, however, was that of a small potato with respect to the decision to use force.[44] Immediately after June 4, Li Peng was the person with whom no American politician and few visiting foreigners wanted their picture taken. Understandable as this reaction may have been, its practical effect was that the senior levels of the U.S. government would not willingly have visible dealings with Premier Li; an invitation for him to visit the United States as an official guest was inconceivable. Washington thus was handicapped in dealing with China's state apparatus run on a daily basis by Premier Li. Furthermore, Li's subordinates did not want to be seen as the darlings of the Americans who were humiliating their boss, so they were reluctant to productively deal with Washington. Finally, Li's willingness to stand up to U.S. pressure, even if many Chinese did not care for him personally, won him a kind of grudging nationalistic admiration in many quarters. Li's natural constituency was of the mind of one agitated Chinese general who in 1990 said to an American group, "Under pressure, China is not *doufu* [bean curd]. It is stone!"

Li, of course, was resentful of the way he was treated by the Americans, a fact that came out clearly in the tone of conversations he had with U.S. visitors during most of the 1990s. Two Chinese interviewees put it to me in nearly identical terms in completely separate conversations: "With respect to views on the United States, there is a difference [between Li Peng and Jiang Zemin], but mostly because of personal treatment rather than more abiding differences. Li Peng knew he would never be invited to the United States and that he was [unfairly in his view] blamed for the Tiananmen violence. Jiang, on the other hand, was relatively well treated by the United States. This was mostly a matter of difference in personal treatment."[45] My notes of a conversation with another Chinese scholar recount the following acidic observations about Americans in the context of their relationship with Li Peng and Chinese more generally: "The Americans are unsophisticated and arrogant, and ignorant, both leaders and the populace. Al Gore was late to a meeting with Li Peng in Copenhagen. Li Peng left. Then Gore had to come to Li Peng's hotel to apologize.... The Americans have a bad habit of being late."[46]

The effects of this strained relationship between the premier and the United States reached beyond sentiment to policy. Li Peng held the position of head of the Foreign Affairs Leading Small Group until at least late 1997. In this position, as explained in the preceding chapter, Premier Li could influence foreign policy in ways that General Secretary Jiang Zemin and Foreign Minster Qian Qichen found difficult to control. It was no accident, therefore, that Jiang could not embark on a more affirmative tack toward the United States until he had wrested control of the foreign policy apparatus from Li.[47] My notes of a conversation with a Chinese official recount: "Li and Liu [Huaqiu of the State Council Foreign Affairs Office, who reported to Li Peng] could order someone in the [Foreign Affairs Ministry's] office of North America and Oceania Affairs to do something and [Minister of Foreign Affairs] Qian might, or might not know about it and in any case the emphasis of what Li/Liu might direct the Bureau to do might be different from what Qian [and Jiang] would prefer. It was not that the line was entirely different, but simply that the tone, emphasis might be different—'Li was more rigid.' But these things matter, because relations with the US are important."[48]

In contrasting Li Peng with Jiang Zemin and Zhu Rongji, one sees how others' perception of an individual leader translates into tangible influence in foreign affairs. When Jiang and Zhu visited the United States (1990,

1997, and 1999), American opinion leaders, government officials, and local leaders tripped over themselves to be seen with them; Li Peng, on the other hand, couldn't even get an invitation to America, much less exercise any influence over such groups or individuals publicly. Nonetheless, American perceptions and sentiments were disconnected from Li's true power at home. Indeed, Americans' visceral dislike of Li blinded them to his considerable power base in China, his skills at domestic policy, and his reputation within China's bureaucracy as an ardent defender of subordinates, China's interests, and the mainland's national dignity.[49] Until his move to the National People's Congress chairmanship in March 1998, Li Peng remained a potent force in Beijing's relations with Washington and, although his power was possibly further diminished in early 1999,[50] he lived to fight another battle.

Li Peng's day came again in the wake of Premier Zhu Rongji's April 1999 visit to the United States, during which the premier had unveiled the earlier-mentioned striking concessions to Washington in the attempt to secure China's accession to the WTO, and with the bombing of the Chinese Embassy in Belgrade, Yugoslavia, on the heels of Zhu's visit. In the wake of that tragedy, Li Peng and other senior leaders (e.g., Qiao Shi and Ding Guan'gen), some of whom had lost out to the Jiang Zemin–Zhu Rongji leadership in 1997 and 1998, sought to enhance their power and policy priorities.[51] They continued to oppose broad concessions to Washington in the ongoing WTO accession negotiations until Jiang Zemin decisively spoke in November 1999.[52] This conservative faction argued that the United States wanted to keep China weak, that its asking price for WTO entry was too high, that Washington had hegemonistic ambitions, that China's military needed more money, and that the U.S. engagement strategy was designed to produce political change on the mainland. This view resonated with many in China's leadership and populace, and though Jiang and Zhu were able to persist in their basic U.S. policy after a period of adjustment, Li Peng's view of America continues to strike responsive chords in China. In this case as in so many others, the skeptics in each society derive political life from the rhetoric, behavior, and missteps of counterparts in the other society. Put crisply, the Patrick Buchanans of America gain life from the Li Pengs of China, and vice versa.

This brings us to the second category of persons who count in the bilateral relationship, namely, those who control the strategic passes of the two policymaking systems.

GUARDIANS OF THE STRATEGIC PASSES

In the preceding pages we looked at a few examples of members of the two nations' governing elites who have had demonstrable effects on the bilateral relationship since 1989. Part of the purpose in so doing was to debunk the notion that in an age of global systems, enormous information and financial flows, and huge national bureaucracies, people don't count. However, in providing one corrective, we may introduce another distortion by implying that only a chosen few people in each system matter. The pages that follow are an antidote to this misconception, though the policy-relevant circle in Beijing is much smaller than that in the United States.

While the importance of a few top policymakers is most evident in both Beijing and Washington during periods of tumult and crisis, the percentage of decisions in the bilateral relationship that are routine, recurrent, and incremental in character has grown. Consequently, previously peripheral players in each system increasingly play significant roles. This category of person is most evident in the U.S. system because of its federal structure, checks-and-balances architecture, dynamic civic society, and transparency. If the Chinese system were more transparent, however, one would doubtless see many more fascinating Chinese counterparts to the Americans mentioned here.

The American system is like a croquet game, inasmuch as to be a winner (to get a policy adopted, bill passed, or policy implemented) you must hit your ball through *all* the wickets in the course. Getting through every wicket but one does not count. In every game of croquet, therefore, there are always one or more players who seek to prevent you from completing the course. Defensive players can marshal their resources to defend a single strategic location. America's political topography has many such strategic locations, and there are organizations and individuals that use that terrain advantageously.

Jesse Helms. Senator Jesse Helms (R-North Carolina) is a classic example of a player who occupies a strategic place in the system and is highly skilled at taking advantage of that location. Helms uses his tactical skills, seniority (elected to the Senate in 1972), chairmanship of a pivotal committee (the Senate Committee on Foreign Relations, since 1995), the rules of the Senate (among which are the right to unlimited debate and the right to place anonymous "holds" on Senate business), the prodigious generation of legislative initiatives, and a tireless staff to play the game of foreign policy politics in a very effective manner.[53] Helms has had a significant effect on U.S.-China relations across a broad range of issues, including:

trade, arms control, Taiwan, Hong Kong, executive branch agency structure, human rights, and personnel appointments (including assistant secretaries of state for East Asian and Pacific affairs and ambassadors to China). We will underscore the impact of this man sometimes known as "Senator No" before moving on to a less well known, but important, figure in U.S.-China relations in the U.S. House of Representatives, Christopher H. Smith (R-New Jersey).

A few examples of Helms's influence are illustrative. Indeed, Helms's priorities are so well known that he often has to do nothing to exercise influence—others simply decide not to challenge him, knowing his views. For example, during the 1999 search for a replacement for Ambassador to China James Sasser, several persons were considered by President Clinton for nomination. However, some names were simply ruled out because it was presumed they would be unacceptable to Senator Helms. If the senator was displeased he could refuse to schedule (or delay) a confirmation hearing. Even potential nominees about whom there was some uncertainty in this regard were problematic. The administration had less than two years left in office and a long, drawn-out confirmation process would mean that the candidate, even if eventually confirmed, would have no time left on post when the process was completed.

Helms is also a master of introducing legislation that, even if it does not become law, affects policy. For example, in March 1999, just before the Clinton administration was coming to the table to discuss possible arms sales with representatives of Taiwan, Senators Helms and Torricelli (D-New Jersey) introduced a piece of legislation (S. 693, the Taiwan Security Enhancement Act) that constituted a shot across the administration's bow as it went into the talks. The bill "authorized" (not *required*) the administration to sell Taiwan almost every military item Taipei had on its most extravagant wish list and *required* the administration to report to Congress on all aspects of the Taiwan weapons sales relationship on a regular basis and develop a plan "for the enhancement of programs and arrangements for operational training and exchanges of personnel between the armed forces of the United States and Taiwan."[54] Some senior officials in the Clinton administration believed that this bill was drawn up with the encouragement of some in Taiwan.[55] In any event, the bill (introduced two months later in the House as H.R. 1838, with Christopher Smith as a cosponsor) helped create an environment in which it became harder for the executive branch to reject some of Taipei's arms purchase requests, including early warning air defense radar. Subsequently, the bill also was discussed as a possible amendment (or piece of companion legislation) to the extension of permanent NTR to China in connection with Beijing's accession to the WTO.

In Beijing, the bill became just one more indication of Washington's true intentions vis-à-vis Taiwan. There are many forces in Beijing that have no incentive to acknowledge the distinction between a "bill" and a "law" in the U.S. legislative process or the difference between legislative branch rhetoric and executive branch policy. In Beijing, beyond the bureaucratic and political calculations that create an incentive to see the worst-case scenario, there is a deeper cultural predisposition to pay the most attention to an interlocutor's intentions. The Taiwan Security Enhancement Act bill became yet another important data point in Beijing's ongoing assessment of U.S. "intentions."

Another example of Senator Helms's influence comes as a result of an agreement between the Reagan administration and the Senate Foreign Relations Committee and the House Committee on International Relations. Those committees of jurisdiction have a period of time to review grants made by what was then the United States Information Agency (and is now a part of the Department of State) to nongovernmental organizations for cultural and educational exchanges, including those involving the PRC. During those review periods, Senator Helms and Christopher Smith on the House International Relations Committee were able to influence the shape and content of some federally funded exchanges with the PRC, particularly with regard to exchanges with China's military, Taiwan, and Hong Kong. Influence was exercised through specific suggestions in the course of raising questions about grants, by asking questions until Helms's and Smith's priorities were accommodated,[56] by directly intervening in an already-approved program, or by threatening a cutoff of funding altogether.

The latter instance involved the visit to the United States of a federally funded delegation of legislators from Hong Kong's Legislative Council (LEGCO). This group was composed entirely of individuals elected by the people of Hong Kong in 1995. Two of these individuals were subsequently named to the Provisional Legislative Council that would replace the previous LEGCO immediately after Hong Kong's retrocession to the PRC on July 1, 1997. Because the two had been appointed to the Provisional Legislative Council through a process widely viewed in the West and many quarters of Hong Kong as undemocratic, Senator Helms (and Senator Craig Thomas, as well as Representative Christopher Smith's office) made it clear to the United States Information Agency (USIA) that this exchange should not proceed with federal money if the two provisional legislators were included in the group. In his April 22, 1997, letter to the director of USIA, Helms wrote, "I wish to make clear that I am unalterably opposed to the use of U.S. taxpayer funds for visits by members of [*sic*] provisional legislature, a body whose creation was engineered by China to take the place of the elected Legislative Council (Legco). I strongly recommend that the provisional legislators be dropped from the program."[57]

In the end, the group came, with the two legislators in question, but was supported by private-sector monies instead of federal funds.

Christopher Smith. New Jersey member of the U.S. House of Representatives Christopher H. Smith often is described as a "blue-collar Republican" (sometimes endorsed by the AFL-CIO)[58]—he is the son of a dairy employee who lost his job when Chris was in grade school.[59] He was first elected to the House in 1980 after leaving his family-owned sporting goods business and after having been director of the New Jersey Right to Life Committee (1976–1978). His district in South Jersey is middle class and racially diverse (12 percent Black, 2 percent Asian, and 5 percent Hispanic origin). Smith is known as a representative with great constituent services, and he wins elections handily (usually with over 60 percent). His voting record (as measured by the *National Journal* ratings) displays a pattern of moderate to slightly "liberal" on "economic" issues, fairly "conservative" on "social" issues, and more "conservative" still on foreign policy matters, although such terms have less meaning than usual in his case.[60] Megan Rosenfeld describes Smith's voting record saying, "He confounds GOP free-market colleagues with his insistence on tying human rights to trade favors, and has opposed many of the welfare cuts that his party wanted to impose on programs for mothers and children, as well as cuts in Medicare."

In trying to explain Smith's policy and voting preferences, *The Almanac of American Politics, 1998* quotes him as saying, "Christ said it in Matthew 25: 'Whatsoever you do to the least of my brethren, you do likewise to me.' That was my motivating scripture through all my years in Right to Life, and it continues to be."[61] It is his Christian religion that analysts assert "is the root of his identity as a man and as a politician."[62] His core commitments are to human rights (including opposition to abortion, which sometimes puts him at odds with other elements of the broad human rights coalition and persons who support the United Nations), freedom of religion, women's and children's rights, and opposition to the persecution of ethnic and religious minorities. Smith, for instance, was part of a congressional effort that directed the U.S. Department of State to issue a report on religious freedom around the world and then used the negative findings to place the spotlight even more brightly on issues of religious freedom in the

PRC. He has also been a long-term, vocal supporter of the cause of a free Tibet, stating in 1998, "Personally, I will not stop working until I meet the Panchen Lama in a free Tibet."[63]

Like Senator Helms, Smith is a master at using congressional hearings to advance his cause. That ability was greatly enhanced when the Republican Party won the majority in the House of Representatives in the 1994 election. He was named chairman of the House Committee on International Relations' Subcommittee on International Operations and Human Rights, which has oversight and/or budget responsibility for the Department of State, the Arms Control and Disarmament Agency, USIA, USAID, and UN funding. In his first year as chairman, for example, he held at least five sets of hearings, which were partly aimed at influencing the ongoing MFN debate, on the following China-related topics: the "Chinese Prison System, 'Laogai'"; "Coercive Population Control in China"; the "United Nations Fourth World Conference on Women"; "Experiences of Harry Wu as a Political Prisoner in the People's Republic of China"; and the "Trial, Conviction, and Imprisonment of Wei Jingsheng: How Should It Affect U.S. Policy?" In addressing that last question, Smith minced no words in a December 18, 1995, hearing when he addressed Wei Jingsheng's sister, Liu Qing:

> If we are willing to trade, as we are right now, with the dictatorship in China, doing the despicable things that they are doing to your brother and others, then why not deal with the Nazis 50 years ago. There isn't one scintilla of evidence ["difference"?] between the two.
>
> I think the time has come to say to our business community that you have been, however unwittingly, accomplices in the misdeeds and the atrocities of the Chinese Government. They have done nothing to stop the kinds of mistreatment and inhuman treatment meted out to Wei Jingsheng.[64]

Often televised, hearings can cumulatively help shape media, congressional, and ultimately popular discourse and create boundaries that the executive branch will itself decide not to transgress. Boundaries of the permissible are invisible lines of popular and political acceptance politicians hesitate to cross. Moreover, hearings can be significant even if those asked to testify refuse to come. On at least two occasions, Smith invited PRC officials to appear before his congressional panels. Both times the invited officials refused, arguing that to do so was "not appropriate"; each time their refusal became the basis for further negative media coverage. In 1997, for example, Smith criticized the Clinton administration after two

Chinese religious affairs officials declined to come to Washington for hearings he was planning. To this refusal Smith replied, "I seriously hope the Clinton administration will do a little more than talk tough on paper when dealing with Beijing. The time has come for firm, decisive action. Religious freedom does not exist in Communist China."[65] In the second case, Smith invited the relatively new Chinese ambassador to Washington, Li Zhaoxing (posted in March 1998), to come to a "meeting" (not a hearing) with members of his subcommittee. After the ambassador first accepted and then, upon further reflection, declined to attend (and with *Congressional Quarterly* reporting that Li would appear as a "witness" at a "hearing"), Smith again publicized what he viewed as an absence of cooperation from China. The *Washington Post* described the incident as follows:

> C-SPAN'S camera was rolling live yesterday to broadcast an unusual event on Capitol Hill: the scheduled appearance before a House International Relations subcommittee of Chinese Ambassador Li Zhao Xing [*sic*]. Ambassadors rarely testify before Congress; nobody could recall that a Chinese ambassador had ever done so. But those expecting a lively exchange between Li and subcommittee Chairman Christopher H. Smith (R-NJ) ... had to settle for a different drama: an angry outburst from Smith when Li canceled at the last minute. "It is very troubling and very, very disturbing that this has happened.... In my 18 years as a congressman, this is the first time I have ever had a no-show at a public meeting."[66]

Smith has been particularly active in the movement to oppose abortion and sterilization in America and around the world. Even as a very junior member of Congress, in 1985 he advocated cutting off contributions to the United Nations Population Fund (UNFPA) because of the organization's operation in China, which was implementing the one-child policy. As Harry Harding explains, "[I]n August 1985 Congress adopted a somewhat looser amendment [than the total ban on U.S. funds for UNFPA Smith was advocating] jointly sponsored by Representative Jack Kemp (R-New York), Senator Daniel Inouye (D-Hawaii), and Senator Jesse Helms (R-North Carolina), which barred U.S. funds from any organization that, as determined by the president, 'supports or participates in the management of a program of coercive abortion or involuntary sterilization.' "[67] Subsequently, Congressman Smith almost single-handedly held up funding for the UN until he extracted a 1999 pledge from the Clinton administration to curtail providing funds to UN agencies that promoted abortions.

In the realm of legislation, in addition to passing laws, members of Congress can flood the legislative in-box with bills until the administration is exhausted. Even if most of the proposed bills stand little chance of becoming law, the administration must devote so much scarce human resources and leadership attention to putting out the brushfires that in its exhaustion it gives in somewhere simply to extinguish the most damaging proposals. In the 105th Congress (1997–1998), for example, the Congressional Research Service had to issue a sixteen-page report just to identify the principal pieces of China-related legislation working their way through Congress.[68]

One example of this strategy occurred in July 1997, in the midst of the annual debate over MFN status and preparations for Chinese President Jiang Zemin's summit with President Clinton, when Chairman Christopher Cox (R-California) of the House Policy Committee announced an eleven-point legislative initiative on "U.S. East Asia Policy." Of the eleven separate pieces of legislation (concerning sanctions on PLA enterprises, slave labor products, Radio Free Asia (RFA), PRC intelligence activities, "subsidies" for the PRC through international financial institutions, theater missile defense sales to Taiwan, WTO accession for the PRC, Chinese proliferation to Iran, freedom for the clergy, forced abortion, and political prisoners), Smith introduced one piece and cosponsored nine others.[69] Concerning the one piece for which he was listed as neither an "introducer" nor "cosponsor" (The Radio Free Asia Act of 1997), "Congressman Smith offered an amendment to the Foreign Policy Reform Act. This authorized $20 million in increased funds for RFA and $10 million for VOA, as well as $10 million for the Broadcasting Board of Governors to complete construction of a transmitter on Tinian Island."[70] Of this batch of proposed legislation, the Clinton administration decided that the price for getting MFN status renewed and killing the most unwelcome of the eleven legislative proposals would be increasing the RFA budget and stationing more diplomats in U.S. posts in the PRC to monitor human rights. The administration chose the options that seemed least damaging.

In the cases of both Helms and Smith, their influence is not felt simply through the legislation they have supported or that bears their names (though each sponsored an above-average volume of legislation in the 1989–1999 decade).[71] Their clout also is felt in their ability to force those who *do* wish to pass legislation, make an appointment, or spend federal funds to take their positions into account—either preemptively or after a long struggle. In speaking of Helms's clout with the political establishment, former Senate Majority Leader Bob Dole put it simply, "They're afraid of him."[72] The influence of legislators like Helms and Smith often is measured as much by what *did not* happen as by the legislation they eventually shepherd into law.

Helms and Smith frequently have expended their power in shaping how executive branch bureaucrats and recipients of federal funds implement existent law or expend federal monies. When combined with the ability to stall legislation or approvals through parliamentary maneuver, all this has great influence on U.S.-China relations.

What are the practical effects that committed individuals such as Senator Helms and Representative Smith can have on policy and behavior? Most important, to be a powerful legislator one does not necessarily need to be the progenitor of landmark law. Rather, one can simply attach amendments to the legislation of others (or to regular authorization and appropriation bills) that the president finds inconvenient, or impossible, to veto. Moreover, in politics as in life, fear can be a powerful force; simply being tough and dedicated *deters* both the executive branch and other legislators from even attempting to pursue certain courses of action. On the House Committee on International Relations, for example, it was well known that Representative Smith's colleagues did not like to go up against him unless the issue involved a core interest of their constituency—it was simply too time consuming and too acrimonious a process. Similarly, as Jesse Helms's colleague, Joseph Biden, described the senator, "He's prepared to be mean. He's prepared to be disliked. He's prepared to be ostracized."[73]

The above tactics aside, however, perhaps the most powerful policy tool wielded by legislators is the oversight function. Through their oversight and budgetary responsibilities, highly motivated legislators can deeply affect policy implementation without writing a single piece of legislation. And further, in addition to the federal bureaucracy's behavior being affected by such oversight, the behavior of recipients of federal funds—private sector contractors—is shaped. If a motivated legislator is willing to threaten the funding agency with retaliation if certain priorities (no matter how worthy or inappropriate they may be) are not pursued, it is likely that those concerns will be addressed. Moreover, in some cases agencies and contractors may not be certain if such pressure represents the views of the member of Congress or those of overzealous staff acting in the member's name. The end result is not only to alter the content of policy on the ground, but circumscribe what bureaucrats even define as feasible. It also sets a broader tone for the bilateral relationship in the media, the public, and with those in Beijing who are monitoring American "intentions."

Americans often point out to Beijing that policymakers in the PRC should recognize that Congress actually has generated relatively little law that is highly inimical to PRC interests, despite the numerous activities that head in that direction. The Chinese acknowledge this but nevertheless maintain their, sometimes justifiable, concerns. A prime example of the latter was President Clinton's decision to authorize Lee Teng-hui's visa in May 1995 (following overwhelming, nonbinding congressional votes). In that situation, Clinton knew (or feared) that if he did not authorize the visa for Lee Congress might pass veto-proof legislation that would be more troublesome still.

Thus we return to the croquet game analogy. One or two players that are willing to be tough and keep hitting your ball away from the wicket can be exceedingly powerful in the U.S.-China relationship.

THE ROLE OF THE SAGE

Beyond those individuals constitutionally empowered to exercise influence over policy and those persons who occupy strategic positions that periodically make them central players in U.S.-China relations, there are the "wise men" or "elders" of each society who periodically exercise influence. Such people are often former officeholders or mentors of those who have subsequently risen to great heights. In the post–cold war United States, Richard Nixon, Henry Kissinger, and former Clinton Secretary of Defense William Perry come to mind.[74] Luminaries aside, there are scores of lesser-known individuals whose advice is sought out in particular circumstances and by a wide variety of policymakers. In post–cold war China, one key elder adviser has been the former mayor of Shanghai, Wang Daohan. Wang was the mayor who preceded Jiang Zemin and Zhu Rongji in Shanghai and who has remained Jiang's informal, trusted adviser on issues related to both the United States and Taiwan policy since Jiang moved to Beijing in 1989.

Richard Nixon. We begin with Richard Nixon, a former policy principal who, after his resignation in 1974, came to play an exceptional role as an elder in the American system until his death about two decades later. Nixon, by virtue of his national interest–based foreign policy framework, his centrality to the rapprochement with the PRC in 1971–1972, and the esteem with which the Beijing leadership held him thereafter, played a unique role in the 1989–1994 period. Interestingly, he played an elder role for *both* George Bush and Bill Clinton, although Clinton drew the most advice from him in connection with Russia. As Clinton said at Nixon's April 27, 1994, funeral in Yorba Linda, California: "For the past year, even in the final weeks of his life, he gave me his wise counsel, especially with regard to Russia."[75]

It was George Bush, however, who drew most often on President Nixon's advice concerning China, though Bush had strong, independent views himself. On Monday morning, June 5, 1989, the first business day after the Tiananmen violence, George Bush records in his diary the following:

> I talked to Nixon at 8:00 AM, and he was saying, "don't disrupt the relationship. What's happened has been handled badly and is deplorable, but take a look at the long haul." I told him I was not going to recall [Ambassador] Lilley, and he thought that was good. He doesn't think we should stop our trade [and should do] something symbolic, but we must have a good relationship in the long run ... and that is what I will try to do while denouncing the violence and abuse of power.... The reports from China are still crazy.... There are rumors that "Li Peng has been shot," and rumors that "Deng was dead." All of this tells me to be cautious, and be calm.[76]

Based on Bush's subsequent actions, Nixon's advice obviously corresponded with his own predisposition. Often advice is sought not so much to generate new ideas as to reinforce the proclivities of the person who is asking for counsel.

Nixon did more than advise following the Tiananmen tragedy; he traveled to Beijing the following fall (late October to early November) and, in so doing, became a bridge in a situation where high-level official exchanges were nominally not possible (the Scowcroft-Eagleburger trip notwithstanding). Indeed, it was Nixon's October 31 meeting with Deng Xiaoping and other top Chinese leaders that helped convince President Bush to send Scowcroft and Eagleburger on their second trip, thinking that they could draw up and implement a road map back to more productive bilateral relations.

In his diary entry of November 5, 1989, Bush recorded that "Nixon came to dinner at the Residence tonight.... Interesting on China—he feels we ought to make some move towards the Chinese.... He thinks the best thing to do is to send [Treasury Secretary Nicholas F.] Brady over there. I'm not sure. I still think that we ought to put it in the context of my meeting with Gorbachev, and making clear to China that we're not overlooking their views or their positions."[77] In his subsequent narrative about this period, Bush wrote, "Based on what I heard from Nixon, I wrote another letter to

Deng suggesting that I send an emissary to Beijing after Malta, to debrief him on the discussions with Gorbachev.... If there was some way to start on the road back before there was serious and lasting damage to the relationship, we should try."[78] While Bush agreed with Nixon on the need to send an emissary to Beijing, he wanted to put it in a more strategic context than the former president was suggesting.

A little more than a week after Bush met with Nixon, Henry Kissinger delivered to the president a letter from Deng Xiaoping proposing a "package solution" to some existing problems (which included Fang Lizhi, the dissident scientist who was still living in U.S. Embassy facilities in Beijing). After his meeting with Kissinger, in which the former secretary of state also suggested sending an emissary to Beijing, Bush concluded, "It was reassuring that Nixon and Kissinger had returned from their separate trips to China with the same analysis of the situation."[79]

Wang Daohan. The variety of individuals who may be consulted by China's senior leadership in various circumstances is veiled in secrecy. Nonetheless, we are able to discern the exceptional role played by one elder, Wang Daohan, the former mayor and party secretary of Shanghai.[80] Though Wang is by no means the only person upon whom President Jiang Zemin relies for advice, Zeng Qinghong being another, Wang's counsel is often solicited and heeded.[81]

Wang Daohan is a courtly gentleman, with a bright smile and gentle voice. He listens carefully to people, likes to be surrounded by intelligent individuals who keep him abreast of the latest currents sweeping the world in fields as diverse as history, biography, literary criticism, philosophy, political science, music, and economic management. His favorite pastime is to go from bookstore to bookstore, whether it is in New York or Shanghai. Born in Anhui Province in 1915, he joined the Chinese Communist Party in 1938; he became known as one of the "four Anhui province prodigies."[82] Wang's post-1949 experience was in economic development (the First Ministry of Machine Building in the early 1950s) and foreign trade (deputy minister of the State Commission for Foreign Economic Relations with Foreign Countries, 1965–1979, and vice chairman of the State Foreign Investment Commission 1979–1980). In the words of the National Committee on U.S.-China Relations, "Thus he was present at the creation of China's open door policy, development of Special Economic Zones, and a host of other critical policy innovations that set the stage for China's phenomenal economic growth of the last fifteen years."[83]

It was in his position as mayor of Shanghai (1981–1985), however, that Wang became more widely known abroad. As mayor he actively solicited outside investment and played a role in bringing in some of the biggest and most advanced foreign projects, including a joint venture between Shanghai Aviation Industry Corporation, the China Aviation Supplies Corporation, and McDonnell Douglas to build modern commercial aircraft (MD-80) in the PRC.[84] In succession, Jiang Zemin and Zhu Rongji followed Wang as mayor of Shanghai.

Jiang and Wang's association dates back to the preliberation period, when Jiang's uncle and foster father (Jiang Shangqing) was an associate of Wang's in northern Jiangsu Province. In about mid-1939, Jiang Shangqing was killed, and thereafter Wang helped the younger Jiang, including sponsoring his studies in Nanjing Central University starting in 1943.[85] In the early-post-1949 era, Jiang started benefiting from Wang's advice and help at key career junctures. Early in the communist era, for instance, Jiang found himself as first deputy director of the China Soap Factory in Shanghai, a position that brought him into contact "with Wang Daohan, the 36-year-old head of the East China Industry Department, to which the newly nationalized soap factory belonged." Bruce Gilley further reports, "It appears that Wang saw something he liked in Jiang very early. Whether because of their historical ties or because Jiang simply impressed him, Wang staked his claim to Jiang right away. It turned out to be Jiang's ticket out of the state factory ghetto. The moment he was made vice-minister of the newly created First Machine-Building Ministry in Beijing in 1952, Wang sent Jiang to the ministry's Number Two Design Bureau in Shanghai as head of a new electrical power equipment department.... It was the beginning of a patronage that would last for four decades."[86]

Skipping ahead to 1989, Jiang sought Wang's advice as he was considering Deng Xiaoping's May offer to become party general secretary. Gilley reports, "As at many times in the past, it fell to Jiang's longtime mentor, Wang Daohan, to dispel Jiang's doubts and embolden his brooding protégé. Jiang telephoned Wang, who was in Beijing at the time.... Wang's response was immediate and unequivocal. The nation was in crisis, he said, and Jiang should take up the baton. Wang was reminded of Lin Zexu, an imperial commissioner appointed by the Qing emperor in 1838 to halt the opium trade in Guangzhou."[87] While Lin Zexu is a paragon of nationalistic virtue and upright service in China, Jiang might also have recalled at this moment that Lin had found it impossible to control the foreign "barbarians" and had been, in his own words, "punished" for his failures.[88]

In the period since 1989, Wang Daohan has overcome substantial health problems and maintained a busy schedule of attending meetings in Beijing, making trips abroad in his role as adviser to Jiang Zemin on both U.S. and Taiwan affairs and as chairman of the nominally nongovernmental Association for Relations across the Taiwan Strait (ARATS), founded in 1991. In April 1993 Wang's role in ARATS took him to Singapore to meet with Taiwan's Koo Chen-fu (chairman of the Straits Exchange Foundation, Taiwan's nominally nongovernmental counterpart to ARATS) in the first high-level, open contact between the PRC and Taipei since 1949. Thereafter, in mid-October 1998 Wang again met with Koo, this time on the mainland. Their third meeting was to occur in Taiwan in the fall of 1999, but did not take place due to mainland outrage with Lee Teng-hui's July 9, 1999, statement asserting that dealings between the PRC and Taiwan were of a "special state-to-state" character. This was a "two Chinas" formula totally unacceptable to the PRC (Chapters 1 and 5).

Parenthetically, Koo Chen-fu, also in his eighties, is a dignified gentleman of similar disposition to Wang. By all accounts both men respect one another and enjoy each other's company, whether in negotiations or at the Beijing Opera.

With respect to Taiwan policy, Jiang Zemin apparently has found it useful to use Wang as a vehicle to loft trial balloons, particularly on the nettlesome definition of "one China." For example, in January 1998 the Chinese president told a group headed by former Defense Secretary William Perry that he was glad the delegation was going to Shanghai to speak with Wang about the issue.[89] Jiang suggested that the group pay careful attention to what the former mayor had to say. When we subsequently met with Wang, we understood him to say that Beijing had flexibility concerning the conditions under which it would resume the discussions with Taiwan that had been broken off in the wake of the 1995 Lee Teng-hui visit to Cornell University. The definition of "one China" (sovereignty) was at the core of the dispute.[90] While we had indications that Wang's intervention was not welcome by elements of the Foreign Ministry and others in Beijing,[91] Wang's meeting with Perry was a modest part of a complex process that ultimately led to the second Wang-Koo talks in the fall of 1998.

Turning to United States-China relations, Wang accompanied Zhu Rongji to the United States as an adviser during his sensitive July 1990 visit. Wang led another group to the United States on a private trip in January 1997. Wang's purpose was to meet key people in the government and private sector and to return to Beijing to provide counsel to Jiang about how to proceed in building the U.S.-China relationship after the Lee Teng-hui visa and missile exercise imbroglio. While in the United States he met with senior NSC, State Department, and Department of Defense officials, and Senator Robb on Capitol Hill.[92] Subsequently, in preparation for his late-1997 summit visit to the United States, Jiang spent about one week in Shanghai running through an hour-by-hour preparation for the U.S. trip. Although Wang was not in Shanghai for the dress rehearsal, he did have associates attend, armed with materials Wang had directed be prepared for the president. Jiang not only worked on his English but also received advice about how to be effective in the United States,[93] rehearsed important speeches, and drilled questions and answers.[94]

In addition to his other roles, Wang also has been designated by Jiang as the nongovernmental interlocutor with former Defense Secretary William Perry in "track two" discussions that focus primarily on issues related to overall U.S.-China relations, military-to-military dialogue, and cross-strait relations.

I have been told by Chinese interviewees that Wang has the privilege of direct communication with Jiang: he often goes to Jiang's Zhongnanhai residence when he is in Beijing, he periodically speaks on the phone with Jiang, and he keeps a steady flow of information going to the president. One event I witnessed indicates the dimensions of this unique relationship. In March 1997 I was staying at a PRC government guesthouse called Tianzhuyuan near the Beijing Capital Airport. I was participating in a conference cochaired by Wang Daohan and former Assistant Secretary of Defense Joseph Nye. One morning I observed that security around the compound had been strengthened considerably and the parking lot was crowded with black limousines. I subsequently learned that Wang had not been feeling as chipper as usual and that the meeting of the Taiwan Affairs Leading Small Group (composed of Jiang Zemin, Wang Zhaoguo, Qian Qichen, and General Xiong Guangkai) had been convened where Wang was rather than in downtown Beijing at a location presumably more convenient for the other leaders.[95]

Jiang's own description of his relationship with Wang suggests an intimate relationship as well. My notes of a January 1998 meeting with the president recount Jiang saying, "Wang Daohan is eleven years older than me but he is still chairman of ARATS and, like me, he also is a graduate of Jiaotong University and he used to be my boss. At Liberation he was 30 years old, but he was a minister of industry in the East China Government and I was a director of a factory. So he is better informed about historical facts than me and I am glad you are going to Shanghai to see him. He was my predecessor as mayor of Shanghai. He is [Jiang searches for the English word] 'Elegant!' [in English] 'Elegant!' [in English]"[96]

In speaking with one well-connected adviser in Shanghai, I gained fascinating insight into how people in Shanghai view the Wang-Jiang relationship. My June 1998 interview notes recount the following:

> Deng Xiaoping always had a big strategic picture in his mind and didn't need to consult with anyone except his bridge partners. Jiang has a different style of listening to advice. Rather broad, and not just in Beijing.... Wang Daohan has a "special hot line" so to speak [to Jiang].... Another important point is that when Deng was there, it was not easy to reach him. So think tanks had only indirect influence. Deng was much more remote. Very few people could approach him. Jiang is more willing to meet more different people.... He has good people.... Jiang relies on Qian Qichen and Wang Daohan. He is clever, he turns to people in Beijing but also gets ideas from other places. This gives him options. We very often say that Shanghai scholars have different views from Beijing. In Beijing when the top leader says something, the departments try to explain why the top leader is correct, but in Shanghai we don't know what the leader says, so we make our own judgement, so we have different ideas. This is good for Jiang.[97]

The primary impact of the wise men or elders in China and the United States has been to broaden the information flowing to senior leaders, multiply the leaders' perceived options, provide conduits through which to discuss possible policy options with the other side without becoming governmentally committed, and sometimes to simply strengthen senior leaders in their initial beliefs.

Nonetheless, the fact that the elder role is by definition outside regular bureaucratic channels frequently generates opposition among bureaucrats in both societies—often in the foreign affairs and national security establishments. These bureaucracies inherently distrust the delivery of messages they do not control and view them as creating static in the regular channels of communication; moreover, each side fears that such informal communication can reveal internal divisions that the other side will exploit. Thus those individuals and organizations who play the elder and intermediary roles in both China and the United States often find that not only do they have opponents in the other society, but they also often face suspicion in their own.

PLAIN, PRIVATE CITIZENS

The United States is known for its highly articulated civic society, active middle class, aggressive press, assertive business community, well-developed philanthropic and nongovernmental organization structures, involved academic community, and broad range of interest groups, and it is not difficult to identify private citizens in each of these realms who have significantly shaped America's interaction with Beijing. In academia, people such as A. Doak Barnett, John King Fairbank, Lucian Pye, Robert Scalapino, and Richard L. "Dixie" Walker, who straddled the cold and post–cold war worlds, come to mind, and they have been succeeded by two generations of involved academics too numerous to mention. In the philanthropic and nonprofit organization worlds, figures such as Houghton "Buck" Freeman, Hank Luce, David Rockefeller, Barber Conable Jr., Jan Berris, Mary Brown Bullock, Chou Wen-chung, Peter Geithner, Sidney Jones, Robert Kapp, Terry Lautz, June Mei, Douglas Murray, Robert Oxnam, Arthur Rosen, and Governor Raymond P. Shafer have played key roles. These and many other individuals have exerted their influence through the written and spoken word, the organizations they have built and nurtured, the students they have trained, and the specific issues to which they have devoted their time, money, and energy.

On the Chinese side, the list is more difficult to compile, although private citizens have had an impact, and their impact is likely to grow and broaden as private businesses and civic organizations multiply and expand. In the meantime, dissidents such as Wei Jingsheng, Fang Lizhi, Wang Dan, Liu Binyan, and a few others have had a tremendous effect on the bilateral relationship, although they often are better known abroad than at home. Indeed, many of these individuals not only became causes célèbres in Washington's interaction with Beijing at various points throughout the 1990s, but once they came to the United States they continued to speak out, thereby aggravating Beijing while shaping American views of China.

Those individuals who have served as China's ambassador to the United States (as well as to Britain, Canada, and the United Nations) not only were influential during their ambassadorships, but often have returned to their country to play significant roles before and after their retirements from public service. In late 1998, for example, Jiang Zemin created a group of about twenty-five such individuals whose foreign policy counsel he seeks on a regular basis. Also important have been some intellectuals in China's institutions of higher education, notably Peking and Fudan universities, and in PRC research institutes such as the Chinese Academy of Social Sciences, other think tanks in Beijing, and institutes in Shanghai.

These examples notwithstanding, the role of private Chinese citizens has been greatly circumscribed up to this point because foreign policy has been tightly controlled by the central elite, autonomous centers of economic power have been exceedingly limited, and civil society is only gradually developing. For now the most obvious influence of private citizens on the bilateral relationship is to be found in the United States. We will, however, look at one remarkable Chinese citizen, Dai Qing, who is a harbinger of things to come in the PRC.

Maurice R. Greenberg. Given the increasing importance of finance and trade in U.S.-China relations in the 1989–2000 period, it is appropriate to look briefly at an individual who has had an enormous impact on bilateral ties—Maurice R. Greenberg, chairman and chief executive officer of the American International Group, the world's leading international insurance organization. Greenberg has had such impact by providing counsel to sitting and former presidents and policymakers in both nations; offering leadership to a broad range of internationally involved nongovernmental organizations in the United States; bringing modern insurance practices, business and management methods, and capital to the PRC; and his key role in lobbying Congress in protracted battles such as the effort to win permanent normal trade relations status for Beijing in May 2000.

Greenberg is perceived, particularly by bruised competitors in the realms of policy dispute or business competition, as a single-minded businessperson motivated by a corporate bottom line that has expanded enormously under his stewardship. But the truth is more complex. The drive and focus we see today are the same that motivated him as a seventeen-year-old to enlist in the army, storm Omaha Beach on D-Day, fight in Europe, muster out of the active military, finish his basic education, attend law school, and then (still in the Army Reserve) help quell a prison camp insurrection of Chinese and North Korean prisoners on the island of Koje-do during the Korean War. Greenberg, like many in his generation, wanted to make America both stronger and more successful. In his particular case, however, the Korean experience led him to conclude that "[o]ur understanding of Asia at the time was very bad.... Americans viewed Asians as little brown brothers and as subhuman, and in return we were not loved."[98] It was this experience of American ignorance of Asia, fused with the twin senses of opportunity and danger in the region, that has made him a dynamo in China policy, at least as much as the narrow corporate interest often ascribed to him.[99]

Greenberg's story, however, did not start in the United States or even with Greenberg, but rather with a young American entrepreneur, C. V. Starr, who in 1919 opened an agency in Shanghai called American Asiatic Underwriters that sold fire and marine insurance. Shortly thereafter, Starr entered the life insurance market by founding the Asia Life Insurance Company, a firm that soon was training local people to sell life policies to the Chinese population. Within a decade Starr had "established offices and agencies across China and in Hong Kong, Indochina, Jakarta, Kuala Lumpur and the Philippines."[100] It was only in 1926 that Starr had an office in the United States.

As a result of domestic unrest and foreign invasion in China and the region, company headquarters were moved to New York in 1939. After World War II, however, "American International was, in fact, the first foreign company to resume business in Shanghai, where operations continued until 1950 when the office was closed. The regional headquarters had been transferred to Hong Kong a year earlier."[101] In 1951 Asia Life became American Life Insurance Company, concentrating much of its effort in the Middle East, Africa, and Japan. By 1962 the company had grown substantially, and its new president, Maurice R. "Hank" Greenberg, restructured the company so that its profitability grew mightily thereafter. In 1967 AIG was formed, going public two years later.

It was only in 1980 that AIG returned to its roots in China, forming a fifty-fifty joint venture with the People's Insurance Company of China (with Greenberg saying at the time, "This is historic. It's never been done before.").[102] It was not until a decade later, however, that AIG could operate in a stand-alone capacity, and only in 1992 did the firm become the first foreign insurer to obtain a license to sell life and general insurance in Shanghai. By 2000, AIG had general insurance operations in Shanghai, Guangzhou, Shenzhen, and Foshan, employing 1,100 Chinese citizens and having an agency force of 10,000. And with the November 1999 bilateral U.S-China agreement on PRC accession to the WTO, and the subsequent May 2000 U.S. House of Representatives approval of permanent normal trade relations for Beijing, there was the prospect that AIG and other American insurers would be able to operate throughout China early in the new millennium.

In the 1980s and 1990s, Greenberg and his colleagues moved simultaneously along three fronts that helped shape U.S.-China relations. The first was the business front. Along this dimension, AIG sought to develop the essential relations of trust with the Chinese and to assist China as it developed a business and investment environment that would make it an attractive partner for foreigners and a rising domestic middle class. Just one part of this effort was Greenberg's work with Shanghai to bring the city the best global business advice; in 1990 then Mayor of Shanghai Zhu Rongji appointed Greenberg chairman of an International Business Advisory Council—a first-of-its-kind body in the PRC. Over the years since its formation the council has held meetings on financial services development, port development, privatization, and other topics.

Moving on the business front meant not only giving advice but also investing capital in Shanghai from the earliest days of the city's outward push. AIG partly financed the fifty-story Shanghai Centre that opened in late 1990, investing some $30 million in the $200 million project that was the city's first truly modern integrated apartment, office, convention, hotel, and shopping complex.[103] Greenberg made sure it was run from day one up to international standards by instituting training, management, and quality assurance procedures that at the time were entirely new to the PRC. Further, Greenberg's commitment to the project did not waiver in the aftermath of June 4, 1989, unlike many other foreign business entities. Given the shock of Tiananmen and the opening of eastern Europe and later Russia, some Fortune 500 companies thought they saw the future—and it was in central Europe and Russia. Yet after a few years experience in Russia, some of these firms had renewed admiration for Chinese accomplishments.

On the second front, Greenberg believed that fickle U.S. government policy and an inadequate understanding of China and American interests in the bilateral relationship at the grassroots level in the United States could undermine both American strategic interests and the climate for business success. Greenberg believed that the United States' national security and economic future required that it deal predictably, sensibly, and on the basis of national interest with the rest of the world.[104]

To that end, he has been a major supporter, leader, and participant in a broad array of internationally oriented nongovernmental, private-sector organizations (several of which this author is associated with). These include: the Council on Foreign Relations, the Center for Strategic and International Studies, the U.S.-China Business Council, the America-China Society, the Asia Society, the National Committee on U.S.-China Relations, the Business Roundtable, the U.S.-Philippine Business Committee, the U.S.-ASEAN Council on Business and Technology, and The Nixon Center.[105] Greenberg has helped these organizations create leadership connections abroad, train talent, and educate public and private sector Americans. In addition, Greenberg was on the President's Advisory Committee for Trade Policy and Negotiation. He almost certainly was the single most influential American business voice on China policy throughout the 1990s, and there are few Asia-oriented academic or nonprofit organizations that have not been affected either directly or indirectly by his attention and support.

Finally, as chairman of the Starr Foundation, Greenberg has supported philanthropic activity through "the disbursement of major financial support to academic, medical, cultural and public policy institutions."[106] On this third front, and with respect to China, the Starr Foundation has used its resources to help train young people as area specialists in some of America's premier educational institutions, to promote academic and policy exchanges with China, and to support research that deepens mutual understanding among leaders and citizens of the two nations. From 1970 through the late 1990s, the foundation made China-related grants totaling $51 million.[107] The Starr Foundation has made its impact on the cultural front in China as well, with *Business Week* recounting the following:

> For more than a year, American International Group Inc. had its eye on 10 stunning pagoda windows. Looted from Beijing's Summer Palace during the Boxer Rebellion, the windows had been hidden away for nearly 80 years until they suddenly surfaced in 1992.... AIG Executive Vice-President Edmund Tse got the Starr Foundation.... to write the Chinese government a check for $515,000 to buy the windows from a Paris antique dealer ...
>
> "People always take things from China," a grateful Beijing official told Tse at a celebration marking the booty's return at the end of 1993. "This is the first time someone returned something."[108]

In short, Greenberg has played a major role by not only pursuing the interests of his firm, but also pushing forward on a much broader front. He has worked with the Chinese as they have transformed their business environment, articulated an internationalist perspective in the United States, and helped develop and nurture the human talent that will make the effective pursuit of an internationalist vision possible in the years ahead.

Greenberg and AIG have their critics both within and outside the business world, but critics often neglect the fact that while AIG has significant interests in the PRC, the firm does more business with Taiwan and Japan by far. Consequently, the firm's definition of its own interests is rather more complex than a caricature might suggest. Nonetheless, while the firm has global, not simply PRC, interests, Greenberg clearly has pursued his China vision tenaciously and effectively. He has made a huge difference, and the real difference is only clear upon reflection. Bringing insurance to China is not simply business: more profoundly, insurance promotes the concept of risk and thereby facilitates the move from a vision of society in which the government is responsible for every life event to a state of mind and reality in which the individual assumes responsibility for his or her own future. An excerpt from a *Washington Post* story is illustrative: " 'In China under the welfare benefits system in the past, everything was provided by the country,' says Karen X.Q. Hu, a former railroad industry employee who is now deputy manager of AIG's Shanghai office. 'Only with the reforms do people think they need the type of security of insurance.'. . . 'People have to understand that there is risk if you set up your own factory, for example,' said Ron Clarke, whose previous post for AIG was in Eastern Europe. 'So this education process is part of China's economic reform process.' "[109]

Dai Qing. While business has provided one among many bases from which private Americans have exerted influence over the U.S.-China relationship, far fewer independent platforms exist in the PRC. Nonetheless, as pluralization of Chinese society proceeds, new power bases will emerge in business and in the arena of civic organizations. Indeed, as the subject of this section, Mme. Dai Qing said to me in 1992, "Economic pluralization is the most important to break down the authoritarian system. Besides economics, there are other dimensions of pluralization—cultural."[110]

Given China's Confucian past that places such importance on "intellectuals" (*zhishi fenzi*), writers, academics, and dissidents have been notable influences on the Sino-American relationship. Sometimes Chinese intellectuals exert their influence within the Communist Party elite through the careful cultivation of personal relationships. Others make their cases and exert their influence by reaching outside the elite to the broader public and, upon occasion, outside China to the world beyond the communist system. Dissidents like Wei Jingsheng, Wang Dan, Fang Lizhi,[111] and Dai Qing (who does not consider herself a dissident, per se) have influenced the U.S.-China relationship. They have done so by appealing to constituencies and organizations outside China, constituencies often found in the U.S. Congress, the Western mass media, and among international nongovernmental organizations and academics.

In the preceding chapter I briefly mentioned Dai Qing in connection with the nascent environmental and NGO movements in the PRC. Nonetheless, her role in the post–cold war period merits additional comment. Her influence has been evident in two complementary and reinforcing directions. First, as China's most well known female journalist, Dai Qing has been an outspoken critic of the PRC's political system, saying in 1999, "Ultimately, all who use their power to hurt freedom of expression will be on the losing side of history."[112] Second, she has been one of the motive forces behind the development of a still weak environmental movement in China and the emergence of nongovernmental forces to promote environmental education and knowledge. More particularly, she has become the human face of opposition to the biggest construction project under way in the world at century's end, the Three Gorges Dam project.

Born in western China, trained in engineering, and a former reporter for the official *Guangming Daily*, Dai Qing is a writer of what the scholar Perry Link terms "literary reportage," "a genre that resembles investigative reporting in the West."[113] Having started this aspect of her career in earnest in the late 1970s, the heady period in which Democracy Wall and the dissident Wei Jingsheng came to world attention, Dai Qing has written a variety of daring pieces dealing with sensitive issues (often historical topics of contemporary relevance) germane to individual and group freedom. Though an extraordinarily brave and frank person, Dai Qing's background as an adopted child who grew up in the privileged setting of Marshal Ye Jianying's home gave her insight into the inner workings of the Chinese Communist Party,[114] as it provided her a certain protection from what otherwise might have been the consequences of her writings. Even with this insulation, however, she spent ten months in Qincheng Prison in the wake of her involvement in the events of June 4, 1989, and after publishing her book *Yangtze! Yangtze! Debate over the Three Gorges Project* in 1989. As Link put it, "Hard facts, reported from her own memory as well as from documentary sources in her possession, would not be easy to refute, and to try to muzzle Dai Qing might only anger her into making more public revelations."[115]

When asked how she visualized what she was doing, Dai told Professor Perry Link, "[Y]ou should imagine living in a dark room with all the shades drawn. If one shade goes up—just a crack—the light that enters is suddenly very interesting. Everyone will rush to look.... Or think of an emperor who has hundreds of concubines, and thus has lost interest in promiscuous sex, and compare him with a deprived man who rushes eagerly when a single opportunity arises."[116]

With this kind of self-defined mission, "to open the shades," Dai Qing has since 1989 taken particular aim at the Three Gorges Dam project, writing and editing two books—*Yangtze! Yangtze!* and *The River Dragon Has Come*[117]—on the subject. The latter volume also lifts the public lid on a huge 1975 series of dam failures in Henan Province that led to between 26,000 and 230,000 deaths (obviously a huge range of estimates, with the first referring to immediate deaths and the latter to all fatalities with any connection to the disaster).[118] These volumes attack the Three Gorges Dam project from a variety of angles—ecological, safety, relocation, and the way in which the decision to proceed with the project was made in the first place. They have had a notable impact among environmental groups, international funding agencies that have decided to eschew controversy by staying away from the project, and those members of the U.S. Congress most concerned with environmental and human rights issues.

Illustrative of the emerging linkage between critics of Chinese policy within the PRC and constituencies abroad, it is no accident that three international NGOs have been particularly vigorous in distributing Dai Qing's work and using it as one part of an intense effort to halt the Three Gorges project. The first organization, Probe International, "is a Toronto-based independent environmental advocacy organization that monitors and exposes the effects of Canadian aid and trade in the Third World."[119] Another NGO, International Rivers Network (IRN), describes itself as "dedicated to developing and assisting a global grassroots movement to protect rivers and watersheds for people and ecosystems dependent upon them. Through research into alternative energy generation, irrigation and flood management schemes, pressure for policy reform at international finance institutions such as the World Bank, and active media and educational campaigns directed at projects around the world, IRN discourages investment in destructive large-scale river development."[120] Finally, Human Rights Watch/Asia has published a widely circulated and critical report on the resettlement aspects of the Three Gorges project.[121]

Dai Qing's work and the outreach capacity of these international NGOs have had an effect. Other environmental organizations, such as Defenders of Wildlife, as well as critics in the U.S. Congress, have used this information to justify their own opposition to the approximately $25 billion project scheduled to be completed in 2009. In turn, this accumulation of opposition contributed to decisions by both the U.S. Export-Import Bank and the World Bank to decline to become directly or indirectly involved in financing the project.

The point here is not that Dai Qing and her international allies have provided a fully balanced assessment of the project's costs and benefits. It is to argue, however, that Dai Qing is a private Chinese citizen who has made a difference in one corner of the U.S.-China relationship.

CONCLUSIONS

Just as in every other human endeavor, individuals count in the United States–China relationship. People count because of the values they hold, the priorities they pursue, their propensity to take risks, and their tenacity or lack thereof. Individuals also count, especially in America, because money, the ability to mobilize talent, and vision are not monopolized by the government. As Amitai Etzioni said, power has its "normative" (ideas and symbolic rewards), "coercive" (physical and psychological force), and "remunerative" (material reward) dimensions,[122] and each of these three types of power is widely dispersed in the United States, and increasingly so in the PRC. Arguably, American academic institutions, nongovernmental organizations, and businesses have been more effective in many realms of dealing with the PRC than has the U.S. government. The Rockefellers used their private wealth to exert enormous impact on U.S.-China relations at the start of the twentieth century,[123] and Hank Greenberg has had a large impact at the close of the century. Decades from now, when the definitive history of China's relations with the United States is written, the roles of China's intellectuals and dissidents will be prominent as well.

9

OF ENDS AND MEANS
Conclusions

The necessity of choosing between absolute claims is then an
inescapable characteristic of the human condition.

Sir Isaiah Berlin

China and the United States must have a very good relationship.
Otherwise, the world will be unpeaceful. The relationship between
these two big nations of the world will be very difficult to handle.

Dr. Li Shenzhi, former director, Institute of American Studies,
Chinese Academy of Social Sciences, July 1999

INTRODUCTION

In 1949–1950, the United States and the newly founded People's Republic
of China were at a fork in the road of their interaction. Mao Zedong and
Harry Truman were constrained by domestic political forces as they made
foreign policy decisions, their choices shaped by layers of inaccurate perceptions. The future costs of their decisions were unclear. Nonetheless,
their choices shaped the next two decades in U.S.-China relations, and
they paid a high price for those decisions—hundreds of thousands of dead
and hundreds of billions of dollars, with the Korean and Vietnam conflicts
being the most expensive episodes in the protracted struggle. In explaining
Vietnam, the author John Updike quoted his college roommate (subsequently a leading CIA analyst of China named Charlie Neuhauser): "No-
body wants it [Vietnam]. We don't want it, Ho Chi Minh doesn't want it;
it's simply a question of annoying the other side."[1]

At the start of the twenty-first century, America and China are once
again at a crossroads in their relationship. The decisions made today and
tomorrow will profoundly shape the lives of peoples in both countries and
people around the world, for decades to come. To understand today's
choices, an abbreviated reflection on more than forty years of cold war experience is instructive.

356

In Mao's eyes, the United States of 1949–1950 was the ascending great power that needed to be balanced with Moscow. Further, America had de facto sided with Chiang Kai-shek's Kuomintang (Nationalists) against the Communist Party during the just-completed civil war, and Washington exercised enormous influence over Japan—China's recently crushed occupier. Finally, as Warren Cohen explains, Mao Zedong had his domestic constituencies to consider: "Although their influence was obviously great, Mao and Chou [Zhou Enlai], like Truman and Acheson, operated under domestic constraints. Rank-and-file Chinese Communists and the commanders of the People's Liberation Army (PLA) were intensely hostile to the United States."[2]

In the United States, President Truman and Secretary of State Dean Acheson also had both internal and external considerations in terms of the China relationship. Throughout his administration, Harry Truman faced a circumstance in which one house of Congress or the other always was dominated by the opposition Republican Party that was highly sympathetic to the defeated Chinese Nationalists, who by late 1949 were in Taiwan. Even so, a plurality of the American public "favored a hands-off policy in China."[3] Public caution aside, predictable rhetoric in the U.S. Congress reinforced anti-American rhetoric and behavior in the PRC. Consequently, a vicious cycle was created in which Chinese anti-American sentiment and action invigorated anticommunist rhetoric and action in the United States that, in turn, fed back into the Chinese system. And finally, because Beijing had "leaned" toward Moscow from the early stages of the cold war, the PRC became a geostrategic threat to which Washington responded with the containment policy. The more threatened Beijing felt, the more it was driven into Moscow's arms and then later into the posture of an isolated, angry nation at war with much of the international system.

In the setting of 1949–1950, Truman and Acheson deferred diplomatic recognition of the PRC, believing that temporizing would somehow make future decisions easier—the expectation was that Taiwan would fall to the communists, thereby eliminating the need for choice. Instead, the momentum of events overtook political leaders in both Beijing and Washington when North Korea's Kim Il Sung launched an attack on South Korea; the ensuing maelstrom sucked America and China into a hot and cold conflict that lasted for the next two decades. And, as Thomas Christensen explains, Truman soon found he needed to give his conservative domestic political opposition its head on China policy so he could maintain support for his principal strategic priority, containment of the Soviet Union and a high defense budget.[4]

A similar combination of leadership deferral, negative and mutually re-inforcing domestic political dynamics, unpredictable third-party-induced events, and a global context of struggle could produce Sino-American conflict again. At a minimum, these processes may diminish the degree to which both nations are able to seize the potential gains of cooperation. The principal agenda of the two nations as they enter a new millennium, there-fore, ought to be to avoid repeating the previous century's errors and to seize the potential material and strategic gains of cooperation. In this con-cluding chapter, I draw upon the preceding chapters to examine alternative futures and explore means by which the U.S.-China relationship can be more effectively managed.

ALTERNATIVE VISIONS: THE FUTURE MUST BE SHAPED; IT IS NOT PREORDAINED

Three factors have shaped the U.S.-China relationship during the 1989–2000 period, and they will continue to do so in the future: (1) the perceptions of American and Chinese leaders concerning their counter-part's interests, intentions, and capabilities; (2) the degree to which there are important areas of cooperation that help moderate inevitable frictions in other domains; and (3) the extent to which there are agreed-upon rules, norms, and institutions to which both sides are committed as they address disputes. Notably, the behavior of both nations today shapes the substance of these variables for tomorrow. There are both hopeful signs and worry-ing indications in the relationship.

If Americans and Chinese can develop shared, nonthreatening percep-tions of one another's fundamental interests and intentions, and impor-tant and tangible areas of cooperation, and develop shared norms and bi-lateral and multilateral institutions that provide a framework in which conflict can be managed, there may be a bright future for the relationship. This is a future that Presidents Clinton and Jiang Zemin in late 1997 dubbed the search for a "constructive strategic partnership," something I simply characterize as a *broadly cooperative* relationship (*guangfan hezuo guanxi*). Conversely, if negative developments occur along each of the three aforementioned dimensions, the prospect for a *conflict-laden* re-lationship is great, perhaps dangerously so. In all probability, the future will be characterized by a *mixed* relationship in which cooperation coexists with significant competition and friction.

The decades ahead probably will be punctuated by stressful times when those managing the relationship will be severely challenged. Chinese and

American leaders and their respective peoples should aspire to cooperation along a wide front, but it is vital to avoid a broadly conflictual relationship.

Scenario One: A Broadly Cooperative Relationship

On October 29, 1997, Presidents Bill Clinton and Jiang Zemin announced that their common objective was to work toward a "constructive strategic partnership" in the twenty-first century.[5] If relations between the United States and China are to achieve such a condition, bilateral ties will have to rest upon compatible perceptions of interests, intentions, and capabilities in both capitals and among each nation's citizens. There will need to be confidence that such a happy circumstance is durable. Moreover, America and China will need to work together to advance common interests across a broad range of policy areas. And finally, Beijing and Washington will need to participate cooperatively in the principal regimes of world governance in the realms of security, economics, the environment, human rights, and other global issues.

As we have seen in preceding chapters, the two countries made tremendous progress during the 1990s in some of these domains, while advances were less dramatic or hardly perceptible in others; along some dimensions there has been retrogression. With respect to intentions, interests, and capabilities, for example, while there is an enormous reservoir of popular goodwill in each nation toward the other, there also are suspicions, fears, and national objectives that make an across-the-board cooperative relationship difficult to achieve. That this mutual confidence will be difficult to realize is apparent from the rhetorical question that a senior Chinese diplomat asked me in June 1999: "Is the United States pursuing a policy of human rights and freedom or power politics and hegemonism?"[6] It was apparent that in his own mind he had already answered this question.

As the twenty-first century begins, China sees an America seemingly committed to a high (and growing) degree of intervention abroad, without recognizing some of the inevitable or self-imposed constraints on U.S. commitments. China's sense of past victimization and its fears make the PRC highly sensitive to hints of a more interventionist posture by Washington. Beijing watches as Washington enhances alliance structures in which China plays no role (NATO and the U.S.-Japan alliance) and wonders whether those alliances could one day be turned against the PRC. As one retired Chinese diplomat put it, "The most important aspect is the development of an interventionist tendency. A trigger-happy superpower has become a menace. I wouldn't say a rogue superpower."[7] In addition, at the core, Chinese are not sure that Americans genuinely desire a strong and prosperous China; U.S. economic sanctions (some in place since 1989) and export controls are the most tangible indications of what they take to be Washington's intentions in this regard. Americans' compulsion to not only interact with China as they find it but to change its society, politics, and culture is another worrisome and offensive indicator of intentions to Chinese officials and citizens alike.

U.S. REASONS FOR DISTRUST OF P.R.C

As for American views, incidents such as the June 1989 violence, the PRC government's hand in anti-American demonstrations in connection with the mistaken bombing of the Chinese Embassy in Belgrade one decade later, missile exercises in the Taiwan Strait in 1995–1996, and island claims in the East and South China Seas propagate an underlying disquiet that an authoritarian government with a nationalistic populace cannot be fully trusted to be a cooperative partner over the long run. Americans worry that once Beijing has acquired the capabilities to act on its resentments, whether it is to reunify forcefully with Taiwan or resolve other irredentist claims unilaterally, it will do so. More fundamentally, America's commitment to oppose the capacity of another country to dominate the region coexists uneasily with the deep-seated Chinese belief that they are entitled to forestall developments in East Asia contrary to their interests. As a very senior Chinese general put it, "Why should we accept the leadership of the United States?"[8] These views are not nationalistic leadership contrivances that the elite employs to blind the populace, but deeply shared beliefs of Chinese leaders and citizens. Consequently, the mutual trust necessary for full bilateral cooperation does not currently exist and will be difficult to achieve in the foreseeable future.

Scenario Two: A Mixed Relationship •• **FEASIBLE + ESSENTIAL**

While a cursory examination of mutual perceptions and national goals reveals that a broadly cooperative relationship of "partnership" will be difficult to achieve any time soon, the productive management of a mixed relationship—sometimes cooperative, sometimes conflictual—is both feasible and essential.

The U.S.-China relationship is a mixture of complementary and competitive interests and diverging perceptions, as demonstrated in the preceding chapters. With respect to security, for example, both Washington and Beijing want to avoid war on the Korean peninsula and prevent the development and deployment of weapons of mass destruction there. And yet when the issue turns from this shared objective to possible reunification of North and South Korea, governed by a South Korean-like regime presumably allied to a United States with a continued American military presence on the peninsula, Chinese anxieties are immediately aroused. Beijing generally sees its security better served by a weak and divided Korea acting as a buffer to separate it from a foreign military presence. Thus, although U.S.-China cooperation on Korean issues during the 1990s was served by the shared fear of instability, future Sino-American friction could be stoked by Beijing's concept of security and a U.S. desire to maintain its forward troop presence in Asia.

The mixed character of the U.S.-China relationship also stems from the multiple purposes to which resources and power can be put. Technology transfer is a prime example. For the PRC, raising its technological level and closing the gap with other military and economic powers is fundamental to its aspirations for national security and economic development. Nonetheless, while Beijing wants to acquire American high technology, it does not wish to become dependent on it or have it become an intrusive wedge either. Thus it is understandable that Beijing resists commercial contracts that permit Americans to oversee the use of technology once it has been purchased (end-user limitations).

Conversely, the United States has an interest in maximizing the volume of high-tech sales to the PRC, yet is simultaneously restrained by the fear of losing control over certain critical technologies. The situation is further complicated, with U.S. business and government knowing that if American firms do not sell the technology in question, adequate substitutes often are available from willing competitors in Europe or Japan. Absent effective multilateral export controls, the question is not whether Beijing obtains the technology but simply which country's workers get the employment and whose stockholders garner the profit. To many Chinese the mere fact that the United States has the debate over what technology to sell to the PRC indicates a desire to keep China weak; it certainly does not signal benign intentions.

Then there is the cultural domain. Chinese deeply admire American innovation, frankness, and power. Nonetheless, they also are deeply anxious about American proclivities to intervene, to exercise their strength in pursuit of their values, and the attractiveness of American pop culture and political ideology around the world. America embodies China's greatest hopes and its greatest nightmares. This ambivalence is nowhere so apparent as in the fact that many of the Chinese students who participated in anti-American demonstrations and stoned the American Embassy in Beijing on May 8–9, 1999, simultaneously planned to continue with advanced study in the United States. The following chanted rhyme (shouted as university students marched by the U.S. Embassy) illustrates the ambivalence. "Close

打
到
美
帝
！
。

down McDonalds; Takeover KFC; Don't Take TOEFL and GRE; Da Dao Mei Di! [Strike down American imperialism]."[9] And, yet, on the way back from these demonstrations that inflicted severe damage on the American Embassy, some students stopped off at Starbucks for a cappuccino—an unsettling cultural juxtaposition.

Looking more broadly at the educational and cultural realm, many of the best and brightest Chinese students wish to come to the United States for study. Many of those students do not return immediately to their homeland upon completion of their studies—some never will. Beijing oscillates between feeling that these individuals eventually will return to China, and thus in the meantime provide a valuable link to the United States, and feeling that it is a waste of money and human resources to provide basic education to those who in the end serve America. Americans harbor ambivalence as well. Visiting Chinese students are greatly admired in the chemistry, mathematics, physics, engineering, and other departments of the top universities in the United States. Some large graduate programs in U.S. universities would have trouble functioning properly without these outstanding Chinese graduate students. However, simultaneously there is a latent concern that American students are not moving into technical fields, making the United States dependent on foreign scientific and engineering talent.[10] And a deeper issue lurks in the shadows of public discussion: to what extent is the United States training technical talent that could be used by a future power that might turn hostile?

In a related vein, the Chinese feel that Americans do not accord significant respect to China's own scientific and technological achievements. This friction became glaringly obvious in May 1999 with the issuance of the three-volume Cox Report by the U.S. Congress (see Chapter 2). The Chinese read the report as a national smear—asserting that every technological breakthrough China has made in the last fifty years resulted from theft of American science and technology, whether the technology was related to missiles, nuclear warheads, or guidance. The Chinese read this as an assertion that they are incapable of innovation and discovery, when in fact they have made indigenously generated strides, including building nuclear-powered submarines.[11]

Consequently, whether the U.S.-China relationship is viewed from the security, economic, or cultural perspective, it is a relationship in which each nation's peoples and leaders see enormous gains to be made but at the same time fear the losses that could be sustained. This ambivalence in both societies animates a process of debate within each country over where its own fundamental interests lie in a broad range of policy areas and generates continual friction between the two nations. This state of affairs is unlikely to fundamentally change for the better in the years ahead.

Scenario Three: A Broadly Conflictual Relationship

If the scenario toward which Beijing and Washington should aspire is one of broad cooperative relations, and the scenario we can expect (and which requires effective management) is a mixed relationship, then the scenario both nations must avoid is one of broad and severe conflict. Leaders of the two nations must not forget the costs that the cold war struggle inflicted on their economies, on their people, and on the world beyond their borders. During the cold war, China and the United States transformed minor conflicts in areas throughout Asia from peripheral brushfires into geostrategic eruptions involving both nations—directly in Korea and more indirectly in Vietnam. Hot and cold conflict between China and the United States diverted valuable resources away from economic development and social progress in both nations for more than twenty years. There were lost opportunities as well—trade was miniscule and each nation's people failed to reap the intellectual and cultural benefits of exchange.

Nonetheless, from the perspective of the year 2000 a return to conflict is a possibility. A number of developments during the 1990s give cause for concern. At the broad strategic level, the 1990s ended on a worrisome note. The Chinese government and many of its citizens believe that the fundamental objective of the United States, as reflected in the enlargement of NATO and the strengthened U.S.-Japan security alliance, is to hem China in (containment) and to retard the rate at which the PRC's strength grows. Beijing, for example, views ongoing economic sanctions and the thirteen-year U.S.-China WTO negotiations as examples of the latter. More worrisome, Chinese often seem to believe that Washington quite simply opposes Beijing's reunification with Taiwan and will do what it can to prevent it, though President Clinton's June 1998 enunciation of the Three No's and his July 1999 reaffirmation of the one-China policy after Lee Teng-hui tried to break out of its confines were reassuring to the PRC. Nonetheless, the fundamental problem of Beijing's determination to move toward reunification, Taiwan's unwillingness to do so, and the United States awkwardly in the middle with somewhat contradictory commitments to the one-China policy, peaceful resolution, and Taiwan's security remains.

In the realm of military power, Beijing has placed its defense bets on limited nuclear deterrence, maintaining capacity to fight a ground campaign on its own territory to deter invasion, being able to assert China's interests in waters close to its shores and in the South China Sea, and developing military capabilities initially designed to deter Taiwan from declaring independence and perhaps to compel reunification in the uncertain future. Two of these four defense objectives are potentially eroded by American plans to proceed with national and theater missile defenses. There is no reason to believe that Beijing will sit idly by and watch while its comparatively small nuclear retaliatory capacity is degraded and its only significant capacity to coerce Taiwan is reduced. Beijing almost certainly will respond by increasing its offensive capacities and military budget, even as it tries to keep its focus on domestic economic modernization. This will spur American countermoves and raise anxiety levels among China's neighbors, particularly residents of Taiwan and Japan. Negotiations to avoid a regional arms spiral are essential but extremely difficult to initiate because of the number of parties involved, disparate force and technology levels, and distrust.

The area of economics, while not so apocalyptic, contains cause for concern as well, though U.S. House of Representatives approval of permanent normal trade relations treatment for the PRC and Beijing's probable entry into the WTO were bright spots in 2000. The 1990s was a decade of unprecedented economic growth in both China and America. Such periods provide politicians in both nations with domestic and foreign policy latitude. In 1999 the United States had a trade deficit with China of nearly $70 billion, and that deficit continues to expand. Although the U.S. government could downplay this huge gap, given that the national unemployment rate in 2000 was the lowest it had been since January 1970 (at 3.9 percent), when unemployment inevitably rises, the deficit will be more difficult to ignore. In an environment of high or rising unemployment, affected industries and organized labor can be expected to powerfully articulate their interests and seek relief from Chinese exports to the United States.

Similarly, in China, the officially reported 9-plus percent average economic growth rate of the 1990s permitted economic and social reform to proceed at a pace that would have been much more difficult to achieve under a circumstance of protracted, slow economic growth. If growth drastically slows for a protracted period, a resentful China mired in economic difficulties would not be an easy partner for the United States. Further, an America protecting domestic economic interests through restrictive trade practices, in the setting of low Chinese economic growth and worker instability, would be a formula for Sino-American friction.

To conclude, while the United States and China may possibly fashion a broadly cooperative relationship, they face the prospect of a difficult mixed relationship, and must avoid highly conflictual relations that are antithetical to their own long-term interests and those of the global community. In order to avoid the latter, the bilateral relationship must be effectively managed, recognizing that domestic concerns and developments will be of overriding importance. No single development will hold more consequence for the relationship than whether China will be able to peacefully deal with the political consequences of the pluralization that is ongoing in its society and governing structure.

GUIDELINES FOR MANAGING U.S.-CHINA RELATIONS IN THE TWENTY-FIRST CENTURY

This book has sought to look at the bilateral relationship and its management through the eyes of both Chinese and Americans. In this concluding section, however, I focus principally on how Americans in positions of responsibility can more productively handle U.S.-China relations in the future, in the full recognition that Chinese have equal obligations in this regard and that many forces are at work in both nations that will make the effectuation of these guidelines difficult, at best.

One: Obtain and Exercise Power without Painting Oneself into a Corner

In the process of electoral competition in the United States, incendiary rhetoric and particularistic promises often are the devices used to attract special interest money, zealous campaign workers, and media attention. Except in time of war or global economic distress, elections usually are dominated by domestic concerns. China, however, is a topic that bridges domestic and foreign policy. Trade issues and human rights, for example, link discussion of the PRC with powerful domestic themes in ongoing national debates on issues such as manufacturing industry job loss and abortion. China's size, nuclear weapons capability, and Communist Party leadership simply make these themes, and the issue of national security, even more powerful in the American setting.

The temptation for political candidates, therefore, is to take policy positions that motivate likely voters, rather than positions that enable the candidate to govern effectively if he or she is fortunate enough to win election. Bill Clinton's first presidential campaign and administration provides a classic example of this problem as it relates to China policy (as does Ronald Reagan's election campaign of 1980). In the effort to differentiate himself, first from his Democratic Party competitors for nomination and then from the incumbent George Bush in the general election of 1992, Clinton adopted rhetoric that was deeply offensive to PRC leaders. Calling the Chinese leadership the "Butchers of Beijing" made it extremely difficult for him to work with them for some time after he was elected. Clinton promised both American voters and the U.S. Congress that he would link improved human rights in China to Beijing's continued eligibility for normal tariff treatment. Though this policy stance did succeed in distinguishing Clinton from Bush, it also set the stage for a long, awkward, costly, and damaging postelection period during which the new president had to disengage himself from a policy that was unworkable.

As former Secretary of State Warren Christopher subsequently put it, "Given the bright line candidate Clinton had drawn, we were, to a certain extent, boxed in on the issue."[12] Former Clinton Secretary of Defense William Perry put it this way: "During the presidential campaign, candidate Clinton had criticized President George Bush for not reacting more strongly to the Tiananmen Square incident and to the Chinese government's abuses of human rights. As president, therefore, Clinton was not initially receptive to the position of those in the administration, including myself, who argued that the only way to influence China in a positive direction was by engaging it."[13] At the end of the protracted adjustment process, Bill Clinton's China policy was very similar in articulation, if not execution, to his predecessor's.

In addition to putting elected officials in an untenable position, there is a more insidious danger in campaign hyperbole, especially when it comes to China. Articulating policy to which one is not committed or that is unsustainable can easily destroy a leader's credibility when the inevitable policy adjustment occurs. Doing policy U-turns can invite both foreign and domestic interlocutors to test one's resolve in inconvenient or dangerous circumstances. As mentioned in Chapters 1 and 2, had Bill Clinton projected a constancy of purpose and vision in China policy (and other areas of foreign policy) in 1993–1994, for example, he *might* not have been challenged in the Taiwan Strait in 1995–1996 with missile exercises.

In China, the absence of a competitive, transparent, mass participatory electoral system suggests that leadership in Beijing does not face this particular set of pressures and dangers. Nonetheless, there are competitive pressures within the elite that are strongest when the ruling group is divided or the process of succession is underway. Moreover, increasingly the elite also must consider a broad range of bureaucratic and social forces. For example, Jiang Zemin's early-1995 soft line on Taiwan was brought into question by Lee Teng-hui's visit to Cornell University later that year. In the context of Deng Xiaoping's deteriorating health and Jiang Zemin's need for military support to guarantee his future power, Jiang may have seen little alternative to a military response to Taipei's actions if he wished to stay credible with the PLA and colleagues at the political center. Thus the struggle for power can lead one down avenues of policy that can prove to be dangerous cul-de-sacs in *both* nations.

Returning to the American system, the trick on the campaign trail is to find methods to speak meaningfully about China without locking oneself into specific short-term policies. While this approach is easier said than done, three suggestions may be useful. One, identify core U.S. interests regarding China (both shared and divergent) and define what is at stake in the short and the long run. Two, emphasize long-term goals, rather than short-term objectives. With a country the size of China, sweeping short-term goals are almost destined to fail. And three, set achievable goals: it is easier to produce change in a country's trade policy than in its political system. It is easier to coerce a small country than a massive one. A mistake that the Clinton administration repeatedly made was to establish unrealistic goals and time horizons for political change in China. Clinton did this when he gave Beijing a one-year deadline for human rights change in 1993, and he made the same mistake in reverse when he was in Hong Kong following his mid-1998 trip to the PRC. He held a news conference in which he exulted over political and social change in the PRC to the point that he established an image of change that subsequent events (i.e., the ongoing arrest of dissidents and religious and quasi-religious adherents) could not sustain. These exaggerated expectations, in turn, became the new baseline by which some Americans judged his policy a failure.

Two: Build an Organizational Structure Capable of Developing and Implementing a Coherent Policy

Having achieved power, the process of organizing that power for the effective formulation and implementation of foreign policy is one of the first issues facing a victorious candidate. As the work of Neustadt, Hess, Rossiter,[14] and many others demonstrates, there is no single formula for building effective organizations that suits all eras, much less all leaders. The optimal structure will depend on a number of considerations, such as the partisan makeup of Congress, the president's own foreign policy and domestic priorities, and the president's decision-making style. Conceding that all of these factors will shape the actual organization of power, from the standpoint of conducting an effective China policy, the preceding chapters reinforce one central conclusion—there is *no substitute* for presidential attention. Presidential attention can be hands-on as it was in the case of George Bush, or Richard Nixon in an earlier era, or it can be delegated as it was under Ronald Reagan when he designated Secretaries of State Alexander Haig and then George Shultz as the primary voices on foreign policy, including China policy.

The most deleterious circumstance is when there appears to be no final policy arbiter in an administration below the president, and the president is disengaged on the issue. The president must expressly delegate authority to someone who is capable of disciplining turf-conscious, interest-specific cabinet-level officials. In the absence of such authority, various cabinet-level and other agencies (Treasury, Commerce, the U.S. Trade Representative, the Department of Defense, and the intelligence community) will go their own way and a disjointed policy will result, thereby confusing Congress, the American public, the Chinese, and allies. In such a cacophony of mixed signals, interest groups will seek to exploit the contradictions, further decreasing the chances for policy constancy.

If there is to be a clear line of responsibility a president must decide early on whether China policy should be run from the Department of State or the White House. Both models can succeed, but when both State and the White House are intense competitors for dominance in China policy, or neither has interest, major difficulties arise. Judging by past experience, one would have to conclude that conducting China policy from the White House has most often produced a coherent outcome (e.g., Kissinger under Nixon, Brzezinski under Carter, Scowcroft under Bush, and Berger under Clinton), because the president tends to become more involved (for reasons of proximity, if nothing else), thus making it easier to enlist the chief executive in resolving interagency conflicts. The antithesis of presidential attention to China policy was most of the first Clinton administration, where no one above the assistant secretary of state took ownership of China policy. In the upper echelons of the executive branch China was seen as a problem to be eschewed, rather than an opportunity to be grasped. Consequently, individual agencies articulated China policies that they found most congenial to their interests, while the White House considered the issue a domestic political problem, to be judged by whether Congress went along and what the effect on interest rates might be. Predictably, China policy only began to become more coherent when in mid-March 1994 policy control shifted from the Senior Steering Group chaired by Winston Lord at the Department of State to the White House.[15] The process of concentrating policy power in the White House reached its zenith under Clinton in the final year of his presidency, when he personally oversaw the fight to extend permanent normal trade relations treatment to Beijing.

In China, although similar principles apply to the making of foreign policy concerning the United States, outsiders have far more difficulty discerning the actual bureaucratic terrain. It is clear, however, that in Beijing there is as great of a need for a final policy arbiter as in Washington. In conversations with foreigners, Chinese President Jiang Zemin refers to the fact that Deng Xiaoping designated him as the person with ultimate responsibility for U.S.-China relations. As we saw in Chapter 7, it was only in 1997–1998 that Jiang succeeded in gaining control of the principal levers of foreign policy control—the Foreign Affairs Leading Small Group being key. It was only in the setting of this control that Jiang could drive his system toward the 1997 and 1998 U.S.-China summits and push forward Premier Zhu Rongji's visit to the United States in April 1999, despite substantial opposition.

Three: Recognize That Resources Are Limited, Define Broad Priorities, and Stay with Them

In his classic book, *Strategies of Containment*,[16] John Lewis Gaddis addresses an enduring issue facing a superpower—where and under what circumstances should the nation make fundamental national security commitments and choose to expend lives and treasure? There is no single answer, but the broad alternatives are clear. On the one hand, commitments of lives and money can be made when vital, traditionally defined national interests are at stake, or one can define one's commitments to particular values (e.g., democracy, human rights, and economic equality) and engage where those values are threatened. Of course, there is the possibility of blending these criteria by, for instance, intervening for humanitarian purposes in areas of core national interest. Using this criterion, one might decide to intervene to stop genocide in Yugoslavia (1999) and not do so in Rwanda (1994), as the Clinton administration decided. Further, this is not to suggest that there always is a conflict between American values and U.S. interests.

But the central issue remains—what are the criteria by which one makes critical national commitments? If one emphasizes humanitarian and values-driven criteria, one can easily end up overcommitted, exhausted, and ultimately ineffectual, because the supply of global tragedy is greater than available resources. There is also the dilemma of double standards when one intervenes in some humanitarian crises and fails to do so in others. And finally, if one defines the defense of universal values as the basis on which national commitments are made, it often is exceedingly difficult to integrate such value-based decisions with economic and security priorities. Yet sitting idly by as humanitarian disasters unfold on CNN renders national leaders vulnerable to the charge of callousness and immorality. And, in an immigrant nation such as America, foreign tragedies often have powerful domestic groups calling for action.

In the past, the PRC also has faced the choice between values-driven and interest-based foreign policy. In the 1960s, Beijing pursued a values-driven foreign policy (global third-world revolution) and by the decade's end the policy was bankrupt and the nation exhausted.

By virtue of its history and the character of the regime, Beijing prefers to deal with a United States that pursues a traditional national-interest-driven definition of priorities versus a values-driven vision. Although by itself, this is not a compelling reason for America to choose the former over the latter, it is a good predictor of what makes U.S.-China relations more or less manageable.

Moving from global to specific priorities in the U.S.-China relationship, it generally is helpful for a president and his administration to be as clear as possible. This is important not only to effectively deal with Beijing but also to effectively deal with domestic interest groups, the U.S. government bureaucracy, and Capitol Hill. Although one might disagree with George Bush's priorities in dealing with the PRC, they could be described, domestic actors understood them, and the Chinese generally had confidence in them. Those priorities included protecting presidential initiative and prerogatives in foreign policy; maintaining productive relations with Beijing out of consideration of regional and global stability; pursuing American security interests such as nonproliferation; fostering economic ties with China; and downplaying public confrontation over human rights issues with the PRC in the belief that quiet, behind-the-scenes interaction would be more effective and that economic change and global involvement were the only long-term guarantors of durable human rights improvement in China.

Being clear about priorities has several advantages. Domestically, the bureaucracy knows the priorities and this, in turn, makes the enforcement of discipline within the administration conceivable. With respect to Congress, one's natural allies can have confidence that if they support the administration's policy they will not be left exposed by a White House that keeps tacking with each shifting breeze. And finally, interest groups are fundamentally opportunistic; they attack where they see indecision and weakness. An inability to establish priorities invites most interest groups to expend resources in an attempt to have the administration embrace its goals.

With respect to the Chinese, if the U.S. administration is unable to establish its own hierarchy of objectives, Beijing can have no confidence that concessions in one area will do anything but produce new demands by Washington in other areas. Priorities provide Beijing some incentive to make concessions. When Washington has defined its core interests, such as nonproliferation, stability on the Korean peninsula, and winning Chinese acquiescence for the Gulf War intervention, Beijing generally has found a way to be at least minimally accommodating.

The fundamental failing of the first-term Clinton administration was its inability to define (and adhere to) realistic priorities in its relationship with the PRC. Human rights, security, and trade interests coexisted uneasily on near equal terms. Ultimately, this fuzziness left domestic interest groups unsatisfied (each feeling it could not count on the administration), and this circumstance minimized the incentives for the Chinese to be accommodating in any area of policy, fearing that concessions in one area would buy them no relief with respect to other issues.

As for Beijing, there was relatively little uncertainty over its foreign policy priorities in the 1990s, which included avoiding a drift toward Taiwan independence; maintaining international relationships that maximized the flow of capital and technology to China; holding off on large-scale defense spending so China's technological and economic base could grow in sophistication and scale, thereby providing the foundation for long-term competitiveness in the defense and trade realms; preventing the formation and strengthening of alliances potentially hostile to the PRC; and achieving a role of equality and dignity in the major institutions of the international system. Taken together, these are national objectives with which the United States, for the most part, can live. It should be a major national objective to avoid pushing Beijing to change its priorities in ways inimical to America's long-term interests.

Four: *Talk Strategically and Define Intentions*

American culture is pragmatic and action oriented. As a consequence, in dealing with another country it is quite natural for Americans to focus on specific problems and solutions. However, before one can effectively address particular problems with the Chinese it is necessary to first establish a framework of interest, principles, and intention against which they can assess particular issues. This frame of reference has several components that, in the aggregate, the Chinese call "mutual understanding." When Americans hear this phrase they are likely to dismiss its significance and think of it as just one more cliché, or verbal ritual ("friendship" and

"strategic relationship" are two more), that seems to be required in dealing with Beijing. To dismiss these concepts, however, is to render oneself
ineffectual.

China still is a Confucian culture. The defining quality of Confucianism
is its attention to "relationships" and the interests and obligations that bind
people together. Before Chinese will have a productive discussion with an
interlocutor on a particular issue they first seek to establish in their own
minds the other party's shared basic common interests with China. Are
fundamental interests compatible? If you have divergent interests and
long-term intentions that are inimical to the PRC's welfare, even a seemingly innocuous deal in the short-run can prove disadvantageous in the future. But if two nations share interests and long-term intentions are benign
or helpful, then resolving immediate issues, or even difficult problems, can
strengthen what is viewed as a beneficial relationship. For example, because
Beijing believed that Lee Teng-hui's objective was independence, no matter
what he said or proposed, Beijing saw virtually no agreement with Taipei to
be in the PRC's interest.

Those who have been most successful in dealing with Beijing have been
those who have invested what to westerners can seem like an inordinate
amount of time talking about trends in the world and within the two societies, mutual relations, and intentions with respect to third parties. Such
broad discussion provides each leadership a mental map of the other. The
greater the Chinese familiarity with an interlocutor's interest map the
greater their confidence in that party's future behavior. Chinese have relatively high confidence in interlocutors when they believe that their behavior and policy derive from a sense of durable, long-term interests. They
have the least confidence when they believe the interlocutor's behavior is
dictated by short-term domestic political calculations that they can barely
discern. From the beginning, Beijing never had much confidence in Bill
Clinton, primarily because he was such a creature of domestic American
politics and he initially spent so little time on the relationship, though this
latter aspect changed dramatically in the final three years of his presidency.

For much of the Clinton presidency, Beijing gave more sustained
thought, at a higher level, to its U.S. policy than vice versa. This is reflected
in the fact that Vice Premier and Foreign Minister Qian Qichen visited the
United States (including visits to the United Nations) repeatedly throughout the 1990s (at least thirteen times from 1990 to 1998). In contrast, Secretary of State Warren Christopher went to China only twice in his four-
year term. Clinton's first-term national security adviser, Anthony Lake,

went to the PRC for the first time only in the last six months of Clinton's first term.

The difference in attention given to the relationship is also reflected in the time that senior Chinese leaders personally devote to it. It is not unusual, for example, for American congressmen, senior corporate executives, and scholars to meet with China's president, premier, or a vice premier and to be given an authoritative recap of Chinese views on visits to the mainland. When Chinese officials visit Washington, however, even individuals of very senior rank find it difficult to see American officials at the cabinet level and frequently have to settle for an assistant secretary of state or comparable official.

Finally, senior Chinese leaders have signaled the importance they attach to the U.S.-China relationship by sending their children to study, travel, and work in the United States. Deng Xiaoping, for example, sent a son to study at the University of Rochester and also sent his youngest daughter, Xiao Rong, to work in the Chinese Embassy in Washington shortly after normalization. Both President Jiang Zemin and Premier Zhu Rongji have sent children to study in the United States. For a combination of strategic, economic, and personal reasons, China's leaders simply pay more sustained attention to the bilateral relationship than have American leaders.

Since the very early 1970s, the periods in which U.S.-China relations have been most productive have been those in which someone at the most senior levels of the executive branch had a strategic, long-term framework (that Beijing substantially shared) and was willing to invest the time in dialogue with the Chinese to build mutual confidence. Certainly Nixon and Kissinger had such an approach to dealing with Beijing, as did Zbigniew Brzezinski in the Carter administration, George Shultz in the Reagan administration, and Brent Scowcroft with George Bush.

The first-term Clinton administration was bereft of such individuals at the most senior levels, except for late in that term when Anthony Lake initiated his "strategic dialogue" with Vice Minister Liu Huaqiu. Secretary of State Warren Christopher did not think in strategic terms, nor did he invest much time in traveling to the PRC or engaging Beijing in anything but problem-oriented discussions. Secretary of the Treasury Robert Rubin put his finger on the problem when he said in September 1997, "We can properly be faulted for vastly under-investing in our relations with Chinese officials up and down the line [and it's no surprise that] we keep having such a hard time understanding each other."[17] In the second term, Lake's successor, Samuel Berger, thought somewhat more strategically and certainly invested more in the relationship's cultivation than his predecessor.

Henry Kissinger and Zbigniew Brzezinski tried to elaborate a common strategic framework with Beijing. In the cold war setting, this framework necessarily involved the Soviet Union and the relationship among the USSR, NATO countries, and China. An August 1972 conversation with Chinese Permanent Representative to the United Nations Huang Hua reveals the detail with which Kissinger, for example, tried to convey the administration's thinking to Beijing at that time.

> We have no interest in maintaining tension in the West [between NATO and the Warsaw Pact], but we have an interest in maintaining our *position* in the West. And if we remain in office, we shall not reduce our forces in Europe unilaterally, as I told the Prime Minister [Zhou Enlai], even by agreement we will not reduce them by much more than 10 percent.
>
> But what we have to try to accomplish before that time period that I mentioned to you is to establish enough of a relationship with you so that it is plausible that an attack on you [by the USSR] involves a substantial American interest. And you would make a great mistake if you thought that we had primarily commercial interests, because with this Administration at least, that's of a third order interest. Our basic strategy is what I mentioned to you.
>
> It is a very complicated policy, but it is a very complicated situation. And we will not participate in any agreements that have the objective tendency of isolating you, or can be directed at you.[18]

Kissinger was clearest about U.S. strategic intentions when he told Chairman Mao on the night of February 17–18, 1973, "If they [the Soviets] attack China, we would certainly oppose them for our own reasons."[19]

There is a misconception in many sectors of America, however, that "talking strategically" is code for a military relationship and big power politics. While in the eras of Kissinger and Brzezinski there was considerable truth to this, it was partially a function of the cold war setting in which the bilateral relationship was conducted. However, there is no generic reason that speaking strategically with the Chinese must involve a heavy military/ security component, though any stable relationship assuredly must involve significant shared security interests and some military-to-military dialogue. In the current world circumstance, for instance, a strategically grounded framework would pay much greater attention to global economic stability, collective peacekeeping, development and environmental concerns, and other transnational issues than was the case in the early 1970s.

The key to "strategically grounded discussion" is not the word *military*, but rather the words *long-term* and *important common interests*.

And this brings me to the last point with respect to strategic dialogue: one must stick with such dialogue through the thick and the thin. One of the most destructive tendencies, in both Beijing and in Washington, has been the reflex to suspend high-level dialogue every time serious problems arise in the relationship. This tendency has different origins in Washington and Beijing. In Washington, the implicit assumption seems to be that to talk to a leadership with which you disagree is to endorse its actions. In Beijing, the tendency to curtail discussion in times of stress seemingly arises from the desire to convey displeasure and from the fact that the Chinese leadership may itself be wrangling about its own posture and not wish to reveal inner division to outsiders.

Whatever the causes of this tendency in both capitals, it is counterproductive. If high-level exchange stops, it is impossible to develop a shared mental map; without such a map, neither side will have much confidence in the other, and the possibilities for miscalculation multiply. Two instances of this destructive reflex were seen in preceding chapters: one occurred in June 1989, when George Bush suspended high-level exchanges, and the other took place a decade later when Beijing curtailed human rights and arms proliferation dialogues with Washington in response to the May 1999 NATO bombing of the Chinese Embassy in Belgrade. In both cases another interesting phenomenon also occurred. In 1989, George Bush sought to telephone Deng Xiaoping in the wake of the Tiananmen tragedy—Deng did not answer the call. Almost exactly a decade later, in May 1999, Bill Clinton sought to reach Jiang Zemin over the "hot line" to discuss the embassy bombing and to apologize. His initial efforts were rebuffed, though eventually the call was scheduled and completed. This behavior does not increase mutual confidence, and a hot line used only when it is not needed is not of much use. It is worthy of note, therefore, that in July 1999 (in the wake of President Lee Teng-hui's July 9 announcement moving away from previous "one China" formulations) Clinton and Jiang spoke by phone (July 18), and this was part of the process by which the minicrisis was managed.

Five: Stay Credible

Although Washington and Beijing are by no means in the same adversarial relationship with each other at the start of the twenty-first century as were the United States and the Soviet Union throughout the cold war era, credibility still counts. As we saw in earlier discussions of the Taiwan Strait tensions of 1995–1996, there was serious doubt among Chinese leaders as to whether and how the United States might react to possible PRC intimidation of Taiwan. Beijing, I believe, was genuinely surprised by the intensity of the American response in March 1996—two aircraft carrier battle groups. Such miscalculation is exceedingly dangerous, and Chinese misjudgments were nurtured by a variety of considerations, including policy vacillations earlier in the Clinton administration and mixed signals from Washington as the period of friction unfolded. In October 1995, a "senior" State Department official publicly discounted the likelihood of an American use of force saying, "You don't really know what would happen until you get there.... [But] we would not be in a position to react with force. We would not elect to do that I'm sure."[20] If Beijing believes, as at least one U.S. Army officer thinks it does, that the United States has "[g]ood equipment, but no stomach to fight," this is exceedingly dangerous.[21]

Clearly, Beijing needs to better understand the determinants of American behavior. At the same time, Washington has an obligation not to foster confusion abroad. The avoidance of making threats upon which one cannot deliver is one way to enhance credibility. Organizing the administration so that it speaks with one voice is another. And finally, having a clear understanding of foreign policy priorities that have been conveyed in ongoing dialogue can further reduce the chance of miscommunication and enhance credibility.

Six: Consider the Domestic Political Circumstance of the Interlocutor

Beijing and Washington have been very uneven in taking the domestic situation of the other into account in developing and implementing bilateral policy. In some cases, leaders in each capital have tried to take the other country's situation into account, as when Jiang Zemin took the risk of letting the visiting Bill Clinton speak to the Chinese people on live television in mid-1998 in order for Clinton to address the concerns of domestic critics back in the United States. Similarly, Jiang Zemin's late-1997 visit to the United States was orchestrated by both sides to play well back in the PRC.

In other cases, however, each side has been tone deaf to the domestic political needs of the other, sometimes weakening those individuals in the other society most predisposed to cooperation. For instance, the April 1999 U.S. unilateral publication of preliminary concessions made by Premier Zhu Rongji on Beijing's behalf in the WTO negotiations weakened Zhu upon his return home. And likewise, China's ongoing arrest of dissidents in March–April, 1999, in anticipation of the tenth anniversary of the Tiananmen tragedy made it much more difficult for the Clinton administration to sustain its "engagement policy." In the same vein, Beijing's domestic need to show its people that China was not isolated in the aftermath of Tiananmen led it to effectively "trap" Brent Scowcroft in photographs as he toasted the Chinese leaders in December 1989. These images enraged many Americans, and the backlash further reduced the Bush administration's capacity to move relations forward. And finally, on February 21, 2000, Beijing released a white paper on Taiwan policy that threatened the possible use of force against Taiwan if Taipei "indefinitely" refused to negotiate about reunification. This threat was articulated in the midst of fierce debate over two pieces of controversial legislation before the U.S. Congress—the Taiwan Security Enhancement Act and the permanent extension of normal trading status to the PRC. Beijing's move weakened the administration in dealing with Capitol Hill, though the Taiwan Security Enhancement Act had not emerged from Senate committee as of mid-2000 and permanent normal trade relations legislation moved through the House of Representatives on May 24, 2000, by a positive vote of 237 to 197.

The rule seems to be that when one's own domestic needs clash with those of a foreign interlocutor, one puts one's own needs first, letting the other side deal with the fallout as best it can. Although this pattern is unlikely to change, one can gain a great deal by, whenever possible, calibrating one's own policies, actions, and the way they are presented to the domestic circumstances and needs of the other.

Seven: Be a Public Educator

The president has a multitude of roles: commander in chief, chief executive, and party leader principal among them. Nonetheless, in the post-cold war era of global mass media saturation, one important job as it relates to China policy—the role of educator—was not performed adequately by either Presidents Bush or Clinton, though Clinton became much more effective in this role in the last months of his presidency, particularly in the spring and summer 2000 fight over extending permanent normal trade relations status to Beijing.

My own experience in speaking to diverse audiences around the United States throughout the 1990s suggests that there is a deep and abiding common sense among the American people. They inherently understand that China is large, significant, and cannot be easily pushed around. Focus group research by the Kettering Foundation and Doble Research Associates clearly shows that Americans are more nuanced than Washington discussion, seeing China as both a "problem" and an "opportunity" rather than either a "friend" or an "enemy."[22] Yet they also have anxieties about the world in general and the role that the PRC may play in the future global order. As the American public sorts through these conflicting impulses, they are looking for leadership.

What the American people are searching for is leadership that can explain the nature of the era they are experiencing, the possible directions in which China could head, the practical limits on American influence, and reasonable policies in light of these considerations. The broad public, as distinct from activists on the left and right, is looking for a stable orientation that reflects a concern for American values that is balanced both by a hardheaded assessment of America's long-term interests and a sober understanding of its capacities. The public opinion expert William Watts, for example, notes that "if you ask [voters or citizens] what they 'like' or 'dislike' you get predictable answers. But if you ask about interests, they say it is important to get along."[23] Leadership involves defining interests as well as assessing (or playing to) desires.

The productive handling of U.S.-China relations is possible—it is essential—and the American people intuitively know this. Leaders who can both explain why this popular intuition is correct and intelligently seek to move the bilateral relationship in more productive directions will serve not only American national interests but their own political interests as well. In this endeavor, American leaders will need to be joined by equally farsighted individuals in Beijing for, as one Chinese vice minister cited earlier said, "It takes two to tango!"[24]

APPENDIX OF TABLES

Table 1. Trade between the United States and Taiwan

	(in millions of US\$, all U.S. government figures)		
	U.S. Exports to Taiwan	*U.S. Imports from Taiwan*	*U.S. Total Trade with Taiwan*
1989	11,323	25,628	36,951
1990	11,560	23,917	35,477
1991	13,191	24,229	37,420
1992	15,205	25,806	41,011
1993	16,250	26,300	42,550
1994	17,078	27,942	45,020
1995	19,295	30,158	49,453
1996	18,413	31,023	49,436
1997	20,388	33,718	54,106
1998	18,157	34,343	52,500

SOURCE: International Monetary Fund, *Direction of Trade Statistics Yearbook* (Washington, D.C. : International Monetary Fund, 1991, 1998, and 1999).

Table 2. U.S.–China Trade and Investment, 1978–1998

(in millions of US$ unless otherwise noted; all U.S. government figures unless otherwise noted)

	Total Trade	% Change from Previous Year	U.S. Exports to China	% of Total U.S. Exports	Chinese Exports to U.S. (PRC fig.)*	% of Total Chinese Exports (PRC fig.)	% of Total Chinese Exports (U.S. fig.)**	Value of U.S. FDI**** Contracts	% Change in FDI Contracts from Previous Year	Value of U.S. FDI Utilized***	% Change in FDI Utilized from Previous Year	Net Chinese Purchase of U.S. Treasury Notes and Bonds
1978	1,181		824	0.6	271	2.8	3.7					--
1979	2,380	101.5	1,724	0.9	595	4.4	4.8					--
1980	4,919	106.7	3,755	1.7	983	5.4	6.4					--
1981	5,665	15.2	3,603	1.5	1,505	7.0	9.6					--
1982	5,414	−4.4	2,912	1.4	1,765	8.1	11.4	281		13		--
1983	4,650	−14.1	2,173	1.1	1,713	7.8	11.2	470	67	5	−62	--
1984	6,385	37.3	3,004	1.4	2,313	9.3	13.6	165	−65	256	5,020	--
1985	8,080	26.5	3,856	1.8	2,336	8.5	15.5	1,152	598	357	39	274
1986	8,347	3.3	3,106	1.4	2,633	8.4	16.7	527	−54	315	−12	122
1987	10,407	24.7	3,497	1.4	3,030	7.7	17.5	342	−35	263	−17	−89
1988	14,278	37.2	5,017	1.6	3,399	7.1	19.4	370	8	236	−10	84
1989	18,708	31.0	5,807	1.6	4,414	8.3	24.4	641	73	284	20	−201
1990	21,103	12.8	4,807	1.2	5,314	8.5	25.9	358	−44	456	61	345
1991	26,592	26.0	6,287	1.5	6,198	8.6	28.2	548	53	323	−29	111
1992	34,883	31.2	7,470	1.7	8,599	10.1	32.1	3,121	470	511	58	3,393
1993	39,950	14.5	8,767	1.9	16,976	18.5	34.0	6,813	118	2,063	304	451
1994	50,649	26.8	9,287	1.8	21,421	17.7	34.2	6,010	−12	2,491	21	12,205
1995	60,270	19.0	11,749	2.0	24,744	16.6	32.6	7,471	24	3,083	24	703
1996	66,387	10.1	11,978	1.9	26,731	17.7	36.0	6,915	−7	3,444	12	14,453
1997	78,637	18.5	12,805	1.9	32,744	17.9	36.0	4,937	−29	3,239	−6	7,688
1998	85,410	8.6	14,241	2.1	37,976	20.7	38.7	6,210	26	3,910	21	2,599

SOURCES: International Monetary Fund, *Direction of Trade Statistics Yearbook* (Washington, D.C.: International Monetary Fund, 1985, 1991, 1998, 1999).

The United States-China Business Council, "China Trade 1998" <http://www.uschina.org/press/tradetable.html> accessed May 1, 2000.

The United States-China Business Council, "Table 1: FDI in China, 1979–1998" <http://www.uschina.org/press/investmarch99.html> accessed May 1, 2000.

The U.S. Census Bureau, "Exports, Imports and Balance of Goods by Selected Countries and Geographic Areas—1998" <http://www.census.gov/foreign-trad...press_releases/December/exh14a.txt> accessed May 1, 2000.

The U.S. Department of Commerce, "Country Commercial Guide—China" <http://www.stat-usa.gov/ccg.nsf/22...fc5e085256758005373f3?OpenDocument> accessed May 1, 2000.

State Statistical Bureau, People's Republic of China, *China Statistical Yearbook*, no. 17 (Beijing: China Statistical Publishing House, 1998).

Financial Management Service, U.S. Department of the Treasury, *Treasury Bulletin*, Winter 1985–June 1999 (various issues).

* The United States claims that the PRC underestimates its exports to the United States by not counting exports channeled through Hong Kong.

** Chinese exports, as recorded by the United States, as a percentage of China's total exports, as reported by the PRC.

*** The 1982 figure is the sum of investment from 1978 to 1982.

****FDI = Foreign Direct Investment

Table 3. Trade Balance between China and the United States

		(in millions of US\$; all US government figures)	
	Chinese Exports to the U.S.	*Chinese Imports from the U.S.*	*Chinese Trade Balance with the U.S.*
1980	1,164	3,755	−2,591
1981	2,062	3,603	−1,541
1982	2,502	2,912	−410
1983	2,477	2,173	304
1984	3,381	3,004	377
1985	4,224	3,856	368
1986	5,241	3,106	2,135
1987	6,910	3,497	3,413
1988	9,261	5,017	4,244
1989	12,901	5,807	7,094
1990	16,296	4,807	11,489
1991	20,305	6,287	14,018
1992	27,413	7,470	19,943
1993	31,183	8,767	22,416
1994	41,362	9,287	32,075
1995	48,521	11,749	36,772
1996	54,409	11,978	42,431
1997	65,832	12,805	53,027
1998	75,109	14,258	60,851

SOURCE: International Monetary Fund, *Direction of Trade Statistics Yearbook* (Washington, D.C. : International Monetary Fund, 1986, 1991, 1998, and 1999).

Table 4. Sino-Russian Trade

(in millions of US$)

	Chinese Government Figures				Russian (USSR) Government Figures			
	Chinese Exports to Russia	Chinese Imports from Russia	Chinese Trade with Russia	Percentage of Chinese Total Trade	Russian Exports to China	Russian Imports from China	Russian Trade with China	Percentage of Russian Total Trade
1989	1,849	2,147	3,996	3.6	1,768	1,869	3,637	3.1
1990	2,048	2,213	4,261	3.7	1,886	1,952	3,838	3.4
1991	1,823	2,081	3,904	2.9	1,917	2,046	3,963	4.2
1992	2,337	3,512	5,849	3.5	2,737	1,669	4,406	5.6
1993	2,692	4,986	7,678	4.0	3,068	2,335	5,403	7.0
1994	1,578	3,466	5,044	2.1	2,838	952	3,790	3.2
1995	1,674	3,799	5,473	2.0	3,377	865	4,242	3.0
1996	1,693	5,156	6,849	2.4	4,670	993	5,663	3.8
1997	2,035	4,084	6,119	1.9	3,982	1,261	5,243	3.4
1998	1,833	3,627	5,460	1.7	3,111	1,142	4,253	3.2

SOURCE: International Monetary Fund, *Direction of Trade Statistics Yearbook* (Washington, D.C.: International Monetary Fund, 1991, 1997, 1998, and 1999).

NOTE: The figures from 1989 to 1991 refer to trade between China and the USSR.

Table 5. Trade Balance between China and Japan

(in millions of US$)

	Japanese Government Figures			Chinese Government Figures*		
	Chinese Exports to Japan	Chinese Imports from Japan	Chinese Trade Balance with Japan	Chinese Exports to Japan	Chinese Imports from Japan	Chinese Trade Balance with Japan
1980	4,346	5,109	−763	4,032	5,169	−1,137
1981	5,283	5,076	207	4,747	6,183	−1,436
1982	5,338	3,500	1,838	4,806	3,902	904
1983	5,089	4,918	171	4,517	5,495	−978
1984	5,943	7,199	−1,256	5,155	8,057	−2,902
1985	6,534	12,590	−6,056	6,091	15,178	−9,087
1986	5,727	9,936	−4,209	5,079	12,463	−7,384
1987	7,478	8,337	−859	6,392	10,087	−3,695
1988	9,861	9,486	375	8,046	11,062	−3,016
1989	11,083	8,477	2,606	8,395	10,534	−2,139
1990	12,057	6,145	5,912	9,210	7,656	1,554
1991	14,248	8,605	5,643	10,252	10,032	220
1992	16,972	11,967	5,005	11,699	13,686	−1,987
1993	20,651	17,353	3,298	15,782	23,303	−7,521
1994	27,569	18,687	8,882	21,490	26,319	−4,829
1995	35,922	21,934	13,988	28,466	29,007	−541
1996	40,405	21,827	18,578	30,888	29,190	1,698
1997	41,827	21,692	20,135	31,820	28,990	2,830
1998	37,079	20,182	16,897	29,718	28,307	1,411

SOURCE: International Monetary Fund, *Direction of Trade Statistics Yearbook* (Washington, D.C.: International Monetary Fund, 1986, 1991,1998, and 1999).
*Trade with Japan is classified by China as trade with Hong Kong if it passed through Hong Kong ports.

Table 6. American Opinion of China

QUESTION: *What is your overall opinion of China—very favorable, mostly favorable, mostly unfavorable, or very unfavorable?* (Asked on form B, 518 respondents, ±5%)

	Very Favorable (%)	Favorable (%)	Unfavorable (%)	Very Unfavorable (%)	No Opinion (%)
99 May 7–9	5	33	38	18	6
99 Mar. 12–14*	2	32	39	20	7
99 Feb. 8–9	8	31	34	16	11
98 July 7–8	6	38	36	11	9
98 June 22–23*	5	34	42	9	10
97 June 26–29	5	28	36	14	17
96 Mar.	6	33	35	16	10
94 Feb.	4	36	38	15	7
93 Nov.	10	43	24	15	8
89 Aug.	5	29	32	22	12
89 Feb.	12	60	10	3	15
87 May	8	57	23	5	7
83 Sept.	6	37	31	21	5
80 Jan.	6	36	30	24	4
79 Feb.	5	25	31	33	6
76 Jan.	3	17	29	45	6
1967	**	5	16	75	4

SOURCE: Frank Newport, "Americans Support Clinton Trip to China," June 27, 1998 <http://www.gallup.com/POLL ARCHIVES/980627.htm> accessed November 13, 1998; Frank Newport, "Americans' Unfavorable Attitudes towards China Unchanged Ten Years after Tiananmen," June 3, 1999 <http://www.gallup.com/poll/releases/pr990603.asp> accessed May 1, 2000.

*Half sample
**Less than 0.5%

Table 7. The U.S. Department of State: Structure and Organization

Year	Position	GB	FB
1960	AS	5	10
	DAS	8	10
1970	AS	5	10
	DAS	17	26
1980	AS	5	13
	DAS	20	46
1990	AS	5	18
	DAS	22	59
1998	AS	6	19
	DAS	16	62

SOURCES: Office of the Federal Register, National Archives and Records Service, General Services Administration, *United States Government Organization Manual 1960/61* (Washington, D.C.: U.S. Government Printing Office, 1960).

Office of the Federal Register, National Archives and Records Service, General Services Administration, *United States Government Organization Manual 1970/71* (Washington, D.C.: U.S. Government Printing Office, 1970).

Office of the Federal Register, National Archives and Records Service, *United States Government Manual 1980/81* (Washington, D.C.: U.S. Government Printing Office, 1980).

Office of the Federal Register, National Archives and Records Service, *United States Government Manual 1998/99* (Washington, D.C.: U.S. Government Printing Office, 1998). Note: Before 1975/1976 issue, its title is *"United States Government Organization Manual."* Afterward, its title is *"United States Government Manual."*

Ann L. Brownson, *1990 Federal Staff Directory* (Mount Vernon: Staff Directories, 1990); U.S. Department of State, *Organization Directory* (Washington, D.C., March 1998); U.S. Department of State, *The U.S. Department of State: Structure and Organization,* <http://www.state.gov/www/about_state/dosstruc.html> accessed May 25, 2000.

NOTE: AS = assistant secretary, including legal adviser, chief financial officers, director general of the foreign service, director of the Foreign Service Institute, chief of protocol, chief information officer, director of intelligence and research (1980); DAS = deputy assistant secretary, including assistant chief of protocol, deputy director of Foreign Service Institute, deputy chief information officer, deputy legal adviser, deputy director general of the foreign service; GB = geographic bureaus; FB = functional bureaus.

Notes

PREFACE

1. Deng Xiaoping made these same points during his early 1992 "southern tour" (*nanxun*). See Deng Xiaoping, "Zai Wuhan, Shenzhen, Zhuhai, Shanghai, dengdi de tanhua yaodian" [Main points of Deng's remarks in Wuhan, Shenzhen, Zhuhai, Shanghai, and other places], in *Deng Xiaoping wenxuan* [Selected essays of Deng Xiaoping], vol. 3 (Beijing: People's Publishing House, 1993), 370–83.

2. Steven Mufson, "Economy of China Is Cooling," *Washington Post*, November 29, 1997, A01.

3. Fang Lizhi, *Bringing Down the Great Wall* (New York: Alfred A. Knopf, 1991), 136.

4. Cited in Ruan Ming, "The Evolution of the Central Secretariat and Its Authority," in *Decision-Making in Deng's China: Perspectives from Insiders*, ed. Carol Lee Hamrin and Suisheng Zhao (Armonk: M. E. Sharpe, 1995), 20.

INTRODUCTION: THE BIG PICTURE

Sources for Chapter Epigraphs:
Qian Qichen, author's notes of meeting, Diaoyutai State Guesthouse, Beijing, September 16, 1997; Robert S. McNamara, James Blight, Robert Brigham, Thomas Biersteker, and Col. Herbert Schandler, *Argument without End: In Search of Answers to the Vietnam Tragedy* (New York: Public Affairs, 1999), 5, 7–8; U.S. senator, author's notes of meeting, July 26, 1999, northern Virginia.

1. I would like to thank Professor Michel Oksenberg for some of the insights in this section.

2. Author's notes of discussion in Beijing (notes on trip of January 10–19, 1998), January 12, 1998.

3. Hu Weixi, "Social Transition and Populism in Modern China," *Strategy and Management*, no. 2 (1995): 23.

4. Hereafter the two terms will be used interchangeably.

5. Bob Woodward, *The Agenda: Inside the Clinton White House* (New York: Simon and Schuster, 1994). The entire book (thirty index entries) was indicative of the president's concern with a bond market conducive to low interest rates. See also David M. Lampton, "America's China Policy in the Age of the Finance Minister: Clinton Ends Linkage," *China Quarterly*, no. 139 (September 1994): 608.

6. George W. Bush, "Remarks at the Yale University Commencement Ceremony in New Haven, Connecticut, May 27, 1991," in *Public Papers of the Presidents of the United States, George Bush, 1991*, Book 1, January 1 to June 30, 1991 (Washington, D.C.: U.S. Government Printing Office, 1992), 565–68.

1. TURNING POINTS: 1989–2000

Source for Chapter Epigraph:
Jin Canrong, "The U.S. Global Strategy in the Post-Cold War Era and Its Implications for Sino-U.S. Relations: The Chinese Perspective," manuscript, Beijing, April 2000.

1. Lee Teng-hui, "Responses to Questions Submitted by *Deutsche Welle*," document provided by Taipei Economic and Cultural Representative Office in the United States, July 9, 1999.

2. George Bush, "Inaugural Address," in *Public Papers of the Presidents: George Bush, 1989*, Book 1, January 20 to June 30, 1989 (Washington, D.C.: U.S. Government Printing Office, 1990), 3–4.

3. Ibid., 2.

4. George Bush and Brent Scowcroft, *A World Transformed* (New York: Alfred A. Knopf, 1998), 91.

5. Ibid.

6. Ibid.

7. Douglas Paal, conversation with author, February 27, 1998.

8. R. W. Apple, "Bush Hails Seoul for Building Ties with N. Korea," *New York Times*, February 22, 1989, A1.

9. George Bush, "Interview with Chinese Television Journalists in Beijing," February 26, 1989, in *Public Papers, 1989*, Book 1, 143.

10. Bush and Scowcroft, *A World Transformed*, 92.

11. Ibid., 97.

12. Ibid., 95–96.

13. Brent Scowcroft, conversation with author, January 1998.

14. Winston Lord, conversation with author, July 26, 1999; for documentation see James Mann, *About Face: A History of America's Curious Relationship with China, from Nixon to Clinton* (New York: Alfred A. Knopf, 1999), 181.

15. Brent Scowcroft, conversation with author, October 7, 1998, The Nixon Center, Washington, D.C. For an account of the American participants in this episode, see Perry Link, *Evening Chats in Beijing: Probing China's Predicament* (New York: W. W. Norton and Co., 1992), 29–32.

16. Bush and Scowcroft, *A World Transformed*, 99.

17. Chuan Chien-ching, "Former Ambassador Lord on Strait Issues" (in Chinese), *Chung-kuo Shih-pao* (Taipei), May 15, 1999, 2, in Foreign Broadcast Information Service, FBIS-CHI-1999-0616.

18. Bush and Scowcroft, *A World Transformed*, 98.

19. James A. Baker III, *The Politics of Diplomacy* (New York: G. P. Putnam, 1995), 98.

20. Ibid., 104.

21. George Bush, *All the Best: My Life in Letters and Other Writings* (New York: Scribner, 1999), 416.

22. Baker, *The Politics of Diplomacy*, 104.

23. Bush and Scowcroft, *A World Transformed*, 98.

24. Kerry Dumbaugh, "An Invitation to Struggle: U.S.-China Policy after the Tiananmen Square Crackdown, 1989–1990," unpublished, n.d., 2–3.

25. Harry Harding, *A Fragile Relationship* (Washington, D.C.: Brookings Institution, 1992), 227; see also Baker, *The Politics of Diplomacy*, 104; see also Bush and Scowcroft, *A World Transformed*, 99–100.

26. Bush, *All the Best*, 428–431, 435–437; Bush and Scowcroft, *A World Transformed*, 100.

27. Former U.S. government official, conversation with author, February 27, 1998. For positional information on Zeng, see Xinhua General Overseas News Service (Beijing), "Jiang Zemin Goes on Visit to DPRK," March 14, 1990, item no. 0314030.

28. George Bush, press conference, June 5, 1989, cited in Dumbaugh, "An Invitation to Struggle," 1.

29. Marianthi Zikopoulos, ed., *Open Doors 1989/90* (New York: Institute of International Education, 1990), 141.

30. Dumbaugh, "An Invitation to Struggle," 7.

31. Bush, *All the Best*, 436.

32. Dumbaugh, "An Invitation to Struggle," 9–10.

33. Ibid., 10.

34. Bush and Scowcroft, *A World Transformed*, 178.

35. Baker, *The Politics of Diplomacy*, 113.

36. Bush and Scowcroft, *A World Transformed*, 174.

37. National Committee on U.S.-China Relations, "Chronology of Sino-American Relations," unpublished, n.d., 41.

38. Bush and Scowcroft, *A World Transformed*, 174.

39. Douglas Paal, conversation with author, February 27, 1998. In their coauthored volume, *A World Transformed*, Bush and Scowcroft explain the "road map": "We hammered out the terms of a 'road map' of reciprocal moves to take us gradually but steadily toward normalization. At the end of this

process was the vague notion of a visit to the United States by General Secretary Jiang Zemin. The plan was set out in general rather than explicit terms.... But the Chinese linked releasing Fang [Lizhi] to the lifting of sanctions—something to which we could not agree" (175).

40. Bush, *All the Best,* 448.

41. Baker, *The Politics of Diplomacy,* 108–9.

42. Bush and Scowcroft, *A World Transformed,* 104.

43. Ibid., 108.

44. George Bush, *Public Papers of the Presidents of the United States: George Bush, 1991,* Book 1 (Washington, D.C.: U.S. Government Printing Office, 1992), 565–68.

45. Mann, *About Face,* 229–31.

46. Baker, *The Politics of Diplomacy,* 111.

47. Xinhua News Agency, "Deng Xiaoping Meets Nixon," October 31, 1989.

48. Joseph Fewsmith, "Reaction, Resurgence, and Succession: Chinese Politics since Tiananmen," in *The Politics of China,* 2d ed., ed. Roderick MacFarquhar (Cambridge: Cambridge University Press, 1997), 485, 473.

49. Jiang Zemin, "Zai qingzhu zhonghua renmin gongheguo chengli sishi zhounian dahui de jianghua," cited in Fewsmith, "Reaction, Resurgence, and Succession," 485.

50. Deng Xiaoping, "The United States Should Take the Initiative in Putting an End to the Strains in Sino-U.S. Relations," in *Deng Xiaoping wenxuan,* vol. 3, 331–32.

51. Baker, *The Politics of Diplomacy,* 112.

52. Benjamin Yang, *Deng: A Political Biography* (Armonk, N.Y.: M.E. Sharpe, 1998), 257. Note that Yang identifies this source as "unofficial sources in Beijing."

53. Lo Ping, "Notes on Northern Journey" (in Chinese), *Cheng Ming* (Hong Kong), no. 167, September 1, 1991, 6, 8, in FBIS-CHI-91-171, 6–8.

54. "In His Own Words: Clinton on China MFN," *China Business Review,* January–February 1993, 18.

55. Former senior Bush administration officials, interviews with author, 1998.

56. Edward Walsh, "Clinton Indicts Bush's World Leadership," *Washington Post,* October 2, 1992, A12.

57. "In His Own Words: Clinton on China MFN," 18.

58. David M. Lampton, "America's China Policy in the Age of the Finance Minister: Clinton Ends Linkage," *China Quarterly,* no. 139 (1994): 600–601.

59. "In His Own Words: Clinton on China MFN," 18; see also Thomas L. Friedman, "Clinton Says Bush Made China Gains," *New York Times,* November 20, 1992, A1.

60. Senior White House official, author's notes of remarks, February 28, 1997.

61. Bob Woodward, *The Agenda: Inside the Clinton White House* (Simon and Schuster: New York, 1994), 62–65. This can be seen from the number of entries in this volume's index dealing with interest rates and the bond market.

62. Anthony Lake, "From Containment to Enlargement," address at the Nitze School of Advanced International Studies, Johns Hopkins University, Washington, D.C., September 21, 1993, from *Department of State Dispatch* 4, no. 39 (September 27, 1993).

63. Warren Christopher, "American Interests and the U.S.-China Relationship," address before the National Committee on U.S.-China Relations and other organizations in New York City, May 17, 1996, 2.

64. Patrick Tyler, *A Great Wall: Six Presidents and China* (New York: Public Affairs, 1999), 229–85. For responses by President Carter and Dr. Brzezinski see "Letters to the Editor," *Foreign Affairs* 78, no. 6 (November/December 1999): 164–66. See also David M. Lampton, "Leaders Count," review of the Tyler book in *The National Interest*, no. 58 (Winter 1999/2000): 127–29.

65. Don Oberdorfer, "U.S. and Taiwan Conclude Talks in Open Discord," *Washington Post*, December 30, 1978, A1.

66. Robert S. Greenberger and Michael K. Frisby, "Clinton's Renewal of Trade Status for China Followed Cabinet Debates, Congress's Sea Change," *Wall Street Journal*, May 31, 1994, A18.

67. Mann, *About Face*, 213.

68. John Barry, with Eleanor Clift, Bob Cohn, and Douglas Waller, "The Collapse of Les Aspin," *Newsweek*, December 27, 1993, 22.

69. Winston Lord, "China and America: Beyond the Big Chill," *Foreign Affairs* 68, no. 4 (Fall 1989): 1.

70. There were thirty-one officials equivalent to or above the level of assistant secretary of state in the Department of State in 1993. See Ann L. Brownson, ed., *1993 Federal Staff Directory/2* (Mount Vernon, Va.: Staff Directories, 1993), 615–43; Richard Holbrooke, *To End a War* (New York: Random House, 1998), 57, mentions this problem, albeit writing about a later period.

71. David M. Lampton, "China Policy in Clinton's First Year," in *Beyond MFN: Trade with China and American Interests*, ed. James R. Lilley and Wendell Willkie II, 16–20 (Washington, D.C.: AEI Press, 1994).

72. U.S. Senate, Committee on Finance, *Hearings on China Most-Favored-Nation Status*, 102d Cong., 1st sess.(Washington, D.C.: U.S. Government Printing Office, 1992), 1–3.

73. Douglas Jehl, "China Breaking Missile Pledge, U.S. Aides Say," *New York Times*, May 6, 1993. This and other sources cited in Lampton, "Clinton's First Year," 155 n. 25.

74. Chinese official, interview with author, April 1993, Beijing, cited in Lilley and Willkie, *Beyond MFN*, 155 n. 33.

75. White House, Office of the Press Secretary, "Report to Congress Concerning Extension of Waiver Authority for the People's Republic of China," May 28, 1993, cited in Lilley and Willkie, 23–24.

76. Mann, *About Face*, 290.

77. *Taiwan Security Enhancement Act,* S. 693, 106th Cong., 1st sess., introduced by Senators Helms and Torricelli, March 24, 1999 <http://web.lexis -nexis.com/congcom...5=199cOae6b635cf5260f523e6e725c79> accessed March 29, 2000; also David M. Lampton, "Enhancing Global, Regional, and Taiwan Security for the Twenty-first Century," testimony before the Senate Committee on Foreign Relations concerning the *Taiwan Security Enhancement Act,* S. 693, August 4, 1999.

78. Barber B. Conable Jr. et al., *United States–China Relations: Current Tensions, Policy Choices,* China Policy Series, no. 12 (New York: National Committee on U.S.-China Relations, 1996), 29.

79. Lena H. Sun, "China Detains Dissident as French Premier Tries to Mend Relations," *Washington Post,* April 9, 1994, A22.

80. Senior White House official, author's notes of remarks, February 28, 1997.

81. Winston Lord, "Emerging Malaise in our Relations with Asia," undated memorandum to Secretary of State Warren Christopher.

82. Lampton, "America's China Policy in the Age of the Finance Minister," 609.

83. Elaine Sciolino, "Clinton and China: How Promise Self-destructed," *New York Times,* May 29, 1994, 1.

84. Xinhua News Agency, "Funeral Service for Nixon Held in California," April 27, 1994, item no. 0427031.

85. Chinese scholar, interview by author, May 4, 1994.

86. President, press conference, May 26, 1994, Office of the Press Secretary, White House.

87. John Pomfret, "Even Up Close, China's Vision of U.S. Is Out of Focus, Defense Officials Indicate," *Washington Post,* February 15, 1998, A11; see also Ashton B. Carter and William J. Perry, *Preventive Defense: A New Security Strategy for America* (Washington, D.C.: Brookings Institution Press, 1999), ch. 3.

88. J. Bruce Jacobs, "A Delicate Balance: The Future of China-Taiwan Relations," *Harvard Asia Pacific Review* (Winter 1997/1998): 46.

89. Michael D. Swaine, "Chinese Decisionmaking toward Taiwan, 1979–97," manuscript (first draft, 1998), 21 n. 27. Swaine notes that Taiwan claimed by 1993 to have unofficial relations with 150 countries, to have ninety offices in 60 countries with which it did not have official diplomatic relations, and that 37 countries with which Taipei did not have diplomatic relations had offices on the island.

90. Jim Mann, "Underestimating China: How Missteps Triggered U.S.-Beijing Confrontations," *Los Angeles Times,* September 9, 1996, A1; see also James Mann, "Between China and the U.S.," *Washington Post,* January 10, 1999, C1–2.

91. Federal Information Systems Corporation, Federal News Service, February 9, 1995, 17.

92. Elaine Sciolino, "Taiwan's Lobbying in U.S.: Mixing Friendship and Hardball," *New York Times,* April 9, 1996, A12; Mann, "Between China and

the U.S.," C2, says, "Cassidy & Associates received a three year, $4.5 million contract to lobby on Taiwan's behalf."

93. Michael Barone and Grant Ujifusa, *The Almanac of American Politics, 1998* (Washington, D.C.: National Journal, 1997), 1020.

94. Ibid., 868.

95. Ibid., 1020.

96. Central News Agency, "Gingrich Says Taiwan Deserves UN Membership," February 4, 1995 <http://web.lexis-nexis.com/univers...5=d5916ac8d3 c82517c858ab8e3134357b> accessed March 30, 2000.

97. Thomas W. Lippman, "GOP-Controlled Foreign Policy Panels Would Reverse Clinton Stands: Administration Sees Revisions as Isolationist Bid to Preempt President," *Washington Post*, May 21, 1995, A7; see also Robert Sutter and Kerry Dumbaugh, "China-U.S. Relations," issue brief. IB94002, Congressional Research Service, Washington, D.C., July 15, 1995.

98. George Gedda, "Christopher Favors Closer Links with Taiwan," Associated Press, February 15, 1995 <http://web.lexis-nexis.com/univers...5= cfc3a3ffbce50a2e896da965d659043> accessed March 30, 2000.

99. Warren Christopher, *In the Stream of History: Shaping Foreign Policy for a New Era* (Stanford, Calif.: Stanford University Press, 1998), 287. Christopher says, "The problem was aggravated by a misunderstanding I had with Vice Premier and Foreign Minister Qian. I had told him when I met with him in April 1995 that we did not intend to make any change in our fundamental policy of only 'unofficial' relations with Taiwan, but I had also warned him that overwhelming congressional support for the Lee visit ... could not be ignored. This warning was intended to alert Qian that a visa might be issued. But he heard only the first half of my statement."

100. Federal News Service, "Hearing of the House International Relations Committee Asia and Pacific Subcommittee," February 9, 1995. See also Federal News Service, "State Department Spokeswoman Christine Shelly Joined by Assistant Secretary of State Winston Lord, State Department Briefing," March 10, 1995.

101. Jim Mann, "How Taipei Outwitted U.S. Policy," *Los Angeles Times*, June 8, 1995, A1.

102. Don Oberdorfer, "Juggling the Two China's: Caught between Beijing and Taiwan, Clinton Dropped the Ball," *Washington Post*, October 22, 1995, C4.

103. Mann, "How Taipei Outwitted U.S. Policy," A1.

104. Jiang Zemin, "President's Speech on Taiwan Reunification," in British Broadcasting Corporation Summary of World Broadcasts, January 31, 1995, pt. 3, Asia-Pacific; China; foreign relations; FE/2215/G.

105. Samuel S. Kim, "Taiwan and the International System: The Challenge of Legitimation," in *Taiwan in World Affairs*, ed. Robert G. Sutter and William R. Johnson, 159, 161 (Boulder, Colo.: Westview Press, 1994).

106. See Winston Lord, assistant secretary of state for East Asian and Pacific affairs, statement before Senate Committee on Foreign Relations, 103d Cong., 2d sess., September 27, 1994, Washington, D.C.

107. The Shanghai Communiqué was issued February 28, 1972, by President Richard Nixon and Premier Zhou Enlai at the Jin Jiang Hotel in Shanghai. Its historic importance lies in the fact that both sides not only elaborated their differences, they also identified common interests, expressed the desire to make progress toward "normalization," and affirmed that neither side sought "hegemony" in the Asia-Pacific region but each would oppose those that did. Most important, the United States said, "The United States acknowledges that all Chinese on either side of the Taiwan Strait maintain there is but one China and that Taiwan is a part of China. The United States Government does not challenge that position. It reaffirms its interest in a peaceful settlement of the Taiwan question by the Chinese themselves."

108. Rough transcript of author's meeting with senior Chinese official, June 14, 1996.

109. Michael D. Swaine, "Chinese Decisionmaking toward Taiwan, 1978–97," in *The Making of Chinese Foreign and Security Policy in the Era of Reform*, ed. David M. Lampton (Stanford, Calif.: Stanford University Press, forthcoming).

110. Patrick E. Tyler, "Tough Stance toward China Pays Off for Taiwan Leader," *New York Times*, August 29, 1995, A8.

111. "U.S. Urged to Return to Three Communiqués" (in Chinese), editorial, *Wen Wei Po*, July 17, 1995, A2, in FBIS-CHI-95-138, 4.

112. Nick Burns (State Department spokesman), "State Department Regular Briefing," Federal News Service, September 14, 1995.

113. John Holdridge, *Crossing the Divide: An Insider's Account of the Normalization of U.S.-China Relations* (Boulder, Colo.: Roman and Littlefield Publishers, 1997), 57–58; see also Robert S. Ross, *Negotiating Compromise* (Stanford, Calif.: Stanford University Press, 1995), 36–42, esp. 38–39.

114. Senior Chinese diplomat, interview with author, August 29, 1995, Washington, D.C.

115. Swaine, "Chinese Decisionmaking toward Taiwan" (first draft, 1998), 31.

116. Mike McCurry, "White House Briefing," Federal News Service, March 7, 1996.

117. Carter and Perry, *Preventive Defense*, 95–97.

118. Barton Gellman, "U.S. and China Nearly Came to Blows in '96: Tension over Taiwan Prompted Repair of Ties," *Washington Post*, June 21, 1998, A1; also author's notes of remarks by senior White House official, February 28, 1997.

119. Carter and Perry, *Preventive Defense*, 96.

120. Senior White House official, author's notes of remarks, February 28, 1997.

121. Anthony Lake, conversation with author, July 18, 1996.

122. Remarks of senior Taiwan official in author's memorandum of visit to Taipei (June 16–18, 1996), June 27, 1996.

123. Warren Christopher, "American Interests and the U.S.-China Relationship," address in New York City, May 17, 1996, 1, 6.

124. Mann, *About Face,* 330.

125. White House, "Joint U.S.-China Statement," October 29, 1997 <http://www.state.gov/www/regions/eap/971029_usc_jtstmt.html> accessed March 30, 2000.

126. Elizabeth Olson, "China Escapes Censure in Vote by UN Human Rights Agency," *New York Times,* April 24, 1999, A5.

127. Xinhua News Agency, "Chinese Official on Falun Gong Practitioners' Gathering," April 27, 1999 <http://web.lexis-nexis.com/univers...5=5bc5a 76779646e5dd55f7136bd7bcf9b> accessed March 30, 2000.

128. James Woolsey, testimony in hearing before the Senate Foreign Relations Committee on the Taiwan Security Enhancement Act, S. 693, August 4, 1999, panel 2 <http://web.lexis-nexis.com/universe/doc...3&_md5 = 7abdo a08206d3da7670ec73eaa907808> accessed March 30, 2000.

129. Tony Blair, "Doctrine of the International Community," speech to the Economic Club of Chicago, April 22, 1999 <http://wwwBritain-info.org /bis/fordom/defence/nato/22ap99–3.stm> accessed March 30, 2000.

130. Zhu Rongji, conversation with congressional group and author, March 31, 1999, Beijing, Great Hall of the People.

131. U.S. House of Representatives, Select Committee, *U.S. National Security and Military/Commercial Concerns with the People's Republic of China,* vols. 1–3 (Washington, D.C.: U.S. Government Printing Office, May 25, 1999).

132. Steven Lee Myers, "Chinese Embassy Bombing: A Wide Net of Blame," *New York Times,* April 17, 2000, A1, A10, carried in State Department, *Washington File,* April 18, 2000, 17–23.

133. Greg McDonald, "President Offers 'Sincere Regret' for Errant Bomb," *Houston Chronicle,* May 9, 1999, A1.

134. James Sasser, conversations with author, June and July 1999, Beijing and northern Virginia.

135. Stanley O. Roth, "The Effects on U.S.-China Relations of the Accidental Bombing of the Chinese Embassy in Belgrade," testimony before the Senate Committee on Foreign Relations, Subcommittee on East Asian and Pacific Affairs, May 27, 1999, Washington, D.C. <http://www.state.gov/www /policy_remarks/1999/990527_roth_china.html> accessed March 30, 2000.

136. Author's notes, PRC, April 26, 2000.

137. Commentator, "A Wanton Blasphemy against Human Civilization," *Renmin Ribao* [People's Daily], May 13, 1999, in FBIS-CHI-1999-0512; also Commentator, "NATO Serious Threat to World Peace," *Renmin Ribao* [People's Daily], May 12, 1999, Xinhua News Agency, May 11, 1999, in FBIS-CHI-1999-0511; and Commentator, "Archcriminal of Humanitarian Disasters," *Renmin Ribao* [People's Daily], May 11, 1999, 1, in FBIS-CHI-1999-0510.

138. Commentator, "*Renmin Ribao* Commentary Blasts Raid on PRC Embassy," *Renmin Ribao* [People's Daily], May 9, 1999, in FBIS-CHI-1999-0509.

139. Leon Harris, "Interview with Thomas Pickering," *CNN Early Edition,* CNN, May 11, 1999, transcript 99051103V08. The interviewer, Leon Harris, said, "[W]hat we're seeing right now is a lifting of the veil of Chinese suspicion, and, in some cases, just outright distrust or hatred of the U.S."

140. "State Department Report on Accidental Bombing of Chinese Embassy," USIS Washington File, July 6, 1999 <http://www.usia.gov/cgi-bin /washfile/di...eea&t=/products/washfile/newsitem.shtml> accessed July 9, 1999.

141. David M. Lampton, "China's U.S. Policy," *Christian Science Monitor,* July 14, 1999, 9. For a PRC account of the postbombing internal debate, see Tao Wenzhao, "A Foreign Policy Debate in China after the Tragic Bombing of the Chinese Embassy in Belgrade," paper presented at conference cosponsored by the Asia Pacific Center for Security Studies and Pacific Forum CSIS, Honolulu, Hawaii, April 19–21, 2000.

142. Lee Teng-hui, "Responses to Questions Submitted by *Deutsche Welle,*" document provided by Taipei Economic and Cultural Representative Office in the United States, July 9, 1999, 2.

2. SECURITY ISSUES

Sources for Chapter Epigraphs:
William Burr, ed., *The Kissinger Transcripts: The Top-Secret Talks with Beijing and Moscow* (New York: New Press, 1999), 100, and Tim Weiner, "Word for Word/Kissinger Transcripts," *New York Times,* January 10, 1999, sec. 4, p. 7; Deng Xiaoping, "Muqian de xingshi he renwu" [The present situation and tasks], in *Deng Xiaoping wenxuan (1975–1982)* [Selected works of Deng Xiaoping, 1975–1982] (Beijing: People's Publishing House, 1983), 204; Wu Fangming and Wu Xizhi, "AMS Journal Views Military Role in Economic Development" (in Chinese), *Guofang* [National Defense] (Beijing), February 15, 1996, in FBIS-CHI-96-203; Qian Qichen, conversation with author, Diaoyutai State Guesthouse, Beijing, September 16, 1997; Chinese scholar, interview by author, June 20, 1998; Dick Morris, "The China-Spy Blame Game," *New York Post,* June 1, 1999, 027.

1. Henry Kissinger, *White House Years* (Boston: Little, Brown and Co., 1979), 164.

2. Ibid., 1062.

3. President Jimmy Carter, conversation with author, November 13, 1996; Jimmy Carter, *Keeping Faith* (New York: Bantam, 1983), 186.

4. Carter, *Keeping Faith,* 187.

5. Ibid., 194.

6. John H. Holdridge, *Crossing the Divide* (New York: Rowman and Littlefield Publishers, 1997), ch. 11.

7. Deng Xiaoping, "Jianshe you Zhongguo tesi de shehuizhuyi" [Building socialism with Chinese characteristics], June 30, 1984, in *Deng Xiaoping wenxuan,* vol. 3, 64.

8. Department of Defense, Office of International Security Affairs, *United States Security Strategy for the East Asia–Pacific Region* (Washington, D.C.: Department of Defense, February 1995), 1, 5.

9. Ming Zhang, *China's Changing Nuclear Posture* (Washington, D.C.: Carnegie Endowment for International Peace, 1999).

10. Barry Naughton, "The Third Front: Defense Industrialization in the Chinese Interior," *China Quarterly*, no. 115 (1988): 353. Incidentally, Mao was not entirely mistaken to see China at risk. A January 27, 1965, memorandum from Assistant Secretary of Defense John T. McNaughton to Secretary Robert McNamara read, "[T]he United States objective in South Vietnam was 'not to help a friend but to contain China.'" Neil Sheehan, Hedrick Smith, E. W. Kenworthy, and Fox Butterfield, *The Pentagon Papers* (New York: Bantam Books, 1971), 342.

11. Su Ruozhou, "A Great Military Reform—Roundup of Strategic Changes in Our Army Building" (in Chinese), *Jiefangjun Bao* (Beijing), December 18, 1998, 1–2, in FBIS-CHI-99-018; also Alexander C. Huang, "The Chinese Navy's Offshore Active Defense Strategy: Conceptualization and Implications," *Naval War College Review* 47, no. 3 (Summer 1994): 15.

12. Yan Xuetong, "In Search of Security after the Cold War: China's Security Concerns" *World Affairs* 1, no. 4 (October–December 1997): 52.

13. Ibid., 53.

14. Michael Pillsbury, ed., *Chinese Views of Future Warfare*, rev. ed. (Washington, D.C.: National Defense University Press, 1998); see Carter and Perry, *Preventive Defense*, 179–80, 198–200, for discussion of the RMA; see also John Wilson Lewis and Xue Litai, *China's Strategic Seapower* (Stanford, Calif.: Stanford University Press, 1995), 101; and Michael Pillsbury, *China Debates the Future Security Environment* (Washington, D.C.: National Defense University Press, 2000).

15. Yan, "In Search of Security after the Cold War," 54.

16. See Wang Shaoguang, "Estimating China's Defense Expenditure: Some Evidence from Chinese Sources," *China Quarterly*, no. 147 (1996): 889–911; see also Roxane D. V. Sismandis, "Modernizing on a Shoestring; Modernization of China's Military: Focus: Military Matters," *China Business Review* 22, no. 6 (1995): 12, who writes, "From 1986–94, the defense budget [official figures] grew 159 percent in nominal terms, but only 4 percent in real terms. This modest increase came even as military expenditures increased at double-digit rates beginning in 1989. Furthermore, defense spending declined as a percentage of gross national product, from 1.9 percent in 1989 to 1.5 percent in 1994." Note: Official figures understate actual military spending by a considerable margin. See also James Mulvenon, *Chinese Military Commerce and U.S. National Security* (Santa Monica, Calif.: RAND Center for Asia-Pacific Policy, June 1997), fig. 2, and Andrew J. Nathan and Robert S. Ross, *The Great Wall and the Empty Fortress* (New York: W. W. Norton and Co., 1997), 148.

17. Information Office of the State Council of the PRC, *White Paper—China's National Defense*, Beijing, July 27, 1998, 10 <http://www.china-embassy.org/Cgi-Bin/Press.pl?wparms> accessed April 27, 2000.

18. Amy P. Celico, "Final Paper, Research Seminar on Chinese Politics" (Johns Hopkins, School of Advanced International Studies, Washington, D.C.,

May 1998), 3. See also Michael Pillsbury, ed., *Chinese Views of Future Warfare* (Washington, D.C.: National Defense University Press, 1997), xxi–xxiii.

19. Robert S. McNamara et al., *Sino-American Military Relations: Mutual Responsibilities in the Post–Cold War Era*, China Policy Series, no. 9 (New York: National Committee on U.S.-China Relations, 1994), 10.

20. Chinese defense analyst, interview with author, June 20, 1998.

21. Xiao Feng, "World Trends under US Global Strategy," pt. 2, *Renmin Ribao* [People's Daily], June 1, 1999, 6, in FBIS-CHI-1999-0601.

22. John W. Lewis, Hua Di, and Xue Litai, "Beijing's Defense Establishment," *International Security* 15, no. 4 (Spring 1991): 92–96.

23. Yi Jan, "Inside Story about Increase in China's Military Spending" (in Chinese), *Ching Pao* (Hong Kong), no. 261 (April 1, 1999): 36–37, in FBIS-CHI-1999-0416.

24. Author's notes of conference, July 1, 1998.

25. John F. Burns, "India Defense Chief Calls U.S. Hypocritical," *New York Times*, June 18, 1998, A10.

26. See, for example, James Webb, "Warily Watching China," *New York Times*, February 25, 1999, A23.

27. Richard Bernstein and Ross H. Munro, *The Coming Conflict with China* (New York: Alfred A. Knopf, 1997), 3.

28. Steven Mufson and John Pomfret, "Chinese Ex-Official Challenges Party," *Washington Post*, June 3, 1998, A16.

29. Shen Weiguang, "Checking Information Warfare" (in Chinese), *Jiefangjun Bao* (Beijing), February 2, 1999, 6, in FBIS-CHI-1999-0217.

30. Notes of "U.S.-PRC Security Cooperation in Northeast Asia," conference, Honolulu, Hawaii, May 26–28, 1998. Statement by Chinese analyst.

31. Chinese international relations scholar, interview with author, June 20, 1998.

32. See, for example, George Bush, "Address Before a Joint Session of Congress on the Persian Gulf Crisis and the Federal Budget Deficit," September 11, 1990, in *Public Papers of the Presidents of the United States, George Bush, 1990*, Book 2, July 1 to December 31, 1990 (Washington, D.C.: U.S. Government Printing Office, 1991), 1219.

33. William Clinton, address at "Dedication of the Roosevelt Memorial," in *Vital Speeches* 63, no. 16 (June 1, 1997): 482.

34. James Schlesinger, "Fragmentation and Hubris," *National Interest*, no. 49 (Fall 1997): 8; see also Charles William Maynes, "The Perils of (and for) an Imperial America," *Foreign Policy*, no. 111 (Summer 1998): 45.

35. Richard N. Haas, "Sanctions Almost Never Work," *Wall Street Journal*, June 19, 1998, A14.

36. Robert S. Greenberger, "States, Cities Increase Use of Trade Sanctions, Troubling Business Groups and U.S. Partners," *Wall Street Journal*, July 1, 1998, A20.

37. Chinese scholar, interview with author, June 20, 1998.

38. "Grumman to Ship Handful of Peace Pearl F-8s to China to Close Program," *Aerospace Daily* 164, no. 57, December 24, 1992, 453; see also Jim Mann, "U.S. Says Israel Gave Combat Jet Planes to China," *Los Angeles Times*, December 28, 1994, A1.

39. Author's notes of conference, July 2, 1998.

40. Author's notes of interview, June 20, 1998.

41. Lake, "From Containment to Enlargement."

42. World Bank, "Country Brief: China," June 1998 <http://www.worldbank.org/html/extdr/offrep/eap/china.htmWorld Bank> 4, accessed July 1, 1998; World Bank, *Sharing Rising Incomes* (Washington, D.C.: World Bank, 1997), 4.

43. David M. Lampton, "Neuhauser Lecture," April 23, 1998, Harvard University, published after delivery as "U.S.-China Relations after the Cold War," *Harvard Asia Quarterly* 2, no. 2 (Winter 1998): 30; see also *China Statistical Yearbook 1997*, no. 16 (Beijing: State Statistical Bureau, 1997), 45.

44. Nicholas R. Lardy, *China in the World Economy* (Washington, D.C.: Institute for International Economics, 1994), 14.

45. Shanghai analyst, cited in Rosemary Foot, "China in the ASEAN Regional Forum," *Asian Survey* 38, no. 5 (1998): 432.

46. Institute of International Strategic Studies, *The Military Balance: 1996/97* (London: Oxford University Press, 1998), 179. The U.S. Defense Intelligence Agency has the higher number of 450; see Rodney W. Jones and Mark G. McDonough, with Toby F. Dalton and Gregory Koblentz, *Tracking Nuclear Proliferation: A Guide in Maps and Charts, 1998* (Washington, D.C.: Carnegie Endowment for International Peace, 1998), 55.

47. For more on the Ministry of Foreign Affairs and the Chinese policy process see Lu Ning, *The Dynamics of Foreign-Policy Decisionmaking in China* (Boulder, Colo.: Westview Press, 1997); also Lampton, *The Making of Chinese Foreign and Security Policy in the Era of Reform.*

48. Shanghai professor, interview by author, June 20, 1998.

49. International affairs analyst, interview by author, June 20, 1998.

50. David M. Lampton, "A Growing China in a Shrinking World: Beijing and the Global Order," in *Living with China*, ed. Ezra F. Vogel (New York: W. W. Norton and Co., 1997), 121.

51. Kent Calder, *Pacific Defense: Arms, Energy, and America's Future in Asia* (New York: Morrow and Co., 1996), 8; see also Mamdough G. Salameh, "China, Oil, and the Risk of Regional Conflict," *Survival* 37, no. 4 (Winter, 1995–96): 133–46.

52. House Select Committee, *U.S. National Security and Military/Commercial Concerns*, vol. 3, 18–19.

53. Winston Lord, in Conable Jr. et al., *Current Tensions, Policy Choices*, 25.

54. Sha Zukang, "Text of Speech" (in English), *Beijing Review*, no. 6 (February 8–14, 1999): 6–8.

55. James Kynge, "China Raises Stakes on US Plan for Asian Missile Shield," *Financial Times*, February 26, 1999, 1.

56. Author's notes of remarks by senior White House official, February 28, 1997.

57. Samuel S. Kim, "The Making of China's Korea Policy in the Era of Reform," draft chapter for Lampton, *The Making of Chinese Foreign and Security Policy in the Era of Reform.*

58. Central Intelligence Agency, Nonproliferation Center, "Unclassified Report to Congress on the Acquisition of Technology Relating to Weapons of Mass Destruction and Advanced Conventional Munitions," January 1–June 30, 1998 <http://www.cia.gov/cia/publications/bian/bian.html> accessed April 26, 2000.

59. On Libya see Bill Gertz, "China Assists Iran, Libya on Missiles," *Washington Times,* June 16, 1998, A1.

60. House Select Committee, *U.S. National Security and Military/Commercial Concerns,* vol. 3, 80–143; also Jeff Gerth and David E. Sanger, "Aircraft Deal with Chinese Is Questioned," *New York Times,* October 30, 1996, A1, A10.

61. House Select Committee, *U.S. National Security and Military/Commercial Concerns,* vol. 1, ii–xxiv.

62. Vernon Loeb, "Ex-Official: Bomb Lab Case Lacks Evidence," *Washington Post,* August 17, 1999, A1.

63. Alastair Iain Johnston, W. K. H. Panofsky, Marco Di Capua, and Lewis R. Franklin (Michael May, ed.), *The Cox Report: An Assessment,* issued December 1999 and cited in Walter Pincus, "Hill Report on Chinese Spying Faulted," *Washington Post,* December 15, 1999, A16. For rebuttal of the Johnston et al. report, see Nicholas Rostow, "The Panofsky Critique and the Cox Committee Report: 50 Factual Errors in the Four Essays," manuscript, n.d. (ca. March 2000).

64. Ministry of Foreign Trade and Economic Cooperation and the National CWC Implementation Office of the PRC, "Regulations of the People's Republic of China on the Administration of the Controlled Chemicals," promulgated by Decree No. 190 of the State Council, December 27, 1995; see also State Council, "Regulations of the People's Republic of China on Control of Nuclear Export," Decree No. 230, September 10, 1997; see also State Administration of Arms Trade of the People's Republic of China, "The Regulations of the People's Republic of China on the Administration of Arms Export," October 22, 1997; and Ministry of Foreign Trade and Economic Cooperation of the People's Republic of China, "Regulations of the People's Republic of China on the Control of Nuclear Dual-Use Items and Related Technologies Export," State Council Decree No. 245, June 1, 1998.

65. Jim Mann, "Threat to Mideast Military Balance: U.S. Caught Napping by Sino-Saudi Missile Deal," *Los Angeles Times,* May 4, 1988, 1.

66. John W. Lewis, Hua Di, and Xue Litai, "Beijing's Defense Establishment: Solving the Arms-Export Enigma," *International Security* 15, no. 4 (Spring 1991): 96.

67. Chinese diplomat, author's conference notes, July 2, 1998.

68. House Select Committee, *U.S. National Security and Military/Commercial Concerns*, vol. 1, ii–vxii. Indeed, a separate evaluation of a CIA "Damage Assessment" undertaken by a committee headed by Admiral David Jeremiah concluded that "China obtained by espionage classified US nuclear weapons information that probably accelerated its program.... We do not know if US classified nuclear information acquired by the Chinese has been passed to other countries." "Intelligence Community Damage Assessment on the Implications of China's Acquisition of US Nuclear Weapons Information on the Development of Future Chinese Weapons (U)," April 21, 1999.

69. Review Panel, "Introductory Note from the Review Panel and Key Findings, The Intelligence Community Damage Assessment on the Implications of China's Acquisition of US Nuclear Weapons Information on the Development of Future Chinese Weapons (U)," April 21, 1999.

70. Eric Schmitt, "New Reports Conflict on Security Breach," *New York Times*, June 6, 1998, A8. Only a year later, the Select Committee on U.S. National Security and Military/Commercial Concerns with the People's Republic of China issued its three-volume unclassified report, concluding that "[t]he PRC has stolen or otherwise illegally obtained U.S. missile and space technology that improves the PRC's military and intelligence capabilities." *U.S. National Security and Military/Commercial Concerns*, vol. 1, xii. Even this report did not quell the debate.

71. Zachary S. Davis, "Proliferation Control Regimes: Background and Status," testimony, Senate Armed Services Hearing on Security Implications of Lowered Export Capabilities, May 11, 1995, Federal Document Clearing House, May 11, 1995, 4–7.

72. House Select Committee, *U.S. National Security and Military/Commercial Concerns*, vol. 3, 6–9.

73. Ibid., 25.

74. Nuclear Proliferation Prevention Act of 1994 (Title VIII, sec. 825, Foreign Relations Authorization Act, FY 1994 and 1995, PL 103–236 [1994]). See Rodney Jones et al., *Tracking Nuclear Proliferation* (Washington, D.C.: Carnegie Endowment for International Peace, 1998), 52–53.

75. House Select Committee, *U.S. National Security and Military/Commercial Concerns*, vol. 3, 168.

76. James N. Thurman, "Why Should US Use Foreign Rockets?" *Christian Science Monitor*, June 18, 1998, 3.

77. Winston Lord, in Conable Jr. et al., *Current Tensions, Policy Choices*, 26.

78. Bill Gertz, *Betrayal: How the Clinton Administration Undermined American Security* (Washington, D.C.: Regnery Publishing, 1999), 273, reproduces an October 23, 1993, letter from Hughes chairman and CEO C. Michael Armstrong to President Clinton asking for the president "to resolve the China sanctions at the upcoming Seattle APEC meeting."

79. Jeff Gerth and David E. Sanger, "Aircraft Deal with Chinese Is Questioned," *New York Times*, October 30, 1996, A10.

80. See R. Jeffrey Smith, "Atomic Club Passwords Were Shared; US, USSR Gave Three Nations Secret Aid," *Washington Post*, March 24, 1994, A22; William Drozdiak and Jeffrey Smith, "Pentagon's Hand in French Arsenal; Washington Helps the 'Independent' Deterrent," *The Guardian* (London), September 20, 1995, 11; Stephen Rosenfeld, "Time to Talk about Israel's Bomb," *Washington Post*, December 1, 1991, C7; and George F. Will, "Innocent of Honor," *Washington Post*, May 21, 1998, A27.

81. Stephen Engleberg and Michael Gordon, "Taipei Halts Work on Secret Plant to Make Nuclear Bomb Ingredient," *New York Times*, March 23, 1988, A1; see also R. Jeffrey Smith and Don Oberdorfer, "Taiwan to Close Nuclear Reactor; U.S. Voiced Concern on Spread of Weapons," *Washington Post*, March 24, 1988, A32.

82. Duncan L. Clarke and Robert J. Johnston, "U.S. Dual-Use Exports to China, and the Israel Factor," *Asian Survey* 39, no. 2 (March–April 1999): 193–213; also Zalmay M. Khalilzad et al., *The United States and a Rising China* (Santa Monica, Calif.: RAND, 1999), 50, 55–56; also Eric Pianin, "Israel-China Radar Deal Opposed," *Washington Post*, April 7, 2000, A28. To further complicate the picture, however, beyond the obvious political implications of pushing Israel to stop revenue-producing transfers may also lie intelligence considerations. For instance, in selling such technology to Beijing, Israel (and consequently perhaps the United States) may acquire information about Chinese forces that would be useful. Also, some of the technology sold to the PRC is older and some analysts would argue that it is better to know another country's technology than to not have such knowledge.

83. Arms Control and Disarmament Agency, *World Military Expenditures and Arms Transfers* (Washington, D.C.: Arms Control and Disarmament Agency 1995), 21.

84. Gary Milhollin, "Made in America?" *Washington Post*, June 7, 1998, C5.

85. Chris Smith, *India's Ad Hoc Arsenal* (New York: Oxford University Press, 1994), 188.

86. Milhollin, "Made in America?" C5.

87. For background and chronology on the missile and satellite issue, see Shirley A. Kan, "China and Possible Missile Technology Transfers from U.S. Satellite Export Policy—Background and Chronology," CRS Report to Congress, Congressional Research Service, February 9, 1999.

88. Reuters, "China Great Wall to Launch 17 Foreign Satellites," November 20, 1998.

89. Xu Dianlong, "Economy Here and There: A Bumper Harvest in Launching Commercial Satellites" (in Chinese), *Liaowang* (Beijing), no. 3, January 18, 1999, 28–29, in FBIS-CHI-January 18, 1999.

90. In December 1988 the "Memorandum of Agreement between the Government of the United States and the Government of the People's Republic of China Regarding Satellite Technical Security" was signed. Xinhua News Ser-

vice, "PRC Executive Comments on Satellites Launched by China" (in English), in FBIS-CHI-98-322.

91. House Select Committee, *U.S. National Security and Military/Commercial Concerns*, vol. 2.

92. Ibid., 250, 252.

93. Samuel R. Berger, "Launching Satellites in China Is Good for the U.S.," *Wall Street Journal,* June 3, 1998, A18.

94. Brent Scowcroft and Arnold Kanter, "What Technology Went Where and Why," *Washington Times,* June 5, 1998, A19.

95. Patricia Wilson, "America Relaxes Sanctions on China," *Daily Telegraph* (London), February 22, 1992, 9.

96. Bill Gertz, "Technology Transfers Detailed for Senate," *Washington Times,* May 22, 1998, A13.

97. Jeff Gerth and David E. Sanger, "How Chinese Won Rights to Launch Satellites for U.S.," *New York Times,* May 17, 1998, A18.

98. Scowcroft and Kanter, "What Technology Went Where and Why," A19.

99. Eric Schmitt, "Helms Says Clinton Tried to Protect China by Waiving Curbs on Satellite Exports," *New York Times,* June 13, 1998, A8.

100. House Select Committee, *U.S. National Security and Military/Commercial Concerns*, vol. 2, 102.

101. Ibid., 107–8.

102. Brian Duffy and Robert S. Greenberger, "Roots of Chinese-Rocket Debate Are in the Reagan Era," *Wall Street Journal,* July 17, 1998, A16.

103. Berger, "Launching Satellites in China Is Good for the U.S.," A18.

104. U.S.-China Business Council, "Satellite Scandal Backgrounder," unpublished memorandum draft, Washington, D.C., n.d., 2.

105. House Select Committee, *U.S. National Security and Military/Commercial Concerns*, vol. 1, xxvii.

106. See, for example, Bill Gertz, "China Assists Iran, Libya on Missiles," *Washington Times,* June 16, 1998, A1.

107. Senate Select Committee on Intelligence, *Report on Impacts to U.S. National Security of Advanced Satellite Technology Exports to the People's Republic of China (PRC), and Report on the PRC's Efforts to Influence U.S. Policy,* S. PRT 106–25, May 1999, 106th Cong., 1st sess. (Washington, D.C.: U.S. Government Printing Office, 1999).

108. House Select Committee, *U.S. National Security and Military/Commercial Concerns*, vols. 1–3.

109. Jeff Gerth, "Satellite Maker Gave Report to China before Telling U.S.," *New York Times,* May 19, 1998, A19.

110. Jeff Gerth, "Democratic Fund-Raiser Said to Name China Tie," *New York Times,* May 15, 1998, A18.

111. Juliet Eilperin, "GOP Says U.S. Gave China Nuclear Edge," *Washington Post,* May 6, 1998, A4.

112. Eric Schmitt, "Chinese Suddenly Improved Rocket Safety, Expert Says," *New York Times,* June 18, 1998, A10.

113. Xinhua News Agency (Beijing), "China Extends Successful Launch Record" (in English), December 19, 1998, in FBIS-CHI-98-353.

114. Jeff Gerth, "Republican Leaders Insist Limits on Satellite Exports Be Kept," *New York Times,* January 8, 1999, A13.

115. David S. Cloud, Helene Cooper, and Andy Pasztor, "U.S. Says China-Satellite Rejection Was One-Time Event, But Chill May Result," *Wall Street Journal,* February 24, 1999, A4; see also Tony Walker and Stephen Fidler, "US Poised to Ban Sale of $450m Satellite to China," *Financial Times,* February 22, 1999, 1, 3.

116. Elaine Sciolino, "Clinton Argues for 'Flexibility' over Sanctions," *New York Times,* April 28, 1998, A1.

117. See David M. Lampton, "China's Foreign and National Security Policy Process: Is It Changing and Does It Matter?" in *The Making of Chinese Foreign and Security Policy in the Era of Reform.*

118. "China Denies U.S. Satellite Technology Allegations," April 10, 2000 <http://dailynews.yahoo.com/h/nm/20000410/tc/china_satellite_1.html> accessed April 10, 2000.

119. "Memorandum of Conversation," Mao Zedong's residence, Beijing, October 21, 1975, in Burr, *The Kissinger Transcripts,* 392.

120. Center for Naval Analyses, "Initial Commentary on Beijing's White Paper—'China's National Defense,'" informal paper, Alexandria, Virginia, August 26, 1998, 5.

121. The TRA (PL 96–8) became law on April 10, 1979, and represented the congressional reaction to the "normalization" of relations with Beijing that had occurred January 1, 1979. The TRA, a law of the United States, sought to ensure that a legal and predictable framework of association was created for the American people and residents of Taiwan. Further, Congress used the instrument of the TRA to express the determination of the United States to continue to provide Taiwan "with arms of a defensive character" "in such quantity as may be necessary to enable Taiwan to maintain sufficient self-defense capability." At bedrock, the TRA was a declaration that "peace and stability in the area are in the political, security, and economic interests of the United States," and that the United States was "to maintain the capacity" "to resist any resort to force or other forms of coercion that would jeopardize the security, or the social or economic system, of the people on Taiwan." The TRA, from which the above citations came, may be found in Richard H. Solomon, ed., *The China Factor* (Englewood Cliffs, N.J.: Prentice Hall, 1981), 304–14.

122. Hung-mao Tien, ed., *Taiwan's Electoral Politics and Democratic Transition: Riding the Third Wave* (New York: M. E. Sharpe, 1996), 115.

123. Ralph N. Clough, "Cross-Strait Relations and U.S. Policy" (draft of paper presented to Workshop on Cross-Strait Relations, University of British Columbia, Vancouver, Canada, August 21–22, 1998), 12.

124. "Public Opinion on Cross-Strait Relations in the Republic of China," Mainland Affairs Council, Executive Yuan, Republic of China, October 1998.

125. Nicholas D. Kristof, "Taiwan Chief Sees Separate Identity," *New York Times,* September 2, 1998, A4.

126. C. F. Koo, "Toward a Constructive Cross-Straits Relationship," May 1998, 1.

127. U.S. Department of Defense, *The Security Situation in the Taiwan Strait: Report to Congress Pursuant to the FY 99 Appropriations Bill,* February 1, 1999, 23 <http://www.defenselink.mil/pubs/twstrait_02261999.html> accessed July 19, 2000.

128. Richard Nixon also offered Premier Zhou Enlai assurances that the United States "won't support Taiwan independence" in 1972 during his first trip to the PRC. See Mann, *About Face,* 46.

129. Jackie Calmes and Craig R. Smith, "Clinton Backs China on Taiwan, Loud and Clear," *Wall Street Journal,* July 1, 1998, C14.

130. "Memorandum of Conversation," October 29, 1976, in Burr, *The Kissinger Transcripts,* 416.

131. White House, Office of the Press Secretary, "Remarks by the President to Students and Community of Beijing University," Beijing, June 29, 1998.

132. Ross Y. Koen, *The China Lobby in American Politics* (New York: Harper and Row, Publishers, 1974).

133. Government Information Office, ROC, "New Members of the Cabinet, 1996" <http://www.roc-taiwan.org/info/chief/index_e.htm> accessed August 28, 1998.

134. Ruth Marcus, "Dole Registers as Taiwan Foreign Agent; Critics Say Arrangement Breaches Terms of Gingrich's Loan," *Washington Post,* January 13, 1998, A5.

135. General organizational literature from FAPA, 538 Seventh Street, S.E., Washington, D.C. 20003.

136. Nigel Holloway, Julian Baum, Charles S. Lee, and Sachiko Sakamaki, "Learned Puppets," *Far Eastern Economic Review,* May 22, 1997, 29–32.

137. On the size of U.S. reexports through Hong Kong see Lardy, *China in the World Economy,* 75.

138. Brian Duffy and Bob Woodward, "FBI Warned 6 on Hill about China Money," *Washington Post,* March 9, 1997, A01; more broadly, see Bob Sutter, "Chinese Government Contacts with Congress—Increased Efforts," *Congressional Research Service Memorandum to China Watchers,* January 6, 1997; also Phillip C. Saunders, "China's America Watchers: Changing Attitudes Towards the United States," *China Quarterly,* no. 161 (March 2000): 51.

139. Connie Cass, "In Addition to Donations, Asian Interests Courted Congress with Trips," Associated Press, December 23, 1996.

140. Ronald Brownstein, "Washington Outlook: Thompson's Charges May Be Buying Trouble for Nation's China Policy," *Los Angeles Times,* July 14, 1997, A5.

141. International relations analyst, interview by author, Shanghai, June 20, 1998.

142. International relations analyst, interview by author, Shanghai, June 20, 1998.

143. From *Nihon Keizai Shimbum* and *Wall Street Journal* surveys, cited in lecture given by Michael Mochizuki, George Washington University, Washington, D.C., April 22, 1997.

144. Secretary of defense, Department of Defense, *Report to Congress Pursuant to Section 1226 or the FY98 National Defense Authorization Act*, Washington, D.C., October 1998.

145. Department of Defense, *Report to Congress on Theater Missile Defense Architecture Options in the Asia-Pacific Region*, Washington, D.C., April 1999; see also Stephen Rademaker, Walker Roberts, and Peter Brookes, House Committee on International Relations, "Memorandum to Benjamin A. Gilman," April 22, 1999, among personal correspondence of author.

3. ECONOMICS AND HUMAN RIGHTS

Sources for Chapter Epigraphs:
Warren Christopher, statement before Senate Foreign Relations Committee, January 13, 1993, in *U.S. Department of State Dispatch* (Bureau of Public Affairs) 4, no. 4 (January 25, 1993) <gopher://dosfan.lib.uic.edu /ooftp:DOSFan:Gophe...:Dispatch%20V.4%20no.%20%20> accessed April 27, 2000; Liu Zhongli, quoted in Thomas L. Friedman, "Deal with China Urged by Bentsen," *New York Times*, March 20, 1994, 20; Patrick J. Buchanan, quoted in Alison Mitchell, "Despite Tensions, Clinton Urges Renewal of China's Trade Status," *New York Times*, May 21, 1996, A6; David E. Sanger, "Rubin and the Great Wall That Is China," *International Herald Tribune*, September 29, 1997, 2; Anne F. Thurston, *Muddling toward Democracy* (Washington, D.C.: United States Institute of Peace, 1998), 2; John M. Goshko, "Dalai Lama Hopeful on Clinton Policy," *Washington Post*, May 1, 1998, A33; John Mintz and Bart Gellman, "U.S. Fears More Extensive Political Crackdown in China," *Washington Post*, January 12, 1999, A13.

1. Peter Montagnon, John Ridding, and Tony Walker, "Comment and Analysis," *Financial Times*, June 11, 1996, 19.

2. Zhang Baoxiang, "A Dangerous New Strategy," *Renmin Ribao* [People's Daily], April 23, 1999, 7, in FBIS-CHI-1999-0423; see also Qian Wenrong, "UN Authority Has Been Damaged," *Renmin Ribao* [People's Daily], April 12, 1999, 7, in FBIS-CHI-1999-0412; see also Luo Renshi, "What Is New about the 'New Gunboat Policy,'" *Jiefangjun Bao* [Liberation Army Daily], May 20, 1999, 5, in FBIS-CHI-1999-0526.

3. "Memorandum of Conversation," Zhongnanhai, February 17–18, 1973, in Burr, *The Kissinger Transcripts*, 93–94.

4. The calculation of jobs is based on Department of Commerce statistics (U.S. Department of Commerce, Economics, and Statistics Administration and U.S. Department of Commerce, Office of International Macroeconomic Analysis) and includes only jobs related to the production of goods/merchandise. The inclusion of "service" exports would raise the job numbers considerably, particularly as time goes on.

5. The 1999 ranking comes from the U.S. Census Bureau <http://www.census .gov/foreign-trade/top/dst/1999/12/balance.html> accessed April 27, 2000; the tenth-place ranking comes from International Monetary Fund, *Direction of Trade Statistics Yearbook, 1991* (Washington, D.C.: International Monetary Fund, 1991), 402–4.

6. Coca-Cola Company, "Fact Sheet: The Coca-Cola Business in China," April 1997, 1.

7. The Boeing Company, "The Boeing Company in China," April 7, 1998, <http://www.boeing.com/companyoffices/aboutus/beochina.html> accessed April 27, 2000.

8. Motorola, "Motorola Asia and the Pacific—Facts 99" <http://www .motorola-asia.com/facts99–3.htm> accessed April 27, 2000.

9. Elisabeth Rosenthal, "China's Middle Class Savors Its New Wealth," *New York Times,* June 19, 1998, A8.

10. Development Research Center of the State Council, "On the Issue of 'Foreign Companies Crowding China's Market'" (in Chinese), *Guanli Shijie* [Management World], no. 68 (September 24, 1996): 77–80, in FBIS-CHI-96-222 (September 24, 1996), Daily Report.

11. Zhongguo Xinwen She, "No Optimism for Exports, Urgent Need for Diversification" (in Chinese), Beijing, June 15, 1998, from British Broadcasting Corporation, *BBC Summary of World Broadcasts,* June 16, 1998, CHINA/FE/D3254/S1.

12. Material supplied by U.S.-China Business Council, January 7, 1998, 3.

13. Zhongguo, "No Optimism for Exports, Urgent Need for Diversification."

14. Xinhua News Agency (Beijing), "U.S. Leading Foreign Investor in China," June 22, 1998, FBIS-CHI-98-173. See also Mainland Affairs Council, *Liang an jingji tongji yue bao* [Cross-strait economic statistics monthly] (Taipei: Mainland Affairs Council, June 1998), 46.

15. Xinhua News Agency (Beijing), "U.S. Leading Foreign Investor in China," June 22, 1998.

16. Jimmy Carter, *Public Papers of the Presidents of the United States: Jimmy Carter, 1979,* Book 2, June 23–December 31, 1979 (Washington, D.C.: U.S. Government Printing Office, 1980), 2000–2005.

17. Edward Walsh, "Buchanan Comes Out Swinging," *International Herald Tribune,* March 3, 1999, 3.

18. Steven Erlanger and David E. Sanger, "On World Stage, Many Lessons for Clinton," *New York Times,* July 29, 1996, A14.

19. U.S. Department of Commerce, as cited by US-China Business Council, "Table 7: China's Trade with the United States."

20. K. C. Fung and Lawrence J. Lau, *The China-United States Bilateral Trade Balance: How Big Is It Really?* (Stanford, Calif.: Asia/Pacific Research Center, 1996).

21. Nicholas R. Lardy, "China and the WTO," Brookings Policy Brief, no. 10, Brookings Institution, Washington, D.C., November 1996, 2–3.

22. Senate Committee, *Hearings on China Most-Favored-Nation Status,* 37.

23. David E. Sanger, "U.S. Business Ties to China Are Far Richer Than Any Diplomatic Links," *New York Times,* October 28, 1997, A14.

24. Business Software Alliance, "Worldwide Business Software Piracy Losses Estimated at Nearly $11 Billion in 1998" <http://www.bsa.org/press box/enforcement/927637266.html> accessed April 27, 2000.

25. Andrew Pollack, "Japan Is Pressed to Extend Music Copyright Protection," *New York Times,* February 6, 1996, D4.

26. Office of the United States Trade Representative, "USTR Mickey Kantor Orders 100% Tariffs on More Than $1 Billion of Chinese Imports," February 4, 1995 <http://www.ustr.gove/releases/1995/02/95-087> accessed March 17, 1998.

27. Ibid., 2.

28. Tiffany Brown, "IPR Talks' Failure 'Won't Greatly Influence' Economy" (in English), AFP (Hong Kong), January 25, 1995, in FBIS-CHI-95-16 (January 25, 1995), 3.

29. Interview by author, Shanghai, June 20, 1998.

30. Michel Oksenberg, Pitman B. Potter, and William B. Abnett, "Advancing Intellectual Property Rights: Information Technologies and the Course of Economic Development in China," Asian/Pacific Research Center, Stanford University, March 1998, 13–14.

31. Business Software Alliance and Software Publishers Association, *1997 Global Software Piracy Report,* June 1998, 6.

32. Pitman B. Potter and Michel Oksenberg, "A Patchwork of IPR Protections," *China Business Review,* January–February 1999, 8–10.

33. Zhao Huanxin, "Call to Stamp Out Software Piracy," *China Daily,* June 25, 1999, 2.

34. Oksenberg, Potter, and Abnett, "Advancing Intellectual Property Rights," 7.

35. Tiffany Brown, "IPR Talks' Failure 'Won't Greatly Influence' Economy" (in English), AFP, in FBIS-CHI-16 (January 25, 1995) Daily Report, 2.

36. Stuart Varney, interview with Mickey Kantor, "News," CNN, February 3, 1995, transcript no. 855-2 <http://web.lexis-nexis.com/univers...5=3537 d02e3e5adcb3d63dd2290733f3e7> accessed May 19, 2000.

37. Oksenberg, Potter, and Abnett, "Advancing Intellectual Property Rights," 8.

38. Office of the United States Trade Representative, "USTR Kantor Says China Must Take Immediate Action to Curb Piracy," December 14, 1995 <http://www.ustr.gov/releases/1995/12/95-92.html> accessed April 27, 2000.

39. Amy Borrus, Dexter Roberts, and Joyce Barnathan, "Counterfeit Disks, Suspect Enforcement," *Business Week,* September 18, 1995, 68.

40. Office of the United States Trade Representative, "Acting USTR Charlene Barshefsky Announces Preliminary Retaliation List on $3 Billion of Chinese Imports," May 15, 1996 <http://www.ustr.gov/releases/1996/05/96-42.html> accessed April 27, 2000.

41. Michel Oksenberg, correspondence with author, October 28, 1999.

42. U.S. Newswire, "Customs Seizes Record-Breaking $54 Million in Counterfeit Imports," February 11, 1998 <Lexis-Nexis.../document? _ansett=GeHauKO-DAARGRUUBRZA-AAUZA-WRARECZYYAARL> accessed April 27, 2000.

43. Kevin Chen, "China's True Brew Stirs Trademark Fight in Taiwan," *Japan Times,* June 18, 1996, 11.

44. *Laogai* means "reform through labor." In the American political debate it has come to stand for all Chinese prison labor exports. For an overview of this issue and prisons more generally, see James D. Seymour and Richard Anderson, *New Ghosts, Old Ghosts: Prisons and Labor Reform Camps in China* (Armonk, N.Y.: M. E. Sharpe, 1998).

45. George Weise, "Statement of George J. Weise, Commissioner, United States Customs Service," before the Senate Committee on Foreign Relations," May 21, 1997 <http://www.usinfo.state.gov/regional/ea/uschina/weise521 .htm> accessed April 27, 2000.

46. Asia Watch, *Prison Labor in China* (New York: Asia Watch, April 19, 1991).

47. Harry Wu, with George Vecsey, *Troublemaker: One Man's Crusade against China's Cruelty* (New York: Random House, 1998).

48. Wu, *Troublemaker,* 135; see also Sarah Henry, "Harry's War," *Los Angeles Times Magazine,* November 17, 1996, 12; see also Carolyn Jung, "Facing Hard Labor in China's Prisons, Harry Wu Is Driven by His Hatred of China's Forced Labor Camps," *Toronto Star,* July 31, 1995, A11.

49. Holly J. Burkhalter, statement before Senate Committee, *Hearings on China Most-Favored-Nation Status,* 51.

50. Paul Blustein, "Can U.S. Point Finger at China? American Inmates Manufacture Products, But Trade Debate Centers on Beijing's Policies," *Washington Post,* June 3, 1997, C1.; see also Dallas Gatewood, "Jailhouse Blues: Oregon Prison-Made Jeans Hit Foreign Markets," *Newsday, News Tribune,* March 23, 1994, C13; see also Gren Manuel, "Fashion Cashes in on Folsom Prison Blues," *South China Morning Post,* May 29, 1995, 20.

51. Jeffrey A. Bader, deputy assistant secretary for East Asian and Pacific affairs, statement before the Senate Foreign Relations Committee, Washington, D.C., May 21, 1997 <http://www.state.gov/www/regions/eap/970521_bader _china_prison.html> accessed April 27, 2000.

52. *Establishing United States Policy toward China,* 104th Cong., 1st sess., H.R. 2058.

53. James Schlesinger, "Fragmentation and Hubris," *National Interest,* no. 49 (Fall 1997): 5.

54. Zhao Haiqing, statement before House Subcommittees on Human Rights and International Organizations, Asian and Pacific Affairs, and on International Economic Policy and Trade, in *Hearings on Most-Favored-Nation Status for the People's Republic of China,* 101st Cong, 2d. sess. (Washington, D.C.: U.S. Government Printing Office, 1990), 66.

55. Marlowe Hood, "Sourcing the Problem: Why Fuzhou?" in *Human Smuggling: Chinese Migrant Trafficking and the Challenge to America's*

Immigration Tradition, ed. Paul J. Smith (Washington, D.C.: Center for International and Strategic Studies, 1997), 83.

56. Du Gangjian and Song Gang, "Relating Human Rights to Chinese Culture," in *Human Rights and Chinese Values*, ed. Michael C. Davis (New York: Oxford University Press, 1995), 35–56; for more on human rights in Chinese foreign policy see Andrew J. Nathan, "Human Rights in Chinese Foreign Policy," *China Quarterly*, no. 139 (September 1994): 622–43; see also Andrew J. Nathan, "China and the International Human Rights Regime," in *China Joins the World: Progress and Prospects*, ed. Elizabeth Economy and Michel Oksenberg (New York: Council on Foreign Relations Press, 1999), 136–60.

57. World Bank, *World Development Indicators 1998*, CD-ROM (Washington: World Bank, 1998); U.S. Department of Education, *1992 National Adult Literacy Survey*, (Washington: National Center for Education Statistics, May 1999). The study was conducted in 1992 and released in 1999.

58. Strobe Talbott, "Democracy and the National Interest," *Foreign Affairs* 75, no. 6 (1996): 55.

59. "Questions for the President: Give and Take with China's Students," *New York Times*, June 30, 1998, A8.

60. *Human Rights in China* (Beijing: Information Office of the State Council, 1991). See also Information Office of the State Council of the PRC, *White Paper—The Progress of Human Rights in China*, December 1995, Beijing. For a broader discussion of these issues, see Davis, *Human Rights and Chinese Values*.

61. James A. Baker III, *The Politics of Diplomacy* (New York: G. P. Putnam's Sons, 1995), 69.

62. Winston Lord, "Emerging Malaise in Our Relations with Asia," undated memorandum to Secretary of State Warren Christopher, 2.

63. Steven Erlanger and David E. Sanger, "On World Stage, Many Lessons for Clinton," *New York Times*, July 29, 1996, A14.

64. Winston Lord, interview by author, August 18, 1999.

65. George Bush, "Inaugural Address," January 20, 1989, in *Public Papers*, vol. 1, 3.

66. Winston Lord, interview by author, August 18, 1999.

67. Elaine Sciolino, "U.S. Showing Frustration over China's Human Rights Policy," *New York Times*, March 9, 1994, 11.

68. Winston Lord, interview by author, August 18, 1999.

69. Warren Christopher, "American Interests and the U.S.-China Relationship," address to National Committee on United States-China Relations and other organizations, May 17, 1996, New York City, Office of the Spokesman, U.S. Department of State.

70. Author's memorandum of conversation, July 18, 1996.

71. Jim Mann and Doyle McManus, "Official Says U.S. Taking Softer Approach to China," *Los Angeles Times*, July 18, 1996, A18.

72. White House, "Joint U.S.-China Statement," October 29, 1997 <http://www.state.gov/www/regions/eap/971029_usc_jstmt.html> accessed July 20, 1998.

73. "The Leaders' Remarks: Hopes for a Friendship, Even If Imperfect," *New York Times,* June 28, 1998, 9.

74. John M. Broder, "President Terms Certain Rights 'Universal,'" *New York Times,* June 29, 1998, A8.

75. Catharin E. Dalpino, "Human Rights in China," Brookings Policy Brief, no. 50, Brookings Institution, Washington, D.C., June 1999.

76. Stanley Lubman, "Sino-American Relations and China's Struggle for the Rule of Law," in East Asian Institute, Columbia University, *Institute Reports,* October 1997, 3.

77. Ibid., 20.

78. Neil J. Diamant, *Revolutionizing the Family* (Berkeley, Calif.: University of California Press, 2000).

79. Wang Jincun, "Global Democratization—Camouflage US Hegemony" (in English), Xinhua News Agency, May 27, 1999, in FBIS-CHI-1999-0526; see also Xiao Feng, "World Trends under US Global Strategy, Part Two of Two," *Renmin Ribao* [People's Daily], June 1, 1999, 6, in FBIS-CHI-1999-0601.

80. Human Rights Watch/Asia, *Death by Default* (New York: Human Rights Watch/Asia, 1996), 5.

81. Ibid., 214.

82. Ibid., 4; for the most balanced account of Chinese orphanages, see Anne F. Thurston, "In a Chinese Orphanage," *Atlantic Monthly,* April 1996.

83. Department of State, *Country Report on Human Rights Practices for 1997: China* (Washington: U.S. Department of State, Bureau of Democracy, Human Rights, and Law, January 30, 1998); see also James Z. Lee and Wang Feng, *One Quarter of Humanity: Malthusian Mythology and Chinese Realities, 1700–2000* (Cambridge: Harvard University Press, 1999); see also "World Briefing," *New York Times,* January 8, 1999, A9.

84. Mariana Wan and Simon Beck, "Organs of Prisoners Used in Ops," *South China Morning Post,* July 25, 1993, 1; see also Christopher Drew, "A Grim Trade in Organs from Chinese Prisoners," *New York Times,* March 1, 1998, Sec. 4, Week in Review, 2.

85. Doug Guthrie, *Dragon in a Three-Piece Suit* (Princeton, N.J.: Princeton University Press, 1999).

86. Observer, "On the New Development of US Hegemonism," *Renmin Ribao* [People's Daily], May 27, 1999, 1, in FBIS-CHI-1999-0527.

87. Tom Lantos, "Statement of Hon. Tom Lantos," House Subcommittee on Trade of the Committee on Ways and Means, *Hearing: United States-China Trade Relations,* 103d Cong., 2d sess., February 24, 1994, 11.

88. Allen Zhuang, "Smuggling of Chinese Illegals on the Increase," *Straits Times* (Singapore), September 25, 1998, 26; see also Central News Agency, "Smuggling of Mainland Illegals on the Rise," September 25, 1998

<http://www.taipei.org/teco/cicc/ne...lish/e-09–25–98/e-09–25–98–10.htm> accessed September 25, 1998.

89. Hood, "Sourcing the Problem: Why Fuzhou?" 80.

90. Ibid., 78.

91. William Booth, "13 Charged in Gang Importing Prostitutes," *Washington Post*, August 21, 1999, A3.

92. Christopher F. Patten, "Hong Kong in Transition," speech before the National Committee on U.S.-China Relations, New York City, May 6, 1993, 6–7.

93. Governor Christopher F. Patten, "Speech to the National Committee on United States-China Relations," New York City, May 6, 1996, 9–10.

94. Ni Shixiong, "A Conceptual Framework for Improving Cross-Straits Relations," paper prepared for the Third Meeting of the New York Roundtable on the U.S.-China and Cross-Straits Relations, July 13–15, 1998, 5.

95. Ministry of Foreign Trade and Economic Cooperation, *Almanac of China's Foreign Economic Relations and Trade*, 1991/92–1996/97. State Statistical Bureau, using MOFTEC figures for 1996 and 1997.

96. Su Yiping, "Mainland-Hong Kong Economic and Trade Relations Enter a New Era," *Zhongguo Tongxun She* (Hong Kong), October 27, 1998, in FBIS-CHI-98-310.

97. Embassy of the People's Republic of China, "Newsletter," no. 98–12 (June 22, 1998): 7.

98. Doug Bereuter, "Third Report," Speaker's Task Force on the Hong Kong Transition, May 22, 1998.

99. Melvyn C. Goldstein, *The Snow Lion and the Dragon: China, Tibet, and the Dalai Lama* (Berkeley: University of California Press, 1997), 83; see also John Kenneth Knaus, *Orphans of the Cold War: America and the Tibetan Struggle for Survival* (New York: Public Affairs, 1999).

100. Warren Christopher, "Hearing of the Senate Foreign Relations Committee: Confirmation Hearing for Warren Christopher," Federal Information System Corporation, January 13, 1993, 23.

101. Michel Oksenberg, "Taiwan, Tibet, and Hong Kong in Sino-American Relations," in Vogel, *Living with China*, 80–81; see also A. Tom Grunfeld, *The Making of Modern Tibet* (Armonk, N.Y.: M. E. Sharpe, 1996).

102. "Questions Pertaining to Tibet," memorandum for the Special Group, Washington, D.C., January 9, 1964, in Department of State, *Foreign Relations of the United States, 1964–1968*, vol. 30, *China* (Washington, D.C.: U.S. Government Printing Office, 1998), 732.

103. Knaus, *Orphans of the Cold War*.

104. "Questions Pertaining to Tibet," 731–33.

105. Central Intelligence Agency, "Memorandum of Conversation between Ambassador McConaughy and Chiang Ching-kuo on 12 February 1968," in Department of State, *Foreign Relations of the United States, 1964–1968*, 660–62.

106. Asia Watch, *Detained in Tibet* (New York: Human Rights Watch, 1994); see also Tibet Information Network and Human Rights Watch/Asia,

Cutting Off the Serpent's Head: Tightening Control in Tibet 1994–1995 (New York: Human Rights Watch, 1996).

107. Xinhua General Overseas News Service, "Hu Yaobang and Wan Li Inspect Tibet," May 31, 1980 <http://web.lexis-nexis.com/univers...5=88a41b2f97c18e45638ff27218c0e2bc> accessed April 27, 2000.

108. Melvyn Goldstein, "The Dragon and the Snow Lion: The Tibet Question in the 20th Century," in *China Briefing, 1990*, ed. Anthony Kane (Boulder, Colo.: Westview Press, 1990), 129.

109. Tibet Information Network and Human Rights Watch/Asia, *Cutting off the Serpent's Head*.

110. International Campaign for Tibet, "Major Congressional and Administration Acts on Tibet," July 1998; chronology supplied by International Campaign for Tibet, Washington, D.C.

111. Public Law 102–138, sec. 355, "China's Illegal Control of Tibet," says, "It is the sense of the Congress that—." This is language that is nonbinding on the executive branch.

112. For an authoritative account of the main contents of the Strasbourg proposals see Office of Tibet, "Tibet Briefing," New York City, 1994, 24; see also Goldstein, *The Snow Lion and the Dragon*, 87–89.

113. Catharin E. Dalpino, *Anchoring Third Wave Democracies: Prospects and Problems for U.S. Policy* (Washington, D.C.: Institute for the Study of Diplomacy, Georgetown University, 1998), 97.

114. For more on the sanctions debate and the executive branch's desire to maintain maximum flexibility in their imposition and use, see Stuart E. Eizenstat, "Statement before the Subcommittee on Trade of the House Ways and Means Committee," Washington, D.C., May 27, 1999 <http://www.state.gov/www/policy_remarks/1999/990527_eizen_sanctions.html> accessed April 27, 2000.

115. Richard N. Haass, "Conclusion: Lessons and Recommendations," in *Economic Sanctions and American Diplomacy*, ed. Richard N. Haass (New York: Council on Foreign Relations, 1998), 197.

4. GLOBAL INSTITUTIONS AND ECONOMIC FLOWS

Sources for Chapter Epigraphs:
William Perry, cited in Mitchel B. Wallerstein, "China and Proliferation: A Path Not Taken?" *Survival* 38, no. 3 (Autumn 1996): 64–65; Zhou Mingwei, Foreign Affairs Office, Shanghai Municipality, cited in Thomas L. Friedman, "The Party's Over," *New York Times*, March 7, 1998, A13; Chinese professor, author's discussion notes, July 9, 1998; Fan Gang, "Impacts of Asia Economic Shake-up on China's Reform and Development," unpublished paper, May 1998; Thomas G. Moore and Dixia Yang, "Empowered and Restrained: Chinese Foreign Policy in the Age of Economic Interdependence," in Lampton, *The Making of Chinese Foreign and Security Policy in the Era of Reform*, forthcoming (Stanford, Calif., Stanford University Press, 2001).

1. Samuel S. Kim, "China and the United Nations," in Economy and Oksenberg, *China Joins the World*, 47; see also Michel Oksenberg and Elizabeth Economy, *Shaping U.S.-China Relations: A Long-Term Strategy* (New York: Council on Foreign Relations, 1997), 7.

2. Union of International Associations, *Yearbook of International Organizations*, vol. 2, 1997/1998 (Munchen: K.G. Saur), table 3, app. 3.

3. Harold K. Jacobson and Michel Oksenberg, *China's Participation in the IMF, the World Bank, and GATT: Toward a Global Economic Order* (Ann Arbor: University of Michigan Press, 1990).

4. Nicholas R. Lardy, "China and the International Financial System," in Economy and Oksenberg, *China Joins the World*, 209.

5. World Bank, "The World Bank and China" <http://wbln0018.worldbank.org/eap/eap.n...06c4b92427852567d1006bf6f1?OpenDocument> accessed April 27, 2000.

6. Asia Development Bank, *Annual Report* <http://www.adb.org/About/Annual_Report> accessed April 27, 2000.

7. Margaret M. Pearson, "The Case of China's Accession to GATT/WTO," in Lampton, *The Making of Chinese Foreign and Security Policy in the Era of Reform*; see also Oksenberg and Economy, *Shaping U.S.-China Relations*, 7–8.

8. For an updated list of the nuclear arms control and nonproliferation agreements to which Beijing is party, see Zhang, *China's Changing Nuclear Posture*, 73–74.

9. Rosemary Foot, "China in the ASEAN Regional Forum: Organizational Processes and Domestic Modes of Thought," *Asian Survey* 38, no. 5 (1998): 425–40.

10. Robert S. Norris, Andrew S. Burrows, and Richard W. Fieldhouse, *Nuclear Weapons Databook*, vol. 5, *British, French, and Chinese Nuclear Weapons* (Boulder, Colo.: Westview Press, 1994), 359; see also Bill Gertz, "China Targets Nukes at U.S.," *Washington Times*, May 1, 1998, 1.

11. Commission to Assess the Ballistic Missile Threat to the United States, "Executive Summary," July 15, 1998 <http://www.fas.org/irp/threat/bm-threat.htm> 3 of 27, accessed October 10, 1998.

12. Jessica Poppele, "The CFC Challenge," *China Business Review* (July–August 1994): 38.

13. Elizabeth Economy, "The Impact of International Regimes on Chinese Foreign Policy Making: Broadening Perspectives and Policies ... But Only to a Point," draft chapter in Lampton, *The Making of Chinese Foreign and Security Policy in the Era of Reform*.

14. World Bank, *Clear Water, Blue Skies* (Washington, D.C.: World Bank, 1997), 11.

15. Elizabeth Economy, "The Environment and Development in the Asia-Pacific Region," in *Fires across the Water*, ed. James Shinn (New York: Council on Foreign Relations Press, 1998), 51.

16. Jim Sheehan, "The Case against Kyoto," *SAIS Review* 18, no. 2 (1998): 121.

17. World Bank, *Clear Water, Blue Skies*, 34.

18. Information Office of the State Council, *Human Rights in China* (Beijing: Information Office of the State Council, 1991).

19. Global Policy Forum, "Changing Patterns in the Use of the Veto in the Security Council" <http://www.igc.org/globalpolicy/security/data/vetotab. htm> accessed April 27, 2000.

20. Kim, "China and the United Nations," 42–89; see also Xinhua News Agency, "Foreign Ministry Spokesman on UN Kosovo Resolution" (in Chinese), October 25, 1998, in FBIS-CHI-98-298; for 1999 data on vetoes see Anthony Goodman, "China Vetoes Renewal of U.N. Force in Macedonia," Reuters, February 25, 1999.

21. Paul Lewis, "China Lifts UN Veto on Guatemala Monitors," *New York Times*, January 21, 1997, 8.

22. Paul Lewis, "China Votes a U.N. Force out of Balkans," *New York Times*, February 26, 1999, A7.

23. Kim, "China and the United Nations," 63, table 2-3.

24. Oksenberg and Economy, *Shaping U.S.- China Relations*, 29.

25. Information Office of the State Council of the PRC, *White Paper— China's National Defense*, July 27, 1998 <http://www.china-embassy.org/ Cgi-Bin/Press.pl?wparms> 17 of 24, accessed April 27, 2000.

26. Barber B. Conable Jr., interview by author, October 4, 1999.

27. Jacobson and Oksenberg, *China's Participation in the IMF, the World Bank, and GATT*, 132.

28. Lardy, "China and the WTO," 5.

29. Commission to Assess the Ballistic Missile Threat to the United States, "Executive Summary," 5 of 27; see also Rodney Jones et al., *Tracking Nuclear Proliferation* (Washington, D.C.: Carnegie Endowment for International Peace, 1998), 53–54.

30. Central Intelligence Agency, Nonproliferation Center, "Unclassified Report of Proliferation-Related Acquisition in 1997—Attachment A" (Washington, D.C.: Central Intelligence Agency, 1998).

31. Ibid., 5.

32. Ibid., 6.

33. Information Office of the State Council of the PRC, *White Paper— China's National Defense*, 23 of 24.

34. Xinhua News Agency, "Spokesman on Nuclear Export Control," September 15, 1997, in FBIS-CHI-97-258; see also Xinhua News Agency, "PRC Regulations on Nuclear Exports" (in Chinese), September 11, 1997, in FBIS-CHI-97-256.

35. Bates Gill, "Two Steps Forward, One Step Back: The Dynamics of Chinese Nonproliferation and Arms Control Policy-Making in an Era of Reform," in Lampton, *The Making of Chinese Foreign and Security Policy in the Era of Reform*; see also Zhang, *China's Changing Nuclear Posture*, 19.

36. Information Office of the State Council of the PRC, *White Paper— China's National Defense*, 3 of 24. For a statement describing how some PRC

scholars view arms control and how it can contribute to China's security, see Zhou Xinhua and Pan Tao, "Post-Cold War International Nonproliferation Mechanism" (in Chinese), *Xiandai Guoji Guanxi* (Beijing), October 20, 1998, 17–18, FBIS-CHI-98-314.

37. Alastair Iain Johnston, "Learning versus Adaptation: Explaining Change in Chinese Arms Control Policy in the 1980s and 1990s," *China Journal*, no. 35 (January 1996): 27–62.

38. Information Office of the State Council of the PRC, *White Paper— China's National Defense*, 2.

39. Bates Gill, "Two Steps Forward, One Step Back," in Lampton, *The Making of Chinese Foreign and Security Policy in the Era of Reform.*

40. U.S. Arms Control and Disarmament Agency, *World Military Expenditures and Arms Transfers 1996* (Washington, D.C.: ACDA, July 1997), 23–24.

41. Yan Kong, "China's Arms Trade Bureaucracy," *Jane's Intelligence Review* 6, no. 2 (February 1, 1994): 80.

42. James Mulvenon, "Chinese Military Commerce and U.S. National Security," (Santa Monica, Calif.: RAND Corporation, June 1997), DRU-1626-CAPP, p. xv.

43. Ian Johnson, "China Fights to End Army-Business Ties," *Wall Street Journal*, August 3, 1998, A11; see also Dexter Roberts, Mark L. Clifford, and Stan Crock, "China's Army under Fire," *Business Week*, August 10, 1998, 36; see also "Can PLA Business Activities Really Be Prohibited?" *Wen Wei Po* (Hong Kong), July 23, 1998, A3, cited in *Inside Mainland China*, September 1998, 30–33.

44. Lampton, "A Growing China in a Shrinking World," 128; Liu Huaqiu, "Evaluation and Analysis of China's Nuclear Arms Control Policy," *Xiandai Junshi* [Contemporary Military Affairs], no. 226 (November 11, 1995), in FBIS-CHI-95-246.

45. Kim, "China and the United Nations," 66.

46. United Nations, "Setting the Record Straight: The UN Financial Crisis" <http://www.un.org/News/facts/finance.htm> 1 of 2, accessed April 27, 2000. For the 1999 figure see Barbara Crossette, "Holbrooke Is (Finally) New Man at U.N.," *New York Times*, August 26, 1999, 10.

47. United Nations, "Resolutions Adopted by the General Assembly," A/RES/52/215, January 20, 1998, 3.

48. Lampton, "A Growing China in a Shrinking World," 130.

49. Chinese scholar, interview by author, Shanghai, June 10, 1996.

50. House Select Committee, *U.S. National Security and Military/Commercial Concerns*, vol. 3, 18.

51. Arms Control and Disarmament Agency, "Missile Technology Control Regime Marks 10th Anniversary" <http://www.ACDA.Gov/FACTSHEET /EXPTCON/MTCRRANNI.HTM> 1, accessed September 16, 1998, and "Com-monly Asked Questions on the Missile Technology Control Regime (MTCR)," November 26, 1997 <http://dosfan.lib.uic.edu/acda/factshee/exptcon/fs.htm> 1 of 4, accessed April 27, 2000.

52. House Select Committee, *U.S. National Security and Military/Commercial Concerns*, vol. 3, 19, 36.

53. Liu, "Evaluation and Analysis of China's Nuclear Arms Control Policy."

54. Ambassador John Holdridge, testimony before Senate Committee on Foreign Relations, *U.S. Policy toward China and Taiwan*, 97th Cong., 2d sess., August 17, 1982, 16–17; see also Kerry Dumbaugh, "Taiwan: Texts of the Taiwan Relations Act, the U.S.-China Communiques, and the 'Six Assurances,' " Congressional Research Service, Library of Congress, Foreign Affairs and National Defense Division, Washington, D.C., May 21, 1998, 18.

55. Stockholm International Peace Research Institute, *SIPRI Yearbook, 1998* (Oxford: Oxford University Press, 1998), 294.

56. Office of the Press Secretary, the White House, "Press Availability by President Clinton and President Jiang," Beijing, June 27, 1998.

57. Central Intelligence Agency, Directorate of Intelligence, *China's Economy in 1995–97*, APLA 97–10008, December 1997, 8.

58. Pearson, "The Case of China's Accession to GATT/WTO."

59. Susan L. Shirk, *How China Opened Its Door: The Political Success of the PRC's Foreign Trade and Investment Reforms* (Washington, D.C.: Brookings Institution, 1994), 73.

60. "Statement by Mike Jendrzejczyk," Senate Foreign Relations Committee Subcommittee on East Asia and Pacific Affairs, *Hearing on U.S. Policy toward Hong Kong*, 105th Cong., 1st sess., April 24, 1997, 5.

61. Nicholas R. Lardy, *China's Unfinished Economic Revolution* (Washington, D.C.: Brookings Institution Press, 1998), 35.

62. *China Statistical Yearbook, 1997* (Beijing: China Statistical Publishing House, 1997), 93; these official unemployment rates are, by all accounts, great underestimates of the actual situation.

63. Ian Johnson and Eduardo Lachica, "China Hinders Its Own Bid for WTO, Adding Trade Barriers as Old Ones Fall," *Wall Street Journal*, May 20, 1997, A15.

64. Pearson, "The Case of China's Accession to GATT/WTO."

65. Chinese scholar, interview by author, August 18, 1998.

66. Pearson, "The Case of China's Accession to GATT/WTO."

67. Chinese scholar, interview by author, August 18, 1998.

68. Pearson, "The Case of China's Accession to GATT/WTO."

69. Gu Yuan, "China: Service Trades Liberalization in Dilemma," *Guoji Shangbao* (Beijing), December 22, 1998, 7, in FBIS-CHI-99-008; see also Ian Johnson, "China's Venture Ban Could Cost Foreign Firms," *Wall Street Journal*, September 23, 1998, A14.

70. Wang Lixin and Joseph Fewsmith, "Bulwark of the Planned Economy: The Structure and Role of the State Planning Commission," in *Decision-Making in Deng's China: Perspectives from Insiders*, ed. Carol Lee Hamrin and Suisheng Zhao (Armonk, N.Y.: M. E. Sharpe, 1995), 51.

71. Yong Wang, "Why China Went for WTO," *China Business Review*, July–August 1999, 43.

72. Author's notes of discussion, July 9, 1998.

73. Chinese scholar, interview by author, October 14, 1998.

74. For the best account of the bureaucratic politics of WTO policymaking, see Yong Wang, "Chinese Accession to WTO: An Institutional Perspective," draft manuscript, June 22, 1999, 12.

75. H. Lyman Miller, "China Regroups: Significance of State Council Reorganization," *China Online* <http://www.chinaonline.com/issues/econ_news /newsarchive/secure/1998/.../en_10.as> accessed April 27, 2000.

76. David M. Lampton, "The Neuhauser Lecture," delivered at Harvard University, April 23, 1998, 5. This cites Lyman Miller's statistics. (Seventeen of twenty-four Politburo members in 1997 were "associated with the coastal backbone of reform. By contrast, only six of the twenty-five members of the 1982 Deng leadership hailed from the coastal provinces and cities.")

77. Zhang Shuguang, Zhang Yansheng, and Wan Zhongxin, *Measuring the Costs of Protection in China* (Washington, D.C.: Institute for International Economics, 1998), 28–29.

78. Chinese scholar, interview by author, August 18, 1998.

79. Nicholas R. Lardy, "U.S. Economic Interests in the Clinton-Jiang Beijing Summit," testimony before the Senate Committee on Foreign Relations, Subcommittee on East Asian and Pacific Affairs, June 18, 1998 <http://www .brook.edu/fp/testimon/lardy/6%2D18%2D98.htm> 1 of 3, accessed April 27, 2000.

80. Chen-yuan Tung, "China's Accession to the WTO and U.S. Policy," unpublished manuscript, Johns Hopkins University—SAIS, Washington, D.C., 2.

81. Eduardo Lachica, "U.S. Firms Say China Sanctions Could Hurt Them," *Asian Wall Street Journal,* January 30, 1995, 8.

82. Charlene Barshefsky, "Renewal of Normal Trade Relations with China," Senate Committee on Finance, July 9, 1998, p. 7; see also the American Chamber of Commerce in Hong Kong, "A Commercially Acceptable China WTO Accession Agreement," position paper, September 25, 1998 <http://www.amcham.org.hk/AmCham_Po..._Papers/Position_Paper -WTO_AA.html> accessed September 25, 1998.

83. Richard W. Stevenson, "U.S. Trade Deficit Grows, But Gap with Japan Slims," *New York Times,* February 29, 1996, D4.

84. Jeffrey Madrick, *The End of Affluence* (New York: Random House, 1995), 71, 88.

85. Terry Oblander, "Nafta Failed, Becker Says; Steel Workers Leaders Says Jobs Go South," *Plain Dealer,* September 18, 1998, 1B.

86. 1997 Bill Tracking H.R. 1140; 105 Bill Tracking H.R. 1140, Date introduced March 20, 1997.

87. Information supplied by Mike Jendrzejczk, Human Rights Watch/Asia, October 1998. For other sources pointing to this linkage between human rights and Beijing's WTO entry, see David E. Sanger, "U.S. Again Tries a Trade Issue as a Carrot and Stick for Beijing," *New York Times,* December 15, 1995, A7; see also International Association of Machinists and Aerospace Workers, "Machinists

Union Opposes Admitting China to WTO without Strong Labor and Human Rights Standards," April 21, 1999 <http://www.iamaw.org/news/releases /April21_99htm> accessed April 27, 2000.

88. Chen Xueyan, "WTO Expert Wang Yaotian Points Out the Need to Treat WTO Entry from the Perspective of the State's Fundamental Interests" (in Chinese), *Guoji Shangbao* (Beijing), April 14, 1999, 1, in FBIS-CHI-1999-0421; see also Peng Gang, "Joining the WTO Is Both Joyful and Worrisome" (in Chinese), *Ta Kung Pao* (Hong Kong), April 20, 1999, A2.

89. This is what Robert Putnam calls a "two-level game." See Robert D. Putnam, "Diplomacy and Domestic Politics: The Logic of Two-Level Games," in *Double-Edged Diplomacy*, ed. Peter B. Evans, Harold K. Jacobson, and Robert D. Putnam (Berkeley: University of California Press, 1993), 431–68.

90. For the most detailed and reliable account of Chinese thinking at this time, see Wang, "Why China Went for WTO," 42–45.

91. Senior U.S. Embassy official, conversation with author, Beijing, June 25, 1999.

92. Helene Cooper and Bob Davis, "Overruling Some Staff, Clinton Denies Zhu What He Came For: Lack of WTO Pact for China Opens Political Dangers for Both Leaders," *Wall Street Journal*, April 9, 1999, A6.

93. William Jefferson Clinton, foreign policy speech at Mayflower Hotel, Washington, D.C., April 7, 1999, White House Office of the Press Secretary <http://www.whitehouse.gov/WH/New/html/19990407–2873.html> accessed April 27, 2000.

94. Cooper and Davis, "Clinton Denies Zhu What He Came For," A1, 6.

95. Senator Joseph Biden, *Taiwan Security Enhancement Act, S. 693: Hearing before the Senate Foreign Relations Committee*, August 4, 1999, panel 2 (Richard Allen, David M. Lampton, Caspar Weinberger, and James Woolsey), 11.

96. Ibid., 11.

97. Helene Cooper, "Rubin Advised against China WTO Deal," *Wall Street Journal*, April 16, 1999, A2.

98. William M. Daley, "Why the U.S. Hung Tough in WTO Negotiations," *Wall Street Journal*, April 15, 1999, A22.

99. "Chinese Premier Zhu Rongji Reflects on U.S.-Chinese Relations," interview, CNN, April 13, 1999 <http://www.cnn.com/TRANSCRIPTS/9904 /13/se/14.html> accessed May 3, 1999.

100. Zhu Rongji, author's notes of meeting, March 31, 1999.

101. Chinese Scholar, interview by author, May 18, 1999; see also Ian Johnson, "Backpedaling Begins in U.S.-China Talks," *Wall Street Journal*, April 23, 1999, A12.

102. Chinese scholar, correspondence with author, June 7, 1999.

103. Michael Richardson, "Financial Crisis Straining Asian Neighbors' Political Ties," *International Herald Tribune*, August 8–9, 1998, 5.

104. Zhang Haitao, "Origin and Characteristics of 'Asian Crisis' and Its Impact on Capitalist World" (in Chinese), *Dangdai Sichao* (Beijing), no. 12 (December 20, 1998): 45–52, in FBIS-CHI-99-011.

105. Gong Wen and Zhang Xiangchen, "Mountain Cannot Block Eastward Flowing Stream—Commentary on General Trend of China Joining WTO," *Renmin Ribao*, May 7, 1999, 1, in FBIS-CHI-1999-0523.

106. See table 3 for the 1990 figure; the 1998 figure is from U.S.-China Business Council, "China's Trade with the United States" <http://www .uschina.org/press/tradetable.html> accessed April 27, 2000.

107. Dexter Roberts and Mark L. Clifford, "Asia's Next Casualty?" *Business Week*, December 15, 1997, 54.

108. Calvin Sims, "Worry over Brazil's Money Chills the Shopping," *New York Times*, November 3, 1997, A3.

109. Thomas L. Friedman, "Falling Bodies," *New York Times*, December 25, 1997, A27.

110. "Meanwhile, Back Where the Wagons Are Circling," *The Economist*, November 29, 1997, 41.

111. John Ridding and James Harding, "Territory Pledges to Defend Peg to US Dollar," *Financial Times*, October 24, 1997, 1.

112. Government of Hong Kong, "1996 External Investments in HK's Non-manufacturing Sectors," April 30, 1998 <http://www.info.gov.hk/censtadt/ hkstat/press/exinv96.htm> accessed September 28, 1998.

113. Government of Hong Kong, Special Administrative Region, "Some Important Facts," September 1997.

114. Zhongguo Xinwen She (Beijing) (internet version), "PBOC Governor Announces Loan to Thailand," August 17, 1997, in FBIS-CHI-97-229.

115. Jakarta Radio Republik Indonesia Network, "Indonesia: PRC Foreign Minister Ends Visit," April 13, 1998, in FBIS-EAS-98-103.

116. Henny Sender, "China Faces Flood of Cheap East Asian Imports," *Wall Street Journal*, July 24, 1998, A12.

117. Former Shanghai Vice Mayor Sha Lin, meeting with author, March 1, 1999.

118. Matthew Miller, "Chongqing Exports Down 36pc Because of Turmoil," *South China Morning Post*, March 4, 1999, 4.

119. Seth Faison, "Beijing on the Brink? Perils of a Giant Economy," *New York Times*, November 27, 1997, A8; Nicholas R. Lardy, "China and the Asian Contagion," *Foreign Affairs*, July–August 1998, 82.

120. Seth Faison, "Chinese Economic Leaders Read a Warning in Asian Crisis," *New York Times*, January 15, 1998, D26.

121. James B. Stepanek, "China's Enduring State Factories: Why Ten Years of Reform Have Left China's Big State Factories Unchanged," U.S. Congress, Joint Economic Committee, *China's Economic Dilemmas in the 1990s*, vol. 2 (Washington, D.C.: U.S. Government Printing Office, 1991), 447.

122. United States–China Business Council, "The U.S.-China Business Council: Forecast '98," January 29, 1998, 1; see also United States–China Business Council, "Foreign Direct Investment in China by Source Country or Region, 1979–1997," table 2 <http//www.uschina.org/bas/invest.html> accessed September 28, 1998.

123. Deborah Kuo, "One Fifth of Taiwan Listed Companies Invest in Mainland," Central News Agency, September 18, 1998 <http://www.taipei.org/teco/cicc/news/english/e-09-18-98-5.htm> accessed September 18, 1998.

124. Liu Changjiu, "The West Is Bright but Not the East," originally published in *Jingji Cankao*, reprinted by Xinhua Hong Kong Service in Chinese, October 21, 1998, FBIS-CHI-98-309. For more on worries concerning FDI, which did decline (actualized FDI) in 1999, see Fan, "Impacts of Asia Economic Shake-up on China's Reform and Development," 4–5.

125. Government of Hong Kong, "Financial Secretary's Speech at Asian Debt Conference," *Daily Information Bulletin*, July 6, 1998 <http://www.info.gov.hk/gia/general/199807/06/0706078.htm> accessed September 3, 1999.

126. Ramkishen S. Rajan, "On the Japanese Economy and Economic Policy in Light of the East Asian Financial Crisis," draft paper, Institute of Policy Studies, Singapore, July 13, 1998, 2.

127. Coordination Burea, Economic Planning Agency, Japanese Government, *The Japanese Economy: Recent Trends and Outlook 1998* (Tokyo: Japanese Government, Coordination Bureau, January 19, 1998).

128. Information Access Company, Comline-Tokyo Financial Wire, "White Collar Workers' Savings Rate Declines," March 19, 1998, 1.

129. Adam Posen, "Some Background Q&A on Japanese Economic Stagnation," briefing memo submitted to the Trade Subcommittee, Committee on Ways and Means, U.S. House of Representatives, July 13, 1998, on Institute for International Economics, "Homepage" <http://207.238.152.36/TESTMONY/japanwm.htm> accessed April 28, 2000.

130. Reuters, "China Paper Assails U.S. Rate Cut as Too Small," October 5, 1998.

131. The 1997 figure is from the International Monetary Fund; the 1998 figure is according to U.S. Department of Commerce figures.

132. Craig S. Smith, "The Outlook: China, of All Places, Sends Capital to U.S.," *Wall Street Journal*, March 30, 1998, A1.

133. David Wessel, "Rubin Presses China on Size of Its Reserves," *Wall Street Journal*, September 29, 1997, 6.

134. "Korea Is Offered $10 Billion Loan," *New York Times*, December 22, 1997, A12.

135. Moore and Yang, "Empowered and Restrained," 33–34.

136. C. Fred Bergsten, "The Asian Monetary Crisis: Proposed Remedies," testimony before House Committee on Banking and Financial Services, 105th Cong., 1st sess., November 13, 1997, 2.

137. Elisabeth Rosenthal, "Beijing Students and Women, Defying Ban, Protest Anti-Chinese Violence in Indonesia," *New York Times*, August 18, 1998, A6.

138. Lardy, "China and the WTO," 3; for the 1996 Chinese figure see *China Statistical Yearbook, 1997;* on Chinese textile worker unemployment, Shi

Miao Miao, division director, Foreign Trade Administration, MOFTEC, interview by author, October 19, 1998.

139. Helene Cooper, "Few CEOs Join Commerce Secretary's Tour to Sell China-WTO Deal to Public," *Wall Street Journal*, May 4, 1999, A24.

140. Information supplied by Daniel F. Leahy, director, Office of External Relations, U.S. International Trade Commission, September 30, 1998.

141. Craig S. Smith, "China's Exporters Press for Yuan's Devaluation," *Wall Street Journal*, July 7, 1998, A11.

142. Lally Weymouth, "Upbeat Jiang on Asia's Woes," *Washington Post*, June 21, 1998, C4.

143. Nicholas D. Kristof, "Asian Democracy Has Two Masters," *New York Times*, December 21, 1997, The World section, p. 4.

144. See for example Lo Ping, "Zhu Rongji Joins CMC Work—He Went to Guangdong in Late October to Handle Major Military, Police, Smuggling Cases" (in Chinese), *Cheng Ming* (Hong Kong), no. 253, November 1, 1998, 6–7, in FBIS-CHI-98-310. See also Lo Ang, *Cheng Ming* (Hong Kong), no. 253, November 1, 1998, 6–7, in FBIS-CHI-98-310.

145. Pamela Burdman, "Web of Corruption Ensnares Officials around the World," *San Francisco Chronicle*, April 28, 1993, A8; see also Paul J. Smith, *Human Smuggling* (Washington, D.C.: Center for International and Strategic Studies, 1997); see also Bertil Lintner, "The Third Wave," *Far Eastern Economic Review*, June 24, 1999, 28–29.

146. Lintner, "The Third Wave," 28–29; see also William Branigan, "Guam's Own 'China Beach,' " *Washington Post*, May 6, 1999, A3–4.

147. Nicholas D. Kristof, "A Sexy Economic Feud of No Interest to the I.M.F.," *New York Times*, June 17, 1999, A4.

148. Lucia Tangi, "ICAC Cracks Syndicate Smuggling Mainlanders Overseas," *Hong Kong Standard*, November 9, 1998, 3, in FBIS-CHI-98-312.

149. Fan, "Impacts of Asia Economic Shake-up on China's Reform and Development"; see also Zhang Yunling, "How to Approach the Issue of Capital Flow," *Renmin Ribao*, November 14, 1998, 5, in FBIS-CHI-98-324.

150. Fan, "Impacts of Asia Economic Shake-up on China's Reform and Development." The impulse to continue reform, even in the difficult SOE sector, was seen in a forum on SOE reform at which Jiang Zemin spoke in April 1999, after Premier Zhu Rongji's trip to the United States had not concluded with an agreement. Beijing Xinhua Domestic Service, "Jiang Zemin on State Enterprise Reform" (in Chinese), April 22, 1999, in FBIS-CHI-1999-0423.

5. THE DILEMMA OF THIRD PARTIES

Sources for Chapter Epigraphs:

Mao and Kissinger dialogue from Tim Weiner, "Word for Word/Kissinger Transcripts," *New York Times*, January 10, 1999, sec. 4, p. 7; Author's note of conversation with senior Hong Kong official, May 1992; "Speech by The Right Hon. Christopher F. Patten," The Plaza Hotel, New York City, May 6, 1996, 14–15. Text of remarks and Q & A provided by Hong Kong Economic and Trade Office, New York City; Gingrich quoted in Steven Mufson, "Gingrich

Tells China: 'We'd Defend Taiwan,'" *Washington Post*, March 31, 1997, 1; Carter and Perry, *Preventive Defense*, 104.

1. From Ken-sheh Weigh, *Russo-Chinese Diplomacy* (Shanghai, 1928), 43, cited in William C. Kirby, "Traditions of Centrality, Authority, and Management in Modern China's Foreign Relations," in *Chinese Foreign Policy*, ed. Thomas W. Robinson and David Shambaugh (New York: Oxford University Press, 1997), 17.

2. U.S. Arms Control and Disarmament Agency, *World Military Expenditures and Arms Transfers* (Washington, D.C.: ACDA, 1997), 5.

3. World Trade Organization, "World Trade Growth Slower in 1998 after Unusually Strong Growth in 1997," April 16, 1999 <http://www.wto.org/wto/intltrad/internat.htm> accessed April 28, 2000.

4. Xinhua News Agency, "Zhu Rongji Warns against Taiwan Independence" (in English), March 15, 2000, in FBIS-CHI-2000-0315.

5. Philip Shenon, "Diplomatic Outsider Lobbies Washington Inner Circle," *New York Times*, April 3, 2000, A12.

6. Lee Teng-hui, conversation with author, Presidential Office, Taipei, Taiwan, June 24, 1999.

7. "Remarks by President, First Lady in Shanghai Roundtable Discussion," White House Press Office, Washington, D.C., June 30, 1998, U.S. Newswire, June 30, 1998.

8. "United States-China Joint Communiqué on United States Arms Sales to Taiwan," in *Public Papers of the Presidents of the United States, Ronald Reagan, 1982*, vol. 2 (Washington, D.C.: Government Printing Office, 1983), 1052–53. The operative phraseology cited here is articulated in light of previous phraseology in which Beijing said that it "would strive for a peaceful resolution to the Taiwan question." The operative passage was as follows: "[T]he United States Government states that it does not seek to carry out a long-term policy of arms sales to Taiwan, that its arms sales to Taiwan will not exceed, either in qualitative or in quantitative terms the level of those supplied in recent years since the establishment of diplomatic relations between the United States and China, and that it intends to reduce gradually its sales of arms to Taiwan, leading over a period of time to a final resolution."

9. Lee Teng-hui, "Responses to Questions Submitted by *Deutsche Welle*," document provided by Taipei Economic and Cultural Representative Office in the United States, July 9, 1999.

10. Nicholas D. Kristof, "Taiwan Chief Sees Separate Identity," *New York Times*, September 2, 1998, A4.

11. Author's notes of meeting, Beijing, September 23, 1997.

12. John Pomfret, "Chinese Missiles Menace Taiwan: U.S. Defense Concept Infuriates Beijing," *Washington Post*, February 11, 1999, A1, 32.

13. Sofia Wu, "ROC Welcomes U.S. House Demand for TMD Coverage for Taiwan," Central News Agency, September 25, 1998.

14. John Pomfret, "Taiwanese Seek U.S. Destroyers," *Washington Post*, December 2, 1998, A37.

15. Ralph N. Clough, *Cooperation or Conflict in the Taiwan Strait* (Lanham: Roman and Littlefield Publishers, 1999), ch. 4.

16. Deborah Kuo, "Taiwan Is Mainland China's Third-Largest Source of Foreign Capital," Central News Agency, November 28, 1998 <.../document?_ansset=6eHauKO-EVERMsSEVERUUARYY-AAZCC-A-WRAARECZEE4/28/00> accessed April 28, 2000. See also Li Zhengyan, "Article Reviews Taiwanese Investment in PRC," Xinhua Domestic Service in Chinese, November 2, 1998, in FBIS-CHI-98-306.

17. Xinhua News Agency, "Trade across the Taiwan Straits Grows 3.3 Percent" (in English), in FBIS-CHI-1999-0327.

18. "ACER Head Proposes Taiwan-Mainland China IT Cooperation," Central News Agency, October 20, 1998, noted that Stan Shih, founder of ACER Computer Company, said in 1998, "[T]he greatest challenge to Taiwan's IT industry is its lack of a huge domestic market ... owning a market as vast as the Chinese mainland is the only way to make any Taiwan products a world-renowned brand name."

19. Kuo, "Taiwan Is Mainland China's Third-Largest Source of Foreign Capital."

20. "Press Conference Given by Prime Minister Thatcher at the Legislative Council Chamber in Hong Kong," Hong Kong television broadcasts, September 27, 1982, in FBIS, Daily Report (China), no. 188 (1982): W1–W8; also, Mark Roberti, *The Fall of Hong Kong* (New York: John Wiley and Sons, 1994), 46–51; see also Christopher Wren, "China Calls Hong Kong Pacts Invalid," *New York Times*, October 1, 1982, A3.

21. Keith B. Richburg, "Hong Kong's Reputation Comes In for a Rough Landing," *Washington Post*, July 15, 1998, A19.

22. Willem van Kemenade, *China, Hong Kong, Taiwan, Inc.* (New York: Alfred A. Knopf, 1997), 75.

23. Aladin Ismail, ed., *Hong Kong 1986* (and volumes for 1987, 1988, 1989, 1990, and 1991) (Hong Kong: Government Information Services).

24. Christopher Patten, *East and West* (New York: Times Books, 1998), 7.

25. John Major, *John Major: The Autobiography* (New York: HarperCollins, 1999), 505.

26. Martin C. Lee, "Still Kowtowing to Beijing," *New York Times*, September 5, 1991, A25.

27. Sheryl WuDunn, "Briton, in China, Calls Ties Normal," *New York Times*, September 4, 1991, A5.

28. Patten, *East and West*, 6–7.

29. Ibid., 42.

30. Ibid., 8.

31. Ibid., 9.

32. Christopher Patten, conversation with author, September 1, 1992.

33. Christopher Patten, "Text of Governor's Televised Policy Address," October 8, 1992, 27–42, in FBIS-CHI-92-196.

34. Kathy Wilhelm, "China Says It Will Replace Hong Kong Government after 1997," Associated Press, March 17, 1993.

35. Kerry Dumbaugh, "Hong Kong's 1998 Elections," CRS report for Congress, Congressional Research Service, Washington, D.C., May 26, 1998, 7. In the end, a Provisional Legislature was installed early the morning of July 1, 1997, and it remained in place until new elections were held under Chinese rules the following May (1998), an election in which the Democratic Party and other democratic-minded parties won a total of nineteen of sixty seats.

36. Christopher Patten, "Speech by The Right Honorable Christopher F. Patten, Governor of Hong Kong" to National Committee on U.S.-China Relations, May 6, 1996, New York City, 9.

37. "U.S. Congress Attacked for Snubbing Legco Visiting Group," *Wen Wei Po* (Hong Kong), April 30, 1997, A16, in FBIS-CHI-97-120; see also "Legislature Faces Puerile Obstacles," *Hong Kong Standard,* April 30, 1997, 10.

38. *Hong Kong Standard,* "Legislature Faces Puerile Obstacles," April 30, 1997, 10.

39. "Hong Kong Paper Says USA Wants to Take Britain's Place" (in Chinese), *Ching Pao* (Hong Kong), July 5, 1995, 1, in British Broadcasting Corporation, *BBC Summary of World Broadcasts,* July 13, 1995, FE/2354/F.

40. Very senior Hong Kong government official, interview by author, May 2, 1992.

41. Xinhua News Agency, "Hong Kong Political Issue Internationalization Doomed to Failure," November 18, 1992, item no. 1118117.

42. Very senior Chinese government representative, interview by author, Hong Kong, May 2, 1992.

43. Jesse Wong and Joanne Lee-Young, "Hong Kong Looks to Mainland for Economic, Political Support," *Wall Street Journal,* July 1, 1998, p. A15.

44. C. H. Tung, interview by author, January 16, 1998.

45. The Honorable Doug Bereuter, chairman, The Speaker's Task Force on the Hong Kong Transition, "Second Report," February 25, 1998, p. 1.

46. Bush and Scowcroft, *A World Transformed,* ch. 4.

47. Boris Savelyev, "Russia, China Discuss Military Cooperation in Far East," ITAR-TASS (Moscow), June 15, 1999, in FBIS-CHI-1999-0615.

48. Moscow Interfax Agency, "Russian, Chinese Defense Ministers Discuss Cooperation" (in English), March 29, 2000, in FBIS-CHI-2000-0329.

49. *Eastern Europe and the Commonwealth of Independent States 1992,* 1st ed. (London: Europa Publications, 1992), 369.

50. U.S. Department of State, "Background Notes: Russia, August 1998" <http://www.state.gov/www/background notes/russia 0898 bgn.html.> accessed October 9, 1998.

51. *Eastern Europe and the Commonwealth of Independent States 1992,* 369; also Lawrence R. Robertson, ed., *Russia & Eurasia: Facts & Figures Annual,* vol. 24 (1998) (Academic International Press, 1998), 40.

52. *The Far East and Australasia 1998,* 29th ed. (Europa Publications), 214; Xinhua News Agency, "Kazakhstan Hails Five-Nation Border Accord," April 26, 1997.

53. Steven Miller, "Western Diplomacy and the Soviet Nuclear Legacy," *Survival* 34, no. 3 (Autumn 1992): 6; Arms Control Association, "Soviet Strategic Nuclear Weapons Outside the Russian Republic," *Arms Control Today* (December 1991): 29.

54. Arms Control Association, "U.S. and Soviet/Russian Strategic Forces," *Arms Control Today* (March 1998) <http://www.armscontrol.org/ACT /march98/factmr.htm.> 2 of 3, accessed April 28, 2000.

55. Annmarie Muth, ed., *Statistical Abstract of the World*, 3d ed. (Detroit: Gale, 1997), 782.

56. Burr, *The Kissinger Transcripts*, 47–48, 51, 69, 138, 142–43.

57. Ibid., 99.

58. Robert S. Ross, *Negotiating Cooperation* (Stanford, Calif.: Stanford University Press, 1995), 33.

59. Ibid., 45.

60. Robert M. Gates, *From the Shadows: The Ultimate Insiders' Story of Five Presidents and How They Won the Cold War* (New York: Simon and Schuster, 1996), 122–23; also Harry Harding, *A Fragile Relationship* (Washington, D.C.: Brookings Institution, 1992), 92; also James Mann, *About Face*, 98; also George Lurdner Jr. and Jeffrey Smith, "Intelligence Ties Endure Despite U.S.-China Strain," *Washington Post*, June 25, 1989, A1.

61. Burr, *The Kissinger Transcripts*, 50–51; see also Mann, *About Face*, 65.

62. James Gerstenzang, "Weinberger Arrives in Peking on Heels of Soviets, All Hoping for Better China Ties," *Los Angeles Times*, October 8, 1986, 11; Harding, *A Fragile Relationship*, 143.

63. Mann, *About Face*, 74.

64. Department of State, unclassified telegram, "Letter from Fonmin DOST Details Allegations of Foreign Intervention," March 1980, from U.S. UN Mission, document USUS N 00954 1608032; see also Secret, Department of State JCS Message Center, August 1986, "SECDEF Travel," which notes Secretary Weinberger's plans to talk with Beijing leaders about Sino-American cooperation vis-à-vis Afghanistan and other matters; see also George P. Shultz, *Turmoil and Triumph* (New York: Charles Scribner's Sons, 1993), 570; see also Patrick Tyler, *A Great Wall: Six Presidents and China* (New York: Public Affairs, 1999).

65. Diego Cordovez and Selig S. Harrison, *Out of Afghanistan: The Inside Story of the Soviet Withdrawal* (New York: Oxford University Press, 1995), 155.

66. Mann, *About Face*, 136–37.

67. Cited in Alexander M. Haig Jr., *Caveat* (New York: Macmillan Publishing Co., 1984), 199.

68. Haig, *Caveat*, 200. For a general overview of the dimensions of strategic cooperation between Washington and Beijing, see John W. Garver, *Foreign Relations of the People's Republic of China* (Englewood Cliffs, N.J.: Prentice Hall, 1993), 92–93, 102.

69. For an overview of the triangular relationship see S. Bilveer, "East Asia in Russia's Foreign Policy: A New Russo-Chinese Axis?" *Pacific Review* 11, no. 4 (1998): 485–503.

70. Cited in Feng Yujun, "Reflections on Sino-Russian Strategic Partnership," *Contemporary International Relations* 8, no. 8 (August 1998): 1.

71. Charlene L. Fu, "China, Russia, Central Asian Republics Sign Border Agreement," Associated Press, April 26, 1996, A.M. cycle.

72. Strategic analyst, interview with author, Shanghai, June 20, 1998.

73. Walter A. McDougall, "The U.S. and Japan: Partners or Else," *New York Times*, August 29, 1993, 15.

74. Hu Yaobang, "Create a New Situation in All Fields of Socialist Modernization," report to the Twelfth National Congress of the Communist Party of China, September 1, 1982, *Beijing Review,* September 13, 1982, 15, 31.

75. David M. Lampton, "China and the Strategic Quadrangle: Foreign Policy Continuity in an Age of Discontinuity," in *The Strategic Quadrangle,* ed. Michael Mandelbaum (New York: Council on Foreign Relations Press, 1995), 66.

76. Cited in Gerald Segal, *Sino-Soviet Relations after Mao,* Adelphi Paper, no. 202 (London: International Institute for Strategic Studies, 1985), 12–13, from FE 7263, A3, 9, and CHI-83–039-Annex.

77. Stephen Blank, "Which Way for Sino-Russian Relations?" *Orbis* (Summer 1998): 354.

78. See International Monetary Fund, *Direction of Trade Statistics, 1991 and 1997;* see also Carla Freeman, *China's Reform Challenge: The Political-Economy of Reform in Northeast China, 1978–1998* (Ph.D. dissertation, Nitze School of Advanced International Studies, Johns Hopkins University, 1998), 244.

79. China Business Information Network, "Chinese Official Calls for Boosting Sino-Russian Trade Ties," January 29, 1999 <.../document?_ansset =GeHauKO-EVERMsSEVERUUARAB-AAZVV-A-WRARECZEBZ4/28/00> accessed April 28, 2000; also Zheng Yu, "China: Sino-Russian Strategic Cooperation Viewed" (in Chinese), *Wen Wei Po* (Hong Kong), September 14, 1998, A7, in FBIS-CHI-98-261; see also John Pomfret, "China, Russia Forging Partnership," *Washington Post*, November 21, 1998, A13.

80. David Shambaugh, "Growing Strong: China's Challenge to Asian Security," unpublished, 17; see also David Shambaugh, "Great Order under Heaven, But Is the Situation Excellent?" unpublished, January 1998, esp. 53–57.

81. Patrick E. Tyler, "Russia and China Sign a Military Agreement," *New York Times,* November 10, 1993, A15.

82. Boris Savelyev, "China Discusses Military Cooperation in Far East," ITAR-TASS (Moscow), June 15, 1999, in FBIS-CHI-1999-0615.

83. John Pomfret, "Russians Help China Modernize Its Arsenal," *Washington Post*, February 10, 2000, A17–18.

84. Feng, "Reflections on Sino-Russian Strategic Partnership," 6; see also Information Office of the State Council of the PRC, *White Paper—China's National Defense.*

85. Xiao Feng, "World Trends under US Global Strategy, Part One of Two" (in Chinese), *Renmin Ribao* [People's Daily], May 31, 1999, 6, in FBIS-CHI-1999-0601.

86. Data from USAID, facsimile dated October 21, 1998.

87. Wang Chongjie, "Complex and Subtle U.S.-Russian Relations" (in Chinese), Beijing Xinhua Domestic Service, September 15, 1993, in FBIS, no. 184 (1993), 8.

88. Thomas W. Lippman, "U.S. Narrows Its Vision of 'Partnership' with Russia," *Washington Post,* November 22, 1998, A33.

89. Wang, "Complex and Subtle U.S.-Russian Relations," 8.

90. Jones et al., *Tracking Nuclear Proliferation,* 54.

91. "Russian Imports Step In to Fill the Arms Gap," *Jane's Defence Weekly* (December 10, 1997): 27; also Pyotr Yudin, "Russian Exports Fall Short … " *Defence News,* December 8–14, 1997, 16; also Dennis J. Blasko, "Evaluating Chinese Military Procurement from Russia," *Joint Force Quarterly,* no. 17 (Fall 1997); see also U.S. Arms Control and Disarmament Agency, *World Military Expenditures and Arms Transfers, 1996* (Washington, D.C.: ACDA, July 1997), 22–23, 116, 139.

92. Pomfret, "China, Russia Forging Partnership," A13.

93. Blank, "Which Way for Sino-Russian Relations?" 351.

94. Stanley Meisler, "Security Council Approves Special Armed Force of 12,500 for Bosnia," *Los Angeles Times,* June 17, 1995, A10.

95. ITAR-TASS News Agency (in English), January 16, 2000, in FBIS-CHI-2000-0116.

96. Craig Turner, "UN Oks Iraq Resolution, Though Support Wanes," *Los Angeles Times,* October 24, 1997, A16; see also John M. Goshko, "U.N. Panel Takes No Action on Iraq's Latest Refusal," *Washington Post,* November 25, 1998, A15.

97. Xinhua News Agency, "Spokesman on UN Kosovo Resolution," October 25, 1998, in British Broadcasting Corporation, *BBC Summary of World Broadcasts,* October 27, 1998, FE/D3368/G.

98. Youssef M. Ibrahim, "U.N. Measure Skirts Outright Threat of Force against Milosevic," *New York Times,* October 25, 1998, sec. 1, p. 6.

99. Xinhua News Agency, "UN Envoy Comments after UN Resolution on Kosovo," October 25, 1998, in FBIS-CHI-98-297.

100. Qian Wenrong, "NATO Attack on FRY Undermines UN Authority," *Renmin Ribao* [People's Daily] (Beijing), April 12, 1999, 7, in FBIS-CHI-1999-0412.

101. Author's notes of meeting of U.S. Members of Congress with Premier Zhu Rongji, Beijing, March 31, 1999.

102. Roger Cohen, "NATO Shatters Old Limits in the Name of Preventing Evil," *New York Times,* October 18, 1998, 3.

103. William Drozdiak, "U.S., European Allies Divided over NATO's Authority to Act," *Washington Post,* November 8, 1998, A33.

104. Feng, "Reflections on Sino-Russian Strategic Partnership," 5–6.

105. Secretary of State Madeleine K. Albright, Secretary of Defense Cohen, Japanese Foreign Minister Obuchi, and Japanese Defense Minister Kyuma, "Press Availability Following the U.S.-Japan Security Consultative Committee Meeting," New York, September 23, 1997, released by Office of the Spokesman, New York, Department of State; see also Steven Lee Myers, "Risking China's Wrath, U.S. and Japan Bolster Military Ties," *New York Times,* September 24, 1997, A7.

106. Yan Xuetong, "In Search of Security after the Cold War: China's Security Concerns," *World Affairs* 1, no. 4 (1997): 56.

107. Feng, "Reflections on Sino-Russian Strategic Partnership," 7.

108. Boris Rumer, "Disintegration and Reintegration in Central Asia: Dynamics and Prospects," in *Central Asia in Transition: Dilemmas of Political and Economic Development,* ed. Boris Rumer (Armonk, N.Y.: M. E. Sharpe, 1996), 14–15; also Oksana Reznikova, "Transnational Corporations in Central Asia," in *Central Asia in Transition,* 82–83, cited in Blank, "Which Way for Sino-Russian Relations?" 354.

109. Paul J. Smith, "East Asia's Economic Transformation and Labor Migration," in *Fires across the Water: Transnational Problems in Asia,* ed. James Shinn (New York: Council on Foreign Relations Press, 1998), 84; see also Elizabeth Wishnick, "Russia in Asia and Asians in Russia," *SAIS Review* 20, no. 1 (Winter–Spring 2000): 87–101.

110. Rajan Menon, "The Strategic Convergence between Russia and China," *Survival* 39, no. 2 (Summer 1997): 105.

111. Carol J. Williams and Rone Tempest, "Yeltsin Talks Tough before Arrival in China," *Los Angeles Times,* April 25, 1996, A10.

112. Personal communication from Russian Far East, fall 1993, cited in Lampton, "China and the Strategic Quadrangle," 84.

113. "Far East: China," CDPP, August 21, 1996, 20–22, cited in Blank, "Which Way for Sino-Russian Relations?" 354 n. 41.

114. Sergei Repko, "Nezavisimoye voyennoe obozreniye" [We'll never be allies], July 25, 1996, 1–2, in *The Current Digest of the Post-Soviet Press* 48, no. 30 (1996): 22.

115. Blank, "Which Way for Sino-Russian Relations?" 347.

116. Li Lingjie, "The Progress of Chinese-Russian Relations: From Friendship to Strategic Partnership," *Far Eastern Affairs* (May/June 1997): 41, cited in Blank, "Which Way for Sino-Russian Relations?" 354.

117. Beijing Xinhua News Agency, "Text of Jiang-Yeltsin Joint Communiqué" (in English), November 24, 1998, in FBIS-CHI-98-328, November 24, 1998.

118. Robert Legvold, "Russia and the Strategic Quadrangle," in Mandelbaum, *The Strategic Quadrangle,* 19.

119. Ibid., 19–20.

120. Lo Ping, "Notes from a Northern Journey" (in Chinese), *Cheng Ming* (Hong Kong), no. 228, (October 1, 1996): 6–8, in FBIS-CHI-96-213.

121. Yan, "In Search of Security after the Cold War," 53.

122. Iris Chang, *The Rape of Nanking: The Forgotten Holocaust of World War II* (New York: Penguin, 1997).

123. Jen Huiwen, "PRC: Column Says U.S., Japan Colluding against PRC" (in Chinese), *Hsin Pao* (Hong Kong), in FBIS-CHI-96-181 (September 13, 1996).

124. Fang Hsiao-yi, "Jiang Zemin's Answers to Questions at Press Conference" (in Chinese), *Wen Wei Po* (Hong Kong), November 29, 1998, A3, in FBIS-CHI-98-337. In Tokyo, Japan Correspondents Club.

125. "Whole Staff of Chinese Foreign Ministry Criticize Tang Jiaxuan for Fawning on Japan" (in Chinese), *Ping Guo Jih Pao* (Hong Kong), December 1, 1998, A24, in FBIS-98-335 (December 1, 1998).

126. Nicholas D. Kristof, "Albright Hugs Wary Tokyo Smarting from Beijing Trip," *New York Times,* July 5, 1998, 4.

127. Jianwei Wang and Xinbo Wu, "Against Us or with Us? The Chinese Perspective of America's Alliances with Japan and Korea" (Asia-Pacific Research Center, Institute for International Studies, Stanford University, May 1998), 20.

128. Liu Jiangyong, "Clinton's China Visit and the New Trends in Sino-U.S.-Japanese Relations," *Contemporary International Relations* 8, no. 7 (July 1998): 10.

129. Ibid.

130. Ni Feng, "The U.S.-Japanese Security Alliance: Impact on Regional Security," draft manuscript, 1998, 9. (Ni is a scholar at the Institute of American Studies, Chinese Academy of Social Sciences, Beijing.)

131. Wu Xinbo, "China and Japan: Looking Warily at Each Other—The Security Dimension of Sino-Japanese Relations" (paper presented to the Second Europe-Northeast Asia Forum: "Japan-China-USA: A Strategic Triangle?" June 11–12, 1999, Stiftung Wissenschaft und Politik, Ebenhausen, Germany).

132. Michael J. Green and Patrick M. Cronin, eds., *The U.S.-Japan Alliance: Past, Present, and Future* (New York: Council on Foreign Relations Press, 1999).

133. Liu, "Clinton's China Visit," 9.

134. Ni, "The U.S.-Japanese Security Alliance," 7–8.

135. Liu, "Clinton's China Visit," 10.

136. Eiko Maruko, "The Limits of American Pressure," *Harvard Asia Quarterly* (Summer 1998): 48–49; also Wang Dajun, "An Important Step in Pursuit of Power Politics" (in Chinese), Xinhua News Agency (Beijing), May 24, 1999, in FBIS-CHI-1999-0526.

137. "The U.S. to Propose Expanded Military Ties," *The Daily Yomiuri,* July 25, 1994, 1 <.../document?_ansset=GeHauKO-EVERMsSEVERUUARDU -AADCA-A-WRARECZEBZ4/28/00> accessed April 28, 2000.

138. James Sterngold, "Some Leaders in Japan Begin to Question U.S. Bases," *New York Times,* August 28, 1994, 16.

139. Carter and Perry, *Preventive Defense,* 100.

140. For summarization of the key points of the declaration see Tsuneo Akaha, "Beyond Self-defense: Japan's Elusive Security Role under the New Guidelines for U.S.-Japan Defense Cooperation," *Pacific Review* 11, no. 4 (1998): 469–70.

141. Nixon-Chou (Zhou En-lai) conversations, declassified in 1999, as cited in Jim Mann, "China Is Old-Hand at Election Watching; Diplomacy: Premier Chou En-lai Expressed Support to Nixon in 1972, Newly Declassified Files Show," *Los Angeles Times,* April 4, 1999, A18.

142. Liang Ming, "A New Trend that Merits Vigilance" (in Chinese) *Jiefangjun Bao* [Liberation Army Daily], June 5, 1999, 4, in FBIS-CHI-1999-0616.

143. Author's notes of meeting, Beijing, September 23, 1997.

144. "Premier Hua Gives Press Conference in Tokyo," *Beijing Review,* June 9, 1980, 12, cited in Wang and Wu, "Against Us or with Us?" 20.

145. An Ding, "Japan-U.S. Summit," *Beijing Review,* May 25, 1981, 13.

146. James Gerstenzang, "Weinberger Starts Trip to Boost U.S. Alliances," *Los Angeles Times,* October 5, 1986, 8; also Wang and Wu, "Against Us or with Us?" 23–24.

147. Note that Chinese and Japanese figures are not fully consistent given how each country treats reexports through Hong Kong.

148. Liang, "A New Trend that Merits Vigilance," 4.

149. Wang and Wu, "Against Us or with Us?" 34.

150. Kensuke Ebata, "Japan Joins USA in Theatre Missile Defence Research," *Jane's Defence Weekly* 30, no. 13 (September 30, 1998).

151. "World/Nation Briefs," *Newsday,* September 21, 1998, A16.

152. Bob Drogin, "Defense Project Strains U.S.-China Ties," *Los Angeles Times,* March 22, 1999, 1.

153. Banning Garrett and Bonnie Glaser, "China and the U.S.-Japan Alliance at a Time of Strategic Change and Shifts in the Balance of Power" (Asia-Pacific Research Center, Institute for International Studies, Stanford University, October 1997), 7.

154. Sofia Wu, "ROC Welcomes US House Demand for TMD Coverage for Taiwan," Central News Agency, September 25, 1998 <.../document?_ansset= GeHauKO-EVERMsSEVERUUBRWAAAYDZ-A-WRADRECZEE4/28/00> accessed April 28, 2000.

155. Liang, "A New Trend that Merits Vigilance," 4.

156. Dow Jones Newswires, *Asia One Year into Crisis,* n.d., 12.

157. Jonathan Fuerbringer, "Deliberately or Not, Rubin Set Up a Fall," *New York Times,* June 18, 1998, D1.

158. Sheryl WuDunn, "Japan's Premier Promises a New Boom at the Banks," *New York Times,* June 19, 1998, A6.

159. Rudi Dornbusch, cited in Bob Davis and Jacob M. Schlesinger, "Weak Yen Stymies U.S. Strategies for Asia," *Wall Street Journal,* June 15, 1998, A2.

160. David E. Sanger, "U.S. Joins Japan in Surprise Move to Shore Up Yen," *New York Times,* June 18, 1998, A1, D5.

161. "Beijing's Toughest Boss," *Newsweek,* May 26, 1997, 41.

6. THE STORIES WE TELL OURSELVES

Sources for Chapter Epigraphs:
Hans J. Morgenthau, foreword to *America's Failure in China, 1941–50,* vol. 1, by Tang Tsou (Chicago: University of Chicago Press, 1969), vii; Anthony Lake, "Confronting Backlash States," *Foreign Affairs* 73, no. 2 (March/April 1994): 45–46; Maynard Parker, "Beijing's Toughest Boss," *Newsweek,* May 26, 1997, 41; Gary L. Bauer, "Clinton's Choice on China," *Washington Post,* October 2, 1997, A15; Commentator, "The Chinese People Cannot Be Bullied," *Renmin Ribao* [People's Daily], May 10, 1999, 1, in FBIS-CHI-1999-0509.

1. David Shambaugh, *Beautiful Imperialist: China Perceives America, 1972–1990* (Princeton, N.J.: Princeton University Press, 1991).

2. William Jefferson Clinton, "Second Inaugural Address," *New York Times,* January 21, 1997, 14; Lee Siew Hua, "I Can Still Play a Role, Says Clinton," *Straits Times,* September 18, 1998, 18; Bob Herbert, "In America," *New York Times,* February 22, 1998, 17; Llewellyn H. Rockwell Jr., "U.S. Deludes Itself as Being Indispensable," *Los Angeles Times,* April 15, 1997, B7; R. Jeffrey Smith, "Push on Bosnia War Crimes Pledged," *Washington Post,* December 9, 1996, A12; and Jonathan Peterson, "Clinton Challenges Congress, Calls for Education Crusade," *Los Angeles Times,* February 5, 1997, A1.

3. William Watts, *Americans Look at Asia* (New York: Henry Luce Foundation, October 1999), 44.

4. Senior Chinese leader, conversation with author, May 9, 1992, Beijing.

5. John King Fairbank, *The United States and China,* 3d ed. (Cambridge: Harvard University Press, 1971), 401–18; Foster Rhea Dulles, *American Policy toward Communist China, 1949–1969* (New York: Thomas Y. Crowell Co., 1972), 6–23; Warren I. Cohen, *America's Response to China,* 3d ed. (New York: Columbia University Press, 1990).

6. Wang Jisi, "The Role of the United States as a Global Pacific Power: A View from China," *Pacific Review* 10, no. 1 (1997): 2–3.

7. Fairbank, *The United States and China,* 402–3.

8. Chinese academic, correspondence with author, May 1999.

9. Hsing Jung, "China Reviews Sino-US Relations: Hierarchy Decides to Accelerate Reform" (in Chinese), *Ching Pao* (Hong Kong), no. 263, June 1, 1999, 22–23, in FBIS-CHI-1999-0614.

10. Wang, "The Role of the United States as a Global and Pacific Power," 3.

11. Jiang Zemin, author's note of meeting, June 14, 1996.

12. Chinese scholar, written remarks not for attribution, Beijing, 1997.

13. Wei Yang, "Column Defends Chinese Patriotism" (in Chinese), *Liaowang* (Beijing), no. 35, August 26, 1996, in FBIS-CHI-179 (August 26, 1996).

14. Allen S. Whiting, "Chinese Nationalism and Foreign Policy after Deng," *China Quarterly*, no. 142 (June 1995): 295.

15. Wen Ming, "Patriotism Is above Criticism" (in Chinese), Beijing Xinhua Domestic Service, November 4, 1996, in FBIS-CHI-96-215, November 4, 1996.

16. Whiting, "Chinese Nationalism and Foreign Policy after Deng," 315.

17. Li Li, "Monster of Dark Civilization and Conspiracy Strategy" (in Chinese), *Jiefangjun Bao* [Liberation Army Daily], May 29, 1999, 4, in FBIS-CHI-1999-0604.

18. See for example T. Christopher Jespersen, *American Images of China, 1931–1949* (Stanford, Calif.: Stanford University Press, 1996); see also Harold Isaacs, *Images of Asia* (New York: Harper and Row, Publishers, 1972); Francis L. K. Hsu, *Americans & Chinese: Passage to Differences*, 3d ed. (Honolulu: University of Hawaii Press, 1981); and Michael Schaller, *The U.S. Crusade in China, 1938–1945* (New York: Columbia University Press, 1979), especially ch. 1.

19. Jespersen, *American Images of China*, 2.

20. Isaacs, *Images of Asia*, 63–64.

21. Frank Newport, "Americans' Unfavorable Attitudes towards China Unchanged Ten Years after Tiananmen," June 3, 1999 <http://www.gallup.com /poll/releases/pr990603.asp> accessed April 28, 2000; see also Watts, *Americans Look at Asia*, 47.

22. Watts, *Americans Look at Asia*, 26.

23. Francis Fukuyama, "The End of History?" *National Interest*, no. 16 (Summer 1989): 3–18.

24. Much has been written about a "new isolationism," but public opinion polling suggests otherwise. As William Watts writes, "Such willingness to remain committed abroad, combined with relatively stable (albeit selective) readiness to come to the defense of friends and allies, does not suggest that Americans are turning inward. There is no isolationist mood sweeping across the land." Watts, *Americans Look at Asia*, 3.

25. John E. Rielly, *American Public Opinion and U.S. Foreign Policy, 1991* (Chicago: Chicago Council on Foreign Relations, 1991), 6.

26. "In His Own Words: Clinton on China MFN," *China Business Review*, 18.

27. Ibid.

28. Lake, "From Containment to Enlargement."

29. Ibid.

30. Morton H. Halperin, "Guaranteeing Democracy," *Foreign Policy*, no. 91 (Summer 1993): 105.

31. Author's notes of discussions in China, April 1–3, 1993.

32. Ibid.

33. Premier Li Peng, author's notes of meeting, Great Hall of the People, Beijing, April 3, 1993.

34. William Kristol, "Time for an Insurrection," *Weekly Standard*, March 10, 1997, 17–18.

35. James Mann, "Framing China," *Media Studies Journal* 13, no. 1 (Winter 1999): 103–4.

36. Watts, *Americans Look at Asia*, 4.

37. Author's notes of the Conference on U.S. Media Coverage of China, sponsored by American University School of Communication, John F. Kennedy School of Government, Harvard University, and the National Committee on U.S.-China Relations, May 6–8, 1998, Washington, D.C.

38. Tony Blair, "Doctrine of the International Community," address to the Economic Club of Chicago, April 22, 1999 <http://www.BRITAIN-INFO-ORG /bis/fordom/defence/nato/22ap99–3.stm> 1 of 2, 9, accessed August 10, 1999.

39. Teresa J. Lawson, *Conference on U.S. Media Coverage of China* (New York: National Committee on U.S.-China Relations, 1998) <http://www .ncuscr.org/conferen.htm> 12 of 21, accessed April 28, 2000.

40. Teresa J. Lawson, *U.S. Media Coverage of China*, National Committee Policy Series, no. 14, June 1998 (New York: National Committee on U.S.-China Relations, 1998), 15.

41. Watts, *Americans Look at Asia*, 11.

42. Lawson, *U.S. Media Coverage of China*, 15; see also Watts, *Americans Look at Asia*, 2.

43. Joan Shorenstein Barone Center on the Press, Politics, and Public Policy, *Turmoil at Tiananmen: A Study of U.S. Press Coverage of the Beijing Spring of 1989* (Cambridge: Harvard University John F. Kennedy School, June 1992), 195.

44. Bridge News Service, Reuters, Associated Press, Economist Intelligence Unit, "China Ready to Ride New Wave of Internet Surfers," *Journal of Commerce*, November 4, 1998, 7A; for somewhat different, Chinese figures, see "China: Internet Users Quadruple in Year to More Than 2 Million" (in English), Beijing Xinhua News Agency, January 22, 1999, in FBIS-CHI-99-022; see also Jiang Jingen, "Internet Users Hit 4-Million Mark," *China Daily*, July 15, 1999, 2.

45. Erik Eckholm, "China Cracks Down on Dissent in Cyberspace," *New York Times*, December 31, 1997, A3.

46. Xinhua News Agency (Beijing), "Ministry Official on Internet's Impact on Chinese Economy" (in English), in FBIS-CHI-2000-0405.

47. Reuter Asia-Pacific Business Report, "Illegal Satellite Dishes Multiply in Shanghai," August 12, 1996.

48. David M. Lampton and Gregory May, *Managing U.S.-China Relations in the Twenty-first Century* (Washington, D.C.: Nixon Center, 1999), 37–38.

49. Eugene Nojek, "U.S. International Broadcasting," Voice of America, January 27, 1999.

50. Agence France Presse, "Witness Atrocities," May 27, 1999, in FBIS-CHI-1999-0527.

51. U.S. administration official, author's notes of conversation, November 9, 1998.

52. Lawson, *Conference on U.S. Media Coverage of China*, 12 of 21.; see also Watts, *Americans Look at Asia*, 11.

53. Watts, *Americans Look at Asia*, 47.

54. Mao Tse-Tung [Mao Zedong], *Selected Works of Mao Tse-Tung*, vol. 4 (Bombay, India: People's Publishing House, 1956), 63–93.

55. Orville Schell, "The Role of the US Media in Sino-US Affairs: A Question of Theory vs. Practice" (paper presented at the Miller Center, University of Virginia, Charlottesville, Va., December 1999), 8.

56. Lawson, *Conference on U.S. Media Coverage of China*, 16 of 21.

57. Joan Shorenstein Barone Center, *Turmoil at Tiananmen*, 203.

58. Tom Korski, "Foreign Ministry Abolishes Use of English at Press Briefings," *South China Morning Post*, July 3, 1996.

59. Lawson, *Conference on U.S. Media Coverage of China*, 10 of 21.

60. Owen Harries, "Virtue by Other Means," *New York Times*, October 26, 1997, sec. 4, p. 15.

61. Author's notes of China Watcher Conference, Washington, D.C., October 8, 1999.

62. Schell, "The Role of the US Media In Sino-US Affairs," 6.

63. Joan Shorenstein Barone Center, *Turmoil at Tiananmen*, 205.

64. Junhao Hong, "Media and U.S.-China Relations: An Analysis on Some Theoretical Aspects," in *Image, Perception, and the Making of U.S.-China Relations*, ed. Hongshan Li and Zhaohui Hong (Lanham: University Press of America, 1998), 101–19.

65. Donald J. Munro, *The Concept of Man in Contemporary China* (Ann Arbor: University of Michigan Press, 1977), 180.

66. Author's notes on the Conference on U.S. Media Coverage of China, May 6–8, 1998, Washington, D.C.

67. Ibid.

68. Ibid.

69. Ibid.

70. Li Xiguang, "It Seems to Me" (in English), *China Daily* (Beijing), December 22, 1995.

71. Lawson, *Conference on U.S. Media Coverage of China*, 14 of 21.

72. See for example "*Renmin Ribao* Commentator on Embassy Bombing," *Renmin Ribao* [People's Daily], internet version in Chinese, May 9, 1999, in FBIS-CHI-1999-0509; also "Commentator Views NATO Bombing as 'Wanton Blasphemy,'" *Renmin Ribao* [People's Daily], internet version in Chinese, May 13, 1999, 1, in FBIS-CHI-1999-0512.

73. Author's notes on the Conference on U.S. Media Coverage of China, May 6–8, 1998, Washington, D.C.; see also Lawson, *Conference on U.S. Media Coverage of China*, 14 of 21.

74. Author's notes on the Conference on U.S. Media Coverage of China, May 6–8, 1998, Washington, D.C.

75. "Zhu Rongji Reportedly under Pressure from Dissatisfied Officials," *Hsin Pao* (Hong Kong), November 20, 1998, 29, *BBC Summary of World Broadcasts*, December 4, 1998, FE/D3401/G.

76. Information Office of the State Council of the People's Republic of China, *History in Focus, October 26–November 2, 1997* (Beijing: China Pictorial, 1997).

77. Policy Planning Staff 39/1, "U.S. Policy toward China," November 23, 1948, in *Foreign Relations of the United States*, vol. 8 (1948), 208, cited in John Lewis Gaddis, *Strategies of Containment* (London: Oxford University Press, 1982), 31.

78. "Zhu Rongji, Vice Premiers Face the Press," British Broadcasting Corporation, *BBC Summary of World Broadcasts*, March 20, 1998, 11, FE/D3180/S1.

79. Seth Faison, "Shanghai Journal: Merry Mayor (No Dour Red He) to Come Calling," *New York Times*, November 7, 1996, A4.

80. Michael Laris, "To Make a Point China Downloads U.S. Arms Data," *Washington Post*, June 1, 1999, A10; see also Zhao Qizheng, "Criticizing the US 'Cox Report'" (in Chinese), *Zhongguo Xinwen She* (Beijing), May 31, 1999, in FBIS-CHI-1999-0531.

7. THE SEAMLESS WEB

Sources for Chapter Epigraphs:
Burr, *The Kissinger Transcripts*, 290; I. M. Destler, Leslie H. Gelb, and Anthony Lake, *Our Own Worst Enemy* (New York: Simon and Schuster, 1984), 268.; American's report on meeting with very senior Chinese official, November 1996; Author's notes of discussion between U.S. senator and visiting Chinese delegation, December 17, 1997; William Jefferson Clinton, "Remarks at PNTR Event," May 9, 2000, White House, Washington, D.C. <Publications-Admin@pub.pub.whitehouse.gov> accessed May 9, 2000.

1. Cited in Lampton, "China and the Strategic Quadrangle," 66.

2. David Easton, *A Framework for Political Analysis* (Englewood Cliffs, N.J.: Prentice Hall, 1965), 50.

3. Harold D. Lasswell, *Politics—Who Gets What, When, How* (New York: McGraw-Hill, 1950).

4. Ambrose Bierce, *The Devil's Dictionary, 1906*, cited in Gorton Carruth and Eugene Erlich, *American Quotations* (New York: Wings Books, 1988), 439.

5. Jen Hui-wen, "Characteristics of Zhu Rongji's Anti-Smuggling Arrangements in South China," *Hsin Pao* [Economic Journal] (Hong Kong), in FBIS-CHI-98-320.

6. Chinese think tank member, interview by author, Washington, D.C., December 1, 1998.

7. Richard H. Solomon, *Chinese Political Negotiating Behavior, 1967–1984* (Santa Monica, Calif.: RAND, 1995), 31.

8. Steven Mufson, "The Go-Between," *Washington Post,* June 16, 1998, A24.

9. Wu Zhong, "Zhu Gives a Crash Course in Diplomacy," *Hong Kong Standard,* April 17, 1999, 11, in FBIS-CHI-1999-0414.

10. John W. Cook et al., *The Rise of Nongovernmental Organizations in China: Implications for Americans,* China Policy Series, no. 8 (New York: National Committee on U.S.-China Relations, 1994).

11. Export-Import Bank of the United States, "Three Gorges Dam in China," transcript of press conference, Washington, D.C., May 30, 1996 <http://www.exim.gov/t3gorges.html> accessed September 18, 1998.

12. Office of the Secretary, United States Senate, Office of Public Records, Washington, D.C., November 5, 1998.

13. *Washington, 1998* (Washington, D.C.: Columbia Books, 1998), 323.

14. Steven M. Teles, "Public Opinion and Interest Groups in the Making of U.S.-China Policy," in *After the Cold War: Domestic Factors in U.S.-China Relations,* ed. Robert S. Ross (Armonk, N.Y.: M. E. Sharpe, 1998), 42.

15. Human Rights Watch/Asia, *Death by Default.*

16. Lester Brown, *Who Will Feed China?* (New York: W. W. Norton and Co., 1995).

17. Morgan Norval, Selous Foundation, undated correspondence, 1997.

18. Hutchison Whampoa Limited, "Company Profile" <http://www.hutchison-whampoa.com/corporate/company_profile.htm> accessed September 23, 1998.

19. Senate Committee on Foreign Relations, "Major Findings and Summary of Events," staff report with cover memo to Senator Jesse Helms by Gina Marie L. Hatheway, May 14, 1997, 25–26.

20. Li Ka-shing, personal resume, 1988. See also Senate Committee, "Major Findings and Summary of Events," 25.

21. Simon Beck, "Congressmen Want Probe into Hutchison Deal," *South China Morning Post,* May 18, 1997.

22. United Press International, "Pentagon: Chinese in Panama No Threat," August 12, 1999, B.C. cycle; see also Tom Raum, "Administration Insists Panama Canal Not Threatened by China Firm," AP, August 12, 1999, P.M. cycle; see also Eloy O. Aguilar, "Panamanians Say Chinese-Owned Port Company Not a Threat," AP, August 28, 1999, A.M. cycle.

23. Jose de Cordoba, "China Undercuts Panama Canal Meeting," *Wall Street Journal,* August 20, 1997, A10.

24. In addition to the aforementioned Senate staff report, see "The Chinese and the Ports: Threat to the Canal?" cable from American Embassy, Panama, June 1998, 98–1936000.

25. Hao Yufan and Zhai Zhihai, "China's Decision to Enter the Korean War," *China Quarterly,* no. 121 (March 1990): 103–8.

26. Lampton, "The Normalization of the Chinese Foreign Policy Process."

27. Roberto Suro, "Not Chinese Agent, Chung Says," *Washington Post,* May 12, 1999, A2.

28. James MacGregor Burns, *Leadership* (New York: Harper and Row Publishers, 1978), 19–20.

29. Shen Caibin, "Zhu Rongji's Personal and Political Connections" (in Japanese), *Chuo Koron* (Tokyo), June 1999, 64–79, in FBIS-CHI-1999-0530, 7.

30. Shi Chen, "Leadership Change in Shanghai: Toward the Dominance of Party Technocrats," *Asian Survey* 38, no. 7 (July 1998): 687.

31. Susan Shirk, "The Domestic Political Dimensions of China's Foreign Economic Relations," in *China and the World*, ed. Samuel S. Kim (Boulder, Colo.: Westview Press, 1984): 65.

32. Gao Guanjiang, "On the Issue of 'Foreign Companies Crowding China's Market'" (in Chinese), *Guanli Shijie* [Management World] (Beijing), September 24, 1996, no. 68, 77–80, in FBIS-CHI-96-222 (September 24, 1996).

33. Fu Xin, "Guangdong Investigates 30 Billion-Yuan Smuggling Cases," *Zhongguo Xinwen She* (Beijing), November 6, 1998, in FBIS-CHI-98-313.

34. Geoffrey Crothall, "Xinhua Forced to Limit Damage of Clampdown," *South China Morning Post*, January 22, 1996, 3; Joseph Kahn, "China's Xinhua Agency Set to Retreat on Curbing News from Foreign Firms," *Wall Street Journal*, October 8, 1997, A19.

35. Walter Pincus, "Top Spy Retiring from CIA," *Washington Post*, July 29, 1999, A27.

36. Winston Lord, interview with author, August 18, 1999.

37. Chinese academic analyst, interview with author, August 18, 1998. For more on the Foreign Affairs Leading Small Group, see Lu Ning, "The Central Leadership, Supraministry Coordinating Bodies, State Council Ministries, and Party Departments," in Lampton, *The Making of Chinese Foreign and Security Policy in the Era of Reform*.

38. Chinese consultant to senior Chinese leaders, interview with author, June 20, 1998.

39. Hedrick Smith, *The Power Game: How Washington Works* (New York: Random House, 1988).

40. John Harwood, "Left, Right, Left," *Wall Street Journal*, July 13, 1998, A1.

41. Bob Sutter, memorandum to "Congressional China Watchers," January 6, 1997, Congressional Research Service, Library of Congress, 2.

42. Marchus Brauchli and Ian Johnson, "Money Flap Undercuts Chinese Lobbying," *Wall Street Journal*, March 11, 1997, A19.

43. See David M. Lampton, "China: Think Again," *Foreign Policy*, no. 110 (Spring 1998): 25–26.

44. Elaine Sciolino, "Campaign Finance Complicates China Policy," *New York Times*, March 10, 1997, A6.

45. Sarah McBride, "Despite Scandal, Foreign Lobbying Isn't What It Was," *Wall Street Journal*, July 18, 1997, A16.

46. James David Barber, *The Presidential Character: Predicting Performance in the White House*, 2d ed. (Englewood Cliffs, N.J.: Prentice Hall, 1977).

47. Robert G. Sutter, "China after Deng Xiaoping—Implications for the United States," CRS report for Congress, Congressional Research Service,

Washington, D.C., April 7, 1995, 11. Note: It is difficult to categorize leaders as simply "provincial"; for example, how does one categorize provincial military leaders? Different studies, therefore, yield somewhat different numbers, but most lead to the same conclusion, namely that the density of central leaders with local experience is becoming greater. See, for instance, Richard Baum, "The Fifteenth National Party Congress: Jiang Takes Command?" *China Quarterly*, no. 153 (March 1998): 154; see also Susan L. Shirk, *The Political Logic of Economic Reform in China* (Berkeley: University of California Press, 1993), 191.

48. H. Lyman Miller and Liu Xiaohong, "The Foreign Policy Outlook of China's 'Third Generation' Elite," in Lampton, *The Making of Chinese Foreign and Security Policy in the Era of Reform*.

49. Paul E. Schroeder, "The Ohio-Hubei Agreement: Clues to Chinese Negotiating Practice," *China Quarterly*, no. 91 (September 1982): 486.

50. Sister Cities International, "78 Cities in China Have Sister City Partnerships" <http://www.sister-cities.org/Direct1/ASIA/CHINA.HTM> accessed September 18, 1998.

51. Author's notes on conference, "United States–China Relations: Where Do We Go from Here?" Airlie House, northern Virginia, July 25–27, 1999.

52. Peter T. Y. Cheung and James T. H. Tang, "External Relations of China's Provinces," in Lampton, *The Making of Chinese Foreign and Security Policy in the Era of Reform*.

53. Mainland Affairs Council, Executive Yuan, *Liang-an Economic Statistical Monthly* (Taipei: Mainland Affairs Council, June 1998), 58.

54. Elaine Sciolino, "Taiwan's Lobbying in U.S.: Mixing Friendship and Hardball," *New York Times*, April 9, 1996, A12.

55. Brauchli and Johnson, "Money Flap Undercuts Chinese Lobbying," A19. There also have been allegations that Taiwan businessmen have made contributions to American state political parties so as to avoid the need to report such contributions nationally. See Judi Hasson and Tom Squitieri, "Clinton Was Pressed to Raise Cash, Records Show," *USA Today* (Asia Pacific Edition), April 3, 1997, 8A. Parenthetically, it is interesting to note that as the 1996–1997 scandal over alleged illegal campaign contributions broke in Washington, three of those most central to the controversy initially had Taiwan connections. Taiwan quickly disassociated itself from its allegedly wayward native sons. See, for example, John Pomfret, "Trio Caught Up in Fund-Raising Probe Called Turncoats in Taiwan," *Washington Post*, March 9, 1997, A14. And, of course, there was the April 1996 fund-raiser that Vice President Gore attended in southern California at a Buddhist temple with Taiwan ties that caused considerable controversy.

56. Haass, "Conclusion: Lessons and Recommendations," 209–210; also Linda Greenhouse, "Justices Weigh Issue of States' Making Foreign Policy," *New York Times*, March 23, 2000, A16.

57. Lynette Holloway, "Vallone Seeks Sanctions on Nations Persecuting Christians," *New York Times*, June 15, 1997, 25.

58. Ibid.

59. Steven Fidler and John Lebate, "Left and Right Unite in Protest over PetroChina Offering," *Financial Times* (London), March 21, 2000, 6.

60. World Bank, *East Asia: The Road to Recovery* (Washington, D.C.: World Bank, 1998), 75.

61. Alan Piazza, *Trends in Food and Nutrient Availability in China, 1950–81*, World Bank Staff Working Papers, no. 607 (Washington, D.C.: World Bank, 1983), 9.

62. Jasper Becker, *Hungry Ghosts* (New York: Free Press, 1996); see also Maurice Meisner, *Mao's China and After*, rev. ed. of *Mao's China* (New York: Free Press, 1986), 250.

63. Lynn T. White III, *Policies of Chaos: The Organizational Causes of Violence in China's Cultural Revolution* (Princeton, N.J.: Princeton University Press, 1989), 276–79; see also Stanley Karnow, *Mao and China: From Revolution to Revolution* (New York: Viking Press, 1972), 215, 239, for Lin Biao quote.

64. Benjamin Yang, *Deng: A Political Biography* (Armonk, New York: M. E. Sharpe, 1998), 257.

65. Deng, *Deng Xiaoping wenxuan*, vol. 3, 298–99.

66. Dr. Frank Newport and Lydia Saad, "Economy Weighs Heavily on American Minds," *The Gallup Poll Monthly*, March 1992, 42.

67. John Rielly, ed., *American Public Opinion and U.S. Foreign Policy, 1991* (Chicago: Chicago Council on Foreign Relations, 1991), 13; for a later view of domestic issues of wide concern, see Frank Newport, "Balanced Budget, Economy Top Priorities for Clinton's Second Term," The Gallup Organization, Princeton, N.J. Gallup Poll Archives <http://www.gallup.com/POLL_ARCHIVES/1996/961207.htm> accessed November 13, 1998.

68. Leslie McAneny, "Huge Majority Backs Shift from International to Domestic Agenda," *The Gallup Poll Monthly*, January 1992, 12.

69. Larry Hugick, "The Peace Dividend," *The Gallup Poll Monthly*, October 1991, 10.

70. Office of the Under Secretary of Defense (Comptroller), "National Defense Budget Estimates for FY 1999," Department of Defense, Washington D.C., March 1998, 4, 64–65, and 201 <http://www.dtic.mil/comptroller.99budget/>.

71. U.S. Department of Commerce, *Statistical Abstract of the United States, 1993*, 113th ed. (Washington, D.C.: Department of Commerce), 332; see also U.S. Department of Commerce, *Statistical Abstract of the United States, 1998*, 118th ed. (Washington, D.C.: Department of Commerce), 342; see also Nigel Holloway, "Numbers Crunch: Budget Cuts Hit U.S. Missions in Asia," *Far Eastern Economic Review*, August 15, 1996, 24.

72. Ambassador James Lilley, conversation with author, July 13, 1999. Moreover, the first visit to Beijing by General Scowcroft and Deputy Secretary of State Lawrence Eagleburger began in the PRC capital on July 1, 1989. See also Bush and Scowcroft, *A World Transformed*, 100–11; see also Baker, *The Politics of Diplomacy*, 107–10.

73. There was subsequent debate over the difference between "exchanges" and "contacts." In his memoirs, Secretary of State Baker said that Bush had

"ordered the suspension of all high-level contacts with Beijing." Baker, *The Politics of Diplomacy,* 107. Also, to some extent there was a bureaucratic explanation for why the "secret trip" proceeded despite an administration policy that was opposed to exchanges. As one administration official at the time explained, "There were post-Tiananmen arrests for ten days and the Chinese Government [made an] effort to look tough, hunting down [people], important story, [lots of] coverage, and it affected our policy. Before [Secretary of State] Baker went up on the Hill he felt more had to be done so he went up [to the Hill] and said no more senior visits, but the Administration had already said to the Chinese that Scowcroft and Eagleburger [were coming]—so this was at cross-purposes." Author's notes of remarks of former Bush administration official, May 8, 1998. Author's notes of May 1998 media conference.

74. Bush and Scowcroft, *A World Transformed,* 174.

75. Ibid.

76. Kerry Dumbaugh, "China's Most-Favored-Nation (MFN) Status: Congressional Consideration, 1989–1998," CRS report for Congress, Congressional Research Service, Washington, D.C., August 1, 1998, 6 n. 7.

77. Mann, *About Face,* 229–30.

78. "Statement of the Honorable Nancy Pelosi on Extension of Most Favored Nation Status to China," testimony, *Most-Favored-Nation Status for the People's Republic of China: Hearing before the Subcommittees on Human Rights and International Organizations, Asian and Pacific Affairs, and International Economic Policy and Trade, of the House Committee on Foreign Affairs,* 101st Cong., 2d sess., May 24, 1990, 209–10.

79. Robert S. Ross, "China," in Haass, *Economic Sanctions and American Diplomacy,* 14.

80. Bush and Scowcroft, *A World Transformed,* 106.

81. Ibid., 108.

82. Deng Xiaoping, "Zai Wuchang, Shenzhen, Zhuhai, Shanghai Deng di de tanhua yaodian" [Keypoints of talks in Wuhan, Wuchang, Shenzhen, Zhuhai and other places], *Renmin Ribao* [People's Daily], November 6, 1993, 1; see also Richard Baum, *Burying Mao* (Princeton, N.J.: Princeton University Press, 1994), 342–44.

83. Chinese Foreign Ministry official, interview with author, May 28, 1996.

84. Beijing Xinhua Domestic Service, "'Main Points' of Deng Xiaoping's Talks" (in Chinese), November 5, 1993, in FBIS-CHI-93-214, 21–26.

85. Wu Jinglian, "Commemorating 20 Years of Reforms and Opening Up" (in Chinese), *Guangming Ribao* (Beijing), November 27, 1998, 6, in FBIS-CHI-98-346 (December 12, 1998).

86. Joseph Fewsmith, "Reaction, Resurgence, and Succession: Chinese Politics since Tiananmen," in *The Politics of China,* 2d ed., ed. Roderick MacFarquhar (Cambridge: Cambridge University Press, 1997), 505–8; see also Allen S. Whiting, "Chinese Nationalism and Foreign Policy after Deng," *China Quarterly,* no. 142 (June 1995): 308–9.

87. Whiting, "Chinese Nationalism and Foreign Policy after Deng," 309.

88. Baum, *Burying Mao,* 364.

89. Baker, *The Politics of Diplomacy,* 107.

90. Patrick J. Buchanan, "Recoup by Playing China Cards," *Los Angeles Times,* March 26, 1997, from USIA Wireless File Staff Supplement, March 27, 1997, 17.

91. Foreign Ministry official, interview with author, December 21, 1998.

8. PEOPLE COUNT

Sources for Chapter Epigraphs:
Burr, *The Kissinger Transcripts,* 64; see also Richard Nixon, *The Memoirs of Richard Nixon,* vol. 2 (New York: Warner Books, 1978), 31; Dai Qing, conversation with author, January 21, 1992; Premier Zhu Rongji, public remarks delivered at Hilton Hotel, New York City, April 13, 1999; senior White House official, author's notes of remarks, February 28, 1997; Ambassador James Sasser, conversation with author, Beijing, June 25, 1999; Craig S. Smith, "2 Lonely, Wavering Lawmakers Are Wined and Dined in China," *New York Times,* May 2, 2000, A1, A8.

1. Zhaohui Hong, "The Role of Individuals in U.S.-China Relations, 1949–1972," in *Image, Perception, and the Making of U.S.-China Relations,* ed. Hongshan Li and Zhaohui Hong (Lanham: University Press of America, 1998), 345–64.

2. Lampton, "China's Foreign and National Security Policy Process."

3. Robert G. Sutter, *U.S. Policy toward China: An Introduction to the Role of Interest Groups* (Lanham: Roman and Littlefield Publishers, 1998), 11.

4. Lu Ning, *The Dynamics of Foreign-Policy Decisionmaking in China* (Boulder, Colo.: Westview Press, 1997); see also David Shambaugh, "Containment or Engagement of China?" *International Security,* no. 21 (Fall 1996): 197–201.

5. See Clark Clifford, with Richard Holbrooke, *Counsel to the President: A Memoir* (New York: Random House, 1991), and Gao Xin, *Jiang Zemin de mu-liao* [Jiang Zemin's counselors] (New York: Mirror Books, 1996), 13–67.

6. Wei Jingsheng, *The Courage to Stand Alone* (New York: Penguin Viking, 1997).

7. Richard L. Berke and John M. Broder, "A Mellow Clinton at Ease in His Role," *New York Times,* December 7, 1997, 1.

8. James A. Baker III, with Thomas M. DeFrank, *The Politics of Diplomacy: Revolution, War & Peace, 1989–1992* (New York: G. P. Putnam's Sons, 1995), 100.

9. Ibid., 44.

10. Ibid., 100.

11. Bush and Scowcroft, *A World Transformed.*

12. Chinese scholar, interview with author, June 20, 1998.

13. American Enterprise Institute, "Biography: James R. Lilley," informal document provided by American Enterprise Institute, Washington, D.C., May 1999.

14. Jason DeParle, "The Man inside Bill Clinton's Foreign Policy," *New York Times,* August 20, 1995, sec. 6, p. 33.

15. Office of the Under Secretary of Defense (Comptroller), "National Defense Budget Estimates for FY 1999," 64, 65.

16. Executive branch, interview by author, June 21, 1994, cited in David M. Lampton, "America's China Policy in the Age of the Finance Minister: Clinton Ends Linkage," *China Quarterly,* no. 139 (September 1994): 614.

17. Senior American official, interview with author, Beijing, November 18, 1994, 1.

18. Woodward, *The Agenda,* 256.

19. William Jefferson Clinton, "Remarks by the President in Foreign Policy Speech," delivered at the Mayflower Hotel, April 7, 1999, Office of the Press Secretary <http://www.whitehouse.gov/WH/New/html/19990407–2873.html> 5 of 7, accessed May 1, 2000.

20. This section is based on the author's experience as president of the National Committee on United States–China Relations in New York City at this time and having accompanied Mayor Zhu Rongji throughout his 1990 trip to the United States.

21. National Committee on U.S.-China Relations, "Final Itinerary: The Delegation of Mayors from the People's Republic of China," available in manuscript from National Committee on U.S.-China Relations, New York, 1990.

22. National Committee on U.S.-China Relations, "Report on the Visit of the Chinese Mayors Delegation," unpublished document, New York, 1990, 4.

23. Analysts of China saw in Zhu's handling of the Shanghai disturbances of mid-1989 a difference from Beijing's and attached particular importance to the following post-Tiananmen statement to the citizens of Shanghai by the mayor: "The event that occurred recently in Beijing is a historical fact, and historical facts cannot be covered up by anybody. The truth will always come out." Steven Mufson, "China's Economic 'Boss': Zhu Rongji to Take Over as Premier," *Washington Post,* March 5, 1998, A26.

24. Premier Zhu Rongji, author's notes of meeting, Beijing, March 31, 1999.

25. Chen Youwei, "China's Perception of US Policy," remarks to the Wilson Center, May 28, 1999 (written text of oral remarks was provided); see also author's notes of meeting with senior White House official, February 28, 1997; see also Chen Youwei, *Tiananmen shijianhou: Zhonggong yu Meiguo waijiao neimu* [The inside stories of the diplomacy between communist China and America after the Tiananmen event] (Taipei: Taiquban, 1999).

26. Chinese official, conversation with author, May 6, 1999; Chinese scholar, interview with author, China, April 4, 1999.

27. Information from Chinese Foreign Ministry.

28. Amy Keller, "Chinese Asked for Feinstein's Help in Boosting Members' Trips to Asia, Congressional Travel Key to China's Lobbying Strategy on Capitol Hill," *Roll Call,* March 13, 1997.

29. Time's editors, "U.S. and China: Ups and Downs," interview with Jiang Zemin, *Time Magazine,* October 27, 1997, 56, 58; "Jiang: 'The Supreme Interest

of China Is Peace and Nation-Building,'" *Washington Post,* October, 19, 1997, A22.

30. Steven Mufson, "Jiang Says China to Sign UN Charter on Rights," *Washington Post,* October 25, 1997, A13.

31. Ann Scott Tyson, "No Snafus: Unscripted Version of Jiang's Visit," *Christian Science Monitor,* November 3, 1997, international section, 1.

32. Chinese official, conversation with author, May 6, 1999.

33. Associated Press, "Exercise in Democracy: Engaging in Dialogue Leads to Some Hostile Questions," *New York Times,* November 2, 1997, 14.

34. President Jiang Zemin, author's notes of meeting, January 13, 1998.

35. President Jiang Zemin, author's notes of meeting, March 5, 1999.

36. Chinese scholar, interview with author, in China, April 4, 1999; also Chinese official, conversation with author, May 6, 1999.

37. Premier Zhu Rongji, author's notes of meeting, Beijing, March 31, 1999.

38. White House, Office of the Press Secretary, "Joint Press Conference of the President and Premier Zhu Rongji of the People's Republic of China," April 8, 1999, 4.

39. "Chinese Premier Zhu Rongji Reflects on U.S.-Chinese Relations," CNN Special Event, April 13, 1999 <http://www.cnn.com/TRANSCRIPTS /9904/13/se.14.html> accessed May 3, 1999.

40. Chen Jian and Su Xiangxin, "Pinning Hopes on the American People," *Zhongguo Xinwen She* (Beijing), 1235 GMT, April 14, 1999, in FBIS-CHI-1999-0415.

41. "Chinese Premier Zhu Rongji Reflects on U.S.-Chinese Relations," interview by Judy Woodruff, CNN, aired April 13, 1999 <http://www.cnn.com/ TRANSCRIPTS/9904/13/se.14.html> accessed May 3, 1999.

42. Chinese scholar/official, interview with author, October 16, 1999.

43. Chen Youwei, "China's Perception of US Policy," remarks to the Wilson Center, May 28, 1999, 3.

44. Chinese official, conversation with author, May 6, 1999.

45. Chinese international affairs specialist, interview with author, December 1, 1998; see also Chinese official, conversation with author, May 6, 1999.

46. Chinese scholar, interview with author, June 20, 1998.

47. "'Sources': Jiang, Li Vie for Foreign Affairs Dominance," *Hong Kong Standard,* November 12, 1996, in FBIS-CHI-96-219.

48. Chinese official, conversation with author, May 6, 1999; see also Mann, *About Face,* 258.

49. Jen Hui-wen, "Beijing Political Situation," *Economic Journal* (Hong Kong), April 2, 1999, 6, in FBIS-CHI-1999-0416.

50. Lo Ping, "Major Changes at Core Level—Formal Establishment of Jiang Zemin-Zhu Rongji Structure," *Cheng Ming* (Hong Kong), no. 258, April 1, 1999, 6–9, in FBIS-CHI-1999-0420.

51. U.S. official, interview with author, May 18, 1999.

52. Chinese scholar/official, interview with author, October 16, 1999.

53. Helms' staff has had employees who are not simply behind-the-scenes, low-key, low-profile associates. Rather, they sometimes have felt able to pub-

licly articulate their own views on key issues in the mass media, views that presumably reflect the senator's. See, for example, Ellen Bork, "The Last Days of Hong Kong," *Weekly Standard* 2, no. 20 (February 3, 1997), 29.

54. Senators Helms and Torricelli, Taiwan Security Enhancement Act (S. 693), March 24, 1999 <http://web.lexis-nexis.com/congcom...5=40d93a35af 114eada1568c1> 5 of 7, accessed May 1, 2000.

55. Executive branch, interviews with author, May 18, 1999, Washington, D.C.

56. Christopher H. Smith, correspondence with federal agency director, May 6, 1996, document in possession of this author.

57. Senator Jesse Helms, correspondence with federal agency director, April 22, 1997, document in possession of this author.

58. Megan Rosenfeld, "The Congressman's Faith Accompli: Don't Accuse Christopher Smith of Being Narrow on Issues: His Principles Are Catholic," *Washington Post*, June 10, 1997, B8.

59. Philip Shenon, "Single-Minded Crusader Who Is Blocking Dues to U.N.," *New York Times*, November 15, 1999, A16.

60. Barone and Ujifusa, *The Almanac of American Politics, 1998*, 920.

61. Ibid., 918.

62. Megan Rosenfeld, "The Congressman's Faith Accompli," *Washington Post*, June 10, 1997, B1.

63. Christopher H. Smith, "Statement, National Day of Action for Tibet," June 15, 1998, on Smith's Web site, News from Congressman Chris Smith <http://www.house.gov/chrissmith/pr980615.htm> accessed May 1, 2000.

64. *Hearing before the Subcommittee on International Operations and Human Rights of the Committee on International Relations, House of Representatives*, 104th Cong., 1st sess., December 18, 1995, 7.

65. Thomas W. Lippman, "U.S. Cites Foreign Foes of Christianity," *Washington Post*, July 23, 1997, A18.

66. "Washington Brief," *Washington Post*, August 6, 1998, A5.

67. Harry Harding, *A Fragile Relationship* (Washington, D.C.: Brookings Institution, 1992), 203.

68. Kerry Dumbaugh, "China Legislation in the 105th Congress," CRS report for Congress, Congressional Research Service, Washington, D.C., September 1, 1998.

69. Republican Policy Committee, U.S. House of Representatives, "China Policy Legislation Update: Introduction and Cosponsors," received by author September 22, 1997.

70. Office of Congressman Christopher Cox, "China Policy Proposals," 2 of 4, document received by author September 22, 1997; see also Office of Chris Smith, "Smith Amendment Triples Radio Free Asia Budget," June 27, 1997 <http://www.house.gov/chrissmith/RFA.htm> accessed May 1, 2000.

71. Bill tracking report, available from Congressional Universe (online service), Bethesda, Md., Congressional Information Service.

72. Richard L. Berke and Steven Lee Myers, "In Washington, Few Trifle with Jesse Helms," *New York Times*, August 2, 1997, 1.

73. Ibid., 1, 8.

74. Carter and Perry, *Preventive Defense*, ch. 3.; see also Mann, *About Face*, 288–89.

75. U.S. Newswire, "Remarks by President Clinton, Dr. Graham, Henry Kissinger, Sen. Dole and Gov. Wilson at Funeral for Richard Nixon," April 27, 1994, 6 of 10.

76. Bush and Scowcroft, *A World Transformed*, 98.

77. Ibid., 157.

78. Ibid.

79. Ibid., 157–58.

80. Gao, *Jiang Zemin de Muliao*, 13–67; also Beijing, Xinhua Hong Kong Service, "News Figure: Chairman Wang Daohan of the Association for Relations across the Taiwan Strait" (in Chinese) in Xinhua News Agency (Hong Kong) October 14, 1998, in FBIS-CHI-98-293.

81. Ling Chen, "When Has Zeng Qinghong, Jiang Zemin's Ambitious Top Advisor, Emerged from behind the Scenes?" *Kai Fang* (Hong Kong), no. 145, January 3, 1999, 35–38, in FBIS-CHI-99-013.

82. National Committee on U.S.-China Relations, biography of Wang Daohan, edition dated May 24, 1999. Unpublished document from files of National Committee on U.S.-China Relations.

83. Ibid.

84. *Zhongguo Xinwen She* (Beijing), "McDonnell Douglas, PRC Join In Airliner Venture," in Chinese, April 12, 1985, in FBIS-CHI-85-073 (April 16, 1985), B2.

85. Chinese academic, interview with author, August 2, 1999; see also Bruce Gilley, *Tiger on the Brink: Jiang Zemin and China's New Elite* (Berkeley: University of California Press, 1998), 17–19.

86. Gilley, *Tiger on the Brink*, 35.

87. Ibid., 134–35.

88. Lin Tse-hsu [Lin Zexu], "A Letter of Lin Tse-hsu Recognizing Western Military Superiority, 1842," in *China's Response to the West: A Documentary Survey, 1839–1923*, by Ssu-yu Teng and John King Fairbank (Cambridge: Harvard University Press, 1967), 28.

89. Jiang Zemin, meeting with delegation of which the author was a member, January 13, 1998, 3.

90. Wang Daohan, conversation with delegation of which the author was a member, Shanghai, January 1998.

91. Chinese academic, interview with author, August 2, 1999.

92. National Committee on U.S.-China Relations, "Final Itinerary for the Visit of the Delegation of the China Foundation for International Strategic Studies, Led by Wang Daohan," January 4–21, 1997, available in unpublished form from National Committee on U.S.-China Relations, New York City. Wang would have met with more members of Congress, but most were out of town for the holiday season.

93. Shanghai analyst, interview with author, August 18, 1998.

94. Chinese academic, interview with author, August 2, 1999.

95. Personal observation by author, March 1997.

96. President Jiang Zemin, meeting with author, Beijing, January 13, 1998.

97. Senior Chinese scholar, interview with author, June 20, 1998.

98. Tom Brokaw, *The Greatest Generation* (New York: Random House, 1998), 323.

99. Anonymous, interview with author, November 15, 1999.

100. American International Group, "AIG History," http://www.aig.com /corpsite/history.html> 1 of 4.

101. Ibid., 2 of 4.

102. Robert J. Cole, "High Risk Insurer," *New York Times*, July 27, 1980, sec. 3, p. 7.

103. P. T. Bangsberg, "U.S.-Backed Project in China Restructures Its Main Financing," *Journal of Commerce*, February 8, 1990, 3A.

104. Maurice R. Greenberg, "Statement Submitted by Maurice R. Greenberg," Joint Hearing on U.S.-China Relations, Committee on International Relations, Subcommittee on Asia and the Pacific, and Subcommittee on International Economic Policy and Trade, U.S. House of Representatives, May 16, 1996, 5.

105. For a partial listing of Greenberg's civic service, see Marquis, *Who's Who in America, 1999* (New Providence, N.J.: Marquis Who's Who, 1998), 1731; also American International Group, "Maurice R. Greenberg," August 1996 biography, faxed document of AIG.

106. American International Group, "Maurice R. Greenberg," August 1996 biography.

107. "AIG In China," brochure produced for Fortune Global Forum in Shanghai, August 1999, 15, available from AIG, New York City.

108. Mark L. Clifford with William Glasgall, "How Beijing Is Boosting AIG," *Business Week*, November 13, 1995, 118 E2.

109. Steven Mufson, "U.S. Insurance Giant Sends Agents to Claim Share of Chinese Market," *Washington Post*, February 15, 1995, A16.

110. Dai Qing, conversation with author, January 21, 1992, 2.

111. Fang Lizhi, *Bringing Down the Great Wall* (New York: Alfred A. Knopf, 1990).

112. Dai Qing, "Guiding Public Opinion," *Media Studies Journal* (Winter 1999): 81.

113. Perry Link, *Evening Chats in Beijing: Probing China's Predicament* (New York: W. W. Norton and Co., 1992), 144.

114. Sheryl Wu Dunn, "Trading Cloak and Dagger for Pen and New Ideals," *New York Times*, December 27, 1991. Ye Jianying was one of the ten marshals of the Chinese army, he had deep taproots into the soil of Guangdong Province, he was the ranking military member of the Communist Party's Military Affairs Commission, he survived the Cultural Revolution with strength enough to protect Deng Xiaoping after Deng's spring 1976 demotion,

and he was a key player in the overthrow of the leftist Gang of Four in late 1976.

115. Link, *Evening Chats in Beijing,* 147.

116. Ibid., 148.

117. Dai Qing, *Yangtze! Yangtze!* (London: Earthscan, 1994); Dai Qing, *The Dragon River Has Come!* (Armonk, N.Y.: M. E. Sharpe, 1998).

118. Dai, *The Dragon River Has Come!* 28.

119. Ibid.—see front matter on "Probe International."

120. Ibid.—see front matter on "International Rivers Network."

121. *The Three Gorges Dam in China: Forced Resettlement, Suppression of Dissent and Labor Rights Concerns,* vol. 7, no. 2, report by Human Rights Watch/Asia, February 1995.

122. Amitai Etzioni, *A Comparative Analysis of Complex Organizations,* rev. ed. (New York: Free Press, 1971), 5.

123. Mary Brown Bullock, *An American Transplant: The Rockefeller Foundation and Peking Union Medical College* (Berkeley: University of California Press, 1980).

9. OF ENDS AND MEANS

Sources for Chapter Epigraphs:
Sir Isaiah Berlin, cited in Owen Harries, "Virtue by Other Means," *New York Times,* October 26, 1997, sec. 4, p. 15; Li Shenzhi, "Friday Letter," July 9, 1999, 2, unpublished document of the Kettering Foundation, Dayton, Ohio.

1. John Updike, "One of My Generation," *Museums and Women and Other Stories* (New York: Alfred A. Knopf, 1972), 180.

2. Cohen, *America's Response to China,* 162–63.

3. Dulles, *American Policy toward Communist China,* 37.

4. Thomas J. Christensen, *Useful Adversaries: Grand Strategy, Domestic Mobilization, and Sino-American Conflict, 1947–1958* (Princeton, N.J.: Princeton University Press, 1996).

5. White House, "Joint U.S.-China Statement," October 29,1997 <http://www.state.gov/www/regions/eap/971029_usc_jtsmt.html> accessed August 10, 1999.

6. Senior Chinese diplomats and scholars, conversation with author, Beijing, June 28, 1999.

7. Ibid.

8. Chinese general, interview by author, Beijing, June 28, 1999.

9. Senior Chinese diplomats and scholars, conversation with author, Beijing, June 28, 1999.

10. Alastair Iain Johnston, W. K. H. Panofsky, Marco Di Capua, and Lewis R. Franklin (Michael May, ed.), *The Cox Committee Report: An Assessment* (Stanford, Calif.: Center for International Security and Cooperation, December 1999).

11. "Nuclear-Powered Submarines: The Aces of Chinese Navy" (in Chinese), *Ta Kung Pao* (Hong Kong), October 19, 1998, D3, in FBIS-CHI-98-299.

12. Warren Christopher, *In the Stream of History* (Stanford: Stanford University Press, 1998), 153.

13. Carter and Perry, *Preventive Defense,* 94.

14. Richard E. Neustadt, *Presidential Power* (New York: John Wiley and Sons, 1960); Stephen Hess, *Organizing the Presidency,* 2d. ed. (Washington, D.C.: Brookings Institution, 1988); and Clinton Rossiter, *The American Presidency* (New York: Harcourt, Brace and Co., 1956).

15. Lampton, "America's China Policy in the Age of the Finance Minister," 617–18.

16. John Lewis Gaddis, *Strategies of Containment: A Critical Appraisal of Postwar American National Security Policy* (New York: Oxford University Press, 1982).

17. David E. Sanger, "Rubin and the Great Wall That Is China," *International Herald Tribune,* September 29, 1997, 2.

18. Burr, *The Kissinger Transcripts,* 73.

19. Ibid., 99.

20. Susan V. Lawrence and Tim Zimmermann, "A Political Test of When Guns Matter," *U.S. News & World Report,* October 30, 1995, 48.

21. John Pomfret, "Even Up Close, China's Vision of U.S. Is Out of Focus, Defense Officials Indicate," *Washington Post,* February 15, 1998, A10.

22. Doble Research Associates, *The Public's Thinking about the China-U.S. Relationship* (Englewood Cliffs, N.J.: Doble Research Associates, April 2000), 16–19.

23. Author's notes of Westfields Conference, held at Westfields, Virginia, February 27–March 1, 1998.

24. Senior Chinese official, conversation with author, Beijing, April 1993, cited in Lampton, "China Policy in Clinton's First Year," 22.

Suggestions for Further Reading

INTRODUCTION: THE BIG PICTURE & CHAPTER 1. TURNING POINTS: 1989–2000

Baker III, James A., with Thomas M. DeFrank. *The Politics of Diplomacy: Revolution, War and Peace, 1989–1992.* New York: G. P. Putnam's Sons, 1995.

Bush, George, and Brent Scowcroft. *A World Transformed.* New York: Alfred A. Knopf, 1998.

Christopher, Warren. *In the Stream of History: Shaping Foreign Policy for a New Era.* Stanford, Calif.: Stanford University Press, 1998.

Christensen, Thomas. *Useful Adversaries: Grand Strategy, Domestic Mobilization, and Sino-American Conflict, 1947–1958.* Princeton, N.J.: Princeton University Press, 1996.

Deng Yong. "The Chinese Conception of National Interests in International Relations." *China Quarterly,* no. 154 (June 1998): 308–29.

Harding, Harry. *A Fragile Relationship: The United States and China since 1972.* Washington, D.C.: Brookings Institution, 1992.

Holdridge, John H. *Crossing the Divide: An Insider's Account of the Normalization of U.S.-China Relations.* Lanham, Md.: Roman and Littlefield Publishers, 1997.

Jia Qingguo and Tang Wei. *Jishou de hezuo: Zhong Mei guanxi de xianzhuang yu qianzhan* [Troublesome cooperation: The status and prospect of Sino-American relations]. Beijing: Wenhua Chubanshe, 1998.

Lampton, David M. "China and the Strategic Quadrangle: Foreign Policy Continuity in an Age of Discontinuity." In *The Strategic Quadrangle,* edited by Michael Mandelbaum, 63–106. New York: Council on Foreign Relations Press, 1995.

———. "China and Clinton's America: Have They Learned Anything?" *Asian Survey* 37, no. 12 (1997): 1099–118.

Madsen, Richard. *China and the American Dream: A Moral Inquiry.* Berkeley: University of California Press, 1995.

Mann, James. *About Face: A History of America's Curious Relationship with China, from Nixon to Clinton.* New York: Alfred A. Knopf, 1999.

Nathan, Andrew J., and Robert S. Ross. *The Great Wall and the Empty Fortress: China's Search for Security.* New York: W. W. Norton and Co., 1997.

Ross, Robert S. *Negotiating Cooperation.* Stanford: Stanford University Press, 1995.

Saunders, Phillip C. "China's America Watchers: Changing Attitudes toward the United States." *China Quarterly,* no. 161 (March 2000): 41–65.

Schlesinger, James R., Charles G. Boyd, Joseph P. Hoar, David E. Jeremiah, Elizabeth D. Knup, David M. Lampton, Thomas R. Morgan, Michael D. Swaine, and John A. Wickham Jr. *Toward Strategic Understanding between America and China.* China Policy Series, no. 13. New York: National Committee on U.S.-China Relations, 1996.

Skidmore, David, and William Gates. "After Tiananmen: The Struggle over U.S. Policy toward China in the Bush Administration." *Presidential Studies Quarterly* 27 (Summer 1997): 514–39.

Swaine, Michael D., and Asley J. Tellis. *Interpreting China's Grand Strategy: Past, Present, and Future.* Santa Monica, Calif.: RAND, 2000.

Tyler, Patrick. *A Great Wall: Six Presidents and China.* New York: Public Affairs, 1999.

Vogel, Ezra F., ed. *Living with China: U.S.-China Relations in the Twenty-first Century.* New York: W. W. Norton and Co., 1997.

Xie Xide and Ni Shixiong. *Quzhe de licheng: Zhong Mei jianji ershi nian* [From normalization to renormalization: Twenty years of Sino-U.S. relations]. Shanghai: Fudan Daxue Chubanshe, 1999.

Yan Xuetong. *Zhongguo guojia liyi fenxi* [The analysis of China's national interest]. Tianjin: Tianjin Renmin Chubanshe, 1996.

Yan Xuetong, Wang Zaibang, Li Zhongcheng, and Hou Roushi. *Zhongguo jueqi: Guoji huanjing pinggu* [International environment for China's rise]. Tianjin: Tianjin Renmin Chubanshe, 1998.

Zhang Jialin. "U.S.-China Relations in the Post-Cold War Period: A Chinese Perspective." *Journal of Northeast Asian Studies* 14 (Summer 1995): 47–61.

2. SECURITY ISSUES

Allen, Kenneth W., and Eric A. McVadon. *China's Foreign Military Relations.* Washington, D.C.: Henry L. Stimson Center, 1999.

Bitzinger, Richard A. "Arms to Go: Chinese Arms Sales to the Third World." *International Security* 17 (Fall 1992): 84–111.

Cambone, Stephen A. "The United States and Theatre Missile Defense in North-East Asia." *Survival* 39 (Autumn 1997): 66–84.

Carter, Ashton B., and William J. Perry. *Preventive Defense: A New Security Strategy for America.* Washington, D.C.: Brookings Institution Press, 1999.

Christensen, Thomas J. "The United States and East Asia's Security Challenges: China, the U.S.-Japan Alliance, and the Security Dilemma in East Asia." *International Security* 23, no. 4 (1999): 49–80.

Clarke, Duncan L., and Robert J. Johnston. "US Dual-Use Exports to China, Chinese Behavior, and the Israel Factor: Effective Controls?" *Asian Survey* 39, no. 2 (1999): 193–213.

Eikenberry, Karl W. "Does China Threaten Asia-Pacific Regional Stability?" *Parameters* 25 (Spring 1995): 82–103.

Garrett, Banning N., and Bonnie S. Glaser. "Chinese Perspectives on Nuclear Arms Control." *International Security* 20 (Winter 1995/1996): 43–78.

Gill, Bates, and Michael O'Hanlon. "China's Hollow Military." *National Interest,* no. 56 (Summer 1999): 55–62.

Hu Fan and Li Daguang. *Da guo de zunyan: Gouzhu ershiyi shiji guojia anquan de jiangu baolei* [The dignity of a great power: Establishing a solid fortress for national security in the twenty-first century]. Shenzhen: Haitian Chubanshe, 1999.

Hyer, Eric. "China's Arms Merchants: Profits in Command." *China Quarterly,* no. 132 (1992): 1101–18.

Johnston, Alastair Iain. "Learning versus Adaptation: Explaining Change in Chinese Arms Control Policy in the 1980s and 1990s." *China Journal,* no. 35 (January 1996): 27–62.

———. "Prospects for Chinese Nuclear Force Modernization: Limited Deterrence versus Multilateral Arms Control." *China Quarterly,* no. 146 (1996): 548–76.

Johnston, Alastair Iain, W. K. H. Panofsky, Marco Di Capua, and Lewis R. Franklin (Michael May, ed.), *The Cox Committee Report: An Assessment.* Stanford, Calif.: Center for International Security and Cooperation, December 1999.

Khalilzad, Zalmay M., Abram N. Shulsky, Daniel L. Byman, Roger Cliff, David T. Orletsky, David Shlapak, and Ashley J. Tellis. *The United States and a Rising China: Strategic and Military Implications.* Santa Monica, Calif.: RAND, 1999.

Lewis, John W., and Hua Di. "China's Ballistic Missile Program: Technologies, Strategies, Goals." *International Security* 17 (Fall 1992): 5–40.

Lewis, John W., Hua Di, and Xue Litai. "Beijing's Defense Establishment: Solving the Arms-Export Enigma." *International Security* 15, no. 4 (Spring 1991): 87–109.

Lin Chong-pin. "The Extramilitary Roles of the People's Liberation Army in Modernization: Limits of Professionalization." *Security Studies* 1 (Summer 1992): 659–89.

Mulvenon, James C., and Richard H. Yang, eds., *The People's Liberation Army in the Information Age.* Santa Monica, Calif.: RAND, 1999.

Pillsbury, Michael. *China Debates the Future Security Environment.* Washington, D.C.: National Defense University, 2000.

———, ed., *Chinese Views of Future Warfare,* revised edition. Washington, D.C.: National Defense University, 1998.

Pollack, Jonathan D. "The Cox Report's 'Dirty Little Secret.'" *Arms Control Today* 29, no. 3 (April/May 1999): 34–35.

Pollack, Jonathan D., and Richard H. Yang. *In China's Shadow: Regional Perspectives on Chinese Foreign Policy and Military Development.* Santa Monica, Calif.: RAND, 1998.

Segal, Gerald. "East Asia and the 'Constrainment' of China." *International Security* 20, no. 4 (1996): 107–35.

Shambaugh, David. "Containment or Engagement of China?" *International Security* 21, no. 21 (Fall 1996): 180–209.

Wallerstein, M. B. "China and Proliferation: A Path Not Taken?" *Survival* 38, no. 3 (1996): 58–66.

Wang Jianwei. "Chinese Perspectives on Multilateral Security Cooperation." *Asian Perspective* 22, no. 3 (1998): 103–32.

Wang Shaoguang. "Estimating China's Defense Expenditure: Some Evidence from Chinese Sources." *China Quarterly,* no. 147 (1996): 889–911.

Wu Xinbo. "Integration on the Basis of Strength: China's Impact on East Asian Security." Working paper, Stanford University Asia/Pacific Research Center, Stanford, Calif., February 1998.

Yan Xuetong. "In Search of Security after the Cold War." *World Affairs* 1, no. 4 (1997): 50–58.

———. "Theater Missile Defense and Northeast Asian Security." *Nonproliferation Review* 6, no. 3 (Spring/Summer 1999): 65–74.

Zhang Ming. *China's Changing Nuclear Posture.* Washington, D.C.: Carnegie Endowment for International Peace, 1999.

3. ECONOMICS AND HUMAN RIGHTS

Chan, Anita. "Labor Standards and Human Rights: The Case of Chinese Workers under Market Socialism." *Human Rights Quarterly* 20 (November 1998): 886–904.

Clarke, Donald C., and James V. Feinerman, "Antagonistic Contradictions: Criminal Law and Human Rights in China." *China Quarterly* 141 (1995): 135–54.

Davis, Michael C., ed. *Human Rights and Chinese Values.* New York: Oxford University Press, 1995.

Fung, K. C., and Lawrence J. Lau. *The China–United States Bilateral Trade Balance: How Big Is It Really?* Stanford, Calif.: Asia/Pacific Research Center, April 1996.

Goldstein, Melvyn C. *The Snow Lion and the Dragon.* Berkeley: University of California Press, 1997.

Guthrie, Doug. *Dragon in a Three-Piece Suit: The Emergence of Capitalism in China.* Princeton, N.J.: Princeton University Press, 1999.

Knaus, John Kenneth. *Orphans of the Cold War: America and the Tibetan Struggle for Survival.* New York: Public Affairs, 1999.

Lee, James Z., and Wang Feng. *One Quarter of Humanity: Malthusian Mythology and Chinese Realities, 1700–2000.* Cambridge: Harvard University Press, 1999.

Lilley, James R., and Wendell L. Willkie II, eds. *Beyond MFN: Trade with China and American Interests.* Washington, D.C.: AEI Press, 1994.

Liu Binyan. *A Higher Kind of Loyalty: A Memoir by China's Foremost Journalist.* New York: Pantheon Books, 1990.

Lubman, Stanley B. *Bird in a Cage.* Stanford, Calif.: Stanford University Press, 1999.

Madsen, Richard, Lourdes Beneria, Roberta Cohen, Karen Gulliver, Gillian Hart, Elizabeth Knup, Virginia Leary, June Mei, and Henry Shue. *Economic Development and Human Rights in China's Interior.* China Policy Series, no. 7. New York: National Committee on U.S.-China Relations, 1993.

Nathan, Andrew J. "Human Rights in Chinese Foreign Policy." *China Quarterly,* no. 139 (September, 1994): 622–43.

———. "China: Getting Human Rights Right." *Washington Quarterly* 20 (Spring 1997): 135–51.

Oksenberg, Michel, Pitman B. Potter, and William Abnett. *Advancing Intellectual Property Rights: Information Technologies and the Course of Economic Development in China.* Stanford, Calif.: Institute for International Studies, March 1998.

Seymour, James D., and Richard Anderson. *New Ghosts, Old Ghosts: Prisons and Labor Reform Camps in China.* Armonk, N.Y.: M. E. Sharpe, 1998.

Thurston, Anne F. "In a Chinese Orphanage." *Atlantic Monthly,* April 1996.

Van Ness, Peter. "Addressing the Human Rights Issue in Sino-American Relations." *Journal of International Affairs* 49 (Winter 1996): 309–31.

Wan, Ming. "Chinese Opinion on Human Rights." *Orbis* 42 (Summer 1998): 361–74.

4. GLOBAL INSTITUTIONS AND ECONOMIC FLOWS

Economy, Elizabeth, and Michel Oksenberg. *China Joins the World: Progress and Prospects.* New York: Council on Foreign Relations Press, 1999.

Funabashi, Yoichi, Michel Oksenberg, and Heinrich Weiss. *An Emerging China in a World of Interdependence.* New York: Trilateral Commission, 1994.

Jacobson, Harold K., and Michel Oksenberg. *China's Participation in the IMF, the World Bank, and GATT.* Ann Arbor: University of Michigan Press, 1990.

Lardy, Nicholas R. *China and the World Economy.* Washington, D.C.: Institute for International Economics, 1994.

———. *China's Unfinished Economic Revolution.* Washington, D.C.: Brookings Institution, 1998.

Naughton, Barry, ed. *The China Circle: Economics and Technology in the PRC, Taiwan, and Hong Kong.* Washington, D.C.: Brookings Institution Press, 1997.

Potter, Pitman B. "Foreign Investment Law in the People's Republic of China: Dilemmas of State Control." *China Quarterly*, no. 141 (1995): 155–85.

Smith, Paul J., ed. *Human Smuggling: Chinese Migrant Trafficking and the Challenge to America's Immigration Tradition*. Washington, D.C.: Center for Strategic and International Studies, 1997.

Wang Yong. "Why China Went for WTO." *China Business Review* (July/ August, 1999): 42–45.

World Bank. *China 2020: Development Challenges in the New Century*. Vol. 1 of *China 2020*. Washington, D.C.: World Bank, 1997.

World Bank. *East Asia: The Road to Recovery*. Washington, D.C.: World Bank, 1998.

5. THE DILEMMA OF THIRD PARTIES

Ash, Robert, and Y. Y. Kueh. "Economic Integration within Greater China: Trade and Investment between China, Hong Kong, and Taiwan." *China Quarterly*, no. 136 (December 1993): 711–45.

Harding, Harry. "The Concept of 'Greater China': Themes, Variations, and Reservations." *China Quarterly*, no. 136 (December 1993): 660–86.

Lampton, David M. "China and the Strategic Quadrangle." In *The Strategic Quadrangle*, edited by Michael Mandelbaum, 63–106 (New York: Council on Foreign Relations Press, 1995).

Tucker, Nancy B. *Taiwan, Hong Kong, and the United States*. New York: Twayne Publishers, 1994.

Yahuda, Michael. "The Foreign Relations of Greater China." *China Quarterly*, no. 136 (December 1993): 687–710.

Yan Xuetong. "In Search of Security after the Cold War." *World Affairs* 50, no. 4 (October–December 1997): 50–58.

Beijing-Taipei-Washington:

Cheng Chu-yuan. "Economic Relations across the Taiwan Straits: Progress, Effects, and Prospects." *American Asian Review* 15 (Spring 1997): 91–118.

Clough, Ralph N. *Reaching across the Taiwan Strait*. Boulder, Colo.: Westview, 1993.

———. *Cooperation or Conflict in the Taiwan Strait?* Lanham, Md.: Roman and Littlefield Publishers, 1999.

Dittmer, Lowell. "China's Taiwan Policy." *American Asian Review* 14 (Winter 1996): 65–96.

Garver, John W. *Face Off: China, the United States, and Taiwan's Democratization*. Seattle: University of Washington Press, 1997.

Gilbert, Stephen P., and William M. Carpenter. *America and Island China*. Lanham, Md.: University Press of America, 1989.

Ji You. "Taiwan in the Political Calculations of the Chinese Leadership." *China Journal*, no. 36 (July 1996): 119–24.

Jia Qingguo. "Reflections on the Recent Tension in the Taiwan Strait." *China Journal*, no. 36 (July 1996): 93–97.

Kuo Cheng-tian. "Economic Statecraft across the Taiwan Strait." *Issues and Studies* 29, no. 10 (October 1993): 19–37.

Leng Tse-kang. "A Political Analysis of Taiwan's Economic Dependence on Mainland China." *Issues and Studies* 34, no. 8 (August 1998): 132–54.

Pollack, Jonathan D. "China's Taiwan Strategy: A Point of No Return." *China Journal*, no. 36 (July 1996): 111–15.

Rigger, Shelley. "Competing Conceptions of Taiwan's Identity." *Journal of Contemporary China* 6, no. 15 (July 1997): 307–17.

Shambaugh, David, ed. *Contemporary Taiwan*, 296–318. Oxford: Clarendon Press, 1998.

Su Ge. *Meiguo: Dui hua Zhengce yu Taiwan wenti* [America: China policy and the Taiwan issue]. Beijing: Shijie Zhishi Chubanshe, 1998.

Tucker, Nancy Bernkopf. "China-Taiwan: U.S. Debates and Policy Choices." *Survival* 40 (Winter 1998/1999): 150–67.

Wachman, Alan M. *Taiwan: National Identity and Democratization*. Armonk, N.Y.: M.E. Sharpe, 1994.

Zhao Suisheng. *Making Sense of Relations across the Taiwan Strait: The Crisis of 1995–1997*. New York: Routledge, 1999.

Beijing-Hong Kong (London)-Washington:

Callick, Rowan. *Comrades and Capitalists: Hong Kong since the Handover.* Sydney: University of New South Wales Press, 1998.

Enright, Michael, David Dodwell, and Edith Scott. *The Hong Kong Advantage.* Hong Kong: Oxford University Press, 1997.

Hook, Brian. "Political Change in Hong Kong." *China Quarterly*, no. 136 (December 1993): 840–63.

Patten, Christopher. *East and West.* New York: New York Times Books, 1998.

Washington-Beijing-Tokyo:

Alexander, Lewis M. "International Perspectives on Maritime Boundary Disputes Involving Korea, Japan, and China." *Korea Observer* 30, no. 1 (Spring 1999): 1–7.

Green, Michael J., and Patrick M. Cronin. *The U.S.-Japan Alliance: Past, Present, and Future.* New York: Council on Foreign Relations Press, 1999.

Green, Michael J., and Benjamin L. Self. "Japan's Changing China Policy: From Commercial Liberalism to Reluctant Realism." *Survival* 38 (Summer 1996): 35–58.

Johnstone, Christopher B. "Japan's China Policy: Implications for US-Japan Relations." *Asian Survey* 38, no. 11 (November 1998): 1067–85.

Liu Jiangyong. "Clinton's China Visit and the New Trends in Sino-U.S.-Japanese Relations." *Contemporary International Relations* 8, no. 7 (July 1998): 1–13.

Mochizuki, Mike, and Michael O'Hanlon. "A Liberal Vision for the U.S.-Japanese Alliance." *Survival* 40 (Summer 1998): 127–34.

Wang Jianwei and Xinbo Wu. "Against Us or with Us? The Chinese Perspective of America's Alliance with Japan and Korea." Asia-Pacific Research

Center, Institute for International Studies, Stanford University, May 1998.

Zhang Yunling. "Changing Sino-U.S.-Japanese Relations." *Pacific Review* 10, no. 4 (1997): 451–65.

———., ed. *Hezuo haishi duikang: Lengzhanhou de Zhongguo, Meiguo he Riben* [Cooperation or confrontation: China, the United States, and Japan after the cold war]. Beijing: Zhongguo Shehui Kexue Chubanshe, 1997.

Washington-Beijing-Moscow:

Bilveer, S., "East Asia in Russia's Foreign Policy: A New Russo-Chinese Axis?" *Pacific Review* 11, no. 4 (1998): 485–503.

Blank, Stephen. "Which Way for Sino-Russian Relations?" *Orbis* 42 (Summer 1998): 345–60.

Blasko, Dennis J. "Evaluating Chinese Military Procurement from Russia." *Joint Force Quarterly*, no. 17 (Fall 1997): 91–96.

Brzezinski, Zbigniew. "The Grand Chessboard: U.S. Geostrategy for Eurasia." *Harvard International Review* 20 (Winter 1997/1998): 48–53.

Burles, Mark. Chinese Policy toward Russia and the Central Asian Republics. Santa Monica, Calif.: RAND, 1999.

Feng Yujun. "Reflections on Sino-Russian Strategic Partnership." *Contemporary International Relations* 8, no. 8 (August 1998): 1–10.

Legvold, Robert. "Russia and the Strategic Quadrangle." In *The Strategic Quadrangle*, edited by Michael Mandelbaum, 16–62 (New York: Council on Foreign Relations Press, 1995).

Lukin, Alexander. "The Image of China in Russian Border Regions." *Asian Survey* 38, no. 9 (Spring 1998): 821–35.

Russett, Bruce, and Allan C. Stam. "Courting Disaster: An Expanded NATO versus Russia and China." *Political Science Quarterly* 113 (Fall 1998): 361–82.

Segal, Gerald. "China and the Disintegration of the Soviet Union." *Asian Survey* 32, no. 9 (1992): 848–68.

Wishnick, Elizabeth. "Russia in Asia and Asians in Russia." *SAIS Review* 20, no. 1 (Winter–Spring 2000): 87–101.

Xu Kui, and Ma Shenglong, eds. *Kua shiji de zhanlue jueze: Jiuling niandai Zhong E guanxi shilu* [Cross-century strategic alternatives: The history of Sino-Russian relations in the 1990s]. Beijing: Xinhua Chubanshe, 1999.

Yuan Jingdong. "Sino-Russian Confidence-Building Measures: A Preliminary Analysis." *Asian Perspective* 22 (Spring 1998): 71–108.

6. THE STORIES WE TELL OURSELVES

Cohen, Warren I. *America's Response to China*, 3d ed. New York: Columbia University Press, 1990.

Dittmer, Lowell, and Samuel S. Kim, eds. *China's Quest for National Identity*. Ithaca, N.Y.: Cornell University Press, 1993.

Issacs, Harold R. *Images of Asia: American Views of China and India.* New York: Capricorn Books, 1962.

Jespersen, T. Christopher. *American Images of China: 1931–1949.* Stanford, Calif.: Stanford University Press, 1996.

MacKinnon, Stephen R., and Oris Friesen. *China Reporting: An Oral History of American Journalism in the 1930s & 1940s.* Berkeley: University of California Press, 1987.

Mann, James. "Framing China: A Complex Country Cannot Be Explained with Simplistic Formulas." *Media Studies Journal* 13 (Winter 1999): 102–7.

Metzger, Thomas A., and Ramon H. Myers. "Chinese Nationalism and American Policy." *Orbis* 42 (Winter 1998): 21–36.

Shambaugh, David. *Beautiful Imperialist: China Perceives America, 1972–1990.* Princeton, N.J.: Princeton University Press, 1991.

Song Qiang, Zhang Changchang, and Qiao Bian. *Zhongguo keyi shuo bu: Lengzhanhou shidai de zhengzhi yu qinggan jueze* [China can say no: The decision between politics and sentiment in the post–cold war]. Beijing: Zhonghua Gongshang Lianhe Chubanshe, 1996.

Wang Jisi. "The Role of the United States as a Global and Pacific Power: A View from China." *Pacific Review* 10, no. 1 (1997): 1–18.

Whiting, Allen S. "Chinese Nationalism and Foreign Policy after Deng." *China Quarterly*, no. 142 (June 1995): 295–316.

———. "The PLA and China's Threat Perceptions." *China Quarterly*, no. 146 (1996): 596–615.

Zhang Xiaogang. "The Market versus the State: The Chinese Press since Tiananmen." *Journal of International Affairs* 47 (Summer 1993): 195–221.

7. THE SEAMLESS WEB

China's Domestic Politics and Foreign Policy:

Baum, Richard. "The Fifteenth National Party Congress: Jiang Takes Command?" *China Quarterly*, no. 153 (March 1998): 141–56.

Burns, John P. "Strengthening Central CCP Control of Leadership Selection: The 1990 Nomenklatura." *China Quarterly*, no. 138 (June 1994): 458–91.

Cook, John W., David M. Lampton, Kevin F. F. Quigley, Peter Riggs, William J. Van Ness Jr., M. Jon Vondracek, and Patricia D. Wright. *The Rise of Nongovernmental Organizations in China: Implications for Americans.* China Policy Series, no. 8. New York: National Committee on United States–China Relations, May 1994.

Fewsmith, Joseph. "Neoconservatism." *Asian Survey* 35, no. 7 (July 1995): 635–51.

———. "Reaction, Resurgence, and Succession: Chinese Politics since Tiananmen." *The Politics of China*, 2d ed., edited by Roderick MacFarquhar. Cambridge: Cambridge University Press, 1997.

Hamrin, Carol Lee, and Suisheng Zhao, eds. *Decision-Making in Deng's China: Perspectives from Insiders.* Armonk, N.Y.: M. E. Sharpe, 1995.

Huang Yasheng. "Web of Interests and Patterns of Behavior of Chinese Local Economic Bureaucracies during Reform." *China Quarterly*, no. 123 (September 1990): 828–43.

Li Cheng and Lynn White. "The Fifteenth Central Committee of the Chinese Communist Party: Full-Fledged Technocratic Leadership with Partial Control by Jiang Zemin." *Asian Survey* 38, no. 3 (March 1998): 231–64.

Li Fan. *Jing qiaoqiao de geming: Zhongguo dangdai shimin shehui* [Silent revolution: Becoming civil society in China]. Ontario, Canada: Mirror Books, 1998.

Lieberthal, Kenneth. *Governing China*. New York: W. W. Norton, 1995.

Lieberthal, Kenneth, and David M. Lampton, eds. *Bureaucracy, Politics, and Decision Making in Post-Mao China*. Berkeley: University of California Press, 1992.

Lu Ning. *The Dynamics of Foreign-Policy Decisionmaking in China*. Boulder, Colo.: Westview Press, 1997.

Pei Minxin. "Chinese Civic Associations: An Empirical Analysis." *Modern China* 24 (July 1998): 285–318.

Robinson, Thomas W., and David Shambaugh. *Chinese Foreign Policy: Theory and Practice*. Oxford: Clarendon Press, 1997.

Ross, Robert S., ed. *After the Cold War: Domestic Factors and U.S.-China Relations*. Armonk, N.Y.: M. E. Sharpe, 1998.

Shambaugh, David, ed. *Is China Unstable?: Assessing the Factors*. Washington, D.C.: Sigur Center for Asian Studies, George Washington University, 1998.

Shirk, Susan L. *The Political Logic of Economic Reform in China*. Berkeley: University of California Press, 1993.

———. *How China Opened Its Door: The Political Success of the PRC's Foreign Trade and Investment Reforms*. Washington, D.C.: Brookings Institution, 1994.

Swaine, Michael D. *China: Domestic Change and Foreign Policy*. Santa Monica, Calif.: RAND, 1995.

———. *The Role of the Chinese Military in National Security Policymaking*, rev. ed. Santa Monica, Calif.: RAND, 1998.

Wu Jinglian. *Dangdai Zhongguo jingji gaige: Zhanlue yu shishi* [China's contemporary economic reforms: Strategy and implementation]. Shanghai: Shanghai Yuandong Chubanshe, 1999.

Yahuda, Michael. "China's Foreign Relations: The Long March, Future Uncertain." *China Quarterly* 159 (1999): 650–59.

American Domestic Politics:

Bush, George. *All the Best: My Life in Letters and Other Writings*. New York: Scribner, 1999.

Dumbaugh, Kerry. "Ten Years in U.S.-China Policy: Non-governmental Organizations and Their Influence, 1989-1999." Paper prepared for conference on Forging a Consensus: Making China Policy in the Bush and Clinton Administrations, University of Virginia, Charlottesville, December 3–5, 1999.

Hichman, John. "Struggle over China Policy: The Clinton Administration and the 105th Congress." *American Asian Review* 17, no. 2 (Summer 1999): 87–115.

Lampton, David M. "America's China Policy in the Age of the Finance Minister." *China Quarterly*, no. 139 (1994): 597–621.

Nye, Joseph S. Jr. *Bound to Lead: The Changing Nature of American Power.* New York: Basic Books, 1991.

Ross, Robert R. *After the Cold War: Domestic Factors and U.S.-China Relations.* Armonk, N.Y.: M. E. Sharpe, 1998.

Smith, Hedrick. *The Power Game: How Washington Works.* New York: Random House, 1988.

Sutter, Robert G. *U.S. Policy toward China: An Introduction to the Role of Interest Groups.* Lanham, Md.: Roman and Littlefield Publishers, 1998.

Woodward, Bob. *The Agenda: Inside the Clinton White House.* New York: Simon and Schuster, 1994.

8. PEOPLE COUNT

Bachman, David. "The Limits on Leadership in China." *Asian Survey* 32, no. 11 (1992): 1046–62.

Dai Qing. *Yangtze! Yangtze!* London: Earthscan, 1989.

Evans, Richard. *Deng Xiaoping and the Making of Modern China.* New York: Penguin Books USA, 1993.

Gao Xin. *Jiang Zemin de muliao* [Jiang Zemin's counselors]. New York: Mirror Books, 1996.

Gilley, Bruce. *Tiger on the Brink: Jiang Zemin and China's New Elite.* Berkeley: University of California Press, 1998.

Goldstein, Avery. "Trends in the Study of Political Elites and Institutions in the PRC." *China Quarterly*, no. 139 (September 1994): 714–30.

Goodman, David G. *Deng Xiaoping and the Chinese Revolution: A Political Biography.* New York: Routledge, 1994.

Hao Yufan and Zhang Yandong. *Wu xing de shou* [An invisible hand]. Beijing: Xinhua Chubanshe, 1999.

Lam, Willy-Wo-Lap. *The Era of Jiang Zemin.* Singapore: Prentice Hall, 1999.

Naughton, Barry. "Deng Xiaoping: The Economist." *China Quarterly*, no. 135 (September 1993): 491–514.

Shambaugh, David. "Deng Xiaoping: The Politician." *China Quarterly*, no. 135 (September 1993): 457–90.

Sutter, Robert G. "American Policy toward Beijing, 1989–1990: The Role of President Bush and the White House Staff." *Journal of Northeast Asian Studies* 9 (Winter 1990): 3–14.

Yahuda, Michael. "Deng Xiaoping: The Statesman." *China Quarterly*, no. 135 (September 1993): 551–72.

Yang, Benjamin. *Deng: A Political Biography*. Armonk, N.Y.: M. E. Sharpe, 1998.

Zang Xiaowei. "Provincial Elite in Post-Mao China." *Asian Survey* 31, no. 6 (1991): 512–25.

Zhao Suisheng. "Deng Xiaoping's Southern Tour: Elite Politics in Post-Tiananmen China." *Asian Survey* 33, no. 8 (1993): 739–56.

Index

Compositor:	Impressions Book and Journal Services, Inc.
Text:	10/13 Aldus
Display:	Aldus and Bank Gothic Medium
Printer:	Edwards Brothers, Inc.
Binder:	Edwards Brothers, Inc.